ArtScroll Mishnah Series®

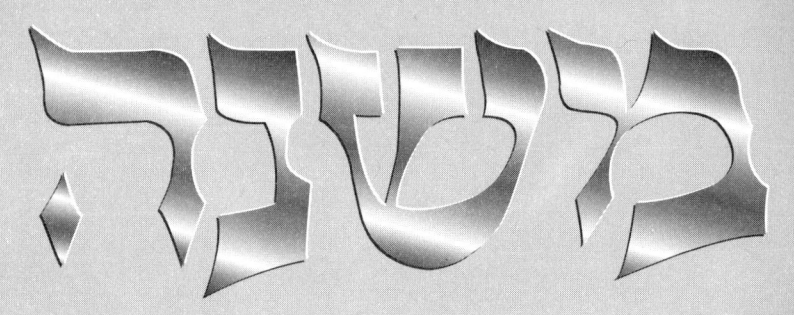

A rabbinic commentary to the Six Orders of the Mishnah

Rabbi Nosson Scherman / Rabbi Meir Zlotowitz

General Editors

שׁשׁה סדרי **מִשְׁנָה**

THE COMMENTARY HAS BEEN NAMED **YAD AVRAHAM**
AS AN EVERLASTING MEMORIAL AND SOURCE OF MERIT
FOR THE *NESHAMAH* OF

אברהם יוסף ע״ה בן הר״ר אליעזר הכהן גליק נ״י
AVRAHAM YOSEF GLICK ע״ה
WHOSE LIFE WAS CUT SHORT ON 3 TEVES, 5735

Published by

Mesorah Publications, ltd

the mishnah

ARTSCROLL MISHNAH SERIES / A NEW TRANSLATION WITH A COMMENTARY **YAD AVRAHAM** ANTHOLOGIZED FROM TALMUDIC SOURCES AND CLASSIC COMMENTATORS.

INCLUDES THE COMPLETE HEBREW TEXT OF THE COMMENTARY OF **RAV OVADIAH BERTINORO**

FIRST EDITION
First Impression . . . September 2001

Published and Distributed by
MESORAH PUBLICATIONS, Ltd.
4401 Second Avenue
Brooklyn, New York 11232

Distributed in Europe by
LEHMANNS
Unit E, Viking Industrial Park
Rolling Mill Road
Jarrow, Tyne & Wear NE32 3DP
England

Distributed in Australia & New Zealand by
GOLDS WORLD OF JUDAICA
3-13 William Street
Balaclava, Melbourne 3183
Victoria Australia

Distributed in Israel by
SIFRIATI / A. GITLER — BOOKS
6 Hayarkon Street
Bnei Brak 51127

Distributed in South Africa by
KOLLEL BOOKSHOP
Shop 8A Norwood Hypermarket
Norwood 2196, Johannesburg, South Africa

THE ARTSCROLL MISHNAH SERIES ®
SEDER ZERAIM Vol. I: *BERACHOS*
© Copyright 2001
by MESORAH PUBLICATIONS, Ltd.
4401 Second Avenue / Brooklyn, N.Y. 11232 / (718) 921-9000 / www.artscroll.com

---

ISBN
1-57819-702-3 (hard cover)

Typography by CompuScribe at ArtScroll Studios, Ltd.
4401 Second Avenue / Brooklyn, N.Y. 11232 / (718) 921-9000

Printed in the United States of America by Noble Book Press
Bound by Sefercraft, Quality Bookbinders, Ltd. Brooklyn, N.Y.

This volume and the
Yad Avraham commentary
to the entire Mishnah Series
are dedicated to the memory of

Avraham Yosef Glick ז״ל

ר׳ אברהם יוסף ז״ל
בן ר׳ אליעזר הכהן ודבורה גליק נ״י
נפטר ג׳ טבת תשל״ה

It is our fervent hope that the hours
spent studying, discussing and reviewing
these volumes within the confines of our world,
will continue to intensify and expand
our connection to the eternal world.

May the learning of this commentary
bring an עליה to the נשמה of
אברהם יוסף בן ר׳ אליעזר הכהן.

תנצב״ה

הנה אמרו ברא מזכה אבא אבא לא מזכה ברא, ומכל מקום מצינו אצל דוד המלך שזיכה לבנו אבשלום ואייתיה לעלמא דאתי (שמואל-ב יט,א ורש"י שם). ביאור הענין הוא שפעולת הבן היא המשך של האב ומשום הכי הבן מזכה להאב מבלי עשיית פעולות מיוחדות למען האב, מה שאין כן בנוגע לאב בעינן או תפילה או פעולה מיוחדת לזכות לבן.

ומטעם זה קמו ר' אליעזר נ"י ונות ביתו דבורה תחי' לעשות פעולה לעילוי נשמת בנם אברהם יוסף ז"ל שתתקיים עד סוף כל הדורות, והרבצת התורה שתצא מפעולה זו של **"יד אברהם"** על ששה סדרי משנה להאיר דרך בלימודו של כל מבין עם תלמיד לא תפסוק עד בְלי ירח.

ר' אברהם יוסף, שנקטף באבו בן כ"ד שנה בדרך נסיעתו לארץ ישראל, היה אדם שמכיריו וידידיו העידו עליו שהיה מתוק. היה מעורב עם הבריות ובעל חסד למופת. היה עושה ומעשה על הצדקה. תפסו אותו כאיש נאמן ואמת אמת תפסוה להאי גברא.

הפירוש **"יד אברהם"** על משנה (אותיות נשמה) אינו פירוש רגיל, אלא כולל פרי עיון בכל סוגיא וסוגיא מהמקרא עד הפוסקים האחרונים, והעידו גדולי תורה על הבהירות והתועלת שיוצאות מההשתמשות בו. זכות תורת חסד (תורה ללמדה זו היא תורה של חסד – סוכה מט, ב) תעמוד לעילוי נשמת אברהם יוסף ב"ר אליעזר הכהן נ"י גליק עד נצח ותנצב"ה אכי"ר.

A PROJECT OF THE

Mesorah Heritage Foundation

✥ Seder Zeraim Vol. I:

מסכת ברכות
Tractate Berachos

Translation and anthologized commentary by
Rabbi Mordecai Rabinovitch

Edited by
Rabbi Reuvein Dowek

Assisted by
Rabbi Yitzchok Stavsky and Rabbi Gidone Lane

Reviewed by
Rabbi Chaim Malinowitz

The Publishers are grateful to

YAD AVRAHAM INSTITUTE

and the

MESORAH HERITAGE FOUNDATION

for their efforts in the publication of the

ARTSCROLL MISHNAH SERIES

הסכמה

הנה ידידי הרב הגאון ר' אברהם יוסף ראזענבערג שליט"א אשר היה מתלמידי החשובים
ביותר וגם הרביץ תורה בכמה ישיבות ואצלינו בישיבתנו בסטעטן אייללנד, ובזמן האחרון
הוא מתעסק בתרגום ספרי קדש ללשון אנגלית המדוברת ומובנת לבני מדינה זו, וכבר
איתמחי גברא בענין תרגום לאנגלית וכעת תרגם משניות לשפת אנגלית וגם לקוטים מדברי
רבותינו מפרשי משניות על כל משנה ומשנה בערך, והוא לתועלת גדול להרבה אינשי
ממדינה זו שלא התרגלו מילדותם ללמוד המשנה וגם יש הרבה שבעזר השי"ת התקרבו
לתורה ויראת שמים כשכבר נתגדלו ורוצים ללמוד שיוכלו ללמוד משניות בנקל בשפה
המורגלת להם, שהוא ממזכי הרבים בלמוד משניות וזכותו גדול. ואני מברכו שיצליחהו
השי"ת בחבורו זה. וגם אני מברך את חברת ארטסקרול אשר תחת הנהלת הרב הנכבד ידידי
מוהר"ר מאיר יעקב בן ידידי הרב הגאון ר' אהרן שליט"א זלאטאוויץ אשר הוציאו כבר הרבה
חבורים חשובים לזכות את הרבים וכעת הם מוציאים לאור את המשניות הנ"ל.

ועל זה באתי על החתום בז' אדר תשל"ט בנוא יארק.

נאום משה פיינשטיין

מכתב ברכה

יעקב קמנצקי

RABBI J. KAMENECKI

38 SADDLE RIVER ROAD

MONSEY, NEW YORK 10952

בע"ה

יום ה' ערב חג השבועות תשל"ס, פה מאנסי.

כבוד הרבני איש החסד שוע ונדיב מקיר רבנן מר אלעזר נ"י בליק שלו' וברכת כל טוב.

מה מאד שמחתי בהודעי כי כבודו רכש לעצמו הזכות שייקרא ע"ש בנו המנוח הפירוש מבואר על כל ששה סדרי משנה ע"י "ארטסקראל" והנה חברה זו יצאה לה מוניטין בפירושה על תנ"ך, והנה נקוה שכשם שהצליחה בתורה שבכתב כן תצליח בתורה שבע"פ. ובהיות שאותיות "משנה" הן כאותיות "נשמה" לפיכך טוב עשה בכוונתו לעשות זאת לעילוי נשמת בנו המנוח אברהם יוסף ע"ה, ומאד מתאים השם "יד אברהם" לזה הפירוש, כדמצינו במקרא (ש"ב י"ח) כי אמר אין לי בן בעבור הזכיר שמי וגו'. ואין לך דבר גדול מזה להפיץ ידיעת תורה שבע"פ בקרב אחינו שאינם רגילים בלשון הקדש. ורד' הטוב יהי' בעזרו ויוכל לברך על המוגמר. וירוה רוב נחת מכל אשר אתו כנפש מברכו.

יעקב קמנצקי

מכתב ברכה

YESHIVAT TELSHE   ישיבת טלז

Kiryat Telshe Stone   קרית טלז־סטוו

Jerusalem, Israel   ירושלים

בע״ה – ד׳ בהעלותך – לבני א״י – תשל״ט – פה קרית טלז, באה״ק

מע״כ ידידי האהובים הרב ר׳ מאיר והרב ר׳ נתן, נר״ו, שלום וברכה נצח!

אחדשה״ט באהבה ויקר,

לשמחה רבה היא לי להודע שהרחבתם גבול עבודתכם בקדש לתורה שבע״פ, בהוצאת המשנה בתרגום וביאור באנגלית, וראשית עבודתכם במס׳ מגילה.

אני תקוה שתשימו לב שיצאו הדברים מתוקנים מנקודת ההלכה, וחזקה עליכם שתוציאו דבר נאה ומתוקן.

בפנותכם לתורה שבע״פ יפתח אופק חדש בתורת ה׳ לאלה שקשה עליהם ללמוד הדברים במקורם, ואלה שכבר נתעשרו מעבודתכם במגילת אסתר יכנסו עתה לטרקלין חדש וישמשו להם הדברים דחף ללימוד המשנה, וגדול יהי׳ שכרכם.

יהא ה׳ בעזרכם בהוספת טבעת חדשה באותה שלשלת זהב של הפצת תורת ה׳ להמוני עם לקרב לב ישראל לאבינו שבשמים בתורה ואמונה טהורה.

אוהבכם מלונ״ח,

מרדכי

מכתב ברכה

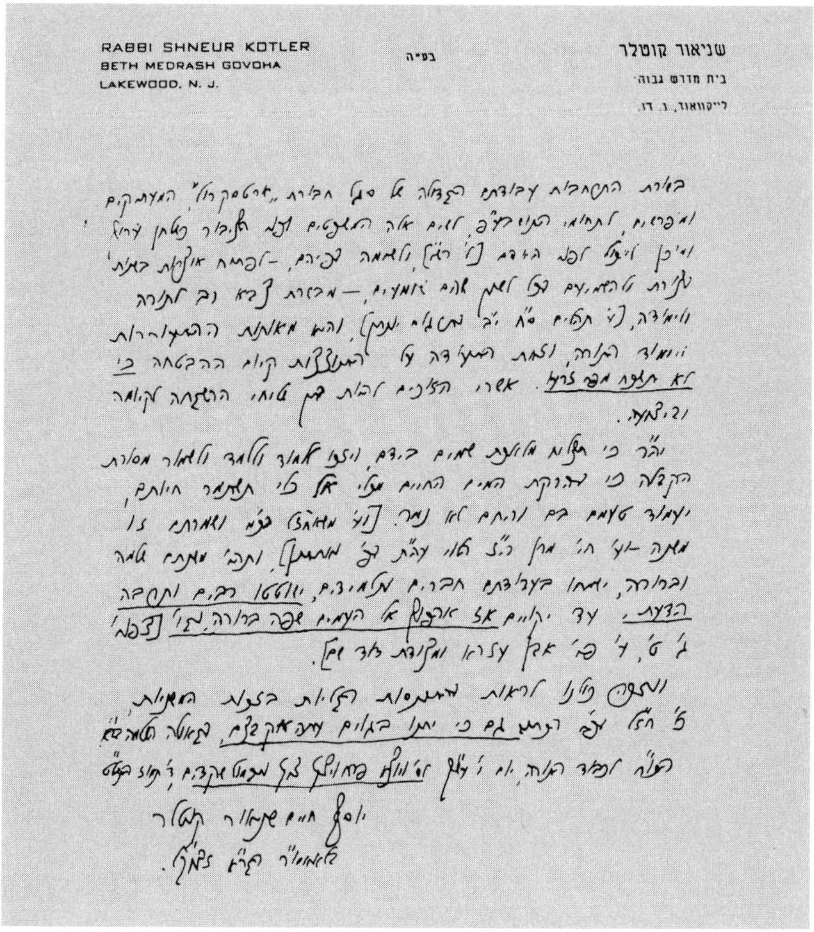

RABBI SHNEUR KOTLER   ב״ה   שניאור קוטלר
BETH MEDRASH GOVOHA
LAKEWOOD, N. J.   בי״ח מדרש גבוה
לייקוואוד, נ. דז.

[handwritten letter text]

בשורת התרחבות עבודתם הגדולה של סגל חבורת ,,ארטסקרול״, המעתיקים ומפרשים, לתחומי
התושבע״פ, לשים אלה המשפטים לפני הציבור כשלחן ערוך ומוכן לאכול לפני האדם [ל׳ רש״י], ולשימה
בפיהם — לפתוח אוצרות בשנות בצורת ולהשמיעם בכל לשון שהם שומעים — מבשרת צבא רב לתורה
ולימודה [ע׳ תהלים ס״ח י״ב בתרגום יונתן], והיא מאותות ההתעוררות ללימוד התורה, וזאת התעודה על
התנוצצות קיום קיום ההבטחה ,,כי לא תשכח מפי זרעו״. אשרי הזוכים להיות בין שלוחי ההשגחה לקיומה
וביצועה.

יה״ר כי תצליח מלאכת שמים בידם, ויזכו ללמוד וללמד ולשמור מסורת הקבלה כי בהרקת המים החיים
מכלי אל כלי תשתמר חיותם, יעמוד טעמם בם וריחם לא נמר. [וע׳ ׳משאחז״ל בכ״מ ושמרתם זו משנה —
וע׳ חי׳ מרן רי״ז הלוי עה״י״ת בפ׳ ואתחנן]. ותהי׳ משנתם שלמה וברורה, ישמחו בעבודתם חברים ותלמידים,
,,ישוטטו רבים ותרבה הדעת״, עד יקויים ,,אז אהפוך אל העמים שפה ברורה וגו׳ ״ [צפני׳ ג׳ ט׳, ע׳ פי׳ אבן
עזרא ומצודת דוד שם].

ונזכה כולנו לראות בהתכנסות הגליות בזכות המשניות, כל׳ חז״ל עפ״י הכתוב ,,גם כי יתנו בגוים עתה
אקבצם״, בגאולה השלמה בב״א.

הכו״ח לכבוד התורה, יום ו׳ עש״ק לס׳ ,,ויוצא פרח ויצץ ציץ ויגמל שקדים״, ד׳ תמוז התשל״ט

יוסף חיים שניאור קוטלר
בלאאמו״ר הגר״א זצוק״ל

מכתב ברכה

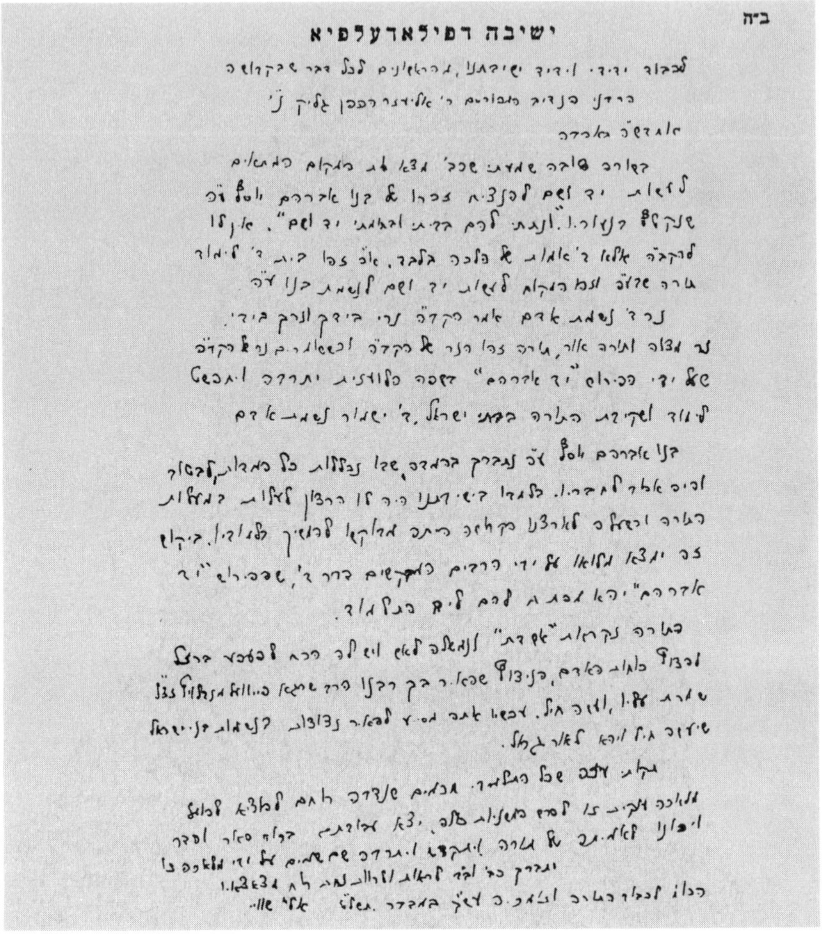

ישיבה דפילאדעלפיא

[handwritten letter in Hebrew script]

ב"ה

לכבוד ידידי וידיד ישיבתנו, מהראשונים לכל דבר שבקדושה
הרבני הנדיב המפורסם ר' אליעזר הכהן גליק נ"י
אחדש"ה באהבה

בשורה טובה שמעתי שכב' מצא את המקום המתאים לעשות יד ושם להנציח זכרו של בנו **אברהם יוסף ע"ה** שנקטף בנעוריו. ,,ונתתי להם בביתי ובחומתי יד ושם''. אין לו להקב"ה אלא ד' אמות של הלכה בלבד. א"כ זהו בית ד' לימוד תורה שבע"פ וזהו המקום לעשות יד ושם לנשמת בנו ע"ה.

נר ד' נשמת אדם אמר הקב"ה נרי בידך ונרך בידי. נר מצוה ותורה אור, תורה זהו הנר של הקב"ה וכשהשומרים נר של הקב"ה שעל ידי הפירוש ,,**יד אברהם**'' בשפה הלועזית יתרבה לימוד ושקידת התורה בבחי ישראל, ד' ישמור נשמת אדם.

בנו אברהם יוסף ע"ה נתברך בהמדה שבו נכללות כל המדות, לב טוב והיה אהוב לחבריו. בלמדו בישיבתנו היה לו הרצון לעלות במעלות התורה וכשעלה לארצנו הקדושה היתה מבוקשו להמשיך בלמודיו. ביקוש זה ימצא מלואו על ידי הרבים המבקשים דבר ד', שהפירוש ,,**יד אברהם**'' יהא מפתח להם לים התלמוד.

התורה נקראת ,,אש דת'', ונמשלה לאש ויש לה הכח לפעול ברול לקצוץ כוחות האדם, הניצוץ שהאיר בך רבנו הרב שרגא פייוועל מנדלוויץ זצ"ל שמרת עליו, ועשה חיל. עכשיו אתה מסייע להאיר נצוצות בנשמות בני ישראל שיעשה חיל ויהא לאור גדול.

תקותי עזה שכל התלמידי חכמים שנדבת רוחם להוציא מפועל מלאכה ענקית זו לפרש המשניות כולה, יצא עבודתם ברוב פאר והדר ויכונו לאמיתה של תורה ויתקדש ויתרבה שם שמים על ידי מלאכה זו.

יתברך כב' וב"ב לראות ולרוות נחת רוח מצאצאיו.

הכו"ח לכבוד התורה ותומכיה עש"ק במדבר תשל"ט

אלי' שוויי

מכתב ברכה

דוד קאהן

ביהמ"ד גבול יעבץ
ברוקלין, נוא יארק

בס"ד כ"ה למטמונים תשל"ט

כבוד רחימא דנפשאי, עושה ומעשה
ר' אלעזר הכהן גליק נטריה רחמנא ופרקיה

שמוע שמעתי שכבר תקעת כפיך לתמוך במפעל האדיר של חברת ארטסקרול — הידוע בכל קצווי תבל
ע"י עבודתה הכבירה בהפצת תורה — לתרגם ולבאר ששה סדרי משנה באנגלית. כוונתך להנציח זכר בנך
הנחמד אברהם יוסף ז"ל שנקטף באבו בזמן שעלה לארץ הקודש בתקופת התרוממות הנפש ושאיפה
לקדושה, ולמטרה זו יכונה הפירוש בשם ,,יד אברהם''; וגם האיר ה' רוחך לגרום עילוי לנשמתו הטהורה
שעי"ז יתרבה לימוד התורה שניתנה בשבעים לשון, על ידי כלי מפואר זה.

מכיון שהנני מכיר היטב שני הצדדים, אוכל לומר לדבק טוב, והנני תקוה שיצליח המפעל הלזה לתת
יד ושם וזכות לנשמת אברהם יוסף ז"ל. חזקה על חברת ארטסקרול שתוציא דבר נאה מתוקן ומתקבל
מתחת ידה להגדיל תורה ולהאדירה.

והנני מברך אותך שתמצא נוחם לנפשך, שהאבא זוכה לברא, ותשבע נחת — אתה עם רעיתך תחיה —
מכל צאצאיכם היקרים אכי"ר

ידידך עז
דוד קאהן

⋟ Publisher's Preface

אָמַר ר׳ יוֹחָנָן, לֹא כָּרַת הקב״ה בְּרִית עִם יִשְׂרָאֵל אֶלָּא עַל תּוֹרָה
שֶׁבְּעַל־פֶּה, שֶׁנֶּאֱמַר ,,כִּי עַל־פִּי הַדְּבָרִים הָאֵלֶּה כָּרַתִּי אִתְּךָ בְּרִית . . .‏״.

R' Yochanan said: The Holy One, Blessed is He, did not seal
a covenant with Israel except because of the Oral Torah, as
it is said (Exodus 34:27): For according to these words have
I sealed a covenant with you . . . (cf. Gittin 60b).

As we present the first Mishnah tractate of תּוֹרָה שֶׁבְּעַל פֶּה, *the Oral Law*,
with the *Yad Avraham* commentary, we once again thank *Hashem
Yisbarach* for having permitted us to bring His Oral Torah — the agency of
His covenant — to His people. It is gratifying that we live in times when there
has been a rebirth of Torah study, not only in the burgeoning number of
yeshivos, but also in homes, synagogues, and offices — and even on buses,
subways, and planes, as the nation of Torah draws closer to the Torah, which
is the heritage and soul of the Jewish people. The Mishnah Series has been an
important component of this upsurge in learning, and we are privileged to
have been its publishers.

Chronologically, this volume is the thirtieth to appear, so that English-
speaking Jewry has been able to evaluate the Series. Its verdict has been a
resounding vote of approval. The crown jewel of the Series is the *Yad Avraham* commentary, compiled and edited by a distinguished group of exceptional *talmidei chachamim* in the United States and Israel. They have blended
the *Gemara*, primary *Rishonim* and *Acharonim*, and Halachic literature to
produce an anthologized commentary that many people, including *gedolei
Yisrael*, have praised as the finest in any language. In fact, many have recom-
mended that it should even be made available in Hebrew.

A look at the Letters of Approbation on the earlier pages evokes feelings
of gratitude and reverent memories. The first four letters are from revered
Torah leaders of the previous generation, our leaders and teachers, the *geonim*
HARAV MOSHE FEINSTEIN, HARAV YAAKOV KAMENETSKY, HARAV MORDECHAI
GIFTER, and HARAV SHNEUR KOTLER זצוק״ל, great men who planted seeds for
the future. They taught and guided us, and their memory inspires us to live up
to their confidence. Their letters testify to their prescience, for they all foresaw
that English would become an important vehicle for the dissemination of
Torah.

HARAV DAVID FEINSTEIN and HARAV SHMUEL KAMENETSKY שליט״א are successors to the mantle of their fathers, in the leadership of *Klal Yisrael* and in the support of our work. Harav Feinstein's encyclopedic knowledge and personal interest are a constant presence in virtually every aspect of our work. Harav Kamenetsky generously provides wise counsel whenever he is called upon. For this we are humbly grateful.

This volume and the entire commentary are sponsored by MR. AND MRS. LOUIS GLICK שיחיו לאי״ט in memory of their son AVRAHAM YOSEF ז״ל. The Glicks are renowned as distinguished supporters of Torah life and education. It is a tribute to their vision that their decision many years ago to support this project has paid enormously rich dividends in the form of learning, knowledge, and almost unprecedented appreciation for the study of Mishnah. When the gaon Maran Harav Yaakov Kamenetsky זצ״ל referred to the ArtScroll Series as the greatest English-language Torah dissemination project in history, this Mishnah Series was one of the factors in his decision. In this sense, Mr. and Mrs. Glick's magnanimity has been truly historic.

As outlined on the dedication page of this volume, Avraham Yosef Glick was an admired and respected young man with a glorious future of service and accomplishment ahead of him. How tragic that he was taken from this life when he was still in his 20's. His parents have kept his name alive with a variety of Torah projects, thus creating memorials that will live on in minds and hearts of this and future generations. This Mishnah Series, with the Yad Avraham commentary, will be the standard in the English-speaking world for decades and generations, and as infinite hours of Torah study flow from it, so will infinite merit for the soul of the young man whose name it carries.

The author of the commentary in this volume is RABBI MORDECHAI RABINOVITCH, an outstanding *talmid chacham* whose name is familiar to students of the Yad Avraham Mishnah and Schottenstein Talmud. Since settling in Israel many years ago, he has become an expert in מִצְוֹת הַתְּלוּיוֹת בָּאָרֶץ, or the agricultural laws of the Land. Thanks to the sponsorship of Mr. and Mrs. Glick, he has written commentaries to most of *Seder Zera'im*, and his writings will appear in forthcoming volumes of the Mishnah Series. We are grateful to him and are proud to be publishing his work.

Regretfully, there were a few years when continuation of the Series was temporarily interrupted. Publication was resumed thanks to the interest and generosity of MR. AND MRS. LESLIE WESTREICH and MR. AND MRS. MOSHE BEINHORN, who dedicated Tractates *Oholos* and *Nega'im*. We are deeply grateful for their friendship and efforts.

HARAV DAVID COHEN שליט״א, in addition to his stature as a major teacher and decisor of Torah law, has been a treasured friend and repository of Torah wisdom from the very first day of the existence of the ArtScroll Series. Another esteemed friend is JUDAH SEPTIMUS, who has unstintingly given of himself and his expertise in too many ways to mention. That the Mishnah Series is now firmly on the way to completion is in great measure thanks to them. We express not only our own gratitude, but that of everyone who will benefit from this great contribution to Torah study.

Many outstanding *talmidei chachamim* took part in editing and preparing this book for publication; we are grateful to them all. RABBI REUVEIN DOWEK was the primary editor of this volume, assisted by RABBI YITZCHOK STAVSKY and RABBI GIDONE LANE. The manuscript was read by RABBI EPHRAIM ZURAVIN and RABBI PESACH GOLDMAN, whose insightful comments were incorporated into this work. The final draft was reviewed in its entirety by RABBI CHAIM MALINOWITZ. Others who assisted were RABBI ELI COHEN, and RABBI MOSHE ROSENBLUM. The editorial process was overseen by RABBI YEHEZKEL DANZIGER. Together with Rabbi Rabinovitch, they are opening the doors of *Seder Zera'im* to countless thousands of our brethren around the world.

The graphics genius of our dear friend and colleague REB SHEAH BRANDER has long since left its stamp on the field of Torah publishing. Every new work in the various ArtScroll Series is another testimonial to his fulfillment of the injunction of Rabbi Akiva Eiger that published works of Torah should be beautiful in their production as well as their content.

MOSHE DEUTCH and YAAKOV HERSH HOROWITZ helped prepare the text of the *Rav* and the pages for print.

CHUMIE ZAIDMAN was primarily responsible for the pagination of the book. Her dedication and skill are much appreciated. RUCHY REINHOLD, CHAYA SURI WOLCOWITZ, and LIBBY ZWEIG did the typing and corrections. MRS. MYRNA STERN and MRS. FAYGIE WEINBAUM proofread with skill and dedication.

We express our appreciation to our esteemed colleague SHMUEL BLITZ, who continues to coordinate the activities of our authors and editors in Israel with dedication and distinction. On this side of the ocean, AVROHOM BIDERMAN does the same, as he shepherds works from manuscripts from computer to print.

As we look back and ahead, we are grateful to *Hashem Yisbarach* for allowing us to be the quill that records His word and we look forward to continuing this sacred task for the benefit of *Klal Yisrael* and the glory of the Torah.

Rabbi Meir Zlotowitz/Rabbi Nosson Scherman

Elul 5761 / September 2001

❧ An Introduction to Mishnah

⊷ The Oral Law and the Mishnah

The Torah consists of two parts, תּוֹרָה שֶׁבִּכְתָב, *the Written Torah*, and תּוֹרָה שֶׁבְּעַל פֶּה, *the Oral Torah*. It is clear from even a superficial reading of the *Chumash* that there had to be "another" Torah, one that complements and explains the Written Torah that was transmitted by Moses. The Oral Torah, too, was given to Moses by God, and was passed down, generation to generation, from Moses to his successors through the ages.

The Oral Torah was to remain just that — oral. It was to be transmitted from teacher to student down through the generations. As *Mabit* explains in *Kiryas Sefer* (Introduction to *Yad HaChazakah*), this oral transmission included more than words and formulas; the teacher-student relationship included also an outpouring of soul. Just as the printed page cannot transmit inflection, nuance, smile and frown, so too it cannot adequately transmit the personality and inner spirit of the teacher.

Oppression and exile eventually eroded the oral process and necessitated that more and more of it be committed to writing. The first instance of this new phenomenon was the Mishnah. The rest of the infinite library of Torah literature flowed from that.

In the following pages we present an outline of the history of the Oral Law and some of its leading teachers and personalities, as it developed into the Mishnah and Gemara. It is taken from *"Mevo She'arim"** by HARAV HAGAON R' MEIR ZVI BERGMAN שליט"א, Rosh HaYeshivah of Yeshivas HaRashbi of Bnai Brak, and supplemented by selections from *"Z'man Nakat,"* by HARAV HAGAON R' DAVID COHEN שליט"א, the distinguished *rav* and *posek* of Brooklyn, N.Y. It is our hope that this will provide the reader with basic background and perspective as he begins the study of the Mishnah.

---

* Translated into English by Rabbi Nesanel Kasnett and published under the title "Gateway to the Talmud" by ArtScroll/Mesorah Publications, Ltd., 1985.

I. The Chain of Transmission

מֹשֶׁה קִבֵּל תּוֹרָה מִסִּינַי, וּמְסָרָהּ לִיהוֹשֻׁעַ, וִיהוֹשֻׁעַ לִזְקֵנִים,
וּזְקֵנִים לִנְבִיאִים, וּנְבִיאִים מְסָרוּהָ לְאַנְשֵׁי כְנֶסֶת הַגְּדוֹלָה.

*Moses received the Torah from Sinai and trans-
mitted it to Joshua, and Joshua to the Elders, and the
Elders to the Prophets, and the Prophets transmitted
it to the Men of the Great Assembly (Avos 1:1).*

A. From Moses Through the Prophets

MOSES RECEIVED THE TORAH FROM SINAI, WHICH MEANS HE RECEIVED
both the Written Law [תּוֹרָה שֶׁבִּכְתָב] and the Oral Law [תּוֹרָה שֶׁבְּעַל פֶּה],
Moses as *Sifra* comments on the verse אֵלֶּה הַחֻקִּים וְהַמִּשְׁפָּטִים
... וְהַתּוֹרֹת, *These are the statutes, judgments and teachings
that Hashem established between Himself and the Children of Israel on
Mount Sinai by the hand of Moses (Leviticus 26:46):* חֻקִּים, *statutes,*
refers to those laws which are not clearly stated in Scripture, but are
derived through the laws of hermeneutics; מִשְׁפָּטִים, *judgments,* refers to
the explicitly stated laws; and the plural term תּוֹרֹת, *teachings,* indicates
that the Jews received two Torahs — one written and one oral.[1] The
continuation of the verse, *on Mount Sinai by the hand of Moses,* teaches
us that the entire Torah — including all its laws, nuances and
interpretations — was given to Moses on Sinai.

The *Gemara (Berachos* 5a) expounds the verse, *And I shall give you
the Tablets of Stone, and the Law, and the Commandment which I have
written, to teach them (Exodus 24:12),* as follows: *Tablets* refers to the
Ten Commandments; *the Law* means the Pentateuch (see *Rashi* ad loc.);
Commandment is the *Mishnah;*[2] *which I have written* denotes the
Prophets and Hagiographa [כְּתוּבִים]; and *to teach them* means the

---

1. As will be evident from the verses adduced below, the term *Oral Law* includes all
teachings of the Torah that are not stated explicitly in Scripture.

2. The Talmud consists of two sections: the Mishnah, which is the collection of laws
compiled by R' Yehudah HaNasi; and the *Gemara,* which explains the Mishnah (see
Section II).

Gemara.[3] The verse teaches us that every facet of Torah was given to Moses on Mount Sinai.

The *Gemara (Megillah* 19b) further states that the verse, *And on them was written according to all the words which Hashem spoke with you on the Mount (Deuteronomy* 9:10), teaches us that God showed Moses fine points of Biblical exegesis,[4] in addition to the latter Sages' interpretations of the teachings of their predecessors.

This verse also teaches that Scripture, Mishnah, Talmud and Aggadah — even those points that an accomplished student would later expound before his teacher — all were previously told to Moses at Sinai (*Yerushalmi* to *Pe'ah* 2:4). Even the ethical teachings in Tractate *Avos* were revealed to Moses at Sinai (*Rav* to *Avos* 1:1).

Many commandments in the Written Torah are incomprehensible without the explicit elucidation provided by the Oral Law. For example, regarding *tefillin* it is stated: *and as* טֹטָפֹת, *ornaments, between your eyes* (*Deut.* 6:8). Without the oral traditions stemming directly from Moses, we would not understand Scripture's intention at all.

In addition, we find that the Torah openly hints at the existence of a parallel body of law, as in the verse וְזָבַחְתָּ מִבְּקָרְךָ, *and you may sacrifice from your herd . . .* כַּאֲשֶׁר צִוִּיתִךָ, *as I have commanded you* (*Deut.* 12:21) [i.e. *in the manner* I have commanded you]. Although the commandment of *shechitah* (ritual sacrifice) is explicitly mentioned in the Written Law, the halachic particulars of its execution are not. The phrase, *as I have commanded you,* obviously suggests the existence of a tradition of comprehensive Oral Law (see *Chullin* 28a; *Rashi* ad loc.).

The commandments which were given to our forefathers before the Giving of the Torah, were reiterated to Moses at Sinai. Indeed, as *Rambam* (*Commentary to Chullin* 7:6) states, all that we abstain from or do today is only because of God's commandment through Moses, and not because the Holy One revealed His will to prophets who lived before Moses. That we do not eat flesh from a living animal is not because God prohibited it to Noah (see *Gen.* 9:4), but because Moses taught us at Sinai that God proscribed this practice. Likewise, we do not circumcise our sons because Abraham circumcised himself and the males in his household (ibid. 17:11), but because God commanded us through Moses to perform the precept of circumcision, just as Abraham did. The same

---

3. The *Gemara* contains the analysis of the mishnayos from which the Halachah is derived (*Rashi* ad loc.).

4. For example, the rule that the terms אֶת (a preposition without parallel in English) and גַּם, *also,* indicate that something else is to be included; and that the terms אַךְ and רַק (both meaning *but* or *only*) indicate that something is excluded (*Rashi* ibid.).

holds true for the prohibition of eating the גִּיד הַנָּשֶׁה (a sinew located in the thigh), which was originally issued to Jacob (ibid. 32:33); yet we are enjoined through Moses's commandment. For, indeed, 613 *mitzvos* were told to Moses at Sinai, and those enumerated above are certainly included in that figure.

The *Gemara* states in *Makkos* 23b: A total of 613 commandments were told to Moses — 365 prohibitions, equaling the number of days in the solar year [which intimates that on each day of the year they warn us not to transgress them (*Rashi*)], and 248 positive commandments, paralleling the number of limbs and organs in the body [hinting that each of a Jew's limbs and organs tell him to perform the commandments (*Rashi*)]. The word תּוֹרָה, *Torah*, in the verse, *The Torah which Moses commanded us* (*Deut.* 33:4), has a numerical value of 611.[5] Add to this number the first two of the Ten Commandments, which the Jews heard directly from the Almighty Himself, and the figure 613 is reached (*Makkos* 23b, 24a).

Tosefos Yom Tov writes in his introduction: Even though Moses transmitted the Oral Law to Joshua clearly and thoroughly, nevertheless, in every subsequent generation, novel interpretations are expounded. This statement does not contradict the *Gemara* in *Megillah* (cited above), which states that the Holy One showed Moses even Biblical interpretations that scholars of later generations would make, inasmuch as Moses never taught these interpretations to anyone else. This solution is apparent from the *Gemara's* wording, which tells us that God *showed* these to Moses, rather than *taught* or *transmitted* them to him. In either of the latter cases Moses would have certainly taught these future interpretations to Joshua, since Moses was extremely generous toward his disciple; for when he was commanded to rest one hand on Joshua in transferring his mantle of Torah greatness to him, Moses in fact rested both (see *Deut.* 34:9). Thus, the *Gemara* tells us that God only *showed* Moses, but He did not give him these interpretations as a legacy for Joshua.

Accordingly, every scholar who merits to conceive a true and original interpretation in the Torah is regarded as though he brought down a part of Torah from the heavens.[6]

---

5. [According to *gematria*, the system of numerology in which each letter of the Hebrew alphabet is assigned a numerical value, ת=400; ו=6; ר=200; ה=5; thus the word תּוֹרָה equals 611.]

6. This explanation will resolve the difficulty posed by *Rambam* in *Sefer HaMitzvos* (*Shoresh* 1): in one place (*Megillah* 19b) the *Gemara* says that God showed the precept of reading the *Megillah* to *Moses*, while in another place (*Shevuos* 39a) it refers to the

Nevertheless, every detail and original thought was included in the Torah that Moses brought down from heaven, as we are taught regarding the verse לֹא בַשָּׁמַיִם הוּא, *It [the Torah] is not in the heavens* (*Deut.* 30:12). "Moses said to Israel, 'Do not say that another Moses will bring us another Torah from heaven, for I am informing you: *It is not in the heavens* — that is, nothing of Torah has been left behind in the heavens!'" (*Midrash Rabbah* ibid.).

In the introduction to his *Commentary on Mishnah, Rambam* explains further that prophecy cannot the Torah or be used to extract the details of the *mitzvos* with the thirteen hermeneutical principles with which the Torah is expounded. Rather, what the prophets like Joshua and Pinchas must do in the matter of analysis and logic is precisely what the Talmudic sages Ravina and R' Ashi do (i.e. interpret the Torah without the benefit of prophecy).

Moses in his lifetime already began to promulgate decrees and regulations (*Shabbos* 30a). He did so not in his capacity as a prophet, but on his own initiative, in order to safeguard the Torah, as it says וּשְׁמַרְתֶּם אֶת מִשְׁמַרְתִּי, *And you shall keep that which I have entrusted you to guard* (*Lev.* 18:30), which the Sages interpret as an admonition to take measures to protect the Torah's precepts from being violated (*Yevamos* 21a). Among his decrees that are known to us: to remove and distance the Nesinites[7] from the main body of the Jewish people (ibid. 79a), and

---

Megillah reading as one of the commandments to be promulgated in the future, after the giving of the Torah.

See also *Ohr HaChayim* to *Leviticus* 13:37, who seeks to reconcile the contradictory statements of the *Gemara*, which in one place (*Megillah* ibid.) says that Moses was given the knowledge of the entire Torah, including even the interpretations of future sages, while elsewhere (*Menachos* 29b) it states that Rabbi Akiva expounded that which was unknown to Moses. He proposes the following resolution:

It is true that all Torah knowledge was bestowed upon Moses and that no other sage can know more than he, and that there will be no original Torah thought from the time of the giving of the Torah until the Messianic age that Moses did not know. Nevertheless, there is one qualification. God taught Moses both the Written and Oral Law, and with His infinite wisdom implanted the Oral Law within the Written Law. Although Moses knew the entire Oral Law, he was not informed of where each of its details was alluded to in the Written Torah. Thus, it became the task of great future sages to pinpoint the sources of these laws in Scripture, giving rise to the books *Toras Kohanim, Sifrei,* etc. Therefore, when the *Gemara* relates that R' Akiva discovered interpretations unknown to Moses, it does not mean to imply that Moses lacked such knowledge, since all Torah came from him. Rather, it means that he did not know the source in Scripture for every law of the Oral Torah.

7. [The Nesinites were Canaanites who, to avoid destruction at the hands of the invading Jewish army, presented themselves to the leaders of Israel as a non-Canaanite people seeking a covenant with Israel. Two groups came; one in the days of Moses (*Tanchuma, Netzavim* 3 cited by *Rashi, Deut.* 29:10), and one in the days of Joshua (*Joshua* Ch. 9). For deceiving Moses, they were made into hewers of wood and drawers of water for the

not to sprinkle the מֵי חַטָאת, *water of purification*, on the Sabbath (*Smag, Asei* 224; see *Pnei Yehoshua* to *Rosh Hashanah* 29b).

Included among Moses's regulations are: (1) the seven days of nuptial festivities [during which the *sheva berachos* (seven blessings) are recited] and the seven days of mourning (*Yerushalmi* to *Kesubos* 1:1; *Rambam, Hilchos Avel* 1:1); (2) the first blessing in *Bircas HaMazon* [Grace After Meals] (*Berachos* 48b); (3) the public reading of the Torah on the Sabbath, Monday and Thursday (*Bava Kamma* 82a); (4) the study of the laws of each festival during that festival (*Megillah* 32a); (5) the division of the *Kohanim* (priests) into eight ministering groups (*Taanis* 27a).[8]

... AND TRANSMITTED IT TO JOSHUA, AS IT IS WRITTEN, AND YOU SHALL put some of your glory upon him (*Numbers* 27:20). Our Sages teach us

Joshua (*Temurah* 16a) that when Moses was about to depart (from this world to Paradise), he said to Joshua, "Ask me (to explain) all the uncertainties you have (in matter of halachah)." He replied, "My teacher, have I ever left you — even for an hour? [I.e. "I have no uncertainties" (*Rabbeinu Gershom* ad loc.).] Did you not write of me, *but his attendant, Joshua, the son of Nun, a lad, never left the tent* (*Ex.* 33:11)?"

Joshua instituted: (1) the second blessing of *Bircas HaMazon* (*Berachos* 48b); (2) the prayer *Aleinu Leshabei'ach*, when the Jews entered *Eretz Yisrael*, to distinguish them from the *families of the earth* and the *nations of the world;*[9] (3) ten enactments when the Land was divided amongst the Tribes.[10]

---

congregation and the Altar (see *Rashi* ibid.). This decree was later reinforced by Joshua (*Josh.* 9:27), who forbade their descendants to intermarry with Jews (see Mishnah *Kiddushin*, p. 86).]

8. *Rambam* (*Sefer HaMitzvos, mitzvas asei* 36) explains that although the concept of separate groups of ministering *Kohanim* is Biblical in origin, it was Moses who divided them into eight groups.

9. *Teshuvos HaGeonim, Shaarei Teshuvah* §44 by *Rav Hai Gaon. Kol Bo* §16 writes that Joshua composed it when the Jews conquered Jericho.

10. Both the *Gemara* (*Eruvin* 17a) and *Rambam* (*Hil. Nizkei Mamon* 5:3) refer to them as תַּקָנוֹת, *enactments*. They are as follows:

(a) that people shall be permitted to graze their cattle in the woods of other people. [See *Rashi* and *Radak* to *II Samuel* 18:6 on the phrase, *in the forest of Ephraim;* although the territory on the east bank of the Jordan River was granted only to the tribes of Reuven, Gad and Menashe (*Num.* 32:32ff.), since Joshua stipulated that one may graze his cattle in the property of others, and since that forest bordered Ephraim's territory, with the Jordan River intervening, the cattle of Ephraim used to graze there and for that reason it was called *the forest of Ephraim*]; (b-c) that wood and grass may be gathered by all in private fields; (d) that shoots may be cut off by all in all places, even private ones; (e) that a new spring may be used by all the townspeople; (f) that fishing with an angle be permitted in

... AND JOSHUA TO THE ELDERS, AS IT SAYS (JUDGES 2:7), AND THE PEOPLE served Hashem all the days of Joshua, and all the days of the Elders,

The Elders *who lived long after Joshua, who saw the great deeds of Hashem (Avos d'Rabbi Nassan).* Rashi (ibid.) comments that the Elders were the rulers and policemen over the Jewish people. There is a dispute in the *Midrash (Bamidbar Rabbah* 3:7) regarding who these Elders were. R' Yehudah Halevi says that they they were the Levites. R' Berachyah maintains that they were Eldad and Meidad; also included among the Elders were Calev, Pinchas and Osniel the son of Kenaz.

The *Gemara (Temurah* 16a) tells us that 1,700 קַל וָחוֹמֶר, *a fortiori arguments;* גְּזֵירוֹת שָׁווֹת, *language similarities;* and דִּקְדּוּקֵי סוֹפְרִים, *Rabbinic interpretations,* were forgotten during the mourning period for Moses, and Osniel the son of Kenaz retrieved them with his learning.[11] He and his colleagues began to collect and organize the laws scattered about the Torah into one cohesive teaching. *Yerushalmi (Shekalim* 5:1) tells us that they were called families of *sofrim,* because they made numbered groups (from the word סָפַר, *sofer* [*to count*]) of the regulations of the Torah — such as: *Five should not separate* [*terumah*] (*Terumos* 1:1); *five species are subject to challah* (*Challah* 1:1); *fifteen women exempt their co-wives* (*Yevamos* 1:1); *there are thirty-six offenses in the Torah whose penalty is* kares [excision; premature death] (*Kereisos* 1:1).

Not always were the particulars of each category located in the same place; often they had to be culled from throughout the Torah. For example, the five who should *not separate terumah* are: (1) a deaf-mute; (2) an insane person; (3) a minor; (4) anyone other than the owner of the produce or his agent; and (5) a gentile. The fourth category is excluded by the verse, *Thus you shall also separate* (*Num.* 18:28), while the other four are exempted by a passage in the Scriptural portion of *Terumah* [*Exodus* Ch. 25] (*Yerushalmi* to *Terumos* 1:1). Because in this case as well

---

the Sea of Tiberias (although it was entirely in the portion of the tribe of Naphtali); (g) that it be permitted to defecate behind a fence (even on private property); (h) that the public may use private paths at certain times; (i) that one who becomes lost in a (private) vineyard may cut his way through, and exit; and (j) that a corpse of a person whose relatives are unknown acquires the right to be buried on the spot where it is found.

These ten regulations are all explained in *Bava Kamma* (80b-82a).

11. The commentators explain that although Joshua was the principal disciple of Moses, he did not restore the forgotten laws himself, but relied on Osniel, because Joshua did not wish to give the mistaken impression that he was transmitting laws as a prophet of God, just as his teacher, Moses, had. [See *Asarah Maamaros,* who states that, for similar reasons, emergency decrees that were permitted for other prophets were forbidden to Joshua.]

as the others they gathered this information from all over the Torah, Solomon called the Sages בַּעֲלֵי אֲסֻפּוֹת, "gatherers" [*Ecclesiastes* 12:11] (see *Netziv* in *Kidmas Ha'emek*).

The Judges were also considered Elders (*Rashi* to *Avos* 1:1; *Meiri* ibid., and in his Introduction to *Avos*). However, some authorities (*Vilna Gaon;* old version of *Avos d'Rabbi Nassan*, Ch. 1) list the order of the Torah's transmission as follows: *Joshua to the Elders, the Elder to the Judges, and the Judges to the Prophets.*

Boaz was a judge. He and his court declared that one should use the Name of God in greeting a fellow Jew (*Ruth* 2:4). We do this when we say *Shalom*, which is one of His Names (*Berachos* 54a, *Makkos* 23b, *Rashi* ad loc.). The Elders and early Prophets instituted the *Kedushah* of *Uva LeTzion* in the morning prayer service (*Tur, Orach Chaim* 132).

... AND THE ELDERS TO THE PROPHETS. ELI THE *KOHEN*, LAST OF THE Judges, transmitted the Torah to Samuel, first of the Prophets.

The Prophets Samuel instituted sixteen groups of ministering Kohanim (*Taanis* 27a).[12] He promulgated the law that a non-*Kohen* may slaughter a sacrificial animal, adducing proofs from Scripture (*Berachos* 31b).[13] From Samuel's court came the tradition that only males from Moab and Ammon are unfit to enter (i.e. marry into) the Congregation of Israel, but that females from these nations may marry into it (*Yevamos* 77a). However, *Rambam* (*Hil. Issurei Biah* 12:18) writes that this is a הֲלָכָה לְמֹשֶׁה מִסִּינַי, *a tradition that Moses received at Sinai.*

The Prophets transmitted the Torah one to another: Samuel gave it to King David.[14] David innovated: (1) twenty-four ministering groups of *Kohanim* (*Taanis* loc. cit.); (2) saying, עַל יִשְׂרָאֵל עַמֶּךְ, וְעַל יְרוּשָׁלַיִם עִירֶךְ, *on Israel, Your people; and on Jerusalem, Your city,* in the third blessing of *Bircas HaMazon* (*Berachos* 48b); (3) the obligation to say one hundred blessings each day (*Tur, Orach Chaim* 45).

He decreed that the prohibition of *yichud* [seclusion of a man with a woman forbidden to him] apply even with an unmarried woman [whom he would be permitted to marry] (*Avodah Zarah* 36b).

The Prophets instituted that *Hallel* be recited when the Jews are rescued from danger (*Pesachim* 117a).

---

12. Rather than the eight previously instituted by Moses (see above, note 8).

13. It is possible that this was one of the laws that was forgotten during the mourning period for Moses; see *Temurah* 16a.

14. See *Midrash Shmuel* 22: Rav Huna, quoting R' Yose, says that on the very night David fled from Saul, he learned from Samuel more than an accomplished student can learn in a hundred years.

David transferred the tradition to Achiyah the Shilonite, in whose days King Solomon's court was functioning (*Makkos* 23b).

Solomon instituted: *eruvin*;[15] the practice of washing the hands (*Eruvin* 21b); saying עַל הַבַּיִת הַגָּדוֹל וְהַקָּדוֹשׁ, *on the great and holy house*, in the third blessing of *Bircas HaMazon* (*Berachos* 48b). He permitted the use of paths that crossed privately owned fields if no produce was growing on them (*Bava Kamma* 81b; *Rambam, Hil. Nizkei Mamon* 5:4); forbade marriage to certain relatives who are otherwise permissible according to the Torah (*Yevamos* 21a); and instituted that the *Bircas Kohanim* (the priestly blessing) be said during the prayers. He also erected two gates in the Temple, one for bridegrooms and the other for mourners (*Pirkei d'Rabbi Eliezer* 17; *Rosh, Moed Katan* §93). Solomon's teacher was Shimi the son of Gera (*Berachos* 8a).

Achiyah the Shilonite transmitted the tradition to Elijah the Prophet,[16] who lived in the era of King Jehoshaphat's court. They forbade a *tevul yom* [a ritually contaminated person who has immersed

<hr />

15. [That is *eruvei chatzeiros* (*Rashi*) — the Rabbinic prohibition to carry on the Sabbath from the private domain of one person to the private domain of another, and the halachic method by which it becomes permitted to do so (see General Introduction to Tractate *Eruvin*).]

16. This follows *Rambam's* view that Pinchas was not later known as Elijah (see *Bava Basra* 121b, *Rashi* ad loc.). However, there is an opinion to the contrary amongst the Sages. In *Malachi* 2:4ff. it is written, *And you shall know ... My covenant of life and peace was with him ... the Law of Truth was in his mouth and iniquity was never found on his lips. He walked with Me in peace and righteousness, and he removed many from sin. For the lips of the Kohen will guard the knowledge, and they will seek Torah from his mouth, for he is an angel of HASHEM, the Lord of Hosts.* R' Velvel of Brisk explained these verses according to the opinion that Pinchas was Elijah, as follows: The transmission of the Torah will always be from sage to sage. Even if there is a hiatus of several generations, it will nevertheless be retransmitted by Elijah, who himself received the Torah for his generation. Thus, *My covenant of life and peace was with him* refers to Pinchas, who received a covenant of peace from God. And: *for the lips of the* Kohen *will guard the knowledge*, inasmuch as Pinchas (who was a *Kohen*) will preserve the Torah and the tradition for the Jewish nation; and *they will seek Torah from his mouth*, since from him the Torah will be sought and restored to the Jewish people.

R' Velvel's father, R' Chaim of Brisk, explains why Pinchas deserved to be the one who safeguards the Torah and tradition throughout the generations and restores it to the Jews. During the incident of Zimri (*Num.* Ch. 25), the appropriate halachah was forgotten, and only Pinchas could recall it. He told Moses, "I learned from you that if a Jew has relations with an Aramean, zealots may kill him" (see *Rashi*, ibid. v. 7). Moses replied that the one who remembers the law should be the one to carry it out. Therefore, just as Pinchas restored the halachah at that time, it is appropriate that he can be the one to restore the law to the Jewish people at the End of Days. Thus, in clear reference to Pinchas, Malachi states, *The law of truth was on his lips* (i.e. Pinchas had immediate recall of the appropriate halachah), and *he removed many from sin* (in that he prevented others from following Zimri's example). Therefore, *the lips of the priest will guard the knowledge and they will seek Torah from him mouth* in the Messianic era as well.

himself in a *mikveh* (ritual pool), but who must await for sunset for his complete purification] to enter the camp of the Levites (*Yevamos* 7b).

Elijah further transmitted the tradition to Elisha, and Elisha to Yehoyada the *Kohen* [he was *Kohen Gadol* (High Priest)]. One of his teachings is found in the Mishnah (*Shekalim* 6:50). Yehoyada gave it over to Zechariah, his son;[17] Zechariah to Hoshea; Hoshea to Amos; and Amos to Isaiah (Yeshaya).[18] Hezekiah (Chizkiyah) and his court functioned during Isaiah's life, and they issued decrees regarding the ritual impurity of idols (*Sanhedrin* 12a; *Rashi, Tos.* ad loc.) and the tithing of vegetables (see *Nedarim* 55a and *Rashi* to *Makkos* 23b). When the Assyrian king Sennacherib besieged Jerusalem [*II Kings* 18:17-19:35], Hezekiah composed the prayer ה׳ אֱלֹהֵי יִשְׂרָאֵל, שׁוּב מֵחֲרוֹן אַפֶּךָ, *Hashem, God of Israel, turn back from Your flaring anger*, which we say every Monday and Thursday as part of *Tachanun* (R' Yaakov of Lisa in *Siddur Derech Chaim*).

Isaiah then transmitted it to Michah; Michah to Joel; Joel to Nahum; Nahum to Habakkuk; Habakkuk to Zephaniah; Zephaniah to Jeremiah (Yirmiyah); Jeremiah to Baruch ben Neriah[19] (*Rambam, Introduction to Yad Hachazakah*); until Haggai, Zechariah and Malachi, who were the last of the Prophets and the first of the Men of the Great Assembly, as is stated: ... *and the Prophets transmitted it to the Men of the Great Assembly* (*Avos* 1:1).

B. The Men of the Great Assembly

THE אַנְשֵׁי כְנֶסֶת הַגְּדוֹלָה, *MEN OF THE GREAT ASSEMBLY*, CONSISTED OF 120 sages, among them Haggai, Zechariah, Malachi,[20] Seraiah, Re'elaiah, Mordechai Bilshan (the Mordechai in the Book of *Esther*), Ezra, Nehemiah ben Chachalyah, Daniel, Chananyah, Mishael and Azariah. They were referred to as Ezra and his court (*Rambam, Introduction to Yad HaChazakah*), since he was the chief judge. They were also called Ezra's groups (*Tanna D'Vei Eliyahu Rabbah* 6).

---

17. He was assassinated. *Pesichta D'Eichah Rabbasi* 23 states that he was the *Av Beis Din* (head of the Court) of his time.

18. His grandson Menashe killed him (*Yevamos* 49b).

19. See below, Section II, that Baruch ben Neriah's disciple was Ezra, who was among the Men of the Great Assembly.

20. There is a dispute in the *Gemara* (*Megillah* 15a) regarding the identity of Malachi. Some contend that he was actually Mordechai; others, that he was Ezra. A third opinion maintains that Malachi was his only name. The *Gemara* concludes that in all probability he was Ezra; *Rambam*, however, follows the third opinion.

Ezra was worthy that the Torah be given to the Jewish nation through him if Moses had not preceded him (*Sanhedrin* 21b). He was the disciple of Baruch ben Neriah (*Megillah* 16b).

They were called the Men of the Great Assembly because they "restored the crown to its rightful place." This refers to the fact that Moses had proclaimed הָאֵל הַגָּדוֹל, הַגִּבּוֹר, וְהַנּוֹרָא, *the great, mighty and awesome God* (*Deut.* 10:17); subsequently, Jeremiah deemed it appropriate to delete the word וְהַנּוֹרָא, *and awesome*, and Daniel deleted הַגִּבּוֹר, *mighty*; the Men of the Great Assembly then reinstated the two terms (*Yoma* 69b).

They also composed blessings, prayers, *kedushos* and *havdalos* (*Berachos* 33a). Under the leadership of Mordechai and Esther they instituted the festival of Purim. In addition, they wrote the Books of *Ezekiel*, the *Twelve Prophets*, *Daniel* and *Esther* (*Bava Basra* 15). Yonasan ben Uziel's Aramaic translation of the *Prophets* originally came from Haggai, Zechariah and Malachi (*Megillah* 3a).[21] The latter were also the source of many halachic decisions in the *Gemara*, transmitted through the generations (see *Chullin* 137b, *Nazir* 53a, *Rosh Hashanah* 19b, *Yevamos* 16a, *Kiddushin* 43a).

We have a tradition from the Men of the Great Assembly that whenever it states in Scripture, . . . וַיְהִי בִּימֵי, *And it happened in the days of* . . ., the intent is to introduce an episode of tribulation (*Megillah* 10b).

The last of this group was Shimon the *Tzaddik* [righteous] (*Rambam* loc. cit.), as the mishnah states, *Shimon the Tzaddik was among the survivors of the Great Assembly* (*Avos* 1:2). Others, however, interpret the mishnah to mean only that Shimon did not live during the first years of the Second Temple in the days of Ezra (*Rashi* ad loc.).

They said three things [i.e. fundamental teachings]: (1) Be deliberate in judgment; (2) raise many disciples; (3) make a protective fence around the Torah (*Avos* 1:1).

Ezra promulgated ten decrees (*Bava Kamma* 82a).[22] Some opine that

---

21. See *Maharsha* (ibid.), who writes that Yonasan ben Uziel was the greatest student of Hillel, who lived a hundred years before the destruction of the Second Temple. Therefore, Yonasan certainly never saw Haggai, Zechariah and Malachi, who lived during the first years of the Second Temple. Rather, the *Gemara* means that Yonasan received the translation from a tradition originating with the earlier Prophets. See also *Meiri*, Introduction to *Avos*, who explains this similarly.

22. They are: (a) to read the Torah during the *Minchah* service on the Sabbath; (b) three men should be called to read three verses of the Torah every Monday and every Thursday; (c) permanent courts of law should convene in every city each Monday and Thursday; (d) clothes should be washed on Thursday in honor of the Sabbath; (e) garlic should be eaten on Friday; (f) on the day a woman is to bake bread, she should rise and

every anonymous regulation in the *Gemara* was enacted by him.

The custom of striking the *aravos* (willow branches) on *Hoshanah Rabbah*, the seventh day of Succos, derives from the prophets Haggai, Zechariah and Malachi (*Succah* 44a).

Among the decrees promulgated by members of the Great Assembly were: Daniel decreed that no Jew may consume gentile oil or wine (*Avodah Zarah* 36a) [oil was subsequently permitted by later sages (ibid.)]; Nehemiah prohibited moving certain types of objects on the Sabbath (*Shabbos* 123b), but this decree applied only to his generation (*Tosafos* to *Bava Kamma* 24b). Haggai, Zechariah, Malachi, Zerubabel and Yehoshua the High Priest forbade Jews from eating Cuthean bread (*Midrash Tanchuma* to *Vayeishev*). Ezra penalized the Levites by declaring that tithes should no longer be given to them (*Yevamos* 86b).

[The decree regarding the impurity of liquids was enacted prior to the era of Haggai and the Great Assembly (*Pesachim* 17a, *Rashi* ad loc.).]

They practiced what they preached. Just as they taught, *Make a protective fence for the Torah*, they were the first to do so.

The very first mishnah in the Talmud (*Berachos* 1:1) speaks about a protective fence for the Torah — the obligation to recite the evening *Shema* prayer before midnight. Thus, the *Mechilta* (*Bo* 6:8) states: Why did the Sages set midnight as the deadline? In order to remove a person from sin, to make a fence around the Torah, and to fulfill the words of the Men of the Great Assembly, who said, *Be deliberate in judgment, raise many disciples, and make a fence for the Torah.*

ANTIGONUS OF SOCHO AND HIS COURT RECEIVED THE TRADITION from them (*Rambam* loc. cit.). Among the members of his court was R'

Antigonus Eliezer ben Charsom, an extremely wealthy man. It was said of him that he subjected all rich men to heavenly judgment, for despite his great wealth his constant occupation was Torah study. Two of Antigonus' students, Tzadok and Boethus (Baysos), became heretics, and from them came the corrupted Sadducees (*Tzedokim*) and Boethusians (*Baysosim*).

---

bake early so that there will be some bread to give to the poor; (g) a woman should wear a petticoat (according to *Rashi*, breeches) for purposes of modesty and chastity; (h) a woman should comb her hair vigorously before immersing herself in the *mikveh*; (i) peddlers should travel from town to town to enable women to buy jewelry and other adornments with which to please their husbands; (j) one who has had an emission of semen may not study Torah until he has immersed himself in a *mikveh* (see *Bava Kamma* 82a).

C. The Pairs

Y OSE[23] *BEN YOEZER OF TZEREIDAH AND YOSE BEN YOCHANAN OF Jerusalem received [it] from them* (Avos 1:4) — from Antigonus and his court (*Rambam* loc. cit.). Some hold that Yose ben Yoezer and Yose ben Yochanan also received the tradition from Shimon the *Tzaddik*, so that *from them* would mean *from Shimon and Antigonus* (*Rabbeinu Yonah* to *Avos* ibid.).

They were the first of the "pairs." Yose ben Yoezer served as *Nasi* [president], while Yose ben Yochanan was the *Av Beis Din* [head of the Sanhedrin (the Supreme Court)] (*Chagigah* 16a,b).

They innovated laws of impurity regarding gentile lands and glass vessels (*Shabbos* 14b).

Yehoshua ben Perachyah and Nitai of Arbel received [it] from them (Avos 1:6). The former was *Nasi* and the latter was *Av Beis Din* (*Chagigah* loc. cit.). Yochanan the *Kohen Gadol*, the Hasmonean, and his sons lived in their days.

The Hasmonean court prohibited and imposed the punishment lashes upon someone who takes a gentile mistress· (*Avodah Zarah* 36b; *Rambam, Hil. Issurei Biah* 12:2). They instituted the eight-day festival of Chanukah, with its mitzvos of lighting candles and giving praise and thanks to God (*Shabbos* 21b). They also began to establish holidays when the Sadducees were defeated, which are mentioned in *Megillas Taanis*.

Later, just prior to the generation of Shemayah and Avtalyon, the Hasmonean court issued prohibitions against a father teaching his son Greek wisdom, and against raising swine (*Sotah* 49b).

Yehudah ben Tabbai and Shimon ben Shatach received [it] from them (Avos 1:8). There are conflicting opinions in the *Gemara* (*Chagigah* 16b) as to which of the two was *Nasi* and which *Av Beis Din*. Shimon ben Shatach's sister was Queen Salome Alexandra, the wife of King Yannai. When Yannai executed all the sages, the world was desolate. Finally, Shimon ben Shatach, through his great knowledge, restored the Torah to its former glory (*Kiddushin* 66a).

---

23. *Rambam* (loc. cit.) refers to him as *Yosef*. He was a *Kohen*, and was called "the pious one among the *Kohanim*." He was killed by the Greeks (*Bereishis Rabbah*).

He also enacted that every Jewish child attend a school of Torah learning (*Yerushalmi, Kesubos* 8:1), and that all of a man's property becomes security for the payment of his wife's *kesubah* [marriage contract] (*Kesubos* 82b).

Authorship of the *Nishmas* prayer, which is part of the Sabbath morning liturgy and the Passover *Haggadah*, is attributed to him (*Siddur Kol Bo*).[24]

Choni Hame'agel ("the circle-maker") lived in the era of this pair.

❖   ❖   ❖

Shemayah and Avtalyon received [it] from them (*Avos* 1:10). Shemayah was *Nasi* and Avtalyon *Av Beis Din* (*Chagigah* loc. cit.). They were proselytes (*Rambam* loc. cit.). *Some of Sennacherib's descendants taught Torah to the public. And who were they? Shemayah and Avtalyon* (*Gittin* 57b).

Akavya ben Mahalalel lived in their generation. It was said regarding him that when the gates of the Temple courtyard were closed while the *pesach* sacrifices were being slaughtered, not one among the crowd of men within the courtyard equaled Akavya's wisdom, purity and fear of God (*Berachos* 19a, *Rashi* ad loc.).

❖   ❖   ❖

Hillel and Shammai received [it] from them (*Avos* 1:12). Hillel was *Nasi* and Shammai was *Av Bein Din* (*Chagigah* 16b). Originally, Menachem was *Av Beis Din*, but he left and Shammai replaced him. Abaye and Rava maintain conflicting views regarding Menachem's fate. Abaye opines that he became a heretic, while Rava holds that he left that high office in order to serve the king (ibid.).

Hillel and Shammai were the last of the "pairs" — there were five in all.

The sons of Beseira occupied the highest positions in the Sanhedrin following the terms of Shemayah and Avtalyon. When they forgot one halachah — whether the *pesach* offering could be brought on the Sabbath — they searched for one of the disciples of Shemayah and Avtalyon who knew the ruling. When they discovered Hillel, they removed themselves from the office and appointed him as *Nasi* (*Pesachim* 66a).

---

24. The verses of the prayer hint at this, for they form an acronym of Shimon's name spelled backwards: נִשְׁמַת וּ=וְאִלּוּ פִינוּ; ע=עַד הֵנָּה עֲזָרוּנוּ; מ=מִי יִדְמֶה לָךְ שׁ=שׁוֹכֵן עַד. [The conjunctive ו precedes the phrase אלּוּ פינוּ in some versions, such as *Nusach Sefard*.]

When the Torah was first forgotten in Israel, Ezra came up from Babylonia and reestablished it; when it was again forgotten, Hillel the Baylonian came up and reestablished it once more (*Succah* 20a).

Controversies and Disagreements: The first legal controversy between sages was whether it was permissible to perform the rite of סְמִיכָה, *leaning* (leaning with one's hands on the head of an offering), on the festivals, since it is ordinarily prohibited to rest one's weight on an animal on the holy days. All five "pairs" wrestled with this problem over a period of two hundred years without resolution (*Chagigah* loc. cit.), until finally the disciples of Hillel and Shammai decided that it was permitted (*Beitzah* 20b).

Yerushalmi (*Chagigah* 2:2) states: Originally, there was only one legal dispute — regarding the rite of leaning.[25] Hillel and Shammai increased them to four.[26] Afterwards, as the Schools of Shammai and Hillel expanded and close contact between master and disciple became increasingly more difficult, the incidence of disagreement in halachah grew and grew. As matters now stand, only the arrival of the Messiah will clarify all the uncertainties.

The Schools of Hillel and Shammai disagreed on over three hundred issues. Usually *Beis Hillel* took the more lenient view, except for those disputes enumerated in Tractate *Eduyos* as the stringencies of *Beis Hillel* and the leniencies of *Beis Shammai*.

For three hundred years the schools of Hillel and Shammai argued, each claiming that the halachah conformed with their opinion. Finally, a heavenly voice proclaimed, "... אֵלּוּ וָאֵלּוּ דִּבְרֵי אֱלֹהִים חַיִּים, *Both these*

---

25. *Tosafos* (*Chagigah* 16a, s.v. יוסי) disputes this, since we find that David and Saul had already argued whether one who offers to betroth a woman with a small coin and with money he has already lent her intends to do so with the loan or with the coin (*Sanhedrin* 19b). *Tosafos Yeshanim* (*Yoma* 59b) also disputes this, for the *Gemara* (ibid.) reports the controversy whether the sprinkling of blood on the Altar was done while walking around the Altar or with circular movement of the hand. Further, in *Sanhedrin* (12a) a controversy is related between King Chizkiyah and the Rabbis.

26. Shammai and Hillel themselves argue about four subjects: (a) Shammai says *challah* [a portion of the dough that is separated and given to a *Kohen*] must be taken from one *kav* of flour and Hillel says from two; (b) Shammai says that nine *kavim* (a certain measure; a *kav* is between 1.5 and 2.6 quarts) of drawn water invalidate a *mikveh*, and Hillel says a *hin* (3 *kav*) of water; (c) Shammai says that menstruating women do not defile retroactively, and Hillel says they do; (d) Hillel says it is permitted to perform the rite of leaning on a sacrifice during a festival, and Shammai says it is not. This fourth dispute predated the era of the pairs. (See *Beitzah* 35a, where a dispute is cited between Hillel and the Rabbis regarding tithing. *Maharatz Chayes* suggests that the Hillel referred to there is the son of R' Gamliel of Yavne. Nevertheless, amongst the students of Hillel and Shammai the incidence of disagreement increased markedly.)

and those are the words of the Living God, but the halachah is like Beis Hillel." Although each group formulated a true concept of the Law, the latter deserved that the halachah follow their view[27] because they were humble and diffident, and because they taught Beis Shammai's opinion as well as their own, even giving precedence to Beis Shammai's ruling (*Eruvin* 13b). R' Yehudah HaNasi (the Prince) followed in the footsteps of his ancestor Hillel, for when he organized the Mishnah he always placed the opinion of Beis Shammai before that of Beis Hillel (*Ritva* ibid.).

Hillel's regulations that are known to us include: (a) The *prozbul*, which allows the needy to acquire loans before *Shemittah* (the Sabbatical Year) by legally circumventing the cancellation of debts that usually takes place on *Shemittah* (*Sheviis* 10:3). (b) An enactment regarding the sale of a house in a walled city. The Torah (*Leviticus* 25:29,30) states that the sale becomes permanent if the purchase price is not returned by the seller within twelve months. Originally, the buyer used to hide from the seller on the last day of the twelve-month period, so the sale would become final. Hillel established that in such situations the seller could deposit the money in a special account, break down the door and reclaim his house (*Gittin* 74b). (c) The order of washing a body before burial (*Gilyon Maharsha* to *Yoreh Deah* 352:1). Likewise, Hillel's opinions are found in many rulings of the Rabbis (see *Bava Metzia* 75a, *Beitzah* 35a, et al.).

Hillel and Shammai decreed that a person's hands must be cleansed even for *terumah* (*Shabbos* 14b, 15a), and also that ritually contaminated metal vessels that were broken and put together again should revert to their prior impurity (ibid. 16a).

When the schools of Hillel and Shammai visited Chananyah ben Chizkiyah ben Garon, they made eighteen decrees (ibid. 13b).[28]

Chananyah ben Chizkiyah and his colleagues, the disciples of Hillel and Shammai, wrote *Megillas Taanis* to commemorate past tribulations (*Shabbos* 13b).[29]

---

27. *R' Yosef Karo* in *Kelalei HaGemara* (in *Halichos Olam*) interprets this to mean that only Beis Hillel deserved to ascertain the truth.

28. [A discussion of the decrees appears in ArtScroll Mishnah, *Shabbos*, pp. 391-394.] See *Rambam's Commentary* (ibid. 1:4) that the elders of the Schools of Hillel and Shammai issued thirty-six decrees.

29. The version of the *Megillas Taanis* in our possession is actually a later integration of two earlier works. The ancient scroll written by the disciples of Hillel and Shammai contained only a calendarlike listing of all the fasts and holidays. The narrative of the actual events and of the miracles which were wrought for our forefathers was never committed to writing, but was transmitted orally in the manner of the mishnayos and

R' Nechunya ben Hakanah lived in their generation. He composed the book *Habahir* on the mysteries of the Torah. The prayer *Ana Becho'ach* is attributed to him.[30] He also composed the prayers which are said upon entering and leaving the house of study (*Berachos* 28b).

D. The Tannaim

Hillel's Successors

R' SHIMON THE SON OF HILLEL RECEIVED [IT] FROM HILLEL AND SHAMMAI (Rambam loc. cit.), and R' Yochanan ben Zakkai received [it] from Hillel and Shammai (Avos 2:8).

Rabban Gamliel I, son of R' Shimon the son of Hillel, was the first to bear the title *Rabban*.[31] He was called Rabban Gamliel the Elder, just as his grandfather was called Hillel the Elder. He received the Torah from his father, R' Shimon.

From the time of Moses until Rabban Gamliel the Torah was studied only in a standing position. After Rabban Gamliel's passing, man began to be weakened by sickness, and henceforth Torah was studied while sitting (*Megillah* 21a). Thus, it is stated, that since the death of Rabban Gamliel the Elder, the honor of Torah has disappeared, and purity and abstinence have departed (*Sotah* 49a).

He established four regulations for the benefit of the public,[32] and another with respect to one who permissibly went beyond the *techum* [Sabbath boundary] (*Rosh Hashanah* 23b).

Rabban Shimon, the son of Rabban Gamliel the Elder, received the tradition from his father. He was the one of the עֲשָׂרָה הֲרוּגֵי מַלְכוּת, the

---

baraisos (see Ch. 3). Later, when the mishnayos were allowed to be written, the oral narrative was added to the ancient *megillah*, which accounts for the mixture of Hebrew and Aramaic in the expanded written version (similar to the use of both languages in the written mishnayos and *Baraisos*). This also explains why the names of later *Tannaim* such as R' Yehoshua ben Karchah and R' Yose ben R' Yehudah are found in *Megillas Taanis* (*Maharatz Chayes, Divrei Neviim Divrei Kabbalah,* Ch. 6).

30. The Kabbalists maintain that this prayer was organized according to the forty-two-letter Name of God referred to in *Kiddushin* 71a. The forty-two-letter Name is revealed only to one who is modest, humble, of middle age, and does not anger, become drunk, or bear a grudge (see *Rashi* ad loc.).

31. *Rabban,* רַבָּן, is comprised of the word רַב, *Rav* (teacher, master), and the final ן, which, in Aramaic, means "our." It indicates that he is the *Rav* of all of us — of the whole nation. Another interpretation is that the final ן indicates a greater level, similar to the word רַגְזָן, an *irritable person,* which stems from רֹגֶז, anger (*Siddur Avodas Yisrael*).

32. Three are mentioned in the mishnayos at the beginning of the fourth chapter in *Gittin,* and another in a *baraisa* there.

ten martyrs killed by the Romans. The *Gemara* (*Shabbos* 15a, according to *Rashi* ad loc.) states: Hillel and (his son) Shimon conducted their presidencies during the one hundred years before the destruction of the Temple.

Rabban Shimon ben Gamliel permitted a woman who must bring five offerings after having given birth five times to bring only one offering (*Kereisos* 8a).[33] Rabban Yochanan ben Zakkai succeeded him as *Nasi*.

Rabban Gamliel ben Rabban Shimon received the tradition from his father. He is known as Rabban Gamliel of Yavneh, and lived at the time of the destruction of the Second Temple. He became *Nasi* after the death of R' Yochanan ben Zakkai, thus restoring the presidency to the family of Hillel.

In Yavneh he added the blessing, *Velamalshinim* (*And for slanderers*), to the *Shemoneh Esrei* prayer[34] (*Rambam, Hil. Tefillah* 2:1).

He and his court inserted the fourth blessing, הַטּוֹב וְהַמֵּטִיב, *Who is good and does good*, into the *Bircas HaMazon*, after permission was granted to bury the victims of Betar. (This is discussed at length in *Avudraham* to *Bircas HaMazon*.)

They forbade the consumption of meat slaughtered by Cutheans (*Chullin* 5b).

Rabban Shimon ben Gamliel received the tradition from his father. He was the father of R' Yehudah HaNasi. The principle that the halachah follows all that R' Shimon ben Gamliel taught in our mishnayos, except for three instances, refers to him, not to the first R' Shimon ben Gamliel.

THE NEXT LINK IN THE CHAIN OF TRADITION WAS R' YOCHANAN BEN Zakkai and his students. R' Yochanan ben Zakkai became *Nasi* after the

R' Yochanan ben Zakkai first R' Shimon ben Gamliel was murdered. He was the least prominent among the disciples of Hillel the Elder, yet he knew the entire Scripture, Mishnah, *Gemara*, Codes, *Aggadah* (the nonlegal portions of Rabbinic

---

33. Although bringing an offering for each birth is a Biblical obligation, Rabban Shimon ben Gamliel was lenient, in accord with the verse, *It is time to do for Hashem; they have breached Your Torah* (*Psalms* 119:126) [which permits a sage to allow a precept to be transgressed in exigent circumstances; in this case, the price for the required offerings had unfairly risen to an exorbitant amount]. R' Shimon ben Gamliel felt that if women did not bring even one offering, this might lead them to eat consecrated food while still ritually unclean. As soon as he announced his decree, however, prices went down and it was rescinded (*Rashi* ad loc.).

34. The *Gemara* (*Berachos* 28b) attributes its authorship to Shmuel HaKatan, because he was the member of Rabban Gamliel's court who actually wrote it.

literature), the rules of hermeneutics, exegesis and numerology, the movements of the sun and the moon, the conversations of the ministering angels, the demons, and the trees, parables, the mysteries of the מַעֲשֵׂה מֶרְכָּבָה, *Visions of the Chariot* (*Ezekiel* 1), and the difficulties that would later perplex Abaye and Rava [in the *Gemara*] (*Succah* 28a, *Rashi* ad loc.).

He issued nine regulations[35] (*Rosh Hashanah* 31b).

Five of R' Yochanan ben Zakkai's disciples were considered among the greatest of the Sages:

(1) R' Eliezer ben Hyrkanos, known as R' Eliezer HaGadol (the Great). His study hall was as large as an arena. One rock was placed there especially for R' Eliezer to sit on. Once, R' Yehoshua entered the study hall and proceeded to kiss the rock, proclaiming, "This rock is like Mount Sinai, and the one who sits upon it — R' Eliezer — resembles the Ark of the Covenant" (*Midrash Shir HaShirim* to 1:2, *Matenos Kehunah* ad loc.).

When R' Eliezer wanted to establish a law according to his own opinion against the majority of Rabbis, his colleagues voted to excommunicate him[36] (*Bava Metzia* 59b).

R' Eliezer was the brother-in-law of R' Gamliel of Yavneh. He compiled the volume of *Baraisos* entitled *Pirkei d'Rabbi Eliezer.*

(2) R' Yehoshua ben Chananya. It is said of him (*Avos* 2:11): "Happy is the one who bore him!" *Yerushalmi* (*Yevamos* 1:6) explains that when his mother was pregnant with him, she would go to each of the twenty-four study halls in her town so that the men would pray for her child to become wise. After he was born she would bring his cradle to the syn-

---

35. They are: (a) Following the destruction of the Temple, he established that the shofar be blown when Rosh Hashanah falls on the Sabbath wherever there is a court; (b) after the destruction of the Temple, that the *lulav* be taken all seven days of *Succos*; (c) following the destruction of the Temple, that the new crop of grain should be forbidden the entire sixteenth day of the month of Nissan; (d) testimony regarding the new moon should be accepted the entire day; (e) that the witnesses of the new moon should go only to the assembly house; (f) that *Kohanim* should not pronounce the priestly blessings while wearing shoes; (g) that witnesses to the new moon should be allowed to desecrate the Sabbath only for the months of Nissan and Tishrei; (h) that a proselyte need not set aside a quarter of a shekel to bring an offering when the Temple will be rebuilt, because of the possibility that he will use it for other purposes; and (i) following the destruction of the Temple, that one need not take the fruit of the vine in its fourth year to Jerusalem, even if it involves only a day's journey, but may redeem the fruit with money and bring that to Jerusalem.

36. *Yerushalmi* (*Moed Katan* 3:1) explains that although R' Eliezer knew that the halachah requires us to follow the view of the majority, he assumed that the rule did not apply to his case. Since they acted disrespectfully to him, he felt it indicated that their opinion was not an objective one, and thus was not subject to this rule.

agogue, so that he become accustomed to hearing the words of Torah.

Onkelos the proselyte[37] received his translation of the Torah from R' Yehoshua ben Chananya and R' Eliezer (*Megillah* 3a).

(3) R' Yose the *Kohen*, who is praised for his piety (*Avos* loc. cit.). The *Gemara* states that his writings were never found in the hand of a gentile, lest they be carried on the Sabbath (*Shabbos* 19a).

(4) R' Shimon ben Nesanel, who is lauded for being one who fears sins (*Avos* loc. cit.). He was wont to teach: Be careful in reading the *Shema* and reciting the *Shemoneh Esrei* prayer, and do not imagine your prayer as a perfunctory act, but as a plea for mercy and grace (ibid. 2:18).

(5) R' Elazar ben Arach, of whom it was said that he outweighs all the Sages (ibid. 2:12).

R' Akiva ben Yosef received [it] from R' Eliezer and R' Yehoshua, and from Nachum Ish Gam Zu. His father was a proselyte (*Rambam*, Introduction to *Yad*). The *Gemara* identifies R' Akiva as a descendant of the Canaanite general Sisera [see *Judges* Ch. 4] (*R' Nissim Gaon* to *Berachos* 27a, quoting *Sanhedrin* 25a).

The Holy One said to Moses, "There will arise a man at the end of several generations — and R' Akiva ben Yosef is his name — who will adduce from the crowns of each letter in the Torah heaps and heaps of laws." Upon which Moses replied to the Holy One, "You have such a man, and You give the Torah through me?" The Holy One answered, "Quiet! Such is My decree!" (*Menachos* 29b).

R' Akiva profoundly understood the mysteries of the מַעֲשֵׂה מֶרְכָּבָה, *Vision of the Divine Chariot* [*Ezekiel* 1]. He entered the פַּרְדֵּס, "*garden*" *of esoteric knowledge*, and emerged safely (*Chagigah* 14b).

No man was ever so fortunate or great in Torah learning or wealth as R' Akiva (*Rabbeinu Gershom* to *Bava Basra* 12b).

He was one of the עֲשָׂרָה הֲרוּגֵי מַלְכוּת, ten martyrs executed by the Romans.[38]

---

37. See *Avodah Zarah* 11a, which implies that Onkelos lived in the days of Rabban Gamliel the Elder. *Hagahos Yaavetz* (ibid.) suggests that the *Gemara* refers to another Onkelos, or, alternatively, to emend the text to read *Rabban Gamliel of Yavneh*. See *Maharatz Chayes*.

38. When R' Akiva was imprisoned he lacked water with which to wash his hands, and so he decided not to eat, saying, "Better that I die on my own account than transgress the enactment of my colleagues" (*Eruvin* 21b).

Chelkas Yoav explains that all his days R' Akiva was concerned about when he would be able to give his life to sanctify God's Name, thus fulfilling the verse in *Shema*: *You shall love Hashem . . . with all your soul.* This, then, is the meaning of "die on my account" — that he was willing to relinquish his great yearning and rather die for a lesser, private cause, in order not to transgress the Rabbinic ruling of washing the hands before eating.

Rabbeinu Nissim Gaon (*Berachos* 57b) writes that R' Akiva's piety exceeded his scholarship, and therefore he was praised for his piety.

He wrote *Mechilta*. The book *Osiyos d'Rabbi Akiva* is attributed to him. He composed the prayer *Avinu Malkeinu* (*Taanis* 25b).

The *Gemara* states in *Yevamos* (16a): *You are Akiva ben Yosef, whose name is renowned from one end of the world to the other.* The numerical value of מִסּוֹף הָעוֹלָם עַד סוֹפוֹ, *from one end of the world to the other,* is 564, equaling the 564 occasions that R' Akiva is mentioned in the Talmud. Further, the numerical value of אוֹצָר בָּלוּם, *a storehouse with compartments,* a term used to describe R' Akiva in *Gittin* 67a, is 375, signifying that the halachah follows R' Akiva's opinion 375 times, like the expression שָׁעָה עוֹמֶדֶת לוֹ (he was successful, שעה=375). According to a variant reading there (*Tos.* ibid.), R' Akiva was called אוֹצָר בָּלוּס, *a mixed storehouse* (i.e., a mind full of all kinds of knowledge); the numerical value of this is identical to that of his name, רַבִּי עֲקִיבָא (*Hagahos Mitzpeh Eisan* to *Yevamos* loc. cit.).

His Talmudic adversary was R' Yishmael, a disciple of R' Nechunya ben Hakanah (*Shevuos* 26a). During the era of the Temple's destruction, while yet a child, R' Yishmael was captured by the Romans, and R' Yehoshua paid a large ransom for his release (*Gittin* 58a). R' Yishmael was exiled along with the Sanhedrin from Yavneh to Usha, as the *Gemara* (*Bava Basra* 28b) says — *Who are the ones who traveled to Usha? — R' Yishmael.* The *Gemara* enumerates five decrees promulgated by the Sages in Usha[39] (*Kesubos* 49b, 50a).

R' Yishmael wrote *Mechilta* (see Ch. 3). The authorship of the book *Heichalos* is attributed to him, and he compiled the list of the Thirteen Hermeneutical Principles with the Torah is which expounded.

The following are the disciples who received the tradition from R' Akiva:

R' Meir, who was the greatest among them.[40] His wife was Berurya, the daughter of R' Chanina ben Teradyon. She once learned three hundred laws from three hundred scholars in one day (*Pesachim* 62b). We even find that she engaged in a legal dispute with the Sages (*Tosefta Kelim* [*Bava Kamma*] 4:9, [*Bava Metzia*] 1:3).

R' Yehudah ben R' Ilai, who was given the privilege of always being the first speaker (*Berachos* 63b; *Shabbos* 33a). He ruled on all questions

---

39. They are: (1) A father must support his small children; (2) one who gives away all his property to his sons is entitled that he and his wife be supported by them; (3) one should not give more than a fifth of his wealth to charity; (4) a child under 12 years of age who refuses to study should be encouraged with soft words; once the child is older, the father should use a strap or withhold food if necessary; (5) if a woman sells her *melog* (usufructuary) property (see General Introduction to *Kesubos* for explanation of this term) while her husband is living, and then she dies, her husband may seize it from the purchasers.

40. See below that R' Meir is the author of every anonymous mishnah.

of halachah for the household of Rebbi [R' Yehudah Hanasi] (*Rashi, Tos.* to *Menachos* 104a), and was praised for his righteousness, being called *the* [anonymous] *pious man* (*Bava Kamma* 103b).

R' Yose ben Chalafta. When Rebbi thought to challenge one of the opinions of R' Yose, he said: We are too lowly to dispute R' Yose, for the disparity between his generation and our own is the difference between the holy of holies and the most profane (*Yerushalmi* to *Yevamos* 6:7). Every anonymous *baraisa* in *Seder Olam* follows his opinion.

R' Shimon bar Yochai composed the *Zohar*.[41]

R' Nechemya.

R' Elazar ben Shamua, the *Kohen*. Rebbi went to him to be examined and to clarify any uncertainties in learning that he had[42] (*Menachos* 18a, *Rashi* ad loc.).

R' Yochanan HaSandlar, who praised himself as one who often attended R' Akiva (*Yerushalmi* to *Chagigah* 3:10). When R' Akiva was imprisoned for engaging in Torah study, which was outlawed by the Romans, R' Yochanan disguised himself as a peddler and passed by the jail, calling, "Who wants to buy needles?" Hidden in this simple query was a halachic question regarding *chalitzah*.[43] R' Akiva then stuck his head out of the window and innocently asked, "Do you have spindles?" — which was in effect a coded response to R' Yochanan's question (ibid., *Yevamos* 12:5).

R' Yochanan came from the city of Alexandria[44] (ibid. *Chagigah* loc. cit.).

Shimon ben Azzai, whose mind was exceedingly sharp, was wont to

---

41. The following passage regarding the *Kabbalah* appears in *Shiyurei Berachah*: "R' Nechunya ben Hakanah was the leading exponent of *Kabbalah* (mystical teachings); he wrote *Habahir*. After him was R' Shimon bar Yochai, who composed the *Zohar*. When R' Shimon and his generation passed away, knowledge of the *Kabbalah* became lost. Finally, the Almighty inspired one eastern monarch to order his servants to dig in a particular spot for reasons of financial gain, and they struck a box which contained a copy of the *Zohar*. When the sages of Tolitola (Toledo, Spain) learned of the discovery, they rejoiced greatly, and from there the *Kabbalah* was disseminated to Israel."

42. Rav called R' Elazar ben Shamua *the happiest of all scholars* (*Kesubos* 40a, *Rashi* ad loc.). The world had been desolate of Torah knowledge and scholarship until R' Akiva came and taught it. Therefore, any of his students who understood the Torah as he did had obviously grasped the halachah, and was aptly called "the happiest of scholars" (*Shitah Mekubetzes*).

43. [When a childless man dies, his brother is obligated either to marry his widow or to perform *chalitzah* (lit., taking off the shoe). See *Deuteronomy* 25:5ff. and General Introduction to Mishnah, *Yevamos*.]

44. *Maharatz Chayes* in *Darkei Moshe* suggests that he was called R' *Yochanan HaSandlar* because he came from Alexandria. However, the early authorities maintain that he was actually a shoemaker, which is the meaning of סַנְדְּלָר, *sandler*.

say, *All the sages of Israel are, in comparison to me, as thin as the husk of a garlic, except for "that bald man"* (a reference to R' Akiva, who was bald). When Abaye was in a cheerful mood he used to say, *I am like Ben Azzai in the markets of Tiberias,* which means: I am open and ready to answer any questions, just like Ben Azzai, who lived in Tiberias and was keen and learned (*Kiddushin* 20a, *Rashi* ad loc.).

R' Elazar ben Chisma, who was an expert in engineering and geometry, could reckon the number of drops of water in the sea (*Horayos* 10a). He used to say: *The laws of bird offerings and the laws regarding the beginning of menstrual periods — these are essential laws; astronomy and mathematics are like the seasonings of wisdom* (*Avos* 3:23).

R' Elazar, the son of R' Yose the Galilean (*Koheles Rabbah* 11:60). Of him, it was said, "Wherever you find a homiletical explanation by R' Elazar, make your ears like a hopper to receive his teachings." He compiled thirty-two rules of Biblical exegesis.

R' Akiva had 12,000 pairs of disciples, from the Gabbas to Antiparas, and all of them died at the same time because they did not treat each other with respect. The world remained desolate [because the Torah had been forgotten (*Rashi*)] until R' Akiva came to our teachers in the South and taught the Torah to them: These were R' Meir, R' Yehudah, R' Yose, R' Shimon and R' Elazar ben Shamua, and it was they who revived the Torah at that time. All of them (the 12,000 pairs) died between Pesach and Shavuos (*Yevamos* 62b).

R' YEHUDAH HANASI (JUDAH THE PRINCE), THE SON OF R' SHIMON BEN Gamliel, known as רַבִּי, *Rebbi,*[45] was also called *Rabbeinu Hakadosh*
Rebbi (our Holy Teacher) because he never permitted his hand to drop below his belt (*Shabbos* 118b). He received the Torah from his father (*Bava Metzia* 84a), from R' Elazar ben Shamua (*Yevamos* 84a), and from R' Shimon bar Yochai and his colleagues, the disciples of R' Akiva. Rava referred to Rebbi as one who drew water from deep wells (*Shevuos* 7a).

Rebbi used to preface his opinions with, "*I say,*"[46] an indication of his humility, as the Mishnah teaches: *When Rebbi died, humility ceased* (*Sotah* 49a; *Horayos* 14a). Rebbi never issued his opinions as absolute

---

45. Even though we find Rebbi and R' Yehudah HaNasi engaged in debate (see *Yerushalmi* to *Peah*, end of Ch. 1), the latter is actually Rebbi's grandson, who is often called R' Yehudah Nesiah.

46. The expression, *Rebbi says, "I say ..."* is often found often in the Babylonian and Jerusalem Talmuds and *Tosefta* (see *Kiddushin* 9b, *Gittin* 38b, 39b, 52a, *Arachin* 17a, 24b, *Taanis* 2b, et al.).

pronouncements of the law, but only that it appeared to him as such, much as today's Talmudic scholars write, *It appears to my impoverished mind (Beis HaOtzar)*.

Rebbi and his court promulgated rules concerning the *sikrikon*, Roman soldiers who threatened to kill Jews unless they would give them their property (*Gittin* 55b), and certain laws regarding a menstruant (*Niddah* 66a). They decreed that even a competent student not decide matters of law without his teacher's permission, even if he is distant from him (*Sanhedrin* 5b). After concluding his prayers Rebbi would add: יְהִי רָצוֹן מִלְפָנֶיךָ, שֶׁתַּצִּילֵנִי מֵעַזֵּי פָנִים וּמֵעַזוּת פָּנִים, *May it be Your will that You rescue me from brazen men and from brazenness . . . (Berachos* 16b). We now recite this as a part of the morning prayers.[47]

Rebbi was the one who organized and edited the Mishnah.

---

47. The *Gemara* (ibid.) comments that Rebbi prayed this even though Antoninus had ordered his soldiers to guard Rebbi and to thrash anyone who attempted to injure him (*Rashi* ad loc.).

II. Foundation of the Mishnah

FROM THE DAYS OF MOSES UNTIL THOSE OF REBBI, THE ORAL LAW WAS never committed to writing for public dissemination. Rather, the leading Torah authority of each generation — whether he was the head of the Sanhedrin or a prophet — used to make personal notes of the teachings he had received from his masters, which he then taught orally to the people. These personal manuscripts[1] contained not only the particulars of the transmitted tradition,[2] but also new laws that were

---

1. See *Shabbos* 6b, which states that Rav found a "secret scroll" of the school of R' Chiya. *Rashi* (ad loc.) explains that when one scholar heard another propound a law that was not taught in the academies, he wrote it down lest he forget it, yet kept it secret since it was not supported by the tradition. In *Bava Metzia* (92a), *Rashi* defines *secret scroll* as a personal manuscript consisting of novel interpretations that the scholar had heard and feared he would forget, and which he concealed because of the prohibition of writing down the Oral Law. (See below, where we discuss the permissibility of committing the Oral Law to writing.) The *Gemara* also mentions *the notebook of Ilfa* (*Menachos* 70a), *the notebook of Levi and the notebook of R' Yehoshua ben Levi* (*Shabbos* 156a).

2. The tradition was principally transmitted from teacher to student. Any legal decision or law repeated by a student in the name of his master to his colleagues in the study hall was accepted as if the master had uttered it — whether to rely on it to determine the practical law, or to question it from a conflicting statement of the teacher. Any legal opinion pronounced by a sage is assumed to have come from his teacher unless explicitly indicated otherwise (see *Yoreh Deah* 242:24).

One who repeats a tradition in the name of the sage who originally said it should imagine that the latter is standing before him, for it says (*Psalms* 39:7) *But in their shadow — a man should walk* (*Yerushalmi*, end of *Shekalim*). On the other hand, one who did not learn a certain halachah from a sage, but cites it in the latter's name, causes the Divine Presence to depart from Israel (end of Tractate *Kallah*). Since the entire goal of our sages' Torah study was to cause the Divine Presence to dwell in our midst, they took great pains not to change, add to, or subtract from what they learned from their teachers.

The disciples highly treasured the traditions of their rabbis. Rav Chisda was once holding two priestly gifts of meat in his hand and called out, "Whoever comes and tells me a new dictum in Rav's name, I shall give these to him" . . . When they related to him yet another saying, he exclaimed, "Did Rav indeed say this? I prefer this second one to the first. If I had another [gift], I would give it to you" (*Shabbos* 10b). On another occasion Rav Kahana said to Rav Ashi, "Did Rav really say that?" He then proceeded to learn it from Rav Ashi forty times, and then knew it as if he had it in his pocket (*Megillah* 7b). In *Chullin* 18b Rav Yosef states: "I studied under Rav Yehudah, who mentioned even the uncertainties of tradition." *Rashi* explains that when Rav Yehudah quoted a tradition by someone who was uncertain of the source, he would say: "I received it from So-and-so, who was unsure if he had received it from So-and-so or So-and-so."

The disciples not only cherished the traditions they personally received from their teachers, but they were even anxious to know if their colleagues had also heard them. R' Ilai said that he had heard certain teachings from R' Eliezer and he questioned all the

advanced at that time using the thirteen hermeneutical rules with which the Torah is expounded, and which were subsequently ratified by the Sanhedrin.

Such was the accepted procedure until Rebbi collected all the decisions, laws, interpretations and explanations that had been heard from Moses (see *Yerushalmi* to *Pe'ah* 2:4), or that the Sanhedrin had innovated, and from this material he composed the Mishnah. He publicly taught this text until it became widely known, written down and disseminated, thus ensuring that the Oral Law would not be forgotten among the Jewish people.

Why did Rebbi not just abide by the status quo? Because he perceived that the level of scholarship was waning, that hardships were approaching, that the power of the Roman government was expanding and that the Jews were being dispersed far and wide. Therefore, he wrote one uniform work for all, to be learned quickly and not forgotten, and he

latter's students, looking for another who had also heard it, but he did not find one (*Eruvin* 83a, *Rashi* ad loc.).

They were careful to quote the opinion precisely, even though a slight variation in wording would not distort the basic ruling. Rav Yehudah, the son of Rav Shmuel ben Shilas, said, quoting Rav, "The guests may not eat anything until the one who breaks bread tasted." Rav Safra explained, "The statement was: '[The guests] may not *taste* etc.'" What practical difference does it make? Only to teach that one must repeat the exact word of his teacher (*Berachos* 47a). In fact, for this reason the students retain their learning, as it says in *Eruvin* (53a): *The sons of Yehudah who chose their words carefully retained their learning.* *Rashi* explains that they were careful to repeat the dictum exactly as the teacher had uttered it.

The mishnah (*Parah* 2:5) teaches, *If [the red cow] has two black or white hairs in one gumah (cavity), it is unfit. R' Yehudah says: "In one kos."* Rav (ad loc.) explains that although there is no halachic dispute between the first *Tanna* and R' Yehudah — since *gumah* and *kos* have the identical meaning — nevertheless, they used different expressions because each was obligated to repeat the exact language of his teacher. Also, the *Gemara* in *Shabbos* (15a) states that Hillel said: "*Drawn water in the amount of a hin invalidates the mikveh*," for one must state a halachah using his teacher's exact phraseology (see *Rashi* there). *Rambam* in his *Mishnah Commentary* to *Eduyos* (1:3) writes that he received a tradition from his teacher, and *Rambam's* teacher from his teacher, that Hillel's masters, the proselytes Shemayah and Avtalyon, because of their inability to enunciate the letter ה (*hei*) correctly, pronounced it as an א (*alef*). Thus, when they said the dictum: *A hin of drawn water invalidates the mikveh*, it sounded like *drawn water does not invalidate* (the word הין, *hin*, sounded like אין, *does not*). Hillel — who could certainly pronounce the letter *hei* — nevertheless employed the phraseology of his teachers. *Vilna Gaon* explains *Rambam's* meaning as follows: Since their inability to pronounce the *hei* in *hin* could very well cause people to think mistakenly that drawn water does not invalidate a *mikveh*, Shemayah and Avtalyon were forced to use the word מלא, *the amount of*, before the word *hin* ["the *amount of* a *hin* of drawn water etc."]. Hillel, who could say *hin* correctly, did not need to add the extra word. Yet, he did so in order to repeat the ruling in his teacher's exact wording (see also *Rashi, Shabbos* ibid. for yet another explanation). Thus, the most basic principle of the transmission of the Oral Law from teacher to student is precision of language.

and the members of his court spent their entire lives teaching the Mishnah to the people (*Rambam*, Introduction to *Yad Hachazakah*).

Writing the Oral Law

REGARDING THE PERMISSIBILITY OF WRITING DOWN SEGMENTS OF THE Oral Law, the *Gemara* (*Gittin* 60b) states: R' Yehudah bar Nachmani, who was Reish Lakish's interpreter, taught as follows: It is written, *Write for yourselves these words* (*Exodus* 34:27). It is also written: . . . *for according to* [עַל פִּי, lit. *by the mouth of*] *these words* (ibid.). The first verse implies that the Torah must be written; the second, that it must be taught orally. How do we resolve this? The answer is that words that are written [i.e. Scripture] may not be recited by heart, and the words which are transmitted may not be committed to writing.

The rationale behind this admonition is that peculiarities in the sentence structure and word formation of the Written Torah contain many hidden meanings and lessons, and if the verses were transmitted orally these interpretations would go unnoticed. Conversely, since the Oral Law is an elucidation of the Written Law, it can be grasped only if a teacher is present to explain its intent. If it were committed to writing, the possibility of misinterpretation would be likely. For that reason it was given orally to Moses at Sinai. However, once the enemy's evil decrees and the numerous difficulties threatened to sunder the people from their Torah, thus posing a situation of עֵת לַעֲשׂוֹת לַה׳, *It is time to do for Hashem* (*Psalms* 119:126), the Sages were compelled to permit the recording of the Oral Law — הֵפֵרוּ תּוֹרָתֶךָ, *they breached Your Torah* (ibid.).[3]

The early authorities are divided as to whether Rebbi was the one who authorized the writing of the Mishnah. *Rambam* maintains that he was; however, *Rashi* contends that while Rebbi arranged the mishnayos and taught them orally, he never wrote them down.[4]

---

3. Similarly, the Sages permitted oral recitation of the Written Torah on certain occasions. For example, the *Kohen Gadol* (High Priest) read one section of the Torah by heart (*Yoma* 68b) so as not to trouble the assembled [by having them wait until the scroll was turned to that portion] (ibid. 70a). See *Tosafos* (*Temurah* 14b), who maintain that the prohibition against reciting the Written Torah applies basically to cases in which one person is reading on behalf of others.

4. See *Eruvin* 62b, where the *Gemara* refers to *Megillas Taanis* as having been written. *Rashi* explains that the *Gemara* specifies *Megillas Taanis* because other than that work, not even one letter of a statement of halachah appeared in written form in those days.

In the period of the Sages of the *Gemara*, during the lifetime of Abaye, the Mishnah had not yet appeared in writing. Proof of this can be found in *Eruvin* 53a and *Avodah Zarah* 2a, where the spelling of certain terms in the Mishnah are disputed. Had the Mishnah

ACTUALLY, LONG BEFORE REBBI, EFFORTS HAD BEEN MADE TO COMPILE and arrange the mishnayos (*Chagigah* 14a). R' Yehudah ben Teima and

Earlier Mishnayos

his colleagues taught six hundred orders of mishnayos (some maintain that it was seven hundred), and Rebbi subsequently reduced them to six orders. However, a responsum from *Rav Sherira Gaon* seems to indicate that Hillel and Shammai fashioned the six orders and that Rebbi only edited and refined them, ultimately producing the work that we have today (*Shem HaGedolim*).[5]

Many tractates of mishnayos were arranged by others before Rebbi, such as *Middos* by R' Eliezer ben Yaakov, and the entire tractate *Keilim* (*Chacham Tzvi*). Wherever it says in the Mishnah, *"even though they said,"* or *"and why did they say,"* or *"because they said"* (*Pesachim* 1:1, *Shabbos* 1:3, et al.), reference is being made to these earlier mishnayos. This is also the intent of the *Gemara* when it mentions a *mishnah rishonah* [earlier mishnah] and *mishnah acharonah* [later mishnah] (*Kesubos* 57a, *Sanhedrin* 27b). Similarly, we find in the *Gemara: This mishnah was taught in the days of Nehemiah ben Chachalyah.*

The first three mishnayos in *Bava Kamma* are unique in their brevity and style. The *Gemara* there (6b) comments, "that *Tanna* is a *Yerushalmi,"* which means that those mishnayos were composed by a sage from Jerusalem who chose to write concisely, and Rebbi subsequently included them — unedited — in his mishnayos (*Maharatz Chayes* ibid.).[6]

---

already been committed to writing, they could have simply looked up the spelling.

Further, the *Gemara* (*Bava Metzia* 85b) reports how R' Chiya orally taught the Six Orders of the Mishnah to six schoolchildren, whereas he taught the Five Books of the Torah to five youngsters from a text. From here we see that in the time of R' Chiya, who was a disciple of Rebbi, the mishnayos were still taught orally.

However, in defense of *Rambam's* opinion, it might be said that the written Mishnah was not yet widely disseminated, and that whoever was still capable of learning it by heart continued to do so, since permission to write it down had been granted only out of great necessity.

5. See *Teshuvos HaGeonim* §20 by *Rav Hai Gaon*, who writes that from the days of Moses until Hillel the Elder six hundred Orders of the Mishnah were extant, just as the Holy One had given them to Moses at Sinai. From Hillel onward the general condition of the world deteriorated, and the honor of Torah diminished, and so Hillel and Shammai established only six orders.

6. Harav Shlomo Min Hahar z"l of Jerusalem suggested that from the style of the mishnayos in the fourteenth chapter of *Zevachim* it appears that their intent was to teach practical halachah and, apparently, they predated Rebbi. Also, the mishnayos which teach the laws of *Yovel* (the Jubilee, of the fiftieth year) must have been disseminated before Chizkiyah, in whose time celebration of *Yovel* was discontinued (this, according to *Rashi*, who maintains that *Yovel* was not observed during the Second Temple period). Even more convincing is the *Gemara* in *Gittin* (48a), which dates the mishnayos con-

Tiferes Yisrael (*Makkos* 3:3, *Zevachim* 5:3) comments on the mishnah concerning offerings that are eaten within the "curtains" of the Temple (i.e. within the Temple enclosure), that the word *curtains* was used in the Mishnah because in Moses' day — when the mishnah was taught — the walls of the Tabernacle were indeed made of curtains. The word was not changed because every mishnah regarding which there is no dispute between *Tannaim* has been taught in the exact language that Moses said it.[7]

R' Nassan, who lived in the generation preceding Rebbi's, also compiled many mishnayos, as it says: *This is the mishnah of R' Nassan*. This is the meaning of the statement: *Rebbi and R' Nassan finalized the Mishnah* (*Bava Metzia* 86a; see *Maharsha* ad loc.) — that is, R' Nassan was the last compiler of the mishnayos before Rebbi.

Rav Sherira Gaon writes in one of his letters that Rebbi edited some mishnayos, while preserving others in their original form. Anonymous mishnayos reflect the opinion of R' Meir. As R' Meir learned the subject and taught it to his students, so did Rebbi establish the lesson as a mishnah, for R' Meir was the greatest of R' Akiva's disciples, as the *Gemara* (*Eruvin* 13b) states: *R' Acha ben Chanina said: It is revealed and known before Him Who spoke and the world came into existence that in the generation of R' Meir there was none equal to him. Why, then, was the halachah not decided according to his views? Because his colleagues could not fathom the depths of his reasoning, for he would declare the ritually impure to be*

---

cerning the first fruits (*bikkurim*) from the time of the first *Yovel. Rashi* (ad loc.) understands this to mean the first *Yovel* the Jewish nation ever observed — in the days of Joshua (see *Meiri* ibid.). Thus we have clear proof that mishnayos were taught as early as Joshua's time, for since then the laws of *bikkurim* have changed. Nevertheless, their original formulation has been retained.

Similarly, *Ohr HaChayim* on the Torah writes that the *baraisa* in *Shabbos* 6b, "Which is a public domain? A highway, a plaza, open alleys and the desert, was originally taught when the Jews were in the Desert [which, as the *Gemara* there explains, was when the Desert was considered a public domain with regard to the Sabbath] (see, however, *Mitzpeh Eisan* there, who avers that the *baraisa* only means if 600,000 men were to walk in the desert today). Also, mishnayos whose meanings were subsequently interpreted differently by other *Tannaim* (Sages of the Mishnah) most probably were written earlier (see *Pe'ah* 4:5, *Kilayim* 2:1,2, et al.). The *Gemara* (*Yoma* 53b) states: It happened that once the *Kohen Gadol* prolonged his prayer [in the Temple on *Yom Kippur*]... They said to him, "Do not make a habit of doing so," for we have learned *He would not pray long, lest he terrify Israel* — which is a mishnah (ibid. 52b). Thus, we see that already in the era of the Temple the mishnayos were being taught. See *Maharatz Chayes* to *Shabbos* (12b), quoting *Vilna Gaon*.

7. [For this reason we read this chapter of *Zevachim* — *Aizehu Mekoman* — each day as part of the morning prayers, because there are no disputes regarding it, and so it has retained its original formulation.]

pure and adduce adequate proof, and the ritually pure to be impure and also supply proof.

Therefore, R' Akiva regarded R' Meir very fondly, even supporting him in his youth. And Rebbi adopted R' Meir's style of teaching — which corresponded to R' Akiva's — in the Mishnah, because it was succinct, lucid, cohesive, and far more precise than those of his colleagues, conveying the desired thought with neither too many nor too few words. Each word that he did select was laden with marvelous implications, which not every sage could fathom. Even though all the *Tannaim* could reason equally well, R' Meir's opinions were preferred to those of his colleagues; therefore, Rebbi selected them, and added later contemporary decisions.

Rebbi also cited minority opinions which are not followed by the halachah, so that if one should claim that view for a support, he can be told that it is a minority opinion and not according to the accepted law (*Eduyos* 1:6).

OFTEN THE *GEMARA* COMMENTS THAT A MISHNAH IS חַסּוֹרֵי מֵיחַסְּרָא, *deficient*. The *Gemara* does not mean to imply that the omission is a

Omissions in the Mishnah

defect in the text, but that Rebbi intentionally deleted that which could otherwise be inferred. That is, since writing down the Oral Law was permitted only because of extreme necessity (*It is time to do for Hashem*), Rebbi was constrained to do so as infrequently as possible. Where he could rely on the student to understand the mishnahs' full import without the missing phrases, he was not permitted to write them.[8]

Some opine that Rebbi's omissions were based on mystical considerations, and they bring support for this view (*Sefer Habris*).

The disciples of *Vilna Gaon* write that their teacher knew all the omissions in the Talmud and did not consider them omissions at all. Rebbi would not have omitted anything from the mishnayos. Rather, *a "deficient" mishnah* is one in which Rebbi followed the opinion of one *Tanna*, and composed the particular mishnah accordingly. The *Gemara*, however, agreed with another disputing *Tanna*, and wished to reconcile the mishnah according to him. This was done by adding words to the mishnah (Introduction to *Pe'as HaShulchan; Aliyos Eliyahu*).

---

8. To be sure, this explanation follows only *Rambam's* view that Rebbi committed Mishnah to writing (see above). *Shelah* quotes *She'eiris Yosef*, who cites R' *Mattisyahu of France*, that Rebbi wrote the Mishnah very concisely, and one can understand the full intent of the *Tanna* from what appears in the Mishnah alone.

The later commentators note that the *Gemara's* expression תְּנֵי הָכִי, *include such and such,* is not synonymous with *the mishnah is deficient.* It merely means to point out that this is indeed the implication of the mishnah (*Yad Malachi,* quoting *Drishah;* but see *Rashi* to *Zevachim* 114b, who does explain this expression to mean *the mishnah is deficient*).

THE MISHNAH WAS WRITTEN IN THE HEBREW LANGUAGE. *RAMBAM* attests to Rebbi's clarity of expression, commenting that he was the most
Language gifted writer in the Holy Language of his time. The Sages even resolved their difficulty understanding obscure words in Scripture by listening to Rebbi's servants speak (see *Megillah* 18a, *Rosh Hashanah* 26b). *Rav Sherira Gaon* writes that Rebbi wrote clearly and succinctly, so that each word was pregnant with an untold number of interpretations and legal implications. His work was obviously accomplished with Divine assistance.

THE DIVISION OF THE SIX ORDERS OF THE MISHNAH INTO INDIVIDUAL tractates was apparently undertaken by Rebbi, for originally there were
The Tractates six or seven hundred orders, as noted above, whereas now we have a total of only sixty-one tractates. Even though the earlier orders were also divided into tractates, as seen in the episode of R' Meir and R' Nassan concerning Tractate *Uketzin* (*Horayos* 13b), Rebbi, nevertheless reorganized them into tractates within the framework of six orders.

The Hebrew word for tractate — מַסֶּכֶת, *masseches* [the Aramaic form מַסֶּכְתָּא is often heard in common speech] — derives from מָסְכָה יֵינָה, *diluted her wine* (*Proverbs* 9:2), for each tractate contains a mixture of disparate laws. The preceding verse in *Proverbs* states: *She* (*Wisdom*) *has hewn out her seven pillars,* which the *Gemara* (*Shabbos* 116a) interprets as referring to the seven books of the Torah.[9] Thus, the Oral Law *dilutes the wine* and *arranges the table* (loc. cit.) of the Written Law, for without the oral tradition no man would dare approach the Written Torah. *Dilutes the wine* has yet another interpretation: that the various laws and ordinances of the Torah are mixed and bound to one another so that the law of one subject may be deduced from one in another area, or that one rule of one subject may be deduced from one

---

9. [The passage *Vayehi Binso'a* . . . (*Num.* 10:35-36) is considered a book unto itself, thus dividing *Numbers* into three books, giving the Torah a total of seven books (*Gem.* ad loc.).]

in another area, or that one rule may be explained or clarified by another. That is why a group of chapters of the Mishnah is called מַסֶּכֶת, from the word מְסִיכָה, *mixture*, just as the word גְּבִירָה, *rich lady*, is related to גְּבֶרֶת, *lady* (Introduction to *Tos. Yom Tov*).

Others explain that *masseches* means *weaving*, like עִם הַמַּסֶּכֶת, *with the web* (*Judges* 16:13), in the story of Samson. Thus, the Oral Law resembles fibers such as wool or flax, which one labors to weave into a cogent entity (*Sefer Chasidim*, Ch. 928).[10]

Still others interpret that the Mishnah represents the warp of the loom and the *Gemara* the woof, for the *Gemara* is the "soul" of the tractate, since one may not decide the law from the Mishnah alone (*Tos. Anshei Shem*).

Alternatively, *masseches* derives from מָסָךְ, *masach*, screen in front of the door (see *Exodus* 26:36, et al.), since the Oral Law is the door through which one enters the Written Law (*Sefer Leket HaKemach*). Another interpretation is that *masseches* stems from כִּיסוּי, *a covering*, to teach us that the Mishnah is hidden and not fathomable without the *Gemara* (*Tos. Anshei Shem*). Also, the numerical value of מַסֶּכֶת is 520; if we add four, corresponding to the number of letters in the word, the total is 524, equaling the number of chapters in the Mishnah (*Chida*).[11]

The tractates are titled according to their subject matter, but occasionally the name is taken from the first word of the opening mishnah, as in Tractate *Beitzah*. Indeed, some refer to *Beitzah* as Tractate *Yom Tov* because it discusses the laws of the Festivals.

The rule is that in regard to two different tractates there is no order to the mishnayos. Thus, if a mishnah containing a dispute between *Tannaim* appears in one tractate, and another mishnah without a dispute and contradicting one of the opinions in the first mishnah appears in a later tractate, we do not say that the halachah follows the second mishnah, as we would if both appeared in the same tractate. This is because Rebbi did not teach the tractates in any particular order, but only according to the interests of his students. However, the final composition of the

---

10. *Tosefos Anshei Shem* demur, arguing that *masseches* refers not to weaving, but to the warp of the loom, which is tightly wound around the pole. However, perhaps we can still say that *masseches* implies something arranged or in one place, and such was the intent of *Sefer Chasidim*.

11. [A well-known mnemonic device for this number is that it is also the numerical value of תַּלְמוּד בַּבְלִי, *the Babylonian Talmud*, although, of course, the Mishnah is the same in the Jerusalem Talmud as well.] However, in his Introduction to *Yad HaChazakah*, *Rambam* states that the Mishnah contains only 523 chapters. Furthermore, the fourth chapter of Tractate *Bikkurim* consists of *baraisos*, not mishnayos; likewise, the sixth chapter of *Avos*.

mishnah was done in a certain order, and therefore explanations must be given as to why each tractate occupies its positions in its order (first *Tosafos* to *Bava Metzia*).

Regarding the Six Orders themselves, some hold that Rebbi taught them in a specific order. Therefore, if a mishnah with a dispute appears in a tractate in one order, and similar mishnah without a dispute appears in a later order, we apply the principle that when a mishnah containing a dispute is followed by one expressing only one opinion on the same subject, the halachah follows the second mishnah (*Kesef Mishneh, Hil. Rotzei'ach*). Others, however, maintain that even regarding the Orders there is really no arrangement (*Tos.* to *Shabbos* 81b).

The Six Orders of the Mishnah are: (1) זְרָעִים, *Zera'im* (Seeds; dealing with agricultural laws), (2) מוֹעֵד, *Moed* (Appointed Time; dealing with the laws of the Sabbath and festivals), (3) נָשִׁים, *Nashim* (Women; dealing with the laws of marriage, divorce, widowhood and related matters), (4) נְזִיקִין, *Nezikin* (Damages; dealing with torts and general monetary law), (5) קָדָשִׁים, *Kodashim* (Sanctities; dealing with Temple and sacrificial law), and (6) טָהֲרוֹת, *Tohoros* (Purities; dealing with the laws of ritual "purity" and "impurity"). The mnemonic acronym is זְמַן נָקָט, *hold on to time* [which implies an appeal to the Jews to recognize and to uphold the Oral Law in all times (*Abarbanel*)].

The *Gemara* (*Shabbos* 31a) teaches: What is meant by the verse, וְהָיָה אֱמוּנַת עִתֶּיךָ חֹסֶן יְשׁוּעוֹת חָכְמַת וָדָעַת, *And the faithfulness of your times, and the strength of salvation will be wisdom and knowledge* (Isaiah 33:6)? *Faithfulness* refers to *Zera'im*;[12] *your times* to *Moed*; the *strength* to *Nashim*;[13] *salvation* to *Nezikin*;[14] *wisdom* to *Kodashim*; and *knowledge* to *Tohoros*. Yet, even so, the verse concludes: יִרְאַת ה' הִיא אוֹצָרוֹ, *the fear of the Lord is [man's] treasure*. The *sine qua non* of all Torah knowledge is the fear of God; without it, there is nothing (see *Maharatz Chayes* to *Shabbos* loc. cit., quoting *Vilna Gaon; Ohr HaChaim* to *Deut.* 13:5).[15]

---

12. *Rashi* explains that only the man of faith will tithe his produce properly. *Tosafos* cite *Yerushalmi* that the Order is so called because one should sow with faith in the Almighty.

13. *Rashi* renders this word in the verse *heirs*, who, of course, are born from women. Some say that the Order of *Nashim* is called *strength*, for indeed it is the strength and the shelter of the Jewish people, since it basically discusses Jewish family life.

14. *Rashi* explains that *Nezikin* helps people by admonishing them not to injure one another, and thereby bring financial obligations upon themselves.

15. The *Midrash* (*Bamidbar Rabbah* 13:18 and to *Psalms* 19:14) expounds a different passage as alluding to the Six Orders of the Mishnah: *Psalms* 19:8-10 states: *The Torah of Hashem is perfect, restoring the soul; the testimony of Hashem is trustworthy, making the simple one wise: the orders of Hashem are upright, gladdening the heart; the command*

The *Midrash* (to *Song of Songs* 6:9) says: *Sixty are royalty* — these are the sixty orders of halachos, i.e. the sixty tractates,[16] as follows:

Zera'im includes: (1) *Berachos*, (2) *Pe'ah*, (3) *Demai*, (4) *Kilayim*, (5) *Sheviis*, (6) *Terumos*, (7)*Maasros*, (8) *Maaser Sheni*, (9) *Challah*, (10) *Orlah*, (11) *Bikkurim*. Some count *Maasros* and *Maaser Sheni* as one, in which case the total number of tractates in *Zera'im* is ten.

Moed includes: (1) *Shabbos*, (2) *Eruvin*, (3) *Pesachim*, (4) *Shekalim*, (5) *Yoma*, (6) *Succah*, (7) *Beitzah*, (8) *Rosh Hashanah*, (9) *Taanis*, (10) *Megillah*, (11) *Moed Katan*, (12) *Chagigah*.

Nashim contains: (1) *Yevamos*, (2) *Kesubos*, (3) *Nedarim*, (4) *Nazir*, (5) *Sotah*, (6) *Gittin*, (7) *Kiddushin*.

Nezikin consists of: (1) *Bava Kamma*, (2) *Bava Metzia*, (3) *Bava Basra*, (4) *Sanhedrin*, (5) *Makkos*, (6) *Shevuos*, (7) *Eduyos*, (8) *Avodah Zarah*, (9) *Avos*, (10) *Horayos*. *Bava Kamma*, *Bava Metzia* and *Bava Basra* are also referred to collectively as *Nezikin*. Some consider them to be one long tractate, which would reduce the total number of tractates in the Order of *Nezikin* to eight. Others consider *Sanhedrin* and *Makkos* as one, further lowering the figure to seven tractates.[17]

Kodashim includes: (1) *Zevachim*, (2) *Menachos*, (3) *Chullin*, (4) *Bechoros*, (5) *Arachin*, (6) *Temurah*, (7) *Kereisos*, (8) *Me'ilah*, (9) *Tamid*, (10) *Middos*, (11) *Kinnim*.

Tohoros contains: (1) *Keilim*,[18] (2) *Ohalos*, (3) *Nega'im*, (4) *Parah*, (5)

---

of Hashem is clear, enlightening the eyes: the fear of Hashem is pure, enduring forever; the judgments of Hashem are true, altogether righteous. The Torah of Hashem is perfect — this is the Order of *Nashim*, as the verse (*Song of Songs* 4:7) states: "Where you will be completely fair, my beloved, *and no blemish will be in you." The testimony of Hashem is trustworthy* — this is the Order of *Zeraim*, for one places his *faith* in Hashem, the Eternal God, and sows his seed. *The orders of Hashem are upright, gladdening the heart* — this is the Order of *Moed*, which contains the laws of *Succah*, *Lulav* and all the festivals of the year, regarding which it says (*Deut.* 16:14): *You shall rejoice on your festival. The command of Hashem is clear, enlightening the eyes* — this is the Order of *Kodashim*, which *enlightens* the eyes of the Sages. *The fear of Hashem is pure* — this is the Order of *Tohoros*, which separates the impure and the *pure*. *The judgments of Hashem are true* — this is the Order of *Nezikin*, which contains all monetary laws.

16. *Meiri* (*Introduction to Avos*) writes that one who knew all sixty tractates was worthy of the title גאון, *Gaon*, whose numerical value is sixty. Regarding the exact number of the tractates, it will be seen in the listing below that there are different ways of listing the tractates, which can yield a total of 60, 61, or 63.

17. *Ri Migash* and *Ritva* opine that those who consider *Nezikin* as one tractate refer to the entire Order and not just to the three "*Bavas.*" According to this opinion, the Order of *Nezikin* contains just one tractate. See *Yad Malachi* §338. See *Maharsha* to *Tosafos*, *Bava Basra* 2a s.v. השותפין.

18. In the *Tosefta*, Tractate *Keilim* is divided into three parts — *Bava Kamma*, *Bava Metzia* and *Bava Basra* — just as *Nezikin* [i.e. the three "*Bavas*"], according to the opinion that it is one tractate.

Tohoros, (6) *Mikvaos*, (7) *Niddah*, (8) *Machshirin*, (9) *Zavim*, (10) *Tevul Yom*, (11) *Yadayim*, (12) *Uketzin*.

The term *mishnah* is similar to מִשְׁנֶה לַמֶּלֶךְ, *mishneh lamelech* (deputy to a king) [*Esther* 10:3], since the Written Torah is the king and the Mishnah is subordinate to it. *Mishnah* also means *to teach*; hence, the masters of the Mishnah are called תַּנָּאִים, *Tannaim*, which is the Aramaic equivalent of teachers,[19] since they taught us the Mishnah.

The Rabbis of the *Gemara* are called אֲמוֹרָאִים, *Amoraim*, since after the Mishnah was finalized no one was allowed to add to or subtract from it in any way. The later sages were permitted only to explain and interpret the mishnayos as they had been taught by their teachers. *Amora* means interpreter in Aramaic.[20]

The students of Rebbi who accepted the tradition from him were: his sons, Shimon and Gamliel, as well as R' Efes, R' Chanina bar Chama, R' Chiya, R' Yannai, Bar Kappara, Rav, Shmuel, R' Yochanan (according to *Rambam*), Levi, R' Bisa, and (according to *Ravad*) R' Chama.

---

19. וְשִׁנַּנְתָּם, *and you shall teach them* (*Deut.* 6:7), is translated by Onkelos as וּתְתַנִּינוּן, of the same root as תַּנָּאִים.

20. As we find in the *Gemara:* Place an *amora* [interpreter] by his side (*Gittin* 43a, *Rashi* ad loc.; *Chullin* 100a; et al.).

III. The Importance of Mishnah Study[1]

T HE *GEMARA* (*TAANIS* 7A-B) STATES: IF YOU SEE A STUDENT WHOSE studies are as hard as iron [i.e. he has difficulty understanding them (*Rashi* ad loc.)], it is because his knowledge of the mishnaic text is not arranged in his mind [in an orderly fashion]. The Mishnah is the foundation of the Oral Law. It contains the basic laws deriving from the commandments found in Scripture. *Gemara* analyzes and elaborates on Mishnah, seeking to establish the underlying principles of the Mishnah's rulings. One cannot properly analyze the Mishnah unless he has command of it. Thus, a student whose knowledge of the Mishnah is deficient will inevitably encounter difficulties in the course of his studies which he cannot resolve.

Thus, the Sages of the Gemara would review the text of the Mishnah numerous times before continuing on to its Talmudic analysis. Reish Lakish would review the Mishnaic text forty times (corresponding to the forty days during which the Torah was transmitted to Moses at Mt. Sinai) before attending the Talmudic lecture of his teacher, R' Yochanan. Rav Adda bar Ahavah would review his Mishnaic text twenty-four times [corresponding to the twenty-four books of Scripture) before attending Rava's Talmudic discourse. For only after having mastered the Mishnah can one arrive at an understanding of its underlying principles.

The *Gemara* (*Horayos* 14a) identifies two types of scholars: "*Sinai*," i.e. one who possesses precise knowledge of the body of Oral Law as it had been presented to Moses at Mt. Sinai; and "*Oker Harim*" (lit. uprooter of mountains), i.e. a sharp-witted scholar who excels at analysis of the laws. The *Gemara* debates which is the superior type of scholar, and concludes that the "*Sinai*" scholar is superior. For "all need the master of wheat," i.e. all must come to the "*Sinai*" scholar for his knowledge of the Mishnah. The basis of all Talmudic analysis is the precise text of the Mishnah. Without it, Talmudic analysis is impossible.

The *Gemara* (*Sanhedrin* 99a) expounds the verse, *For he despised the word of Hashem* (*Numbers* 15:31), to refer to one who does not take proper heed of the Mishnah. *Maharal* (ad loc.) explains: The Mishnah,

---

1. This section is based largely on *Z'man Nakat*, by HaRav HaGaon R' David Cohen שליט"א.

which delineates the mitzvos of the Torah, is considered "the word of Hashem." *Pilpul* (Talmudic debate that is not based on the Written Law) is not "the *word* of Hashem" because it emanates from the rational human mind. Hence, one who engages in excessive *pilpul* and ignores the study of Mishnah is viewed as a person who "despises the word of Hashem."

The Midrash (*Vayikra Rabbah* 7:3) states: The Holy One, Blessed is He, says, "When you engage in the study of Mishnah, it is as if you offer a sacrificial offering [in the Temple]." The Midrash (ibid.) states further that the ingathering of the exiles at the coming of the Messiah will be in the merit of Mishnah study.

The letters of the word משנה are the same as נְשָׁמָה, *soul*. This signifies the beneficial spiritual effects Mishnah study has on one's soul (see *ba'er Heitiv*, *Orach Chaim* 1:6). For this reason, it is customary to study Mishnah in memory of someone who has passed away, for the merit of Mishnah study serves to elevate the soul of the deceased in Heaven.[2]

The study of Mishnah is looked upon very favorably in Heaven. As is well known, R' Yosef Karo, author of *Shulchan Aruch*, merited that a heavenly angel came to study with him. R' Yosef Karo compiled a collection of the teachings of this angel, called *Maggid Meisharim*. Throughout this book, the angel makes numerous references to the study of Mishnah, enjoining R' Yosef Karo to scrupulously devote time to its study.

A *baraisa* (*Bava Metzia* 33a) authored by Rebbi states: "Those who engross themselves in the study of Scripture accomplish a measure, but it is not a large measure. Those who engross themselves in the study of Mishnah accomplish a large measure, and they receive reward for studying it. As for the study of the Talmud, there is no greater measure than this — yet one should always run to study Mishnah more than Talmud." The Gemara questions the seeming contradiction in the *baraisa*. First the *baraisa* states that there is no greater measure than Talmud study, implying that it is more important than the study of Mishnah. Yet the *baraisa* concludes that one should run to study Mishnah more than Talmud!" The Gemara explains: Initially, Rebbi taught that Talmud study is preferable to the study of Mishnah. However, when he saw that people pursued the study of Talmud, neglecting the Mishnah, he declared: "One should always run to study Mishnah more than Talmud."

---

2. It is customary to recite a short prayer after studying mishnayos for the merit of the deceased. The text of this prayer appears at the end of this volume.

◆§ Seder Zeraim Vol. I:

מסכת ברכות
Tractate Berachos

Translation and anthologized commentary by
Rabbi Mordecai Rabinovitch

Edited by
Rabbi Reuvein Dowek

Assisted by
Rabbi Yitzchok Stavsky
Rabbi Gidone Lane

Reviewed by
Rabbi Chaim Malinowitz

ᴥ§ Introduction to Seder Zera'im

The Mishnah consists of six *Sedarim* [orders; sing.: *Seder*]. The first of these is the order of זְרָעִים, *Zera'im* ["Seeds"], which deals with the laws governing agriculture, primarily in the Land of Israel. The *Gemara* in *Shabbos* (31a) homiletically expounds *Isaiah* 33:6 as alluding to the six orders of the Mishnah. The verse reads: וְהָיָה אֱמוּנַת עִתֶּיךָ חֹסֶן יְשׁוּעֹת חָכְמַת וָדָעַת יִרְאַת ה' הִיא אוֹצָרוֹ, *And the faithfulness of your times and the strength of salvations will be wisdom and knowledge and the fear of Hashem is [man's] treasure.*[1] "Faithfulness" alludes to the Order of *Zera'im*, whose laws rely on the integrity of the farmer to separate the requisite tithes.[2] Moreover, unlike other occupations, in which success tends to breed arrogant self-reliance, farming develops one's faith in God, on Whom the farmer must rely to provide all that is necessary to make the crops grow.[3] *"Your times"* refers to the Order of *Moed; "the strength"* refers to the Order of *Nashim; "salvations"* refers to the Order of *Nezikin; "wisdom"* refers to the Order of *Kodashim;* and *"knowledge"* refers to the Order of *Tohoros.*[4] But, as the verse concludes, even beyond the study of Torah is *the fear of Hashem, which is [man's] treasure.*

Appropriately, *Zera'im* is the inaugural order of the Mishnah, because agriculture is the basis of all sustenance, and no service of God [which is the essence of the entire Torah — Written and Oral] is possible without physical sustenance (*Rambam, Introduction to the Mishnah*).[5]

---

1. Translation follows *Radak* ad loc.; cf. *Rashi* there.

2. *Rashi* to *Shabbos* ad loc.

3. See *Tosafos* there.

4. See above, *"An Introduction to Mishnah"* for explanations of how these respective orders are alluded to in these words.

5. [Moreover, in light of the verse expounded by the *Gemara* in *Shabbos* (cited above), it is the Order of "Faithfulness" — human integrity and faith in God — that represents the fundamental principles upon which all study of Torah and service of God must be founded (cf. *Tos. Yom Tov, Preface*).]

Why *Berachos* is contained in and in fact begins the order of *Zera'im* will be discussed in the tractate introduction (below). The ensuing tractates of this order are: *Pe'ah* (dealing with the portions of the crop that must be left for the poor); *Demai* (dealing with the treatment of produce that might not have been fully tithed); *Kilayim* (dealing with the laws of forbidden hybrids); *Sheviis* (dealing with the laws of the *Shemittah* year); *Terumos* (dealing with the portion of the crop that the farmer must give to the Kohen); *Maasros* (dealing with the tithe of the crop that the farmer must give the Levi); *Maaser Sheni* (dealing with the "second tithe," which the farmer eats in Jerusalem); *Challah* (dealing with the portion of bread dough that one who bakes gives to the Kohen); *Orlah* (dealing with the laws regarding a fruit tree's early years); and *Bikkurim* (regarding the first fruits that a farmer separates and brings to the Temple).

✎§ General Introduction to Tractate Berachos

✎§ The Tractate

Berachos ["Blessings"], as its name implies, deals primarily with the assorted blessings that are recited at various times and occasions. In essence, a בְּרָכָה, *blessing* (which invariably begins and/or ends with the formula בָּרוּךְ אַתָּה ה׳, *Blessed are You, Hashem*), is an acknowledgment of God as the Creator of the phenomenon beheld, the Commander of the mitzvah performed, or Provider of the benefit enjoyed. Sometimes, a blessing simply acknowledges; at times it also implores. Always, it serves to heighten our awareness of our Heavenly Father and His intimate closeness to us.[1] *Deuteronomy* 10:12 declares: וְעַתָּה יִשְׂרָאֵל מָה ה׳ אֱלֹהֶיךָ שֹׁאֵל מֵעִמָּךְ כִּי אִם־לְיִרְאָה אֶת־ה׳ אֱלֹהֶיךָ לָלֶכֶת בְּכָל־דְּרָכָיו וּלְאַהֲבָה אֹתוֹ וְלַעֲבֹד אֶת־ה׳ אֱלֹהֶיךָ בְּכָל־לְבָבְךָ וּבְכָל־נַפְשֶׁךָ, *And now, O Israel, what does Hashem, your God, ask of you? Only to fear Hashem, your God, to go in all His ways and to love Him, and to serve Hashem, your God, with all your heart and with all your soul.* From here, the Sages derive that one must recite a hundred blessings every day — expounding the verse as if it read: "מֵאָה" ה׳ אֱלֹהֶיךָ שֹׁאֵל מֵעִמָּךְ, *"one hundred" does Hashem, your God, ask of you.*[2] Indeed, this exposition of the Sages is in full harmony with the plain meaning of the verse. For the Sages have issued a prescription for how to attain the lofty ideal set forth in the verse: By thoughtfully blessing and acknowledging God on one hundred occasions throughout the day, one cultivates a profound awareness and awe of the Creator, and learns to go in His ways and love and serve Him with the totality of heart and soul.[3]

---

1. See *Rambam, Hil. Berachos* 1:3-4. [Regarding the precise meaning of the word בָּרוּךְ (generally translated as "blessed"), see below.]

2. *Menachos* 43b with *Rashi*; cf. *Tosafos* there, and *Baal HaTurim* to *Deuteronomy* ad loc. and to *Genesis* 14:19.

3. It is for this reason that *Rambam* includes the laws of blessings and Prayer in *Sefer Ahavah* (*Book of Love*) of his halachic code. For these obligations serve as a constant

This tractate consists of nine chapters, covering four basic themes:[4] *Krias Shema* — the acknowledgment of God's Oneness and sovereignty — and its associated blessings (Chapters 1-3); *Tefillah*, i.e. the *Shemoneh Esrei* prayer (Chapters 4-5); blessings for benefits enjoyed [בִּרְכוֹת הַנֶּהֱנִין] (Chapters 6-8); and blessings which acknowledge that God is the author of all natural phenomena and all that happens to us [בִּרְכוֹת הוֹדָאָה] (Chapter 9).

Rambam (*Commentary to the Mishnah, Preface*) explains Rebbi's choice of *Berachos* as the first tractate of the Mishnah[5] as follows: In seeking to preserve the well-being of a healthy person, the expert doctor will first prescribe the proper diet and means of preparing food. Now, the recitation of a blessing over food is indeed an essential "preparation" of that food, since it is forbidden to partake of it without a blessing. [And — as explained in the *Seder* introduction (above) — the reason that the Mishnah begins with the Order of *Zerai'm* in the first place is that food and physical sustenance are the prerequisites for all service of God.] Therefore, the first laws to be detailed are those concerning blessings.[6]

↵§ Blessings

The texts of the various blessings were formulated by Ezra and his court, the Men of the Great Assembly (see *Gem.* 33a; *Rambam, Hil. Krias Shema* 1:7). The *Bircas HaMazon*, the Grace After Meals, is an exception. The first of the four blessings contained in the *Bircas HaMazon*, known as בִּרְכַּת הַזָּן, *Bircas HaZan*, was formulated by Moses in the Desert, at the time the Manna first fell from Heaven; the second, known as בִּרְכַּת הָאָרֶץ, *Bircas Haaretz*, was formulated by

---

reminder of God and his Providence, and promote a reciprocal feeling of love for Him on our part.

4. Based on *Meiri, Preface*.

5. *Meiri* (*Introduction*) remarks that in the times of the Geonim, Talmudic study among the people focused on the Orders of *Moed, Nashim* and *Nezikin*, to the virtual neglect of *Zerai'm, Kodashim* and *Tohoros*, which deal primarily with topics that are not practically relevant in exile. Because of this, the *Geonim* removed from the neglected Orders the three more relevant tractates — *Berachos* (from *Zera'im*), *Chullin* (from *Kodashim*) and *Niddah* (from *Taharos*) — placing the first two in *Moed* and the third in *Nashim*, so that those tractates would be mastered along with the three "relevant" orders. [It is already many centuries, though, that these tractates have been restored to their original orders.]

6. *Meiri* (*Introduction*) further accounts for the primacy of *Berachos* on the basis of its dealing with the fundamentals of our faith — the Oneness of God, prayer to Him, and our need to declare His praise and express our gratitude to Him. Moreover, it is fitting to treat these mitzvos first because of their daily and nearly constant application.

Joshua when the Jewish Nation entered Eretz Yisrael; the third blessing, בּוֹנֵה יְרוּשָׁלַיִם, *Bonei Yerushalayim*, was composed partly by David and partly by Solomon; the last blessing, הַטּוֹב וְהַמֵּטִיב, *Hatov Ve'hameitiv*, was formulated by the Sages of Yavneh some time after the destruction of the Second Temple (*Gem.* 48b).

Another difference between the *Bircas HaMazon* and other blessings is that it is a Biblical obligation, derived from *Deuteronomy* 8:10,[7] whereas all other blessings are Rabbinical obligations. According to some authorities, there is also a Biblical obligation to utter a blessing before studying Torah, the בִּרְכַּת הַתּוֹרָה, *Bircas HaTorah* (*Ramban, addendum to Sefer HaMitvos, Asei* §15; *Chinuch mitzvah* 430; *Rashba* to 48b s.v. הא דאפליגו).

⊰ The *Shema*

The first topic dealt with in the tractate is the laws of the *Shema* and its associated blessings (Ch. 1-3). *Rambam* (Introduction to *Mishnah Comm.*) explains that in presenting the laws of blessings, which encompass both blessings over food and those recited upon the performance of a mitzvah, Rebbi begins the tractate with the laws of the *Shema* and its associated blessings, since recitation of the *Shema* is the only mitzvah incumbent on every man every day.[8] The Mishnah deals with the *Shema* before discussing its blessings because it is only fitting to detail the laws of the *Shema* itself before those of the blessings that the Sages instituted upon its recitation. R' Yeshayah Acharon (cited in *Shiltei HaGiborim* to the beginning of this tractate), however, writes that since *the beginning of wisdom is fear of Hashem* (*Psalms* 111:10), our holy Sages placed at the Mishnah's outset the laws of the *Shema*, which require man to declare every morning and evening the Oneness of Hashem and the acceptance of His sovereignty, Torah and mitzvos.

There is an obligation to recite the *Shema* twice daily, once in the evening and once in the morning. The *Shema* consists of three Scriptural passages. The first, which begins with the verse: שְׁמַע יִשְׂרָאֵל ה' אֱלֹהֵינוּ ה' אֶחָד, *Hear O Israel, Hashem is our God, Hashem is the One and Only*, consists of the verses in *Deuteronomy* 6:4-9. The second, which begins with the words וְהָיָה אִם־שָׁמֹעַ, *And it will be if you*

---

7. However, the Torah does not mandate a specific text to be recited. The actual texts of the blessings were formulated by Moses, Joshua, David and Solomon, as noted above (see *Rashba* to 48b s.v. הא דאמרינן).

8. See *Rambam, Hil. Tefillah* 1:1; see also *Beur Halachah* to 1:2.

hearken..., consists of the verses in *Deuteronomy* 11:13-21. The third passage, which begins with the word וַיֹּאמֶר, *And [Hashem] said...*, consists of the verses in *Numbers* 15:37-41, and refers to the laws of *tzitzis* and the Exodus from Egypt. The term *Shema*, which technically refers to the first of these three passages, is also used to refer to all three passages together. The obligation to recite the first of these passages is based on the verse in the passage which states: וְשִׁנַּנְתָּם לְבָנֶיךָ וְדִבַּרְתָּ בָּם בְּשִׁבְתְּךָ בְּבֵיתֶךָ וּבְלֶכְתְּךָ בַדֶּרֶךְ וּבְשָׁכְבְּךָ וּבְקוּמֶךָ, "And you shall teach them thoroughly to your children, and you shall speak of them, while you sit in your home and while you go on the way, *and when you retire and when you arise*" (*Deuteronomy* 6:7). Similarly, the second passage states: וְלִמַּדְתֶּם אֹתָם אֶת־בְּנֵיכֶם לְדַבֵּר בָּם בְּשִׁבְתְּךָ בְּבֵיתֶךָ וּבְלֶכְתְּךָ בַדֶּרֶךְ וּבְשָׁכְבְּךָ וּבְקוּמֶךָ, "You shall teach them to your children to discuss them, while you sit in your home, while you walk on the way, *when you retire and when you arise*" (ibid. 11:19). These verses are understood to refer to the passages in which they are written. The obligation to recite the third passage of the *Shema* — *Vayomer* — derives from the commandment [stated in *Exodus* 13:3 and *Deuteronomy* 16:3] to verbally refer to the Exodus, mention of which is contained in this passage, on a twice-daily basis. This passage also refers to the mitzvah of *tzitzis*. *Tzitzis* serve as a reminder of our obligation to observe all the Torah commandments (see *Numbers* 15:39). Thus, the passage was deemed suitable for incorporation into the *Shema*, which contains similar statements of obedience to God's commands (*Gem.* 12b).

The *Gemara* (21a) debates whether the recitation of the *Shema* is a Biblical obligation or a Rabbinical obligation. According to R' Elazar, there is a Biblical requirement to recite the *Shema*, derived from the aforementioned verses in the *Shema*. Rav Yehudah, however, contends that the obligation is Rabbinic. According to Rav Yehudah, these verses refer to Torah study in general. They are merely Scriptural *allusions* [אַסְמַכְתָּא] to this Rabbinical enactment (see *Tosafos* ad loc. s.v. ההוא).[9] Some authorities rule in accordance with Rav Yehudah that the recitation of the *Shema* is a Rabbinical obligation (*Tosafos* to *Bava Kamma* 87a s.v. וכן and to *Menachos* 43b s.v. ואיזו; see also *Tosafos* to *Sotah* 32a s.v. קרית; *Teshuvos HaRosh* 4:21). In the opinion of the majority of authorities, however, there is a Biblical obligation to recite

---

9. *Shaagas Aryeh* (§1) contends that even according to Rav Yehudah there is a Biblical obligation to recite Scriptural passages morning and evening, as the verse indicates. However, Biblically, one may recite any Biblical passage. The requirement to fulfill the Biblical obligation by reciting the specific passages of the *Shema* is a Rabbinical enactment.

the *Shema* (*Rambam, Sefer HaMitzvos, Asei* §10; *Rif* 12b; *Rosh* 1:15, et al.).

However, even those who maintain that the recitation is Biblically mandated disagree regarding the extent of the Biblical obligation. According to some, Biblically one is only required to recite the first verse of the *Shema*: שְׁמַע יִשְׂרָאֵל ה׳ אֱלֹהֵינוּ ה׳ אֶחָד [*Deuteronomy* 6:6] (*Teshuvos HaRashba* I:320; *Chinuch mitzvah* 420; *Beis Yosef, Orach Chaim* 63 s.v. וכתב רבינו יונה). Others maintain that the recitation of the entire first passage is a Biblical obligation (*Rabbeinu Yonah* 9a-b; *Yereim HaShalem* §252; see also *Rashi* to 2a s.v. עד סוף). A third opinion maintains that the recitation of the first *two* passages is Biblically mandated (*Pri Chadash, Orach Chaim* 67), while the third is a Rabbinic obligation.[10] Yet another view contends that all three passages are Biblically mandated (*Chareidim*, Ch. 1, *mitzvah* 14,15; *Pri Megadim, General Introduction, Hil. Kerias Shema*).[11]

❧ The Blessings of the *Shema*

The Rabbis formulated specific blessings to be recited together with the *Shema*. Two blessings are recited before both the morning and evening *Shema* — *Yotzeir Ohr* (giving praise to God for the creation of light) and *Ahavah Rabbah*[12] (thanking God for giving us His Torah, the ultimate manifestation of His love for us, and beseeching Him to grant us the wisdom to understand it properly) in the morning, and *Maariv Aravim* (similar to *Yotzeir Ohr*, but with changes that reflect its nighttime recitation) and *Ahavas Olam* (like *Ahavah Rabbah*, thanking God for the gift of the Torah) in the evening. One blessing is recited following the morning *Shema*, *Emes VeYatziv* (concentrating on the kindness God did for us in redeeming us from Egyptian bondage). The evening *Shema* is followed by two blessings, *Emes Ve'Emunah* (similar to *Emes VeYatziv*) and *Hashkiveinu* (a supplica-

---

10. The obligation to verbally mention the Exodus — in fulfillment of which we recite the third passage of the *Shema* — is undoubtedly Biblical [although *Pri Megadim* (*General introduction, Hil. Krias Shema*) notes that *Rambam* does not include this commandment in his listing of the mitzvos; see there for possible explanations]. However, Biblically, any verbal reference to the Exodus suffices. The requirement to discharge one's Biblical obligation with the specific passage of *Vayomer* is, according to these opinions, a Rabbinical institution.

11. For detailed discussions regarding these various opinions, see *Minchas Kohen, Mevo HaShemesh, maamar sheni* Ch. 13; *Einayim LeMishpat* to *Berachos* 21a.

12. According to some authorities, this blessing begins with the words *Ahavas Olam* (see further comm. to mishnah 1:4 s.v. בשחר).

tory blessing that God guard us through the night). Although the Rabbis instituted these blessings to be recited with the *Shema*, they do not *depend* on the *Shema*. Thus, although ideally they should be recited together with the *Shema* as the Rabbis intended, if one recites the *Shema* without these blessings, he may recite them later. Similarly, if one failed to recite the morning *Shema* within its allotted time, he may nevertheless recite these blessings (see mishnah 1:2; *Gem.* 10b).

The Rabbis formulated blessings to be recited before performing most positive commandments, known as בְּרְכוֹת הַמִּצְוֹת, *bircos hamitzvos*. The standard form of these blessings is: בָּרוּךְ אַתָּה ה' אֱלֹהֵינוּ מֶלֶךְ הָעוֹלָם אֲשֶׁר קִדְּשָׁנוּ בְּמִצְוֹתָיו וְצִוָּנוּ..., *Blessed are You, Hashem, our God, Who has sanctified us with His commandments and commanded us.* ... Nowhere do we find a requirement to recite such a formula before performing the mitzvah of the *Shema*. However, some authorities maintain that the blessing immediately preceding the *Shema* (*Ahavah Rabbah* in the morning, *Ahavas Olam* at night) was formulated to replace the standard *bircas hamitzvah* for the commandment of reciting the *Shema*. According to this view, if one recited the blessings of the *Shema* without reciting the *Shema* itself, he must repeat the *Ahavah Rabbah/Olam* blessing when he later recites the *Shema* (*Rabbeinu Yonah* 1a-b s.v אלא). *Ramban* (to 2a, ed. Dickman) subscribes to this view, and therefore decries the common practice of interjecting the phrase אֵל מֶלֶךְ נֶאֱמָן, *God, trustworthy King*, between *Ahavah Rabbah/Olam* and the *Shema*, for any interruption between a *bircas hamitzvah* and the performance of the mitzvah for which it is recited invalidates the blessing.[13] Others, however, contend that the Rabbis did not institute any *bircas hamitzvah* for the *Shema*. These authorities argue that it is evident that neither the *Ahavah Rabbah/Olam* blessing nor the other blessings associated with the *Shema* are *bircos hamitzvah* of the *Shema*, for they do not follow the standard form of such blessings, nor do they refer to the *Shema* in any way. Rather, the blessings of the *Shema* are all independent expressions of praise to God which the Rabbis instituted to be recited with the *Shema*. According to this view, if one recited the blessings without reciting the *Shema*, he need not recite these blessings [nor a standard *bircas hamitzvah*] when he later recites the *Shema* (*Teshuvos HaRashba* I:47, 63, 319). *Meiri* (to 11b s.v והרי למדת) takes another view. Indeed, the mitzvah of reciting the *Shema* warrants a *bircas hamitzvah*. However, the *Ahavah*

---

13. However, *Meiri* (*Magen Avos* Ch. 1; see also v. to 13a s.v אלה הן בין הפרקים) disputes *Ramban's* assertion that interjecting this phrase is considered an interruption

Rabbah/Olam blessing, while formulated primarily as a blessing of praise and thanks, fulfills the function of a *bircas hamitzvah*, rendering a *bircas hamitzvah* of the standard form superfluous. However, if for some reason one cannot recite this blessing before the *Shema* (e.g. he has no prayerbook and he does not know its text by heart), he would instead recite the standard text of a *bircas hamitzvah* — "Blessed are You... Who has sanctified us with His commandments and commanded us *to recite the Shema.*" [14]

⛤ Prayer

Chapters Four and Five detail the laws of Prayer. As used by the mishnah, the term *Prayer* refers to the *Shemoneh Esrei*. The *Shemoneh Esrei* is also known as the *Amidah*, since it must be recited in a standing position (see mishnah 4:5). There is a Rabbinic obligation to recite the *Shemoneh Esrei* three times daily, in the morning [*Shacharis*], the afternoon [*Minchah*], and at night [*Maariv*] (see mishnah 4:1). The *Gemara* (27b) debates whether praying *Maariv* is obligatory or discretionary (see *Rif* 19a; *Meiri* to 26a s.v. תפילת הערב). Although the halachah follows the view that *Maariv* was instituted as a discretionary prayer, the authorities state that nowadays *Maariv* is no longer optional, since Jews everywhere have accepted it as a binding obligation (*Rambam, Hil. Tefillah* 1:6; see *Rif* ibid.).

The authorities debate whether there is a Biblical obligation to pray. *Rambam* (*Sefer HaMitzvos, Asei* §5) maintains that there is a Biblical obligation, deriving from the verse (*Deuteronomy* 11:13) which enjoins us: וּלְעָבְדוֹ בְּכָל־לְבַבְכֶם, *to serve Him with all your heart*. *Ramban* (*Hasagos* ad loc.), however, disagrees, contending that the verse does not refer specifically to Prayer, but to Divine service in general, commanding us to serve God wholeheartedly. Alternatively, *Ramban* suggests that the verse only mandates Prayer in times of distress, such as wartime. At other times, however, there is no Biblical obligation to pray.

However, even *Rambam* agrees that the number of daily prayers, the text of Prayer (i.e. the *Shemoneh Esrei*) and the requirement that these Prayers be recited at specific times of day are Rabbinical institutions (see *Rambam, Hil. Tefillah* 1:1).

The weekday *Shemoneh Esrei* is divided into three sections. The first three blessings are blessings praising God; the last three blessings are

---

14. *Rabbeinu Yonah* (loc. cit.), however, rejects the notion that the Rabbis formulated a standard *bircas hamitzvah* for the *Shema* in addition to *Ahavah Rabbah/Olam*.

expressions of thanksgiving. The middle section consists of blessings of supplication (see *Rambam, Hil. Tefillah* 1:2). This structure is based on Scriptural precedent (see *Gem.* 32a; *Lechem Mishneh, Hil. Tefillah* 1:2).

⋖ Blessings Recited Before Eating

Most of Chapter 6 deals with the laws of blessings recited before eating. The obligation to recite these blessings is Rabbinical, and is based on the logical presumption that before benefiting from an item, one should acknowledge and thank God, Who provided the item. Thus the Rabbis decreed: It is forbidden for a person to derive benefit from this world without [first reciting] a blessing (*Gem.* 35a). Accordingly, the Rabbis formulated blessings, בִּרְכוֹת הַנֶּהֱנִין, *bircos hanehenin*, to be recited before eating and drinking. The various blessings the Rabbis formulated for food and drink are discussed in mishnayos 1-3.

Another benefit for which the Rabbis instituted a blessing is the smelling of fragrant aromas (see *Gem.* 43b). There are many other pleasant sensations, however, for which the Rabbis did not mandate blessings. One is not required to recite a blessing before experiencing an enjoyable sight or sound. *Ramban* (to Ch. 8) and *Tosafos* (to *Pesachim* 53b s.v. אין) explain that the Rabbis stipulated that a blessing be recited only for benefits one ingests. Thus, eating or drinking requires a blessing. Similarly, one must recite a blessing when smelling an aromatic substance, since he inhales the aroma. Benefits one enjoys through the senses of sight, hearing and touch do not enter the body, and, therefore, do not warrant a blessing.[15]

⋖ Blessings After Eating

The last mishnah of Chapter 6 discusses the *Bircas HaMazon*, the Grace After Meals. In contrast to the obligation to recite blessings before eating, which is Rabbinical, the obligation to recite the *Bircas HaMazon* is Biblical (*Gem.* 21a), deriving from Deuteronomy 8:10, which states: וְאָכַלְתָּ וְשָׂבָעְתָּ וּבֵרַכְתָּ אֶת־ה' אֱלֹהֶיךָ עַל־הָאָרֶץ הַטֹּבָה אֲשֶׁר נָתַן־לָךְ, *You will eat and you will be satisfied, and bless Hashem, your God, for the good Land that He gave you* (*Rambam, Sefer HaMitzvos, asei* §19).

---

15. The blessing of בּוֹרֵא מְאוֹרֵי הָאֵשׁ, *Who creates the illuminations of the fire*, which we recite after the Sabbath, as part of the *Havdalah* service, upon seeing a lit candle is not a *bircas hanehenin* for benefiting from the light, but rather a blessing of *praise* to God for *creating* light. It is similar to the blessing *Yotzeir Ohr*, the first of the morning *Shema* blessings, which is also an expression of praise to God for creating the light of day (*Ramban ibid.*).

According to some, one is Biblically obligated to recite the *Bircas HaMazon* only if he ate enough to satisfy his hunger (*Rambam, Hil. Berachos* 1:1; *Rashi* to 20b s.v. שיעורא and to 48a s.v. עד). According to others, even an amount of bread the size of an olive Biblically obligates the *Bircas HaMazon* (*Hasagos HaRavad, Hil. Berachos* 5:15; *Ramban, Milchamos Hashem*, 12a of *Rif* folios).

There is a Tannaitic dispute whether this obligation applies only after eating bread, after eating a member of the Seven Species,[16] or after eating any food (see mishnah 6:8). The halachah follows the view that the full *Bircas HaMazon* is only recited after eating bread. After eating one of the Seven Species, a one-blessing abridgment of the *Bircas HaMazon* is recited. After eating other foods, a short blessing — *Borei Nefashos* — is recited. There is a difference of opinion regarding the nature of the one-blessing abridgment of the *Bircas HaMazon*. Some maintain that it is Biblically mandated (*Ramban* to 49b s.v. ר' מאיר; *Rashba* to 44a s.v. ורבנן). According to others, it is a Rabbinical obligation (*Rambam, Hil. Berachos* 8:12 and *Kesef Mishneh* ad loc.; cf. *Kesef Mishneh* to ibid. 1:2 s.v. וכן). All agree, however, that the *Borei Nefashos* blessing is not Biblically mandated (*Rambam* ibid. 8:12).

⚜ The collective *Bircas HaMazon*

Chapter 7 of the tractate is devoted to the laws of the Collective *Bircas HaMazon* (*zimun*). This is the formula mandated when a group of at least three people eat a meal together. One of the company is appointed the reader, and following a prescribed formula (see mishnah 7:3), he summons the others to participate in the *Bircas HaMazon*. The reader then recites the *Bircas HaMazon* out loud on behalf of the entire company, who must listen to him in silence, or recite it along with him quietly (*Shulchan Aruch, Orach Chaim* 183:7; see also *Rama, Orach Chaim* 200:2). The *Gemara* (45a) appears to derive this requirement from Scripture. Nevertheless, some maintain that it is a Rabbinic obligation.[17]

---

16. These are the seven species of agricultural produce for which Scripture praises Eretz Yisrael. They are: wheat, barley, grapes, figs, pomegranates, olives and dates (see *Deuteronomy* ibid. v. 8).

17. According to *Ravad* (cited by *Tur, Orach Chaim* 188), the *zimun* requirement is Biblical (see also *Hasagos HaRavad* to *Baal HaMaor* 44a of *Rif* folios, §2). *Re'ah* (to 45a s.v. אמר רב אסי) and *Meiri* (to 45a s.v. וענין הזימון) contend that it is a Rabbinical obligation. *Pri Megadim* (cited by *Shaarei Tziyun* 197:16) asserts that the majority of authorities are of the opinion that *zimun* is a Rabbinical obligation. However, *Chazon Ish* (*Orach Chaim* 31:1) questions this assertion.

⋖ Blessings Recited on Special Occasions

Chapter 8 of the tractate concludes the discussion of laws relating to meals. Chapter 9 turns to blessings formulated for specific occasions. These range from blessings recited upon seeing a site at which notable events occurred (mishnah 1) to blessings recited upon witnessing striking natural phenomena and landmarks (mishnah 2), to blessings recited on joyous and sad occasions (mishnahs 2,3).

⋖ The Meaning of בָּרוּךְ

Generally, the word בָּרוּךְ is translated as "blessed" (and the word בְּרָכָה as "a blessing"). And when used in reference to God, "blessed" is meant in the sense of "praised" or "acknowledged with praise."[18] Some Rishonim,[19] however, object that this rendering does not capture the root meaning of ברך, which is "addition" and "increase."[20] Rather, they assert, the fundamental meaning of בָּרוּךְ said in reference to God is that He is the Infinite Source of limitless goodness and bounty.[21] Indeed, our blessings do nothing for *God*, Who is perfect, and categorically beyond the need for anything from His creatures or creation. Rather, the benefit of blessings is for *us*, who acknowledge God's providence and goodness and thereby becoming fitting receptacles for an effusion of His beneficence.[22]

---

18. See *Ibn Ezra* to *Genesis* 9:26; *Radak, Shorashim* ברך 'ע; *Chizkuni* to *Genesis* 24:27.

19. *Rashba* in *Chidushei Agados* to the *Gemara* below, 7a, and in *Teshuvos* 5:51; *Rabbeinu Bachya* in *Kad HaKemach* ברכה 'ע.

20. As in the verse וּבֵרַךְ אֶת־לַחְמְךָ וְאֶת־מֵימֶיךָ, *and He will give increase to your bread and your water* (*Exodus* 23:25). [*Ibn Ezra* (cited in note 8), though, seems to account for this by rendering *"additional" praise.*]

21. See also *Sefer HaChinuch* §430. These Rishonim add, however, that while they are explaining בָּרוּךְ on its simple level, it actually embodies profound secrets of the Torah.

[*Sefer HaIkkarim* (2:26) explains that the word בָּרוּךְ can refer either to the *source* of bounty or to its *recipient*; hence, it is used to describe God as well as the person He has blessed.]

22. *Rabbeinu Bachya* and *Sefer HaChinuch* loc. cit.

See also an alternative explanation of בָּרוּךְ in *Sforno* to *Genesis* 14:20 and *Commentary of R' Samson Raphael Hirsch* to *Genesis* 9:27 ברוך ה"ד. [It has also been suggested that בָּרוּךְ comes from בֶּרֶךְ, *knee*, and means: *the One to Whom the knee is bent.*]

⋖§ Acknowledgments

If not for the support and encouragement of the Yad Avraham Institute, and its patrons, Mr. and Mrs. Louis Glick, this work could not have been undertaken. I pray that Hashem grant them all that is good forever and ever. Special thanks are due to R' Paltiel Lipshitz, who followed the course of this commentary from its inception. And finally, the assistance of my dear wife Chana must be properly credited. Not only does she liberate me from household obligations, but she actively shows an interest in my work and its progress. If not for her help, I could never have put pen to paper. May Hashem grant us the strength and ability to raise all our family in His way.

At a time when the fate of the Jewish community in the Land of Israel hangs in the balance, it is only appropriate to end with the immortal words of King David (*Psalms* 29:11), which conclude the Talmudic Tractate *Berachos* (*Gem.* 64a): ה' עֹז לְעַמּוֹ יִתֵּן ה' יְבָרֵךְ אֶת־עַמּוֹ בַשָּׁלוֹם, "Hashem will give might to His nation, Hashem will bless His nation with peace."

Mordecai Rabinovitch
18 Elul 5761

פרק ראשון ❧
Chapter One

There is a Biblical obligation to recite the *Shema* twice daily: once when we lie down at night and once when we arise in the mornings, as the verse (*Deuteronomy* 6:7) states: וּבְשָׁכְבְּךָ וּבְקוּמֶךָ . . . וְדִבַּרְתָּ בָּם, *and you shall speak of them . . . when you lie down and when you arise.* This obligation, however, is not tied to the moment that the individual goes to sleep or gets up. Rather, it relates to the time when it is customary for people to engage in these activities, whether the individual in question does so or not (see below, mishnah 3). The following mishnah delineates the time period in which the evening *Shema* may be recited.

[א] מֵאֵימָתַי קוֹרִין אֶת שְׁמַע בְּעַרְבִית?
מִשָּׁעָה שֶׁהַכֹּהֲנִים נִכְנָסִים

פרק ראשון – מאימתי. (א) מאימתי קורין. משעה שהכהנים נכנסין לאכול בתרומתן. כהנים שנטמאו וטבלו, אין יכולים לאכול בתרומה עד שיעריב שמש, דהיינו צאת הכוכבים. והא דלא תני משעת צאת הכוכבים, מלתא אגב אורחיה קא משמע לן שאם נטמאו הכהנים בטומאה שטהרתן תלויה בקרבן כגון זב ומצורע, אין הכפרה מעכבתן מלאכול בתרומה, דכתיב (ויקרא כב: ז) ובא השמש וטהר ואחר יאכל מן הקדשים, ביאת שמשו מעכבתו מלאכול בתרומה, ואין כפרתו מעכבתו מלאכול בתרומה: **עד סוף האשמורה הראשונה.** שליש הראשון של לילה, שהלילה נחלק לשלש משמרות. ומשם ואילך לא מקרי תו זמן קריאת שמע דשכיבה, ולא קרינא ביה בשכבך. ומקמי צאת הכוכבים נמי יממא הוא ולאו זמן שכיבה. והמקדימים וקורים קריאת שמע של ערבית מבעוד יום, סומכים אהא דרבי יהודה דאמר לקמן בפרק תפלת השחר תפלת המנחה עד פלג המנחה, שהוא שעה ורביע קודם הלילה. וקיימא לן דעבד כרבי יהודה עבד, ומיד כשכלה זמן המנחה מתחיל זמן קריאת שמע של ערבית:

1.

מֵאֵימָתַי קוֹרִין אֶת שְׁמַע בְּעַרְבִית? — *From when may we recite the Shema in the evening?*

What is the earliest time of night that can be classified as בְּשָׁכְבְּךָ, *when you lie down?*

The obligation to recite the *Shema* is stated in the Torah. Presuming the reader to be familiar with the topic to which it refers (*Rashi* to 2a s.v. אקרא קאי), the mishnah, without preamble, discusses the precise time limits for fulfilling the evening *Shema* obligation (*Gemara* 2a).

The mishnah first deals with the evening *Shema*, and afterwards with the morning *Shema* (below, mishnah 2). This order follows the Torah (*Deuteronomy* 6:7), which mentions the obligation to recite *Shema* in the evening before the obligation to do so in the morning (*Tos. Yom Tov*, from *Gem.* 2a). Alternatively, this order is adopted because in general the Torah regards the night as preceding the day, as the verse (*Genesis* 1:5) states: *And there was evening and there was*

morning, one day (*Meleches Shlomo*, from *Gem.* 2a; see *Tosafos* there s.v. אי הכי and *Tzlach* s.v. ליתני שחרית ברישא).

The mishnah's discussion relates only to the first two sections of the *Shema* — שְׁמַע (*Deuteronomy* 6:4-9) and וְהָיָה אִם שָׁמֹעַ (*Deuteronomy* 11:13-21). It is only concerning these passages that the Torah stipulates that they be recited בְּשָׁכְבְּךָ, *when you lie down* (*Deuteronomy* 6:7, 11:19), the precise definition of which the mishnah seeks to clarify. The obligation to recite the third section of the *Shema* — וַיֹּאמֶר (*Numbers* 15:37-41) — does not derive from the verse וּבְשָׁכְבְּךָ וּבְקוּמֶךָ, but from an entirely separate obligation to remember the exodus from Egypt each day and night (see below, mishnah 5). Thus, the times for its recital depend simply on the times of night and day as defined by halachah, and not on the times of "lying down" and "arising." Thus, while the exact time limits for reciting the first two sections of *Shema* require clarification (and are the subject of dispute, as will soon be seen), it is clear that the obligation to recite the third section starts at nightfall and extends until the morning (*Tos. Anshei Shem* from

1. From when may we recite the *Shema* in the evening? From the time that the *Kohanim* enter

YAD AVRAHAM

Shaagas Aryeh §8-9; cf. *Rabbeinu Yonah* p. 1a[1] s.v. אלא כך הוא העניין).

Note that the verb קורין, which commonly means "we read" (i.e. we read from a text), has been translated as "we recite." It cannot mean "we read" since there is no obligation to read the *Shema* from a scroll or book (see *Orach Chaim* 49:1; *Tosafos* to *Temurah* 14b s.v. דברים שבכתב). In mishnaic Hebrew, the verb *to read* is used idiomatically for the recitation of anything that is written, whether it is actually read or recited by heart [see *Yoma* 7:1] (*Tos. Anshei Shem*). Alternatively, the term here is used in the sense of "calling out," and reflects the custom of reciting the first verse of *Shema* out loud (see *Orach Chaim* 61:4), as a means of enhancing one's concentration (*Tif. Yisrael; Shulchan Aruch* [ibid. §26] notes the custom of many to recite the entire *Shema* out loud).

מִשָּׁעָה שֶׁהַכֹּהֲנִים נִכְנָסִים לֶאֱכֹל בִּתְרוּמָתָן, — *From the time that the Kohanim enter to eat their terumah.*

That is, from the time that a *Kohen* who had been *tamei*, and hence forbidden to eat *terumah*, attains the state of purification that allows him to once again partake of *terumah* (see *Maharsha* to 2b s.v. משעה שהעני). This occurs at the time when stars become visible at night (*Rav*).

Terumah is the portion that is set aside from agricultural produce of *Eretz Yisrael*, and given to a *Kohen*. It may be eaten only by *Kohanim* who are *tahor* (see *Leviticus* 22:1-7; *Yevamos* 74a-75a). With most forms of *tumah*, a state of complete purity is attained by immersing in a *mikveh* on

the designated day and then awaiting nightfall. Certain types of *tumah* necessitate the bringing of a set of sacrificial offerings to complete the purification process (see *Kereisos* 2:1). One who has not yet brought these offerings is forbidden to eat sacrificial foods, since he has not yet achieved a state of complete *taharah*. Nevertheless, a *kohen* is permitted to partake of *terumah* on the night following his immersion, regardless of whether he is still obligated to offer sacrifices to complete the purification process (*Negaim* 14:3). This is derived from the verse (*Leviticus* ibid. v.7) which states: וּבָא הַשֶּׁמֶשׁ וְטָהֵר וְאַחַר יֹאכַל מִן הַקֳּדָשִׁים, *After the sun has set and the sky shall be clear [from light], thereafter he may eat from the holies,* which teaches that regardless of the type of *tumah* for which he immersed, a *Kohen* may eat *terumah* (*the holies*) upon nightfall (*Yevamos* ibid.; translation of the verse follows *Rambam, Hil. Terumos* 7:2; see *Rashi* to 2b s.v. אדכי for a somewhat different interpretation). The appearance of three medium-sized stars in the sky signals the definite advent of night. This is known as צֵאת הַכּוֹכָבִים, *the emergence of the stars.* Thus, the time at which a *Kohen* who had been *tamei* would enter his home to partake of *terumah* is *the emergence of the stars.* The mishnah teaches that, likewise, the earliest time at which the evening *Shema* may be recited is the *emergence of the*

---

1. This commentary is more precisely known as *Talmidei Rabbeinu Yonah*, since it was compiled by *Rabbeinu Yonah's* students based on his teachings. Throughout our commentary, we will refer to it simply as *Rabbeinu Yonah*, the name by which it is commonly known. All citations of this commentary refer to the folios of *Rif*.

יד אברהם

stars[1] (Rav, Rambam Comm.).

The exact time of *the emergence of the stars* is a subject of dispute among the authorities. In the opinion of *Rabbeinu Tam*, this occurs four *mil* after sunset.[2] (A *mil* is two thousand *amos*. In terms of time, a *mil* is defined as the amount of time required to walk two thousand *amos*.) In practical terms, this is between seventy-two and ninety minutes after the sun sets beyond the horizon [depending on the different opinions regarding the length of a *mil* as defined as a unit of time] (see *Sefer Ha-Yashar* §121, *Tosafos* to *Shabbos* 35a s.v. תרי). This is the view followed by *Shulchan Aruch* (*Orach Chaim* 261:2). Others, however, maintain that it occurs three-quarters of a *mil* — between fourteen and eighteen minutes — after sunset (see *Teshuvos Maharam Alshakar* §96, *Gra* in *Shenos Eliyahu* here and *Beur HaGra* to *Orach Chaim* ibid.).[3]

The word בְּשָׁכְבְּךָ, *when you lie down*, teaches that the earliest time one may recite the evening *Shema* is when people go to sleep. Accordingly, one cannot fulfill the evening obligation

before *the emergence of the stars*, since that is not yet a time for sleeping (*Rav, Rashi*).

Rav notes the common custom of reciting the *Maariv* prayers, including the *Shema*, in the synagogue before *the emergence of the stars*. According to our mishnah, however, one cannot fulfill his *Shema* obligation at this time. *Rav* (following *Rabbeinu Tam*, quoted by *Tosafos* to 2a s.v. מאימתי) explains that those who do not repeat the *Shema* later, after nightfall, rely on the view of R' Yehudah, who maintains (below, 4:1) that *Minchah* can be prayed only up to an hour and a quarter before nightfall (a period known as *plag haminchah*). It follows that immediately after the time for praying *Minchah* expires, the time for *Maariv* and the evening *Shema* begins. Although the Rabbis disagree and contend that the *Minchah* prayer may be recited until nightfall, the *Gemara* (27a) rules that one may follow either view.[4]

Tosafos (ibid.) challenge the explanation of *Rabbeinu Tam* on many grounds. *Rosh* (1:1) maintains that R' Yehudah's statement refers only to the time for *prayer*; the

1. Strictly speaking, the emergence of three medium-sized stars is a sign of definite nightfall (see *Shabbos* 35b). However, since we are not certain what is considered a "medium"-sized star, in practice we wait until the appearance of three small stars (see *Rabbeinu Yonah* 1b s.v. והא דאמרינן, *Orach Chaim* 235:1 and *Mishnah Berurah* §1; see also 293:2).

2. It should be noted that in terms of halachah, "sunset" is defined as the time when the sun disappears beyond the western horizon, and not when the line of the horizon bisects the orb of the sun, as it is scientifically defined. The latter time precedes the halachic sunset by some two to three minutes (see *Tif. Yisrael* to mishnah 2, §14).

3. A detailed discussion of the bases of these opinions is beyond the scope of this work. We will note, however, that the *Gemara* in *Pesachim* (94a) places the time of *the emergence of the stars* at four *mil* after sunset, whereas in *Shabbos* (34b-35b) it rules that it occurs three-quarters of a *mil* after sunset. The conflicting opinions of the authorities result from the different resolutions of this contradiction. Furthermore, the authorities disagree regarding the length of a *mil* as a unit of time, with opinions ranging from between eighteen minutes and twenty-four minutes. In addition, the exact time of *the emergence of the stars* depends on the latitude of a given location, and the time of year (see *Beur HaGra* to *Orach Chaim* 459:2, *Beur Halachah* 261 s.v. שהוא).

4. However, one cannot rely on the view of the Rabbis and pray *Minchah* after *plag haminchah*, and then pray *Maariv* before nightfall based on R' Yehudah's opinion, for this is contradictory (see *Tosafos* ibid.; *Orach Chaim* 233:1).

1
1

to eat their *terumah*. [And We may recite it].
Until the end of the first watch. [These are]

obligation to recite the evening *Shema*, however, is not contingent on the time for prayer, but on the time when "you lie down" (see also *Tos. R' Akiva* §2). *Ri* (cited in *Tosafos* ibid.) explains that this custom is based on other views cited in the *Gemara* (2b), according to which the time for reciting the evening *Shema* begins before nightfall. However, *Rashi*, citing *Yerushalmi* (1:1), maintains that indeed one does not fulfill his obligation by reciting the *Shema* before *the emergence of the stars*. According to *Rashi*, the purpose of the *Shema* recited in the synagogue is so that our supplications (in the *Shemoneh Esrei*) should follow the reading of a Torah passage. Accordingly, those who pray before *the emergence of the stars* have an obligation to repeat the *Shema* later. The view of *Rashi* is widely shared. It is the view of *Rav Amram Gaon* and *Rav Hai Gaon* (cited in *Rosh* ibid.), as well as *Rif*, *Rambam* (*Hil. Krias Shema* 1:9), *Rabbeinu Yonah*, *Rashba* and others. *Shulchan Aruch* (*Orach Chaim* 235:1), as well, rules in accordance with *Rashi*.[1]

It seems strange that the mishnah defines the starting time for the evening *Shema* in terms of the time for eating *terumah* rather than stating directly that it may be recited from *the emergence of the stars*. The *Gemara* (2a) explains that the mishnah does this in order to teach incidentally that even those *Kohanim* whose *tumah* requires the bringing of sacrifices, e.g. a *zav* or a *metzora* (see *Leviticus* 14:10-32 and 15:14-15), are permitted to eat *terumah* upon nightfall of the day they immersed in a *mikveh*, although they are forbidden to eat sacrificial foods until they offer their sacrifices (*Rav, Ram-*

bam Comm.; see above s.v. משעה שהכהנים). By not specifying that the *Kohanim* to which it refers are those who are not required to bring sacrificial offerings the next day, the *Tanna* indicates that *all Kohanim* are permitted to partake of *terumah* at this time, regardless of any additional requirement to offer sacrifices the next day (*Rashba* 2a s.v. הא קמ"ל).

[The mishnah speaks of the time when the *Kohanim* come in to eat תְּרוּמָתָן, "their *terumah*," rather than simply saying *terumah*. *Shenos Eliyahu* explains that the mishnah wishes to stress that it is referring only to the *terumah* that is separated for the *Kohen* from agricultural produce of the Land of Israel, and not to certain sacrificial foods that are also known as *terumah* (e.g. the loaves of the *todah* offering; see *Leviticus* 7:14). As noted above, a *Kohen* who must still bring a purification offering is not permitted to eat sacrificial foods upon the nightfall following his immersion, but rather must wait until he offers the necessary sacrifices on the next day. The mishnah implies that it does not refer to such *terumah* by speaking of "his (i.e. the *Kohen's*) *terumah*." *Terumah* from agricultural produce that is given to a *Kohen* is considered his personal property. Sacrificial *terumah*, however, is not the *Kohen's* property; the Torah merely allows him to eat it. Hence, it cannot be referred to as "his" *terumah* (see *Meleches Shlomo* s.v.לאכול from *Teshuvos HaRama Mifano* §1 for a similar explanation; for other explanations, see *Tos. Yom Tov*; *Rashash* and *Chiddushei R' Zelig Reuven Benges*, II:2).]

עַד סוֹף הָאַשְׁמוּרָה הָרִאשׁוֹנָה. דִּבְרֵי רַבִּי אֱלִיעֶזֶר. — [*And we may recite it*] *until*

---

1. *Rashi* maintains that one can discharge his obligation by repeating the first portion of the *Shema*, which is customarily recited in bed before going to sleep (see *Gemara* 4b). However, *Rabbeinu Yonah* rules that the first two sections need to be repeated. *Mishnah Berurah* (235:11, citing *Shaagas Aryeh*) states that it is proper to recite all three sections.

ברכות דִּבְרֵי רַבִּי אֱלִיעֶזֶר. וַחֲכָמִים אוֹמְרִים: עַד חֲצוֹת.
א/א רַבָּן גַּמְלִיאֵל אוֹמֵר: עַד שֶׁיַּעֲלֶה עַמּוּד הַשַּׁחַר.

ר' עובדיה מברטנורא

עד שיעלה עמוד השחר. דכל הלילה מקרי זמן שכיבה. והלכה כרבן גמליאל, שגם חכמים מודים
לו, ולא אמרו עד חצות אלא אלא כדי להרחיק את האדם מן העבירה. ומיהו לכתחילה משהגיעה זונת

יד אברהם

the end of the first watch. [These are]
the words of R' Eliezer.

Having answered the mishnah's
opening question concerning the start
of the time for reciting the evening
Shema, the mishnah goes on to discuss
the end of the time allotted for this
recitation (Shenos Eliyahu s.v. מאימתי;
cf. Yesh Seder LeMishnah; see also
Meleches Shlomo s.v. מאימתי).

The night is divided into three equal
shifts or watches, in each of which a
different group of heavenly angels
sing praises to God (Tos. Yom Tov,
from Rashi to 3a s.v. אי קסבר). Hence,
the end of the first watch is the end of
the first third of the night (Rav, Rambam Comm.).

The expression used by the Torah to
describe the period of time during
which the evening Shema is recited,
when you lie down, is ambiguous. It
can be understood to mean the time
when a person goes to sleep (i.e. toward
the beginning of the night), or it can
mean the time when one is asleep (i.e.
the entire night). With regard to the
start of the allotted time, there is no
difference between the two interpretations, for the time one goes to sleep is
the same as when he actually sleeps.
Regarding the end of the designated
time, however, this ambiguity gives
rise to differing views.

R' Eliezer understands the expression when you lie down to mean the
time when people go to sleep (Rashi to
3a s.v. לאו ר' אליעזר היא). He therefore

rules that one may fulfill his obligation
to recite the evening Shema only during the first third of the night, for only
this period can be characterized as a
time during which people go to sleep
(Rav, Rashi). By the end of this period,
anyone who plans on going to sleep
for the night has already done so
(Rashi to 4a s.v. לימרו כר' אליעזר).

The attribution "these are the words of
R' Eliezer" refers only to the statement
"until the end of the first watch," and not
to the preceding ruling "from the time that
the Kohanim enter to eat their terumah"
(Shenos Eliyahu s.v. מאימתי; cf. Rabbeinu
Yonah 1a s.v. ואיפסיקא; see Gem. 3a, where
this point is debated). Indeed, according to
a Baraisa cited by the Gemara (2b), R'
Eliezer maintains that the time for reciting
the evening Shema begins even earlier
than nightfall.

וַחֲכָמִים אוֹמְרִים: עַד חֲצוֹת. — But the
Sages say: Until midnight.

The Sages maintain that the evening Shema may be recited until the
halfway point of the night. [This is not
necessarily 12 a.m. For example, if the
night begins at 8 p.m. and ends at 5
a.m., the halfway point of the night is
12:30 a.m.]

The Sages disagree with R' Eliezer's
interpretation of the phrase when you
lie down as meaning the time when
people go to sleep. Rather, they define it
as the time that people are asleep. Accordingly, the Torah allows for the recitation of the evening Shema the entire night. However, as a safeguard to
ensure that people do not procrastinate

1   the words of R' Eliezer. But the Sages say: Until midnight.
1   Rabban Gamliel says: Until the light of dawn rises.

YAD AVRAHAM

— rationalizing that much time remains in which to fulfill their obligation — and inadvertently come to miss the Biblical deadline, the Rabbis enacted that one must recite the *Shema* before midnight (*Gemara* 4b).

It would seem that since this midnight deadline is of Rabbinic origin, one who failed to recite the evening *Shema* before midnight, although he has transgressed a Rabbinical enactment, may still fulfill his Biblical obligation until morning. This, in fact, is the ruling of *Rambam* (*Hil. Krias Shema* 1:9) and *Ramban* (*Milchemes Hashem*, 2a of folios of *Rif*), and is the view followed by *Shulchan Aruch* (*Orach Chaim* 235:3). *Rabbeinu Yonah* (cited in *Meleches Shlomo*), however, maintains that one who misses the midnight deadline cannot fulfill his obligation even on a Biblical level. According to *Rabbeinu Yonah*, the Rabbis abolished the Biblical deadline entirely, something they were empowered to do, in certain circumstances, in the interest of distancing a person from a transgression (see *Yevamos* 90a-b). This is similar to the Rabbinical restriction against taking a *lulav* on the Sabbath of Succos (*Succah* 4:1). Once the Rabbis promulgated this decree, taking a *lulav* on that day no longer fulfills any commandment. Thus, once the Rabbis instituted a midnight deadline for reciting the evening *Shema*, the Biblical obligation applies only until that time. However, as will be seen below (s.v. אמר להם), if one's failure to recite the *Shema* before midnight was not the result of intentional disregard of this Rabbinically imposed deadline, all agree that he may recite the *Shema* up until the end of the night even according to the Sages.

רַבָּן גַּמְלִיאֵל אוֹמֵר: עַד שֶׁיַּעֲלֶה עַמּוּד הַשַּׁחַר.

— *Rabban Gamliel says: Until the light of dawn* (lit. *the morning beam*) *rises.*

The first rays of light to dawn in the east toward the end of night expand until they appear as a column or beam of light known as עַמּוּד הַשַּׁחַר, *the morning beam* (*Rambam Comm.*; ed. *Kafich*; see *Mishnah Berurah* 89:2). The morning is considered to begin at this time (see *Megillah* 2:4). According to one opinion, this point in time (commonly referred to as עֲלוֹת הַשַּׁחַר) occurs approximately an hour and a half before sunrise (*Tosafos to Pesachim* 11b s.v. אחד אמר, *Beur HaGra* to *Orach Chaim* 459:2). Others maintain that this is approximately an hour and twelve minutes before sunrise (*Rambam Comm.*; for a detailed discussion of these two views, see *Shenos Eliyahu*).[1]

Some identify עֲלוֹת הַשַּׁחַר with הָאִיר פְּנֵי הַמִּזְרָח, *the illumination of the eastern horizon*, i.e. the spread of light across the entire eastern horizon, which occurs a bit later (*Shenos Eliyahu*; see *Beur Halachah* to 89:1 s.v. ואם התפלל).

Rabban Gamliel interprets the term *when you lie down* as do the Sages, to mean the time during which people are asleep, i.e., the entire night (*Rav, Rashi*). Unlike the Sages, Rabban Gamliel does not feel it necessary to impose any Rabbinical safeguards. Thus, he maintains that one may recite the evening *Shema* at any time during the night until the light of dawn rises, the time at which people awaken, which cannot be classified as a "time of lying down."

---

1. The basis of this dispute is the two opinions mentioned in *Pesachim* (94a) regarding the length of time between dawn and sunrise. According to one opinion, this is five *mil*. Another view maintains that it is four *mil* (see *Magen Avraham* 89:2).

מַעֲשֶׂה שֶׁבָּאוּ בָנָיו מִבֵּית הַמִּשְׁתֶּה. אָמְרוּ לוֹ: לֹא קָרִינוּ אֶת שְׁמַע. אָמַר לָהֶם: אִם לֹא עָלָה עַמּוּד הַשַּׁחַר חַיָּבִין אַתֶּם לִקְרוֹת.

קריאת שמע של ערבית דמתניתין, דהיינו מלאת הכוכבים, אסור לסעוד וכל שכן לישן עד שיקרא קריאת שמע ויתפלל. **בני רבן גמליאל שמעינהו שבאו בניו מבית המשתה.** ברבן דאמרי עד חלות, והכי קאמרי ליה, הא דפליגי רבנן עלך, דוקא קאמרי עד חלות והו לא, ויחיד ורבים הלכה כרבים, או דלמא רבנן כוותך סבירא להו, והאי דקאמרי עד חלות, כדי להרחיק את האדם מן העבירה. ואמר להו, רבנן כוותי סבירא להו, והאי דקאמרי עד חלות, כדי להרחיק את האדם מן העבירה, וחייבים אתם לקרות:

יד אברהם

However, even Rabban Gamliel agrees that ideally one should discharge his *Shema* obligation as soon after *the emergence of the stars* as possible. Indeed, one may not start a meal or lie down to sleep before reciting the *Shema*, for fear that he will come to miss the deadline (*Rav, Rosh* §9; see *Orach Chaim* 235:3 and *Mishnah Berurah* §26).

The *Gemara* (8b) decides the halachah in accordance with the view of Rabban Gamliel. It is not clear, however, whether the *Gemara* refers to Rabban Gamliel's contention that there is no Rabbinically imposed midnight deadline, or only to his dispute with R' Eliezer regarding the interpretation of the expression *when you lie down* to include the entire night, an interpretation with which the Sages also agree (see *Rav, Rambam Comm.*; for the reason why this interpretation is attributed to R' Gamliel rather than to the Sages, see Beur Halachah 235, s.v. וזמנה (עד חצי הלילה. Some authorities maintain that we follow Rabban Gamliel's view allowing the evening *Shema* to be recited even Rabbinically the entire

night (*Rosh* 1:9, *Rashba* to 9a s.v. ובני (רבן גמליאל. Others, however, rule that we follow the majority opinion of the Sages, according to which the *Shema* must Rabbinically be recited before midnight (*Rambam, Hil. Krias Shema* 1:9). This is the view followed by *Shulchan Aruch* (*Orach Chaim* 235:3).

According to a Baraisa cited in the *Gemara* (8b), in extenuating circumstances, e.g. if one was sick and could not recite the *Shema* earlier, one may fulfill his obligation until sunrise. Although with regard to all matters of halachah night is defined as ending at dawn (see *Megillah* 2:4), the Torah did not make recitation of the evening *Shema* dependent on night, but rather on the time when people are asleep. Since there are people who sleep past dawn, it can be categorized as a time of "lying down." This view is followed in halachah (*Orach Chaim* 235:4).[1] However, since the majority of people are awake at this time, it is only considered a time of "lying down" in extenuating circumstances. Rabban Gamliel's ruling allowing the evening *Shema* to be recited only until dawn refers to usual circumstances (*Rashba* to 8b s.v. איכא דמתני לה אסיפא, *Rosh* 1:9; see further *Mishnah Berurah* 235:30).

מַעֲשֶׂה שֶׁבָּאוּ בָנָיו מִבֵּית הַמִּשְׁתֶּה. אָמְרוּ לוֹ:

---

1. However, at that time one should not recite the blessing of הַשְׁכִּיבֵנוּ (*Gemara* 9a), which relates specifically to a time when the majority of people are asleep (*Tosafos* there s.v. ובלבד שלא יאמר).

1
1

It happened that his sons came [home] from a banquet. They said to him: We have not [yet] recited the *Shema*. He said to them: If the light of dawn has not yet risen, you are obligated to recite.

לֹא קָרִינוּ אֶת שְׁמַע. — *It happened that his sons came [home] from a banquet* (lit. *house of drinking*). *They said to him: We have not [yet] recited the Shema.*

The phrase בֵּית הַמִּשְׁתֶּה refers to any gathering in which drinking wine figures prominently (*Rambam Comm.*). *Tos. Yom Tov* (*Eruvin* 8:1) states that wherever the term בֵּית הַמִּשְׁתֶּה is used, it refers to a wedding. [See *Beis Yosef, Orach Chaim* 99 for a practical difference between these two interpretations.]

Rabban Gamliel's sons returned home after midnight from a banquet. Due to their preoccupation with the banquet, they had neglected to recite the evening *Shema* (*Rosh* 1:9, *Rashba*). Since the midnight deadline of the Sages had already passed, they were unsure if they were still able to discharge their obligation. They realized that the majority opinion of the Sages ought to prevail over their father's view that the time for reciting the *Shema* extends through the entire night. However, they were uncertain how the Sages' opinion should be understood: Do the Sages dispute Rabban Gamliel's interpretation of the phrase *when you lie down* [and maintain, as does R' Eliezer, that it refers to the time when people go to bed, which they contend includes the entire first half of the night? (*Rashi* to 9a s.v. ורבנן פליגי)]. If so, their midnight deadline is Biblical in nature, and Rabban Gamliel's sons, who were required to follow the Sages' ruling, would be unable to fulfill their

obligation. Or do the Sages agree with Rabban Gamliel [that the term includes the entire time that people sleep (*Rashi* to 9a s.v. או דילמא)], in which case their midnight deadline represents a Rabbinic safeguard designed to ensure that people do not neglect their obligation? As such, one would still be able to fulfill his Biblical obligation after midnight (*Rav*, from *Gemara* 9a). Unsure of the Sages' reasoning, the sons sought their father's guidance.

As noted above (s.v. וחכמים אומרים), *Rabbeinu Yonah* maintains that as a result of the Sages' precautionary enactment, one cannot discharge his *Shema* obligation after midnight even on a Biblical level. This, however, applies only to one who intentionally ignored the Rabbinic deadline, relying on the fact that Biblical law allows him to fulfill his obligation until dawn. The sons of Rabban Gamliel did not willfully ignore the Sages' injunction, but simply forgot to recite the *Shema* earlier. Hence, if in fact the Sages' ruling was the result of a Rabbinically imposed safeguard, they would be able to recite the *Shema* after midnight as well (*Tos. Anshei Shem* s.v. בר"ב סד"ה מעשה; for alternative solutions, see *Mishnas R' Yosef*).

אָמַר לָהֶם: אִם לֹא עָלָה עַמּוּד הַשַּׁחַר חַיָּבִין אַתֶּם לִקְרוֹת. — *He said to them: If the light of dawn has not yet risen, you are obligated to recite.*

Rabban Gamliel answered his sons that the Sages agree to his interpretation of the phrase *when you lie down* to imply the entire night; their ruling represents a Rabbinical safeguard. Thus, even according to the majority opinion of the Sages, the obligation to

וְלֹא זוֹ בִלְבַד, אֶלָּא כָּל מַה שֶּׁאָמְרוּ חֲכָמִים עַד
חֲצוֹת – מִצְוָתָן עַד שֶׁיַּעֲלֶה עַמּוּד הַשָּׁחַר. הֶקְטֵר
חֲלָבִים וְאֵבָרִים – מִצְוָתָן עַד שֶׁיַּעֲלֶה עַמּוּד
הַשָּׁחַר. וְכָל הַנֶּאֱכָלִין לְיוֹם אֶחָד – מִצְוָתָן עַד

─────── ר' עובדיה מברטנורא ───────

וְלֹא זוֹ בלבד. כולה מילתא דרבן גמליאל היא דאמר לבניו: הקטר חלבים
ואיברים. של עולה תמיד של בין הערבים שנזרק דמו ביום, מלוה להעלות הנתחים כל
הלילה, דכתיב (ויקרא ו: ב) היא העולה על מוקדה על המזבח כל הלילה עד הבקר:

יד אברהם

recite the evening *Shema* was still in
effect (*Rav* from *Gemara* 9a).

As noted above (s.v. רבן גמליאל אומר),
if one failed to recite the evening *Shema*
before dawn due to extenuating circumstances, he may fulfill his obligation until
sunrise. Nevertheless, Rabban Gamliel did
not state that if it was not yet *sunrise*, the
obligation to recite the evening *Shema* is in
effect. This is because his sons' failure to
recite the *Shema* was not the result of extenuating circumstances but of negligence
(*Rosh* 1:9, *Rashba* to 9a s.v. ולענין פסק הלכה).

וְלֹא זוֹ בִלְבַד, אֶלָּא כָּל מַה שֶּׁאָמְרוּ חֲכָמִים
עַד חֲצוֹת – מִצְוָתָן עַד שֶׁיַּעֲלֶה עַמּוּד
הַשָּׁחַר. — *And not only this, but all
things about which the Sages said
"Until midnight," [the time for fulfill-
ing] the commandment extends until
the light of dawn rises.*

This is all part of Rabban Gamliel's
answer to his sons (*Rav*, from *Gemara*
9a). Rabban Gamliel pointed out that
the evening *Shema* is not the only
commandment regarding which the
Rabbis instituted a midnight deadline
as a safeguard. Indeed, wherever midnight is given as a deadline for fulfilling a commandment, it is a Rabbinically decreed precautionary measure;
Biblical law, however, allows the entire night for fulfilling the commandment.

Rabban Gamliel now proceeds to

demonstrate this assertion by listing
examples of commandments regarding which we find midnight deadlines, although clearly Biblical law allows their fulfillment the entire night.

הֶקְטֵר חֲלָבִים וְאֵבָרִים – מִצְוָתָן עַד שֶׁיַּעֲלֶה
עַמּוּד הַשָּׁחַר. — *[For] the burning of the
sacrificial fats and limbs [on the Altar, the time for fulfilling] the commandment extends until the light of
dawn rises;*

Certain parts of every animal sacrifice are burned on the Altar. These
consist primarily of its hard fats [חֵלֶב]
(see *Leviticus* 3:3,9,14). In the case of
olah (burnt offering), the entire animal is burned on the Altar (ibid. 1:6-9,
12-13). Although sacrificial offerings
can only be offered by day (*Zevachim*
56a; *Rambam, Hil. Maaseh HaKorbanos* 4:1), their fats, as well as the
limbs of the *olah* offerings, may be
placed on the Altar at any time during
the night to be burned, up until dawn
of the next day, when they become
disqualified. This is derived from the
verse (ibid. 6:2) which states: הוּא הָעֹלָה
עַל מוֹקְדָה עַל־הַמִּזְבֵּחַ כָּל־הַלַּיְלָה עַד־
הַבֹּקֶר, *it is the olah [that stays] on the
flame, on the Altar, all night until the
morning.* This is understood to mean
that the limbs of the *olah* may be
placed on the Altar at any time during

1
1

And not only this, but all things about which the Sages said "Until midnight," [the time for fulfilling] the commandment extends until the light of dawn rises. [For] the burning of [the sacrificial] fats and limbs [on the Altar, the time for fulfilling] the commandment extends until the light of dawn rises; and [for] all [the sacrificial parts] that are eaten for one day, [the time for fulfilling] the commandment extends until the

the night (*Rav, Rambam Comm.*).[1]

Rabban Gamliel could not have meant to demonstrate from this example that all midnight deadlines are of Rabbinic origin, for nowhere do we find a midnight time limit with regard to placing the fats and limbs on the Altar. Indeed, the mishnah in *Megillah* (2:6) lists the burning of these portions on the Altar among the commandments that can be fulfilled throughout the entire night. Rather, Rabban Gamliel wished to establish the rule that nighttime obligations are generally applicable throughout the entire night, as the mishnah (ibid.) rules (*Rav, Rashi*). It follows, then, that Biblical law allows the recitation of the evening *Shema* the entire night, and the Sages' ruling limiting its recitation to the first half of the night is a Rabbinic stringency (see below s.v. אם כן).

Rambam (*Comm., Hil. Maaseh HaKorbanos* 4:2), however, maintains that these portions must be placed on the Altar before midnight. Accordingly, Rabban Gamliel cites this example in support of his assertion that such deadlines are of Rabbinic origin, for clearly Biblical law allows these portions

to be placed on the Altar throughout the entire night.[2] According to *Rambam*, the mishnah in *Megillah* refers only to the *Biblical* time limit concerning nighttime obligations (see *Rambam Comm.* there).

וְכָל הַנֶּאֱכָלִין לְיוֹם אֶחָד – מִצְוָתָן עַד שֶׁיַּעֲלֶה עַמּוּד הַשַּׁחַר. — *and [for] all [the sacrificial parts] that are eaten for one day, [the time for fulfilling] the commandment extends until the light of dawn rises.*

The meat of most sacrifices is eaten. Certain offerings may be eaten for two days and the intervening night, e.g. the *shelamim* (peace offering). Other sacrifices may be eaten only for one day, i.e. the day they were offered and the following night. These are the *chatas* (sin offering), and *asham* (guilt offering) which are eaten by the Kohanim; and the *todah* (thanksgiving offering) portions of which may be eaten by non-Kohanim. Biblical law allows these to be eaten until the morning of the following day, at which point they be-

1. *Rav* mentions specifically the עוֹלַת תָּמִיד, *the daily olah offering*. This is because this offering is the subject of the verse. However, the same law applies to all other offerings (*Meleches Shlomo*).

2. From *Rambam* (*Comm.* to *Zevachim* 9:6) it would seem that this midnight deadline is alluded to in that mishnah (see also *Shenos Eliyahu*; for an alternative source, see *Tos. Yom Tov*). However, *Rashi* (*Yoma* 20a s.v. אחר חצות) explains that mishnah differently, in a manner consistent with his view here that the Rabbis never limited the time allotted for placing these portions on the Altar.

שֶׁיַּעֲלֶה עַמּוּד הַשַּׁחַר. אִם כֵּן, לָמָה אָמְרוּ חֲכָמִים
עַד חֲצוֹת? כְּדֵי לְהַרְחִיק אָדָם מִן הָעֲבֵרָה.

[ב] מֵאֵימָתַי קוֹרִין אֶת שְׁמַע בְּשַׁחֲרִית?

ר' עובדיה מברטנורא

וכל הנאכלין ליום אחד. כגון תודה וחטאת ואשם וכיוצא בהם שהם נאכלים ליום ולילה,
זמן אכילתן עד שיעלה עמוד השחר והוא המביא לידי נותר: **אם כן למה אמרו חכמים
עד חצות.** בקריאת שמע ובאכילת קדשים, אבל בהקטר חלבים ואיברים לא אמרו בו חכמים
עד חלות כלל, ולא נקט ליה הכא אלא להודיע שכל דבר שמלותו בלילה כשר כל הלילה: **בדי
להרחיק את האדם מן העבירה.** שלא יבא לאכלן אחר שיעלה עמוד השחר ויתחייב כרת. וכן
בקריאת שמע, שלא יאמר עדיין יש לי שהות, ותעבור עונתה:

יד אברהם
---

come נוֹתָר, *leftovers* [which are forbidden to be eaten under penalty of *kares*
(excision)] (*Rav*). This is derived from
the verse (*Leviticus* 7:15) regarding the
todah, which states: לֹא־יַנִּיחַ מִמֶּנּוּ עַד־
בֹּקֶר, *he shall not leave any of it until
morning* (*Rambam Comm.*). The law
pertaining to *chatas* and *asham* is
derived from the law of *todah* (*Rashi*).
Nevertheless, the mishnah (*Zevachim*
5:3,5,6) rules that these sacrifices must
be eaten before midnight of the night
following their offering. Clearly, this
mishnah refers to a Rabbinically imposed deadline, and not a Biblical one.

אִם כֵּן, לָמָה אָמְרוּ חֲכָמִים עַד חֲצוֹת? — *If
so, why did the Sages say: "Until
midnight"?*
If indeed by Biblical law nighttime
obligations can be performed the entire
night, why did the Sages impose a
midnight time limit for reciting the
evening *Shema* and for eating the sacrificial offerings? (*Rav, Rashi*; see
above s.v. הקטר חלבים ואיברים).

כְּדֵי לְהַרְחִיק אָדָם מִן הָעֲבֵרָה. — *In order to
distance a person from transgression.*

The Rabbis instituted precautionary
safeguards so that people would not
come to miss the Biblical deadline for
reciting the evening *Shema*, or inadvertently come to eat of the meat of the
sacrifices after dawn.

The Sages were concerned that were
one to rely on the Biblical deadline for
reciting the evening *Shema* — dawn
— he would push off the recitation until later, reasoning that much time yet
remains in which to fulfill his obligation. He might thus forget entirely to
recite the *Shema* until it is too late. To
ensure that people do not procrastinate,
the Sages set a much earlier deadline
for the recitation of the evening *Shema*.

With regard to the meats of the sacrifices, the Rabbis were concerned that
one would not notice the coming of
dawn, and inadvertently eat of them
after the night had ended, a transgression which (when committed willfully) carries the severe penalty of
kares. Thus, they forbade these meats
to be eaten well before they become
Biblically prohibited (*Rav, Rashi*).[1]

Eating the meats of the sacrifices is a

---

1. The Rabbis did not limit the time allotted to eat the *shelamim*. This is because the
shelamim is eaten until sunset of the day following its offering. Sunset is an event
unlikely to be overlooked, and there is no reason for concern that one will think that the

1 light of dawn rises. If so, why did the Sages say: "Until
2 midnight"? In order to distance a person from transgression.

2. From when do we recite the *Shema* in the morning?

YAD AVRAHAM

mitzvah (see *Rashi* to *Pesachim* 59a s.v.
בשאר; *Ramban, Sefer HaMitzvos*, addenda
to *mitzvos aseh* §1). It thus seems strange
that the commentaries explain the midnight deadline instituted by the Rabbis as a
means to prevent inadvertent eating of
נותר. Why not explain that, just as with regard to the *Shema*, the Rabbis were concerned that one would procrastinate and
not fulfill the commandment of eating the
sacrificial meats? *R' Akiva Eiger* explains
that indeed this reason suffices according to
the Sages who imposed a midnight deadline for reciting the evening *Shema*. Just as
they were concerned that one would not
fulfill his *Shema* obligation, so they were
concerned that one might not fulfill his
obligation to eat these sacrificial meats. But
this does not explain why Rabban Gamliel,
who was *not* concerned that one might neglect to fulfill his *Shema* obligation, agrees
to the Rabbinically imposed deadline with
regard to eating the sacrificial meats (as evident from his silence on the subject). Evidently, there was more reason for concern
regarding the sacrificial meats than with
regard to the *Shema*. Therefore, the commentaries explain that Rabban Gamliel
agrees to this restriction because eating the

sacrificial meats after dawn carries a very
severe penalty. Moreover, failure to recite
the *Shema* represents a sin of *omission*,
whereas eating the sacrificial meats after
dawn is a sin of *commission*, which is a
more serious violation (*Tos. R' Akiva* §5; for
a different approach, see *Tif. Yisrael*).

As noted above (s.v. הקטר חלבים) *Rashi*
and *Rav* maintain that the Rabbis did not
limit the time allotted to place on the Altar
those portions which are required to be
burned. This begs the question: Why, in
fact, did the Rabbis not institute a precautionary deadline to ensure that the *Kohanim* charged with this duty not procrastinate and allow the Biblically mandated
deadline to elapse? *R' Yoel Chasid* suggests
that the Rabbis were not concerned that
the *Kohanim* would allow the deadline to
pass because *Kohanim* are known to be
scrupulous in fulfilling their duties (see
Shabbos 20a), and the Rabbis assumed that
they would discharge their obligation in a
timely manner. The obligation of *Shema*,
on the other hand, is incumbent even on
non-*Kohanim*. Similarly, the *todah* offering is eaten in part by non-*Kohanim*. Thus,
the concern exists that they will come to
transgress[1] (*Chidushei Maharich*).

2.

The following mishnah discusses the recitation of the morning *Shema*. The
period of time during which one can fulfill this obligation is set forth by the
Torah (*Deuteronomy* 6:7, 11:19) as: וּבְקוּמֶךָ, *when you arise*, i.e. the period of time
when people awaken and rise from bed. Precisely what period of time is
included in this term is the subject of the mishnah.

מֵאֵימָתַי קוֹרִין אֶת שְׁמַע בְּשַׁחֲרִית? — *the morning?*
From when do we recite the Shema in   What is the earliest time of day that

sun has not set and the sacrificial meats are still permitted. The advent of עֲלוֹת הַשַּׁחַר,
however, is not as noticeable (*Tosafos* to *Zevachim* 57b s.v. להרחיק).

1. The Rabbis imposed a precautionary deadline with regard to the *chatas* and *asham*,
even though they are eaten only by *Kohanim*, so as not to differentiate between different
types of offerings. See *Tif. Yisrael* who answers this point somewhat differently.

מִשֶּׁיַּכִּיר בֵּין תְּכֵלֶת לְלָבָן. רַבִּי אֱלִיעֶזֶר אוֹמֵר:
בֵּין תְּכֵלֶת לְכַרְתִּי. וְגוֹמְרָהּ עַד הָנֵץ הַחַמָּה.

ר' עובדיה מברטנורא

(ב) בין תכלת ללבן. בין חוטי תכלת לחוטי לבן שבטלית. פירוש אחר, גיזת צמר שצבעה
תכלת ויש בה מקומות שלא נקלטה הצבע יפה ונשאר לבן: **בין תכלת לכרתי.** לבע התכלת
קרוב לגוון של כרתי שקורין פורוש בלע"ז:

יד אברהם

can be characterized as וּבְקוּמֶךָ, *when you arise?* (*Rabbeinu Yonah;* see comm. below, s.v. רבי אליעזר אומר).

מִשֶּׁיַּכִּיר בֵּין תְּכֵלֶת לְלָבָן. — *From when one can distinguish between techeiles and white.*

When it is light enough to distinguish between the *techeiles* strings and the white strings in the coils of *tzitzis*, one may recite the morning *Shema* (*Rav,* first explanation; *Rambam Comm.;* the source of this interpretation is *Yerushalmi* 1:2).

The Torah (*Numbers* 15:38) stipulates that *tzitzis* consist of strings of white wool and strings of תְּכֵלֶת, *techeiles*, wool dyed with a special dye (the exact number of strings dyed is the subject of dispute among the authorities; see *Rambam, Hil. Tzitzis* 1:6; *Raavad* ad loc.; *Tosafos* to 9b s.v. אלא). In the opinion of many, this dye is a shade of blue (see *Tif. Yisrael, Tosafos* to *Succah* 31b s.v. הירוק). Others maintain that it is a shade of green (*R' Shlomo Sirilio*, cited in *Meleches Shlomo;* this seems to be the view of *Yerushalmi* 1:2, cited by *Tosafos* ibid., as well as *Rashi* — see below, s.v. רבי אליעזר אומר).

First a white string and then a *techeiles* string are wrapped around the other strings, forming a coil of white and blue [or green] (*Rambam* ibid. 1:7). When one can distinguish between the blue (or green) and white in this coil, one may recite the morning *Shema* (*Rashba, Meiri*).

Alternatively, the mishnah refers to a fleece that had been colored with this special dye, which did not dye the fleece to a uniform color. When it is

light enough to distinguish between the dyed patches of the fleece and those parts that were not well dyed, one may recite the morning *Shema* (*Rav,* second explanation; *Rashi*).

The mishnah cannot be referring to two *separate* pieces of wool, one of which is dyed and the other not, for the difference between the two can be discerned even at night! (*Gemara* 9b). Starlight or the early light of dawn, however, does not suffice to distinguish between the white and the *techeiles* strings of the coils of *tzitzis* (*Rashba, Meiri*). Similarly, it requires more light to distinguish between the dyed and undyed portion of the same fleece.

רַבִּי אֱלִיעֶזֶר אוֹמֵר: בֵּין תְּכֵלֶת לְכַרְתִּי. — *R' Eliezer says: between techeiles and leek.*

R' Eliezer maintains that the morning *Shema* may not be recited until one can distinguish between the color of *techeiles* and the green color of leek (*Rav; Rambam Comm;* see also *Kafich* ed.; *Rashi; Tiferes Yisrael;* see also *Aruch* s.v. כרת), which is very similar to the color of *techeiles* (*Rav*).

R' Eliezer's statement would seem to imply that *techeiles* is a shade of green, similar to leek, and not a shade of blue (see above, s.v. משיכיר בין תכלת ללבן). This seems to be the understanding of *Rashi* and *Rav.* However, it is possible that *techeiles* is in fact blue. In the semidarkness of dawn it is difficult to distinguish between shades of green and blue (see *Tif. Yisrael*). *Meiri* explains that in the early morning light it is difficult to distinguish between any two colored items. Moreoever, *Rav's* interpretation of

1
2

From when one can distinguish between *techeiles* and white. R' Eliezer says: between *techeiles* and leek. And one must finish it by sunrise.

כָּרָתִי as *leek* is not universally accepted. *Tosafos* (*Chullin* 47b s.v. אלא and *Succah* 31b s.v. הירוק) and *Rabbeinu Yonah* maintain that it is indigo. Since indigo and *techeiles* are both shades of blue, it is difficult to distinguish between the two without sufficient light.

More light is needed to distinguish between *techeiles* and leek (or indigo) than is neeeded to distinguish between *techeiles* and white. Hence, according to R' Eliezer, the period during which one may recite the morning *Shema* begins later than it does according to the first *Tanna* of our mishnah (*Meiri; R' Shlomo Sirilio*, cited in *Meleches Shlomo*).

A *baraisa* cited by the *Gemara* (9b) states that one may recite the *Shema* from the time when "one can recognize his friend from a distance of four *amos*." The *Gemara* rules accordingly. *Yerushalmi* (1:2) notes that this is identical to the time when a person can distinguish between the white strings and the *techeiles* strings of *tzitzis*. Thus, the halachah follows the view of the first *Tanna* of our mishnah (*Orach Chaim* 58:1; *Mishnah Berurah* there # 2).

A different *baraisa* cited in the *Gemara* (8b) implies that one may recite the morning *Shema* from עֲלוֹת הַשַּׁחַר, *the rise of the light of dawn*. Since some people awaken at that time, it can be classified as a time "when you arise." However, this *baraisa* does not contradict our mishnah, which gives a later

time. One can discharge his obligation from dawn only in extenuating circumstances, e.g. if one must set out on a journey and will therefore be unable to recite the *Shema* at the proper time (see *Rif* 2b). Since most people are still asleep at dawn, it is considered a time "when you arise" only in exceptional circumstances (see *Aruch HaShulchan, Orach Chaim* 58:6).[1] Our mishnah refers to the time when the *majority* of people arise, which is the earliest time one may recite the morning *Shema* in *ordinary* circumstances (*Rosh* 1:9, *Rashba* to 8b s.v. ולעניין פסק). *Tosafos* (8b s.v. לא לעולם) interpret that Baraisa differently, and maintain that one can never discharge his obligation before the times listed in our mishnah.

וְגוֹמְרָהּ עַד הָנֵץ הַחַמָּה. — *And one must finish it by sunrise.*

The end of the period during which the morning *Shema* may be recited is sunrise (*Shenos Eliyahu, Tif. Yisrael*).

Some interpret the term וְגוֹמְרָהּ as "he *reads* it (i.e. the *Shema*)" by sunrise. According to either version the mishnah states the *Shema* must be reicted by sunrise. Other versions of the text do not include the word וְגוֹמְרָהּ at all (see *Tos. Yom Tov, Meleches Shlomo*).

This is part of R' Eliezer's statement (*Rambam Comm.*). In R' Eliezer's opinion, the time for reciting the morning *Shema* ends with הָנֵץ הַחַמָּה, "sunrise." This term (which derives from a root meaning "to blossom") refers to the

---

1. This is the ruling of *Shulchan Aruch* (*Orach Chaim* 58:3) as well. As noted in mishnah 1 (s.v. אמר להם), one who, due to extenuating circumstances, had not recited the evening *Shema* before dawn, may recite it until sunrise, since the period between dawn and sunrise can be categorized as a time "when you lie down." However, even in extenuating circumstances, one cannot recite the evening *Shema* after dawn and then recite the morning *Shema* before sunrise. For by reciting the evening *Shema* at this time he has defined this period as a time "when you lie down"; he cannot now classify it as a time "when you arise" (*Orach Chaim* ibid. §5; see *Mishnah Berurah* §21 who notes that not all agree to this ruling; see also *Rashba* to 8b s.v. הכי גרסינן. See further *Shaarei Tziyun* §14).

רַבִּי יְהוֹשֻׁעַ אוֹמֵר: עַד שָׁלֹשׁ שָׁעוֹת, שֶׁכֵּן
דֶּרֶךְ בְּנֵי מְלָכִים לַעֲמֹד בְּשָׁלֹשׁ שָׁעוֹת.

─── ר' עוֹבַדְיָה מִבַּרְטֶנּוּרָא ───

עַד שָׁלֹשׁ שָׁעוֹת. בַּיּוֹם, עַד סוֹף שָׁעָה שְׁלִישִׁית שֶׁהוּא רְבִיעַ הַיּוֹם בַּזְּמַן שֶׁהַיָּמִים וְהַלֵּילוֹת שָׁוִים. וּלְעוֹלָם זְמַן קְרִיאַת שְׁמַע הוּא עַד רְבִיעַ הַיּוֹם, בֵּין שֶׁהַיָּמִים אֲרוּכִים בֵּין קְצָרִים. וְכֵן הוּא דְּתָנַן לְקַמָּן (פֶּרֶק ד' מִשְׁנָה א') תְּפִלַּת הַשַּׁחַר עַד אַרְבַּע שָׁעוֹת בַּיּוֹם, הַיְנוּ עַד שְׁלִישׁ הַיּוֹם. וְאַרְבַּע שָׁעוֹת דְּנָקַט, לְפִי שֶׁשְּׁלִישׁ הַיּוֹם הוּא אַרְבַּע שָׁעוֹת בַּזְּמַן שֶׁהַיָּמִים וְהַלֵּילוֹת שָׁוִין. וְכָל מָקוֹם שֶׁנִּזְכַּר בַּמִּשְׁנָה כָּךְ וְכָךְ שָׁעוֹת בַּיּוֹם,

יד אברהם

emergence of the upper edge of the ball of the sun on the horizon (see *Rashi* to 9b s.v. שמש עם; see *Tos. Yom Tov* from *Rabbeinu Yonah* and *Mishnah Berurah*, *Beur Halachah* 58:1 s.v. כמו). R' Eliezer maintains that sunrise signifies the end of the "time of rising," during which the morning *Shema* must be recited, since most people have awakened by this time (*Tos. R' Akiva* §7).

However, even according to R' Eliezer, one who rises from bed after sunrise is still able to fulfill the obligation of reciting the *Shema* to some degree, although he cannot fulfill it in a complete and timely manner. This is similar to reciting the morning prayers after their allotted time; one who does so is not rewarded as one who recited the prayers at the proper time; nevertheless he does receive reward for his prayers [see *Gemara* 26a] (*Rashba*). Alternatively, the period until sunrise is meant only as the *ideal* time for the recitation of *Shema*. The period after sunrise is also a legitimate time for its recitation, albeit not ideally (*Rabbeinu Yonah*, 4b s.v. עד הנץ החמה). However,

R' Akiva Eiger (*Tos. R' Akiva* ibid.) implies that according to R' Eliezer, one cannot fulfill his *Shema* obligation at all after sunrise.

R' — רַבִּי יְהוֹשֻׁעַ אוֹמֵר: עַד שָׁלֹשׁ שָׁעוֹת, *Yehoshua says: By three hours,*

[R' Yehoshua maintains that the time "when you arise" extends] until the end of the third hour of the day (*Rav*), as he will immediately explain.

Some authorities maintain that R' Yehoshua refers to the *start* of the third hour, not its end (see *Meleches Shlomo* s.v. עד ג' שעות).

R' Yehoshua does not refer to sixty-minute hours but to שָׁעוֹת זְמַנִּיּוֹת, *seasonal hours*; i.e. the units obtained by dividing the day into twelve equal segments, each of which is called an "hour." The length of a "seasonal hour" varies according to the length of the day. Hence, the mishnah's three hours actually represent a quarter of any given day (*Rav*, *Rambam Comm.*).[1] Accordingly, on a short winter day, the period of time during

---

1. There is some question as to when these three hours begin. *Magen Avraham* (58:1) reckons the day from עֲלוֹת הַשַּׁחַר until צֵאת הַכּוֹכָבִים. This span is divided into twelve "hours," and the time for reciting the morning *Shema* ends three "hours" after עֲלוֹת הַשַּׁחַר. *Gra* (see *Shenos Eliyahu* to mishnah 1 s.v. ר"ג אומר, *Beur HaGra* to Orach Chaim 459:2) maintains that the "day" (in this context) begins at sunrise and ends at sunset. It is this span that is divided into twelve "hours." The time for reciting the morning *Shema* concludes three "hours" after sunrise. This represents a later deadline than *Magen Avraham's*.

R' Yaakov Emden suggests that R' Yehoshua's deadline is based neither on the time of עֲלוֹת הַשַּׁחַר nor the time of sunrise. Rather, it is dependent on the time of midday, i.e. when the sun is at its apex. The day is defined as beginning six sixty-minute hours before this time, and ending six hours later. This length of the "day" is fixed at twelve hours, regardless of the times of dawn and nightfall. A short winter "day" begins before dawn

1
2

R' Yehoshua says: By three hours, for such is the way of princes, to rise by three hours.

which one can fulfill his morning *Shema* obligation will be far shorter than on a long summer day (see *Mishnah Berurah* 58:5).

Tosafos HaRosh (to 3b s.v. כיון) appears to understand the "hours" of the mishnah to be sixty-minute hours. This is also the opinion of *P'nei Yehoshua* (*Mahadura Basra* to *Berachos*).

שֶׁכֵּן דֶּרֶךְ בְּנֵי מְלָכִים לַעֲמֹד בְּשָׁלֹשׁ שָׁעוֹת. — *for such is the way of princes, to rise by three hours.*

R' Yehoshua maintains that the time which qualifies as "when you arise" is not defined by the habits of the majority. Rather, it continues until *all* have arisen (*Rav, Rambam Comm.*; see *Tos. R' Akiva* #8).

The halachah is decided in accordance with R' Yehoshua's view (*Orach Chaim* 58:1). The custom of the וְתִיקִין, *the scrupulous ones,* i.e. those who held mitzvos in great esteem, was to recite the *Shema* immediately before sunrise, so that they could begin the *Shemoneh Esrei* with the rise of the sun. The *Gemara* (9b) states that one should emulate this practice. Thus, ideally one should recite the *Shema* before sunrise (*Orach Chaim* 58:1).

As noted in the previous mishnah (comm. s.v. רבן גמליאל אומר and s.v. וחכמים אומרים), the Sages and Rabban Gamliel interpret the expression "when you lie down" to mean the entire period of time during which people are lying in bed, i.e. the entire night, and thus rule that the Torah allows for the recitation of the evening *Shema* through the night. No *Tanna*, however, interprets the phrase "when you arise" to mean the entire period of time during which people are

awake, i.e. the entire day. All agree that this expression refers only to the time during which people awaken and rise from bed. R' Eliezer and R' Yehoshua disagree only regarding the period of time which can be thus defined. [It is understandable that R' Eliezer interprets the phrase to mean the time when people awaken, for he also defines the phrase "when you lie down" as the time during which people go to sleep (comm. to Mishnah 1, s.v. רבי אליעזר אומר). But why do the Sages and Rabban Gamliel not rule that the morning *Shema* may be recited throughout the day (at least according to Biblical law), as they maintain regarding the evening *Shema*?] Meiri (to first mishnah) explains that this is because in Hebrew, the term קִימָה, *arising,* denotes one who arises from a sitting or laying position. The state of *being* in a standing position is referred to as עֲמִידָה, *standing.* Therefore, all agree that the expression "when you arise" relates only to the time during which people awaken and arise from bed (see also *Pri Chadash, Orach Chaim* 58:1 s.v. ואיכא למידק; *Taz* ad loc.).

Kesef Mishnah (*Hil. Krias Shema* 1:13), however, maintains that those who allow the recitation of the evening *Shema* the entire night indeed interpret the expression "when you arise" similarly to mean the entire day. The obligation to recite the morning *Shema* within the first quarter of the day is a Rabbinical enactment, decreed to ensure that one recite the *Shema* before the morning *Shemoneh Esrei*, which, according to the view followed by halachah, must be recited before the end of the fourth hour of the day (below, 4:1). See *Minchas Kohen* (*Mevo Hashemesh* 2:12) and *Magen Avraham* (58:7), who raise many objections to this understanding.

and ends well after nightfall; in the summer, the "day" will begin after sunrise and end before sunset. According to this interpretation, one may fulfill his morning *Shema* obligation until three sixty-minute hours before midday, regardless of the actual length of the day (*Lechem Shamayim*; this interpretation is based on *Zohar*).

הַקּוֹרֵא מִכָּאן וָאֵילָךְ לֹא הִפְסִיד; כְּאָדָם הַקּוֹרֵא בַּתּוֹרָה.

[ג] **בֵּית שַׁמַּאי** אוֹמְרִים: בָּעֶרֶב כָּל אָדָם יַטּוּ וְיִקְרָאוּ, וּבַבֹּקֶר יַעֲמֹדוּ,

---

ר' עובדיה מברטנורא

על דרך זה אתה צריך לחשב ולדון. זו הבנתי מפירושי הרמב"ם ונתקבל לי. וטעמא דרבי יהושע דאמר עד שלש שעות ביום, שכן דרך בני מלכים שאין עומדין ממטתם עד סוף שעה שלישית. ורחמנא דאמר ובקומך, עד שעה שכל בני אדם עומדים ממטתם קאמר. והלכה כרבי יהושע. ומיהו לכתחלה צריך לכוין לקרות קריאת שמע עם הנץ החמה כמו שהיו וותיקין עושים: **לא הפסיד**. כלומר לא הפסיד מלברך לפניה ולאחריה, אלא אף על פי שעברה עונתה קורא ומברך לפניה ולאחריה: **כאדם הקורא בתורה**. אף על פי שלא יצא ידי חובת קריאת שמע בעונתה, יש לו קבול שכר כקורא בתורה: (ג) **יטו**. על צדיהם, דכתיב בשכבך דרך שכיבה: **יעמדו**. דכתיב ובקומך דרך קימה:

יד אברהם

One — הַקּוֹרֵא מִכָּאן וָאֵילָךְ לֹא הִפְסִיד; *who recites from then and onward does not lose;*

I.e. he has not lost the ability to recite the blessings associated with the morning *Shema* (below, mishnah 4). [These are the two blessings that precede the morning *Shema* and the one that follows it.] Thus, although one no longer fulfills his *Shema* obligation after the third hour, his recitation serves the purpose of enabling him to recite the accompanying blessings (*Rav, Rambam Comm.*, from *Gemara* 10b).

Although the allotted time for reciting the morning *Shema* expires at the end of the first quarter of the day, the blessings that are recited together with the morning *Shema* are not subject to the same deadline. These blessings are not בְּרְכוֹת הַמִּצְוָה, *birchos hamitzvah*, blessings recited when fulfilling a positive commandment. [This is evident from the formula of these blessings. They make no mention of the commandment of reciting the *Shema*. A בִּרְכַּת הַמִּצְוָה, on the other hand, takes the form of "Blessed are

You... Who has sanctified us with His commandments and commanded us to recite ... (*Rashba*, Responsa I:47, 69, 319; see General Introduction).] Rather, these blessings are independent prayers of thanksgiving and praise to God that are recited *along* with the *Shema* (*Meiri* to 11b s.v. והרי למדת; *Rashba* ibid.; see below, mishnah 2:2 s.v. בין ברכה ראשונה). As such, they are not bound by the time limits that apply to the *Shema* obligation.

There is a disagreement as to whether the blessings are subject to the same deadline as the morning prayers (see below 4:1), or if they may be recited the entire day. *Rosh* (1:10), citing *Rav Hai Gaon*, rules that these blessings are subject to the same deadline as prayers. Reciting these blessings afterward is a violation of the prohibition against uttering Hashem's Name in vain. This is the ruling brought in *Shulchan Aruch* (*Orach Chaim* 58:6). According to *Rambam* (*Comm.* and *Hil. Kerias Shema* 1:13), the blessings may be recited any time during the day.

As noted in the previous mishnah (s.v. מאימתי), the obligation to recite the third section of the *Shema* — וַיֹּאמֶר — is not subject to the times "when you lie down"

One who recites from then and onward does not lose; [he is] like a person reading from the Torah.

3. Beis Shammai say: In the evening all people must lie down and recite [the *Shema*], and in the morning they must stand, for it is

YAD AVRAHAM

and "when you arise," but rather to halachically defined day and night. Accordingly, one who recites this passage at any time during the day has fulfilled his obligation (*Shaagas Aryeh* §10).

בְּאָדָם הַקּוֹרֵא בַּתּוֹרָה. — *[he is] like a person reading from the Torah.*

Although one who recites the *Shema* after the third hour of the day has not fulfilled his obligation to recite the morning *Shema*, it is nevertheless not a meaningless act. Since *Shema* is made up of passages from Scripture, their recitation has the value of reading from the Torah (*Rav, Rambam Comm.* from *Gem.* 10b).

It seems strange that the mishnah informs us that one who recites the *Shema* is like a person reading from the Torah. Surely, everyone is aware that the *Shema* consists of Torah passages. [The point cannot be simply that the person may still recite the benedictions associated with the *Shema*, for this is already seen from the Mishnah's statement that one who recites the *Shema* after the deadline "has not lost."]

R' *Shlomo Min Hahar* (quoted by Rab-

beinu Yonah 5a s.v. לא הפסיד and cited in *Tos. R' Akiva* 9) explains this statement as follows: It is normally forbidden to recite Scriptural passages from memory (see *Gittin* 60b). The recitation of *Shema*, however, is an exception to this rule, because this restriction does not apply to passages whose recitation fulfills a religious obligation (cf. *Tosafos* to *Temurah* 14b s.v. דברים). One might presume that *Shema* recited after the allotted time cannot be recited by heart, since one fulfills no obligation with this recitation. This, however, is not the case. Since it is permissible to recite the *Shema* by heart in fulfillment of one's obligation, it is permitted when there is no obligation to recite it, as well. It is this law that the mishnah teaches by stating that one who recites *Shema* after the third hour is "like a person reading from the Torah." Although he recites it by heart, it is permitted as if he has read it from a Torah scroll. However, *Tos. R' Akiva* (ibid.) notes that others have a different explanation why the *Shema* may be recited by heart, according to which there is no reason to presume that *Shema* recited after the allotted time cannot be recited by heart (see *Beis Yosef, Orach Chaim* 49; *Shulchan Aruch* and *Mishnah Berurah* ad loc.).

3.

The following mishnah discusses the issue of whether or not one must assume a specific position while reciting the *Shema*.

בֵּית שַׁמַּאי אוֹמְרִים: בָּעֶרֶב כָּל אָדָם יַטּוּ וְיִקְרְאוּ, וּבַבֹּקֶר יַעֲמֹדוּ, — *Beis Shammai say: In the evening all people must lie down and recite [the Shema], and in the morning they must stand,*

Beis Shammai maintain that one

must recite the evening *Shema* while lying down, in a sleeping position, as will be explained below [s.v. שנאמר ובשכבך ובקומך] (*Rav, Rashi*; see *Rambam Comm.,* Kafich ed.). The morning *Shema* must be recited while standing.

שֶׁנֶּאֱמַר: "וּבְשָׁכְבְּךָ וּבְקוּמֶךָ." וּבֵית הִלֵּל
אוֹמְרִים: כָּל אָדָם קוֹרֵא כְּדַרְכּוֹ, שֶׁנֶּאֱמַר:
"וּבְלֶכְתְּךָ בַדֶּרֶךְ." אִם כֵּן, לָמָּה נֶאֱמַר: "וּבְשָׁכְבְּךָ

— ר' עובדיה מברטנורא —

כדרכן. בֵּין בְּקִימָה בֵּין בִּישִׁיבָה בֵּין בִּשְׁכִיבָה בֵּין בַּהֲלִיכָה:

יד אברהם

Thus, in the evening, someone who had been standing must lie down to recite the *Shema*; in the morning, one who was sitting must stand up to recite it (see *Meleches Shlomo*).

Rav and *Rashi* comment that Beis Shammai require the evening *Shema* to be recited while lying *on one's side*. This is because the *Gemara* (13b) states that one may not recite the *Shema* while lying on his back (see *Rashi* there, s.v. פרקדן; alternatively, the *Gemara* means while one is lying on his stomach — see *Aruch* ערך פרקד). This is because reciting the *Shema* — which constitutes an acceptance of God's absolute sovereignty (see below, 2:2) — must be performed with great respect. Reciting it in a supine position smacks of haughtiness (*Shoshanim LeDavid*).

Some maintain that the *Gemara* means to forbid reciting the *Shema* even while lying on one's side, for reciting the *Shema* in *any* horizontal position is considered disrespectful (*Rabbeinu Yonah* 15a s.v. שנים שהיו ישנים; see further footnote to s.v. ובית הלל אומרים). According to this view, Beis Shammai must be understood to mean that the evening *Shema* is to be recited in a *sitting* position, while *reclining* on one's side (*Tif. Yis., Kol HaRamaz*). [This latter explanation, however, seems to be contradicted by the *Gemara* (11a), which implies that Beis Shammai require the evening *Shema* to be recited בְּשְׁכִיבָה מַמָּשׁ, *while actually lying down* (*Shoshanim LeDavid, Tiferes*

Yaakov).] Although some sanction for this view can be found in *Rambam Comm.* [Vilna edition] (see *Shoshanim LeDavid*; see also *Meiri*, Dickman ed.), it is not supported by the Kafich edition of *Rambam Comm.*

שֶׁנֶּאֱמַר: "וּבְשָׁכְבְּךָ וּבְקוּמֶךָ." — *for it is stated: "When you lie down and when you arise"* (Deuteronomy 6:7.)

Beis Shammai understand the Torah's stipulation that the *Shema* be recited *when you lie down and when you arise* as a directive that the evening *Shema* be recited in the position one assumes while sleeping, i.e. a lying position, and the morning *Shema* in the position one assumes when he arises from his bed, i.e. a standing position. Although the purpose of this phrase is to teach the eligible times for reciting the evening and morning *Shema* (see prefatory comments to mishnah 1), Beis Shammai contend that this cannot have been the sole intent of the Torah; had the verse only intended to give the times during which the morning and evening *Shema* are to be recited, it would have simply stated, בָּעֶרֶב וּבַבֹּקֶר, *in the evening and in the morning*, or, בַּלַּיְלָה וּבַיּוֹם, *at night and by day* (see *Rashba* to 11a s.v. אם כן).[1] The formulation *when you lie down*

---

1. Evidently, Beis Shammai interpret the phrase "when you lie down" to refer to the time during which people are asleep, i.e. the entire night (see comm. to mishnah 1, s.v. וחכמים אומרים and s.v. רבן גמליאל אומר). Thus, the Torah could have specified the time limits for the recitation of the evening *Shema* simply by stating that it must be recited at night (*Tzlach* to 11a, s.v. בבקר ובערב). Regarding the implication of the term "the morning" (or "the day") for

1
3

stated: *When you lie down and when you arise* (*Deuteronomy 6:7*). But Beis Hillel say: Every person recites according to his [preferred] manner, for it is stated (ibid.): *While you walk on the way.* If so, why is it stated: *When you lie down*

YAD AVRAHAM

and when you get up, then, must be intended to teach an additional law — that the evening *Shema* must be recited in a sleeping position, and the morning *Shema* in the position one assumes upon arising (*Gemara 11a;* see also *Meiri, Tif. Yis. [Boaz] §2*).

וּבֵית הִלֵּל אוֹמְרִים: כָּל אָדָם קוֹרֵא כְּדַרְכּוֹ, שֶׁנֶּאֱמַר: "וּבְלֶכְתְּךָ בַדֶּרֶךְ." — *But Beis Hillel say: Every person recites according to his [preferred] manner, for it is stated: "While you walk on the way"* (*Deuteronomy 6:7.*)

Beis Hillel contend that the Torah does not stipulate that the *Shema* be recited in any particular position. They derive this from the Torah's statement (*Deuteronomy 6:7*) that the *Shema* may be recited וּבְלֶכְתְּךָ בַדֶּרֶךְ, *while you walk on the way,* which is understood to mean, "in whatever position you happen to be" (*Rambam Comm.; Tiferes Yisrael*). Alternatively, this statement demonstrates that there is no requirement to recite the *Shema* while lying down or standing up, for the verse allows the recitation even while walking (*Meiri*). Hence, Beis Hillel

maintain that one may recite the *Shema* in any position he prefers (*Meiri*), whether standing or sitting, lying down[1] or walking (*Rav, Rashi*).

Although Beis Hillel permit the recitation of *Shema* while walking, they nevertheless require that one pause and stand in his place while reciting the first verse of the *Shema*. This stipulation results from the special concentration needed while reciting the first verse, and not from any particular posture requirement (*Meleches Shlomo,* from *Gemara 13a-b*).[2] Therefore, one need not *stand;* he may sit as well. Indeed, it is preferable to sit, since one can thus better concentrate (*Rabbeinu Yonah* 20b s.v. בין כך ובין כך; see also *Rosh 2:3*, citing *Yerushalmi*).

— אִם כֵּן, לָמָּה נֶאֱמַר: "וּבְשָׁכְבְּךָ וּבְקוּמֶךָ"? — *If so, why is it stated: "when you lie down and when you arise"?* (*Deuteronomy ibid.*)

Since Beis Hillel maintain that the phrase *when you lie down and when you arise* was only intended to teach the proper times for reciting the *Shema,* why did the Torah not simply state *in the evening and in the morning* (or *at night and by day*), which denotes the same time periods? (*Tif. Yis.*).

the exact period during which the morning *Shema* may be recited), see *Shaagas Aryeh §5.*

1. However, as noted above (s.v. בית שמאי אומרים), he may not recite it while lying on his back (or stomach), and according to some, even while lying on his side (see *Orach Chaim 63:1* with *Rema;* see also *Beur Halachah* s.v. מאחר שכבר שכוב). However, if it is difficult for one to change positions, it suffices to incline a bit on his side (*Shulchan Aruch* ibid.).

2. This requirement also includes the verse בָּרוּךְ שֵׁם כְּבוֹד מַלְכוּתוֹ לְעוֹלָם וָעֶד, which is recited immediately after the first verse of the *Shema* (*Magen Avraham 63:5*). According to some, one should stand still until after the verse of וְהָיוּ הַדְּבָרִים הָאֵלֶּה אֲשֶׁר אָנֹכִי מְצַוְּךָ הַיּוֹם עַל-לְבָבֶךָ (*Meiri;* see *Rosh 2:3, Mishnah Berurah 63:11*). However, one who recites these verses while walking fulfills his obligation and need not repeat them (*Mishnah Berurah §9*).

וּבְקוּמֶךָ"? בְּשָׁעָה שֶׁבְּנֵי אָדָם שׁוֹכְבִים וּבְשָׁעָה שֶׁבְּנֵי אָדָם עוֹמְדִים.

אָמַר רַבִּי טַרְפוֹן: אֲנִי הָיִיתִי בָא בַדֶּרֶךְ, וְהִטֵּיתִי לִקְרוֹת כְּדִבְרֵי בֵית שַׁמַּאי, וְסִכַּנְתִּי בְעַצְמִי מִפְּנֵי הַלִּסְטִים. אָמְרוּ לוֹ: כְּדַי הָיִיתָ

ר' עובדיה מברטנורא

כדי היית. ראוי היית ליהרג, ואם היית מת היית מתחייב בנפשך:

יד אברהם

בְּשָׁעָה שֶׁבְּנֵי אָדָם שׁוֹכְבִים וּבְשָׁעָה שֶׁבְּנֵי אָדָם עוֹמְדִים. — *At the time when people* go to *sleep and at the time when people get up.*

Beis Hillel argue that the term ערב can connote the afternoon (see *Numbers* 9:3). The term בקר denotes the entire morning [or until the end of the fourth hour of the day] (see *Gem.* 27a). The time for the evening *Shema*, however begins at צֵאת הַכּוֹכָבִים, *the emergence of the stars* [mishnah 1], and the morning *Shema* may be recited, according to the latest opinion only until the end of the third hour [mishnah 2] (*Kol HaRamaz*). Thus, the Torah could not have written *in the evening and in the morning* to teach the exact parameters of the times during which the evening and morning *Shema* are to be recited; the Torah must write *when you lie down and when you arise.* Hence, there is no basis to derive from this verse a requirement to recite the *Shema* while in a particular position, as Beis Shammai maintain.

The mishnah explains why Beis Hillel dispute Beis Shammai's derivation from

the phrase *when you lie down* etc. of a stipulation that the *Shema* be recited in a particular position; they maintain that the sole intent of the verse was to teach the exact times during which the *Shema* may be recited. But how do Beis Shammai refute Beis Hillel's proof from the phrase וּבְלֶכְתְּךָ בַדֶּרֶךְ, *while you walk on the way*, which seemingly implies that the *Shema* may be recited while in any position?

The *Gemara* (11a) explains that Beis Shammai contend that this phrase is not intended to teach that the *Shema* may be recited while walking. Rather, the phrase (which translates literally as, *and during your going on the way*) teaches an entirely different law; viz. that the recitation of *Shema* is not obligatory on one occupied with the performance of a mitzvah (see below, mishnah 2:5). The expression "during your going" implies that the recitation of *Shema* is obligatory only on one who is involved in his *personal* business. If, however, he is engaged in performing a *mitzvah*, he is exempt from the commandment of reciting the *Shema*.[1]

Beis Hillel agree that the phrase teaches that one involved in fulfilling a mitzvah is exempt from the *Shema* obligation. However, they argue that the phrase still indicates that the *Shema* may be recited

---

1. This phrase is the source of the rule that הָעוֹסֵק בְּמִצְוָה פָּטוּר מִן הַמִּצְוָה, *one involved in per-forming a mitzvah is exempt from [fulfilling] another mitzvah* (see *Succah* 26a). This rule, however, applies only if one cannot fulfill both commandments at the same time (see *Rema, Orach Chaim* 38:8, *Mishnah Berurah* there §29 and *Beur Halachah* s.v. אם צריך לטרוח).

1
3

and when you arise (Deuteronomy 11:19)? At the time when people go to sleep and at the time when people get up.

R' Tarfon said: I was coming on the road, and I lay down to recite in accordance with the words of Beis Shammai, and I endangered myself on account of the bandits. They said to him: It would have been

while walking, for the verse clearly states that when one *is* engaged in his own, discretionary business — and hence obligated to recite the *Shema* — he may recite it even while "going on the way," i.e. while walking. Thus, both teachings are implied in the verse: a) that there are no posture requirements; and b) that someone engaged in the performance of a mitzvah is exempt from the *Shema* obligation (*Rambam Comm.*; see *Tos. Yom Tov* s.v. והוא; *Tos. Anshei Shem* s.v. והוא).

As with all matters of dispute between Beis Shammai and Beis Hillel, the halachah follows the view of Beis Hillel (*Orach Chaim* 63:1), for, as the Gemara (*Eruvin* 13b) states, their opinions were declared authoritative by a בַּת קוֹל, *a heavenly voice*. Whether one is allowed to follow the view of Beis Shammai if he wishes is the subject of the rest of our mishnah.

אָמַר רַבִּי טַרְפוֹן: אֲנִי הָיִיתִי בָא בַדֶּרֶךְ, — וְהִטֵּיתִי לִקְרוֹת כְּדִבְרֵי בֵית שַׁמַּאי, R' Tarfon said: I was coming on the road, and I lay down to recite in accordance with the words of Beis Shammai,

R' Tarfon was riding on his animal when the time to recite the evening *Shema* arrived. Although Beis Hillel permit one to recite the *Shema* in any position, even while riding, R' Tarfon wished to discharge his obligation in a manner acceptable to Beis Shammai as well. Therefore, he dismounted and lay down to recite the evening *Shema* (*Rambam Comm*).

וְסִכַּנְתִּי בְּעַצְמִי מִפְּנֵי הַלִּסְטִים. — *and I*

endangered myself on account of the bandits.

R' Tarfon related that by dismounting and lying down he placed himself in danger from bandits who would attack travelers on the highway (*Rambam Comm.*). He placed his personal safety at risk in order to fulfill his *Shema* obligation in a manner acceptable according to Beis Shammai.

Some infer from R' Tarfon's reference to "*the* bandits" that he was referring to a particular band of criminals. These highwaymen had *already* attacked him and had stolen all his possessions but had not harmed him personally. Despite the danger that these bandits might return at any moment and cause him physical harm, R' Tarfon dismounted to satisfy Beis Shammai's opinion (*R' Ephraim Ashkenazi*, as explained by *Meleches Shlomo*). R' Tarfon related this incident to demonstrate the lengths to which he would go to satisfy even Beis Shammai's opinion (see *Tif. Yis.* §25).

Although it is forbidden for one to place himself in a position of danger (*Choshen Mishpat*, 427:10), even to fulfill a commandment of the Torah (see *Rambam, Hil. Yesodei HaTorah* 5:1), R' Tarfon relied on the merit of his fulfilling the mitzvah of reciting the *Shema* to protect him from harm [see *Sotah* 21a] (see *Tif. Yis.*, loc. cit.).

Alternatively, R' Tarfon related that while he was *lying down* and reciting the *Shema*, he was attacked by bandits, who threatened his life. He saw this incident as a heavenly punishment for transgressing the ruling of the Rabbis that in all disputes between Beis Shammai and Beis Hillel, the halachah follows Beis Hillel. R' Tarfon recounted his frightening experience to demonstrate that one must follow the view of Beis Hillel (*Tif. Yis.*, loc. cit.; see also *Chiddushei HaGra*; see further below, s.v. אמרו לו).

אָמְרוּ לוֹ: כְּדַי הָיִיתָ לָחוּב בְּעַצְמְךָ, שֶׁעָבַרְתָּ עַל דִּבְרֵי בֵּית הִלֵּל. — *They said to him: It would have been fitting for you to come to harm, for you transgressed the words of Beis Hillel.*

[Although Beis Hillel allow the recitation of the *Shema* while lying down, R' Tarfon's dismounting and reciting the *Shema* while lying down was clearly in order to satisfy Beis Shammai's opinion, for according to Beis Hillel, one may recite the *Shema* while riding as well. Thus, R' Tarfon is considered to have "transgressed" the ruling of Beis Hillel.]

R' Tarfon's fellow Sages replied that he was wrong to endanger himself in order to accommodate the view of Beis Shammai. He could not rely on the merit of his performance of the mitzvah to protect him, since according to Beis Hillel, whose view is accepted by halachah (see above, s.v. בשעה שבני אדם שוכבים), he could have fulfilled his *Shema* obligation without dismounting (*Rishon L'Tziyon*). Thus, by dismounting, he placed himself in needless danger, which itself warranted that he be punished by coming to harm. Had R' Tarfon been killed,

his colleagues said, he would have been responsible for his own death (*Rav, Rambam Comm.*; see *Rishon L'Tziyon*).

According to the explanation that R' Tarfon himself realized that he was punished for following the view of Beis Shammai (see above, s.v. וסכנתי בעצמי), the Sages stressed that he was not being punished merely for needlessly placing himself in danger to fulfill Beis Shammai's opinion; even had he been in the safety of his own home, his actions would have warranted severe punishment, since he transgressed the Rabbis' decree that one must follow the rulings of Beis Hillel (*Chiddushei HaGra, Tif. Yis.*).

These two interpretations reflect the two opinions cited in the *Gemara* (11a) regarding the permissibility of following the more stringent view of Beis Shammai in cases where Beis Hillel agree that the mitzvah can be fulfilled in this manner, e.g. the case of the *Shema*, which Beis Hillel allow to be recited either standing or while lying down. According to a Baraisa taught by the amora Rav Yechezkel, one may follow the view of Beis Shammai and lie down to recite the evening *Shema*, or stand up to recite it in the morning, since it is acceptable to recite the *Shema* in this manner even according to Beis Hillel. According to this opinion, R' Tarfon's colleagues could not have meant that he was deserving of death simply because he followed the view of Beis Shammai. Rather, he was guilty of placing himself in needless danger, since according to the halachah he was not required to lie down (*Rishon L'Tziyon, Kol HaRamaz*). Rav Yosef and Rav Nachaman bar Yitzchak, however, maintain that the Rabbis forbade following the views of Beis

1
3

fitting for you to come to harm, for you transgressed the words of Beis Hillel.

Shammai, since the rulings of Beis Hillel were declared authoritative by a heavenly voice (see above, s.v. comm. בשעה שבני אדם שוכבים). Thus, even had R' Tarfon not been in a place of danger, he was deserving of death for favoring Beis Shammai's ruling. Indeed, Rav Nachaman bar Yitzchak cites R' Tarfon's incident to prove his point (*Tos. Anshei Shem*, citing *Mishnas R' Nassan*).

The silence of *Rambam* (*Hil. Krias Shema* 2:2) regarding the *Gemara's* dispute indicates that he is of the opinion that one may fulfill the *Shema* obligation in a manner acceptable to Beis Shammai if he wishes. [This is consistent with *Rambam's* explanation (above) that R' Tarfon's colleagues criticized his actions only because he needlessly placed himself at risk (*Tos. Anshei Shem*).] *Shulchan Aruch* (*Orach Chaim* 63:2), however, rules in accordance with the view of Rav Yosef and Rav

Nachaman bar Yitzchak that it is forbidden to follow the opinion of Beis Shammai.[1] Therefore, one may not change the position in which he finds himself to accommodate the opinion of Beis Shammai. One who does so is considered a "transgressor," although this does not invalidate his recitation. Thus, in the morning, one who is sitting may not stand up to recite the *Shema*. Even if he wishes to stand for other reasons, e.g. to better concentrate, he may not do so, since it *appears* as if his purpose is to satisfy Beis Shammai's requirement (*Mishnah Berurah* §5). However, in the morning, one who is already standing need not sit down before reciting the *Shema* simply to demonstrate that the halachah follows the opinion of Beis Hillel, nor need one stand up before reciting the evening *Shema* (*Rabbeinu Yonah*, 5a s.v. כדברי בית שמאי; *Meleches Shlomo;* see *Shulchan Aruch* ibid., §1-2).

4.

The following mishnah focuses on the blessings associated with the morning and evening *Shema*. These blessings were instituted by the Rabbis to be recited with the *Shema* (*Rambam, Hil. Krias Shema* 1:6). Stylistic differences in the structure of the various blessings lead to a discussion of certain rules regarding the wording of blessings in general.

1. This rule, however, applies only with regard to disputes where, in certain respects, the opinion of Beis Shammai represents somewhat of a leniency. For example, according to Beis Hillel, one should preferably not recite the *Shema* in a lying position, since a standing or sitting position demonstrates greater respect. Thus, one who follows Beis Shammai's view and recites the evening *Shema* lying down has not fulfilled his obligation in the manner considered ideal by Beis Hillel. However, in cases where Beis Shammai's view entails no leniency, one may be stringent and follow their rulings. Thus, the *Gemara* (53b) describes how a certain student followed the view of Beis Shammai and returned to the place of his repast to recite the *Birkas HaMazon*, which he had forgotten to recite previously, although Beis Hillel do not require him (see below, mishnah 8:7). As the *Gemara* relates, this student was rewarded by heaven for his actions (*Teshuvos Rema* §91, cited in *Tos. R' Akiva*). Others explain that this scholar was permitted to follow Beis Shammai's view because Beis Hillel agree that Beis Shammai's ruling there represents the *preferred* course of action, although Beis Hillel do not require one to act thus (*Rabbeinu Yonah*, 40a s.v. חד עבד בשוגג; *Rosh* 8:5, cited in *Tos. R' Akiva; Shenos Eliyahu*).

[ד] בַּשַּׁחַר מְבָרֵךְ שְׁתַּיִם לְפָנֶיהָ וְאַחַת לְאַחֲרֶיהָ, וּבָעֶרֶב שְׁתַּיִם לְפָנֶיהָ

ר' עובדיה מברטנורא

(ד) **שתים לפניה.** יוצר אור ואהבה: **ואחת לאחריה.** אמת ויציב: **ובערב מברך שתים לפניה.** מעריב ערבים ואהבת עולם:

יד אברהם

בַּשַּׁחַר מְבָרֵךְ שְׁתַּיִם לְפָנֶיהָ וְאַחַת לְאַחֲרֶיהָ, — In the morning one recites two blessings before [the Shema] and one after it,

The two blessings recited before the morning Shema are יוֹצֵר אוֹר, Yotzeir Or, and אַהֲבָה רַבָּה, Ahavah Rabbah (or, according to some authorities, אַהֲבַת עוֹלָם, Ahavas Olam; see below, footnote to comm., s.v. ובערב).[1] The blessing recited following the morning Shema is אֱמֶת וְיַצִיב, Emes VeYatziv[2] (Rav, Rambam Comm.).

Note that the mishnah uses the singular form ("In the morning one recites") when referring to the obligation to recite the blessings of Shema. With regard to the Shema obligation, however, the mishnah uses the plural ("from when may we recite the Shema in the evening" — mishnah 1; "from when may we recite the Shema in the morning" — mishnah 2). Shenos Eliyahu (mishnah 1 s.v. קורין) explains that the use of the singular form in our mishnah reflects the law that one may discharge his obligation regarding the blessings of the

Shema by hearing them recited by another, as long as both the reader and the listener intend to thereby discharge the listener's obligation (see Rama, Orach Chaim 59:4).[3] The mishnah's use of the singular form indicates that only one person in a group need actually recite these blessings; the others can discharge their obligation by listening to his recitation. This is not the case with regard to the Shema. One cannot fulfill his obligation merely by hearing the Shema recited by another; each individual must recite it himself [for the reason for this law, see Eliyah Rabbah 62:2, citing Maharam Alshakar; Avudraham, p. 31]. Thus, the previous mishnayos refer to the recitation of the Shema in the plural, to indicate that its recitation is incumbent on all the individuals in a group. [See Ritva (Megillah 2a s.v. מגילה), who also suggests that the use by the previous mishnayos of the plural reflects the idea that each person must recite the Shema independently.][4]

וּבָעֶרֶב שְׁתַּיִם לְפָנֶיהָ וּשְׁתַּיִם לְאַחֲרֶיהָ; — and in the evening [one recites] two [blessings] before [the Shema] and two after it;

---

1. In its count of the blessings associated with the Shema, the mishnah does not include the blessing of יִשְׁתַּבַּח, Yishtabach, which precedes the Shema in the morning prayer service. This blessing does not relate to the Shema but rather to פְּסוּקֵי דְזִמְרָא, Pesukei D'Zimra, the introductory passages of praise to God recited at the beginning of the service (Rashi to 11b s.v. יוצר אור).

2. The word emes, although it is recited together with the last passage of the Shema (see Gemara 14a-b, Rashi to 14b s.v. וה' אלהים אמת), is not part of the Scriptural passage of וַיֹּאמֶר, but is the first word of the blessing which follows.

3. This law applies to all other blessings as well, with the exception of the blessings of the Shemoneh Esrei. One can fulfill his Shemoneh Esrei obligation in this manner only if he is incapable of reciting it himself (Orach Chaim 124:1; see Mishnah Berurah § 1).

4. However, many authorities disagree, and rule that one can discharge his Shema obligation by hearing it recited (see Magen Avraham 61:16, Mishnah Berurah §40).

4. In the morning one recites two blessings before [the *Shema*] and one after it, and in the evening [one recites] two [blessings] before [the *Shema*]

YAD AVRAHAM

The two blessings that precede the evening *Shema* are מַעֲרִיב עֲרָבִים, *Maariv Aravim*, and אַהֲבַת עוֹלָם, *Ahavas Olam*.[1] The two blessings that follow the evening *Shema* are אֱמֶת וֶאֱמוּנָה, *Emes VeEmunah*, and הַשְׁכִּיבֵנוּ, *Hashkiveinu* (*Rav, Rambam Comm.*).[2]

Our mishnah discusses the blessings associated with the morning *Shema* before discussing those related to the evening *Shema*. This is in contrast to the mishnah's discussion of the *Shema* itself, in which the evening *Shema* is mentioned (mishnah 1) before the morning *Shema* (mishnah 2). In general, when discussing obligations that apply at different times of the day, it is more appropriate for the mishnah to discuss the morning obligation first, since the

Torah adopts this order with regard to the daily *tamid* offering (*Numbers* 28:4). However, as the *Gemara* (2a) explains, a discussion of the *Shema* more appropriately begins with the evening obligation, since this follows the order of the Torah with regard to the *Shema* (see comm. to mishnah 1 s.v. מֵאֵימָתֵי קוֹרִין). This Scriptural precedent does not apply to the blessings of the *Shema*, which are not derived from that verse, for they are not of Scriptural origin (see prefatory comments above). Therefore, our mishnah follows the order used by the Torah regarding the *tamid* offering, and refers to the morning blessings first (*Tos. Yom Tov*, based on *Tosafos* to 2a s.v. לֵיתְנֵי and s.v. אִי הָכִי). Alternatively, the mishnah first mentions the morning blessings because its previous discussion of the *Shema* ended at this point [mishnah 2] (*Gemara* ibid.; for

1. The exact wording of the opening phrase of both the evening and morning versions of the second blessing is the subject of a dispute in the *Gemara* (11b). R' Elazar maintains that it begins with the expression אַהֲבָה רַבָּה, while the Rabbis, basing themselves on Scripture, are of the opinion that it starts with the phrase אַהֲבַת עוֹלָם. *Rif* (5a), *Rambam* (*Hil. Krias Shema* 1:6) and others rule in accordance with the view of the Rabbis that the blessing begins with the words אַהֲבַת עוֹלָם. This version is followed by *nusach Sefard. Tosafos* (ad loc. s.v. ורבנן) and *Rosh* (1:12, citing the ruling of the *geonim*) maintain that both views should be followed. In the evening one should begin this blessing with the words אַהֲבַת עוֹלָם, and in the morning, with the words אַהֲבָה רַבָּה (see *Mishnah Berurah* 60:2 for the reason why אַהֲבָה רַבָּה is the more appropriate morning version of the blessing). *Rosh* notes that this was the custom throughout France and Germany, and indeed this is the version of *nusach Ashkenaz* (see *Orach Chaim* 60:1 with *Rama*). However, even according to *Rosh* and *Tosafos*, one who begins the morning blessing with the words *ahavas olam* fulfills his obligation (*Mishnah Berurah* loc. cit.).

2. In the Diaspora, an additional blessing is recited following these two blessings — יִרְאוּ עֵינֵינוּ, *Yir'u Eineinu*. The mishnah does not include this blessing in its count of the blessings of the *Shema* because it does not relate to the *Shema* at all. Rather, it was instituted by the Rabbis to allow latecomers more time to catch up to the congregation. In Mishnaic times, synagogues were commonly located outside the city, and the Rabbis were concerned lest a latecomer be left alone at night in an unpopulated area after the rest of the congregation departed (*Tos. Yom Tov*, from *Tosafos* to 2a s.v. מברך שתים). Some authorities maintain that this blessing was first instituted in Talmudic times (see *Maadanei Yom Tov* to *Rosh* 1:5, אות ש), or possibly even later, in the Geonic era (see *Rosh* to *Megillah* 3:5 with *Korban Nesanel* אות ג).

וּשְׁתַּיִם לְאַחֲרֶיהָ; אַחַת אֲרֻכָּה וְאַחַת קְצָרָה.

ר' עובדיה מברטנורא

ושתים לאחריה. אֱמֶת וֶאֱמוּנָה וְהַשְׁכִּיבֵנוּ: **אחת ארוכה ואחת קצרה.** חֲמֵסֵים שֶׁלְּפָנֶיהָ
קָאֵי, יוֹצֵר אוֹר אֲרוּכָה שֶׁפְּתוּחָה בְּבָרוּךְ וַחֲתוּמָה בְּבָרוּךְ, וְכֵן מַעֲרִיב עֲרָבִים. אַהֲבָה קְצָרָה, שֶׁחוֹתֶמֶת

יד אברהם

the reason, according to this explanation, that Beis Shammai in mishnah 3 refer to the evening *Shema* and then the morning *Shema*, see *Tzlach* to 2a s.v. ארדקאי).

Altogether, there are seven blessings recited with the *Shema*, of which three are recited in the morning, and four in the evening. *Yerushalmi* (1:5) explains that this number corresponds to the number of praises of God the psalmist would utter daily, as the verse (*Psalms* 119:164) states: שֶׁבַע בַּיּוֹם הִלַּלְתִּיךָ, *Seven times a day I have praised You* (*Tos. Yom Tov* from *Rashi*).

The three blessings recited with the morning *Shema* and the first three evening blessings parallel each other, with certain textual differences that reflect their daytime and nighttime recitations respectively (see *Meiri* to 12a s.v. ברכות הנתקנות). However, the *Hashkiveinu* blessing recited at night has no corresponding morning blessing. This is because *Hashkiveinu* is essentially a prayer that God watch over us and protect us from harm. The Rabbis only instituted this blessing to be recited at night, for then, a person is asleep and helpless and requires a greater degree of Divine protection (*Rashi* in *Sefer HaPardes* §57). Alternatively, the reason why the Rabbis did not institute a fourth daytime blessing was because these blessings are intended to correspond to the seven daily praises of the psalmist, as noted above. In dividing these seven blessings between the evening and the morning, the Rabbis instituted that the majority of these blessings — four of them — be recited with the evening *Shema*, which precedes the morning *Shema*. This is in accordance with the principle that one should attempt to fulfill the Torah's commandments expeditiously

(*Levush HaTecheiles* 58:1, cited in *Meleches Shlomo*).

אַחַת אֲרֻכָּה וְאַחַת קְצָרָה. — *one lengthy [blessing] and one brief [one]*.

A "lengthy" blessing is one that begins and concludes with the formula בָּרוּךְ אַתָּה ה', *Blessed are You, Hashem*. A "brief" blessing is one that concludes with this formula but does not begin with it (*Rav*).

It should be noted that *Rav's* definition of the terms "lengthy" and "brief" as regards blessings is one of many proposed by the commentators. This dispute affects the interpretation of the mishnah's following clauses as well. We will first explain the rest of the mishnah as understood by *Rav*, and will then present the interpretations of some of the other commentators.

The mishnah refers to the blessings recited before the *Shema* in the morning and in the evening. The first of these — *Yotzeir Or* in the morning and *Maariv Aravim* in the evening — are "lengthy" blessings, because they contain the phrase *Blessed are You, Hashem* both at the beginning and end. The second of the blessings recited before the *Shema* — *Ahavah Rabbah* (or *Ahavas Olam*) in the morning and *Ahavas Olam* in the evening — are "brief" blessings, because they conclude, but do not begin, with the words *Blessed are You, Hashem* (*Rav*).

According to this interpretation, the mishnah does not discuss the blessings that are recited *after* the *Shema* (see *Meiri*). As defined above, these are classified as "brief" blessings, since they conclude, but do not begin, with the words *Blessed are You, Hashem* (*Rashba* 11a s.v. אחת ארוכה).

1
4

and two after it; one lengthy [blessing] and one brief [one].

YAD AVRAHAM

In determining the forms the various blessings take, the Rabbis followed certain basic guidelines. Generally, a blessing begins and ends with the words *Blessed are You, Hashem*. There are, however, exceptions. One of these exceptions is a בְּרָכָה הַסְּמוּכָה לַחֲבֶרְתָּה, *a blessing which follows another [blessing]* in a series (for example, all the blessings of the *Shemoneh Esrei* after the first one). Such blessings do not begin with the words *Blessed are You, Hashem* (see *Gemara* 46a). These words at the beginning of the first blessing in the series suffice for all the blessings that follow (*Rashi* to 46b s.v. ויש מהן, *Tos. R' Akiva* §11; cf. *Tosafos* to *Pesachim* 104b s.v. חוץ מברכה הסמוכה לחבירתה, who maintain that these words at the *conclusion* of each blessing in the series serve as the opening clause for the blessing which follows). Thus, the first of the *Shema* blessings — *Yotzeir Or* and *Maariv Aravim* — begin with the clause *Blessed are You, Hashem*, while the blessings that follow conclude, but do not begin, with this clause. The *Shema* recited between the second and the third blessings is not considered an interruption of the series; therefore the blessings that follow the *Shema* also do not contain this clause at their beginning (*Rashi* loc. cit., *Meiri*, *Tos. R' Akiva* loc. cit.; see also *Orach Chaim* 60:1). [Other guidelines followed by the Rabbis will be discussed below (s.v. ושלא לחתום).]

Rashba rejects this explanation for the formulations of the blessings of the *Shema*. He argues that the mishnah defines the second blessing of the *Shema* as a "brief" blessing because it does not begin with the words *Blessed are You, Hashem*. But if the reason this blessing does not begin with this clause is simply because it follows another blessing, then it cannot be classified as "brief," for in effect it *does* begin with this clause. As noted above, this clause at the beginning of the first of a series of blessings serves as the opening clause for each of the subsequent blessings in the series (see also *Re'ah*). Moreover, the *Gemara* (12a) rules that it is not essential to recite the blessings of *Shema* in any particular order (see also *Orach Chaim* 60:3). Thus, it is possible to recite the blessing of *Ahavah Rabbah* before *Yotzeir Or*. Indeed, as explained by the *Gemara* (ibid.), a Baraisa states that this was the practice of the *Kohanim* who were involved in the Temple service. According to the aforementioned explanation, when the order of the first two blessings is reversed, the blessing of *Ahavah Rabbah*, which opens the series of blessings, should begin with the words *Blessed are You, Hashem*, and *Yotzeir Or*, which follows, should not. Yet the mishnah states that *Yotzeir Or* and *Maariv Aravim* are "lengthy" blessings, whereas *Ahavah Rabbah* and *Ahavas Olam* are "brief" blessings, implying that the former *always* begin with the words *Blessed are You, Hashem*, and the latter *never* begin with them, regardless of the actual order in which they are recited.[1] Evidently, the forms of the various blessings of the *Shema* have nothing to do with the order in which they are recited. Rather, the Rabbis deemed it appropriate, for whatever reason, to formulate *Yotzeir Or* and *Maariv Aravim* as "lengthy" blessings, i.e. to open and close with the words *Blessed are You, Hashem*, and the other blessings as "brief." For a resolution of the second objection raised by *Rashba*, see *Kesef Mishneh, Hil. Krias Shema* 1:8 s.v. הקדים.

1. See, however, *Meiri* (to 11b s.v. ובסוגיא זו), who contends that when *Ahavah Rabbah* is recited before *Yotzeir Or*, it *does* begin with the words *Blessed are You, Hashem*. The mishnah's statement that *Yotzeir Or* is a "lengthy" blessing and *Ahavah Rabbah* is "brief" does not present a difficulty to *Meiri*, who defines these terms differently than *Rashba* and *Rav* (see comm. below, s.v. ושלא לחתום).

מָקוֹם שֶׁאָמְרוּ לְהַאֲרִיךְ, אֵינוֹ רַשַּׁאי לְקַצֵּר;
לְקַצֵּר, אֵינוֹ רַשַּׁאי לְהַאֲרִיךְ. לַחְתֹּם, אֵינוֹ רַשַּׁאי
שֶׁלֹּא לַחְתֹּם; וְשֶׁלֹּא לַחְתֹּם, אֵינוֹ רַשַּׁאי לַחְתֹּם.

─────────── ר' עובדיה מברטנורא ───────────

בברוך ואֵינה פותחת בברוך: **לחתום. בברוך: שלא לחתום.** כגון ברכת הפירות וברכת המצות:

יד אברהם

— מָקוֹם שֶׁאָמְרוּ לְהַאֲרִיךְ, אֵינוֹ רַשַּׁאי לְקַצֵּר;
Where they said to recite a lengthy [blessing], one may not shorten [it];

The mishnah now enumerates some rules regarding the proper recitation of the various blessings.

A proper understanding of this and the following statements of the mishnah necessitates some explanatory comments. The precise wording of the various blessings, although formulated by the Rabbis, is not essential for proper recitation. It is acceptable to recite a version which is not faithful to the exact text formulated by the Rabbis (*Rashba* to 11a, s.v. ארוכה אחת).[1] However, the basic *form* of a blessing *is* essential for its proper recitation. As we have seen, the Rabbis constructed the blessings in different forms. Some were constructed as "lengthy" blessings, while others were formulated in a "brief" form. Other defining characteristics of the various blessings will be mentioned by the mishnah below. Every blessing must be recited in the form in which it was constructed by the Rabbis. Thus, one has no license to tamper with the text of a particular blessing in a manner which affects the essential components by which it is defined.[2]

The mishnah's statement that *Where they said to recite a lengthy [blessing], one may not shorten [it],* refers to a blessing which opens and

closes with the phrase *Blessed are You, Hashem* (see above, s.v. ארוכה אחת). This form of blessing may not be shortened by omitting the opening formula (*Tos. Yom Tov* in explanation of *Rav*). For example, one may not omit these words at the beginning of the blessing of *Yotzeir Or*. These words are the defining characteristic of a "lengthy" blessing; omitting them causes the blessing to be classified as "brief."

לְקַצֵּר, אֵינוֹ רַשַּׁאי לְהַאֲרִיךְ. — *[where they said] to recite a brief [blessing], one may not lengthen [it].*

One may not add the words *Blessed are You, Hashem* to the beginning of a blessing formulated by the Rabbis in a "brief" form, i.e. one that concludes, but does not begin, with these words (*Rav*, as explained by *Tos. Yom Tov*). Thus, one may not begin the blessing of *Ahavas Olam* with the words *Blessed are You, Hashem.* Since a "brief" blessing is defined by its lack of this opening formula, the addition of these words at the beginning of the blessing changes it from a "brief" to a "lengthy" blessing.

לַחְתֹּם, אֵינוֹ רַשַּׁאי שֶׁלֹּא לַחְתֹּם; — *[Where they said] to conclude [a blessing] with a closing formula, one may*

---

1. However, it is certainly preferable to follow the exact text formulated by the Rabbis (see *Kesef Mishneh, Hil. Berachos* 1:5; *Mishnah Berurah* 187:4).

2. The authorities dispute whether one who alters the basic form of a blessing fulfills his obligation (see *Rambam, Hil. Krias Shema* 1:8; *Milchemes Hashem* 6b of folios of *Rif* s.v. אמר הכותב כבוד רבינו שלמה; *Chiddushei HaRe'ah* to mishnah; *Orach Chaim* 187:1; *Beur HaGra* ad loc. and *Mishnah Berurah* §4).

1

4

Where they said to recite a lengthy [blessing], one may not shorten [it]; [where they said] to recite a brief [blessing], one may not lengthen [it]. [Where they said] to conclude [a blessing] with a closing formula, one may not conclude [the blessing] without the closing formula; and [where they said] not to conclude [a blessing] with a closing formula, one may not conclude [the blessing] with a closing formula.

YAD AVRAHAM

not conclude [the blessing] without the closing formula;

[Translation follows *Rav;* cf. *Rambam Comm.;* see further below, s.v. ושלא לחתום.] One may not omit the phrase *Blessed are You, Hashem* from those blessings which conclude with it (*Rav,* from *Rashi*). This refers both to "lengthy" blessings and "brief" ones, for both types conclude with these words. Just as adding or deleting this phrase at the *beginning* of a blessing changes its basic form, so too deleting this phrase at the *end* of a blessing affects its form (see *Tos. Yom Tov*).

וְשֶׁלֹא לַחְתֹּם, אֵינוֹ רַשַּׁאי לַחְתֹּם. — *and [where they said] not to conclude [a blessing] with a closing formula, one may not conclude [the blessing] with a closing formula.*

The mishnah now introduces a classification of blessing which it has not previously discussed — a blessing which begins with the words *Blessed are You, Hashem* but does not conclude with these words (see *Tos. Yom Tov* s.v. להאריך; see also *Shoshanim LeDavid,* cited below, s.v. ושלא לחתום). Examples of this type of blessing include that recited before eating fruit [*Blessed are You, Hashem, our God, King of the universe, Who creates the fruit of the tree*] and those recited before performing a mitzvah [for example, the blessing

recited upon donning *tzitzis: Blessed are You, Hashem. . . Who has sanctified us with His commandments and has commanded us to wrap ourselves in tzitzis*] (*Rav, Rashi*). This type of blessing is defined by its *lack* of the concluding formula, *Blessed are You, Hashem.* Thus, one may not add these words to the end of the blessings, since this changes its basic form.

These blessings do not contain a concluding formula because they consist only of a single short sentence of thanks to God [for creating the fruit or for granting the specific mitzvah] (*Pesachim* 105a). Therefore, it is unnecessary to repeat the clause *Blessed are You, Hashem* after the brief praise (*Rashbam* ad loc. s.v. הא נמי; see also *Tos. R' Akiva* §12).

The foregoing is *Rav's* interpretation of the mishnah, according to which a "lengthy" blessing is one which begins and ends with the phrase *Blessed are You, Hashem,* and a "brief" blessing is one which concludes with this phrase but does not begin with it. A blessing which begins with this phrase but does not end with it, e.g. a blessing recited before performing a mitzvah, is *not* classified as "brief," but rather as a blessing without a חֲתִימָה, *a concluding formula* (see *Tos. Yom Tov* s.v. להאריך).

As noted above (s.v. אחת ארוכה), many commentators dispute *Rav's* definition of these terms. One objection to *Rav's* interpretation is raised by *Shoshanim LeDavid* (cited in *Tos. Anshei Shem*). He reasons that any blessing which does not meet the criteria of a "lengthy" blessing should, by default, be categorized as "brief." Since, as *Rav* maintains, a "lengthy" blessing is one which contains the words *Blessed are You, Hashem* at its beginning and at its conclusion, a blessing which begins with these words but does not end with them should be categorized as a "brief" blessing. This, in fact, is how *Yerushalmi* (1:5, cited by *Tos. Yom Tov*) classifies a "brief" blessing, as does *Rambam* (*Comm.*) and *Rashba* (11a s.v. אחת ארוכה). *Rashi* offers yet another definition of "lengthy" and "brief." Although these commentators agree with the *laws* that emerge from the mishnah as explained by *Rav*, they do not necessarily derive them from the same clauses of the mishnah. We will now explain the mishnah as understood by these commentators.

Rambam (*Comm.*) understands the mishnah's statement that the blessings of the *Shema* contain *one lengthy [blessing] and one brief [one]* as does *Rav*, to be referring to the blessings that are recited before the *Shema*. However, *Rambam* interprets the mishnah's next statement, *Where they said to recite a lengthy [blessing], one may not shorten [it]; [where they said] to recite a brief [blessing], one may not lengthen [it]*, differently. Whereas *Rav* understands this clause to be discussing revising the *beginning* of a blessing, *Rambam* (in accordance with his definition of "lengthy" and "brief" — see above) interprets this clause to mean that one may tamper neither with the beginning *nor* the ending of a blessing by adding or omitting the words *Blessed are You, Hashem* (*Kesef Mishneh, Hil. Krias Shema* 1:7).

According to *Rambam*, the mishnah has thus far dealt with the issue of revising the beginning and ending formulae of blessings. Thus, the mishnah's next clause, לַחְתֹּם, אֵינוֹ רַשָּׁאי שֶׁלֹּא לַחְתֹּם; וְשֶׁלֹּא לַחְתֹּם, אֵינוֹ רַשָּׁאי לַחְתֹּם, cannot be referring to a bless-

ing's closing formula. Rather, *Rambam* understands the term לַחְתֹּם to mean *to insert*. Accordingly, the mishnah reads: *[Where they said] to insert an addition, one may not omit the addition; and [where they said] not to insert an addition, one may not insert an addition.* This refers to passages that are inserted into certain blessings on special occasions, such as the passage of יַעֲלֶה וְיָבֹא, *Ya'aleh VeYavo*, which is inserted in the blessing of רְצֵה, *Retzei*, on *Rosh Chodesh* and holidays. The mishnah rules that such additions may not be omitted where the Rabbis legislated that they be inserted. Where insertions into the text were not authorized by the Rabbis, they may not be added to the text of the blessing (see *Shoshanim LeDavid*, cited in *Tos. Anshei Shem*).

Thus, according to *Rambam*, the mishnah discusses two separate issues; 1) the changing of the basic form of a blessing by revising its opening or concluding formula, and 2) the insertion of unauthorized additions into a blessing's text. Neither of these changes is permitted.

Rashba (who, as noted above, agrees with *Rambam's* definition of a "brief" blessing as one which does not both begin and end with the words *Blessed are You, Hashem*) explains this last clause differently. Since a blessing is considered "brief" whether the words *Blessed are You, Hashem* are found only at its beginning or only at its end, one might think that the words *Blessed are You, Hashem* at the beginning of a "brief" blessing may be transferred to its end. This revision should not affect the classification of the blessing, for either version is considered "brief." However, the mishnah teaches that this is not so; the position of these words in the blessing is also a defining characteristic. Thus, reciting these words at the end of a blessing rather than at the beginning, or vice versa, changes the blessing's basic form, and is therefore not permitted.

Rashi explains that the mishnah's

reference to *one lengthy [blessing] and one brief [one]* refers to the two blessings recited *following* the evening *Shema*. The first of these blessings — *Emes VeEmunah* — is classified as a "lengthy" blessing; the second — *Hashkiveinu* — falls in the category of a "brief" blessing.

According to this interpretation, the opening and closing formulae are not the determining factors in the categorization of a particular blessing as "lengthy" or "brief," for both *Emes VeEmunah* and *Hashkiveinu* do not begin with the words *Blessed are You, Hashem*. Rather, the *content* of the blessing determines its classification. A blessing which deals with many topics is considered "lengthy," one which concentrates on a single issue is considered "brief." Thus, *Emes VeEmunah* — which refers to the Exodus from Egypt, God's dominion over the world, the splitting of the Red Sea, the smiting of the first-born Egyptians and the concept of God as the Redeemer of Israel — is classified as a "lengthy" blessing. *Hashkiveinu*, which concentrates on the single theme of God's protection of His nation Israel, is considered a "brief" blessing (*Meiri, Rashba,* loc. cit., in explanation of *Rashi;* see also *Re'ah, Shenos Eliyahu*).

Tosafos (11a s.v. ארוכה אחת) understand *Rashi* to mean that *Emes VeEmunah* is considered a "lengthy" blessing because of its actual length, while *Hashkiveinu* is a "brief" blessing because it is short. While *Tosafos* agree with *Rashi's* definition of "lengthy" and "brief" (as they understand it), they object to *Rashi's* interpretation that

the mishnah refers to *Emes VeEmunah* and *Hashkiveinu*. They argue that *Hashkiveinu* is actually quite lengthy, and on occasion made lengthier still by the insertion of various פִּיּוּטִים, *piyutim* (hymns), into the text. Moreover, *Tosafos* note, in Mishnaic and Talmudic times, the third passage of the *Shema* — וַיֹּאמֶר — was often not recited (see *Gemara* 14b, comm. to mishnah 1:5 s.v. מזכירין). At such times, *Emes V'Emunah* was replaced with a condensed version of the blessing (which begins with the words מוֹדִים אֲנַחְנוּ לָךְ, *Modim anachnu lach* — see *Gemara,* loc. cit.). This alternate version is even shorter than the blessing of *Hashkiveinu*. How, then, can the mishnah state that the first blessing recited after the evening *Shema* is always a "lengthy" one? *Rabbeinu Tam*, therefore, explains the mishnah to be referring *only* to the blessing of *Emes VeEmunah*. According to *Rabbeinu Tam*, the mishnah's statement, אַחַת אֲרֻכָּה וְאַחַת קְצָרָה, means that there are *two* versions of this blessing — a lengthy version (*Emes V'Emunah*) and a brief version (*Modim Anachnu Lach*). The mishnah rules that either version is acceptable. [See *Rashba* (loc. cit.) for another interpretation by *Rabbeinu Tam* of the mishnah's statement.]

According to *Rashi*, the mishnah's statement, *Where they said to recite a lengthy [blessing], one may not shorten [it]; [where they said] to recite a brief [blessing], one may not lengthen [it]*, means that one may not omit any of the topics referred to in a "lengthy" blessing, nor include topics other than the single theme dealt with in a "brief" blessing[1] (*Meiri*).

Rashi explains the next clause of the mishnah, *and [where they said] not to conclude [the blessing] with a closing formula, one may not conclude [the blessing] with a closing formula, as*

---

1. The practice of inserting *piyutim* into the service does not contravene this law, since these *piyutim* are consistent with the theme of the blessing itself. Similarly, it is permitted to add a personal petition while reciting the blessing in the *Shemoneh Esrei* which relates to that matter (*Meiri, Rashba* loc. cit., see *Orach Chaim* 119:1). Alternatively, these additions are permitted because they are not intended to be permanent additions to the text (*Re'ah*).

[ה] **מַזְכִּירִין** יְצִיאַת מִצְרַיִם בַּלֵּילוֹת. אָמַר רַבִּי אֶלְעָזָר בֶּן עֲזַרְיָה: הֲרֵי אֲנִי כְּבֶן שִׁבְעִים שָׁנָה, וְלֹא זָכִיתִי

ר' עובדיה מברטנורא

(ה) מזכירין יציאת מצרים בלילות. פרשת ציצית אומרים אותה בקריאת שמע של ערבית, אף על פי שאין בלילה זמן ציצית דכתיב וראיתם אותו פרט לכסות לילה, אומרים אותה בלילה מפני יציאת מצרים שבה: **כבן שבעים שנה.** היה נראה זקן, ולא זקן ממש אלא שהלבינו שערותיו יום שמינו אותו נשיא כדי שיראה זקן ורואי לנשיאות, ואותו היום דרש בן זומא מקרא זה: **ולא זכיתי** לא נלחתי להכמים. ודומה לו בש"ס בפרק בנות כותים (לח: ג) בהא זכנהו רבי אלעזר לרבנן כלומר נלחם:

יד אברהם

does *Rav* (see above, s.v. לחתום), to mean that one may not omit the words *Blessed are You, Hashem* from those blessings that conclude with this formula, nor add these words to the end of those blessings that do not contain them.

However, whereas according to *Rav* this clause complements the preceding clause, which discusses revisions at the *beginning* of the blessings (see above, s.v. מקום שאמרו להאריך), according to *Rashi* — who defines "lengthy" and "short" blessings differently — this clause introduces a concept which the mishnah has not previously mentioned.

5.

The third section of the *Shema* — וַיֹּאמֶר — is recited in fulfillment of the Torah's command that we mention the Exodus from Egypt every day. This obligation is derived from the verse (*Exodus* 13:3): זָכוֹר אֶת הַיּוֹם הַזֶּה אֲשֶׁר יְצָאתֶם מִמִּצְרַיִם, *Remember this day on which you departed from Egypt* (*Rashi*, ad loc.; cf. *Rambam, Hil. Krias Shema* 1:3; see also *Minchas Chinuch* §21). The commandment is repeated in *Deuteronomy* (16:3): לְמַעַן תִּזְכֹּר אֶת יוֹם צֵאתְךָ מֵאֶרֶץ מִצְרַיִם כֹּל יְמֵי חַיֶּיךָ, *So that your will remember the day of your departure from the land of Egypt all the days of your life.* Biblically, any verbal reference to the Exodus suffices. However, for various reasons, the Rabbis instituted that we discharge our obligation with the passage of וַיֹּאמֶר (*Numbers* 15:37-41), which concludes with the verse: אֲנִי ה' אֱלֹהֵיכֶם אֲשֶׁר הוֹצֵאתִי אֶתְכֶם מֵאֶרֶץ מִצְרַיִם לִהְיוֹת לָכֶם לֵאלֹהִים אֲנִי ה' אֱלֹהֵיכֶם, *I am Hashem, your God, Who has removed you from the land of Egypt to be a God unto you; I am Hashem your God.* One of these reasons is because this passage discusses the commandment of *tzitzis.* As the verse (v. 39) states, *tzitzis* serve as a reminder of our obligation to observe all the Torah's commandments. Thus, it was deemed suitable for incorporation into the *Shema,* which contains similar statements of obedience to God's commands [see mishnah 2:2 with comm. s.v. אלא כדי] (*Gemara* 12b).

Unlike the first two sections of the *Shema,* which the Torah explicitly stipulates are to be recited in the evening and the morning (see prefatory comments to mishnah 1), the Torah does not clearly state that the Exodus must be mentioned twice daily, by day and by night. The following mishnah deals with the issue of whether the obligation to mention the Exodus applies only during the daytime, or at night as well.

5. **W**e mention the Exodus from Egypt at night.
R' Elazar ben Azaryah said: Behold, I am
like a seventy-year-old man, yet I did not prevail

YAD AVRAHAM

מַזְכִּירִין יְצִיאַת מִצְרַיִם בַּלֵּילוֹת. — *We mention [lit. we cause to be mentioned] the Exodus from Egypt at night.*

That is, we recite the passage of וַיֹּאמֶר, which contains a reference to the Exodus, as part of the evening *Shema*. Although the mention of *tzitzis* is not relevant at night, since the commandment applies only during the day (see *Shabbos* 27b, *Menachos* 43a), the passage must be recited because of its concluding verse, which refers to the Exodus from Egypt. This obligation, the mishnah rules, is obligatory at night as well as by day (*Rav*, *Rambam Comm.*, *Rashi*).

As noted in the prefatory comments to this mishnah, the Rabbis legislated that we recite this particular passage to discharge our obligation to mention the Exodus because of its reference to the commandment of *tzitzis*. Since this reason is not relevant at night, when there is no *tzitzis* obligation, it would seem that there is no reason why we must fulfill our nighttime obligation with this passage rather than with any of the many Scriptural passages that refer to the Exodus, or with a mere verbal reference to the Exodus. Nevertheless, the Rabbis instituted that we discharge even our nighttime obligation with the passage of וַיֹּאמֶר because people are accustomed to reciting this passage as part of the *Shema* in the morning (*Tos. Yom Tov* s.v. שנאמר למען תזכור).

Many authorities dispute this interpretation of the mishnah's statement as referring to the passage of וַיֹּאמֶר. They argue that it is apparent from the *Gemara* (14b) that in fact there is no Rabbinical requirement to recite this passage at night, since its main topic — *tzitzis* — is not relevant at night (see *Rashi* ad loc. s.v. אמרי במערבא and s.v. לא יתחיל). Indeed, as the *Gemara* there states, in Eretz Yisrael they commonly did *not* recite the

passage of וַיֹּאמֶר at night. Rather, they discharged the nighttime obligation to mention the Exodus with their recitation of the first of the blessings that follow the evening *Shema* — *Emes VeEmunah*, which also contains a reference to the Exodus. These authorities therefore explain that our mishnah's statement [*We mention the Exodus of Egypt at night*] does not refer to a specific Scriptural passage. Rather, the mishnah simply states that the obligation to mention the Exodus is incumbent at night as well as by day. The manner in which we fulfill this obligation, however, is not discussed by the mishnah, but rather is a subject of debate in the *Gemara* [ibid.] (*Piskei HaRid*, ed. Mechon HaTalmud p.27; *Shenos Eliyahu*; *Shaagas Aryeh* §9 s.v. וכדי שתביין הדברים; see also *Yerushalmi* 1:6, cited by *Meleches Shlomo*; *Commentary of Rabbeinu Hillel* to *Sifrei*, Numbers 16:3).

אָמַר רַבִּי אֶלְעָזָר בֶּן עֲזַרְיָה: הֲרֵי אֲנִי כְּבֶן שִׁבְעִים שָׁנָה, — *R' Elazar ben Azaryah said: Behold, I am like a seventy-year-old man,*

R' Elazar ben Azaryah was not actually seventy years old at this time. Rather, he was *like* a seventy-year-old man, i.e., his appearance was that of a seventy-year-old, but he was actually much younger. As the *Gemara* (28a) relates, this was the result of a miracle which occurred to him. The Sages wished to appoint R' Elazar ben Azaryah president of the Sanhedrin at the youthful age of eighteen [*Yerushalmi* (4:2, cited by *Meleches Shlomo*) states that he was sixteen at the time]. His wife advised him not to accept the position, for it was unbefitting for a man of his youth to expound in front of the Sages. A miracle occurred and his hair turned white, giving him the

שֶׁתֵּאָמֵר יְצִיאַת מִצְרַיִם בַּלֵּילוֹת, עַד שֶׁדְּרָשָׁה
בֶּן זוֹמָא: שֶׁנֶּאֱמַר: לְמַעַן תִּזְכֹּר אֶת יוֹם
צֵאתְךָ מֵאֶרֶץ מִצְרַיִם כֹּל יְמֵי חַיֶּיךָ. יְמֵי חַיֶּיךָ
– הַיָּמִים – כֹּל יְמֵי חַיֶּיךָ – הַלֵּילוֹת.

יד אברהם

distinguished appearance of a man seventy years old.

R' Elazar ben Azaryah's reference to his appearance serves as an introduction to his following statement regarding his dispute with the Sages (see below, s.v. ולא זכיתי). R' Elazar ben Azaryah related that although the miracle which occurred to him attested to his halachic competence, nevertheless he was not able to convince the Sages to accept his view (Tos. Yom Tov).

Rambam (*Comm.*; see *Rosh Yosef*) suggests that R' Elazar ben Azaryah's elderly appearance was rooted in natural causes. R' Elazar ben Azaryah's tremendous exertions in his studies caused premature aging.

According to this interpretation, R' Elazar ben Azaryah related that despite his mastery of the Torah that resulted from his enormous efforts, as evidenced by his premature aging, he was unsuccessful in his attempts to convince the Sages of his view (Tos. Yom Tov).

וְלֹא זָכִיתִי שֶׁתֵּאָמֵר יְצִיאַת מִצְרַיִם בַּלֵּילוֹת, עַד שֶׁדְּרָשָׁה בֶּן זוֹמָא: — *yet I did not prevail [with my argument] that the Exodus from Egypt should be mentioned at night, until this was expounded by Ben Zoma:*

[Translation follows *Rav*; see further below.]

R' Elazar ben Azaryah was of the opinion that the Torah requires that the Exodus be mentioned both by day and by night, as the mishnah rules in its opening statement. However, the Sages disputed his view. R' Elazar ben Azaryah related that he was unable to convince the Sages of his view, and es-

tablish the halachah in his favor (*Rav, Meiri, Aruch* s.v. זך). The halachah thus remained undecided until Ben Zoma expounded a verse in support of R' Elazar ben Azaryah's opinion.

Some commentators explain that the Sages maintain that there is no requirement to mention the Exodus at night at all. According to the Sages, one need not recite the passage of וַיֹּאמֶר as part of the evening *Shema* [nor refer to the Exodus in the blessing of *Emes VeEmunah* — see above, s.v. מזכירין] (*Rashba*). Others say that even the Sages agree that there is a requirement to mention the Exodus at night, as the mishnah rules in its opening statement. However, whereas in the opinion of R' Elazar ben Azaryah this is a Biblical obligation, the Sages contend that it is a Rabbinical enactment. By expounding a Scriptural verse, Ben Zoma demonstrated that this obligation is of Biblical origin (*Ravad*, cited by *Meiri* and *Rashba*; *Meleches Shlomo*).

It is evident from R' Elazar ben Azaryah's statement that even before hearing Ben Zoma's exposition, he had already formed his opinion that the Exodus must be mentioned at night. He arrived at this conclusion based on the following reasoning: Presumably, the obligation to mention the Exodus applies in the part of the day in which the Exodus occurred. As the *Gemara* (9a) explains, there were actually two stages to the Exodus. The first stage occurred on the night after the fourteenth of *Nissan*, when Pharaoh granted the Jews permission to leave (see *Exodus* 12:31). The second phase was their actual departure from Egypt, which took place the following morning (see *Numbers* 33:3). Certainly, the more important phase of the Exodus was the actual departure of the Jews, and

1
5

[with my argument] that the Exodus from Egypt should be mentioned at night, until this was expounded by Ben Zoma: For it is stated: *So that you will remember the day of your departure from the land of Egypt all the days of your life (Deuteronomy 16:3.).* The days of your life — [this means] the days; *all the days of your life* — [this includes] the nights [also].

there is no question that the Exodus must therefore be mentioned by day. However, R' Elazar ben Azaryah contends that the events of the previous night were also an integral part of the Exodus. Therefore, mention of the Exodus must also be made at night. [This is consistent with his opinion regarding the time limit for eating the *korban pesach*, as explained by the *Gemara* there.] The Sages, however, maintain that since the Jews actually departed only in the morning, the Biblical obligation to mention the Exodus only applies by day (*Meiri; P'nei Yehoshua* s.v. מזכירין, cited in *Tos. Anshei Shem;* see also *Tos. R' Yehudah HaChassid;* see also *Maharsha* to 12b s.v. ימי חייך).

Rav and *Rashi* comment that Ben Zoma expounded this law on the day R' Elazar ben Azaryah was appointed president of the Sanhedrin (see above, s.v. אמר רבי אלעזר בן עזריה). Their comments are apparently based on the *Gemara* (28a), which states that the day of R' Elazar ben Azaryah's appointment saw a tremendous influx of students in the Academy, which led to such intensified study and discussion that not a single question of halachah was left unresolved. Presumably, the issue of the nighttime obligation to mention the Exodus was also resolved this day (*Tos. Yom Tov*).

Rambam (Comm.) interprets the phrase לא זָכִיתִי to mean *I did not merit.* R' Elazar ben Azaryah related that he

did not merit to know the Scriptural source of the Biblical obligation to mention the Exodus at night until Ben Zoma expounded a verse to this effect.

According to this explanation, there was no dispute regarding the obligation to mention the Exodus at night. All agree that there is such an obligation, as the mishnah rules in its opening statement. R' Elazar ben Azaryah simply stated that he was unaware of the Biblical source of this obligation until he heard Ben Zoma's exposition (*Tzlach* to 12b, s.v. מוכירין; cf. *Tos. Yom Tov* s.v. עד שדרשה, who implies that there is a dispute even according to *Rambam;* see *Tos. Anshei Shem* to *Tos. Yom Tov* ibid.).

שֶׁנֶּאֱמַר: לְמַעַן תִּזְכֹּר אֶת יוֹם צֵאתְךָ מֵאֶרֶץ מִצְרַיִם כֹּל יְמֵי חַיֶּיךָ. — *For it is stated: So that you will remember the day of your departure from the land of Egypt all the days of your life (Deuteronomy 16:3).*

[Ben Zoma expounded this verse, which is a source of the obligation to mention the Exodus (see prefatory comments), to include a nighttime obligation to mention the Exodus in addition to the daytime requirement.]

יְמֵי חַיֶּיךָ — הַיָּמִים, כֹּל יְמֵי חַיֶּיךָ — הַלֵּילוֹת. — *The days of your life — [this means] the days; all the days of your life — [this includes] the nights [also].*

[Ben Zoma, who was famous for his powers of exposition (see *Sotah* 49a

וַחֲכָמִים אוֹמְרִים: יְמֵי חַיֶּיךָ – הָעוֹלָם הַזֶּה. כֹּל
יְמֵי חַיֶּיךָ – לְהָבִיא לִימוֹת הַמָּשִׁיחַ.

יד אברהם

with *Rashi* s.v. הדרשנים), points out a superfluity in the wording of the verse. Rather than simply stating "remember the day of your departure from the land of Egypt the days of your life," the verse writes "all the days of your life." Ben Zoma expounds the superfluous term *all* (כֹּל) to include a requirement to mention the Exodus, once by day and once again at night.]

וַחֲכָמִים אוֹמְרִים: יְמֵי חַיֶּיךָ – הָעוֹלָם הַזֶּה, כֹּל יְמֵי חַיֶּיךָ – לְהָבִיא לִימוֹת הַמָּשִׁיחַ. — *But the Sages say: The days of your life — [this means] this world; all the days of your life — [this comes] to include the days of the Messiah.*

The Sages maintain that the superfluity in this verse is not intended to teach a nighttime obligation to mention the Exodus, but that this requirement will remain in effect even after the arrival of the Messiah. Regarding

the Messianic era, Scripture (*Jeremiah* 23:7-8) states: *Behold, days are coming — the word of Hashem — when people will no longer swear, "As Hashem lives, Who brought the Children of Israel up from the land of Egypt": But rather, "As Hashem lives, Who brought up and brought back the offspring of the House of Israel from the land of the North and from all the lands wherein He dispersed them."* This passage seems to imply that after the Final Redemption, the Exodus from Egypt will no longer be mentioned. Our verse teaches that indeed there will still be an obligation to mention the Egyptian Exodus. However, it will be secondary to the mention of the Final Redemption (*Meiri*, from *Gem.* 12b).

Thus, the Sages dispute Ben Zoma's exposition. This begs the question: Since the Sages countered Ben Zoma's exposition, why did R' Elazar ben Azaryah state

1
5
But the Sages say: The days of your life — [this means] this world; *all* the days of your life — [this comes] to include the days of the Messiah.

that it enabled him to prevail in his argument? *Tos. Yom Tov* (s.v. ולא זכיתי) explains that, as a *baraisa* cited in the *Gemara* (loc. cit.) states, Ben Zoma refuted the Sages' exposition, arguing that the aforementioned passage in *Jeremiah* indeed implies that there will be no obligation to mention the Egyptian Exodus after the Final Redemption. Although the Sages responded that the passage means that the Egyptian Exodus will not be of *primary* importance, the simple meaning of the passage accords with Ben Zoma's understanding. Therefore, the halachah was decided in his — and R' Elazar ben Azaryah's — favor.

Alternatively, R' Elazar ben Azaryah was unaware of the Sages' counterexposition. Thus, he thought that Ben Zoma brought convincing Scriptural proof in his support. However, Rebbi, the redactor of the mishnah, noted that just as the Sages disputed R' Elazar ben Azaryah's opinion, they contested Ben Zoma's exposition as well (*Chidushei HaGra;* for another solution to this question, see *Shoshanim LeDavid*, cited in *Tos. Anshei Shem.*).

According to *Rambam* (see above, s.v. לא זכיתי), the Sages agreed with R' Elazar ben Azaryah that the Exodus must be mentioned at night. However, they maintained that this obligation does not derive from the verse expounded by Ben Zoma.

Shenos Eliyahu suggests that the different expositions proposed by Ben Zoma and the Sages result from different understandings of the word כל. This word can mean *the entire* and it can mean *all* (as we have translated it). Ben Zoma understands it to mean *the entire*; accordingly, the verse states that the obligation to remember the Exodus applies the "entire" day, i.e., during both the daytime segment and the nighttime segment. The Sages, on the other hand, understand the term to mean *all.* Thus, the verse states that the obligation to mention the Exodus applies "all" the days of our lives, i.e., for eternity.

פרק שני ~§

Chapter Two

[א] **הָיָה** קוֹרֵא בַתּוֹרָה וְהִגִּיעַ זְמַן הַמִּקְרָא, אִם כִּוֵּן לִבּוֹ – יָצָא; וְאִם לָאו – לֹא יָצָא.

ר' עובדיה מברטנורא

פרק שני – היה קורא. (א) היה קורא בתורה. פרשת קריאת שמע: והגיע זמן. קריאת שמע: אם כיון לבו יצא. לדברי האומר מצות צריכות כונה, צריך לפרש אם שיהא מתכוין לצאת ידי חובתו, והאומר מצות אין צריכות כונה מפרש אם כיון לבו לקרות כהלכתן וכהלכתן, לאפוקי קורא להגיה שאינו קורא התיבות כנקודתן אלא קורא ככתיבתן כדי להבין בחסרות ויתרות, דבקריאה כזו לא יצא. ואנן קיימא לן כמאן דאמר מצות צריכות כונה:

יד אברהם

1.

The following mishnah discusses the concentration one must have when reciting the *Shema*. In addition, it delineates the laws regarding interrupting the recitation of the *Shema*.

הָיָה קוֹרֵא בַתּוֹרָה וְהִגִּיעַ זְמַן הַמִּקְרָא, — *[If] one was reading from the Torah and the time arrived for the* recital [*of the Shema*],

A person was reading aloud from a Torah scroll a passage containing a section of the *Shema* (e.g. the sixth chapter of *Deuteronomy*). When he reached the verse which marks the beginning of the *Shema* section, it was time for reciting the *Shema* (*Rav; Rashi; Tos. Anshei Shem*).

אִם כִּוֵּן לִבּוֹ – יָצָא; וְאִם לָאו – לֹא יָצָא. — *if he directed his mind [properly], he has discharged his obligation; but if not, he has not discharged his obligation.*

[Since this person recited the text of the *Shema* only incidently, as part of his reading of Scripture, he did not necessarily read the verses in the manner required for a valid recitation of the *Shema* (the valid manner for reciting the *Shema* will be discussed below). Thus, he can only discharge his obligation with this recitation if he concentrated (*directed his mind*) on reciting the relevant passages as required. If he did not concentrate, merely reading the words of the *Shema* does not constitute a valid recitation.]

The *Shema* consists of three separate sections of the Torah. The first part is the passage of *Deuteronomy* 6:4-9, the second part is ibid. 11:13-21, and the third is *Numbers* 15:37-41. In our mishnah's case, the person is presumably reading the Torah sequentially, which perforce means that he is reading the intervening sections as well. It is thus evident from our mishnah that even if one pauses for a lengthy period of time between the sections of the *Shema*, he fulfills his obligation (*Rashba* to 13a s.v. היה קורא בתורה, cited by *Tos. Anshei Shem*; see *Orach Chaim* 65:1). It also emerges that that failure to recite the blessings with the *Shema* does not invalidate the recitation, for the person was engaged in reading the Torah and did not recite the blessings before he read the relevant passages (*Rashba* ibid., from *Yerushalmi*; see *Orach Chaim* 60:2 with *Mishnah Berurah* §3,4; cf. *Tosafos* ad loc. s.v. היה קורא and *Rav Hai Gaon*, cited by *Rashba* to 12a ושמע מינה, who maintain that *Yerushalmi* only applies this leniency to an individual; a congregation, however, must recite the blessings before and after the *Shema*). Ideally, however, one should recite the blessings with

2
1

1. [[I]f] one was reading from the Torah and the time arrived for the recital [of the *Shema*], if he directed his mind [properly], he has discharged his obligation; but if not, he has not discharged his obligation.

YAD AVRAHAM

the *Shema*, as instituted by the Rabbis (see *Rashba* to 14a s.v. רבי יהודה אומר).

In addition, we can derive from our mishnah that one fulfills his *Shema* obligation even if he does not follow the order in which the Rabbis arranged its sections. For the person in our mishnah presumably recited the sections of the *Shema* in their Scriptural sequence, in which the last section (*Numbers* 15:37-41) precedes the first two sections (*Rashba* to 13a s.v. היה קורא בתורה, Oraysa ed.; see further comm. to mishnah 2:3 s.v. הקורא למפרע).

The mishnah does not define the sort of concentration to which it refers. The *Gemara* (13a) suggests two different definitions, in accordance with the two opinions regarding the issue of whether or not מִצְוֹת צְרִיכוֹת כַּוָּנָה, *commandments require intent* [i.e. whether the valid fulfillment of a mitzvah requires that the mitzvah act be performed with the specific intent to thereby discharge the obligation imposed by the Torah] (see *Eruvin* 95b, *Rosh Hashanah* 28a-29a, *Pesachim* 114b). According to those *Amoraim* who maintain that a mitzvah must be performed with the intent to discharge one's obligation, our mishnah refers to this intent. If the reader intends to fulfill his obligation of reciting the *Shema* with this recitation, his reading constitutes a valid recitation. If, however, he intends merely to read this particular Scriptural passage, without intending specifically to fulfill the Torah's command to recite the *Shema*, then he has not discharged his obligation, despite having recited the exact text of the *Shema*.

According to those *Amoraim* who

contend that the performance of a mitzvah does not require intent to meet one's obligation, the *Gemara* explains that our mishnah refers to one who is inspecting a Torah scroll for mistakes. Since he reads the text merely to help him detect missing or extra letters in the text, he does not necessarily pronounce the words with the correct vowels, because the vowels of a word are in any case not included in the text of the Torah. Consequently, he may read the word לְטֹטָפֹת, *l'totafos*, as לְטַטְפָת, *l'tatfas*, or מְזוּזֹת, *mezuzos*, as מְזוּזָת, *mezuzas*. According to this opinion, the mishnah means that if he concentrated on pronouncing each word correctly as he is reading, he fulfills his *Shema* obligation. However, if he does not pay heed to the proper pronunciation, he has not discharged his obligation, since proper vocalization is essential to a valid recitation. According to this interpretation, the mishnah does not refer to a type of *intent*, but to *concentrating* on the correct pronunciation of the words he recites (*Rav; Tosafos* to 13a s.v. בקורא; *Meiri*).

Some commentators explain this second definition of the *Gemara* to mean that this person unwittingly articulated the words of the passage as he was comparing this scroll to an accurate text. He cannot fulfill his *Shema* obligation in this manner, even if he pronounced the words correctly, because he did not recite the words as a conscious and deliberate act. This person is considered a מִתְעַסֵּק, *a preoccupied individual* — i.e. one who while performing one act unintentionally performs another. His recitation is analogous to exhaling into a *shofar* on *Rosh*

בַּפְּרָקִים – שׁוֹאֵל מִפְּנֵי הַכָּבוֹד וּמֵשִׁיב,

─────────── ר' עובדיה מברטנורא ───────────

בפרקים. לקמן במתניתין מפרש מה הם הפרקים: **שוֹאֵל מפני הכבוד.** שואל בשלום אדם נכבד שראוי להקדים לו שלום כגון אביו או רבו או שגדול ממנו בחכמה: **ומשיב.** ואין צריך לומר שמשיב

───────────

יד אברהם

Hashanah without intending to produce any sound at all. As the *Gemara* (*Rosh Hashanah* 28b) states, all agree that even if he inadvertently produces a sound that conforms to the ritual specifications of the mitzvah of *shofar*, he does not discharge his *shofar* obligation. For even if it is not necessary to perform a mitzvah with specific intent to fulfill the Torah's commandment, the *act* of the mitzvah must be performed intentionally. Our mishnah states that if this proofreader concentrated on reading the text, i.e. he recited the relevant passages as a conscious act of reading, he discharges his *Shema* obligation. If his reading was unintentional, he has not discharged his obligation (*Rabbeinu Yonah* 7a s.v. קורא היה, cited by *Tos. R' Akiva; Meiri; Rashba* to 13a s.v. היה קורא להגיה).

Many authorities decide the halachah in accordance with the view that one can discharge his obligation without specific intent to fulfill the commandment [אֵין מִצְוֹת צְרִיכוֹת כַּוָּנָה] (see *Shulchan Aruch, Orach Chaim* 60:4). *Rav*, however, comments that the halachah follows the view that one must have specific intent to fulfill the commandment of the Torah [מִצְוֹת צְרִיכוֹת כַּוָּנָה]. This opinion is shared by many authorities (see *Milchemes Hashem, Rosh Hashanah* 7a of folios of *Rif,* s.v. ועוד; *Rosh, Rosh Hashanah* 3:11; see *Rambam, Hil. Shofar* 2:4 with *Magid Mishneh* and *Lechem Mish-*

nah; Shenos Eliyahu), and is declared decisive by *Shulchan Aruch* (ibid.).[1]

The authorities that rule that one must have intent to fulfill the Torah's commandments bring a proof from a Baraisa cited by the *Gemara* (13b), which states that one must concentrate while reciting the first verse of the *Shema.* The Baraisa clearly is not referring to concentrating on pronouncing the words correctly (or to reciting them as a conscious act). Rather, these commentators maintain that the Baraisa refers to concentrating on fulfilling one's *Shema* obligation (*Lechem Mishneh* loc. cit., in explanation of *Rambam; Milchemes Hashem* loc. cit.; see *Milchemes Hashem* for the reason the Baraisa rules that this intent is not required for the entire *Shema*). Others, however, contend that the Baraisa does not mean that this verse must be recited with intent to fulfill one's obligation, but rather that one must concentrate on the *meaning* of the words of the first verse and their significance. Since reciting this verse constitutes acceptance of God's sovereignty (see next mishnah), it cannot be said mechanically [see mishnah 2] (*Rashba* to 13b s.v. שמע, cited by *Tos. Anshei Shem; Shitah Mekubetzes* to 13b s.v. ת"ר שמע; see also *Re'ah* to 13a-b and *Rambam, Moreh Nevuchim* III:51).[2] This interpretation of the Baraisa is followed by *Shulchan Aruch* (ibid.). Thus, *Shulchan Aruch* rules that, in

───────────

1. There is some question as to whether one must also have this intent when fulfilling Rabbinical commandments (see *Mishnah Berurah* 60:10, *Beur Halachah* s.v. וכן הלכה).

2. *Ramban* in *Milchemes Hashem* (loc. cit.) rejects this understanding of the Baraisa. He argues that if in fact there is a special requirement to concentrate on the meaning of the words of the first verse, the *Gemara* should have suggested that our mishnah's ruling that one can only fulfill his *Shema* obligation by reading from the Torah if he concentrates refers to the special concentration needed when reciting the first verse. However, *Rashba* (loc. cit.) explains that our mishnah cannot be referring to this type of concentration, because it is only required for the first verse, whereas the mishnah requires the one reading from a Torah to concentrate for the entire recitation.

At junctures [between sections of the *Shema* or its blessings] one may greet [another] out of respect, and he may reply [to a greeting]; but in the

addition to reciting the entire *Shema* with intent to thereby discharge his obligation (see above), one must also concentrate on the meaning and significance of the first verse[1] (see *Orach Chaim* 60:4-5 and *Mishnah Berurah* ibid. §11).

⋙ **Interrupting the Shema to greet people**

Generally, one may not interrupt his recital of the *Shema* or its blessings.[2] In certain circumstances, however, it is permissible to interrupt the *Shema* to initiate a greeting or respond to the greeting of another. In circumstances that permit one to initiate a greeting, he may certainly respond to a greeting (*Gem.* 13b). However, as will be seen in the mishnah, circumstances that allow him to respond to a greeting do not necessarily permit him to initiate a greeting.[3]

בַּפְּרָקִים — שׁוֹאֵל מִפְּנֵי הַכָּבוֹד וּמֵשִׁיב,
At junctures [between sections of the

Shema or its blessings] one may greet [another] out of respect, and he may reply [to a greeting];

[The translation of בַּפְּרָקִים as *at junctures* follows *Shenos Eliyahu* and *Tos. Anshei Shem;* see comm. to next mishnah s.v. אלו הן.]

If one is at a point in between the paragraphs of the *Shema* or its associated blessings (these points will be defined in the following mishnah), he may initiate a greeting to someone whom the Torah obligates him to honor, such as his father, his teacher or someone who possesses greater Torah knowledge than he (*Rav, Rambam Comm.;* see *Rav* s.v. רבי יהודה אומר; *Rambam, Hil. Krias Shema* 2:15). Certainly, at this point one may reply to a greeting extended by one of these people (*Rav, Rambam Comm.,* from *Gem.* 13b).[4]

Rosh (2:5) and *Rashba* (to 13b s.v. בפרקים)

1. This requirement also includes the declaration that follows the first verse — בָּרוּךְ שֵׁם כְּבוֹד מַלְכוּתוֹ לְעוֹלָם וָעֶד (*Mishnah Berurah* 63:12), since this statement continues our affirmation of acceptance of the yoke of Heaven (see *Mishnah Berurah* 66:11).

2. This includes pausing for the amount of time it takes this person to recite the three sections of the *Shema* (see *Magen Avraham* 65:1). As noted above (s.v. אם כוון לבו), an interruption does not invalidate the recitation (*Orach Chaim* 65:1; see *Beur Halachah* s.v. בין בדבור). However, if the interruption was involuntary, and lasted the length of time it takes one to recite the *Shema*, the recitation *is* invalid (see *Rama, Orach Chaim* 65:1; *Mishnah Berurah* §2,6).

3. It should be noted that the language used when interrupting the *Shema* is irrelevant. Where an interruption is forbidden, it is forbidden even in Hebrew (*Rav* s.v. ומשיב שלום; *Tosafos* to 13a s.v. ובאמצע). Where it is permitted, one may speak in any language (*Meiri* to 13a s.v. ורבי יהודה; *Kesef Mishneh, Hil. Krias Shema* 2:17).

4. *Nimmukei Yosef* (*Bava Basra* 58a of folios of *Rif,* s.v. והלכתא תוך כדי דיבור) states that one must limit his greeting to the minimum necessary to show proper respect, e.g. one greeting to his teacher may not exceed the words שָׁלוֹם עָלֶיךָ רַבִּי וּמוֹרִי, *Peace unto you, my master and teacher* (see also *Ramban* to *Bava Basra* 129b s.v. והילכתא). *Tos. R' Yehudah Chassid* (cited by *Beur Halachah* 66 s.v. ומשיב) rules that one should limit his greeting to the single word,

וּבָאֶמְצַע — שׁוֹאֵל מִפְּנֵי הַיִּרְאָה וּמֵשִׁיב; דִּבְרֵי
רַבִּי מֵאִיר. רַבִּי יְהוּדָה אוֹמֵר: בָּאֶמְצַע —
שׁוֹאֵל מִפְּנֵי הַיִּרְאָה וּמֵשִׁיב מִפְּנֵי הַכָּבוֹד;

ר' עובדיה מברטנורא

לָהֶם שָׁלוֹם אִם הִקְדִּימוּ לוֹ: **וּבָאֶמְצַע. הַפֶּרֶק: שׁוֹאֵל מִפְּנֵי הַיִּרְאָה.** אָדָם שֶׁהוּא יָרֵא מִפָּנָיו שֶׁמָּא יַהַרְגֶנּוּ, וְאֵין צָרִיךְ לוֹמַר שֶׁמֵּשִׁיב לוֹ שָׁלוֹם. אֲבָל מִפְּנֵי הַכָּבוֹד לֹא: **רַבִּי יְהוּדָה אוֹמֵר בָּאֶמְצַע.** הַפֶּרֶק שׁוֹאֵל בְּשָׁלוֹם מִי שֶׁהוּא יָרֵא מִמֶּנּוּ, וּמֵשִׁיב שָׁלוֹם לְמִי שֶׁמּוּטָל עָלָיו לְכַבְּדוֹ:

יד אברהם

dispute the inclusion of one's father or teacher among those whom one may greet מִפְּנֵי הַכָּבוֹד, *out of respect*. They maintain that these people are included in the mishnah's next category — those whom one may greet מִפְּנֵי הַיִּרְאָה, *out of fear*, with regard to whom interruptions are treated more leniently (see *Shenos Eliyahu*; see further below, s.v. וּבָאֶמְצַע). *Rashba* contends that the people one is permitted to greet מִפְּנֵי הַכָּבוֹד, *out of respect*, are people superior to him in Torah knowledge. Elsewhere, however, *Rashba* (*Teshuvos*, I:321) implies that someone superior in Torah knowledge is also included in the category of those whom one may greet out of fear (see *Divrei Chamudos* 2:18; see also *Tzror HaChaim*, ed. S. Yerushalmi, p. 6 s.v. ולעניין; see further below, footnote to s.v. וּבָאֶמְצַע). Accordingly, one who may be greeted *out of respect* perforce refers to a person whom etiquette dictates be shown respect, such as a person distinguished by his wealth or age (see *Maadanei Yom Tov* to Rosh 2:5 §3; see also *Rashi*; *Kesef Mishneh*, Hil. Krias Shema 2:15, in explanation of Rosh 2:5). This definition is followed in halachah (*Orach*

Chaim 66:1; see *Mishnah Berurah* there §3).

וּבָאֶמְצַע — שׁוֹאֵל מִפְּנֵי הַיִּרְאָה וּמֵשִׁיב, דִּבְרֵי רַבִּי מֵאִיר. — *but in the middle [of a section] he may greet [another only] out of fear and he may reply. [These are] the words of R' Meir.*

The middle of a section of the *Shema* or its blessings [as defined by the next mishnah] is treated more stringently than between sections. At this point, a person may initiate a greeting only to one whom he fears would kill him were he not to extend a greeting (*Rav, Rashi*). Certainly, at this point, he may respond to the greeting of a person he fears (*Rav, Rambam Comm.*, from Gem. 13b).[1]

Many commentators reject *Rav's* and *Rashi's* definition of "fear" as fear for one's life. They argue that the mishnah cannot have intended to teach that one is permitted to interrupt his recitation for fear of his life, for it is obvious that one need not — indeed, may not — place his life in danger to recite the *Shema* uninterrupted (*Rosh* 2:5, *Rashba*

"Shalom" — the Hebrew equivalent of, "Hello." *Tos. Yom Tov* (s.v. בפרקים) writes it is proper to greet one's teacher with the more respectful salutation, but should limit his greeting of others to, "Shalom."

1. In circumstances in which it is permitted to interrupt the *Shema* in the middle of a section, one may interrupt even in the middle of a verse (*Tosafos* to 13a s.v. ובאמצע; *Meiri*, citing *Yerushalmi*), although some require that the interruption of the verse be at a logical pause in the verse (*Rabbeinu Manoach*, cited by *Kesef Mishneh*, Hil. Krias Shema 2:15). However, even in such circumstances one may not interrupt the opening verse of the *Shema* (*Ramach*, cited by *Kesef Mishneh* ibid.), or the following declaration of בָּרוּךְ שֵׁם כְּבוֹד מַלְכוּתוֹ לְעוֹלָם וָעֶד, unless failure to do so would put his life in danger (*Orach Chaim* 66:1; see *Mishnah Berurah* there §11,12).

2 middle [of a section] he may greet [another only]
1 out of fear and he may reply. [These are] the
words of R' Meir. R' Yehudah says: In the middle [of a section] he may greet [another only]
out of fear but he may reply out of respect;

to 13b s.v. בפרקים; see also *Teshuvos Ha-Rashba* I:321). Rather, these commentators explain the term יִרְאָה, *fear*, in the sense of *awe*. According to this definition, the mishnah refers to those whom the Torah obligates him to treat with awe — one's father (see *Leviticus* 19:3) and one's primary teacher (see *Bava Kamma* 41b, *Avos* 4:12). *Shulchan Aruch* (*Orach Chaim* 66:1) rules in accordance with this view.[1]

In defense of *Rashi* (and *Rav*), *Taz* (*Orach Chaim* 66:1) explains that the mishnah does not refer to a situation where one's life would actually be endangered were he not to interrupt his recitation. Presumably, the person whom he may greet out of fear will not kill him once he explains that he failed to extend a greeting because he was involved in paying homage to God (see *Gem.* 32b). However, in this situation, the one reciting the *Shema* is certainly *presently* in fear of his life until he can explain his failure to greet the other. Therefore, the mishnah allows him to extend a greeting. For further defense of this opinion, see *Bach* (*Orach Chaim* 66 s.v. בין הפרקים); *Rashash*.

Alternatively, the mishnah does not refer to a *life-threatening* situation, but to a case where one fears that his failure to greet a person would provoke that individual to cause him physical or monetary harm (see *Beur Halachah* 66 s.v. או אנס), e.g. the failure to greet an extortionist or an informer (*Rambam Comm.*), or a king (*Rambam, Hil. Krias*

Shema 2:16 and *Kesef Mishneh* 2:15; *Meiri; Re'ah*; see also *Rishon LeTzion*).

רַבִּי יְהוּדָה אוֹמֵר: בָּאֶמְצַע – שׁוֹאֵל מִפְּנֵי הַיִּרְאָה וּמֵשִׁיב מִפְּנֵי הַכָּבוֹד; — *R' Yehudah says: In the middle [of a section] he may greet [another only] out of fear but he may reply out of respect;*

R' Yehudah is more lenient regarding responding to a greeting than regarding initiating a greeting (*Rashba* to 14a s.v. רבי יהודה אומר). Thus, while R' Yehudah agrees with R' Meir that one may only interrupt the *Shema* in the middle of a passage to greet someone he fears, he contends that at this point, one may respond to a greeting issued by someone he is obligated (or toward whom it is proper) to show respect (*Rav*; see above s.v. בפרקים).

Certainly, one must show no less respect to God than to a mortal of flesh and blood. Thus, according to R' Yehudah (whose view is accepted by halachah; see below, s.v. בפרקים) it is certainly permitted to interrupt the *Shema* in the middle of a section to respond to the *chazzan's* recital of קָדִּיש, Kaddish, and קְדֻשָּׁה, Kedushah. *Rabbeinu Yonah* (7b s.v. רבי יהודה אומר) adds that it is also permitted to respond to מוֹדִים, *Modim* (although he rules that one should only recite the words מוֹדִים אֲנַחְנוּ לָךְ, *Modim anachnu lach* — see *Mishnah Berurah* 66:20), and בָּרְכוּ, *Borchu* (see further *Tos. R' Akiva* §15).

1. As noted above (s.v. בפרקים), *Rashba* (*Teshuvos*, I:321) includes in this category one who possesses superior Torah knowledge. However, *Mishnah Berurah* (ibid. §7) notes that the consensus of the authorities is that this person is classified as one whom may be greeted *out of respect*. However, the premier Torah scholar of the generation is treated as one's primary teacher, and one may greet him even while in the middle of a paragraph of the *Shema* (see *Tosafos* to *Bava Kamma* 41b s.v. לרבות).

בְּרָכוֹת בַּפְּרָקִים – שׁוֹאֵל מִפְּנֵי הַכָּבוֹד וּמֵשִׁיב שָׁלוֹם לְכָל אָדָם.

ב/ב

[ב] **אֵלוּ** הֵן בֵּין הַפְּרָקִים: בֵּין בְּרָכָה רִאשׁוֹנָה לִשְׁנִיָּה, בֵּין שְׁנִיָּה לְ,,שְׁמַע'', וּבֵין ,,שְׁמַע'' לְ,,וְהָיָה אִם־שָׁמֹעַ'', בֵּין ,,וְהָיָה אִם־שָׁמֹעַ''

— ר' עובדיה מברטנורא —

וּמֵשִׁיב שָׁלוֹם לְכָל אָדָם. שֶׁהִקְדִּים לוֹ שָׁלוֹם. וַהֲלָכָה כְּרַבִּי יְהוּדָה. וּבְכָל מָקוֹם שֶׁאָסוּר לְהַפְסִיק, כָּךְ אָסוּר לְדַבֵּר בִּלְשׁוֹן הַקּוֹדֶשׁ כְּמוֹ בִּשְׁאָר לְשׁוֹנוֹת:

יד אברהם

בַּפְּרָקִים – שׁוֹאֵל מִפְּנֵי הַכָּבוֹד וּמֵשִׁיב שָׁלוֹם לְכָל אָדָם. — *at junctures [between sections], he may greet [another] out of respect and he may reply with a greeting to any person.*

R' Yehudah agrees with R' Meir's opinion that between sections of the *Shema* one may initiate a greeting only due to respect. However, he maintains that at these points, one may reply to anyone's greeting (*Rav*), even the greeting of someone he is not obligated to respect (*Rashi* to 13b s.v. לכל אדם).

The halachah is decided in accordance with R' Yehudah's view. Therefore, between sections of the *Shema* and its blessings, one may initiate a greeting out of respect and respond to anyone's greeting. In the middle of a section, he may initiate a greeting out of fear, and respond out of respect (*Orach Chaim* 66:1). However, this applies only where failure to greet a person would cause resentment. One should not interrupt the *Shema* or its blessings to greet a person who will feel no ill will if a greeting is not extended (*Mishnah Berurah* there §2).

2.

The following mishnah identifies which points in the *Shema* and its blessings are considered "between the sections," where interruptions are treated more leniently than the middle of sections. The mishnah then explains the significance of the order in which the three sections of the *Shema* are recited.

אֵלוּ הֵן בֵּין הַפְּרָקִים: — *These are between the sections [of the Shema and its blessings]:*

[The following points constitute junctures between the various sections of the *Shema* and its blessings, where one may interrupt his recitation to initiate a greeting out of respect.]

Note that in the previous mishnah we have translated the term פְּרָקִים as *junctures*. That mishnah uses this term to refer to the point between sections; thus, the term translates as *junctures* [or *joints*], i.e. the juncture of two paragraphs or sections. Our mishnah

refers to the juncture between sections as בֵּין הַפְּרָקִים, *between the* פְּרָקִים; in this context, the term פְּרָקִים means *sections* (see *Tos. Anshei Shem* to previous mishnah s.v. בפרקים).

בֵּין בְּרָכָה רִאשׁוֹנָה לִשְׁנִיָּה, בֵּין שְׁנִיָּה לְ,,שְׁמַע'' — *Between the first blessing and the second [blessing]; between the (end of the) second [blessing] and [the passage of] "Shema"* (Deuteronomy 6:4-9);

Each of the blessings of the *Shema* constitutes a separate and distinct section. Thus, someone who has completed the first blessing but has not yet

at junctures [between sections], he may greet [another] out of respect and he may reply with a greeting to any person.

2. These are between the sections [of the *Shema* and its blessings]: Between the first blessing and the second [blessing]; between the second [blessing] and [the passage of] *"Shema"* (*Deuteronomy 6:4-9*); and between *"Shema"* and [the passage of] *"Vehayah im shamoa"* (*Deuteronomy 11:13-21*); between *"Vehayah im shamoa"* and [the passage

started the second blessing, or someone who completed the second blessing but has not yet begun the first section of the *Shema*, שְׁמַע יִשְׂרָאֵל, *Shema Yisrael*, is considered to be "between the sections." [In the context of our mishnah, the term *"Shema"* refers not to the three Scriptural passages that constitute what is commonly called *Shema*, but only to the first of these passages, beginning with the words שְׁמַע יִשְׂרָאֵל.]

The Rabbis formulated blessings to be recited before performing most positive commandments. These blessings are known as בִּרְכוֹת הַמִּצְוֹת, *Birchos HaMitzvos*. However, the Rabbis did not formulate a *birchas hamitzvah* for fulfilling the commandment to recite the *Shema*. Although the second *Shema* blessing immediately precedes the *Shema*, it is not a *birchas hamitzvah*. This is evidenced by the fact that our mishnah classifies the second of the *Shema* blessings and the first passage of the *Shema* as two distinct and separate sections, and in certain circumstances allows interruptions between the two. A *birchas hamitzvah*, on the other hand, relates to the commandment to which it refers, and thus must be recited immediately before performing that commandment; there can be no interruption between the blessing and the performance of the commandment. The

wording of the blessing, which does not follow the form of a *birchas hamitzvah* (*Blessed are You, Hashem, our God, King of the universe, Who has sanctified us with His commandments and has commanded us. . .*), also shows that it is not a *birchas hamitzvah*. Rather, this blessing is an expression of thanksgiving and praise to God for the favor He has shown us by giving us His Torah and His precepts, and is a prayer that He grant us wisdom to understand them. It was incorporated with the *Shema* in the daily service because it parallels the concepts that are contained in the verses of *Shema* (*Re'ah*; see comm. to mishnah 1:2 s.v. הקורא; see General Introduction).

Meiri implies that the second *Shema* blessing does fulfill the function of a *birchas hamitzvah*. Nevertheless, since this is not the primary purpose of this blessing, the Rabbis were more lenient with regard to interruptions between the blessing and the *Shema*.

וּבֵין ,,שְׁמַע" לְ,,וְהָיָה־אִם שָׁמֹעַ", בֵּין ,,וְהָיָה אִם־שָׁמֹעַ" לְ,,וַיֹּאמֶר", — *and between "Shema" and [the passage of] "Vehayah im shamoa" (Deuteronomy 11:13-21); between "Vehayah im shamoa" and [the passage of] "Vayomer" (Numbers 15:37-41);*

The mishnah designates the three Scriptural passages which constitute

לְ,,וַיֹּאמֶר", בֵּין ,,וַיֹּאמֶר" לְ,,אֱמֶת וְיַצִּיב". רַבִּי
יְהוּדָה אוֹמֵר: בֵּין ,,וַיֹּאמֶר" לְ,,אֱמֶת וְיַצִּיב" לֹא
יַפְסִיק.

─────── ר' עובדיה מברטנורא ───────

(ב) בין ויאמר לאמת ויציב לא יפסיק. דכתיב וה' אלהים אמת (ירמיה י), הלכך אין מפסיקין

יד אברהם

the *Shema* by their opening words. Each of these passages is considered a distinct section of the *Shema*. Thus, someone who concluded the first of these three passages [which begins with the words שְׁמַע יִשְׂרָאֵל, *Shema Yisrael*], but has not yet begun the next passage [which begins with the words וְהָיָה אִם־שָׁמֹעַ, *Vehayah im shamoa*], or who has concluded the passage of *Vehayah im shamoa* but has not begun the third passage [which begins with the words וַיֹּאמֶר ה' אֶל־מֹשֶׁה, *Vayomer Hashem el Moshe*], is considered to be between sections.

The mishnah's specification of the exact points in the *Shema* and its blessings that are "between the sections" seems unnecessary. Obviously, each blessing or Scriptural passage is a distinctly separate section. *Shenos Eliyahu* explains that the mishnah lists the junctures between the various sections to emphasize that no other points in the *Shema* are classified as "between the sections." One might have thought that the first verse of the passage of *Shema Yisrael* is considered a separate section, for, as the *Gemara (Pesachim 56a)* states, one must pause briefly after reciting this verse to distinguish it from the other verses of the passage. [The brief pause is because this verse reflects a concept distinct from the rest of the passage; it is one's acceptance of God's sovereignty, while the following verses speak of the commandment to love God and other basic commandments.] By listing the points between

the various sections, the mishnah underscores that the juncture between the first and the second verses of the "*Shema*" passage is *not* considered "between the sections," but rather is subject to the laws regarding interruption in the middle of sections. See *Shenos Eliyahu* for another example of a point which might have been thought to be "between the sections."

בֵּין ,,וַיֹּאמֶר" לְ,,אֱמֶת וְיַצִּיב". — *between* "*Vayomer" and [the blessing of]* "*Emes Veyatziv.*"

One who has completed the passage of *Vayomer* [which concludes with the word אֱלֹהֵיכֶם] and has not yet begun the blessing of *Emes Veyatziv*, which is the lone blessing recited after the morning *Shema*, is considered to be "between the sections."

As previously noted (comm. to mishnah 1:5 s.v. מזכירין), the authorities dispute whether or not there is an obligation to recite the passage of *Vayomer* as part of the evening *Shema*. Some commentators see in the mishnah's reference to the blessing of *Emes Veyatziv* — rather than referring to "the third blessing," a term which would denote both the morning and evening versions of the blessing — an indication that there is no requirement to recite *Vayomer* at night. According to their view, our mishnah only refers to the juncture between the conclusion of the morning *Shema* and *Emes Veyatziv*, since this juncture is not applicable with regard to the evening *Shema* and the blessing of *Emes Ve'emunah* (*Rashash; see also Kol HaRamaz*).[1] Those who

---

1. Even those authorities who contend that there is no obligation to recite *Vayomer* at night agree that, in practice, it is recited (see *Gem.* 14b). However, in light of the fact that

of] *"Vayomer"* (*Numbers* 15:37-41); between *"Vayomer"* and [the blessing of] *"Emes Veyatziv."* R' Yehudah says: Between *"Vayomer"* and *"Emes Veyatziv"* one may not interrupt.

YAD AVRAHAM

maintain that there is an obligation to recite *Vayomer* at night will explain that the mishnah refers to *Emes Veyatziv* simply because it uses the morning *Shema* as its frame of reference when listing the points in the *Shema* that are "between the sections." The purpose of defining the various sections of the *Shema* and its blessings is to demonstrate where an interruption to greet a person is treated more leniently, and this law is more relevant to the morning *Shema*, because greetings are commonly extended at the beginning of the day (*Beis David*; for another explanation, see *Tos. Chadashim*). For whichever reason the mishnah refers to the morning *Shema*, the junctures listed by the mishnah apply to the corresponding points in the evening *Shema* as well [with the possible exception of *Emes Ve'emunah*] (see *Magen Avraham* 236:1).

Because the mishnah refers to the morning *Shema*, it only mentions the first three of the *Shema* blessings. The mishnah does not discuss the juncture between the third evening blessing (*Emes Ve'emunah*) and the fourth evening blessing (*Hashkiveinu*). The status of this juncture is disputed by the authorities. Some maintain that the juncture between these two blessings is considered "the middle of a section." They base this assertion on the *Gemara* (4b), which explains that, although the *Shemoneh Esrei* should immediately follow the *Shema* blessing referring to the Redemption from Egypt (*Emes Veyatziv* in the morning and *Emes Ve'emunah* at night), *Hashkiveinu* is not considered to interrupt between *Emes Ve'emunah* and the *Shemoneh Esrei*, because it also relates

to the theme of the Redemption (see *Rabbeinu Yonah* 2b s.v. ואעג for elaboration). Thus, these authorities reason that (with regard to interrupting the *Shema*) *Hashkiveinu* is to be considered part of the same section as *Emes Ve'emunah* (*Shoshanim LeDavid*, cited in *Tos. Anshei Shem*). Others, however, contend that any point between separate blessings or Scriptural passages is classified as "between the sections," regardless whether the two paragraphs share a common theme. Thus, the point between the two separate blessings of *Emes Ve'emunah* and *Hashkiveinu* is considered "between the sections" (*Beur Halachah* to 66:5, s.v. ואלו הן בין הפרקים).

רַבִּי יְהוּדָה אוֹמֵר: בֵּין,,וַיֹאמֶר" לְ,,אֱמֶת וְיַצִיב" לֹא יַפְסִיק. — R' *Yehudah says: Between "Vayomer" and "Emes Veyatziv" one may not interrupt.*

R' Yehudah maintains that the point between the word אֲלֵיכֶם (at the end of the passage of *"Vayomer"*) and the following blessing of *Emes Veyatziv* (or *Emes Ve'emunah*) is treated even more stringently than the middle of a section. At this juncture, one may not interrupt for any reason, unless there is actual danger to his life (*Rosh* 2:8; *Rabbeinu Yonah* 8a s.v. אלו הן בין הפרקים; *Orach Chaim* 66:5; see *Mishnah Berurah* there §28; see *Meleches Shlomo*). According to R' Yehudah, one must recite the words אֲלֵיכֶם and אֱמֶת together, to conform to the verse (*Jeremiah* 10:10) which connects these two words: וַה' אֱלֹהִים

according to this view there is no *obligation* to recite *Vayomer* at night, there is some question whether the entire passage is considered "between the sections," and is treated more leniently than other sections (*Beur Halachah* to 66:5, s.v. ואלו הן בין הפרקים).

אָמַר רַבִּי יְהוֹשֻׁעַ בֶּן קָרְחָה: לָמָּה קָדְמָה ,,שְׁמַע" לְ,,וְהָיָה אִם־שָׁמֹעַ"? אֶלָּא כְּדֵי שֶׁיְּקַבֵּל עָלָיו עֹל מַלְכוּת שָׁמַיִם תְּחִלָּה, וְאַחַר כָּךְ יְקַבֵּל עָלָיו עֹל מִצְוֹת. ,,וְהָיָה אִם־שָׁמֹעַ" לְ,,וַיֹּאמֶר"?

--- ר' עובדיה מברטנורא ---

בֵּין אֲנִי ה' אֱלֹהֵיכֶם לֶאֱמֶת. וְכֵן הֲלָכָה. **והיה אם שמוע** נוֹהֵג בֵּין בַּיּוֹם בֵּין בַּלַּיְלָה. דִּכְתִיב בָּהּ (דברים יא) וְלִמַּדְתֶּם אֹתָם אֶת בְּנֵיכֶם, וְתַלְמוּד תּוֹרָה נוֹהֵג בֵּין בַּיּוֹם וּבֵין בַּלַּיְלָה:

יד אברהם

אֱמֶת, *But Hashem, God, is true (Rav, from Gem. 14a-b).*[1]

Rambam (Hil. Krias Shema 2:17) understands R' Yehudah to mean that this point is not considered "between the sections," but rather "the middle of a section." Thus, one may not interrupt to initiate a greeting out of respect or reply to anyone's greeting. However, one may initiate a greeting out of fear or reply to a greeting out of respect (see also *Shenos Eliyahu*; see comm. to mishnah 2:1, footnote 1 to s.v. ובאמצע).

R' Yehudah's requirement applies only when one recites the *Shema* and its blessings in the usual order, in which the blessing of *Emes Veyatziv* (or *Emes Ve'emunah*) follows the section of *Vayomer*. Since in this case the word אֱמֶת follows the word אֱלֹהֵיכֶם, R' Yehudah requires that the two be recited together without interruption. However, if one recites the sections of the *Shema* in an order in which *Emes Veyatziv* (or *Emes Ve'emunah*) does not immediately follow the section of *Vayomer* (see comm. to previous mishnah s.v. אם כוון לבו), R' Yehudah's ruling that the words אֱלֹהֵיכֶם and אֱמֶת must be recited together does not apply (*Rabbeinu Yonah* 8b s.v. הקורא למפרע).

אָמַר רַבִּי יְהוֹשֻׁעַ בֶּן קָרְחָה: — *R' Yehoshua ben Korchah said:*

Many commentators identify R' Yehoshua ben Korchah with R' Yehoshua, the son of R' Akiva (see *Shevuos 6a, Pesachim 112a*). R' Akiva was called *kore'ach* (see *Bechoros 58a*)

on account of his baldness (קֵרֵחַ; see *II Kings 2:23*), and his son became known as R' Yehoshua ben Korchah [lit. — the son of the baldhead] (*Rashi* to *Shevuos 6a* s.v. רבי יהושע בנו של רבי עקיבא, *Rabbeinu Gershom* to *Bechoros 58a* s.v. חוץ מן הקרח; *Ri*, cited by *Tosafos* to *Bava Basra 113a* s.v. ומטו בה). Other commentators dispute this contention, for it is unlikely that the Rabbis of the mishnah would perpetuate R' Akiva's derogatory nickname by referring to his son as "the son of the baldhead." Moreover, other references in the Talmud to R' Yehoshua ben Korchah indicate that he was too old to have been the R' Yehoshua who was R' Akiva's son (*Rabbeinu Tam*, cited in *Tosafos* to *Bava Basra* loc. cit. and to *Shabbos 150a* s.v. ורבי יהושע בן קרחה היא; see *Meleches Shlomo*).

לָמָּה קָדְמָה ,,שְׁמַע" לְ,,וְהָיָה אִם־שָׁמֹעַ"? — *Why does [the passage of] "Shema" precede [the passage of] "Vehayah im shamoa"?*

Why did the Men of the Great Assembly (אַנְשֵׁי כְּנֶסֶת הַגְּדוֹלָה), who established the order in which the passages of the *Shema* are recited, arrange the passage of שְׁמַע יִשְׂרָאֵל before the passage of וְהָיָה אִם־שָׁמֹעַ? (*Meleches Shlomo*).

---

1. Accordingly, one should not even pause between the two words (*Mishnah Berurah 66:29*).

<table>
<tr><td>**2**</td><td rowspan="2">R' Yehoshua ben Korchah said: Why does [the passage of] *"Shema"* precede [the passage of] *"Vehayah im shamoa"*? Only so one will first accept upon himself the yoke of Heaven's sovereignty, and afterward accept upon himself the yoke of [the] commandments. And [why does] *"Vehayah im shamoa"* [precede the passage of] *"Vayomer"*?</td></tr>
<tr><td>**2**</td></tr>
</table>

YAD AVRAHAM

Although the passage of שְׁמַע יִשְׂרָאֵל (*Deuteronomy* 6:4-9) precedes the passage of וְהָיָה אִם־שָׁמֹעַ (ibid. 11:13-21) in the Torah, this cannot be the reason why it is recited first, for the passage of וַיֹּאמֶר (*Numbers* 15:37-41) precedes both other passages of the *Shema* in the Torah, yet it is recited last. Obviously, the Scriptural sequence of these passages does not dictate the order of their recitation. It would, therefore, seem more appropriate for the passage of וְהָיָה אִם־שָׁמֹעַ, which is written in the plural form and addresses all of Israel collectively, to be recited *before* the passage of שְׁמַע יִשְׂרָאֵל, which is written in the singular form (*Tos. Yom Tov*, from *Tosafos* to 14b s.v. למה קדמה; see also *Meiri*).

אֶלָּא כְּדֵי שֶׁיְּקַבֵּל עָלָיו עֹל מַלְכוּת שָׁמַיִם — תְּחִלָּה, וְאַחַר כָּךְ יְקַבֵּל עָלָיו עֹל מִצְוֹת. *Only so one will first accept upon himself the yoke of Heaven's sovereignty, and afterward accept upon himself the yoke of [the] commandments.*

[The word אֶלָּא, *only*, seems superfluous. Indeed, many editions of the mishnah do not contain this term (see *Shinuyei Nuschaos* note 14).][1]

The *Shema* section begins with the verse (*Deuteronomy* 6:4): *Hear, O Israel, Hashem is our God, Hashem is the One and Only*. This declaration affirms the existence and absolute unity of God, and constitutes a recognition and acceptance of His sovereignty. The passage of וְהָיָה אִם־שָׁמֹעַ begins with the verse (ibid. 11:13): *And it will be if you hearken to My commandments that I command you today, to love Hashem your God, and to serve Him with all your heart and with all your soul*. Our recital of this passage expresses our commitment to obey God's commandments, such as the *mitzvos* of *tefillin*, *mezuzah* and the study of Torah, to which the passage refers. Accepting God's sovereignty logically precedes the acceptance of His dictates. Only one who views himself as a subject of the King will obey His commands (see *Mechilta* to *Exodus* 20:3 s.v. לא). Therefore, the Rabbis instituted that the passage of שְׁמַע be recited before the passage of וְהָיָה אִם־שָׁמֹעַ (*Meiri*).

וְהָיָה אִם שָׁמֹעַ לְ,,וַיֹּאמֶר"? — *And [why does] "Vehayah im shamoa" [precede the passage of] "Vayomer"?*

If the passage of שְׁמַע is recited before

1. *Kol HaRamaz* (cited in *Tos. Anshei Shem*) suggests that the mishnah is stressing that the passage of וְהָיָה אִם־שָׁמֹעַ contains all the commandments mentioned in the passage of שְׁמַע יִשְׂרָאֵל, with the exception of acceptance of God's sovereignty. Thus, the *only* reason the passage of שְׁמַע יִשְׂרָאֵל is recited first is so that a person accept the yoke of the kingdom of Heaven before accepting the yoke of the commandments.

שֶׁ,,וְהָיָה אִם־שָׁמֹעַ" נוֹהֵג בַּיּוֹם וּבַלַּיְלָה; ,,וַיֹּאמֶר"
אֵינוֹ נוֹהֵג אֶלָּא בַּיּוֹם.

[ג] **הַקּוֹרֵא** אֶת שְׁמַע וְלֹא הִשְׁמִיעַ לְאָזְנוֹ —

ר' עובדיה מברטנורא

ויאמר אינו נוהג אלא ביום. דאית ביה פרשת ציצית שאינה נוהגת בלילה, דכתיב בלילה, דכתיב (במדבר טו)
וראיתם אותו:

יד אברהם

the passage of וְהָיָה אִם־שָׁמֹעַ because it contains an affirmation of God's sovereignty, then seemingly the passage of וַיֹּאמֶר should also precede וְהָיָה אִם־שָׁמֹעַ, for it, too, conveys this concept, as the concluding verse of the passage states: *I am Hashem your God, Who has removed you from the land of Egypt to be a God unto you; I am Hashem your God (Tos. Yom Tov).*

There is a fundamental controversy regarding which verses of the *Shema* must be recited by Biblical law. According to some, the Biblical obligation applies only to the first section of the *Shema* — the passage of שְׁמַע יִשְׂרָאֵל. Others maintain that the first two sections are Biblically required, but not the passage of וַיֹּאמֶר (see General Introduction).

It would seem that a recitation which is Biblically mandated should precede one which is only a Rabbinical obligation. This gives rise to the question: According to the opinion that only the passage of שְׁמַע יִשְׂרָאֵל is Biblically mandated, why does R' Yehoshua ben Korchah question its institution as the first passage to be recited? And according to the view that the passage of וְהָיָה אִם־שָׁמֹעַ is Biblically mandated, but not the passage of וַיֹּאמֶר, why does R' Yehoshua ben Korchah question the institution of וַיֹּאמֶר after וְהָיָה אִם־שָׁמֹעַ? This difficulty leads *Shoshanim LeDavid* (cited in *Tos. Chadashim*) to conclude that, indeed, the Biblical obligation includes all three passages (see also *Pri Chadash, Orach Chaim 67*). However, *Shaagas Aryeh* (§2, cited in *Tos. Anshei Shem*) refutes the

premise that a recitation which is Biblically mandated should precede one which is a Rabbinical obligation.

שֶׁ,,וְהָיָה אִם־שָׁמֹעַ" נוֹהֵג בַּיּוֹם וּבַלַּיְלָה; — *Because "Vehayah im shamoa" applies by day and by night,*

That is, the commandment of Torah study referred to in this passage applies by day and by night (*Rav; Rashi; Meiri*; see, however, further s.v. וַיֹּאמֶר).

,,וַיֹּאמֶר" אֵינוֹ נוֹהֵג אֶלָּא בַּיּוֹם. — *[whereas] "Vayomer" applies only by day.*

I.e. the commandment which constitutes the central theme of the passage of וַיֹּאמֶר — *tzitzis* — only applies during the day (*Rav; Rashi; Rambam Comm.; Meiri*; see comm. to mishnah 1:5 s.v. מזכירין). This is derived from the verse (*Numbers 15:39*) which states: *It shall constitute tzitzis for you, that you may see it.* The phrase *that you may see it* implies that the commandment of *tzitzis* applies only during the day, when they can be seen (see *Menachos 43a*; see *Orach Chaim 18:1* for two views regarding this exposition).

The simple meaning of the mishnah seems to imply that the *recital* of וַיֹּאמֶר does not apply at night. This, in fact, is how *Yerushalmi* (1:6, cited by *Meleches Shlomo* to mishnah 1:5 s.v. מזכירין) understands the mishnah's statement. However, the aforementioned commentators are of the opinion that there is an obligation to recite the passage of וַיֹּאמֶר at night (see comm. to mishnah 1:5 s.v. מזכירין). Accordingly,

2 Because *"Vehayah im shamoa"* applies by day and
3 by night, [whereas] *"Vayomer"* applies only by day.

3. [If] one recites the *Shema* and does not make
[it] audible to his ears, he has discharged [his

YAD AVRAHAM

the mishnah's statement cannot be referring to the *recital* of וְהָיָה אִם־שָׁמֹעַ and
וַיֹּאמֶר. Rather, the mishnah refers to the
themes these passages discuss. However,
according to those authorities who contend
that there is no requirement to recite וַיֹּאמֶר at
night, the mishnah does indeed mean that
whereas there is an obligation to recite וְהָיָה
אִם־שָׁמֹעַ at night, there is no such obligation with regard to וַיֹּאמֶר (see *Shenos
Eliyahu; Shaagas Aryeh* §9).

A Baraisa cited by the *Gemara* (14b)

gives an additional rationale for the order
of the sections: The section of שְׁמַע יִשְׂרָאֵל
logically precedes וְהָיָה אִם־שָׁמֹעַ because it
commands us to *learn* the Torah, to *teach*
the Torah to others, and to *fulfill* the
Torah's commandments, whereas the passage of וְהָיָה אִם־שָׁמֹעַ only commands us to
teach the Torah and to fulfill its commandments. The passage of וְהָיָה אִם שָׁמֹעַ precedes וַיֹּאמֶר because the latter refers only to
fulfilling a commandment of the Torah (i.e.
tzitzis).

3.

The mishnah enumerates several laws pertaining to the recital of the *Shema*.

הַקּוֹרֵא אֶת שְׁמַע וְלֹא הִשְׁמִיעַ לְאָזְנוֹ, יָצָא.
— *[If] one recites the Shema and does
not make [it] audible to his ears, he
has discharged [his obligation].*

This refers to someone who articu-
lates the words of the *Shema*, but does
not hear the words he recites (*Shiltei
HaGibborim*, 8b of folios of *Rif* §3; see
also *Rosh* 3:14).

Rashba (to 15a s.v. וְרַבִּי יוֹסֵי; see *Chazon
Ish, Orach Chaim* 14:1) suggests that an
inaudible recitation is the equivalent of a
mere *mental* recitation [for the purpose of
speech is to make one's thoughts heard
(*Chazon Ish* ibid.)]. Accordingly, the mishnah refers not only to an inaudible recitation of the *Shema*, but also to a recitation in
one's thoughts as well (see also *Riaz*, cited
in *Shiltei HaGibborim* loc. cit.; *Pnei Yehoshua* ad loc. s.v. הקורא). However, it is

evident from the words of *Rashi* (to 15a s.v.
בלבו) that he disputes this interpretation
(see also *Rosh* loc. cit.). This dispute has
halachic ramifications, for the *Gemara*
(15b) decides the halachah in favor of this
first *Tanna* of our mishnah. *Shulchan
Aruch* (*Orach Chaim* 62:3) rules that although an inaudible verbal recitation is
valid, one cannot discharge his obligation
with a mere *mental* recitation (see *Mishnah
Berurah* there §6; *Beur Halachah* s.v. יצא,
who states that this is the opinion of the
vast majority of *Rishonim*; see further
comm. to mishnah 3:4).

The mishnah's terminology [If one recites... he has discharged his obligation]
implies that even according to this *Tanna*,
an inaudible recitation is valid only after
the fact. Ideally, however, one should hear
the words he is reciting (*Meleches Shlomo*,
from *Gem.* 15b; see *Orach Chaim* loc. cit.).[1]

1. There is some question whether this is a Biblical or Rabbinical requirement. *Ravad*
(cited in *Rashba* to 15b s.v. אמר רב יוסף) maintains that Biblically one should ideally hear
the words he utters. *Rosh* (3:14) indicates that this is required only Rabbinically (see also
Tos. Anshei Shem s.v. רבי יוסי, in explanation of *Rav*). See *Shaagas Aryeh* §7 for a practical
difference between these two views.

יָצָא.   רַבִּי יוֹסֵי אוֹמֵר: לֹא יָצָא.
קָרָא וְלֹא דִקְדֵּק בְּאוֹתִיּוֹתֶיהָ, רַבִּי יוֹסֵי אוֹמֵר:
יָצָא. רַבִּי יְהוּדָה אוֹמֵר: לֹא יָצָא.
הַקּוֹרֵא לְמַפְרֵעַ – לֹא יָצָא.

ר' עובדיה מברטנורא

(ג) **רבי יוסי אומר לא יצא.** דכתיב שמע, השמע לאזנך מה שאתה מוציא מפיך. ותנא קמא
סבר, שמע בכל לשון שאתה שומע. והלכה כתנא קמא: **ולא דקדק באותיותיה.** להוליכן בשפתיו
יפה, בשתי תיבות שהתיבה השניה מתחלת באות שהתיבה הראשונה נגמרת, כגון על לבבך, עשב
בשדך, ואבדתם מהרה, אם אינו נותן ריוח ביניהם להפרידם נמצא קורא אותם שתי אותיות כאות
אחת: **רבי יוסי אומר יצא.** והלכה כרבי יוסי. מיהו לכתחלה צריך לדקדק באותיותיה, וכן יזהר
שלא יניח יניע הנד ולא נד ולא ירפה החזק ולא יחזק הרפה. וגריך להתיז זיי"ן של תזכרו שלא
יהא נראה כאומר תשכרו בשי"ן כלומר כדי שתרבו שכר, שהרי אין ראוי לשמע את הרב על מנת
לקבל פרס: **הקורא למפרע.** הקדים פסוק שלישי לשני ושני לראשון וכיוצא בזה: **לא יצא.** דכתיב
והיו הדברים, בהווייתן יהו, כלומר כמו שהן סדורין בתורה. ומיהו אם הקדים פרשה פרשת לפרשת

יד אברהם

רַבִּי יוֹסֵי אוֹמֵר: לֹא יָצָא. — R' Yose says:
He has not discharged [his obligation].

R' Yose asserts that the Torah stipulates one must hear the words of the
Shema he utters. R' Yose derives this
from the first verse of the Shema
which states: Hear [שְׁמַע], O Israel,
Hashem is our God, Hashem is the
One and Only (Deuteronomy 6:7).
The word Hear implies that one must
hear his recital (see Tos. Yom Tov).
Accordingly, R' Yose maintains that a
valid recitation requires that one
"make heard" to his ears the words of
the Shema that his mouth utters (Rav,
from Gem. 15a).

Some explain that R' Yose derives his
view by expounding the word שְׁמַע as if it
was written שַׁמַּע, make heard. Thus, the
verse implies that one must be able to hear
his recitation (MelecheS Shlomo; Rashash).

The Tanna Kamma, who maintains
that an inaudible recitation is valid af-

ter the fact, expounds the word שְׁמַע
differently, i.e. to teach that one may
recite the Shema in any language
which he "hears," i.e. any language he
understands.[1] Thus, according to the
Tanna Kamma, there is no basis to
invalidate a recitation one does not
hear (Rav, from Gem. 15a; see Tos.
Anshei Shem).

קָרָא וְלֹא דִקְדֵּק בְּאוֹתִיּוֹתֶיהָ, — [If] he recited [the Shema] but was not meticu-
lous in [enunciating] its letters,

This refers to one who does not pronounce the last letter distinctly when
reciting a word which ends with the
same letter that begins the next word.
For example, if one does not pause between the words בְּכָל־לְבַבְכֶם, the first
ל will often not be articulated. This
makes the two words sound like one
— בְּכָלְבַבְכֶם (Rav; Rashi, printed with
Rif 8b s.v. ולא דקדק).

---

1. However, he may not recite the Shema in a language he does not understand, with the
exception of Hebrew, in which he may fulfill his obligation even if he does not understand it (see Mishnah Berurah 62:3). In any case, it is preferable to recite the Shema in
Hebrew (Bach, Orach Chaim 193, cited by Mishnah Berurah ibid.).

2	obligation]. R' Yose says: He has not discharged
3	[his obligation].

[If] he recited [the *Shema*] but was not meticulous in [enunciating] its letters, R' Yose says: He has discharged [his obligation]. R' Yehudah says: He has not discharged [his obligation].

[If] one recites [the *Shema*] out of sequence, he has not discharged [his obligation].

YAD AVRAHAM

Rabbeinu Yonah (8b s.v. הקורא את שמע, cited in *Meleches Shlomo*) disputes the aforementioned interpretation of the mishnah, for it seems from the *Gemara* (15b) that the topic of the proper enunciation of such words is a separate issue introduced in a Baraisa cited by the *Gemara*. Apparently, our mishnah refers to some other type of indistinct pronunciation. *Rav*, however, understands that the Baraisa cited by the Gemara *elaborates* on our mishnah, which does not describe the sort of indistinct enunciation to which it refers (see *Tos. Yom Tov*; see also *Rashi* to *Rif* loc. cit.).

Rabbeinu Yonah explains our mishnah to mean that one did not pronounce the letters properly, i.e. he did not enunciate a *dagesh* ("hard sound") letter (e.g. בּ, which is pronounced as a "B") when required, or a *rafeh* ("soft sound") letter (e.g. ב, which is pronounced as a "V") when required. Or he swallowed letters, e.g. swallowing the ה and the א of וְחָרָה אַף, pronouncing the words as וְחָרָף. See below s.v. רבי יוסי אומר for other examples of improper pronunciation.

רַבִּי יוֹסֵי אוֹמֵר: יָצָא. רַבִּי יְהוּדָה אוֹמֵר: לֹא יָצָא. — *R' Yose says: He has discharged [his obligation]. R' Yehudah says: He has not discharged [his obligation].*

[R' Yose maintains that even if the pronunciation of the words was inarticulate it is a valid recitation. In R' Yehudah's opinion, those words which

were not enunciated correctly are considered not to have been recited.]

The halachah accords with the view of R' Yose that such a recitation is valid. However, this is only after the fact. Initially, one must take care to pronounce each word of the *Shema* distinctly and properly (*Rav*, from *Gem.* 15b).[1] *Rav* adds that one should be careful to differentiate between a שְׁוָא נָע, *sh'va na* (which is pronounced like the "i" in "this"), and a שְׁוָא נָח, *sh'va nach* (which is silent). Also, one must take care to stress the ז of the word תִּזְכְּרוּ, *tizkiru* (*you may remember*) [in the verse (*Numbers* 15:40) which states: לְמַעַן תִּזְכְּרוּ וַעֲשִׂיתֶם אֶת־כָּל־מִצְוֹתָי, *So that you may remember and perform all of My commandments*], so that it should not sound like תִּשְׂכְּרוּ, *tiskiru* (*you may be rewarded*), which would imply that the purpose of fulfilling the commandments is to receive reward, a concept which is incompatible to the proper approach to serving God [see *Avos* 1:3] (see *Tos. Yom Tov*, who explains that this reason is in addition to the reason that in general he must properly enunciate the words of the *Shema*).

הַקּוֹרֵא לְמַפְרֵעַ, לֹא יָצָא. — *[If] one recites [the Shema] out of sequence, he has not discharged [his obligation].*

I.e. if he reversed the Scriptural order of the verses, e.g. he recited the third verse of a section before the second, and the second verse before the

---

1. *Mishnah Berurah* (62:1) states that one should be *extremely* careful in this regard.

קָרָא וְטָעָה, יַחֲזֹר לַמָּקוֹם שֶׁטָּעָה.

[ד] **הָאֱמָנִין** קוֹרִין בְּרֹאשׁ הָאִילָן אוֹ
בְּרֹאשׁ הַנִּדְבָּךְ, מַה שֶׁאֵינָן

ר' עובדיה מברטנורא

והיה אם שמוע, ופרשת והיה אם שמוע לשמע, נראה דאין זה חשוב למפרע, וילא, שהרי אינן סדורות כן זו לאחר זו בתורה: **יחזור למקום שטעה.** אם בין פרק לפרק טעה, שאינו יודע באיזה פרק הפסיק ולראש ולראש הפסיק, חוזר להפסק ראשון שהוא והיה אם שמוע. והרמב"ס אומר שהוא ואהבת את ה', ואם באמלע הפרק פסק, שיודע הפרק שפסק בו, אבל אינו יודע באיזה מקום מפנותו פרק פסק, חוזר לראש אותו הפרק. היה קורא וכתבתם, ואינו יודע אם הוא בוכתבתם של שמע או בוכתבתם של והיה אם שמוע, חוזר לוכתבתם של שמע, ואם נסתפק לאחר שהתחיל למען ירבו, אינו חוזר, שעל הרגל לשונו הוא הולך: [ד] **נדבך.** שורה של בנין אבנים, כמו נדבכין די אבן גלל בעזרא (ו). ואף על גב דמסתפי דלמא נפלי ולא מלו מכווני, לא הגריכוס חכמים לרדת, דקריאת שמע לא בעי כוונה אלא פסוק ראשון בלבד:

יד אברהם

first, he has not discharged his obligation (*Rav; Rambam Comm.*). The *Gemara* (13a) derives the requirement to recite the verses in their Scriptural sequence from the words of the first section of the *Shema* (Deuteronomy 6:6), which state: וְהָיוּ הַדְּבָרִים הָאֵלֶּה, *These words shall be...* The term וְהָיוּ (*shall be*) is understood to mean "they shall be as they are," i.e. in the order in which they are found in the Torah. This teaches that when these verses are recited in fulfillment of the commandment of *Shema*, they must follow the Scriptural order (*Rav*).

The Mishnah does not refer to one who recites the three *sections* of the *Shema* out of sequence, e.g. if he recited the section of *Vayomer* before the section of *Shema Yisrael*. The order of the three *Shema* sections does not in any case follow the Scriptural sequence, but is rather the order instituted by the Rabbis [see comm. to previous mishnah s.v. למה קדמה] (*Rav; Rambam, Hil. Kerias Shema* 2:11), and the Rabbis did invalidate a recitation which does not follow their arrangement (*Rosh* 2:12; see comm. to mishnah 2:1 s.v. אם כוון).

[*Rashi* (to 13a s.v. מדברים) explains the

mishnah to mean that one recited the *words* in a particular verse out of sequence. For example, instead of saying מזוזת ביתך ובשעריך (*Deuteronomy* 6:9), he said ובשעריך ביתך מזוזת. It seems strange that an exposition should be needed to invalidate such an incoherent reading (*Turei Even* to *Megillah* 17a s.v. שלא יקרא למפרע).]

קָרָא וְטָעָה, יַחֲזֹר לַמָּקוֹם שֶׁטָּעָה. — [If] one recited [the Shema] and erred, he must return to the place where he erred.

This refers to someone who forgets where he is up to in his recitation of the *Shema*. He must return to the point in the *Shema* which he does not remember reciting, and resume his recitation from there (*Rav*, as understood by *Tos. Anshei Shem*). Thus, if he knows that he completed a section of the *Shema*, but does not remember which section, he must continue his recitation from the beginning of the second section (*Gem.* 16a), i.e. the section of *Vehayah im shamoa* (*Rav, Rashi* to 16a s.v. יחזור). He does not need to start from the beginning of the first section, because he is certain that he completed at least one section (see *Beis Yosef* 64,

[If] one recited [the *Shema*] and erred, he must return to the place where he erred.

4. **W**orkers may recite [the *Shema*] on top of a tree or on top of a wall, which they are not

cited by *Tos. Yom Tov*).

Rambam (Hil. *Krias Shema* 2:13, cited by *Rav*), however, states that where one remembers completing a section, "the place where he erred" is the second verse of the section of *Shema Yisrael*, i.e. the verse of וְאָהַבְתָּ אֵת ה׳ אֱלֹהֶיךָ. Since one must pause briefly after declaring בָּרוּךְ שֵׁם כְּבוֹד מַלְכוּתוֹ לְעוֹלָם וָעֶד (*Orach Chaim* 61:14; see comm. to mishnah 2 s.v. ובין שמע), this juncture seems to a reader to be the end of a section. It is possible, then, that although he remembers concluding a section, he had actually only recited the first verse of *Shema Yisrael* and בָּרוּךְ שֵׁם כְּבוֹד (*Beis Yosef* ibid., cited by *Tos. Yom Tov*).

If he knows which section he was reciting, but does not remember which verse, he must return to the beginning of that section (*Rav*, from *Gem.* 16a). However, if he is certain that he recited the opening verses of

that section, he resumes his recitation from the point of doubt (*Tos. Yom Tov*, from *Rosh* 2:12). If he was reciting the verse of וּכְתַבְתָּם עַל־מְזֻזוֹת בֵּיתֶךָ וּבִשְׁעָרֶיךָ, which is written in both the first and the second section of the *Shema*, and he is uncertain whether he was reciting the verse in the first section of *Shema* or the second section, he must return to the verse in the first section and continue from there. However, if he had already begun reciting the verse of לְמַעַן יִרְבּוּ, which follows the verse of וּכְתַבְתָּם in the second section, he need not return to the first section. The fact that he recited the verse following וּכְתַבְתָּם in the second section indicates that it was indeed the וּכְתַבְתָּם of the second section that he had recited (*Rav*, from Gem. 16a; cf. *Rashi* ad loc. s.v. סרכיה נקט).

4.

The *Shema* should ideally be recited in a manner conducive to concentration (see *Gem.* 13b). However, in certain circumstances, it may — even initially — be recited under conditions that make it difficult to concentrate. The following mishnah discusses such a circumstance, and contrasts the law regarding the *Shema* with the law regarding *Shemoneh Esrei*.

הָאֻמָּנִין קוֹרִין בְּרֹאשׁ הָאִילָן אוֹ בְּרֹאשׁ הַנִּדְבָּךְ, — *Workers may recite [the Shema] on top of a tree or on top of a wall,*

These workers were engaged in their labors on top of the tree or wall, picking the fruit or building the wall, when the time for reciting the *Shema* arrived (*Rashi*). Although fear of falling detracts from their ability to concentrate on the meaning of the

words of *Shema*, the mishnah does not require these workers to descend the tree or wall to recite the *Shema*. One need only concentrate on the meaning and significance of the first verse of the *Shema* for the recitation to be valid (see *Gem.* 13b; comm. to mishnah 2:1), and the mishnah considers it possible for these workers to meet the minimum requirements of concentration for the duration of a single verse (*Rav*).

רַשָּׁאִין לַעֲשׂוֹת כֵּן בַּתְּפִלָּה.

מה שאינן רשאין לעשות כן בתפלה. דצלותא רחמי היא ובעי כוונה, הלכך יורדין למטה ומתפללין:

יד אברהם

Although these are certainly not ideal locations in which to properly concentrate, the Rabbis did not trouble workers to descend from the tree or wall to recite the *Shema* (see *Meiri*).

Although the Rabbis do not obligate a worker to descend from a tree or wall to recite the *Shema*, they do require that he interrupt his labors while reciting the entire first section (*Gem.* 16a). This is not so that he can concentrate on the recitation, for, as noted above, only the first verse requires special concentration. Rather, he must stop working because the first section of the *Shema* may not be recited in a casual, offhand manner [see *Yoma* 19b] (*Rif* 9b; *Rosh* 2:13; *Rambam, Hil. Krias Shema* 2:4; see *Rashba* to 16a s.v. לא קשיא, who explains why this law does not apply to the other sections of the *Shema*; see also *Rabbeinu Yonah* 9a-b s.v. למימרא). Others, however, explain that indeed the reason one must cease work is so that he can concentrate properly. The *Gemara's* ruling that he must stop for the entire first section reflects the view of R' Akiva (*Gem.* 13b), who maintains that one must concentrate for the entire first section. Accordingly, the view which maintains that concentration is needed only for the first verse — which is the opinion followed in halachah — requires one to desist from work only for the first verse (*Baal HaMaor* 9a of folios of *Rif*, s.v. רמי; *Tosafos* to 16a s.v. הא; see also *Meiri* to 16a s.v. האומנין and to 13b s.v. כוונה אי זו).

The term אָמָּנִין (which we have translated as *workers*) generally means *craftsmen*. As such, it is perforce used by the mishnah to refer to the skilled workers building a wall, inasmuch as picking fruit

off a tree is not a craft. Accordingly, *Yerushalmi* emends the mishnah to read: "הַפּוֹעֲלִים, *Laborers,* may recite [the *Shema*] on top of a tree, וְהָאָמָּנִין, *and craftsmen,* may recite [the *Shema*] on top of a wall."

The mishnah's reference to אָמָּנִין, which connotes hired professional workers, indicates that it allows only employees to recite the *Shema* while standing on top of a tree or wall, but not the employer. Since these employees are paid by the day, including the time they recite the *Shema*, the mishnah allows a recital under less than ideal conditions, to avoid a financial loss to their employer. However, no such consideration was given to their employer, who is not in the pay of others (*Shenos Eliyahu;* see *Rashi* to 16a s.v. יורד ומתפלל and s.v. לפי). Others explain that the mishnah specifies *craftsmen* because they are engaged in work while on top of the tree or wall. Therefore, we do not require them to interrupt their work to descend. Their employer, on the other hand, often ascends the tree or wall simply to oversee his workers. Since requiring him to descend does not interrupt the work being done, he may not take advantage of the same leniency extended to those actually performing labor (*Rabbeinu Manoach,* cited by *Kesef Mishneh, Hil. Krias Shema* 2:4). However, if the employer *is* participating in the work, he, too, is not required to descend to recite the *Shema* (*Orach Chaim* 63:8). Yet another opinion maintains that there is no distinction between employee and employer; neither is required to descend (*Rashba* to 16a s.v. בעל הבית; *Rabbeinu Yonah* 9a s.v. תנו רבנן, cited in *Meleches Shlomo; Meiri* to 16a s.v. אע"פ).[1]

1. It is possible, however, that this leniency applies only to an employer who is himself an experienced craftsman, and is accustomed to maintaining his balance on top of walls and trees. But if he is not used to standing in such places, his fear of falling prevents him from concentrating at all on the words of the *Shema*, and he is required to descend (see *Meiri*

YAD AVRAHAM

A נִדְבָּךְ (which we have translated as *wall*) is a structure of brick or stone (*Rav; Rashi*). *Rambam Comm.* (here and to *Keilim* 20:5) defines נִדְבָּךְ as an upright panel of a wooden frame used to construct a wall. *Rashi* and *Rav* cite a verse in *Ezra* (6:4) to corroborate their interpretation. However, this same verse also uses the word נִדְבָּךְ with reference to a wooden structure, as *Rambam* understands the term (see *Hagahos Maharatz Chayes* to *Gem.* 16a).

מַה שֶׁאֵינָן רַשָׁאִין לַעֲשׂוֹת כֵּן בַּתְּפִלָּה. — *which they are not permitted to do with regard to prayer.*

[The mishnah refers to the prayer of *Shemoneh Esrei*.]

Although a worker may recite the *Shema* while on top of a tree or wall, this leniency does not apply to reciting the *Shemoneh Esrei*. The blessings of the *Shemoneh Esrei* are supplications to God for assistance and mercy (see *Gem.* 20b). As such, the *Shemoneh Esrei* should be recited with concentration on the words one says, not by rote (see *Gem.* 30a). It is, therefore, forbidden to engage in any activity which will detract from one's concentration (see *Gem.* 23b with *Rashi* s.v. לא יאחז). Since a person on top of a tree or wall is concerned with maintaining his balance, it is not possible for him to concentrate on his prayers for the entire course of the *Shemoneh Esrei*. [This is in contrast to the *Shema*, which only requires concentration for the first verse.] Therefore, he must descend to pray (*Rav; Rashi*).

The wording of the mishnah — "which

they are not permitted to do with regard to prayer" — seems convoluted. The mishnah could have simply stated: הָאֻמָּנִין קוֹרִין בְּרֹאשׁ הָאִילָן... אֲבָל לֹא מִתְפַּלְלִין, "Craftsmen may recite on the top of a tree... but they may not pray [in this fashion]." Possibly, the mishnah wishes to imply that although one is not permitted to pray on the top of a tree or wall, if he did so the prayer is valid after the fact (*Meleches Shlomo*; see also *Shoshanim LeDavid*).

The *Gemara* (16a) cites a Baraisa which qualifies the mishnah's ruling forbidding praying the *Shemoneh Esrei* while on top of a tree. The Baraisa states that a hired worker working in an olive tree or a fig tree may recite the *Shemoneh Esrei* while in the tree. This is because these trees have many branches, and a worker can stand comfortably there without fear of falling (*Rashi* ad loc. s.v. ומתפללין). Alternatively, the presence of many branches makes it difficult to climb down from these trees. Were workers required to do so, they would be taking undue time away from their jobs (*Rabbeinu Yonah* 9a s.v. תנו רבנן, based on *Yerushalmi* 2:5). Others explain that the maintenance of these trees is very expensive. If workers would constantly descend in order to pray, many branches would be broken, causing considerable monetary loss to the tree's owner (*Meiri* to 16a s.v. אע"פ, in explanation of *Yerushalmi* ibid.; *Rabbeinu Yehonasan*, cited by *Meleches Shlomo*).

This leniency only applies to employees of the tree's owner. The owner himself must descend to pray (*Gem.* 16a). This is because he is not as accustomed as his employees to maintaining his balance even in trees with many branches. Consequently, he is not able to pray there with the proper concentration (*Meiri* loc. cit.). Moreover, we are only lenient with regard to hired

ibid.; *Rashash* to 16a s.v. ובעל הבית). Perhaps the mishnah refers to אֻמָּנִין to indicate that its ruling applies only to people such as experienced craftsmen, who are accustomed to standing on walls and trees.

— ר' עובדיה מברטנורא —

(ה) **חתן.** שֶׁנָּשָׂא בְתוּלָה, פָּטוּר מִקְּרִיאַת שְׁמַע לַיְלָה רִאשׁוֹנָה, מִשּׁוּם דְּטָרִיד שֶׁמָּא לֹא יִמְצָאֶנָּה בְתוּלָה. וְאֲנִי שְׁמַעְתִּי שֶׁמְּתִירָא שֶׁמָּא יַעֲשֶׂה כְּרוּת שָׁפְכָה בִּבְעִילָתוֹ, וְטָרְדָא דְּמִצְוָה הִיא, וְרַחְמָנָא אָמַר וּבְלֶכְתְּךָ בַדֶּרֶךְ, בִּלְכַת דִּידָךְ הוּא דְּמִחַיְּבַתְּ, הָא דְּמִצְוָה פְּטִירַת:

יד אברהם

workers, since requiring them to descend would cause a monetary loss to their employer, who must pay them for their time. The owner himself, however, is not in the pay of others. Therefore, we do not extend to him the same leniency as to hired workers (*Rashi* to 16a s.v. יורד ומתפלל; *Meiri* loc. cit.; cf. *Rashash* to 16a s.v. בעל הבית, who suggests that if the owner of the tree is an experienced craftsman accustomed to standing in such places, he is permitted to pray there).

5.

The following mishnah discusses a case where one is exempt from reciting the *Shema*.

חָתָן פָּטוּר מִקְּרִיאַת שְׁמַע — *A bridegroom is exempt from the Shema recital*

The mishnah refers to a bridegroom who marries a virgin, and has not yet consummated the marriage. One who marries a widow, however, is obligated to recite the *Shema*, even before consummating the marriage (see *Rav*, from *Gem.* 16a).

A bridegroom who marries a virgin is distracted by anxiety regarding consummation of the marriage. He is concerned that he may discover that his bride is actually not a virgin [and might possibly therefore be forbidden to him][1] (*Rav*, first explanation; *Rambam Comm.*). Alternatively, he is worried that the act of cohabitation with a virgin might mutilate his member in a manner that would render him halachically unfit for marriage[2] (*Rav*, second explanation; *Talmidei Rabbeinu Yonah* 9b s.v. חתן פטור).

The Torah specifically exempts a bridegroom who marries a virgin from the obligation to recite the *Shema*. This law is derived from the verse in the first section of *Shema*

1. According to Biblical law, marriage consists of two stages. The first stage is known as אֵרוּסִין, *erusin* (also called קִדּוּשִׁין, *kiddushin*), while the second stage is called נִשּׂוּאִין, *nisuin*. After *erusin*, the wife may not wed anyone else; intimate relations with any other man is considered adultery. However, during this stage of marriage, the couple is Rabbinically forbidden to engage in marital relations (see *Rambam, Hil. Ishus* 10:1). In earlier times, *nisuin* would usually be performed a year after *erusin* (see *Kesubos* 5:2). Our mishnah refers to one who has taken his wife in *nisuin*. If he discovers that she is not a virgin, the possibility exists that she had engaged in an adulterous relationship after *erusin*. An adulterous wife is forbidden to her husband (see *Kesubos* 9a).

2. A person with a mutilated member is known as a כְּרוּת שָׁפְכָה, *khrus shafchah*. He is forbidden from marrying and cohabiting with an ordinary Jewish woman (see *Deuteronomy* 23:2; *Yevamos* 75a-b; for further details see *Rambam, Hil. Isurei Biah* Ch. 16; *Shulchan Aruch, Even HaEzer* 5). The bridegroom in our mishnah is concerned that in his haste to consummate the marriage, he will penetrate the hymen of his virgin bride in a manner that will injure his member.

YAD AVRAHAM

(*Deuteronomy* 6:7) which states: וְדִבַּרְתָּ בָּם... וּבְלֶכְתְּךָ בַדֶּרֶךְ, "And you shall speak of them... *and during your going on the way.*" The expression "*during your* going on the way" implies that only one engaged in discretionary activities ("*your* going") is obligated to recite the *Shema*, but one who is preoccupied with a mitzvah is exempt. This exposition is understood to exempt a bridegroom, whose mental distraction results from his impending performance of a mitzvah — namely, the mitzvah of procreation (*Rambam Comm.*; see *Tzlach*, cited by *Tos. Anshei Shem*, who explains which mitzvah is involved if the bridegroom has already fulfilled the mitzvah of procreation with a different wife). Hence, the mishnah rules that a bridegroom who has not yet consummated his marriage to a virgin is not obligated to recite the *Shema* (*Rav*, from *Gem.* 16a-b).

The law is that a person engaged in *any* mitzvah is exempt from performing another mitzvah (הָעוֹסֵק בְּמִצְוָה פָּטוּר מִן הַמִּצְוָה). The source of this exemption is the same verse from which we derive the exemption of a bridegroom, from the preceding words, "and you shall speak of them *during your sitting in your home.*" The expression "*during your* sitting" implies that the obligation of *Shema*, or any mitzvah, applies only when one is involved in his own affairs, as opposed to being involved in the performance of a mitzvah (see *Gem.* 11a, 16a, *Succah* 25a; see also *Tosafos* to *Succah* 25a s.v. ובלכתך). Nevertheless, a separate exposition is required to teach that a bridegroom is exempt. This is because a bridegroom who will soon be consummating his marriage is not *occupied* in *performing* a mitzvah, but is merely mentally *distracted* by its eventual fulfillment. A special exposition is therefore needed to teach that even *distractions* resulting from a mitzvah are

reason to exempt one from the *Shema* obligation (*Rashi* to 11a s.v. ובלכתך).

A person marrying a widow or divorcee is obviously not concerned that he will discover his bride is not a virgin. [Nor need he be concerned that the act of cohabitation may possibly render him halachically unfit for marriage.] Thus, the impending consummation of his marriage does not distract him as it does one who marries a virgin. Therefore, the exemption which applies to the bridegroom of a virgin does not apply to him (*Rambam Comm.*).

In light of the general exemption from other mitzvos of one involved in a mitzvah, many authorities maintain that even one marrying a widow is exempt from the *Shema* obligation while he is occupied with the wedding, since marrying a wife is also part of the mitzvah of procreation. According to these authorities, the distinction the *Gemara* draws between one who marries a virgin (and is therefore exempt from reciting the *Shema*) and one who marries a widow (who is not exempt) refers to the period *after* the marriage ceremony. Since at that time the bridegroom of a widow is neither actively fulfilling the mitzvah of getting married nor distracted by thoughts of consummating the marriage, he is not considered involved with a mitzvah. The bridegroom of a virgin, on the other hand, is considered involved in a mitzvah even after the marriage ceremony, since he is preoccupied with thoughts of consummating the marriage (see *Rashba* to 11a s.v. בלכתך; *Meiri* to 16a s.v. זהו ביאור המשנה).

Others, however, contend that the distinction drawn by the *Gemara* between the bridegroom of a virgin and the bridegroom of a widow refers even to the time during which the bridegroom is actively involved in marrying. According to this interpretation, the *Gemara* is differentiating between performing a mitzvah which involves

הָרִאשׁוֹן עַד מוֹצָאֵי שַׁבָּת, אִם לֹא עָשָׂה מַעֲשֶׂה.
מַעֲשֶׂה בְּרַבָּן גַּמְלִיאֵל שֶׁקָּרָא בַּלַּיְלָה הָרִאשׁוֹן

ר' עובדיה מברטנורא

אם לא עשה מעשה. אם לא בעל עד מוצאי שבת שהם ארבעה לילות, פטור. ומשם ואילך לבו
גם בה ותו לא טריד, ואף על פי שלא עשה מעשה חייב בקריאת שמע:

יד אברהם

mental preoccupation (in which case we apply the principle of הָעוֹסֵק בְּמִצְוָה פָּטוּר מִן הַמִּצְוָה) and performing a mitzvah which does not cause distraction (in which case the principle of הָעוֹסֵק בְּמִצְוָה פָּטוּר מִן הַמִּצְוָה does not apply). Since marrying a widow does not generate any mental distraction, the bridegroom of a widow is always obligated to recite the *Shema* (*Rav Hai Gaon*, cited by *Rashba* and *Meiri* ibid.; *Rambam Comm.*; *Rashi* to *Succah* 25a s.v. כונס אלמנה; see also *Rambam, Hil. Krias Shema* 4:1).

Some authorities maintain that the exemption from other mitzvos when one is occupied with a mitzvah applies only to those other mitzvos whose fulfillment would interfere with the performance of the mitzvah at hand (see *Tosafos* to *Succah* 25a s.v. שלוחי מצוה; *Rosh, Succah* 2:6; see also *Rashi* to *Succah* 25a s.v רטריד and s.v. כונס אלמנה with *Aruch LaNer* ad loc.; cf. *Meiri*, loc. cit., who understands *Rashi's* view differently). According to this view, a bridegroom who has not yet consummated his marriage to a virgin is exempt only from the obligation to recite the *Shema* or similar mitzvos requiring concentration (e.g. prayer; see comm. to previous mishnah s.v. מה שאינו רשאי). Performing these mitzvos would require the bridegroom to abolish all thoughts of his impending fulfillment of the mitzvah of consummating

the marriage. However, mitzvos which do not necessitate concentration can easily be performed by a bridegroom; they are therefore not subject to this exemption (*Meiri* loc. cit.). Others, however, contend that the exemption applies even where performing of the second mitzvah would *not* impede performance of the mitzvah at hand (see *Ran* to *Succah*, 11a in folios of *Rif*, s.v. ואיכא למידק). Accordingly, the bridegroom in our mishnah is exempt not only from reciting the *Shema*, but from all other mitzvos as well (see *Rambam, Hil. Krias Shema* loc. cit.; see further comm. to mishnah 3:1 s.v. ופטור).

בַּלַּיְלָה הָרִאשׁוֹן עַד מוֹצָאֵי שַׁבָּת, אִם לֹא עָשָׂה מַעֲשֶׂה. — *on the first night [of his marriage] until [the night following] the departure of the [ensuing] Sabbath, if he did not [yet] perform the act [of consummating the marriage].*

The mishnah refers to a bridegroom who married a virgin on Wednesday, as was the practice in Mishnaic times (see *Kesubos* 2a).[1] Accordingly, our mishnah teaches that a bridegroom who has not yet consummated the marriage remains exempt from the *Shema* obligation through the fourth night following the wedding [from

---

1. This was because in the times of the Mishnah, the courts convened twice a week, on Mondays and Thursdays. The Rabbis therefore instituted that a virgin should be married on Wednesday, so if, upon consummating the marriage that night, her husband discovers that she is in fact not a virgin — a state of affairs calls into question her permissibility to him — his anger at her, which will not cool off over the course of one night, will ensure that he will go to court the next morning to clarify her status (see *Kesubos* 1:1; see *Gem.* there 2a, which explains why the Rabbis did not institute that virgins should be married on Sundays). Now that the courts convene on the other days of the week as well, this enactment no longer applies (*Gem.* ibid. 3a).

on the first night [of his marriage] until [the night following] the departure of the [ensuing] Sabbath, if he did not [yet] perform the act [of consummating the marriage].

It happened that Rabban Gamliel recited [the *Shema*] on the first night [after] he married.

YAD AVRAHAM

Wednesday night until Saturday night — *the departure of the Sabbath*] (*Rabbeinu Yonah* 9b s.v. הֹחתן). After the fourth night, however, he is no longer exempt, even if he has not yet consummated the marriage. By this time, he has developed a fondness for his wife, and is no longer distracted by thoughts of consummating the marriage (*Rav; Rambam Comm.*). Even if he finds that his wife is not a virgin, he will forgive her and chose to ignore the question of her permissibility to him. Nor is he concerned that the act of cohabitation will render him halachically unfit for marriage, for, having grown accustomed to his wife, he will not be embarrassed to perform the act slowly, eliminating the possibility of injuring his member (*Tos. Yom Tov*).

There is a difference of opinion among the authorities as to whether the bridegroom is exempt from both the evening *Shema* and the morning *Shema* (*Rabbeinu Yonah* 9b s.v. חתן; *Tosafos Rabbeinu Yehudah Chassid; Tosafos HaRosh*), or only from the evening *Shema* (*Meiri* to 16a s.v. מה; *Rabbeinu Manoach*, cited by *Kesef Mishneh, Hil. Krias Shema* 4:2; *Radvaz*, cited by *Shitah Mekubetzes* to *Kesubos* 6a s.v. מתיב; see also *Hagahos Mareh Kohen* to 16a, in explanation of *Rashi, Sefer HaPardes*). Those who exempt him only from the evening *Shema* reason that he is not distracted during the day, because he certainly does not intend to consummate the marriage during the daytime, when

marital relations are inappropriate (*Tos. Yom Tov*)

Tos. Yom Tov suggests that the wording used by the mishnah — בַּלַּיְלָה הָרִאשׁוֹן עַד מוֹצָאֵי שַׁבָּת, "*on the first night until the departure of the Sabbath,*" as opposed to "*from the first night etc.*" — indicates that the exemption applies only during each of the four *nights* until Saturday night (see also *Tif. Yis.* §28). However, *Tos. Yom Tov* notes that it is possible that the phrase *on the first night* is not connected to the mishnah's statement *until the departure of the Sabbath*. Rather, the mishnah issues a ruling that applies to *every* bridegroom of a virgin, that on the night of his marriage, he is exempt. The mishnah then discusses a bridegroom who did not consummate the marriage immediately, and rules that he is exempt up until Saturday night. The mishnah, then, should be understood as follows: *A bridegroom is exempt from the Shema recital on the first night [of his marriage]. If he did not [yet] perform the act [of consummating the marriage], [he is exempt] until the departure of the [ensuing] Sabbath.* According to this understanding, the mishnah implies that the exemption which starts at marriage continues uninterrupted through the fourth night.

מַעֲשֶׂה בְּרַבָּן גַּמְלִיאֵל שֶׁקָּרָא בַלַּיְלָה הָרִאשׁוֹן שֶׁנָּשָׂא. — *It happened that Rabban Gamliel recited [the Shema] on the first night [after] he married.*

[Rabban Gamliel married a virgin. Although he had not yet consummated the marriage, he did not take advantage of the exemption granted in this circumstance.]

שֶׁנָּשָׂא. אָמְרוּ לוֹ תַלְמִידָיו: לֹא לִמַּדְתָּנוּ, רַבֵּנוּ,
שֶׁחָתָן פָּטוּר מִקְּרִיאַת שְׁמַע בַּלַּיְלָה הָרִאשׁוֹן?
אָמַר לָהֶם: אֵינִי שׁוֹמֵעַ לָכֶם לְבַטֵּל מִמֶּנִּי
מַלְכוּת שָׁמַיִם אֲפִלּוּ שָׁעָה אֶחָת.

יד אברהם

אָמְרוּ לוֹ תַלְמִידָיו: לֹא לִמַּדְתָּנוּ, רַבֵּנוּ, שֶׁחָתָן
פָּטוּר מִקְּרִיאַת שְׁמַע בַּלַּיְלָה הָרִאשׁוֹן? — *His
students said to him: Did you not teach
us, our master, that a bridegroom is exempt from the Shema recital on the
first night [of his marriage]?*

[Rabban Gamliel's students did not
understand why he recited the *Shema*.
He was obviously aware of a bridegroom's exemption, for he had taught
them this law! Why, then, did he seemingly contradict his own teaching?]

The students questioned Rabban Gamliel's actions in an indirect manner (*Did you
not teach us, our master*). This is in accordance with the law that when a student
sees his teacher acting in a manner contrary to halachah, he must inform him of
this in a respectful manner, by calling his
attention to the relevant law (*Maharatz
Chayes* to 16b s.v. למדתנו; see *Rambam,
Hil. Talmud Torah* 5:9).

אָמַר לָהֶם: אֵינִי שׁוֹמֵעַ לָכֶם לְבַטֵּל מִמֶּנִּי
מַלְכוּת שָׁמַיִם אֲפִלּוּ שָׁעָה אֶחָת. — *He said
to them: I will not listen to you to
abrogate from myself [the acceptance
of the sovereignty of] the kingdom of
heaven for even one moment.*

Rabban Gamliel did not dispute his
students' assertion that a bridegroom
is exempt from reciting the *Shema*.
Nevertheless, he replied that he was
not willing to forgo the opportunity to
declare his acceptance of the sovereignty of God (see *Tos. R' Akiva* §19;
P'nei Moshe to *Yerushalmi* 2:9 s.v.
אמר ליה). He declared that he was not
even willing to postpone reciting the
Shema until later that night, after con-

summating his marriage (*Tif. Yis.*).
Judging himself capable of properly
concentrating on the *Shema* despite
the distractions of a bridegroom (see
Meiri), he recited the *Shema* even
though he was not obligated to do so
(*Rambam Comm.*).

The mishnah records this incident to
teach that if a bridegroom is of sufficient
stature that he is confident of reciting the
Shema with the proper concentration despite his preoccupation, and is renowned
for his piety so that his actions will not be
construed as haughty, he may recite the
Shema if he so wishes. The issue of
whether an ordinary person may recite the
Shema despite his exemption is disputed in
a later mishnah [mishnah 8] (*Tos. Yom Tov,*
from *Tosafos* to 16a s.v. מעשה בר"ג; see *Tos.
R' Akiva* §20; see further comm. to mishnah 2:8 s.v. רבן שמעון בן גמליאל אומר).

Alternatively, the mishnah relates this
incident because the statement of Rabban
Gamliel's students (*Did you not teach us,
our master, that a bridegroom is exempt. . .*)
supports the mishnah's ruling that a bridegroom is not obligated to recite the *Shema*
(*Tos. R' Akiva* §19; see also *Chiddushei
Maharich*).

Yerushalmi (2:9) cites a Baraisa which
states that one who is exempt from an obligation and nevertheless performs it is considered foolish [הֶדְיוֹט]. However, *Yerushalmi* explains that reciting the *Shema* is
an exception to this rule, because it constitutes acceptance of the sovereignty of
Heaven. Thus, Rabban Gamliel defended
his recitation of the *Shema* on the grounds
that he wished to affirm God's sovereignty
(see *P'nei Moshe* loc. cit.; see also *Tif. Yis*
§36). Alternatively, an extralegal stringency is improper only where it leads to a

2
5

His students said to him: Did you not teach us, our master, that a bridegroom is exempt from the *Shema* recital on the first night [of his marriage]? He said to them: I will not listen to you to abrogate from myself [the acceptance of the sovereignty of] the kingdom of heaven for even one moment.

YAD AVRAHAM

leniency (for example, eating in a *succah* when it is raining, since this desecrates the honor of the holiday). However, no le-

niency will result from reciting the *Shema* (*Tif. Yis.* §30; see also *Beur Halachah* to 639:7 s.v. וכל הפטור).

6.

The previous mishnah related an incident in which Rabban Gamliel's students questioned his actions, which seemed to contradict his own teachings. The next two mishnayos record other instances where Rabban Gamliel's students questioned his actions on the basis of his teachings. These incidents have nothing to do with the *Shema* recital (*Meiri; Beis David*, cited by *Tos. Anshei Shem* s.v. רחץ).

The following mishnah records an incident which occurred when Rabban Gamliel was in mourning for his wife. Upon the death of one's seven closest relatives (i.e. one's father, mother, brother, sister, son, daughter or spouse), a person enters two consecutive states of mourning. The first state, which is Biblical in origin, is called אֲנִינוּת, *aninus* (see *Deuteronomy* 26:14); it begins immediately after the death of the relative. The length stipulated by the Torah for this period of mourning is the subject of a Tannaic dispute (see *Zevachim* 99b-101a). Some *Tannaim* maintain that by Biblical law *aninus* lasts only until the end of the day on which the relative died, but was extended through the following night by Rabbinical decree. Other *Tannaim* are of the opinion that the night following the death is included in the Biblical period of *aninus*.

The second state of mourning, which is known as אֲבֵלוּת, *aveilus*, begins (according to most authorities; see below s.v. רחץ) with the burial and lasts seven days. In the opinion of most authorities, this state of mourning is a Rabbinical enactment (see *Rif* 9b-10a; *Rosh* 2:15). Among the activities prohibited for an *aveil* (i.e. one who is in a state of *aveilus*) are washing his hands, face and feet with hot water, or bathing the entire body even with cold water (*Yoreh Deah* 381:1). Many authorities are of the opinion that these restrictions are Biblically mandated during the period of *aninus* (see *Rif* 10a; the opinion of the *Geonim*, cited by *Rosh* loc. cit.; *Rambam, Hil. Aveil* 1:1 with *Kesef Mishneh*). Others, however, contend that Biblical law only forbids an *onein* (i.e. one who is in a state of *aninus*) to partake of מֵעֲשֵׂר שֵׁנִי, *maasar sheni* (*the second tithe; see Deuteronomy* ibid.) and the meat of sacrificial offerings, as these are the only two prohibition specifically mentioned by the Torah with regard to *aninus* [see *Leviticus* 10:19 with *Rashi; Deuteronomy* loc. cit.] (*Tosafos* to 16b s.v. אנינות לילה; see also *Rosh* ibid.; *Rabbeinu Yonah* 9b s.v. מאי טעמא).

[ו] רָחַץ לַיְלָה הָרִאשׁוֹן שֶׁמֵּתָה אִשְׁתּוֹ.
אָמְרוּ לוֹ תַלְמִידָיו: לֹא לִמַּדְתָּנוּ,
רַבֵּנוּ, שֶׁאָבֵל אָסוּר לִרְחֹץ? אָמַר לָהֶם: אֵינִי
כִשְׁאָר כָּל אָדָם; אִסְטְנִיס אָנִי.

ר' עובדיה מברטנורא

(ו) רחץ לילה הראשון שמתה אשתו. ואף על פי שהאבל אסור ברחיצה: אסטניס אני. קר
וּמֶלֹוֹן — לשון לינה —, וּמִכֵּאן לַעְרֵבָא אם לֹא הִיָה רוחֵץ. ואין אסור בימי אבלו אלא רחיזה של תענוג.

יד אברהם

רָחַץ לַיְלָה הָרִאשׁוֹן שֶׁמֵּתָה אִשְׁתּוֹ. — [Rabban Gamliel] washed on the first night that his wife died.

On the night following his wife's death, while he was in a state of aveilus, Rabban Gamliel washed himself, although an aveil is forbidden to wash his body (Rav; Rashi; see prefatory comments).

Rambam (Comm.) comments that Rabban Gamliel washed himself with hot water. Rambam evidently understands the term רָחַץ (he washed) to mean that Rabban Gamliel washed only part of his body, i.e. his hands, face and feet. This is only forbidden with hot water; the prohibition against washing oneself with cold water during aveilus applies only to the entire body (see prefatory comments). Since it is evident from the continuation of the mishnah that Rabban Gamliel's actions seemed to contravene the laws of aveilus, Rambam explains that he washed with hot water (Tos. Yom Tov; see there for another explanation of Rambam's comment).

Rashi explains that Rabban Gamliel's wife was buried on the day of her death. Apparently, Rashi concurs with the view of the authorities who maintain that the laws of aveilus (e.g. the prohibition against washing) first take effect after the deceased is buried (see Rambam, Hil. Aveil 1:2; R' Yitzchak Ibn Gei'us, cited by Tur, Yoreh Deah 341; see prefatory comments above). Accordingly, Rabban Gamliel's washing must have occurred after his wife's burial, or his actions would not have seemed to be

in violation of the laws of aveilus (Einayim LaMishpat). Others, however, contend that most of the laws of aveilus (including the prohibition against washing oneself) take effect at the time of death (Ramban, Toras HaAdam, cited by Tur ibid.). According to this view, it is possible that Rabban Gamliel's wife had not yet been buried when this incident occurred.

Washing is prohibited for the entire seven days of aveilus. See below (s.v. אמר להם) for the reason the mishnah mentions that this incident took place on the first night after the death of Rabban Gamliel's wife.

אָמְרוּ לוֹ תַלְמִידָיו: לֹא לִמַּדְתָּנוּ, רַבֵּנוּ, שֶׁאָבֵל אָסוּר לִרְחֹץ? — His students said to him: Did you not teach us, our master, that a mourner is forbidden to wash?

[The students could not understand Rabban Gamliel's conduct, which seemed to contradict the laws of aveilus.]

[See comm. to previous mishnah s.v. אמרו לו תלמידיו for the reason why Rabban Gamliel's students phrased their question in such a roundabout way.]

אָמַר לָהֶם: אֵינִי כִשְׁאָר כָּל אָדָם; אִסְטְנִיס אָנִי. — He said to them: I am not like all other people; I am a delicate individual.

[The translation of אִסְטְנִיס follows Rashi; see also Aruch s.v. אסתניס

6. [**R**abban Gamliel] washed on the first night that his wife died. His students said to him: Did you not teach us, our master, that a mourner is forbidden to wash? He said to them: I am not like all other people; I am a delicate individual.

YAD AVRAHAM

(cited by *Rishon LeTziyon*). *Rav* follows *Rambam Comm.*, who relates this word to a root meaning "cold" and explains that Rabban Gamliel suffered from the cold; washing with hot water alleviated his discomfort. *Kol HaRamaz* (cited by *Tos. Anshei Shem*) suggests that according to *Rav* the word אִסְטְנִיס is a general term which denotes one who suffers from one of a wide variety of physical infirmities. The specific condition from which Rabban Gamliel suffered resulted from the cold.]

Rabban Gamliel's response was that washing during the period of *aveilus* is only forbidden for pleasure. Since he washed himself only to alleviate the discomfort caused by his delicate nature, his washing was permitted (*Rav; Tosafos* to 16b s.v. אסטניס; cf. *Rabbeinu Chananel*, cited by *Rabbeinu Yonah* 9b s.v. רחץ בלילה). Thus, although most people may not wash during *aveilus*, he was permitted to wash to ease his discomfort.

As noted in the prefatory comments, the *Tannaim* dispute whether the state of *aninus* on the night following the death of one's relative is of Biblical or Rabbinic origin. The *Gemara* (16b) explains that Rabban Gamliel's actions were predicated on the view that on the night following the death, the state of *aninus* is Rabbinical. Similarly, the *aveilus* restrictions are then only Rabbinically mandated, and in cases where not washing would cause acute discomfort, the Rabbis were lenient and did not forbid it. On the day of the death, however, when

all agree that the state of *aninus* is of Biblical origin, there is no room for leniency, and one may not wash himself for any reason. The commentators suggest that the reason the mishnah notes that Rabban Gamliel washed on the *first* night after his wife's death is to demonstrate this point — that Rabban Gamliel maintains that at this time the Biblically mandated state of mourning (*aninus*) is no longer in effect (*Meleches Shlomo;* see also *Tos. Anshei Shem*).

The *Gemara* seems to imply that during the Biblical state of *aninus*, washing or bathing is prohibited by Biblical law, and is therefore forbidden in all cases. This understanding of the *Gemara* corroborates the view of those who maintain that on the day of death, during the Biblically mandated period of mourning (*aninus*), the *aveilus* restrictions are also Biblical in nature (*Meiri;* see above, prefatory comments).

Others, however, contend that even on the day of death there is no Biblical prohibition against washing oneself. In their opinion, the only Biblical restrictions that apply during *aninus* are those specifically mentioned by the Torah — partaking of *maasar sheni* and eating the meat of sacrificial offerings (see prefatory comments). According to this view, the *Gemara* does not mean that washing to alleviate discomfort is forbidden on the day of death because of a *Biblical* prohibition, but rather, that the *Rabbis* were more stringent regarding the state of *aveilus* they imposed after burial when a parallel Biblical state of *aninus* exists. Thus, Rabban Gamliel was permitted to wash only on the night following his wife's death, when, in his opinion, the Biblical state of *aninus* had already ended (*Tosafos* to 16b s.v. אסטניס; see also *Rosh* 2:15; *Rabbeinu Yonah* 9b s.v. מאי טעמא).

[ז] וּכְשֶׁמֵּת טָבִי עַבְדּוֹ, קִבֵּל עָלָיו תַּנְחוּמִין.
אָמְרוּ לוֹ תַלְמִידָיו: לֹא לִמַּדְתָּנוּ,
רַבֵּנוּ, שֶׁאֵין מְקַבְּלִין תַּנְחוּמִין עַל הָעֲבָדִים? אָמַר
לָהֶם: אֵין טָבִי עַבְדִּי כִּשְׁאָר כָּל הָעֲבָדִים; כָּשֵׁר הָיָה.

יד אברהם

7.

The incident recorded in the following mishnah involves Tavi, the Canaanite slave (עֶבֶד כְּנַעֲנִי) of Rabban Gamliel. Tavi was a most unusual slave. In *Succah* 2:1 Rabban Gamliel refers to Tavi as a Torah scholar, and the *Gemara* (*Yoma* 87a) states that Tavi was worthy of ordination (see *Kesubos* 28a-b). *Yerushalmi* (*Succah* 2:1) records that Tavi wore *tefillin*, a mitzvah not generally observed by slaves (*Rashi to Gittin* 40a s.v. שהניח, *Kesubos* 96a s.v. מנו).

וּכְשֶׁמֵּת טָבִי עַבְדּוֹ, קִבֵּל עָלָיו תַּנְחוּמִין. — *And when Tavi his slave died, he accepted condolences for him.*

Upon returning from a funeral, it was customary for the mourners to stand in place while others would form rows and pass in front of them to offer words of comfort (see *Rashi* to 16b s.v. אין עומדין). This demonstrates respect for the deceased, as it shows that his passing engenders sorrow. This practice was not followed at the funeral of a slave (see below s.v. אמרו לו תלמידיו). However, Rabban Gamliel thought so highly of his slave, Tavi, that he felt him worthy of this final honor. Therefore, Rabban Gamliel stood in his place after the funeral while the people passed in front of him to offer him words of comfort (*R' Shlomo Sirilio*, cited by *Meleches Shlomo*).

אָמְרוּ לוֹ תַלְמִידָיו: לֹא לִמַּדְתָּנוּ, רַבֵּנוּ, שֶׁאֵין מְקַבְּלִין תַּנְחוּמִין עַל הָעֲבָדִים? — *His students said to him: Did you not teach us, our master, that we do not accept condolences for slaves?*

Rabban Gamliel had taught his students that one may not accept condolences for the loss of a Canaanite slave. A Baraisa cited by the *Gemara* (16b)

elaborates: After the funeral, we do not form rows to comfort those who mourn the slave's passing (see above, s.v. וכשמת); we do not pronounce the condolence blessings that are usually recited during the mourners' first postfuneral meal (see *Kesubos* 8b); and we do not console the mourners with the same formula used to console a mourner for the passing of a free man. The reason we do not follow any of the usual mourning practices is the concern that people who are unaware of the identity of the deceased might see the final honor being accorded him and will mistakenly assume that he was a full-fledged Jew, rather than a Canaanite slave. This assumption can have serious halachic consequences, for a slave is forbidden to marry a Jewess (see *Rambam, Hil. Issurei Biah* 12:11-13). If people suppose that the deceased was a Jew, they will presume that his children are also Jewish, when in fact they have the status of slaves, and are forbidden to marry Jewesses (*Tif. Yis.*, from *Tosafos* to 16b s.v. אין עומדין).

The law is that a child's status as a slave or Jew is determined by his mother's status. The children of a female slave are slaves,

7. **A**nd when Tavi his slave died, he accepted condolences for him. His students said to him: Did
you not teach us, our master, that we do not accept
condolences for slaves? He said to them: Tavi my slave
is not like all other slaves; he was a worthy [person].

YAD AVRAHAM

even if the father is a Jew; the children of a
Jewess are Jews, even if the father is a slave
(*Rambam, Hil. Issurei Biah* 15:3-4). The
question thus arises: What halachic problems can possibly occur from mistaking a
deceased slave's status? This mistake will
not cause confusion regarding his children's status, for this is not contingent on
his status as a slave or Jew, but on their
mother's status. Certainly, were the slave
alive, confusion regarding his status could
result in his marrying a Jewess, which is
forbidden. But why were the Rabbis concerned that a mistake could occur after his
death?

The answer is that, indeed, with regard
to a *male* slave, there is no concern that this
demonstration of respect upon his death
will cause such problems. However, with
regard to a *female* slave, there can be serious halachic consequences. Since the status
of her children is determined according to
her status, if someone were to assume that
she was Jewish, they would then assume
that her children are Jewish as well. Thus,
there is reason to forbid the usual mourning practices with regard to a female slave.
Once the Rabbis forbade these customs,
they did not differentiate between mourning for female slaves and male slaves
(*Tzlach* to 16b s.v. עומדין אין ה"ד; see *Sma*
279:14 for another possible solution to this
question).

Alternatively, Rabban Gamliel had
not taught his students that it is *forbidden* to accept condolences for a
slave, but that it is *not proper* to feel
such grief at his passing that one
needs to be consoled. As the Baraisa
cited in the *Gemara* (ibid.) states, one
should feel no more grief over the

death of a slave than over any financial loss (*Meiri*).

אָמַר לָהֶם: אֵין טָבִי עַבְדִּי כִּשְׁאָר כָּל
הָעֲבָדִים; כָּשֵׁר הָיָה. — *He said to them:
Tavi my slave is not like all other
slaves; he was a worthy [person].*

Rabban Gamliel justified his behavior on the grounds that Tavi was an
extraordinary person. Slaves are generally steeped in immoral behavior
(see *Gittin* 13a); Tavi was different —
he was extremely virtuous (*Meleches
Shlomo*). Moreover, he was a Torah
scholar, and even worthy of being ordained (*Tif. Yis.*; see prefatory comments).

According to the explanation that it is
not *appropriate* to accept condolences on
the death of a slave, Rabban Gamliel explained that Tavi was so exceptional that
Rabban Gamliel's grief at his passing was
warranted (see *Meiri* to mishnah). According to the explanation that it is *forbidden* to
accept condolences for a slave, lest people
mistake the deceased for a Jew, Rabban
Gamliel answered that in deference to
Tavi's Torah scholarship, it was permitted
to practice the usual mourning customs at
his funeral (*Tif. Yis.* ibid.). Since there is no
real concern that problems will arise from
mistakenly assuming that a deceased male
slave is a Jew (see above s.v. לו אמרו), the
Rabbis made an exception in the case of a
slave who was a Torah scholar (*Tzlach* loc.
cit.).

Rabban Gamliel's students only questioned why he accepted condolences for
a Canaanite slave, in apparent contradiction to his teaching. However, there is another reason to question Rabban Gamliel's

[ח] חָתָן אִם רָצָה לִקְרוֹת קְרִיאַת שְׁמַע לַיְלָה הָרִאשׁוֹן, קוֹרֵא. רַבָּן שִׁמְעוֹן בֶּן גַּמְלִיאֵל אוֹמֵר: לֹא כָל הָרוֹצֶה לִטֹּל אֶת הַשֵּׁם יִטֹּל.

(ח) **לא כל הרוצה ליטול את השם יטול.** אם לא הוחזק חכם ופרוש בשאר דברים, אין [זה] אלא גאוה שמראה בעצמו שיכול לכוין לבו. ואין הלכה כרבן שמעון בן גמליאל. וחזינן לקצת מרבותינו דאמרי דהאידנא דהכל אדם כל אדם קריאת שמע שמע בלילה הראשון, שכיון שבדורות הללו אין מכוונים כל כך בשאר ימים, אם לא יקרא בלילה ראשון מיחזי יותר כיוהרא, שמראה בעצמו שהוא מכוין בכל שעה אלא השתא אלא משום דטריד במצוה:

actions — namely, Tavi was not Rabban Gamliel's relative! One observes the laws and customs of mourning only for the death of a close relative. *Rashba* (cited in *Meleches Shlomo*; *Tos. R' Akiva* §21) cites a *Yerushalmi* which answers that a student is as precious to his teacher as a son. A faithful servant is also as highly regarded by his master as a son. Thus, Rabban Gamliel mourned the death of Tavi, who was both his close student and faithful servant. *Meiri* notes, however, that, Rabban Gamliel did not actually observe the laws of *aveilus*, since Tavi was not his relative (see prefatory comments to previous mishnah). *Shenos Eliyahu* explains that Rabban Gamliel's students questioned his actions on two accounts: Why did he accept con-

dolences for the death of his slave, contrary to his teaching that such behavior is forbidden (or inappropriate); and why did he mourn the passing of one who was not his relative? Rabban Gamliel answered that his behavior was correct on both accounts. To the question of why he accepted condolences for a slave Rabban Gamliel replied, "Tavi my slave is not like all other slaves," i.e. my teaching applies to other slaves, not to Tavi (as explained above). The second part of Rabban Gamliel's response ("he was a worthy [person]") was intended to explain why he mourned someone to whom he was not related. Rabban Gamliel answered that one must mourn the passing of a worthy person even if he is not his relative (see *Shabbos* 105b).

8.

The mishnah returns now to its previous discussion regarding a bridegroom's exemption from reciting the *Shema* (see mishnah 5). As seen from the incident involving Rabban Gamliel recorded in that mishnah, one who is renowned for his piety and meticulous performance of mitzvos may forgo the exemption of a bridegroom and recite the *Shema* (see comm. there s.v. אמר להם). Our mishnah debates whether other people may also do so (*Tos. R' Akiva* §20).

חָתָן אִם רָצָה לִקְרוֹת קְרִיאַת שְׁמַע לַיְלָה הָרִאשׁוֹן, קוֹרֵא. — **If a bridegroom wishes to perform the Shema recital [on] the first night [of his marriage], he may recite [the Shema].**

Although a bridegroom is not obligated to recite the *Shema* because he is involved in a mitzvah (see mishnah 2:5), if he is confident of his ability to

recite it with the proper concentration, he may forgo his exemption. As seen from the statement of Rabban Shimon ben Gamliel which the mishnah cites presently, one might think that a bridegroom is *forbidden* to recite the *Shema*, because, inasmuch as it demonstrates his confidence in his ability to banish the mental distrac-

8. If a bridegroom wishes to perform the *Shema* recital [on] the first night [of his marriage], he may recite [the *Shema*]. Rabban Shimon ben Gamliel says: Not everyone who desires to acquire a reputation [for piety] may acquire [it].

YAD AVRAHAM

tions affecting a bridegroom and concentrate properly on the *Shema*, it can be construed as an act of haughtiness. The *Tanna Kamma* of our mishnah therefore teaches that a bridegroom *is* permitted to recite the *Shema*. [See below for the reason the mishnah specifically mentions the *first* night of marriage, although a bridegroom's exemption can last as long as four nights after the wedding (see mishnah 2:5).]

רַבָּן שִׁמְעוֹן בֶּן גַּמְלִיאֵל אוֹמֵר: לֹא כָל הָרוֹצֶה לְטֹל אֶת הַשֵּׁם יִטֹּל. — *Rabban Shimon ben Gamliel says: Not everyone who desires to acquire a reputation* (lit. *to take the name*) *[for piety] may acquire [it].*

I.e. not everyone who wishes to follow the practices of saintly people, and perform a mitzvah from which he is exempt, may do so. Rabban Shimon ben Gamliel maintains that unless a bridegroom is renowned as a Torah scholar and a pious man, he is *forbidden* to recite the *Shema* on the night of his wedding. Rabban Shimon ben Gamliel argues that reciting the *Shema* in such circumstances is indeed construed as an act of haughtiness, since the bridegroom misleadingly presents himself as one who can maintain the proper level of concentration despite the distractions engendered by his marriage (*Rav; Rashi,* printed on 17b s.v. לֹא כל הרוצה; cf. *Rashi* to *Pesachim* 55a s.v. ליטול לו). Alternatively, he will recite the *Shema* out of a desire to acquire a reputation

as a saintly person, and not for the sake of fulfilling the mitzvah (*Rambam Comm.*).

Rabban Shimon ben Gamliel agrees that his father — Rabban Gamliel— was permitted to recite the *Shema* on his wedding night (see mishnah 2:5). However, whereas according to the *Tanna Kamma* the incident with Rabban Gamliel proves that a bridegroom may forgo his exemption, Rabban Shimon ben Gamliel maintains that this incident only demonstrates that one renowned for his scholarship and scrupulous observance of mitzvos, like Rabban Gamliel, may recite the *Shema* despite his exemption, for his behavior is certainly not pretentious (*Yerushalmi* 2:9, cited by *Meleches Shlomo;* see prefatory comments).

The dispute between the *Tanna Kamma* and Rabban Shimon ben Gamliel pertains only to the night of the marriage. Rabban Shimon ben Gamliel agrees that after the first night, a bridegroom may recite the *Shema* even if he is still exempt (see mishnah 2:5). After the first night, the bridegroom's recitation does not imply haughtiness, for people will simply assume that he has already consummated the marriage and is no longer exempt from reciting the *Shema* (*Tos. Chadashim; Tos. R' Akiva;* see *Tif. Yis., Boaz* §2).

The *Gemara* (17b) questions the views of the *Tanna Kamma* and R' Shimon ben Gamliel, citing a mishnah in *Pesachim* (4:5), in which the views they express seem to contradict their respective opinions here. The *Tanna Kamma* of that mishnah states

יד אברהם

that in locales where people customarily perform work on *Tishah B'Av*, one should work and not set himself apart from the community, except a Torah scholar, who must refrain from working, since he should feel the loss of the Temple more keenly than others do (see *Meiri* to *Pesachim* 54b s.v. מקום שנהגו). Rabban Shimon ben Gamliel rules that everyone should act like Torah scholars, i.e. they should refrain from work. Evidently, the *Tanna Kamma* maintains that only true Torah scholars may refrain from work; others would be guilty of pretentious behavior for demonstrating more grief than ordinary people feel at the destruction of the Temple. R' Shimon ben Gamliel, on the other hand, is not concerned by the fact that such behavior seems haughty. These views apparently contradict the respective views of the *Tanna Kamma* and R' Shimon ben Gamliel in our mishnah, in which the *Tanna Kamma* is not concerned that one's behavior will be construed as haughty, whereas R' Shimon ben Gamliel is concerned.

The *Gemara* presents two solutions to this difficulty. One *Amora* answers that,

indeed, the views of the two *Tannaim* have been erroneously reversed in one of these two mishnayos.[1] Another *Amora* differentiates between the two mishnayos. With regard to the *Shema*, the *Tanna Kamma* maintains that it is not pretentious for a bridegroom to forgo his exemption, because his actions do not stand out. He is behaving no differently than the vast majority of people who recite the *Shema*. In contrast, sitting idly while others work is conspicuous — and hence, pretentious — behavior. Rabban Shimon ben Gamliel, on the other hand, maintains that since everyone is aware that a bridegroom finds it difficult to concentrate on the *Shema*, reciting the *Shema* flaunts one's ability to summon the requisite concentration even under distracting circumstances; thus, it is an act of haughtiness. Not working on *Tishah B'Av*, however, does not necessarily lead people to assume that one is mourning excessively; they will presume that this person simply has no work to perform.

The authorities disagree regarding which opinion is accepted by halachah. *Rav*, following *Rif* (10a) and *Rambam* (*Hil. Krias Shema* 4:7), rules

---

1. *Rashi* to *Pesachim* (55a s.v. מוחלפת השיטה) implies that it is not known which of these two mishnayos is in error. *Beis Yosef* (*Orach Chaim* 70 s.v. ואם רצה), however, states that it is *our* mishnah which mistakenly attributes the opinions of the *Tanna Kamma* and Rabban Shimon ben Gamliel. Accordingly, Rabban Shimon ben Gamliel is not concerned that one's behavior seems pretentious, while the *Tanna Kamma* does take this into account. See *Tzlach* (to 17b s.v. מוחלפת השיטה), who explains *Beis Yosef's* assumption; see next footnote.

that any bridegroom may forgo his exemption. *Tosafos* (17b s.v. רב שישא) decides the halachah in accordance with the view that only one renowned for his righteousness may recite the *Shema* on the night of his wedding.[1]

In practice, however, all agree that in our times, bridegrooms should recite the *Shema*. Since in any case we do not generally recite the *Shema* with a level of concentration that would be affected by the distractions of the impending consummation of a marriage, *not* reciting the *Shema* implies haughtiness. For it demonstrates a belief that in usual circumstances, one *does* attain the proper level of concentration (*Rav*, from *Tosafos* to 17b s.v. רב שישא; see *Orach Chaim* 70:3).[2]

1. *Tosafos* base their ruling on the view of the *Amora* (cited above) who maintains that the opinions of the *Tanna Kamma* and Rabban Shimon ben Gamliel are correctly attributed both here and in *Pesachim*. Accordingly, Rabban Shimon ben Gamliel is the one who maintains that, unless they are renowned for their piety, bridegrooms may not forgo their exemption and recite the *Shema*. *Tosafos* state that there is a general rule that wherever Rabban Shimon ben Gamliel is cited in a mishnah, the halachah is decided in accordance with his view (see *Kesubos* 77a). Hence, the law is that ordinary people are forbidden to recite the *Shema* when they are exempt. *Beis Yosef* suggests that those who rule that a bridegroom *is* permitted to recite the *Shema* also follow Rabban Shimon ben Gamliel. They, however, base their ruling on the *Amora* who contends that the views in our mishnah must be reversed; hence, *Rabban Shimon ben Gamliel* is actually the one who maintains that a bridegroom may forgo his exemption (see previous footnote). See, however, *Meleches Shlomo*, who cites many authorities who dispute the assertion that the halachah generally follows Rabban Shimon ben Gamliel; see also *Tos. Yom Tov* (*Peaschim* 4:5); see *Tzlach* (loc. cit.) for a different explanation of the two views of the authorities.

2. Some authorities maintain that in our times a bridegroom is actually *obligated* to recite the *Shema*. For since our level of concentration is such that the distractions of a bridegroom would not detract from it, the exemption of one involved in a mitzvah no longer applies (*Maharam MiRothenburg*, cited by *Tur*, *Orach Chaim* 70, as understood by *Perishah* §5; see *Mishnah Berurah* §14). *Rav*, however, implies that even nowadays a bridegroom is exempt from reciting the *Shema*; nevertheless, he should not take advantage of this exemption, since doing so is construed as an act of haughtiness (see *Perishah* ibid.).

פרק שלישי ﴾
Chapter Three

T he present chapter continues the discussion begun in the previous chapter (mishnayos 5 and 8) of exemptions from the *Shema* obligation (see *Tosafos* to 17b s.v. מי שמתו; *Meiri*, introduction to chapter).[1] The following two mishnayos focus on the exemptions that result from a death and burial.

---

1. *Tosafos* (ibid.) note that in *Rashi's* version of the mishnah, the order of this and the following chapter is reversed. *Tosafos*, however, argue that our mishnah, with its discussion of those exempt from reciting the *Shema*, is the logical continuation of the end of the previous chapter, which revolves around this issue. *Meleches Shlomo* points out that *Rashi's* comments in our mishnah (see s.v. מי שמתו) indicate that he, too, followed our order of the mishnah. Evidently, *Tosafos* possessed a different edition of *Rashi*.

[א] **מִי** שֶׁמֵּתוֹ מֻטָּל לְפָנָיו – פָּטוּר מִקְּרִיאַת
שְׁמַע, מִן הַתְּפִלָּה וּמִן הַתְּפִלִּין.

─────────── ר' עוֹבַדְיָה מִבַּרְטֶנוּרָא ───────────

פרק ג – מי שמתו. (א) **מי שמתו מוטל לפניו.** אחד מן הקרובים שחייב להתאבל עליהם
מוטל עליו לקברו: **פטור מקריאת שמע.** משום דטריד טרדא דמצוה:

─────────── **יד אברהם** ───────────

3.

מִי שֶׁמֵּתוֹ מֻטָּל לְפָנָיו — *One whose dead [relative] lies before him*

That is, the body is awaiting burial. The mishnah refers to the death of one's close relative, for whom he is obligated to mourn. The mourner, known as an אוֹנֵן, onein (see prefatory comments to mishnah 2:6), is charged by the Torah with ensuring that his relative receives a proper burial. Until the burial, an *onein* is subject to certain exemptions (and restrictions), as the mishnah will presently rule (*Rav; Rambam Comm.*).

The mishnah does not intend the expression מֻטָּל לְפָנָיו, "lies before him," in its literal sense, i.e. that one is actually in the presence of the corpse. Rather, the mishnah refers to a case where the body awaits burial, the arrangements for which are the responsibility of the relatives of the deceased. In the words of the *Gemara* (18a): If he is responsible to bury [the body], it is as if it lies before him (*Rav*; see *Rambam Comm.*; see also *Kol HaRamaz*, cited by *Tos. Anshei Shem* s.v. מי שמתו; see below, s.v. פטור).

Although it is the responsibility of *all* the mourners to ensure that their deceased relative is buried, some authorities maintain that the mishnah refers only to the relative with the *primary* responsibility to arrange

the burial (e.g. the husband of the deceased, as opposed to her brothers). The other relatives are not subject to the exemptions (or restrictions) of an *onein*, since, under the circumstances, they are not "responsible to bury [the body]" (*Rabbeinu Tam*, cited by *Tosafos* to 17b-18a s.v. ואינו מברך, *Rosh* 3:3 and *Tur, Yoreh Deah* 341; see also *Rav* s.v. מי שמתו). Others, however, contend that the mishnah refers to *any* relative required to mourn the deceased, regardless of whether or not he arranges the burial (*Rambam Comm.; Rosh* 3:3 and *Rosh to Moed Katan* 3:55; *Shulchan Aruch, Orach Chaim* 71:1; see *Beur HaGra* ad loc.; see further *Taz* ad loc. §1 with *Levushei Serad*).

פָּטוּר מִקְּרִיאַת שְׁמַע, מִן הַתְּפִלָּה וּמִן הַתְּפִלִּין. — *is exempt from the recitation of the Shema, from Prayer and from [donning] tefillin.*

Since the Torah obligates the *onein* to arrange the burial of his deceased relative, until the burial he is viewed as someone preoccupied with a mitzvah (*Rav*), i.e. the mitzvah of burying his relative. Accordingly, just as the bridegroom of a virgin is exempt from other mitzvos due to the distractions engendered by the impending consummation of his marriage (see mishnah 2:5), so an *onein* is exempt from other mitzvos (*Rashi; Rivav*, 10a of *Rif* fol., s.v. מי שמתו; see *Yerushalmi* 1:1, second explanation).[1] Alternatively, an *onein* is

─────────────────────────────

1. See comm. to mishnah 2:5 (s.v. חתן פטור) for the Scriptural source of this exemption. *Yerushalmi* (3:1, cited by *Tosafos* to 17b s.v. פטור) cites a different source for the exemption of an *onein*. See *Peirush Miba'al Sefer Charedim* to *Yerushalmi* ad loc s.v. בון אמר ר' and *Pnei Yehoshua* to *Tosafos* ibid., who explain why *Yerushalmi* does not derive this exemption

1. One whose dead [relative] lies before him is exempt from the recitation of the *Shema,* from Prayer and from [donning] *tefillin.* The

YAD AVRAHAM

granted this exemption because respect for the deceased demands that, until the burial, the *onein* focus his thoughts on the loss of his relative (*Yerushalmi* ibid., first explanation, as understood by *Re'ah* and *Ritva* to 17b s.v. מי שמתו).

The law is that a mourner is exempt from donning *tefillin* the entire first day of *aveilus,* even after the burial (see *Shulchan Aruch, Yoreh Deah* 388:1), for it is inappropriate for one in mourning to wear *tefillin,* which Scripture describes as "your glory" (see *Gem.* 11a). Accordingly, *Yerushalmi* (3:1) and *Rashba* (to 17b s.v. הא דקתני, cited by *Tos. R' Akiva* §23) explain that our mishnah perforce includes the exemption of an *onein* from *tefillin* only incidentally, since this exemption is not limited to the time before the burial. Others, however, explain, that the exemption of a mourner from donning *tefillin* because of its description as "your glory" applies only after the burial, when the various *aveilus* restrictions take effect (see prefatory comments to mishnah 2:6). Our mishnah teaches that an *onein* is exempt from the mitzvah of *tefillin* even before the burial, due to his preoccupation with the burial (*Meiri; Tif. Yis, Boaz* §1).

Regarding the exemption of a bridegroom, we have seen (mishnah 2:8) that all agree that one renowned for his saintly practices may forgo his exemption and recite the *Shema.* According to the *Tanna Kamma* of that mishnah, others may also forgo this exemption.

Rashi (to 17b s.v. ואינו מברך) implies that the same is true regarding an *onein's* exemption. This is also the ruling of *Rambam* (*Hil. Krias Shema* 4:7). However, *Tosafos* (ad loc. s.v. ואינו מברך), citing *Yerushalmi* (1:1), contend that it is *forbidden* for an *onein* to recite the *Shema* or fulfill other commandments, either because performing other mitzvos will cause the *onein* to neglect the burial arrangements, or because respect for the deceased dictates that the *onein* not involve himself in matters which distract him from contemplating the death of his relative (see above s.v. מי שמתו; see *Meseches Semachos* 10:1, which only cites the reason of respect for the deceased). The practical difference between these two reasons lies in a case where there are others who arrange the burial.

Most authorities follow *Yerushalmi's* second reason, and rule that an *onein* may not forgo his exemption even if the burial is arranged by others (*Rabbeinu Yonah* 10a-b s.v. מי שמתו; see *Rosh* 3:1). Others, however, maintain that since *Yerushalmi* does not decide between these two reasons, one may be lenient and forgo his exemption, provided there are others who arrange the burial (*Ravyah,* cited by *Mordechai* §57). *Shulchan Aruch*

from the same source as a bridegroom's exemption.

Although the mishnah only discusses the exemption of the relatives of the deceased from mitzvah obligations, the exemptions listed by the mishnah extend also to the others involved in the burial, since they, too, are occupied with the mitzvah of burying the dead. Thus, one who guards the body before it is buried is exempt from reciting the *Shema.* [If there are *two* people watching the body, however, they should take turns reciting the *Shema* while the other guards the body] (*Gem.* 18a; see *Shulchan Aruch, Orach Chaim* 71:3,4). Those who dig the grave, as well, are granted this exemption (*Gem.* 14b; see *Shulchan Aruch* ibid. §5).

נוֹשְׂאֵי הַמִּטָּה וְחִלּוּפֵיהֶן וְחִלּוּפֵי חִלּוּפֵיהֶן,
אֶת שֶׁלִּפְנֵי הַמִּטָּה וְאֶת שֶׁלְּאַחַר הַמִּטָּה:
אֶת שֶׁלַּמִּטָּה צֹרֶךְ בָּהֶן – פְּטוּרִין, וְאֶת שֶׁאֵין

──────── ר' עובדיה מברטנורא ────────

וחלופיהן. שכן דרך שמתחלפין, לפי שהכל רוצים לזכות במטוה: **את שלפני המטה.** המזומנים
לנשאה כשתגיע המטה אללם. כלומר בין אותם שלפני המטה ובין
אותם שלאחר המטה, אם המטה צריכה להם פטורים. ואותן שאין המטה צריכה להן, כגון ההולכים
ללוות את המת בלבד לכבודו, חייבין:

──────── יד אברהם ────────

(Orach Chaim 71:1) rules that one should not forgo his exemption under any circumstances; however, we need not protest if an onein forgoes his exemption in cases where others are arranging the burial, since this is permitted according to Ravyah [and certainly according to Rashi and Rambam] (see Mishnah Berurah there §5,6; see Yoreh Deah 341:1).

Our version of the mishnah lists only three mitzvos from which an onein is exempt — Shema, Prayer (i.e. the Shemoneh Esrei) and tefillin.[1] A Baraisa cited by the Gemara (18a) rules that he is exempt from all mitzvos, in accordance with the principle that one involved in a mitzvah is exempt from all other mitzvos. Some authorities (cited by Meiri; Rabbeinu Yonah 10b s.v. ועל כן) contend that our mishnah disputes this point. In the opinion of these authorities, the mishnah only exempts an onein from the three mitzvos listed, because each requires a degree of concentration impossible for an onein, with his mental distraction regarding the burial, to attain. Most authorities, however, maintain that the mishnah does not intend to limit the onein's exemption to these three mitzvos. Rather,

the mishnah lists these three mitzvos to teach that the exemption granted an onein applies even to these mitzvos. It might have been thought that the importance of affirming God's sovereignty — which, as the Gemara (14b-15a) states, is ideally accomplished by reciting the Shema while wearing tefillin and then praying the Shemoneh Esrei — dictates that even an onein is obligated in these mitzvos despite his preoccupation with the death of his relative. The mishnah therefore teaches that an onein is exempt from them, and certainly from other mitzvos (Tos. Yom Tov, from Rabbeinu Yonah ibid.). Alternatively, one might think that an onein is obligated in these three mitzvos because they are easily performed even by an onein involved with the burial. The mishnah therefore teaches that the exemption of an onein includes these three mitzvos (Rashba; Meiri; see also Re'ah; see Maadanei Yom Tov to Rosh 3:1 §1, from Tosafos to 14b s.v. ומכל מצות, for another reason one might think that an onein is obligated to recite the Shema).

Many of the authorities who exempt an onein from all mitzvos nevertheless maintain that a bridegroom is only

───────────────────────

1. Some versions of our mishnah (including the one printed in the Gemara), however, include the following phrase: וּמִכָּל מִצְוֹת הָאֲמוּרוֹת בַּתּוֹרָה, "and [he is exempt] from all the commandments stated in the Torah" (Shinuyei Nuschaos; see Meleches Shlomo s.v. ומן התפלה).

3
1

pallbearers, and those who replace them, and those who replace their replacements, those in front of the bier and those behind the bier: those needed [to carry] the bier are exempt [from reciting the *Shema*], and those not needed

exempt from those mitzvos that require concentration, e.g. reciting the *Shema* or *Shemoneh Esrei* (see comm. to mishnah 2:5 s.v. חתן פטור). According to these authorities a bridegroom is obligated in any mitzvah which does not require concentration because its performance will not affect his ability to fulfill the mitzvah of consummating the marriage. Since it is possible to fulfill both mitzvos, the second mitzvah is not subject to the exemption of one involved in the performance of a mitzvah (see *Meiri* to 16a s.v. מה שפטרנו). In contrast, an *onein* who is distracted by performing other mitzvos might possibly neglect to properly arrange the burial (for which reason *Yerushalmi* forbids an *onein* to perform other mitzvos — see above). Since *any* mitzvah will interfere with his performance of the mitzvah at hand, all mitzvos are included in the exemption granted an *onein* (*Meiri*; for an alternative explanation, see *Tos. Anshei Shem*, citing *Taz*).

נוֹשְׂאֵי הַמִּטָּה וְחִלּוּפֵיהֶן וְחִלּוּפֵי חִלּוּפֵיהֶן, — *The pallbearers, and those who replace them, and those who replace their replacements,*

[The mishnah now discusses the exemptions of nonrelatives of the deceased, who participate in his funeral.]

It is a mitzvah to take part in burying the deceased. Hence, it is common at funerals for people to take turns carrying the bier, since everyone wishes to share in this mitzvah. Thus, there are

many sets of pallbearers at a funeral (*Rav; Rashi*). Alternatively, it was the practice to prepare alternate pallbearers to replace the original pallbearers when they grew weary (*Rambam Comm.*). The following ruling applies to all who participate in carrying the bier.

אֶת שֶׁלִּפְנֵי הַמִּטָּה וְאֶת שֶׁלְאַחַר הַמִּטָּה: — *those in front of the bier and those behind the bier:*

That is, those who line the funeral route ahead of the bier, as they await their turn to carry the bier (*Rav; Rashi*), and those who have already carried the bier and now join the procession behind it (*Rashi*). Regarding these people ...

אֶת שֶׁלַּמִּטָּה צֹרֶךְ בָּהֶן — פְּטוּרִין, — *those needed [to carry] the bier are exempt [from reciting the Shema],*

Anyone who intends to carry the bier is exempt from reciting the *Shema*, and from other mitzvos, as well. Whether he is still awaiting his turn to carry the bier, or if he has already carried it but intends to carry it again, he is subject to the exemption of one involved in a mitzvah (see *Rav; Rambam, Comm.* and *Hil. Krias Shema* 4:4; *Meiri*; see *Beis Yosef, Orach Chaim* 72 s.v. נושאי המטה).

Although those who await their turn to carry the bier may have time to recite the *Shema* before the bier reaches them, they are nevertheless exempt while they await their turn, since their assistance might be required at any time (*Rabbeinu Yonah* 10b s.v. נושאי מטה).

לְמַטָּה צֹרֶךְ בָּהֶן – חַיָּבִין. אֵלּוּ וָאֵלּוּ פְּטוּרִין מִן הַתְּפִלָּה.

[ב] **קָבְרוּ** אֶת הַמֵּת, חָזְרוּ, אִם יְכוֹלִין

<hr>

ר' עובדיה מברטנורא

ואלו ואלו פטורים מן התפלה. דלאו דאורייתא היא כמו קריאת שמע. ואיכא דאמרי מפני שהיא צריכה כוונה יתירה:

<hr>

יד אברהם

— and
those not needed [to carry] the bier are
obligated.

Those people who attend the funeral
only to accompany the deceased to his
final resting place, but do not intend to
carry the bier [or those who have already carried it and do not intend to
carry it again], are obligated to recite
the *Shema* (*Rav; Rambam Comm.*).
Although it is a mitzvah to participate
in a funeral procession, these people are
not exempt from the *Shema* obligation.
This is because reciting the *Shema* does
not hinder one's ability to fulfill the
mitzvah of accompanying the deceased to his final resting place (*Tos.
Yom Tov*). Although one must stand
still while reciting the first verse of the
Shema (see comm. to mishnah 1:3 s.v.
ובית הלל אומרים), the minimal amount
of time required to recite the first verse
does not interfere with the mitzvah of
following the funeral procession (*Rabbeinu Yonah* 10b s.v. אלו ואלו; *Meiri*;
Lechem Shamayim, cited by *Tos. Anshei Shem*; see below, s.v. אלו ואלו).

Rashi had a different reading of our
mishnah (which is also the version of the
mishnah found in the *Gemara*), according
to which the mishnah rules that those behind the bier, who have already carried it,
are obligated to recite the *Shema* even if
their assistance will be required again. This
is because, having already fulfilled the
mitzvah of carrying the bier, they are no
longer so preoccupied with the mitzvah as

to become exempt from other mitzvos
(*Mordechai* §56). A similar version is found
in *Yerushalmi* (cited by *Rabbeinu Yonah*),
which interprets the mishnah to obligate all
those behind the bier because, in practice,
they will not get another opportunity to
carry the bier. *Tosafos* (to 17b s.v. הכי גרים)
have a version of *Rashi* which explains the
mishnah like *Yerushalmi*, an interpretation
which *Tosafos* reject. The ruling of
Shulchan Aruch (*Orach Chaim* 72:1) follows *Rambam* and *Rav*.

אֵלּוּ וָאֵלּוּ פְּטוּרִין מִן הַתְּפִלָּה. — *Both these
and these are exempt from Prayer.*

Both those who participate in carrying the bier and those who merely accompany the procession are exempt
from praying *Shemoneh Esrei*. Whereas reciting the *Shema* is a Biblical obligation, the obligation to pray the *Shemoneh Esrei* is *Rabbinic* in nature (see
General Introduction). Therefore, the
prayer obligation is treated more leniently; even those merely accompanying the funeral procession — who
are obligated to recite the *Shema* — are
exempt from prayer due to their involvement in a mitzvah (*Rav*, first explanation; *Rashi*).

Alternatively, the funeral participants are exempt from prayer but not
from the *Shema* obligation because
the *Shemoneh Esrei* requires a greater
degree of concentration than the
Shema, which is difficult to attain under the circumstances (*Rav*, second explanation; *Rambam Comm.*).

3
2

[to carry] the bier are obligated. Both these and these are exempt from Prayer.

2. [W]hen] they have buried the deceased [and] are returning [from the grave], if they can

YAD AVRAHAM

Rabbeinu Yonah (10b s.v. אלו ואלו) suggests that the exemption from prayer stems from the fact that *Shemoneh Esrei* must be recited while standing in place. This requirement certainly interferes with the mitzvah of accompanying the funeral procession. The *Shema*, on the other hand, may be recited while walking, with the exception of the first verse. See *Bach* (*Orach Chaim* 106 s.v. כל), who interprets *Rambam Comm.* in a similar manner.

In light of the exemptions generated by a funeral, a Baraisa cited by the *Gemara* (19a) states that a funeral should not begin close to the time prescribed to recite the *Shema*, out of concern that the funeral will take longer than anticipated and the participants will miss the opportunity to recite the *Shema*. However, if the funeral has already begun, it should not be interrupted to allow for the recitation of the *Shema* and *Shemoneh Esrei*, since, during the funeral, the participants are exempt from one or both of these obligations. *Rabbeinu Yonah* (11b s.v. אין מוציאין) adds that if the time to recite the *Shema* has already arrived, the funeral procession should be delayed until it may be reasonably assumed that the participants have already recited the *Shema* and *Shemoneh Esrei*.

2.

After the burial, the mourners gather at a place some distance from the grave to accept condolences from the other funeral participants. There, the mourners stand in place, and those who wish to comfort them form lines and offer condolences as they file past (see *Rambam, Hil. Aveil* 13:1; *Ramban*, cited by *Tur, Yoreh Deah* 376; see *Beis Yosef* there s.v. והרמב"ן). These ranks are known as the שׁוּרָה, *row* (see comm. to mishnah 2:7 s.v. וכשמת). At one point, the Rabbis instituted that the *mourners* pass through the rows of people to accept condolences. However, this enactment was subsequently abolished (see *Sanhedrin* 19a; cf. *Yerushalmi* end of 3:2, cited by *Meleches Shlomo*, but see *P'nei Moshe* to *Yerushalmi* ad loc. s.v. משנה אחרונה; see further below, s.v. העומדים בשורה).

Comforting a mourner is a Biblically mandated mitzvah (cf. *Rambam, Hil. Aveil* 14:1; see further below s.v. ואם לאו). As such, one occupied with consoling a mourner is exempt from the *Shema* obligation, in accordance with the principle that one involved in performing one mitzvah is exempt from other mitzvos (*Rabbeinu Yonah* 11b s.v. קברו את המת, cited by *Tos. Yom Tov*). However, this exemption applies only insofar as reciting the *Shema* conflicts with the mitzvah of offering condolences. If one's recitation of the *Shema* will not interfere with his offering condolences to the mourner, he is obligated to recite the *Shema*. The following mishnah discusses the effect attendance at the "row" has on one's *Shema* obligation.

קָבְרוּ אֶת הַמֵּת, חָזְרוּ, — *[When] they have buried the deceased [and] are returning [from the grave],*

If, as the funeral participants are returning from the burial and are proceeding to the "row" to offer

לְהַתְחִיל וְלִגְמֹר עַד שֶׁלֹּא יַגִּיעוּ לַשּׁוּרָה – יַתְחִילוּ; וְאִם לָאו – לֹא יַתְחִילוּ.

ר' עובדיה מברטנורא

(ב) להתחיל ולגמור. פרשה אחת של קריאת שמע: **לשורה.** שהיו עושים שורות סביב האבל לנחמו בשובם מן הקבר: **ואם לאו.** שהיה הדרך קרוב מן הקבר עד המקום שבו עושים השורה, ואין פנאי להתחיל ולגמור עד שלא יגיעו לשורה:

יד אברהם

condolences to the mourners, the time for reciting the *Shema* arrives, the following law applies (*Meiri*).

אם יְכוֹלִין לְהַתְחִיל וְלִגְמֹר עַד שֶׁלֹּא יַגִּיעוּ לַשּׁוּרָה – יַתְחִילוּ; — *if they can begin and finish [their recitation] before they reach the "row," they should begin [the recitation]*;

The mishnah does not mean that they have time to recite the *entire Shema*. Rather, if they have time to finish a *portion* of the *Shema*, even if only the first verse, before they arrive at the "row" to console the mourners,[1] they should recite that portion (*Rambam, Hil. Krias Shema* 4:6 and *Comm.*, ed. Kafich, from *Gem.* 19a).

As long as they are not yet at the "row," reciting the *Shema* does not conflict with the mitzvah of consoling the mourners. Thus, they must recite whatever portion of the *Shema* they are able before they reach the "row" (see prefatory comments). Once they arrive at the "row," their recitation does conflict with the mitzvah of offering condolences, and is, therefore, interrupted (*Meiri* to 19a s.v. המשנה השלישית; *Tur, Yoreh Deah* 376; but see further below).

Rav, as well as *Rambam Comm.* (ed.

Vilna), interpret the mishnah as referring to a case when there is sufficient time to recite the first *section* of the *Shema*. This understanding is at variance with the *Gemara*, which explains our mishnah to be referring to the first *verse* of the *Shema* (see *Eliyah Rabbah, Orach Chaim* 72:5). *Tos. Yom Tov* suggests that *Rav* and *Rambam* are actually referring to the first verse, as the *Gemara* explains. They describe this verse as the first "section" because, in certain respects, it is considered a separate section (see comm. to 2:3 s.v. קרא וטעה).

The commentators offer various explanations for the mishnah's ruling requiring this abbreviated recitation. Some, following the view that one can fulfill his Biblical *Shema* obligation by reciting the first verse (see General Introduction), explain that the purpose of this recitation is to at least discharge the *Biblical* obligation (*R' Y. F. Perla, Commentary to Sefer Hamitzvos of Rasag*, vol. I p. 141). Others explain that there is a Rabbinical obligation, distinct from the *Shema* obligation, to affirm God's sovereignty by reciting the first verse of the *Shema*. Usually, one discharges this obligation while fulfilling his obligation to recite the entire *Shema*. However, in the case of our mishnah, where

---

1. Although one must stand still while reciting this first verse (see comm. to mishnah 1:3 s.v. ובית הלל אומרים and above 3:1 s.v. ואת שאין למטה), in which case they will certainly finish reciting it by the time they reach the "row," the concern here is that the people and the mourners should reach the "row" simultaneously so that the mourners should not have to wait for them. Therefore, they only stop to recite the first verse if they will surely reach the "row" before or at the same time as the mourners (*Beur Halachah* to 72:4 s.v. וכל העם; for an alternative solution see *Aruch HaShulchan* ibid.).

3
2
begin and finish [their recitation] before they reach the "row", they should begin [the recitation]; but if not, they should not begin.

one does not have enough time to recite the entire *Shema* before reaching the "row," the mishnah rules he should, nevertheless, recite the first verse, in fulfillment of this Rabbinical obligation (*Shaagas Aryeh* §2 s.v. והא דתנן).

Both *Rashba* (19a s.v. הכי נמי) and *Meiri* (loc. cit.) have a version of *Rashi* which interprets the mishnah to rule that if there is sufficient time to recite at least a portion of the *Shema* before reaching the "row," one should not interrupt his recitation upon arriving at the row, but rather should recite the *Shema* in its entirety. The reasoning behind this ruling is that, having begun his recitation, he is now occupied with *that* mitzvah, and is thus exempt from the mitzvah of consoling the mourners (*Meiri* ibid.; see also *Beis Yosef*, *Orach Chaim* 72 s.v. קברו, citing *R' Yitchak Aboab*). However, our edition of *Rashi* contains no such comment. In any case, most authorities dispute this interpretation (see *Mishnah Berurah* 72:12 and *Shaarei Tziyun* §16).

According to the view that one interrupts his recitation upon arriving at the "row," even if he has only recited the first verse, the following question arises: We have seen that one may initiate a greeting in the middle of a section of the *Shema* only out of fear (see mishnah 2:1). Why, then, is one allowed to interrupt his recitation after the first verse — which is reckoned as the middle of a section (see mishnah 2:2) — to offer condolences to a mourner? Even if offering condolences is the equivalent of issuing a greeting out of respect, it should nevertheless be forbidden while one is in middle of a section of the *Shema*. The answer is that since the mourners attend the "row" in order to receive condolences, their mere presence is tantamount to initiating a greeting. Thus, the condolences offered by the people in the "row" are considered *responses* to a greeting, and according to R'

Yehudah (see mishnah 2:1), whose view is accepted by halachah, one may respond to a greeting in middle of a section even out of respect (*Meiri; Tif. Yis.* §11).

וְאִם לָאו — לֹא יַתְחִילוּ. — *but if not, they should not begin.*

If the gravesite is not far enough from the "row" to allow even a partial recitation of the *Shema*, the people should not begin reciting *Shema* (*Rav, Rambam Comm.*). In this case, reciting even a portion of the *Shema* conflicts with the mitzvah of consoling the mourner. Thus, we apply the principle that one involved in a mitzvah (comforting mourners) is exempt from another mitzvah (reciting the *Shema*).

Although the people have not yet arrived at the row and begun offering condolences, they are nevertheless viewed as being occupied with a mitzvah and are thus exempt from reciting the *Shema*. This is because consoling a mourner demonstrates respect for the deceased (see *Rambam, Hil. Aveil* 14:7). As such, it is considered a continuation of the mitzvah of burying the deceased, and the funeral participants are viewed as being occupied with the mitzvah of paying homage to the deceased from the beginning of the funeral until after they console the mourners (see *Re'ah; Shitah Mekubetzes*, cited by *Tos. Anshei Shem* s.v. לא יתחילו; *Meiri*).

Rambam (*Hil. Krias Shema* 4:6), however, implies that those on their way to the "row" are not *exempt* from the *Shema* obligation; they are merely allowed to *postpone* the recitation until after they offer condolences. However, if the deadline for reciting the *Shema* will have passed by the time they finish consoling the mourners, they

הָעוֹמְדִים בַּשׁוּרָה: הַפְּנִימִים פְּטוּרִים,
וְהַחִיצוֹנִים חַיָּבִין.

— ר' עובדיה מברטנורא —

הַפְּנִימִים. הָרוֹאִים [פְּנֵי] הָאֲבֵלִים: וְהַחִיצוֹנִים. שֶׁאֵינָם רוֹאִים פְּנֵי הָאֲבֵלִים:

יד אברהם

are obligated to recite the *Shema* before offering condolences (see *Kesef Mishneh* ad loc.; *Rama, Orach Chaim* 72:4). *Magen Avraham* (72:4) explains that according to *Rambam,* these people are not considered to be involved with the mitzvah of consoling the mourners until they *arrive* at the "row." Thus, they are not *exempt* from the *Shema* obligation while walking to the row. The mishnah only allows them to recite the *Shema* later.

Alternatively, *Rambam's* ruling is based on his view that consoling a mourner is only a Rabbinical mitzvah (see *Rambam, Hil. Aveil* 14:1). According to *Rambam,* involvement in a Rabbinical mitzvah does not exempt one from mitzvos of Biblical origin. Thus, *Rambam* rules that fulfillment of the Biblical obligation to recite the *Shema* can be *delayed,* but not *superseded,* by the Rabbinical mitzvah of comforting the mourners (*Tos. Anshei Shem* ibid.; see *Meiri* loc. cit., who seems to understand *Rambam* in a similar manner).[1]

הָעוֹמְדִים בַּשׁוּרָה: הַפְּנִימִים פְּטוּרִים,
וְהַחִיצוֹנִים חַיָּבִין. — *[Regarding] those standing in the row: the inner ones are exempt, while the outer ones are obligated.*

As noted above (see prefatory comments), at one time, the Rabbis instituted that the funeral attendees form ranks through which the mourners pass to receive condolences. Our mishnah refers to this enactment, which was subsequently revoked (see *Yeru-*

shalmi 3:2, cited by *Meleches Shlomo* s.v. יתחילו). In this arrangement, the row of comforters is sometimes many ranks deep, and those in the back of the row are not able to speak to the mourners and offer condolences. They attend the "row" out of respect for the mourners, for a large crowd at the "row" demonstrates greater respect (*Tif. Yis.*).

The "inner ones" are those people who can see the mourners' faces from where they are standing in the "row." The "outer ones" are those whose view of the mourners is blocked by the people in front of them (*Rav; Rambam, Hil. Krias Shema* 4:6; see *Gem.* 19b; see *Rambam Comm.*). Those who see the mourners are able to offer condolences and are therefore exempt from reciting the *Shema.* Those who cannot see the mourners are not considered occupied with the mitzvah of consoling mourners, since they are not able to offer condolences. Thus, they are obligated to recite the *Shema* (*Meiri* to 19b s.v. הגיעו).

Even those who find themselves at the back of the "row," however, are exempt from the *Shema* obligation while *walking* to the "row." Since it is not known at this time who will stand at the front of the "row" and be able to offer condolences and who will stand in back, the exemption of one occupied with a mitzvah is granted to *all* the funeral participants (*Meiri* ibid.).

1. According to *Magen Avraham's* explanation of *Rambam,* if one is actually occupied with consoling the mourners, he *is* exempt from reciting the *Shema,* even if he will not have time to recite it later. *Mishnah Berurah* (72:13) rules in accordance with this view. [It thus emerges that, according to *Magen Avraham,* performance of a Rabbinical mitzvah (e.g. comforting mourners, according to *Rambam's* opinion) *does* exempt one from Biblical obligations (*Pri Megadim* ad loc.).]

<table>
<tr><td>**3**</td><td rowspan="3">[Regarding] those standing in the "row": the inner ones are exempt [from the *Shema* obligation], and the outer ones are obligated.</td></tr>
<tr><td>**2**</td></tr>
</table>

3	[Regarding] those standing in the "row": the
2	inner ones are exempt [from the *Shema* obliga-
	tion], and the outer ones are obligated.

YAD AVRAHAM

3.

The previous mishnayos have discussed *situations* which exempt a person who is otherwise obligated to recite the *Shema*. The following mishnah identifies people who are *never* subject to the *Shema* obligation. The mishnah issues rulings regarding other commandments, as well — the requirement to don *tefillin*, to pray, to affix a *mezuzah* and to recite the Grace After Meals. Although the primary focus of our mishnah is the *Shema* obligation, these rulings are included here because each relates to the *Shema* in some way.[1]

A mishnah (*Kiddushin* 1:7) states that women are obligated in all commandments incumbent on men, with the exception of positive commandments that must be fulfilled in a specific period of time [מִצְוֹת עֲשֵׂה שֶׁהַזְּמַן גְּרָמָא]. Examples of time-bound commandments from which women are exempt are the obligation to wear *tzitzis*, which only applies during the daytime (see comm. to mishnah 2:2 s.v. ויאמר); to take a *lulav*, which applies only on Succos; and to hear the sound of a *shofar*, which we are only commanded to do on Rosh Hashanah (*Gem.* ibid. 33b-34a; see there for the source of this rule). However, there are exceptions to this general rule. For example, women are obligated to recite *Kiddush* on the Sabbath, although this commandment applies only on this one day of the week (see *Gem.* 20b). Conversely, women are not commanded to study Torah, although this obligation applies at all times (see below s.v. ומן התפילין).

An עֶבֶד כְּנַעֲנִי, *Canaanite slave*, i.e. a non-Jew who was acquired by a Jew and has undergone circumcision and immersion in a *mikvah*, has a quasi-Jewish status; he is obligated in those commandments in which women are obligated. Thus, slaves, too, are exempt from most positive commandments that are confined to specific periods of time (see *Chagigah* 4a for the source of this law; see also *Tos. R' Akiva* §28; *Shaar HaMelech*, *Hil. Milah* 1:1 for details regarding this rule).

By Biblical law, minors (i.e. children who have not yet grown the two pubic hairs considered by halachah as a sign of adulthood) are exempt from all commandments. However, with regard to most positive commandments, the Rabbis decreed that when a minor has reached the age at which he can be trained to perform a certain mitzvah, his father is obligated to see to it that he performs that mitzvah. The age at which this Rabbinical obligation takes effect varies with the particular child and the particular mitzvah (see *Tosafos* to *Succah* 28b s.v. כאן בקטן).[2]

1. The commands to don *tefillin* and affix a *mezuzah* are mentioned in the text of the *Shema* (*Deuteronomy* 6:8-9, 11:18,20); the Grace After Meals is alluded to in the second section of the *Shema* (ibid. 11:15); prayer (i.e. the *Shemoneh Esrei*) is recited after the recitation of the *Shema* and its blessings in the evening and the morning (*Rashba* to 20a s.v. נשים ועבדים; *Meiri*).

2. There is some question as to whether, in addition to the obligation the Rabbis imposed on the father to train his child in the performance of mitzvos, there is a Rabbinical obligation incumbent on the minor to fulfill them, as well. *Rashi* (to 48a s.v. עד שיאכל; see also *Ramban*, cited by *Ran* to *Megillah*, 6b of *Rif* fol. s.v. רבי יהודה) maintains that the child

─────────── ר' עובדיה מברטנורא ───────────

(ג) נשים ועבדים פטורים מקריאת שמע. אף על פי שהיא מצות עשה שהזמן גרמא וכל
מצות עשה שהזמן גרמא נשים פטורות, סלקא דעתך אמינא לחייבן הואיל ואית בה מלכות
שמים, קא משמע לן. ותפילין מצות עשה שהזמן גרמא הם, דלילה ושבת לאו זמן תפילין נינהו,
וסלקא דעתך אמינא הואיל ואתקיש ואתקש תפילין למזוזה, נשים נחייבו, קא משמע לן: **קטנים**. אפילו
קטן שהגיע לחינוך לא הטילו על אביו לחנכו בקריאת שמע, לפי שאינו מצוי תמיד אצלו בעונת
קריאת שמע. ולא בתפילין, משום דסתם קטן אינו יודע לשמור תפיליו שלא יפיח בהן:

יד אברהם

**נָשִׁים וַעֲבָדִים וּקְטַנִּים פְּטוּרִין מִקְּרִיאַת
שְׁמַע** — Women, slaves and minors
are exempt from the recitation of the
Shema

The Shema is a time-bound positive commandment, for the evening
Shema may only be recited at night,
during the time people are usually
asleep (see mishnah 1:1), while the
morning Shema obligation is limited
to the time when people arise from bed
(see mishnah 1:2). Thus, women are
not obligated to recite the Shema, in
accordance with the rule that women
are exempt from time-bound positive
commandments [see prefatory com-
ments] (Rif 11b; Rosh 3:13; see Rav
and Rashi from Gem. 20b).[1] Similarly,

himself is not even Rabbinically obligated in mitzvos. Tosafos (ad loc. s.v. עד שיאכל; see
also Tosafos to Megillah 19b s.v. ורבי יהודה מכשיר), however, contend that there is a
Rabbinical obligation on the child to fulfill those mitzvos his father must train him to
perform (see Kehillos Yaakov §24).

1. In the opinion of Kesef Mishneh (Hil. Krias Shema 1:13), the time limits imposed for
reciting the morning Shema are Rabbinical in nature; Biblical law allows the entire day
for the recitation (see comm. to mishnah 1:2 s.v. הקורא מכאן ואילך). Magen Avraham (58:7)
raises various objections to this view, among them the argument that our mishnah exempts women from reciting the Shema because it is a positive commandment confined to
a specific time period. But according to Kesef Mishneh, there is no time during the day or
night when — Biblically — the commandment to recite the Shema does not apply! In
defense of Kesef Mishneh, Shaagas Aryeh (§12 s.v. וראיתי לבעל מגן אברהם) explains that
the morning and evening Shema are two separate and distinct obligations. As such, each
is time bound, for the evening Shema applies only at night, and the morning Shema only
by day (see Mishnah Berurah 70:2).
    This dispute between Magen Avraham and Shaagas Aryeh has ramifications regard-
ing the obligation of women in the commandment to mention the Egyptian Exodus by
day and by night — in fulfillment of which we recite the third section of the Shema, וַיֹּאמֶר
(see prefatory comments to mishnah 1:5). As previously noted, the daytime obligation
may be fulfilled at any time during the day, and the entire night is acceptable for fulfilling
the nighttime obligation (see comm. to mishnah 1:1 s.v. מאימתי). Thus, there is no time
during the day or night when the commandment to mention the Exodus does not apply.
According to the understanding of Magen Avraham, this means that the obligation to
mention the Exodus is not a time-bound commandment, and is therefore incumbent on
women. Shaagas Aryeh (ibid.), however, maintains that it is a time-bound positive commandment from which women are exempt, for the daytime obligation is confined to the
day, and the nighttime obligation applies only by night. See Mishnah Berurah (ibid.)
concerning this and related issues.

YAD AVRAHAM

Canaanite slaves are exempt from the *Shema* obligation, since they are only obligated in those commandments that are incumbent on women [see prefatory comments] (see *Tos. Yom Tov*).[1]

Although the rule that women (and hence Canaanite slaves) are not obligated in time-bound positive commandments is already stated in a different mishnah (*Kiddushin* 1:7), it is necessary for our mishnah to specifically exempt women and slaves from the *Shema* obligation. One might think that the *Shema* is an exception to the general rule that women are exempt from such commandments, due to the significance of the declaration of faith it embodies — the affirmation of God's sovereignty and unity. Our mishnah must therefore teach that women (and Canaanite slaves) are nevertheless exempt (*Rav*, from *Gem.* 20b; see *Shoshanim L'David*, cited by *Tos. Anshei Shem* s.v. ואית בה מלכות שמים).[2]

Minors are Biblically exempt from reciting the *Shema* just as they are not obligated in any of the Torah's commandments. Nor did the Rabbis require a father to train his minor child to perform this mitzvah as they did with regard to other commandments (see prefatory comments). This is because a child is unlikely to be near his father when the obligation to recite the *Shema* is at hand. Thus, a minor need not recite the *Shema*, even if he has reached the age of training (*Rav; Rashi*).

Tosafos (to 20a s.v. וקטנים) argue that a father *is* Rabbinically obligated to train his son to recite the *Shema*, for the *Gemara* (*Succah* 42a) states that as soon as a child is able to speak, his father should teach him to recite the *Shema*. Rather, *Tosafos* explain our mishnah to be referring only to a very young child, who has not yet reached the age at which he can be trained to perform this mitzvah (see *Mishnah Berurah* 70:6). An older minor, however, would indeed be required to recite the *Shema* (see also *Rambam, Hil. Krias Shema* 4:1; *Meiri*; see below s.v. וזמן התפלין). In the opinion of *Rav* and *Rashi*, however, the requirement mentioned in the *Gemara* in *Succah* derives from the obligation to teach one's son Torah, and not from an obligation to train one's child to fulfill the mitzvah of the *Shema* (*Beur HaGra* to *Orach Chaim* 37:3 and 70:2).

The views of both *Rashi* (and *Rav*) and *Rabbeinu Tam* are cited by *Shulchan Aruch* (*Orach Chaim* 70:2), who concludes that, although, strictly speaking, the halachah follows *Rashi* and *Rav* (see *Mishnah Berurah* there §9), it is proper to be stringent and train a minor to recite the *Shema*, in accordance with the view of *Rabbeinu Tam*.

1. *Yerushalmi* (3:3) derives the exemption of Canaanite slaves from the *Shema* obligation from the opening verse of the *Shema*, which states (*Deuteronomy* 6:4): *Hear, O Israel, Hashem our God, Hashem is One* (i.e. our one and only Master). A Canaanite slave cannot proclaim God as his sole Master, for he is subject to the authority of his owner (see *Chagigah* 4a, where a similar exposition is made with regard to the obligation to visit the Temple during the Three Festivals). See *Tos. R' Akiva* §27 for a practical difference between the two sources of a Canaanite slave's exemption.

2. However, although they are not *obligated* to recite the *Shema*, it is proper for women (and slaves) to accept upon themselves the sovereignty of Heaven (*Shulchan Aruch, Orach Chaim* 70:1) by reciting at least the first verse (*Rama* ad loc.; see *Mishnah Berurah* §4).

ר' עובדיה מברטנורא

וחייבין בתפלה. דתפלה רחמי היא, ומדרבנן היא, ותקנוה אף לנשים ולחנך בה הקטנים:

יד אברהם

וּמִן הַתְּפִלִּין, — *and from [donning] tefillin,*

Women, slaves and minors are exempt from the obligation to wear *tefillin*. Since there is no obligation to wear *tefillin* at night or on the Sabbath, the mitzvah of *tefillin* is classified as a time-bound commandment. Accordingly, we apply the rule that women (and slaves) are not obligated in mitzvos that apply only to specific periods of time (*Rav; Rashi; see Gem.* 20b). [It should be noted that the issue of whether or not there is an obligation to wear *tefillin* at night or on the Sabbath is the subject of a Tannaitic dispute (see *Eruvin* 95b-96b). The *Tanna* of our mishnah follows the view that there is no obligation at these times (*Rashi*).]

Although the mitzvah of *tefillin* is a time-bound commandment, it is by no means obvious that this mitzvah is included in the ruling in *Kiddushin* (1:7) exempting women (and therefore slaves) from such obligations. *Tefillin* might have been thought to be an exception to the general exemption granted to women from time-bound positive commandments because, in the first section of the *Shema*, the Torah juxtaposes the commandment to don *tefillin* [וּקְשַׁרְתָּם לְאוֹת עַל־יָדֶךָ וְהָיוּ לְטֹטָפֹת בֵּין עֵינֶיךָ, *Bind them as a sign upon your arm and let them be totafos* (i.e. *tefillin*) *between your eyes* (Deuteronomy 6:8)] with the commandment of *mezuzah* [וּכְתַבְתָּם עַל־מְזֻזוֹת בֵּיתֶךָ וּבִשְׁעָרֶיךָ], *And you shall write them on the doorposts of your house and upon your gates* (ibid v. 9)]. The commandment of *mezuzah is* incumbent on women (as the mishnah presently rules). One might think that the juxtaposition of these two commandments teaches that

women are obligated in *tefillin* as they are obligated in *mezuzah*. Our mishnah must therefore teach that the mitzvah of *tefillin* is in fact included in the general exemption from time-bound positive commandments granted women (*Rav; Rashi* to *Gem.* 20b s.v. מהו דתימא).

The reason we do not derive from *mezuzah* that women are obligated to don *tefillin* is because the verse *preceding* the Torah's command to don *tefillin* deals with the commandment to teach Torah to one's children. *Deuteronomy* 6:7 states: וְשִׁנַּנְתָּם לְבָנֶיךָ, *You shall teach them* (i.e. the words of Torah) *thoroughly to your children.* This juxtaposition occurs in the second section of the *Shema* as well: וּקְשַׁרְתֶּם אֹתָם לְאוֹת עַל־יֶדְכֶם וְהָיוּ לְטוֹטָפֹת בֵּין עֵינֵיכֶם, *You shall bind them for a sign upon your arm and let them be totafos between your eyes* (Deuteronomy 11:18). The next verse deals with the commandment to teach Torah to one's son: וְלִמַּדְתֶּם אֹתָם אֶת־בְּנֵיכֶם לְדַבֵּר בָּם, *You shall teach them to your sons to discuss them.* This double juxtaposition teaches that just as women are exempt from Torah study (as the verse states: "you shall teach them to your *sons*"— implying: but not to your *daughters*; see *Kiddushin* 29b), so, too, they are exempt from the obligation to don *tefillin.* This exposition is more compelling than the one linking *tefillin* and *mezuzah* because the juxtaposition of Torah study and *tefillin* occurs twice, whereas *tefillin* is juxtaposed with *mezuzah* only once, in the text of the first section of the *Shema* (*Tos. Yom Tov,* from *Kiddushin* 34a; see *Tos. R' Akiva* §24; *Tos. Anshei Shem* s.v. דלילה).

There is no obligation, even Rabbinically, for minors to don *tefillin.* The Rabbis did not require fathers to train their children in this mitzvah because the sanctity of *tefillin* demands that one carefully control his bodily

YAD AVRAHAM

functions while wearing them. Specifically, one must take care not to pass gas while wearing *tefillin.* Since minors are deemed incapable of being careful in this regard, the Rabbis did not stipulate that they be trained in the performance of this commandment (*Rav; Rashi*).[1]

Tosafos (loc. cit.) argue that a father *is* obligated to train his son in the mitzvah of *tefillin,* for the *Gemara* in *Succah* (42a) states that once a child matures sufficiently to guard *tefillin* with proper deference, his father must purchase a pair for him. Accordingly, *Tosafos* interpret our mishnah to be referring to minors who have not yet reached this trainable age (see above s.v. נשים). *Rav* and *Rashi,* however, understood that *Gemara* to be referring to exceptional cases, where a child has demonstrated the ability to conduct himself properly while wearing *tefillin.* Our mishnah refers to the majority of minors, who have not proven themselves disciplined enough to guard the sanctity of *tefillin,* even though they are capable of being trained in other commandments (*Rashba* to 20a s.v. נשים; see also *Rabbeinu Yonah* 11b s.v. נשים).

וְחַיָבִין בִּתְפִלָּה — *but they are obligated in prayer,*

That is, women and slaves are obligated to pray, and fathers are obligated to train their children to pray (*Rav*). The prayer obligation is a Rabbinic enactment (see *Gem.* 21a; General Introduction). In instituting this obligation, the Rabbis did not differentiate between men and women (and slaves), because the essence of prayer is the request for Divine mercy, something equally needed by both men and women (*Rav; Rashi;* see *Gemara* 20b).

Rabbinical enactments are not subject to the rule exempting women from timebound positive commandments. Thus, the fact that each of the three prayers is confined to a specific time of the day — *Shacharis* in the morning, *Minchah* in the afternoon and *Maariv* at night — is not a reason to exempt women from the prayer obligation (*Rashi* to 20b s.v. הכי גרסינן; cf. *Tosafos* ad loc. s.v. בתפלה).

In the opinion of *Rambam* (*Sefer Ha-Mitzvos, mitzvos aseh* §5; *Hil. Tefilah* 1:1), the obligation to pray is *Biblical* (see General Introduction). However, even according to *Rambam,* the obligation to pray thrice daily, at set times and following a prescribed text, is a Rabbinical enactment; by Biblical law, one may discharge his obligation by articulating some form of prayer at some unspecified point during the day. Since the *Biblical* prayer obligation is not confined to a specific time during the day, it is not classified as a time-bound positive commandment, and is, therefore, incumbent on women and slaves as well as on men (ibid. 1:2; see *Meiri* to 20b s.v. מחלוקת גדולה; see *Rabbeinu Yonah* 11b s.v. ותפילה for another reason why the prayer obligation is not subject to the exemption of timebound positive commandments).[2]

Although the Rabbis did not obligate a father to train his son to recite

---

1. Indeed, it is *forbidden* for a minor to don *tefillin* unless he is capable of behaving in a manner befitting their sanctity (see *Mishnah Berurah* 37:8).

2. One consequence of the dispute between *Rashi* (and *Rav*) and *Rambam* relates to the extent of a woman's prayer obligation. According to *Rashi* — who maintains that women are obligated in prayer because they were included in the Rabbinical enactment of prayer — women are required to pray *Shacharis* and *Minchah,* with the prescribed text, just as men are (however, they are not obligated to pray *Maariv,* which was originally instituted as a discretionary prayer, not as an obligation — see *Gem.* 27b). However, according to *Rambam* — who maintains that women are obligated in prayer because of a Biblical

— ר' עובדיה מברטנורא —

ובמזוזה. דמהו דתימא הואיל ואתקש לתלמוד תורה, כי היכי דנשים פטורות מתלמוד תורה דכתיב (דברים יא) ולמדתם אותם את בניכם ולא בנותיכם, הכי נמי נפטרו ממזוזה אף על פי שהיא מצות עשה שלא הזמן גרמא, קא משמע לן: **ובברכת המזון.** מיבעיא לן אי חייבות בברכת המזון מדאורייתא כיון דכתיב (שם ח) ואכלת ושבעת וברכת הויא ליה מצות עשה שלא הזמן גרמא, או שמא אין חייבות מדאורייתא משום דכתיב (שם) על הארץ הטובה אשר נתן לך, והארץ לא נתנה

יד אברהם

the *Shema* because the son is often not in his father's presence during the time eligible for reciting the *Shema* (see above, s.v. נשים), the Rabbis did obligate him to train his son to pray. The time for the morning *Shema* lasts only until the end of the third hour of the day. The time for prayer, on the other hand, lasts until the end of the *fourth* hour of the day (see mishnah 4:1), and a son is usually found with his father at some point during this time period (*Meiri* s.v. ויש מפרשים).

As noted above (s.v. נשים, s.v. ומן התפילין), *Tosafos* maintain that our mishnah refers to minors who have not yet reached the age at which they can be trained to perform commandments. However, the mishnah's present statement cannot be understood to obligate a father to train such a young child to fulfill the mitzvah of prayer (or the other commandments that our mishnah will list presently). Accordingly, *Rabbeinu Tam* (cited by *Tosafos* ibid.) explains that the "minors" referred to in the mishnah (i.e. minors who are not old enough to be trained) are included in the rulings of our

mishnah only with regard to the *exemptions* the mishnah lists in its first clause. The rulings regarding *obligations*, however, refer only to women and slaves, but not to the minors previously mentioned.[1] However, the father of a minor who has reached the age of training *is* obligated to train him in these mitzvos.

וּבִמְזוּזָה — *and in mezuzah*,

The obligation to affix a *mezuzah* to one's doorposts applies at all times. Since it is not a time-bound commandment, it is incumbent on women (and slaves) as well as on men [see prefatory comments] (*Rashi*). As with regard to most commandments (the *Shema* and *tefillin* obligations being exceptions to the rule, for the reasons explained above), fathers are Rabbinically obligated to train their children in the performance of this mitzvah. Thus, if a minor has a dwelling of his own, his father must train him to affix a *mezuzah* to his doorposts (*Rambam, Hil. Mezuzah* 5:10; see *Kesef Mishneh* ad loc.).

obligation which is is not time bound — it is possible that women were never included in the Rabbinical enactment instituting a fixed version of prayer at specific times of the day. Accordingly, women can discharge their obligation by uttering a simple request to God at any time during the day (see *Tif. Yis.* §17; *Mishnah Berurah* 106:4).

1. *Meiri* (to our mishnah s.v. ויש מפרשים) also maintains that the latter clause of the mishnah does not refer to minors, but for a different reason: There is no Rabbinical obligation incumbent on the child himself to perform mitzvos, but rather on his father to train him in their fulfillment. Thus, the latter clause, which refers to one's *personal* obligation, cannot be referring to minors. However, as previously noted (see prefatory comments, footnote 1), some authorities are of the opinion that there *is* a Rabbinical obligation on the child himself, in addition to his father's requirement to train him in mitzvah performance.

and in *mezuzah,* and in the Grace After Meals.

The rule that women are obligated in commandments that are not time bound is mentioned in the mishnah in *Kiddushin* (1:7). Nevertheless, our mishnah must specifically include women and slaves in the *mezuzah* obligation, for one might think that this mitzvah is an exception to the rule. This is because the *mezuzah* obligation is juxtaposed with the obligation of Torah study. *Deuteronomy* 11:19 states: וְלִמַּדְתֶּם אֹתָם אֶת בְּנֵיכֶם, *You shall teach them to your sons.* The next verse states: וּכְתַבְתָּם עַל־מְזוּזוֹת בֵּיתֶךָ וּבִשְׁעָרֶיךָ, *And you shall write them on the doorposts of your house and upon your gates.* It might have been thought that this juxtaposition teaches that women are exempt from the obligation of *mezuzah* just as they are not obligated to study Torah (see above, s.v. וּמִן התפילין). Our mishnah therefore teaches that women *are* obligated in *mezuzah*, as they are obligated in all other positive commandments that are not time bound (*Rav; Rashi* to 20b s.v. נקיש, from *Gem.* there).

The reason this juxtaposition is not expounded to exempt women from the *mezuzah* obligation is because the Torah states that one who fulfills this mitzvah is granted long life, as it is written (ibid. v. 20-21): וּכְתַבְתָּם עַל־מְזוּזוֹת בֵּיתֶךָ וּבִשְׁעָרֶיךָ. לְמַעַן יִרְבּוּ יְמֵיכֶם, *And you shall write them on the doorposts of your house and upon your gates: In order to prolong your days* etc. Since women have as much need of long life as men, the Gemara (*Kiddushin* 34a) concludes that men and women are equally obligated in *mezuzah* (*Tos. Yom Tov,* from *Rashi* ibid.).

וּבְבִרְכַּת הַמָּזוֹן. — *and in the Grace After Meals.*

Women and slaves are obligated to recite the Grace After Meals, and a father is obligated to train his minor children in its recitation.

The *Gemara* (20b) is uncertain whether a woman's obligation to recite the Grace After Meals is Biblical in nature, as is a man's obligation, or only Rabbinical. On one hand, this obligation — which is derived from the verse (*Deuteronomy* 8:10): וְאָכַלְתָּ וְשָׂבָעְתָּ וּבֵרַכְתָּ אֶת־ה' אֱלֹהֶיךָ עַל־הָאָרֶץ הַטֹּבָה אֲשֶׁר נָתַן־לָךְ, *You will eat and you will be satisfied, and bless Hashem, your God, for the good Land that He gave you* — is not a time-bound positive commandment, for it applies whenever a person eats the requisite amount of food.[1] As such, the Biblical requirement would seem to apply to women as well. On the other hand, since the Torah characterizes the Grace as a blessing of thanksgiving for the Land of Israel (*and bless Hashem... for the good Land that He gave you*), it is possible that the verse does not refer to women, who were not granted a share in the Land (*Rav; Rashi* to 20b s.v. או דרבנן; see *Tosafos* ad loc. s.v. נשים and *Rashba* s.v. בעא מיניה for a different basis for the *Gemara's* uncertainty).

This question has ramifications with regard to the halachic ability of a woman to recite the Grace After Meals on behalf of a man who is Biblically obligated to recite the Grace. As a rule, one who is unable to recite the Grace himself can discharge his obligation by hearing the recitation of another who is similarly obligated. However, if a woman's obligation is Rabbinical in nature, a man who is

---

1. Although the Torah (*Exodus* 16:8) states: בְּתֵת ה' לָכֶם בָּעֶרֶב בָּשָׂר לֶאֱכֹל וְלֶחֶם בַּבֹּקֶר לִשְׂבֹּעַ, *When, in the evening, Hashem gives you meat to eat and bread to satiety in the morning,* these fixed times for eating do not render the obligation to recite the Grace After Meals a time-bound positive commandment (*Gem.* ibid.).

בְּרָכוֹת [ד] **בַּעַל** קֶרִי מְהַרְהֵר בְּלִבּוֹ, וְאֵינוֹ מְבָרֵךְ

לנקבות, ולא אפשיטא: **(ד) בעל קרי.** עזרא תקן שלא יקרא בעל קרי בתורה — בין
שראה קרי לאונסו בין לרצונו — עד שיטבול. ולא מפני טומאה וטהרה, שאין דברי תורה מקבלין
טומאה, אלא כדי שלא יהיו תלמידי חכמים מצויין אצל נשותיהן כתרנגולים. **קריאת**
שמע בלבו כשהגיע זמן המקרא: **מהרהר.**

Biblically obligated cannot discharge
his obligation by hearing the recitation of a woman, since she is not obligated to the same degree as he is (*Gem.
ibid.*).

Another practical difference between
the two possibilities emerges in a case
where a woman is unsure if she had already recited the Grace. If a woman is Biblically obligated to recite the Grace, then in
cases of doubt she must recite it, in accordance with the principle that when in
doubt concerning Biblical obligations, one
must act stringently. However, if her obligation is Rabbinical in nature, she need not
recite the Grace, in accordance with the
rule that when in doubt with regard to
Rabbinical obligations, one acts leniently
(see *Mishnah Berurah* 186:3).

Since the *Gemara* does not issue a ruling
with regard to this question, many authorities maintain that the issue remains unre-

solved (see *Rambam, Hil. Berachos* 5:1;
Shulchan Aruch, Orach Chaim 186:1).
Others, however, decide the issue in favor
of the view that women are *Biblically* obligated to recite the Grace After Meals
(*Rashba* to 20b s.v. ולעניין פסק; *Meiri* to 20b
s.v. מה שביארנו; see *Beur Halachah* to 186:1
s.v. אלא מדרבנן).

The *Gemara* does not discuss the nature
of a slave's obligation to recite the Grace
After Meals. Some authorities maintain
that the status of his obligation is subject to
the same uncertainty as that of a woman
(*Rambam* loc. cit.; *Tashbatz* I:169, cited by
Gilyon HaShas to 20b). Others, however,
contend that the obligation of a slave is
undoubtedly Biblical in nature. Although
slaves did not themselves receive a share in
the Land, they are part of a general group
— males — which did receive a share of the
Land (*Rashba* to 20b s.v. בעא; *Meiri* loc. cit.;
Shitah Mekubetzes to 20b s.v. נשים; see also
Ramban to Bava Basra 81a s.v. והכתיב).

4.

The *Gemara* (*Bava Kamma* 82a) records ten edicts instituted by Ezra the
Scribe. Among these is the enactment that a בַּעַל קֶרִי, *baal keri* (i.e. one who
experienced a seminal emission), is prohibited from articulating words of Torah
until he purifies himself by immersing in a *mikveh*[1] (see ibid. 82b).

Although a *baal keri* is *tamei* (see *Leviticus* 15:16), it was not his state of
tumah which led Ezra to prohibit Torah study for a *baal keri*; Ezra did not
forbid the study of Torah for one who is *tamei* with any other type of *tumah*
(see *Gem.* 22a). Rather, this enactment was intended to ensure that Torah
scholars not excessively engage in marital relations at the expense of Torah
study. The burden of immersing in a *mikveh* after each act of intimacy deters
Torah scholars from engaging in marital relations excessively (*Rav,* from *Gem.*

1. In certain cases, it suffices if nine *kabin* of water are poured on the *baal keri* [in
contemporary terms, this is approximately 3.4 gallons, or, according to others, approximately 5.7 gallons; see *Middos VeSheurei Torah* 17:30] (see *Gem.* 22b).

YAD AVRAHAM

ibid; *Rambam, Hil. Tefillah* 4:4). Another reason Ezra prohibited a *baal keri* from studying Torah before he purifies himself is because inadvertent seminal emissions are often the consequence of levity, an attitude inconsistent with the feelings of awe and respect necessary to study God's sacred Torah (*Meiri; Tur, Orach Chaim* 88; see *Gem.* 22a with *Rashi* s.v. מכאן).

As will be seen in the coming mishnah, some *Tannaim* maintain that a *baal keri* is also forbidden to pray or to recite the *Shema*.[1] The coming mishnah discusses how a *baal keri* deals with obligatory recitations such as the *Shema* and the various blessings.[2]

בַּעַל קֶרִי מְהַרְהֵר בְּלִבּוֹ, — *A baal keri contemplates [the text of the Shema] in his mind,*

A *baal keri* who has not purified himself by the time for reciting the *Shema* should not articulate the text of the *Shema*, but rather should recite it mentally (*Rambam Comm.; Rabbeinu Yonah* 12a s.v. בעל קרי).

As a result of Ezra's enactment, one who experiences a seminal emission is forbidden to recite the *Shema* (see prefatory comments). However, he is not entirely exempt from the *Shema* obligation. Although he cannot recite the *Shema* orally, the Rabbis required him to recite the text in his mind (see *Rav; Rashi*). [Mental recitation of

words of Torah was not prohibited by Ezra's decree (see *Gem.* 20b).]

The reason a *baal keri* must recite the *Shema* in his mind is the subject of a dispute in the *Gemara* (20b) between the *Amoraim* Ravina and Rav Chisda. In Ravina's opinion, the mishnah's ruling reflects the view that a mental recitation of the *Shema* is the halachic equivalent of an oral recitation [הַרְהוּר כְּדִבּוּר דָּמֵי] (although, as noted above, mental recitation of Torah was not included in Ezra's decree; see *Tosafos* to 20b s.v. כדאשכחן). Under normal circumstances, a mental recitation is valid only after the fact. However, since a *baal keri* is forbidden to verbally recite the *Shema*, he may *initially* fulfill his obligation with a mental recitation (see *Baal Ha-Maor* 12a in fol. of *Rif*, s.v. מתני׳).[3] According to Ravina, the purpose of a *baal keri's*

1. According to some authorities, the prohibition against praying was not part of Ezra's enactment, but was instituted later by the Rabbis (*Rambam, Hil. Tefillah* 4:4; see *Kesef Mishneh* ad loc.; *Pri Chadash, Orach Chaim* 88). Others contend that the prohibition against prayer was included in Ezra's original edict (see *Meiri; Rosh* to *Bava Kamma* 7:19).

2. It should be noted that the laws delineated in our mishnah are no longer applicable, as Ezra's decree was annulled in Talmudic times (see *Gem.* 22a; *Rav* s.v. לפניו ואינו מברך; *Rambam, Hil. Krias Shema* 4:8). Nevertheless, even nowadays, one who conducts himself in accordance with Ezra's decree is praiseworthy, provided that this does not adversely affect his fulfillment of his obligations [e.g. immersing in a *mikveh* will cause him to miss the deadline for reciting the *Shema*] (*Mishnah Berurah* 88:2,4). Indeed, *Rambam* (*Hil. Tefillah* 4:6) notes the widespread custom of *baalei keri* to purify themselves before praying.

3. *Raavad* (*Hasagos* to *Baal HaMaor* ad loc.) maintains that under normal circumstances, Ravina *invalidates* a mental recitation of the *Shema*. He allows it only in extenuating circumstances, such as a *baal keri* who does not have access to a body of water in which to purify himself.

לֹא לְפָנֶיהָ וְלֹא לְאַחֲרֶיהָ. וְעַל הַמָּזוֹן מְבָרֵךְ
לְאַחֲרָיו, וְאֵינוֹ מְבָרֵךְ לְפָנָיו. רַבִּי יְהוּדָה

─────────── ר' עובדיה מברטנורא ───────────

ואינו מברך לפניה ולאחריה. ואפילו בהרהור, כיון דברכות לאו דאורייתא לא אברכוהו רבנן:
ועל המזון מברך לאחריו. דחיובא דאורייתא הוא: **ואינו מברך לפניו.** דלאו חיובא דאורייתא
היא. וכבר נפסקה ההלכה דבטלוה לטבילותא, ובעלי קריין קורין קריאת שמע כדרכן וטובלקין

───────────────────
יד אברהם

mental recitation is to discharge his *Shema* obligation.

Rav Chisda, however, contends that one can never discharge his *Shema* obligation — or, for that matter, any obligation which calls for reciting a prescribed text — with a mental recitation [הַרְהוּר כְּדִבּוּר דָּמֵי]. According to Rav Chisda, the purpose of requiring a *baal keri* to mentally recite the text of the *Shema* is only so that he should not sit idle while others are involved with its recitation.[1] However, after he purifies himself, he must repeat the *Shema* orally if the deadline for its recitation has not yet passed (*Hasagos HaRaavad*, 12a in fol. of *Rif* s.v. יצא בדיעבד).

The halachah is decided in accordance with Rav Chisda that a mental recitation is not the equivalent of an oral recitation (*Tosafos* to 20b s.v. ורב חסדא; *Rosh* 3:14 et al.). Thus, if for some reason one cannot articulate the text of the *Shema*, he should recite it mentally, as our mishnah rules with regard to a *baal keri* (*Shulchan Aruch, Orach Chaim* 62:4), but should repeat it orally when he is able (*Mishnah Berurah* 62:7; see *Beur Halachah* s.v. יצא).

וְאֵינוֹ מְבָרֵךְ לֹא לְפָנֶיהָ וְלֹא לְאַחֲרֶיהָ. —

but he does not recite the blessings [of the *Shema*], neither [the blessings] preceding it nor [those] following it.

That is, a *baal keri* does not even make a *mental* recitation of the blessings associated with the *Shema* (*Rav*; *Rashi*).

In contrast with the *Shema*, the recitation of which is Biblically mandated, the blessings of the *Shema* are of Rabbinic origin (see prefatory comments to mishnah 1:4). Therefore, the Rabbis did not require even a mental recitation for a *baal keri* (*Rav*; *Rashi*, from *Gem.* 21a).

According to the view that the *Shema* obligation is also only Rabbinically mandated (see General Introduction), the distinction between the *Shema* and its blessings is a consequence of the importance the Rabbis attached to the *Shema* as a declaration of God's sovereignty (*Gem.* ibid.).

Rav and *Rashi* imply that the Rabbis did not *require* a *baal keri* to mentally recite the blessings of the *Shema*; he is, however, *permitted* to contemplate these blessings, since mental recitation of prayer is not

1. As noted previously (comm. to mishnah 2:3 s.v. הקורא את שמע), some commentators maintain that the issue of whether one can discharge his *Shema* obligation with a mental recitation is a corollary of the dispute in mishnah 2:3 between the *Tanna Kamma* and R' Yose regarding whether one can discharge his obligation with an *inaudible verbal* recitation of the *Shema* (see *Rashba* to 15a s.v. ורבי יוסי אמר). Others, however, maintain that the dispute in that mishnah refers *only* to an inaudible recitation of the *Shema* (see *Baal HaMaor* loc. cit.; *Shitah Mekubetzes* to 21a s.v. ולענין הלכתא). *Rosh* (3:14) understands the dispute between Ravina and Rav Chisda to revolve around this very point: Ravina maintains that according to the *Tanna Kamma* of that mishnah, a mental recitation is valid. Thus, Ravina interprets our mishnah in accordance with the view of the *Tanna Kamma*. Rav Chisda, however, contends that the *Tanna Kamma* only allows an inaudible verbal recitation. Thus, there is no basis to assume that a mental recitation of the *Shema* is valid.

3	[of the *Shema*], neither [the blessings] preceding it nor
4	[those] following it. And with regard to food, he recites the blessings that follow [a meal], but he does not recite the blessings preceding [a meal]. R' Yehudah

forbidden as a result of Ezra's decree (see *P'nei Yehoshua* to 20b s.v. כדאשבחן בסיני). However, other commentators imply that a *baal keri* is *forbidden* to contemplate the text of the blessings (see *Tosafos* to 20b s.v. בעל קרי and to 21a s.v. הא; *Rabbeinu Yonah* 12a-b s.v. רבי יהודה אומר; see also *Shenos Eliyahu*; see further *Pri Chadash, Orach Chaim* 88).

וְעַל הַמָּזוֹן מְבָרֵךְ לְאַחֲרָיו, וְאֵינוּ מְבָרֵךְ לְפָנָיו. — *And with regard to food, he recites the blessings that follow [a meal], but he does not recite the blessings preceding [a meal].*

[I.e. a *baal keri* must mentally recite the Grace After Meals, but not the blessings recited before eating.]

The requirement to recite the Grace After Meals is a Biblical obligation (see comm. to previous mishnah s.v. ובברכת המזון). Hence, the Rabbis required a *baal keri* to mentally recite it just as they obligated him to mentally recite the *Shema*. The blessings recited before eating were instituted by the Rabbis; thus, they did not require even a mental recitation, just as they did not require a *baal keri* to mentally recite the blessings of the *Shema* (*Rav* and *Rashi*, from *Gem.* ibid.).[1]

The foregoing interpretation follows the *Gemara's* understanding of our mishnah, according to which the first words of the mishnah (*A baal keri contemplates in his mind*) refers to the text of the *Shema*. Accordingly, the following words (*but he does not recite the blessings [of the Shema]* etc.) must perforce teach that a *baal keri* does not even make a *mental* recitation of these blessings (see *Rabbeinu Yonah* 12a s.v. ואינו מברך).

Yerushalmi (3:4, cited by *Meleches Shlomo*), however, interprets the entire first clause of the mishnah (*A baal keri contemplates in his mind, but he does not recite the blessings*) to be referring to the blessings of the *Shema*. According to *Yerushalmi*, our mishnah does not allow a *verbal* recitation of these blessings, but *does* require a mental recitation. As for the *Shema* itself, *Yerushalmi* maintains that since its recitation is Biblically mandated, it is not subject to Ezra's decree; it is recited *verbally*. Similarly, the Biblically obligated Grace After Meals is articulated by a *baal keri*, whereas the blessings before eating are mentally recited.[2]

Shenos Eliyahu adopts *Yerushalmi's* understanding of the mishnah. He interprets the relevant passages in the *Gemara* in a manner consistent with this approach (see also *Rabbeinu Chananel*, ed. D. Metzger, editorial note 77,86).

---

1. Although the last of the four blessings which constitute the Grace After Meals — הַטּוֹב וְהַמֵּטִיב, *Hatov Vehameitiv* — is recited in fulfillment of a *Rabbinical* obligation (see *Gem.* 46a), the Rabbis instituted that this blessing always be recited together with the other blessings of the Grace (*Tos. R' Akiva* §31, citing *Pri Chadash*; see *Shaagas Aryeh* §14).

2. This ruling that Biblically mandated recitations may be performed verbally by a *baal keri*, whereas Rabbinical obligations are recited mentally, is actually the view of the *Tanna* R' Meir (see *Gem.* 22a). According to *Yerushalmi*, the *Tanna Kamma* of our mishnah is R' Meir. According to the understanding of the *Gemara*, however, R' Meir's view represents an opinion not cited by our mishnah (see *Shenos Eliyahu*; see also *P'nei Yehoshua* to 20b s.v. במשנה).

אוֹמֵר: מְבָרֵךְ לִפְנֵיהֶם וּלְאַחֲרֵיהֶם.

[ה] **הָיָה** עוֹמֵד בִּתְפִלָּה וְנִזְכַּר שֶׁהוּא בַעַל קֶרִי, לֹא יַפְסִיק, אֶלָּא יְקַצֵּר.

ר' עובדיה מברטנורא

בתורה ומתפללין ומברכין כל הברכות, ואין מטרטר בדבר: **(ה) לא יפסיק.** תפלתו לגמרי, אלא

יד אברהם

רַבִּי יְהוּדָה אוֹמֵר: מְבָרֵךְ לִפְנֵיהֶם וּלְאַחֲרֵיהֶם.
— R' Yehudah says: He recites the
blessings before them and following
them.

That is, a *baal keri* may *articulate*
both the blessings associated with the
Shema and the blessings pronounced
before eating. Certainly, R' Yehudah
allows a *baal keri* to verbally recite the
Biblically mandated *Shema* and Grace
After Meals (*Rabbeinu Yonah* 12a-b
s.v. רבי יהודה אומר).

R' Yehudah agrees that, due to
Ezra's enactment, a *baal keri* must purify himself before uttering words of
Torah. However, he contends that
Ezra's decree only forbids articulating
those words of Torah which require
that one become engrossed in his
learning, e.g. intricate, detailed halachic issues. It is, however, permitted to
utter straightforward and simple laws,
which require no mental exertion. R'
Yehudah maintains that the various
recitations discussed by our mishnah
fall in this latter category (*Rabbeinu
Yonah* ibid., from *Gem.* 22a).

Some commentators understand the

Gemara to mean that according to R' Yehudah, Ezra's decree only prohibits the articulation of Biblical texts (e.g. the three
sections of the *Shema*). Texts formulated
by the Rabbis, such as the blessings associated with the *Shema*, do not contain the
same degree of sanctity as Biblical ones,
and their recitation was therefore not included in Ezra's prohibition. Included in
the category of Rabbinical texts is the
Grace After Meals, for although the obligation to recite the Grace is Biblical, the
text of the blessing was formulated by the
Rabbis. According to this interpretation of
R' Yehudah's view, a *baal keri's* obligation
with regard to Rabbinical texts (e.g. the
blessings of the *Shema*) is *greater* than the
obligation regarding Biblical texts (such as
the *Shema*) — i.e. the former are articulated, while the latter is only contemplated;
in contrast, whereas the *Tanna Kamma*
obligates a *baal keri* to mentally recite the
Shema and other Biblical obligations, he
exempts a *baal keri* from any type of recitation of the blessings of the *Shema* and
similar Rabbinical obligations (*Shitah
Mekubetzes* to 22a s.v. אמר רב נחמן; *Lechem Shamayim* to mishnah 3:6, cited by
Tos. Anshei Shem there s.v. זב; see *Rashi* to
22a s.v. עשאן ר' יהודה and *Meleches Shlomo*
s.v. מהרהר בלבו).

5.

The following mishnah continues the discussion begun in the previous mishnah regarding the ways in which Ezra's decree affects obligatory recitations.
This leads to a discussion concerning factors which prohibit one from reciting
the *Shema*.

הָיָה עוֹמֵד בִּתְפִלָּה וְנִזְכַּר שֶׁהוּא בַעַל קֶרִי,
[If] one was standing in prayer and he

remembered that he is a baal keri,

As previously noted (see prefatory

3
5

says: He recites the blessings before them and following them.

5. [I]f] one was standing in prayer and he remembered that he is a *baal keri*, he should not stop
[praying]; rather, he should shorten [his prayer].

comments to previous mishnah), one who experiences a seminal emission is forbidden by Rabbinical decree to pray (i.e. to recite the *Shemoneh Esrei*). Since prayer is a Rabbinical obligation, a *baal keri* does not even mentally recite the text of the *Shemoneh Esrei* (*Meiri*, from *Gem.* 21a; see *Tosafos* ad loc. s.v. הא, cited by *Meleches Shlomo*; see comm. to previous mishnah s.v. ואינו מברך).[1] However, this ruling applies only if the *baal keri* has not yet started the *Shemoneh Esrei*. If he remembered that he is a *baal keri* only after beginning the *Shemoneh Esrei*, the following law applies:

לֹא יַפְסִיק, אֶלָּא יְקַצֵּר. — *he should not stop [praying]; rather, he should shorten [his prayer].*

Since he has already begun saying the *Shemoneh Esrei*, the *baal keri* may continue his verbal recitation, but should shorten each of the remaining blessings (*Rav; Rashi*) by reciting only their beginnings and ends [e.g. אַתָּה חוֹנֵן לְאָדָם דַּעַת בָּרוּךְ אַתָּה ה' חוֹנֵן הַדָּעַת] (*Meiri; Tos. Yom Tov;* see comm. to mishnah 4:3 s.v. רבי יהושע אומר).

Prayer is essentially a petition for Heavenly mercy. Due to the impor-

tance of appealing for Divine assistance, the Rabbis allow a *baal keri* to continue his recitation of the *Shemoneh Esrei*, albeit in an abridged form (see *Tos. Yom Tov* s.v. אלא יקצר).

In our mishnah's specific reference to the *Shemoneh Esrei,* some authorities see an indication that a *baal keri* who inadvertently began reciting the blessings of the *Shema* does interrupt his recitation. He does not even continue with a mental recitation, in accordance with the law that a *baal keri* does not even mentally recite Rabbinically mandated recitations (see previous mishnah). Since the blessings of the *Shema* are essentially expressions of thanksgiving rather than supplications for Divine aid, the Rabbis did not make the same allowance for these blessings as they did for the *Shemoneh Esrei* (see *Tos. Yom Tov* loc. cit.; *Tif. Yis.* §25; see also *Tos. Anshei Shem* s.v. בתוי"ח ד"ה אלא).

Others, however, contend that there is no difference between the *Shemoneh Esrei* and the blessings of the *Shema*. The blessings of the *Shema* also contain elements of supplication. In their view, a *baal keri* may continue his verbal recitation of the blessings of the *Shema* just as he may continue reciting the *Shemoneh Esrei*. Our mishnah refers to the *Shemoneh Esrei* simply to teach that *even* the *Shemoneh Esrei*, which consists of numerous blessings, may be completed in abridged form by a *baal keri* who mistakenly began to recite it. Certainly, one

1. Even according to *Rambam* (who maintains that there is a Biblical obligation to pray — see comm. to mishnah 3:3 s.v. וחייבין בתפלה), the obligation to pray at specific times of the day (i.e. in the morning, afternoon and evening) is Rabbinical. Thus, one is not *Biblically* obligated to recite a particular Prayer (*Meiri* ibid. and to 20b s.v. והמשנה החמישית).

יָרַד לִטְבֹּל: אִם יָכוֹל לַעֲלוֹת וּלְהִתְכַּסּוֹת וְלִקְרוֹת
עַד שֶׁלֹּא תָנֵץ הַחַמָּה, יַעֲלֶה וְיִתְכַּסֶּה וְיִקְרָא. וְאִם

─────── ר' עובדיה מברטנורא ───────

יקרא כל ברכה וברכה: ולקרות עד שלא תנץ החמה. שהותיקין מדקדקים על עלמן
לגמור קותה עם הנץ החמה, דכתיב (תהלים עב) ייראוך עם שמש:

יד אברהם

may continue reciting — in an abbreviated form —the relatively few blessings of the Shema (Pri Chadash, cited by Tos. Chadashim s.v. אלא יקצר; Chazon Nachum).

What the mishnah definitely *does* imply is that a baal keri may not continue a verbal recitation of the Shema he inadvertently started. Rather, he must recite the remainder of the Shema in his mind, as prescribed in the previous mishnah (Tosafos Yom Tov loc. cit.; Tif. Yis. §25; Lechem Shamayim).

The text of the Shemoneh Esrei was formulated by the Rabbis, so they can replace it with an abridged version at their discretion. The text of the Shema, on the other hand, is Biblical. It is therefore not subject to abridgment; one can only discharge his Shema obligation by reciting the complete text. Since a baal keri may not verbally recite the full text of the Shema, the law is that he continues his recitation in his mind (see Tos. Yom Tov ibid.).

◆§ Environments in which the Shema may not be recited

By Biblical law, it is forbidden to contemplate, and certainly forbidden to articulate, דְּבָרִים שֶׁבִּקְדֻשָׁה, *words of sanctity* (e.g. the various blessings, the Shema and words of Torah), in the proximity of excrement. This prohibition is derived from the verse (Deuteronomy 23:13-15): וְיָד תִּהְיֶה לְךָ מִחוּץ לַמַּחֲנֶה... וְכִסִּיתָ אֶת צֵאתֶךָ... וְהָיָה מַחֲנֶיךָ קָדוֹשׁ וְלֹא־יִרְאֶה בְךָ עֶרְוַת דָּבָר, You shall have a place outside the camp [in which to relieve yourself]... and you shall cover your excrement... so your camp shall be holy, so that He (i.e. God) shall not see a shameful thing among you. This teaches that words of sanctity may only be contemplated when "your camp (i.e. the area immediately surrounding a person) is holy," i.e. it contains no uncovered excrement (see Rashi to Shabbos 150a s.v. והיה מחניך קדוש). This prohibition includes contemplating words of sanctity in the presence of a foul odor that emanates from a tangible source [רֵיחַ רַע שֶׁיֵּשׁ לוֹ עִיקָּר] (see Shulchan Aruch, Orach Chaim 79:8; Mishnah Berurah §29). By Rabbinical decree, it is forbidden to contemplate words of sanctity where urine is present, even if the urine does not emit a bad odor (see Gem. 25a).

The concluding words of the passage (so that He shall not see a shameful thing among you) constitute a prohibition forbidding one to articulate words of sanctity when his or someone else's genitalia are visible to him (see Gem. 25b; Bava Metzia 114b with Rashi s.v. ערות דבר). [However, under these conditions, it is permitted to contemplate words of sanctity.] By Rabbinical enactment, this is forbidden, even if one's body is covered, if there is no physical separation (e.g. a belt) between his upper body and his genitalia (see Gem. ibid.).[1]

1. The nature of our commentary does not allow for a detailed treatment of the laws derived from this verse. We have therefore limited our comments to those aspects of these laws that are necessary for a proper understanding of our mishnah. The reader is referred to the preface of Beur Halachah to Orach Chaim 74 and 79 for a synopsis of the details of these laws.

3
5

[If] he went down to immerse [in a *mikveh*]: If he is able to go up [from the *mikveh*], cover himself, and recite [the *Shema*] before sunrise, he should go up, cover himself, and recite [it]. But if

YAD AVRAHAM

יָרַד לִטְבֹּל: — *[If] he went down to immerse [in a mikveh]:*

If the *baal keri* went to immerse himself in a *mikveh* so that he could verbally recite the *Shema* (*Meiri*), and it was time to recite the morning *Shema* . . .

אִם יָכוֹל לַעֲלוֹת וּלְהִתְכַּסּוֹת וְלִקְרוֹת עַד שֶׁלֹּא תָנֵץ הַחַמָּה, יַעֲלֶה וְיִתְכַּסֶּה וְיִקְרָא. — *If he is able to go up [from the mikveh], cover himself, and recite [the Shema] before sunrise, he should go up, cover himself, and recite [it].*

If there is sufficient time for the *baal keri* to emerge from the *mikveh*, cover his genitalia (see prefatory comments above), and recite the *Shema* before sunrise, he should do so.

The reference to "sunrise" does not imply that our mishnah follows the view of R' Eliezer that the deadline for reciting the morning *Shema* is sunrise (see mishnah 1:2). Rather, our mishnah refers to the practice of the וָתִיקִין, *vasikin* (the scrupulous ones), who always time their recitation of the *Shema* to finish with the rise of the sun (*Rambam Comm.*, from *Gem.* 25b; see further below, s.v. וְאִם לָאו).

The basis for this practice is the verse (*Psalms* 72:5): יִירָאוּךָ עִם־שָׁמֶשׁ, *They will fear You* (i.e. God) *with [the rising of] the sun,* which is understood to mean that we should demonstrate our awe of God — by accepting His sovereignty with our recitation of the *Shema* — at sunrise[1] (*Rav; Rashi* to 9b s.v. דכתיב).

Rabbeinu Yonah (4b s.v. תניא) implies that the verse in *Psalms* does not teach that one should complete the *Shema* by sunrise, but that one should *begin* his *Prayer* (i.e. the morning *Shemoneh Esrei*) with the rise of the sun. According to this view, this verse is the reason why the *vasikin* delay their recitation of the *Shema* until immediately before sunrise. Rather than performing this mitzvah at the earliest possible time (as is their custom with regard to other mitzvos), they delay its recitation in order to recite the *Shemoneh Esrei* (which ideally should be recited immediately after the final blessing of the *Shema* — see *Gem.* 4b) as the sun rises (*Tos. R' Akiva* §32; see also *Meiri; Tosafos* to 9b s.v. לקריאת שמע כותיקין and to *Yoma* 37b s.v. א"ל אביי; *Rosh* 1:10).

Rabbeinu Yonah comments further that the expression עִם־שָׁמֶשׁ, *with the sun,* does not connote the precise time of sunrise, but includes the period from sunrise until the sun begins to cast its light over the world, which is a few minutes after sunrise. Thus, one who prays the *Shemoneh Esrei* within this period of time also fulfills the ideal expressed in *Psalms.* The reason the *vasikin* were careful to complete their recitation of the *Shema before* sunrise and pray *at* sunrise is because the *Shema* should ideally be recited before sunrise; the period after sunrise is a *secondary* (*bedi'avad*) time to recite the *Shema.*

---

1. The full verse reads: יִירָאוּךָ עִם־שָׁמֶשׁ וְלִפְנֵי יָרֵחַ דּוֹר דּוֹרִים, and its literal meaning is: *They will fear You as long as the sun and moon endure, generation after generation.* In this context, the expression עִם־שָׁמֶשׁ does not refer to the *rise* of the sun. However, since the expression עִם־שָׁמֶשׁ literally means "*with* the sun," the verse is also understood to mean "They will fear You *with* the sun," i.e. as the sun rises.

לַאו, יִתְכַּסֶּה בַמַּיִם וְיִקְרָא. אֲבָל לֹא יִתְכַּסֶּה לֹא
בַמַּיִם הָרָעִים וְלֹא בְמֵי הַמִּשְׁרָה, עַד שֶׁיָּטִיל לְתוֹכָן

ר' עובדיה מברטנורא

יתבסה במים. ודוקא מיס עכורים שאין לבו רואה את הערוה, אבל צלולים לא: **במים הרעים.** מיס סרוחים: **במי המשרה.** מיס ששורין בהס פשתן: **עד שיטיל לתוכן מים.** חסורי מחסרא והכי קתני, ולא יקרא אלא מי רגלים עד שיתן לתוכן מים, ושיעור המיס שיטיל למי רגלים

יד אברהם

וְאִם לָאו, יִתְכַּסֶּה בַמַּיִם וְיִקְרָא. — But if not, he should cover himself with the water and recite the [Shema].

If time does not suffice for the baal keri to emerge from the mikveh, cover his genitalia, and complete his recitation of the Shema before sunrise, he should recite the Shema in the mikveh while submerged in its water. Since there is not enough time before sunrise to cover himself properly and recite the Shema, he may rely on the covering provided by the waters of the mikveh.

Although the Shema may be recited after sunrise, our mishnah extends this leniency so that one can fulfill the ideal of reciting the Shema before sunrise. However, Rashi (to 25b s.v. דילמא) implies that only those who are always careful to follow the optimal practice of the vasikin, to recite the Shema before sunrise, may rely on the cover provided by the mikveh waters to recite the Shema before sunrise. One who usually recites the Shema after sunrise may rely on the mishnah's leniency only if the time for reciting the Shema will have expired (i.e. the end of the third hour of the day — see mishnah 1:2) by the time he clothes himself.

However, Rabbeinu Yonah (loc. cit.; 13b s.v. היה עומד) maintains that the reason the mishnah makes allowances to enable one to recite the Shema before sunrise is because ideally the Shema should be recited before sunrise (see above s.v. אם יכול). Since this initial deadline applies to everyone, even those who do not follow the practice of the vasikin should recite the Shema in the mikveh if this is necessary in order to recite the Shema before sunrise (see also Tif. Yis. §26; see Rambam, Hil. Krias Shema 2:7).

Indeed, Rabbeinu Yonah notes that one who recites the Shema while in the mikveh will not be able to fulfill the ideal of reciting the Shemoneh Esrei immediately following the Shema (which, according to Rabbeinu Yonah, is the reason the vasikin delayed reciting the Shema until sunrise — see above s.v. אם יכול). By the time he emerges from the mikveh and clothes himself, the opportunity to fulfill this ideal will have passed. Nevertheless, the importance of reciting the Shema within the ideal time period outweighs this consideration.[1]

Assuming the water to which our mishnah refers to be clear, the Gemara (25b) asks: Granted that the water in which the person is submerged constitutes a covering of his genitalia,[2] it does not constitute a separation between his genitalia and his upper body (see prefatory comments above).

---

1. Meiri, however, implies that one may take advantage of the mishnah's leniency only if he will pray the Shemoneh Esrei immediately after the Shema. Evidently, Meiri does not consider the brief period needed to clothe oneself to be an interruption between the Shema and the Shemoneh Esrei.

2. Although his genitalia are visible through the transparent water, since they are submerged in the water, it suffices to avert his gaze from them (Raavad, cited by Rashba to 25b s.v. והלא).

3

5

not, he should cover himself with the water and recite [the *Shema*]. But he may not cover himself with foul water, nor with water used for soaking [flax], unless he pours [clean] water into [it].

How, then, can he rely on the covering provided by the water of the *mikveh* to recite the *Shema*? The *Gemara* answers that our mishnah refers to water that is murky. Such water *is* considered a separation between one's genitalia and his upper body. If the water is transparent, he may only recite the *Shema* if he stirs up mud from the bottom of the *mikveh* to cloud the water (see *Rav*).

Rama (*Darkei Moshe, Orach Chaim* 74:1 and *Hagahos* to *Shulchan Aruch, Orach Chaim* 74:2, cited by *Tif. Yis.* §27) infers from *Rashba* (to 25b s.v. והלא) and *Rabbeinu Yonah* (16b s.v. אבל צלולין) that the requirement that the waters of the *mikveh* not be transparent applies only when one is submerged up to his neck in the water. Since in this case both his genitalia and his upper body are in the same domain (the water of the *mikveh*), there is considered to be no separation between the two if the water is clear. However, if only the person's *lower body* is in the water, the water which covers his lower body is considered a separation between his genitalia and his upper body, and he may recite the *Shema* (cf. *Mor U'Ketziah* to *Tur Orach Chaim* 74 s.v. וכתב הרשב"א).

אֲבָל לֹא יִתְכַּסֶּה לֹא בַּמַּיִם הָרָעִים וְלֹא בְּמֵי הַמִּשְׁרָה, — *But he may not cover himself with foul water, nor with water used for soaking [flax],*

Although one may rely on the covering provided by water to recite the *Shema*, the water cannot be rancid. It is

forbidden to recite the *Shema* (or any other words of sanctity) where there is a foul odor (see prefatory comments above). Foul water, or water used for soaking flax, emits an unpleasant odor (*Rav*; *Rambam Comm.*).

עַד שֶׁיָּטִיל לְתוֹכָן מַיִם. — *unless he pours [clean] water into [it].*

The mishnah cannot be referring to pouring clean water into foul water or water used for soaking flax, for they are still malodorous even after clean water is poured into them (*Rashi*, from *Gem.* 25b). Rather, the mishnah refers to urine, the presence of which prohibits one from reciting the *Shema* even if the urine does not emit an odor [see prefatory comments above] (*Rav* and *Rashi*, from *Gem.* ibid.; see *Tos. Anshei Shem* s.v. עד שיטיל).[1] Our mishnah teaches that pouring clean water into the urine nullifies the urine, allowing one to recite the *Shema* (or other words of sanctity) in its vicinity.

The amount of water required to nullify urine is a *reviis*[2] for the product of each urination (*Gem.* 25b, as understood by *Rav*; *Rambam, Hil. Krias Shema* 3:10; *Shulchan Aruch, Orach Chaim* 77:2; see *Kesef Mishneh* ad loc.).

However, *Rashba* (to 25b s.v. כמה, as understood by *Beur HaGra* to *Orach Chaim* 77:2 and *Chacham Tzvi* §102) interprets the *Gemara* to mean that a single *reviis* of

---

1. The term לְתוֹכָן literally means *into them*. Our mishnah uses the plural pronoun when referring to urine because the Hebrew term for urine — מֵי רַגְלַיִם — is plural.

2. *A reviis* is a liquid measure variously estimated at from three to a bit more than five ounces.

ברכות
ג/ה

מַיִם. וְכַמָּה יַרְחִיק מֵהֶם וּמִן הַצּוֹאָה? אַרְבַּע
אַמּוֹת.

שֶׁל פֶּטֶס אַחַת, רְבִיעִית: וְכַמָּה ירחיק מהם. מִן הַמֵּי רַגְלַיִם שֶׁלֹּא הִטִּיל לְתוֹכָן מַיִם, וּמִן
הַצּוֹאָה: אַרְבַּע אַמּוֹת. וְדַוְקָא כְּשֶׁהֵיא לְנֶגְדּוֹ אוֹ לְאַחֲרָיו, אֲבָל לְפָנָיו מַרְחִיק כִּמְלֹא עֵינָיו:

water suffices to nullify *any* amount of urine.

Generally, the law of nullification requires that the nullifying element constitute the greater part of the mixture. However, since the prohibition against reciting words of sanctity in the presence of urine is only Rabbinical (see prefatory comments above), the Rabbis were lenient and ruled that a *reviis* of water nullifies even a greater amount of urine (*Rashba* ibid.).

וְכַמָּה יַרְחִיק מֵהֶם וּמִן הַצּוֹאָה? — *And how far must he distance himself from [it] and from excrement?*

At what distance from undiluted urine or excrement is one no longer considered to be in their proximity (*Rav; Rashi; Rambam Comm.*), and therefore permitted to recite the *Shema* and other words of sanctity?

The prohibition forbidding contemplating or articulating words of sanctity where there is uncovered excrement is derived from the verse, *So your camp shall be holy* (see prefatory comments above). Hence, the prohibition applies only when excrement is in the immediate proximity of the person reciting the words of sanctity ("your camp"). Thus, our mishnah inquires: At what distance is the excrement (or urine) not considered in "the camp" of this person?

Rav, Rashi and *Rambam* interpret the mishnah's inquiry to be referring to excre-

ment and urine. This implies that with regard to other foul-smelling objects, the prohibition against contemplating or articulating words of sanctity is not dependent on their presence in "your camp" (see *Beis Yosef* and *Bach, Orach Chaim* 86; *Aruch HaShulchan* 86:2). *Magen Gibborim* (*Shiltei HaGibborim* 86:1) posits that according to these authorities, one need only distance himself to the point at which the foul odor can no longer be detected.

However, *Yerushalmi* (cited by *Meleches Shlomo*) interprets the mishnah to be referring also to the foul-smelling water and the water used to soak flax previously mentioned by the mishnah (see also *Re'ah* to 25b s.v. ולא יתבסה; *Meiri*; *Tur* and *Shulchan Aruch, Orach Chaim* 86:1). According to this interpretation, the ruling our mishnah presently issues applies to all foul-smelling objects (see *Beis Yosef* and *Bach* ibid.).

אַרְבַּע אַמּוֹת. — *Four amos.*

A person's "camp" extends four *amos*. Thus, if one distances himself four *amos* from the excrement or undiluted urine, he may recite words of sanctity.[1]

There is a dispute in the *Gemara* (25a) concerning the point from which these four *amos* are measured. Rav Huna holds that the four *amos* are measured from the source of the odor, whereas Rav Chisda holds that they are measured from the point at which the stench can no longer be detected. According to Rav Chisda, if the odor is detectable up to two *amos* from the

1. There is some question as to whether our mishnah refers to a radius of four *amos* around a person, or an area four *amos* by four *amos* (see *Sheyorei Korban* to *Yerushalmi, Eiruvin* 4:1 s.v. מתפלל לוכסן; *Sheilas David, Yoreh Deah* 16:4).

3	And how far must he distance himself from [it]
5	and from excrement? Four *amos*.

pollutant, one may only recite words of sanctity six *amos* from the pollutant.

Rambam (*Hil. Krias Shema* 3:12) rules in accordance with Rav Huna that one may recite words of sanctity four *amos* away from the pollutant [provided that the stench does not reach that far (cf. *Rashi* to 25a s.v. מרחיק)]. *Shulchan Aruch* (*Orach Chaim* 79:1), however, rules in accordance with Rav Chisda that one must distance himself four *amos* from where the stench can no longer be detected (see *Tif. Yis.* §33).

If the pollutant is in a location that is ten *tefachim* higher or lower than where the person is standing, he may recite words of sanctity. In this case, the pollutant is considered to be in a separate domain, and not in "your camp" (*Gem.* 25a). Similarly, one may recite words of sanctity if the pollutant is in a separate room, even if it is within four *amos* (see *Rosh* 3:46; *Shulchan Aruch, Orach Chaim* 79:2).

The mishnah's ruling applies only if the excrement or urine is behind him or to his side, where he does not see it. If the pollutant is in front of him, he may not recite words of sanctity as long as it is within his field of vision (*Rav* and *Rambam Comm.*, from *Gem.* 26a).

One's field of vision is considered his "camp." As such, if the pollutant is within one view, his "camp" is not "holy," and he is subject to the prohibition forbidding the contemplation or articulation of words of sanctity in unclean places. However, if the pollutant is on a level either ten *tefachim* higher or ten *tefachim* lower than the person, or is in a different room, one may recite words of sanctity. Since the pollutant is in an entirely separate domain, it is not considered to be in his "camp," even though it is visible to him (*Rosh* loc. cit.).

Alternatively, the reason one may not recite words of sanctity when the pollutant is within his field of sight is because the concluding words of the verse in *Deuteronomy* 13:15 (*So that He shall not see a shameful thing among you*), from which we derive that one may not articulate words of sanctity when one's genitalia are visible (see prefatory comments above), refer also to excrement and other pollutants. Thus, just as it is forbidden to articulate words of sanctity within view of exposed genitalia, so it is prohibited to recite words of sanctity within view of excrement. Accordingly, even if the pollutant is in a separate domain, one may not recite words of sanctity, since the pollutant is nevertheless visible (*Rashba* to 25a s.v. היה מקום; see *Beur Halachah*, preface to *Orach Chaim* 79). [However, it is permissible to *contemplate* words of sanctity in this case, just as one may contemplate words of sanctity when one's genitalia are visible (*Beur Halachah* to 79:2 s.v. דוקא; see prefatory comments above).]

6.

The mishnah returns to its discussion of Ezra's decree requiring a *baal keri* to purify himself before articulating words of Torah or praying. The following mishnah discusses situations in which the *baal keri* is subject to an additional type of *tumah*, from which he cannot yet purify himself. The mishnah examines whether Ezra requires a *baal keri* to remove the *tumah* of *keri* even though the *baal keri* will remain *tamei* as a result of the other *tumah* he contracted, from which he cannot yet be purified. [As previously noted (see prefatory comments to mishnah 4), any *tumah* other than *keri* does not forbid Torah study and Prayer (see *Rif* 17b).]

[ו] זָב שֶׁרָאָה קֶרִי, וְנִדָּה שֶׁפָּלְטָה שִׁכְבַת זֶרַע, וְהַמְשַׁמֶּשֶׁת שֶׁרָאֲתָה נִדָּה

ר' עובדיה מברטנורא

(ו) **זב שראה קרי.** אַף עַל פִּי שֶׁטּוּמְאַת שֶׁבְּטֶבַע מִשּׁוּם זִיבָה וְאֵין טְבִילָה זוֹ מְטַהַרְתּוֹ, אֲפִילוּ הָכִי צָרִיךְ טְבִילָה לְדִבְרֵי תוֹרָה עֶזְרָא כְּתִקְנַת עֶזְרָא מִשּׁוּם קֶרִי. וְכֵן נִדָּה אִם בָּאָה לְהִתְפַּלֵּל וּפוֹלֶטֶת שִׁכְבַת זֶרַע הֲרֵי הִיא כְּבַעַל קֶרִי. וְשִׁכְבַת זֶרַע מְטַמֵּא הָאִשָּׁה בְּפָלִיטָתוֹ כָּל שְׁלשָׁה יָמִים לְאַחַר תַּשְׁמִישׁ, וּלְאַחַר מִכָּאן כְּבָר הִסְרִיחַ בַּגּוּפָהּ וְאֵין רָאוּי עוֹד לִהְיוֹת וָלָד נוֹצָר מִמֶּנּוּ. וְהָכִי פֵּירוּשׁוֹ, נִדָּה שֶׁפָּלְטָה עַתָּה תַשְׁמִישׁ שֶׁשִּׁמְּשָׁה אֶתְמוֹל קוֹדֶם שֶׁרָאֲתָה, וְהַמְשַׁמֶּשֶׁת מִטְּתָהּ שֶׁרָאֲתָה נִדָּה לְאַחַר שֶׁשִּׁמְּשָׁה, צְרִיכִין טְבִילָה:

יד אברהם

זָב שֶׁרָאָה קֶרִי, — *A zav who experienced a seminal emission,*

A *zav* is a male who experiences an irregular seminal discharge, known as a זִיבָה, *zivah* (lit. *a flow*), arising from a disorder of the male genitalia (see *Niddah* 35b; *Rambam, Hil. Mechusrei Kapparah* 2:1 for details regarding the type of seminal discharge classified as a *zivah*). After a single *zivah*, the *zav* becomes *tamei*. He may immerse in a *mikveh* immediately and becomes completely pure the evening following his immersion. One who experiences *two zivos* remains *tamei* until he counts seven "clean" days (i.e. days in which he is free from discharges), and then immerses in a spring. A *zav* who experiences *three* such discharges must also bring a set of sacrificial offerings to complete the purification process (see *Leviticus* 15:1-15).

Our mishnah refers to a *zav* who experienced two or more *zivos*, whose *tumah* therefore lasts for at least seven days. In addition, during this seven-day period, he experienced a seminal emission and became a *baal keri*. Thus, even if he were to immerse immediately to remove the *tumah* of

keri, he would still remain *tamei* as a *zav* (see *Rav; Rashi*).

וְנִדָּה שֶׁפָּלְטָה שִׁכְבַת זֶרַע, — *and a niddah who emits semen,*

A *niddah* is a woman who has menstruated. She is *tamei* for seven days, after which she immerses in a *mikveh* (see *Leviticus* 15:19). Besides the regular laws that apply to one who is *tamei*, a *niddah* is forbidden to engage in intimate relations until she purifies herself (ibid. 18:19).

A woman who emits viable semen (i.e. it is still capable of causing fertilization) becomes *tamei* to the same degree as a *baal keri* (see *Mikvaos* 8:3; *Shabbos* 9:3).[1] She is also subject to Ezra's decree forbidding a *baal keri* to articulate words of Torah and Prayer (*Rav; Rashi*).

With regard to the *Shema*, Ezra's decree is of little practical consequence to women, who are not obligated to recite the *Shema* (see mishnah 3). The principal effect of Ezra's decree on women concerns the prohibition regarding Prayer, an obligation which *is* incumbent on them [see ibid.] (see *Rav; Rambam Comm.;* see *Shoshanim L'David,* cited by *Tos. Anshei Shem* s.v. בר"ב ד"ה זב). The prohibition against Torah study also has a practical effect on

---

1. There is a difference of opinion regarding the length of time after intercourse the semen is considered fertile and therefore capable of rendering the woman *tamei*. The opinions range from as little as one full day and the fraction of a day to three full days [i.e. seventy-two hours] (see *Shabbos* 86a; *Mikvaos* 8:3).

3
6

6. **A** *zav* who experienced a seminal emission, and a *niddah* who emits semen, and a woman who had intercourse and saw *niddah* [blood]

women, for although women are not obligated in Torah study *per se* (see comm. to mishnah 3 s.v. ומן התפילין), they *do* study the laws of those commandments that apply to them (*Tif. Yis.* §37).

As previously noted (see prefatory comments to mishnah 4), Ezra's enactment was aimed primarily at Torah scholars, to deter them from engaging excessively in marital relations at the expense of their religious activities. Ezra included women in his decree because the requirement that she immerse in a *mikveh* before praying will cause a wife to discourage her husband from engaging in intimate relations inordinately (*Tos. Yom Tov* s.v. שפלטה).

Our mishnah refers to a woman who became a *niddah* and soon afterward emitted some of the semen she received through a previous act of intercourse. Even if she immerses to remove the *tumah* caused by her emission of semen, she will still remain *tamei* as a *niddah* (*Rav; Rashi; Rambam Comm.*).

As will soon be seen (s.v. והמשמשת), the act of intercourse itself renders a woman *tamei* like a *baal keri*, and thus subject to Ezra's decree. The present case of the mishnah deals with a woman who had immersed immediately after intercourse to remove the *tumah* of *keri*. Thus, her current status as a *baal keri* results from the semen she emitted after she became a *niddah* (*Rambam Comm.; Meiri*). The significance of this point will be discussed below (s.v. והמשמשת).

וְהַמְשַׁמֶּשֶׁת שֶׁרָאֲתָה נִדָּה — *and a woman who had intercourse and saw niddah [blood]*

The very act of intercourse renders a woman *tamei* as a *baal keri*, even if she does not emit any of the semen

(*Tos. Yom Tov*). This is derived from the verse (*Leviticus* 15:18): וְאִשָּׁה אֲשֶׁר יִשְׁכַּב אִישׁ אֹתָהּ שִׁכְבַת־זָרַע וְרָחֲצוּ בַמַּיִם וְטָמְאוּ עַד־הָעָרֶב, *A woman with whom a man will have carnal relations, they shall immerse themselves in the water and remain tamei until evening* (see *Rambam, Hil. Shaar Avos HaTumos* 5:9). Similarly, a woman who engages in intercourse is subject to Ezra's decree prohibiting Prayer and the articulation of Torah until she purifies herself (see *Tos. Yom Tov*).

Our mishnah refers to a case in which a woman engaged in intercourse and had not yet immersed when she became a *niddah*. In her present state, even after immersing in a *mikveh* to remove the *tumah* of *keri*, she will remain *tamei* as a *niddah* (see *Rav*; cf. *Rambam Comm.*, who apparently understands the mishnah to mean that the woman became a *niddah during* intercourse; see also *Ritva* to 26a s.v. איבעיא להו).

The principal difference between this case and the previous ones is which *tumah* came first. In the case of a *zav* who later had a seminal emission or a *niddah* who emitted semen, the person was first subject to the lengthier *tumah* (*zivah* or *niddah*), and only afterward became subject to the *tumah* of *keri*. In the latter case, the woman became a *baal keri* (as a result of intercourse) *before* contracting the lengthier *tumah* of *niddah*. The two types of cases represent two different aspects of the question of whether Ezra's decree applies in situations when the *baal keri* will remain

צְרִיכִין טְבִילָה. וְרַבִּי יְהוּדָה פּוֹטֵר:

ורבי יהודה פוטר. אַף בְּמִשַׁמֶּשֶׁת שֶׁרָאֲתָה נִדָּה פָּטַר רַבִּי יְהוּדָה, וְאַף עַל גַּב דְּמַטְיַקְרָא בַּת טְבִילָה הֲוָת וְאֵיכָא לְמֵימַר דְּלֹא פָּקְעָה חוֹבַת טְבִילָה מִינָהּ. וּכְבָר כָּתַבְנוּ לְעֵיל דְּבָטְלוּהָ לְטְבִילוּתָא מִפְּנֵי שֶׁהָיְתָה תַּקָּנָה שֶׁאֵין רוֹב הַצִּבּוּר יְכוֹלִין לַעֲמוֹד בָּהּ:

יד אברהם

tamei even after removing the *tumah* of *keri*. In the first two cases of the mishnah, the issue under consideration is whether the person's subsequent status as a *baal keri* subjects him to Ezra's decree in the first place. In the mishnah's third case, where the woman first became a *baal keri* (through intercourse), there was a period of time — before she became a *niddah* — during which she was undoubtedly subject to Ezra's decree. In this case, the question is whether the subsequent lengthier *tumah* abrogates the immersion requirement to which she had previously been subject (see *Gem.* 26a).

The mishnah could have easily illustrated the case of one who contracted the lengthier type of *tumah after* becoming a *baal keri* with the example of a *man* who experienced a seminal emission which subjected him to Ezra's decree, and afterward experienced a *zivah*. The reason the mish-

nah chooses to give the example of a woman who engaged in intercourse and afterward became a *niddah* is to teach incidentally that a woman becomes a *baal keri* simply by engaging in intercourse (*Tos. Yom Tov*, as explained by *Tos. R' Akiva* §33).

צְרִיכִין טְבִילָה. — *require immersion [in a mikveh].*

In all the aforementioned cases — even when he (or she) contracted the lengthier *tumah* first (see *Tif. Yis.*) — the *baal keri* is forbidden to pray or recite words of Torah until he (or she) immerses in a *mikveh* to remove the *tumah* of *keri*.

The *Tanna Kamma* maintains that Ezra's decree is not contingent on the *baal keri's* ability to purify himself, but rather on his ability to remove the *tumah* of *keri* for which Ezra instituted his enactment. Since immersion *will* remove the *tumah* of *keri*, if not the lengthier *tumah*, this *baal keri* is

3 require immersion [in a *mikveh*]. But R' Yehudah
6 exempts [them].

subject to the restrictions regarding Prayer and the recitation of words of Torah until he immerses (*Rav; Rashi; Rabbeinu Chananel; Ritva* to 20b s.v. ורמינהו; see *Rambam, Hil. Tefillah* 4:5).

וְרַבִּי יְהוּדָה פּוֹטֵר. — *But R' Yehudah exempts [them].*

In all the mishnah's cases, R' Yehudah exempts the *baal keri* from the requirement to immerse in a *mikveh* before reciting words of Torah. Even when the *tumah* of *keri preceded* the lengthier *tumah* — in which case the *baal keri* was certainly subject to Ezra's decree at one time — R' Yehudah maintains that the subsequent lengthier *tumah* abolishes the immersion requirement to which the *baal keri* had previously been subject [see above s.v. והמשמשת] (*Rav*; see *Gem.* 26a).

R' Yehudah contends that Ezra required immersion only where the *baal keri* can thereby attain a *complete* state of purity. Since in our mishnah's cases, the *baal keri* would remain *tamei* even after immersing, he is not subject to Ezra's decree and may recite

words of Torah in his present state (*Rabbeinu Yehonasan MiLunel* s.v. זב שראה; see also *Rabbeinu Chananel; Shitah Mekubetzes* to 21b s.v. תנן והזב; see *Shaarei Yosher* 2:21 for a different interpretation of the dispute of the *Tanna Kamma* and R' Yehudah).

As previously noted (comm. to mishnah 4 s.v. רבי יהודה אומר), most commentators maintain that according to R' Yehudah, Ezra's decree only prohibits articulating those words of Torah that cause one to become engrossed in his learning. According to these commentators, R' Yehudah issues his ruling here only with regard to such Torah study; for according to R' Yehudah, even a *baal keri* who is *not* subject to a lengthier type of *tumah* is permitted to recite the *Shema* and the *Shemoneh Esrei* (see *Tos. Yom Tov; Tos. R' Akiva* §33).

Others, however, maintain that R' Yehudah only allows a *baal keri* to recite texts that are of Rabbinical origin, but forbids the articulation of Biblical texts, such as the *Shema* (see comm. ibid.). According to this understanding, R' Yehudah issues his ruling with regard to the *Shema* as well (*Lechem Shamayim*, cited by *Tos. Anshei Shem*).

פרק רביעי ﴾₪﴿
Chapter Four

[א] **תְּפִלַּת** הַשַּׁחַר עַד חֲצוֹת. רַבִּי יְהוּדָה
אוֹמֵר: עַד אַרְבַּע שָׁעוֹת.

───────── ר' עובדיה מברטנורא ─────────

פרק ד – תפלת השחר. (א) תפלת השחר עד חצות. שכן תמיד של שחר קרב עד
חצות לרבנן, ולרבי יהודה אינו קרב אלא עד ארבע שעות ביום. ועד ארבע שעות היינו עד סוף
שעה רביעית שהוא שליש היום היום בזמן שהיום שתים עשרה שעות, וכן זמנה לעולם עד סוף
שליש היום לפי אורך הימים וקוטנן כדכתבינן לעיל גבי קריאת שמע. והלכה כרבי יהודה:

יד אברהם

1.

Having completed its discussion of the laws of the *Shema*, the mishnah turns
to the laws of Prayer, i.e. the *Shemoneh Esrei*.

The various Prayers were instituted by the Rabbis to correspond to the communal sacrifices that were offered in the Temple.[1] The Morning Prayer
(*Shacharis*) and Afternoon Prayer (*Minchah*) correspond to the daily *tamid*
offerings (see *Numbers* 28:1-8) that were offered at these times, as the verse (ibid.
v.4) states: אֶת־הַכֶּבֶשׂ אֶחָד תַּעֲשֶׂה בַבֹּקֶר וְאֵת הַכֶּבֶשׂ הַשֵּׁנִי תַּעֲשֶׂה בֵּין הָעַרְבָּיִם, *The one
lamb shall you make in the morning and the second lamb shall you make in the
afternoon.* The Evening Prayer (*Maariv*) corresponds to the burning on the
Altar of the fats and limbs of the afternoon *tamid*, which burned throughout the
night (see *Rambam, Hil. Tefillah* 1:6; *Tur, Orach Chaim* 235; cf. *Rashi* to 26b s.v.
אברים and s.v. ופדרים). The *Mussaf* (lit. *additional*) Prayer, which is recited on
the Sabbath, Rosh Chodesh and Holidays, corresponds to the additional sacrifices (known as *mussafim*) that were obligatory on these days [see *Numbers*
28:9-29:39] (*Gem.* 26b; see General Introduction).

The following mishnah delineates the time limits for reciting the various
Prayers. The period of time allotted for a particular Prayer is based on the time
during which its corresponding sacrifice was offered (see *Gem.* ibid.).[2]

תְּפִלַּת הַשַּׁחַר עַד חֲצוֹת. — *The Morning
Prayer [may be recited] until midday.*

The *Tanna Kamma* of our mishnah
maintains that the entire morning is

───────────────

1. According to one opinion cited by the *Gemara* (26b), the concept of thrice-daily Prayer
originated with the Patriarchs, each of whom instituted one of the Daily Prayers of
Shacharis, Minchah and *Maariv*. However, even this opinion agrees that the practice of
the Patriarchs was not binding on their descendants. The *obligation* to recite the three
Prayers was instituted later, by the Rabbis, based on the Temple sacrifices (see *Gem.* ibid;
Ritva ad loc. s.v. ואסמכינהו; *Maharitz Chayes* ad loc.; cf. *Tzlach* ad loc. s.v. ואסמכינהו).

2. In common parlance, the term "Prayer" is used to refer to the entire prayer service.
However, the mishnah generally uses the term in reference to the *Shemoneh Esrei*, which
is the portion of the service recited in fulfillment of the Rabbinical institution of thrice-
daily prayer. Similarly, our mishnah's discussion of the time limits for the various prayers
relates to the *Shemoneh Esrei* segment of each of these services. Other portions of the
service are subject to different time limits (e.g. the morning *Shema*, which may not be
recited before the time at which one can distinguish between *techeiles* and white wool, and
must be completed by the end of the third hour of the day — see mishnah 1:2).

1. The Morning Prayer [may be recited] until midday. R' Yehudah says: Until four hours [into

YAD AVRAHAM

acceptable for reciting the *Shemoneh Esrei* of *Shacharis*. This opinion reflects the view that the morning *tamid* sacrifice may be offered until midday (*Rav* and *Rambam Comm.*, from *Gem.* 26b; see prefatory comments).

As the source of the view that the deadline for offering the morning *tamid* sacrifice (and hence the deadline for the *Shemoneh Esrei* of *Shacharis*) is midday, *Yerushalmi* (4:1, cited by *Meiri*) cites the verse (*Numbers* 28:3) which states concerning the *tamid* offerings: שְׁנַיִם לַיּוֹם עֹלָה תָמִיד, *two a day, as a continual olah.* The expression "two a day" is expounded to mean that the day is divided into two equal parts regarding the *tamid* offerings. The first half of the day (from dawn until midday) is the time during which the morning *tamid* may be offered, and the second half of the day (from midday until evening) is the time during which the afternoon *tamid* may be offered.

The mishnah does not discuss the earliest time for reciting *Shacharis*. *Rosh* (4:1, cited by *Meleches Shlomo*) postulates that the earliest one may pray *Shacharis* is dawn, as that is the earliest point at which the morning *tamid* may be offered (see *Yoma* 3:1, *Tamid* 3:2; see comm. to mishnah 1:1 s.v. רבן גמליאל אומר for the halachic definition of "dawn"). Indeed, *Rosh* explains that, having indicated that *Shacharis* and the morning *tamid* offering are linked (by giving midday as the deadline for reciting *Shacharis*), the mish-

nah felt it unnecessary to explicitly mention the earliest time one may recite *Shacharis*, for it is self-evident that this depends on the start of the period during which the morning *tamid* may be offered.[1]

Rosh adds, however, that the *Shemoneh Esrei* of *Shacharis* should preferably be recited at sunrise.[2] This is the practice of the *vasikin*, the scrupulous ones, who conclude the morning *Shema* and its associated blessings at sunrise and immediately begin the *Shemoneh Esrei*, in fulfillment of the verse, *They will fear You with [the rising of] the sun* [*Psalms* 72:5] (see *Gem.* 26a; comm. to mishnah 3:5 s.v. אם יכול לעלות).

רַבִּי יְהוּדָה אוֹמֵר: עַד אַרְבַּע שָׁעוֹת. — R' *Yehudah says: Until four hours [into the day].*

That is, until the *end* of the fourth hour (*Rav*, from *Gem.* 27a).

The mishnah refers here to שָׁעוֹת זְמַנִּיּוֹת, *seasonal hours,* i.e. the units of time obtained by dividing the day into twelve equal segments, the length of which vary according to the length of the day (see comm. to mishnah 1:2 s.v. רבי יהושע אומר; see footnote there regarding the definition of "day" in this regard). Thus, R' Yehudah's deadline represents a third of any given day (*Rav; Rambam Comm.*).

In R' Yehudah's opinion, the deadline for bringing the morning *tamid*

1. The reason the mishnah demonstrates the connection between the morning *tamid* and *Shacharis* by giving the *latest* time for reciting *Shacharis*, rather than the *earliest* time, is because the mishnah must refer to the deadline for *Shacharis* in any case, since it is the subject of a dispute, as will soon be seen (*Maadanei Yom Tov* ad loc. §3).

2. Indeed, most authorities maintain that in normal circumstances, Prayer before sunrise is valid only after the fact. Only in extenuating circumstances may one initially pray before sunrise (see *Shulchan Aruch* 89:1 with *Mishnah Berurah* §4). Another factor to be considered is that although Prayer after dawn is valid, one who prays before the time when he is able to distinguish between *techeiles* and white wool (the earliest time one may recite the *Shema* — see mishnah 1:2) is unable to fulfill the ideal of reciting the *Shema* and its blessings before the *Shemoneh Esrei* [see *Gem.* 4b] (*Beur Halachah* ad loc. s.v. יצא).

תְּפִלַּת הַמִּנְחָה עַד הָעֶרֶב. רַבִּי יְהוּדָה אוֹמֵר: עַד

תפלת המנחה עד הערב. עד שתחשך:

יד אברהם

offering is the end of the fourth hour of the day. Accordingly, he rules that *Shacharis* must be recited before this time (*Rav, Rambam Comm.*).

R' Yehudah's ruling is based on his view that as used in Scripture, the term "morning" connotes the period from dawn until the end of the fourth hour of the day (*Yerushalmi* 4:1; see *Gem.* 27a). Accordingly, the morning *tamid* sacrifice — regarding which the verse (*Numbers* 28:4) states: "The one lamb shall you make in the *morning*" — must be brought before the end of the fourth hour of the day (*Yerushalmi* ibid.; *Meiri*).

The halachah is decided in favor of R' Yehudah (*Rav*, from *Gem.* 27a; see *Shulchan*

Aruch, Orach Chaim 89:1). However, even R' Yehudah agrees that one who recites the *Shemoneh Esrei* between the end of the fourth hour and midday, discharges his *Shacharis* obligation, although not the obligation to recite the *Shacharis Shemoneh Esrei* within the time period established by the Rabbis (*Rambam, Hil. Tefillah* 3:1; *Meiri*; see also *Rif* 18a; *Rosh* §1). Therefore, if one missed R' Yehudah's deadline, even if willfully, he should recite *Shacharis* until midday. After midday, he should not recite *Shacharis* (*Shulchan Aruch* ibid. and *Rama*); rather, he should recite an additional *Shemoneh Esrei* when praying *Minchah* (see *Gem.* 26a; below s.v. ושל מוספים), but only if his failure to pray *Shacharis* was inadvertent (*Mishnah Berurah* ad loc. §7).

⇐§ *Minchah Gedolah* and *Minchah Ketanah*

A proper understanding of our mishnah's next clause requires an explanation of the terms מִנְחָה גְדוֹלָה, *minchah gedolah* (lit. *the greater minchah*), and מִנְחָה קְטַנָּה, *minchah ketanah* (lit. *the smaller minchah*).

With regard to the *Minchah* Prayer, the afternoon is divided into two segments, *minchah gedolah* and *minchah ketanah*. *Minchah gedolah*, the first portion of the afternoon, begins a (seasonal) half-hour after midday and lasts three (seasonal) hours, i.e. until nine and a half hours into the day. The time remaining until the end of the day — two and a half (seasonal) hours — is called *minchah ketanah* (see below s.v. תפילת המנחה regarding when the day is considered to end as regards *Minchah*).

This division of the afternoon is based on the time when the afternoon *tamid* was usually offered. Technically, the afternoon *tamid* may be offered beginning six and a half hours into the day (i.e. half an hour after midday). In practice, however, it was usually slaughtered at eight and a half hours into the day, and offered on the Altar an hour later (see *Pesachim* 5:1). This was done to allow the public more time for their voluntary offerings, which may not be slaughtered after the afternoon *tamid* (see *Gem.* ibid. 58a). On the Fourteenth of *Nissan*, the afternoon *tamid* was slaughtered an hour earlier, to allow extra time to bring the *korban pesach*, which must be offered *after* the afternoon *tamid*. On the rare occasions when the Fourteenth of *Nissan* came out on a Friday, the afternoon *tamid* would be slaughtered at the earliest time possible (six and a half hours into the day), to allow time to roast the *korban pesach*, which could not be done on the night of the Sabbath (*Pesachim* 5:1 and *Gem.* ibid.). *Minchah gedolah*

4
1

the day]. The *Minchah* Prayer [may be re-
cited] until evening. R' Yehudah says: Until

YAD AVRAHAM

represents the period of time during which it is permissible, but not usual, to offer the afternoon *tamid*. *Minchah ketanah* begins at the time in the afternoon when the *tamid* was usually offered on the Altar.

תְּפִלַּת הַמִּנְחָה עַד הָעֶרֶב. — *The Minchah prayer [may be recited] until evening.*

That is, it may be recited until the onset of darkness (*Rav; Rashi*), i.e. until צֵאת הַכּוֹכָבִים, *the emergence of the stars* (the appearance of three middle-sized stars in the sky), at which time halachah considers night to begin [see comm. to mishnah 1:1 s.v. משעה שהכהנים] (see *Shulchan Aruch, Orach Chaim* 233:1).[1]

The *Minchah* Prayer corresponds to the afternoon *tamid* offering, and the deadline for its recitation is therefore linked to the deadline for offering this sacrifice (see prefatory comments). The *Tanna Kamma* maintains that the afternoon *tamid* can be offered until evening (see *Gem.* 26b).

Many commentators, however, argue that the term "evening" cannot be referring to night, but rather to sunset. These authorities contend that all sacrifices, including the *tamid* offering to which the *Minchah* Prayer is linked, must be offered by sunset.

Afterward, the blood of the offering becomes unfit to sprinkle on the Altar — a part of the service essential to the validity of the offering (see *Tosafos* to *Zevachim* 56a s.v. מנין לדם, citing *Rabbeinu Tam*). Since the deadline for reciting *Minchah* depends on the deadline for offering the afternoon *tamid* sacrifice, these authorities maintain that the *Tanna Kamma's* deadline for praying *Minchah* is sunset[2] (*Rabbeinu Yonah* 18a s.v. תפילת המנחה; see also *Rambam Comm.* and *Hil. Tefillah* 3:4; *Meiri*; cf. *Shaagas Aryeh* §17, who argues that it *is* possible to offer sacrifices after sunset).

Shulchan Aruch and *Rama* (*Orach Chaim* 233:1) follow the view that one may recite *Minchah* until nightfall. However, *Mishnah Berurah* (§14) notes that it is certainly desirable to pray before sunset, in accordance with those who maintain that *Minchah* after sunset is invalid.

The commentators offer various explanations as to why the afternoon Prayer is given the appellation "the *Minchah* Prayer." *Rambam Comm.* explains that the term *minchah* is the name given to the last two and a half (seasonal) hours of the

---

1. Actually, the deadline for reciting *Minchah* is somewhat earlier than *the emergence of the stars*. The period before these stars appear is known as בֵּין הַשְּׁמָשׁוֹת, *twilight*, and its halachic status as day or night is uncertain. Since this period may possibly no longer be day, one must recite *Minchah* before this time begins (see *Mishnah Berurah* 233:14).

The authorities disagree regarding the start of this twilight period. Some maintain that it begins at sunset (see *Teshuvos Maharam Alshakar* §96, citing *Rav Hai Gaon* and *Rav Shereira Gaon; Beur HaGra* to *Orach Chaim* 261:2). According to this view, *Minchah* must be recited before sunset. According to others, this twilight period begins three-quarters of a *mil* (between fourteen and eighteen minutes — see *Beur Halachah* to *Shulchan Aruch* ibid. s.v. מתחילת השקיעה) before *the emergence of the stars* (see *Rabbeinu Tam*, cited by *Tosafos* to *Pesachim* 94a s.v. רבי יהודה אומר). Accordingly, *Minchah* may be recited for some time after sunset (see *Mishnah Berurah* ibid. §9).

2. As noted above (see previous footnote), many authorities maintain that the deadline for reciting *Minchah* is sunset for a different reason; because the period of twilight — which may possibly be night — begins at sunset.

עַד פְּלַג הַמִּנְחָה. זְמַן מִנְחָה קְטַנָּה הוּא מִתְּשַׁע שָׁעוֹת וּמֶחֱצָה עַד הַלַּיְלָה, שֶׁהֵם שְׁתֵּי שָׁעוֹת וּמֶחֱצָה, נִמְצָא פְּלַג הַמִּנְחָה שֶׁהוּא חֲצִי שִׁעוּר זֶה שָׁעָה וּרְבִיעַ. וּפָסַק הַהֲלָכָה בָּזֶה, דְּעָבַד כְּמַר עָבַד וְדַעֲבַד

יד אברהם

afternoon (i.e. *minchah ketanah*). Since the afternoon Prayer should ideally be recited during this time (as will be seen below), the Prayer became known as "the *Minchah* Prayer," i.e. the Prayer recited during the time known as *Minchah*. [However, *Rambam* does not explain why this period of time is called *Minchah*.] In a similar vein, *Tos. Yom Tov* notes that *Ramban* (to *Exodus* 12:6) interprets the term מִנְחָה, *minchah*, to mean *rest*, and explains that it refers to the gradual setting of the sun that begins at noon. Thus, the afternoon is known as *Minchah*.

Tosafos (to *Pesachim* 107a s.v. סָמוּךְ, cited by *Tos. Yom Tov*) understand the term *minchah* to be a reference to the *korban minchah* (meal-offering) which was brought together with each of the *tamid* offerings (see *Numbers* 28:5). Based on the *Gemara* (*Berachos* 6b), *Tosafos* suggest that the time at which the meal-offering of the afternoon *tamid* is brought is a particularly propitious time for reciting the Afternoon Prayer. Thus, the Prayer became known as "the Prayer of the *Minchah*" (see also *Shenos Eliyahu*).

As by *Shacharis*, the mishnah does not mention the earliest time one may recite *Minchah*. A Baraisa cited by the *Gemara* (26b) sets this time at six and a half hours into the day (i.e. *minchah gedolah*), which is the earliest point at which the afternoon *tamid* may be offered.[1]

Rambam (*Hil. Tefillah* 3:2) rules that although Prayer during the period of *minchah gedolah* is valid, ideally one should not recite *Minchah* before *minchah ke-*

tanah, since this was the time the *tamid* was usually offered on the Altar. *Tur* (*Orach Chaim* 233), however, does not seem to differentiate between *minchah gedolah* and *minchah ketanah* (see *Beis Yosef* ad loc. s.v. וּמִדִּבְרֵי רַבֵּינוּ). *Shulchan Aruch* (*Orach Chaim* 233:1) follows the view of *Rambam*.

רַבִּי יְהוּדָה אוֹמֵר: עַד פְּלַג הַמִּנְחָה. — *R' Yehudah says: Until plag haminchah.*

The term פְּלַג הַמִּנְחָה (lit. *half-minchah*) is the name given to the midway point between the beginning of *minchah ketanah* and the end of the day, i.e. one and a quarter (seasonal) hours before the end of the day (*Rav; Rambam Comm.;* see *Gem.* 27a).

R' Yehudah disputes the position of the *Tanna Kamma* that *Minchah* may be recited the entire afternoon. In his view, the deadline for reciting *Minchah* is one and a quarter hours before the end of the day, i.e. until ten and three-quarter hours into the day.

In a Baraisa cited by the *Gemara* (26b), R' Yehudah states that his *plag haminchah* deadline for reciting *Minchah* is based on the time when the afternoon *tamid* was offered. *Meiri* understands this to mean that R' Yehudah disputes the view of the *Tanna Kamma* that the afternoon *tamid* may be offered until evening. According to R' Yehudah, the deadline for offering the *tamid* is *plag haminchah* (see *Meiri* for the Scriptural source of this view). Thus, *Minchah* — which is linked to this offering — may also only be recited until this time.[2]

---

1. Although the afternoon begins after midday, the afternoon *tamid* may not be offered until half an hour later. According to some, this half-hour is a Rabbinical safeguard to ensure that the *tamid* not be inadvertently slaughtered before midday (see *Magen Avraham* 89:5, 233:1; *Pri Chadash* to *Orach Chaim* 233:1; see also *Yerushalmi* 4:1, cited above s.v. תפלת השחר). However, *Rashi* (to 26b s.v. מנחה גדולה and to *Pesachim* 58a s.v. אלא; see also *Mishnah Berurah* 233:1; but see *Rashi* to *Pesachim* 93b s.v. חמשה עשר) implies that Biblical law prohibits the offering of the afternoon *tamid* before half an hour after noon.

2. *Hashlamah* takes a somewhat different approach. He suggests that R' Yehudah

Shenos Eliyahu, however, implies that R' Yehudah agrees that, strictly speaking, the deadline for the afternoon *tamid* is evening. Nevertheless, practically, it was not feasible to bring the *tamid* after *plag haminchah*, because the various Temple services which followed the *tamid* also had to be performed before evening. R' Yehudah based his *plag haminchah* deadline for reciting *Minchah* on the *practical* deadline for offering the afternoon *tamid*.

Tosafos (to 26b s.v. עד as explained by *Lechem Mishneh, Hil. Tefillah* 3:2) reject the notion that R' Yehudah's deadline for reciting *Minchah* is linked to the afternoon *tamid*. Rather, *Tosafos* explain that *plag haminchah* is the time when the afternoon incense was usually burned on the Inner Altar of the Temple (see *Exodus* 30:8). In R' Yehudah's opinion, the Rabbis linked the *Minchah* Prayer not with the afternoon *tamid* itself, but with the offering of this incense which *followed* the *tamid* (see *Yoma* 3:5),[1] and based the deadline for reciting *Minchah* on the time this incense was usually offered. [However, it is not clear how *Tosafos* know that this incense was usually offered at *plag haminchah* (*Meleches Shlomo*; see also *Pnei Yehoshua* to 26b s.v. בתוס׳ בד״ה עד פלג and s.v. בגמרא מ״ט אמרו).]

The time for *Maariv* begins after the deadline for praying *Minchah*. Thus, the dispute between the *Tanna Kamma* and R' Yehudah pertains, as well, to the earliest time one may recite

Maariv. According to the *Tanna Kamma*, one may not recite *Maariv* before evening. According to R' Yehudah, one may recite *Maariv* beginning after *plag haminchah* (see *Rav* s.v. עד פלג; *Shenos Eliyahu*).

The *Gemara* (27a) is uncertain whether the halachah is decided in accordance with the *Tanna Kamma* or R' Yehudah. Consequently, the *Gemara* rules that one may follow whichever view he wishes. However, one must be consistent. Thus, if one prays *Maariv* after *plag haminchah* in accordance with R' Yehudah, he should not recite *Minchah* on another occasion after *plag haminchah* in accordance with the *Tanna Kamma*, since this contradicts his usual practice (*Rav*; *Rabbeinu Yonah* 18b s.v. דעבד כמר עבד; *Rosh* §4 et al.).

However, in such a case, his Prayer is valid after the fact. In extenuating circumstances, he may even initially recite *Minchah* after *plag haminchah*, even if he usually follows the view of R' Yehudah (*Shulchan Aruch, Orach Chaim* 233:1).[2] However, even in extenuating circumstances he may not recite *Maariv* before evening on the same day he recited *Minchah* after *plag haminchah*, since he thereby contradicts his practice of the very same day (see *Mishnah Berurah* 233:11).

expounds the verse (*Numbers* 28:3) which states regarding the *tamid*, "two a day, as a continual *olah*," to teach that the Torah allots the same amount of time for the afternoon *tamid* as the morning *tamid* — four hours (see above s.v. רבי יהודה אומר עד ארבע שעות). Since the earliest point at which the afternoon *tamid* may be offered is six and a half hours into the day, the deadline for the afternoon *tamid* according to R' Yehudah is actually ten and a *half* hours into the day. The extra fifteen minutes R' Yehudah allots for *Minchah* corresponds to the additional time it takes to place on the Altar the two logs that were added after the afternoon *tamid* (see *Yoma* 2:5). [Evidently, *Hashlamah* is of the opinion that *Biblically* the afternoon *tamid* may not be offered earlier than a half-hour after midday (see previous footnote).]

1. The connection between the incense offering and the *Minchah* Prayer is based on the verse (*Psalms* 141:2): תִּכּוֹן תְּפִלָּתִי קְטֹרֶת לְפָנֶיךָ מַשְׂאַת כַּפַּי מִנְחַת עָרֶב, *Let my prayer stand as incense before You; the lifting of my hands as an afternoon offering* (*Tosafos* ibid.; see also *Yerushalmi* 4:1).

2. Another exception to this rule is the Friday-night *Maariv*. Even one who customarily recites *Minchah* after *plag haminchah* in accordance with the *Tanna Kamma* may recite

---

ר' עוֹבַדְיָה מִבַּרְטְנוּרָא

כְּמַר עֲבַד, וּהֲרוֹצֶה לַעֲשׂוֹת כְּדִבְרֵי חֲכָמִים וּלְהִתְפַּלֵּל תְּפִלַּת הַמִּנְחָה עַד הָעֶרֶב יַעֲשֶׂה, וּבִלְבַד שֶׁלֹּא יִתְפַּלֵּל עַרְבִית בַּזְּמַן הַזֶּה, שֶׁכֵּיוָן שֶׁמֵּחֲשִׁיב אוֹתוֹ יוֹם לְעִנְיַן שֶׁמִּתְפַּלֵּל בּוֹ מִנְחָה אֵינוֹ יָכוֹל לְהַחֲשִׁיבוֹ לַיְלָה וּלְהִתְפַּלֵּל בּוֹ עַרְבִית. וְאִם בָּא לַעֲשׂוֹת כְּדִבְרֵי רַבִּי יְהוּדָה שֶׁלֹּא לְהִתְפַּלֵּל מִנְחָה אֶלָּא עַד פְּלַג הַמִּנְחָה שֶׁהוּא שָׁעָה וּרְבִיעַ קֹדֶם הַלַּיְלָה עוֹשֶׂה וּמִשָּׁם וְאֵילָךְ יוּכַל לְהִתְפַּלֵּל עַרְבִית: **אֵין לָהּ קֶבַע.** זְמַנָּהּ כָּל הַלַּיְלָה. וְהָא דְתָנֵי אֵין לָהּ קֶבַע וְלֹא קָתָנֵי כָּל זְמַנָּהּ כָּל הַלַּיְלָה, לְאַשְׁמְעִינַן דִּתְפִלַּת עַרְבִית רְשׁוּת, לְפִי שֶׁהִיא כְּנֶגֶד הַקְרָבַת אֵיבָרִים וּפְדָרִים שֶׁקְּרֵבִים כָּל הַלַּיְלָה, וְהַךְ רְשׁוּת גִּינְהוּ שֶׁכֵּיוָן שֶׁזָּרַק הַדָּם נִגְרָסֶה הַקָּרְבָּן אַף עַל פִּי שֶׁנִּטַמְּאוּ אֵיבָרִים וּפְדָרִים אוֹ שֶׁאָבְדוּ. וּמִיהוּ הָאִידְנָא קַבְּלוּהָ עֲלֵיהֶם כְּחוֹבָה: **וְשֶׁל מוּסָפִין בָּל הַיּוֹם.** אִם מֵחֲרָה אַחַר שֶׁבַע יָצָא, אֲבָל נִקְרָא פּוֹשֵׁעַ. וְכֵן הֲלָכָה:

יד אברהם

תְּפִלַּת הָעֶרֶב אֵין לָהּ קֶבַע. — *The Evening Prayer has no set [time].*

That is, the evening *Maariv* Prayer may be recited at any time during the night (*Rav, Rashi*). This Prayer corresponds to the placing and burning of fats and limbs of the afternoon *tamid* on the Altar (see prefatory comments), which burned throughout the night. Therefore, the Rabbis allotted the entire night to recite *Maariv* (see *Rav*, from Gem. 26b).

Alternatively, the Rabbis were more lenient with regard to the *Shemoneh Esrei* of *Maariv* and did not set a time limit for its recitation, because the burning of the fats and limbs of an offering are not essential to its validity (*Rambam Comm.*; cf. *Rabbeinu Yonah* 18b-19a s.v. מאי אין לה קבע, cited by *Tos. Chadashim*).

The mishnah could have simply stated, "The Evening Prayer [may be recited] the entire night." The mish-

nah's choice of terminology indicates a fundamental aspect of the *Maariv* prayer that distinguishes it from the morning and *Minchah* prayers — viz. the *Shemoneh Esrei* of *Maariv* is an optional, not an obligatory, prayer. The expression אֵין לָהּ קֶבַע (lit. *it has no set*) implies not only that the *time* for reciting the *Maariv Shemoneh Esrei* is not restricted to a particular time of night, but also that there is no set obligation to recite this Prayer at all (see *Rabbeinu Yonah* loc. cit.).[1]

The reason the Rabbis did not institute *Maariv* as an obligation is because the sacrificial service to which it is linked — the burning of the fats and limbs of the *tamid* on the Altar — is not essential to the validity of the sacrificial offering. As long as the blood of the offering is properly sprinkled on the Altar, the offering is valid, even if its parts are lost or disqualified and

the Friday-night *Maariv* before evening (provided he recited the Friday-afternoon *Minchah* before *plag haminchah*, so that his practice is not contradictory on the very same day). The basis for this leniency is that once one accepts the Sabbath early (as indeed we are commanded to do) he may consider it nighttime in regard to praying, as well (*Mishnah Berurah* 267:3). The practice of praying *Maariv* early on Friday night is very common in the summertime in the more northerly latitudes, where waiting until dark to pray would mean not commencing the Friday-night meal until quite late.

1. Again, we stress that our mishnah discusses only the *Shemoneh Esrei* of the evening service, which it refers to as *Maariv*. The *Shema* that is part of the evening service is recited in fulfillment of a Biblical obligation and is in no way discretionary.

4
1

plag haminchah. The Evening Prayer has no set
[time]. And the *Mussaf* Prayer [may be recited]

therefore not burnt on the Altar (*Rav*, from *Gem.* 27b; *Rashi* to Shabbos 9b s.v. למאן דאמר).

There are two different understandings of the optional nature of *Maariv*. *Tosafos* (to 26a s.v. טעה and to 27b s.v. הלכה) explain that the *Gemara* does not mean one can forgo reciting *Maariv* at will. Rather, if one must choose between performing a mitzvah whose time will pass or reciting *Maariv*, then due to the less rigid nature of the *Maariv* obligation, he should perform the mitzvah rather than recite *Maariv*. The *Gemara* means that in relation to another mitzvah, *Maariv* is discretionary.

Others maintain that indeed the Rabbis instituted *Maariv* as a voluntary prayer. However, reciting *Maariv* even once constitutes an acceptance to recite it always, and it takes on the force of a binding obligation (see *Rif* 19a and *Shiltei HaGibborim* §1; *Meiri*).

However, Jews everywhere have always prayed *Maariv* and have accepted it as a binding obligation; thus, one is not permitted to forgo its recitation (*Rav*; see also *Rambam, Hil. Tefillah* 1:6 and 9:9).

Nevertheless, certain vestiges of *Maariv's* original elective nature remain. For example, the *chazzan* does not repeat the *Shemoneh Esrei* of *Maariv* as he does for the *Shemoneh Esrei* of the other Prayers (see *Mishnah Berurah* 237:1).

וְשֶׁל מוּסָפִין כָּל הַיּוֹם. — *And the Mussaf Prayer [may be recited] the entire day.*

The *Mussaf* Prayer recited on the Sabbath, Holidays and *Rosh Chodesh* corresponds to the additional sacrifices (*mussafim*) offered in the Temple on these occasions [see *Numbers* 28:9-29:39] (see *Gem.* 26b with *Rashi* s.v. תפלת המוספין).

The *Tanna Kamma* maintains that these additional sacrifices are valid if offered at any time of the day (see *Megillah* 20b for the Scriptural source of this view), and thus one may recite the corresponding *Mussaf* Prayer throughout the day (*Gem.* 26b; *Megillah* ibid.). However, the *Gemara* (28a, as explained by *Rambam, Hil. Tefillah* 3:5; cf. *Ramach*, cited by *Kessef Mishneh* ad loc.) qualifies this ruling by stating that one who recites the *Mussaf* Prayer after the seventh hour of the day (i.e. an hour after midday) is considered negligent, although he discharges his obligation (*Rav;* see *Shulchan Aruch, Orach Chaim* 286:1). This is because the preferred time for offering the *mussaf* sacrifice is within seven hours (see *Mishnah Berurah* ad loc. §2, citing *Levush*).

The linkage between the *mussaf* offering and the *Mussaf* Prayer leads to other qualifications of the *Tanna Kamma's* ruling. The first sacrifice offered in the Temple every day is the morning *tamid* (see *Menachos* 49a). Thus, one should recite *Shacharis*, which corresponds to the morning *tamid*, before *Mussaf* (*Rabbeinu Yonah* 18a s.v. תפילת המנחה, cited by *Tos. Yom Tov* s.v. כל היום). [However, since a *mussaf* sacrifice offered before the morning *tamid* is valid after the fact (see *Menachos* 49b), one who recites *Mussaf* before *Shacharis* discharges his obligation (*Rashba* to *Megillah* 20b s.v. המוספים; *Rama, Orach Chaim* 286:1).]

Similarly, one may not offer any sacrifice after the afternoon *tamid* (see *Yoma* 33a; *Rambam, Hil. Temidim U'Mussafim* 1:3) [with the exception of the *korban pesach*, which must be offered *after* the *tamid*]. Therefore, one should pray *Mussaf* before *Minchah*, which corresponds to the afternoon *tamid* (*Meiri; Rashba* ibid.). [Here, too, one who recites *Mussaf* after

כָּל הַיּוֹם. רַבִּי יְהוּדָה אוֹמֵר: עַד שֶׁבַע שָׁעוֹת.

[ב] **רַבִּי** נְחוּנְיָא בֶּן הַקָּנָה הָיָה מִתְפַּלֵּל בִּכְנִיסָתוֹ לְבֵית הַמִּדְרָשׁ וּבִיצִיאָתוֹ תְּפִלָּה קְצָרָה. אָמְרוּ לוֹ: מַה מָּקוֹם לִתְפִלָּה זוֹ? אָמַר לָהֶם: בִּכְנִיסָתִי אֲנִי מִתְפַּלֵּל שֶׁלֹּא תֶאֱרַע תַּקָּלָה עַל יָדִי,

—————— ר' עובדיה מברטנורא ——————

(ב) **מה מקום.** כלומר, מה טיבה: **שלא תארע תקלה.** שלא יצא מכשול על ידי, כדמפרש

יד אברהם

R' — רַבִּי יְהוּדָה אוֹמֵר: עַד שֶׁבַע שָׁעוֹת.
Yehudah says: Until seven hours [into the day].

R' Yehudah maintains that the *mussaf* sacrifice may only be offered until the end of the seventh hour of the day. Accordingly, he rules that the corresponding *Mussaf* Prayer must be recited before this time (*Gem.* 26b).

It is not clear what R' Yehudah's basis is for disqualifying a *mussaf* sacrifice offered after the seventh hour. *Meiri* (to the mishnah s.v. של מוספין) implies that R' Yehudah's deadline is a Rabbinic precaution intended to ensure that enough time remains to offer the afternoon *tamid*, which (as noted above s.v. ושל מוספים) is offered after the *mussaf* sacrifice.

Many versions of our mishnah (including the one found in *Yerushalmi*) do not include R' Yehudah's ruling regarding the deadline for *Mussaf* (see *Tosafos* to 27a s.v. תא שמע, cited in *Tos. Yom Tov*; *Meleches Shlomo*). Although R' Yehudah's ruling is cited in a Baraisa in the *Gemara* (26b), the commentators explain that Rebbi — the redactor of the mishnah — did not include R' Yehudah's view in the mishnah out of concern that citing it would be construed as an indication that his view regarding *Mussaf* is followed in halachah, just as halachah accepts his view regarding the deadlines for *Shacharis* (see רבי יהודה אומר עד ארבע שעות above s.v.

Minchah discharges his obligation, since a *mussaf* sacrifice offered after the afternoon *tamid* is valid (*Rashba* ibid.; see *Tosafos* to *Rosh Hashanah* 30b s.v. ונתקלקלו). Indeed, the *Gemara* (28a) rules that if one had not yet recited *Mussaf* by the time allotted for *Minchah*, he should first recite *Minchah* and then recite *Mussaf*, in accordance with the principle that one should discharge a more frequent obligation before performing an obligation that is less common (see *Shulchan Aruch, Orach Chaim* 286:4 for details regarding this ruling).]

It should be noted that there is a fundamental difference between *Mussaf* and the three daily Prayers of *Shacharis, Minchah* and *Maariv*. Although the daily Prayers relate to the daily *tamid* offerings, their basic purpose is to plead for Heavenly assistance. One always requires Divine aid, and thus the rationale for reciting a particular Prayer applies throughout the day. Therefore, one may compensate for his inadvertent failure to recite one of these Prayers by reciting an additional *Shemoneh Esrei* after the next scheduled Prayer (see *Gem.* 26a). The purpose of *Mussaf*, on the other hand, is to verbally commemorate the *mussaf* sacrifices that were offered in the Temple. This purpose is only accomplished during the time these sacrifices were offered. Thus, one who fails to recite *Mussaf* cannot compensate by reciting an additional *Shemoneh Esrei* later (*Tosafos* to 26a s.v. איבעיא להו; see further, prefatory comments to mishnah 7).

4
2

the entire day. R' Yehudah says: Until seven
hours [into the day].

2. R' Nechunyah ben HaKannah would pray,
upon entering and leaving the study
hall, a short prayer. They said to him: What
place is there for this prayer? He said to
them: When I enter [the study hall], I pray
that a mishap not come about through me,

<hr>

YAD AVRAHAM

and — to a certain extent — *Minchah* [see
above s.v. רבי יהודה אומר עד פלג המנחה]
(*Tosafos* ibid., as explained by *Ramaz*, cited
in *Tos. Anshei Shem; Chiddushei Maharich*). Others, however, reject this ratio-

nale, arguing that in fact, R' Yehudah's
deadline is accepted to some extent, for ideally one should recite *Mussaf* by the end of
the seventh hour [see above s.v. ושל מוספים]
(*Ramaz* ibid.).

2.

After completing the morning prayers in the synagogue, one should ideally
devote time to Torah study in the study hall (*Shulchan Aruch, Orach Chaim*
155:1; see *Gem.* 64a). Accordingly, after having mentioned the times for the
daily Prayers in the previous mishnah, our mishnah proceeds to discuss a law
relevant to entering and leaving the study hall (*Tif. Yis.* §8).

רַבִּי נְחוּנְיָה בֶּן הַקָּנָה הָיָה מִתְפַּלֵּל בִּכְנִיסָתוֹ
— לְבֵית הַמִּדְרָשׁ וּבִיצִיאָתוֹ תְּפִלָּה קְצָרָה.
*R' Nechunyah ben HaKannah would
pray, upon entering and leaving the
study hall, a short prayer.*

The concept of Prayer is not restricted to the thrice-daily formal
Prayers instituted by the Rabbis.
Whenever one is faced with a situation in which he feels the need for
Divine assistance, he should utter a
prayer beseeching God for aid. Thus,
R' Nechunyah ben HaKannah would
recite a prayer invoking Heavenly assistance before pursuing his studies, as
the mishnah will soon explain (*Meiri*).

Although the term "prayer" is generally
used by the mishnah to refer specifically
to the *Shemoneh Esrei* (see prefatory
comments to previous mishnah, footnote 2), our mishnah uses the term in its
more general sense, to refer to any plea

directed to God (*Rambam Comm.*).

אָמְרוּ לוֹ: מַה מָּקוֹם לִתְפִלָּה זוֹ? — *They
said to him: What place is there for
this prayer?*

I.e. what is the nature of this prayer
(*Rav; Rashi;* see *Yerushalmi's* version
of our mishnah). R' Nechunyah ben
HaKannah's students (see *Shinuyei
Nuschaos*) inquired as to the purpose
of this prayer.

Alternatively, they asked him at which
point during the day this prayer should be
recited (*Shenos Eliyahu*).

אָמַר לָהֶם: בִּכְנִיסָתִי אֲנִי מִתְפַּלֵּל שֶׁלֹּא תֶאֱרַע
תַּקָּלָה עַל יָדִי, — *He said to them: When
I enter [the study hall], I pray that a
mishap not come about through me,*

That is, may a mishap not occur to
my colleagues on my account (*Rav*).

R' Nechunyah answered that his
prayer was a request that he not err in

וּבִיצִיאָתִי אֲנִי נוֹתֵן הוֹדָיָה עַל חֶלְקִי.

───────── ר' עובדיה מברטנורא ─────────

בברייתא שלא אכשל בדבר הלכה וישמחו חבירי, הרי רעה שתבא על ידי שאגרום להם
שיענשו: **אני נותן הודיה על חלקי.** מודה על הטובה שחלק לי שם חלקי מיושבי בית
המדרש. ושתי תפלות הללו בכניסתו לבית המדרש וביציאתו חובה על כל איש ואיש לאמרן,
דהכי אמרינן בברייתא בכניסתו מה הוא אומר וביציאתו מהו אומר, משמע דחובה דחייבו למימרינהו:

יד אברהם

deciding a matter of halachah, potentially causing his colleagues to rejoice
at his mistake. He would then be the
cause of the Heavenly punishment
they would surely receive as a result
(*Rav;* see *Rashi* to 28b s.v. ולא אכשל).
In addition, the incorrect ruling, itself,
would cause a mishap, for those who
relied on R' Nechunyah's decisions
would transgress (see *Rashi* ibid.; *Tos.
Yom Tov*).

According to the interpretation that R'
Nechunyah's students inquired as to the
correct time for reciting this prayer (see
above s.v. אמרו לו), he answered that there
is no set time; rather, it is recited whenever
one enters (and leaves) the study hall
(*Shenos Eliyahu*).

A Baraisa cited by the *Gemara* (28b)
elaborates: "Upon entering the study
hall what does one say? *May it be
Your will, Hashem, my God, that a
mishap not come about through me.
And may I not stumble in a matter of
law and [cause] my colleagues to rejoice over me. And may I not say regarding something which is tamei
that it is tahor, and not regarding
something which is tahor that it is
tamei. And may my colleagues not
stumble in a matter of law and I
[would be led to] rejoice over them."*[1]

Our translation of this Baraisa follows

Rav and *Rashi*, who understand the reference to "rejoicing" to be a transgression
caused as a result of one's error in his studies
or the errors of his colleagues. Some commentators, however, understand this to be a
request that his colleagues derive pleasure
("rejoice") from his correct Torah insights.
According to this interpretation, this prayer
embodies two requests: 1) that one not err in
his studies, and 2) that his colleagues derive
enjoyment from his Torah insights. Similarly, the end of this prayer contains requests that one's colleagues not err in their
rulings, and that he rejoice in their accurate
Torah insights (*Bach, Orach Chaim* 110 s.v.
הנכנס; see also *Maharsha, Chiddushei Ag-
gados* to 28b s.v. וישמחו בי). Accordingly,
the Baraisa would translate as follows:
"And *may* my colleagues rejoice *with* me...
And *may* I rejoice *with* them."

According to the interpretation of *Rav*
and *Rashi*, the entire prayer is a request on
one's own behalf, i.e. that he not be responsible for causing others to sin (by causing
them to rejoice in his errors), nor be guilty
of sinning himself (by rejoicing in the errors of others). According to the second interpretation of the Baraisa, the last part of
this prayer is a request on behalf of one's
colleagues, that they not err in their studies,
and that they merit to find the truth in
Torah, causing him to rejoice (see *Tif. Yis.,
Boaz* §2).

וּבִיצִיאָתִי אֲנִי נוֹתֵן הוֹדָיָה עַל חֶלְקִי. — *and
when I exit I give thanks for my lot.*

───────────────

1. There are various readings of this Baraisa. We have cited the version printed in the
Gemara; however, *Rav* seems to follow the version of *Rif* (19a), which omits some of the
elements found in our version (see *Tos. Anshei Shem* s.v. שלא). *Yerushalmi* (4:1) presents
yet a different version of this prayer. See *Mishnah Berurah* 110:35 regarding the optimal
formula one should recite.

and when I exit I give thanks for my lot.

YAD AVRAHAM

Upon leaving the study hall, I thank God for His goodness in establishing my portion in life among those who are to be found in the study hall (*Rav*).

The Baraisa (cited above s.v. אמר להם) elaborates: "Upon exiting what does one say? *I thank You, O Hashem, my God, that You have established my lot with those who dwell in the study hall, and You have not established my portion with idlers. For I arise early and they arise early; I arise early for words of Torah, and they arise early for words of idleness. I toil and they toil; I toil and receive reward, and they toil and do not receive reward. I run*

and they run; I run to the life of the World To Come, and they run to the pit of destruction."

The fact that the Baraisa introduces the texts of these prayers with the words, "what *does* one say," rather than inquiring, "what *did* he (i.e. R' Nechunyah ben HaKannah) say," indicates that the recital of this prayer is obligatory on everyone, and was not merely the private practice of R' Nechunyah ben HaKannah[1] (*Rav*, from *Rambam Comm.*; see also *Shulchan Aruch, Orach Chaim* 110:8; *Mishnah Berurah* §36; cf. *Shitah Mekubetzes* to 28b s.v. רבי נחוניא).

3.

The following mishnah discusses whether one must recite the full text of the *Shemoneh Esrei* to fulfill his prayer obligation, or if he may, instead, recite an abridged version which touches upon all the matters included in the complete version.

The text of the *Shemoneh Esrei* was composed by the אַנְשֵׁי כְנֶסֶת הַגְּדוֹלָה, *the Men of the Great Assembly*, in the time of Ezra the Scribe (*Megillah* 17b; *Rambam, Hil. Tefillah* 1:4). The name *Shemoneh Esrei* ("eighteen") derives from the fact that as originally formulated, this prayer consisted of eighteen blessings. In later years, at the behest of Rabban Gamliel, the president of the Sanhedrin in Yavneh after the destruction of the Second Temple, the Rabbis composed an additional blessing for the *Shemoneh Esrei* (*Gem.* 28b-29a). This blessing (which in many versions of the *Shemoneh Esrei* begins with the words וְלַמַּלְשִׁינִים אַל תְּהִי תִקְוָה, *And for slanderers let there be no hope*, and is known as בִּרְכַּת הַמִּינִים, *the Blessing of Heretics* — see *Gem.* ibid.) contains a plea that God destroy the heretics, whose activities posed a great threat to the Jewish nation during the time of Rabban Gamliel (*Rambam, Hil. Tefillah* 2:1). Although the *Shemoneh Esrei* now contains *nineteen* blessings, the original name remained.[2]

1. The recitation of these prayers is not contingent on one's studying Torah in the study hall among his colleagues. One who learns in private (e.g. at home) should also recite these prayers, before and after his studies (*Mishnah Berurah* 110:35,36).

2. According to *Yerushalmi* (4:3, as emended by *Gra* in *Shenos Eliyahu*), the blessings of בּוֹנֵה יְרוּשָׁלַיִם, *Bonei Yerushalayim*, and מַצְמִיחַ קֶרֶן יְשׁוּעָה, *Matzmiach keren yeshuah* (the fourteenth and fifteenth blessings in our version of the *Shemoneh Esrei*), combine to form a single blessing. Thus, the original text of the *Shemoneh Esrei* contained *seventeen* blessings. With the addition of the *Blessing of Heretics*, the *Shemoneh Esrei* [according to *Yerushalmi*] now consists of eighteen blessings (cf. *Pnei Moshe* ad loc., who maintains

[ג] **רַבָּן** גַּמְלִיאֵל אוֹמֵר: בְּכָל יוֹם מִתְפַּלֵּל אָדָם שְׁמוֹנֶה עֶשְׂרֵה. רַבִּי יְהוֹשֻׁעַ אוֹמֵר: מֵעֵין שְׁמוֹנֶה עֶשְׂרֵה. רַבִּי עֲקִיבָא אוֹמֵר: אִם שְׁגוּרָה תְפִלָּתוֹ בְּפִיו – יִתְפַּלֵּל שְׁמוֹנֶה עֶשְׂרֵה; וְאִם לָאו – מֵעֵין שְׁמוֹנֶה עֶשְׂרֵה.

—— ר' עובדיה מברטנורא ——

(ג) **מעין שמונה עשרה.** ליח מפרשי בגמרא שאומר מכל ברכה וברכה מן האמלעיות בקולר וחותם על כל אחת ואחת. ואית דאמרי, הביננו ה' אלהינו לדעת דרכך, שהיא ברכה אחת שיש בה מעין כל הברכות האמלעיות של שמונה עשרה, וחותם ברוך אתה ה' שומע תפלה: **שגורה תפלה.** שהוא למוד ורגיל בה. והלכה כרבי עקיבא שמי שאין תפלתו שגורה בפיו, או בשעת הדחק, מתפלל אדם שלש ראשונות ושלש אחרונות והביננו באמלע שהיא מעין כל האמלעיות, חוץ מימות הגשמים שאינו מתפלל הביננו מפני שלריך לומר שאלה בברכת השנים, וחוץ ממולאי שבתות וימים טובים

יד אברהם

The blessings of the *Shemoneh Esrei* fall into three categories. The first three blessings consist of praises to God. The next thirteen blessings are requests to God concerning our needs. The *Shemoneh Esrei* concludes with three blessings expressing thanksgiving to Him (see *Rambam* ibid. 1:4).

רַבָּן גַּמְלִיאֵל אוֹמֵר: בְּכָל יוֹם מִתְפַּלֵּל אָדָם שְׁמוֹנֶה עֶשְׂרֵה. — *Rabban Gamliel says: Every day a person must pray the eighteen [blessings of the Shemoneh Esrei].*

That is, [every prayer of every day] must consist of the complete, unabridged text of the *Shemoneh Esrei*; one cannot discharge his obligation with an abridged version (*Meiri*).

Rabban Gamliel issued this ruling before the בְּרְכַּת הַמִּינִים, *the Blessing of the Heretics*, was instituted in Yavneh at his behest (see prefatory comments). Thus, he refers to the *eighteen* blessings of the *Shemoneh Esrei*, rather than the *nineteen* of which it now consists (*Tos. Yom Tov; Tif. Yis.*).

רַבִּי יְהוֹשֻׁעַ אוֹמֵר: מֵעֵין שְׁמוֹנֶה עֶשְׂרֵה. — *R' Yehoshua says: [He may recite] an abridgment of the eighteen [blessings].*

R' Yehoshua maintains that one can discharge his obligation by reciting an

abbreviated version of the *Shemoneh Esrei*. Certainly, it is preferable to recite the complete text. However, if one is preoccupied with other matters and finds it difficult to pray the entire *Shemoneh Esrei*, he may recite an abridged version of the *Shemoneh Esrei*, even though he is capable of concentrating properly on the full text (see *Meiri*).

The form of this abridged version is the subject of a dispute between the *Amoraim*, Rav and Shmuel. Both agree that the first three blessings of the *Shemoneh Esrei* (the blessings praising God) and the last three blessings (the blessings of thanksgiving) are recited in full (see *Rambam Comm.*). The dispute concerns the middle blessings (which represent our requests to God). Rav maintains that each of these blessings is shortened by reciting only

that subsequently, the combined blessing of מַצְמִיחַ קֶרֶן יְשׁוּעָה and בּוֹנֵה יְרוּשָׁלַיִם was divided into two).

4
3

3. R abban Gamliel says: Every day a person must pray the eighteen [blessings of the *Shemoneh Esrei*]. R' Yehoshua says: [He may recite] an abridgment of the eighteen [blessings]. R' Akiva says: If his prayer is fluent in his mouth, he must pray the eighteen [blessings]; but if not, [he should pray] an abridgment of the eighteen.

YAD AVRAHAM

its opening and concluding words (e.g. אַתָּה חוֹנֵן לְאָדָם דַּעַת בָּרוּךְ אַתָּה ה' חוֹנֵן הַדָּעַת). According to Shmuel, all the middle blessings are condensed into a single blessing (known as הֲבִינֵנוּ, *Havineinu*, after its opening words) which contains allusions to each of the blessings it replaces. This abridgment concludes with the blessing בָּרוּךְ אַתָּה ה' שׁוֹמֵעַ תְּפִלָּה, *Blessed are You, Hashem, Who hears prayer* (*Rav*, from *Gem.* 29a; see *Gem.* for the text of the *Havineinu* blessing; see below s.v. ואם לאו regarding which of these opinions is followed by halachah).

We have seen (mishnah 3:5) that if one remembers that he is a *baal keri* after he has begun reciting the *Shemoneh Esrei*, he should complete his recitation in an abridged form. The commentators interpret this to mean that he should shorten each blessing, reciting only its beginning and end (see comm. there s.v. לא יפסיק), as Rav explains our mishnah. The commentators do not suggest that that mishnah refers to Shmuel's abridged version of the *Shemoneh Esrei*, the *Havineinu* prayer. Possibly, this is because the ruling in that mishnah includes a case where one remembered he was a *baal keri* after reciting the first of the middle group of blessings (i.e. the fourth blessing of the *Shemoneh Esrei*, חוֹנֵן הַדָּעַת). In such a situation, he would need to revise the text of *Havineinu* to omit the words that correspond to the blessing already recited. Since this can easily disconcert the *baal keri* and detract from his concentration, even Shmuel agrees that in this case, the *baal keri*

should recite each blessing in an abbreviated form (*Kol HaRamaz* to mishnah 3:5, cited by *Tos. Anshei Shem* there s.v. אלא; see *Tzlach* to 22b s.v. אלא יקצר who maintains that in this case the remaining blessings *cannot* be substituted with *Havineinu*, which was formulated to replace *all* the middle blessings). However, according to Shmuel, if one remembers he is a *baal keri before* he begins the fourth blessing, indeed he should recite the shorter *Havineinu* prayer (*Tzlach* ibid.).

רַבִּי עֲקִיבָא אוֹמֵר: אִם שְׁגוּרָה תְּפִלָּתוֹ בְּפִיו — יִתְפַּלֵּל שְׁמוֹנֶה עֶשְׂרֵה; — *R' Akiva says: If his prayer is fluent in his mouth, he must pray the eighteen [blessings];* I.e. he is accustomed to its text (*Rav*), and can, therefore, recite the prayer without stumbling over the words (*Tos. Yom Tov*, from *Rav* to mishnah 5:5: s.v. אם שגורה). [Thus, he can concentrate properly on the words he recites.]

R' Akiva maintains that preoccupation with other matters is not sufficient reason to allow substituting *Havineinu* for the complete text of the *Shemoneh Esrei*. As long as one is capable of reciting the full text of the *Shemoneh Esrei* with the proper level of concentration, he may not recite an abridged version (*Meiri*).

וְאִם לָאו — מֵעֵין שְׁמוֹנֶה עֶשְׂרֵה. — *but if not, [he should pray] an abridgment of the eighteen.* If one is not well versed in the text

[ד] רַבִּי אֱלִיעֶזֶר אוֹמֵר: הָעוֹשֶׂה תְּפִלָּתוֹ קֶבַע — אֵין תְּפִלָּתוֹ תַּחֲנוּנִים.

—— ר' עובדיה מברטנורא ——

שְׁצָרִיךְ לוֹמַר הַבְדָּלָה בְּחוֹנֵן הַדָּעַת: (ד) הָעוֹשֶׂה תְּפִלָּתוֹ קֶבַע. שֶׁתְּפִלָּתוֹ דּוֹמֶה עָלָיו כְּמַשּׂאוֹי. וּלְשׁוֹן קֶבַע, שֶׁאוֹמֵר חוֹק קָבוּעַ עָלַי לְהִתְפַּלֵּל וְצָרִיךְ אֲנִי לָצֵאת מִמֶּנָּה:

יד אברהם

of the *Shemoneh Esrei*, and, hence, is not capable of concentrating properly on the long version, he may instead recite the shorter, abridged version. Similarly, if he is distracted by other matters to such an extent that he cannot concentrate properly for the entire *Shemoneh Esrei*, he may discharge his obligation with the abridged version (*Meiri; Rambam, Hil. Tefillah* 2:2). It is preferable to recite the shorter, less comprehensive *Havineinu* prayer with proper concentration than the more detailed, but longer, *Shemoneh Esrei* without proper concentration (*Meiri*).

The halachah is decided in accordance with R' Akiva. Therefore, one who is not fluent in the text of the *Shemoneh Esrei* [and can thus not attain the proper level of concentration], or one in extenuating cir-

cumstances (e.g. while traveling on the road, one fears that his prayer will be interrupted — see *Shulchan Aruch, Orach Chaim* 110:1 and *Mishnah Berurah* §2), may recite an abridgment of the *Shemoneh Esrei*. The abridged version one recites is *Havineinu* (*Rav*; see *Shulchan Aruch* ibid.).[1] However, there are times when the *Shemoneh Esrei* cannot be replaced by *Havineinu*. During the winter season one is required to insert a request for abundant rainfall (the addition of וְתֵן טַל וּמָטָר) in the blessing of בָּרֵךְ עָלֵינוּ. Similarly, the *Shemoneh Esrei* of the *Maariv* at the conclusion of a Sabbath or Holiday contains the addition of *Havdalah* [אַתָּה חוֹנַנְתָּנוּ לְמַדַּע תּוֹרָתֶךְ] in the blessing of אַתָּה חוֹנֵן. The text of *Havineinu* makes no allowance for the insertion of these additions, and, therefore, it may not replace the *Shemoneh Esrei* at these times (*Rav*, from *Gem.* 29a; see *Shulchan Aruch* ibid.).[2]

4.

Prayer is a unique opportunity to present our desires to God, the Sole Provider (see *Mishnah Berurah* 98:8). This should be reflected in the manner in which one recites the *Shemoneh Esrei*; with sincerity, imploring God to provide

1. *Beur Halachah* (to 110:1 s.v. אֹו שֶׁלֹּא יוּכַל) notes that today, the custom is not to take advantage of this leniency, but rather to recite the full *Shemoneh Esrei* even in situations where one cannot concentrate. *Beur Halachah* suggests that this is because we are equally incapable of concentrating properly on *Havineinu*. Thus, replacing the *Shemoneh Esrei* with *Havineinu* would accomplish nothing (see *Meiri* cited above). Alternatively, *Beur Halachah* explains that, due to the constant distractions we face, were we to rely on the *Havineinu* prayer whenever we are not able to concentrate, we would never pray the complete unabridged version of the *Shemoneh Esrei*.

2. However, it would seem that one who recites *Havineinu* at the conclusion of the Sabbath or holiday does discharge his obligation after the fact, since failure to recite *Havdalah* does not invalidate one's prayer (see *Beur Halachah* to *Shulchan Aruch* ibid. s.v. וְאִינּו). [Failure to recite וְתֵן טַל וּמָטָר, however, *does* invalidate one's prayer (*Shulchan Aruch, Orach Chaim* 117:4).]

4. R' Eliezer says: [If] one makes his Prayer fixed, his Prayer is not a supplication.

YAD AVRAHAM

his needs and requirements. The following mishnah discusses the consequences of reciting the *Shemoneh Esrei* in a manner which is not consistent with its supplicatory nature. The mishnah also discusses the law concerning circumstances in which it is impossible to concentrate on one's Prayer at all.

רַבִּי אֱלִיעֶזֶר אוֹמֵר: הָעוֹשֶׂה תְפִלָּתוֹ קֶבַע —
— *R' Eliezer says: [If] one makes his Prayer fixed,*

The term קֶבַע connotes a burdensome duty which one seeks to be done with (*Gem.* 29b). One who makes his Prayer "fixed" is one who only recites the *Shemoneh Esrei* in order to discharge his obligation (*Rav, Rashi* to 29b s.v. כמשוי; *Rambam Comm.*), but does not sincerely implore God to grant him his needs (see *Magen Avraham* 98:4).

This inappropriate attitude is demonstrated when one prays at a hurried pace, thus indicating that he recites his Prayer to relieve himself of an onerous obligation, but does not feel a need for that for which he prays (*Bach, Orach Chaim* 98 s.v. מחשבתו, based on *Tur* ad loc. and *Rabbeinu Yonah* 20a s.v. ורבנן אמרי; *Eliyah Rabbah* 98:4). One also demonstrates this improper mindset by turning to other activities immediately upon concluding his Prayers (*Rambam, Hil. Tefillah* 4:16; *Meiri* to 32b s.v. המתפלל).[1]

The *Gemara* cites the foregoing interpretation in the name of R' Oshaya. A different interpretation cited by the *Gemara* — in the name of the Rabbis — is that the mishnah refers to one who does not pray in a supplicatory

manner, i.e. in pleading tones, with a humble spirit and a broken heart (see *Rabbeinu Yonah* to *Avos* 2:13), as befits one appealing for mercy. Rather, he recites the "fixed" formula of Prayer by rote (see *Yerushalmi* 4:4 with *Peirush MiBaal Sefer Ha-Chareidim* s.v. ובלבד).[2]

Rambam (loc. cit.) and *Shulchan Aruch* (*Orach Chaim* 98:3) rule in accordance with *both* interpretations: One should pray with sincerity, not simply to discharge his obligation, and one should also pray in supplicatory tones. Evidently, these authorities maintain that R' Oshaya and the Rabbis do not argue with regard to the halachah; they only dispute the *meaning* of the term קֶבַע, but agree that Prayer should be recited in accordance with both interpretations (see *Kessef Mishneh* ad loc.; see also *Shoshanim L'David*, cited by *Tos. Anshei Shem* s.v. העושה). However, *Rav Hai Gaon* (cited by *Rabbeinu Yonah* 20a s.v. ורבנן) and *Rabbeinu Chananel* (cited by *Rosh* §18) imply that this dispute *does* have halachic ramifications (see further below, s.v. אין תפלתו).

אֵין תְּפִלָּתוֹ תַחֲנוּנִים. — *his Prayer is not a supplication.*

I.e. the Prayer he recites is not considered true Prayer, because it does not fulfill the requirement of being a supplication to God (see *Rav Hai Gaon* loc.

1. *Meiri* (ibid.). comments that the purpose of reciting the liturgical composition of עָלֵינוּ, *Aleinu*, after reciting the *Shemoneh Esrei* of Minchah and Maariv is to ensure that one tarry a bit after reciting his Prayer.

2. *Shoshanim L'David* (cited by *Tos. Anshei Shem* s.v. העושה) is at a loss to explain why *Rav* ignores the interpretation of the Rabbis, and cites only the interpretation of R' Oshaya. However, *Tos. Yom Tov* notes that *Rav*, in his commentary to *Avos* (2:13), does cite both interpretations.

רַבִּי יְהוֹשֻׁעַ אוֹמֵר: הַמְהַלֵּךְ בִּמְקוֹם
סַכָּנָה – מִתְפַּלֵּל תְּפִלָּה קְצָרָה; אוֹמֵר:
„הוֹשַׁע הַשֵּׁם אֶת עַמְּךָ אֵת שְׁאֵרִית יִשְׂרָאֵל;
בְּכָל פָּרָשַׁת הָעִבּוּר יִהְיוּ צָרְכֵיהֶם לְפָנֶיךָ.

———— ר' עובדיה מברטנורא ————

מתפלל תפלה קצרה. ומה היא תפלה קצרה, שאומר הושע ה' את עמך וגו': **בכל פרשת**
העבור. אפילו בשעה שהם פורשים לעבירה, יהיו צרכיהם גלוים לפניך לרחם עליהם. פרשת, לשון
פרישה. העבור, של עבירה. ואין הלכה כרבי יהושע, אלא התפלה שמתפללים במקום סכנה היא צרכי
עמך מרובים וכו'. ומתפלל אותה אדם כשהוא מהלך, ואינו מתפלל לא ג' ראשונות ולא ג' אחרונות.
וכשיעבור מקום הסכנה ותתיישב דעתו, צריך לחזור ולהתפלל תפלה כתקנה אם לא עברה עונתה:

———— יד אברהם ————

cit.; *Rabbeinu Chananel* loc. cit.). Consequently, one who prays in such a
manner does not discharge his obligation, and he must repeat the *Shemoneh
Esrei* (see *Beis Yosef* and *Bach, Orach
Chaim* 98; *Eliyah Rabbah* ibid.).

Rav Hai Gaon rules that one's Prayer is
invalid only if he does not pray in supplicatory tones, in accordance with the interpretation of the Rabbis (see *Mishnah Berurah*
98:9 and *Beur Halachah* s.v. יתפלל). However, even the Rabbis agree that ideally, one
should pray with sincerity, and not simply
to relieve himself of the Prayer obligation,
although such an attitude does not invalidate one's Prayer (see *Beis Yosef* ibid.).

Alternatively, because his Prayer is
not a genuine supplication, it is not
favorably accepted by God. However,
he *does* discharge his obligation (see
Re'ah; Shitah Mekubetzes to 29b s.v.
כל שאינו יכול; *Tif. Yis.; Kol HaRamaz,*
cited by *Tos. Anshei Shem* s.v.
תחנונים).[1]

In light of the opinion that one who does
not pray in supplicatory tones does not discharge his obligation, *Mishnah Berurah*
(ibid.; see also *Beur Halachah* ibid.) states
that one must be extremely careful to recite

his Prayers in the proper tone. However,
since many other authorities maintain that
one does discharge his obligation if he
prays in this improper manner, one who
does not pray in supplicatory tones should
not repeat the *Shemoneh Esrei.*

רַבִּי יְהוֹשֻׁעַ אוֹמֵר: הַמְהַלֵּךְ בִּמְקוֹם סַכָּנָה –
מִתְפַּלֵּל תְּפִלָּה קְצָרָה; — *R' Yehoshua
says: One traveling in a dangerous
place prays a short prayer;*

[I.e. rather than reciting the *Shemoneh Esrei*, he recites a short prayer
in its stead.]

The Rabbis exempted one from the
Prayer obligation in situations where
reciting the *Shemoneh Esrei* — or
even *Havineinu* — would entail danger; for example, when one is traveling on the highway and is at risk of
being attacked by bandits or wild animals while praying. However, to prevent a total absence of Prayer, he recites a short prayer (*Rambam, Hil.
Tefillah* 4:19; *Meiri;* see *Mishnah
Berurah* 110:13).

Rambam Comm. implies that this prayer
is recited whenever one's mind is unsettled
and he finds it extremely difficult to con-

1. According to this latter interpretation, *Ramaz* suggests that the term תַּחֲנוּנִים derives
from the root חֵן, *favor.* The mishnah states that prayer which manifests an improper
attitude does not *find favor* in the eyes of God (see also *Tif. Yis.* ibid.).

4
4

R' Yehoshua says: One traveling in a dangerous place prays a short prayer. He says: Save, Hashem, Your nation, the remnant of Israel. Even when [they] turn away [from You] in sin, may their needs be before You.

centrate. The mishnah's reference to one traveling in a dangerous place is merely an illustration of such a circumstance (see *Mishnah Berurah* ibid.).

אוֹמֵר: — *He says:*

The mishnah now presents the text of the short prayer one recites in dangerous places (*Rav; Rashi; Rambam Comm.*).

,,הוֹשַׁע הַשֵּׁם אֶת עַמְּךָ אֶת שְׁאֵרִית יִשְׂרָאֵל; — *"Save, Hashem, Your nation, the remnant of Israel;*

These words are taken from *Jeremiah* 31:6 (*Tos. Yom Tov*).

בְּכָל פָּרָשַׁת הָעִבּוּר יִהְיוּ צָרְכֵיהֶם לְפָנֶיךָ. — *Even when [they] turn away [from You] in sin, may their needs be before You.*

Even when the nation is not worthy, may You supply their needs, so that they remain self-sufficient and do not become dependent on other nations for support (*Rabbeinu Yonah* 20a s.v. בכל פרשת העבור).

Our translation of the term פָּרָשַׁת הָעִבּוּר follows *Rav*, and is based on one interpretation cited by the *Gemara* (29b), according to which the term עבור relates to the term עֲבֵרָה, *transgression*. The term פָּרָשַׁת is understood to derive from the word פָּרוּשׁ, *turned away*. Hence, the expression פָּרָשַׁת הָעִבּוּר is understood to mean: *when they* (i.e. Israel) *turn away from You* (i.e. God) *in sin*.

Another interpretation cited by the *Gemara* assigns a dual meaning to the term עבור, relating it to the word

עֶבְרָה, *anger*, and the word עוּבָּרָה, *pregnant*, which conveys the concept of *fullness* (as the body of a pregnant woman is *full* with a fetus). The term פָּרָשַׁת is understood in the sense of פֵּרוּשׁ, *explanation*. According to this interpretation, the expression literally means, "the [various] explanations of [the term] עבור" (i.e. *anger* and *full*), and refers to a time when God is *full* of *anger* toward Israel (*Rashi* to 29b s.v. אפי׳ בשעה, as explained by *Maharsha*; cf. *Meleches Shlomo*, who interprets *Rashi* differently; see *Rambam Comm.*, ed. Kafich, for a different explanation of the *Gemara*).

Both these interpretations actually refer to the same situation, for the sins of Israel are the cause of Divine anger (*Rabbeinu Chananel*). Since it is indelicate to mention in prayer the possibility of Israel's sinning, this prayer is worded obscurely (*Ritva* to 29b s.v. בכל פרשת).

Yerushalmi (4:4) understands this prayer to be a reference to the recitation of the *chazzan* who leads the Prayers in the synagogue. Evidently, *Yerushalmi's* version of our mishnah reads פָּרָשַׁת הָעִבּוּר. The term עבור, *he who passes*, is an allusion to the *chazzan*, to whom the mishnah often refers as "the one *who passes* before the Ark [to lead the Prayers]" (see mishnah 5:3). The term פָּרָשַׁת is derived from a root meaning "to articulate." Thus, the expression פָּרָשַׁת הָעִבּוּר is rendered "the articulation of the *chazzan*." Since the person traveling in a dangerous location is not able to pray himself, he beseeches God to hearken to the Prayer recited by the *chazzan* in the synagogue (*R'Shlomo Sirilio*, cited by *Meleches Shlomo*).

בָּרוּךְ אַתָּה ה', שׁוֹמֵעַ תְּפִלָּה".

[ה] **הָיָה** רוֹכֵב עַל הַחֲמוֹר – יֵרֵד. וְאִם אֵינוֹ
יָכוֹל לֵירֵד – יַחֲזִיר אֶת פָּנָיו. וְאִם

─── ר' עוֹבַדְיָה מִבַּרְטְנוּרָא ───

(ה) **הָיָה רוֹכֵב עַל הַחֲמוֹר יֵרֵד.** אֵין הֲלָכָה כִּסְתָם מִשְׁנָה זוֹ, אֶלָּא בֵּין יֵשׁ לוֹ מִי שֶׁיֹּאחַז חֲמוֹרוֹ
בֵּין אֵין לוֹ מִי שֶׁיֹּאחַז חֲמוֹרוֹ לֹא יֵרֵד, מִפְּנֵי שֶׁאֵין דַּעְתּוֹ מְיֻשֶּׁבֶת עָלָיו כְּשֶׁהוּא יוֹרֵד: **יַחֲזִיר אֶת פָּנָיו.**
לְצַד יְרוּשָׁלַיִם, שֶׁנֶּאֱמַר (מלכים־א ח) וְהִתְפַּלְלוּ אֵלֶיךָ דֶּרֶךְ אַרְצָם:

יד אברהם

בָּרוּךְ אַתָּה ה', שׁוֹמֵעַ תְּפִלָּה". — *Blessed
are You, Hashem, Who hears prayer."*
This blessing concludes the short
prayer of R' Yehoshua.

A Baraisa cited by the *Gemara* (29b)
lists several alternative versions of the
prayer recited when traveling in a
dangerous place. The *Gemara* rules
that we do not recite R' Yehoshua's
version, but rather one that reads: *The
needs of Your nation are many, but
their minds are limited. May it be
Your will, Hashem, our God, that You
give each and every one enough for
his sustenance, and to each and every
body what it lacks. Blessed are You,
Hashem, Who hears prayer* (*Rav;
Rambam Comm.*; see *Shulchan
Aruch, Orach Chaim* 110:3).

We have seen another example of a
Prayer one recites when it is difficult to
concentrate on the *Shemoneh Esrei* —
Havineinu (see previous mishnah). However, there is a fundamental difference between *Havineinu* and the prayer mentioned
by our mishnah. *Havineinu* is an abridged
version of the *Shemoneh Esrei*, and was designed to *replace* the full version. One who
recites *Havineinu* discharges his Prayer

obligation; he is not required to repeat the
complete *Shemoneh Esrei* later, when he is
able to concentrate. The short prayer of our
mishnah, on the other hand, does not allude
to the requests contained in the *Shemoneh
Esrei*, and was not designed to replace the
Shemoneh Esrei. One cannot discharge his
Prayer obligation with this short prayer,
and when the danger passes, he must recite
the complete *Shemoneh Esrei* (*Rav, Rambam Comm.*, from *Gemara* 30a, see *Rashi* ad
loc. s.v. וכי מטי).[1]

The difference between *Havineinu* and
the prayer of our mishnah is evidenced by
the fact that *Havineinu* is subject to the
laws of *Shemoneh Esrei*, while this short
prayer is not. *Havineinu* must be prefaced
with the same three introductory blessings
of praise recited at the beginning of the
Shemoneh Esrei, and the three concluding
blessings of thanksgiving found at the end
of the *Shemoneh Esrei* (see comm. to previous mishnah s.v. רבי יהושע אומר). The short
prayer of our mishnah does not begin or
conclude with these blessings. Furthermore,
while *Havineinu* must be recited while
standing, as is the law regarding *Shemoneh
Esrei* (see prefatory comments to next mishnah), the short prayer of our mishnah may
be recited while walking or riding (*Rav,
Rambam Comm.*, from *Gem.* 30a).

5.

No matter where one prays, the site of the Temple in Jerusalem, and specifically the Chamber of the Holy of Holies there, is the conduit through which

---

1. And if the time for that particular Prayer has passed, he must compensate for that Prayer
by praying twice at the time of the next Prayer, as is the law when one inadvertently
forgets to recite a Prayer (*Rama, Orach Chaim* 110:3; see *Mishnah Berurah* §15).

Blessed are You, Hashem, Who hears prayer.

5. **[**I**f]** one was riding on a donkey, he should dismount [to pray]. But if he is not able to dismount, he should turn his face [and pray]. And

YAD AVRAHAM

Prayer ascends heavenward, as it were (see *Pirkei D'Rabbi Eliezer* Chap. 35; *Menoras HaMaor* 3:100). Thus, in the prayer he uttered upon completing the Temple, Solomon referred to Prayer directed toward the Holy of Holies: *If the heavens are restrained and there be no rain, for they* (i.e. the Jewish nation) *have sinned against You, and they pray toward this place* (i.e. the Holy of Holies). . . *may You hear from Heaven* etc. (*I Kings* 8:35-36). Regarding those who are in Jerusalem but not in the Temple precincts — and who, therefore, cannot face in the precise direction of the Holy of Holies — Solomon stated (*II Chronicles* 6:32): *and they will pray toward this House* [i.e. the Temple]. Concerning those who are not in Jerusalem, but are in Eretz Yisrael, Solomon said (*I Kings* 8:44): *and they will pray to Hashem by way of the city that You have chosen* (i.e. Jerusalem). Regarding those who are outside of Eretz Yisrael, Solomon stated (ibid. v. 48): *and they will pray to You by way of their land* [i.e. Eretz Yisrael] (see *Maharsha* to 30a s.v. היה עומד). Based on these verses, the Rabbis instituted that when reciting the *Shemoneh Esrei* outside of Eretz Yisrael, one should face toward Eretz Yisrael. In Eretz Yisrael, one should pray facing toward Jerusalem. In Jerusalem, one should pray facing the site of the Temple. One who is in the Temple precincts should pray facing the Holy of Holies (*Gem.* 30a; see *Tosafos* ad loc. s.v. היה עומד; *Aruch HaShulchan, Orach Chaim* 94:2,8). Thus, those who live to the west of Eretz Yisrael (e.g. in America) should recite the *Shemoneh Esrei* facing east (*Rama, Orach Chaim* 94:2).[1]

In addition, the Rabbis instituted that the *Shemoneh Esrei* be recited while standing (see *Rambam, Hil. Tefillah* 5:1,2). The following two mishnayos discuss the law in situations which make it difficult or impossible to stand for the *Shemoneh Esrei* and face in the proper direction.

הָיָה רוֹכֵב עַל הַחֲמוֹר — יֵרֵד. — *[If] one was riding on a donkey, he should dismount [to pray].*

If one was riding on a donkey when the time for Prayer arrived, he should not recite the *Shemoneh Esrei* while on the donkey. Rather, he should dismount, so he can pray while standing (*Meiri*).

וְאִם אֵינוֹ יָכוֹל לֵירֵד — יַחֲזִיר אֶת פָּנָיו. — *But if he is not able to dismount, he should turn his face [and pray].*

That is, if he will not be able to concentrate on the *Shemoneh Esrei* if he dismounts; for example, there is no one else to hold his animal's reins, and holding them himself would disrupt his concentration (see *Gem.* 30a). In

---

1. *Rabbeinu Yonah* (20b s.v. היה עומד) states that even outside of Eretz Yisrael one is required to face Jerusalem, the Temple and the Holy of Holies. Since he cannot do this in a physical sense, he should picture himself facing these locations (see also *Shulchan Aruch, Orach Chaim* 94:1 and *Mishnah Berurah* §3; cf. *Perishah, Orach Chaim* 94:1, cited by *Tos. Anshei Shem*; see below s.v. יכוין את לבו).

[ו] הָיָה יוֹשֵׁב בִּסְפִינָה אוֹ בְקָרוֹן אוֹ בְאַסְדָּא –
יְכַוֵּן אֶת לִבּוֹ כְּנֶגֶד בֵּית קֹדֶשׁ הַקֳּדָשִׁים.

ר' עובדיה מברטנורא

יכוין את לבו כנגד בית קדשי הקדשים. שנא' (שם) והתפללו (אליך) אל המקום [הזה]:
(ו) באסדא. עצים הרבה קשורים ומהודקים יחד, ומשיטים אותם בנהר ובני אדם הולכים
עליהם. ובלשון מקרא (דברי הימים-ב ב) קרוין רפסודות:

יד אברהם

such a case, he should not dismount,
but should halt his animal and recite
the *Shemoneh Esrei* while seated.
However, he must turn his face toward Eretz Yisrael (or Jerusalem or the
Temple), in accordance with the law
that one should face in that direction
while reciting the *Shemoneh Esrei* [see
prefatory comments] (*Meiri*).

In a Baraisa cited by the *Gemara* (30a),
Rebbi disputes the view that one should dismount and pray if he is able to so. In Rebbi's
opinion, a traveler should never dismount
to pray, for he can concentrate better while
he is traveling than when he dismounts [for
he is distracted by thoughts of the travel
time he is losing (see *Rashi* ad loc. s.v. שאין
דעתו)]. The halachah is decided in accordance with Rebbi (*Rav*, from *Gem.* ibid.).
According to most authorities, Rebbi does
not even require the traveler to halt his animal to recite the *Shemoneh Esrei* (see *Rambam Comm.*; *Tosafos* to 30a s.v. הלכה כרבי;
Beis Yosef, *Orach Chaim* 94 s.v. וטעמא דרבי;
cf. *Rabbeinu Yonah* 20b s.v. בין כך), since
obligating him to interrupt his journey
would hinder rather than enhance his concentration (*Meiri*, based on *Rashi* ibid.).

וְאִם אֵינוֹ יָכוֹל לְהַחֲזִיר אֶת פָּנָיו — *And
if he is unable to turn his face,*

If one is not even able to stop the
animal and turn toward Eretz Yisrael

— e.g. his fellow travelers refuse to
wait for him to pray, and he is afraid
to travel unaccompanied — then ...
(*Meiri*).

יְכַוֵּן אֶת לִבּוֹ כְּנֶגֶד בֵּית הַקֳּדָשִׁים. — *he
should concentrate his thoughts toward
the Chamber of the Holy of Holies
[while praying].*

[I.e. he should picture himself facing the Holy of Holies.] When one is
able, he should pray in the direction of
the Holy of Holies, as the verse (*I
Kings* 8:35) states: *and they pray toward this place* (*Rav*; see prefatory
comments). If he cannot face the Holy
of Holies in a physical sense, he
should at least *imagine* himself to be
facing in this direction, in fulfillment
of this verse (see *Tos. Anshei Shem*).

Rambam Comm. (as explained by
Lechem Mishneh, Hil. Tefillah 5:3) interprets the mishnah's statement (*concentrate
his thoughts toward the Chamber of the
Holy of Holies*) to mean that one should
concentrate his thoughts toward *He Who
resides*, as it were, in the Holy of Holies, i.e.
God. According to *Rambam*, one is not required to *imagine* himself facing in a particular direction. If he cannot physically face
in the proper direction, he should merely
direct his thoughts toward God (see also
Rambam, Hil. Tefillah 5:3).[1]

1. *Rambam's* interpretation is apparently based on a Baraisa cited by the *Gemara* (30a),

4
6

if he is unable to turn his face, he should concentrate his thoughts toward the Chamber of the Holy of Holies [while praying].

6. **[**I**f]** he was sitting in a boat or a wagon, or on a raft, he should concentrate his thoughts toward the Chamber of the Holy of Holies [while praying].

6.

The following mishnah is a continuation of the previous mishnah.

הָיָה יוֹשֵׁב בִּסְפִינָה אוֹ בְקָרוֹן אוֹ בְאַסְדָּא, — *[If] he was sitting in a boat or a wagon, or on a raft,*

One was traveling in a boat, wagon or raft when the time for Prayer arrived, and was unable to determine the correct direction to face while reciting the *Shemoneh Esrei* (*Meiri*, second explanation; see below, s.v. יכון).

Our translation of אַסְדָּא as *raft* follows *Rav*, who explains an אַסְדָּא to be a collection of logs that are tied together and floated down a river. This is one of two interpretations suggested by *Rashi* (printed on 28b).

In his other interpretation, *Rashi* explains אַסְדָּא to mean *stocks*, used to immobilize prisoners. [According to this interpretation, the person cannot face toward Eretz Yisrael because he is physically incapable of turning in that direction.]

Others explain an אַסְדָּא to be a small boat [as opposed to סְפִינָה, which connotes a larger boat] (*Rambam Comm.*; *Meiri*).

From a Baraisa cited by the *Gemara* (30a) it emerges that in these situations, one does not stand to recite the *Shemoneh Esrei*, but

rather recites it sitting down. This is because these conveyances shake considerably while in motion, making it difficult to stand and recite the *Shemoneh Esrei* (*Tos. Yom Tov*, from *Beis Yosef, Orach Chaim* 94 s.v. ומי"ש רבינו אם היה בספינה). Moreover, one who stands in a boat or raft is distracted by the fear of falling overboard (*Rashi* to 30a s.v. בקרון ובספינה), making it difficult for him to properly concentrate on the *Shemoneh Esrei* (*Tif. Yis.* §23).[1]

יְכַוֵּן אֶת לִבּוֹ כְּנֶגֶד בֵּית קֹדֶשׁ הַקֳּדָשִׁים. — *he should concentrate his thoughts toward the Chamber of the Holy of Holies [while praying].*

Since it is not possible to face in the proper direction, one should recite the *Shemoneh Esrei* as he is, but should envisage himself facing the Holy of Holies (*Meiri*; see comm. to previous mishnah s.v. יכוין את לבו; cf. *Rambam Comm.*, cited there). [However, if one *is* aware of the direction of Eretz Yisrael, and] it is possible to turn and face in that direction while praying, one

which states that one who is unable to discern the correct direction in which to pray should "direct his heart to his Father in Heaven." Evidently, there is no requirement in this case to picture himself facing in the proper direction (*Tos. Anshei Shem*).

1. However, this is not a blanket exemption. If it *is* possible to concentrate on the *Shemoneh Esrei* while standing, one must do so (*Rambam, Hil. Tefillah* 5:2; *Shulchan Aruch, Orach Chaim* 94:4). At the very least, if at all possible he should stand up at the points in the *Shemoneh Esrei* which call for bowing, and at the beginning and end of the *Shemoneh Esrei*, so that he can take the three steps backward and forward at these points (*Shulchan Aruch* ibid.; *Rama* ad loc.).

[ז] רַבִּי אֶלְעָזָר בֶּן עֲזַרְיָה אוֹמֵר: אֵין תְּפִלַּת הַמּוּסָפִין אֶלָּא בְּחֶבֶר עִיר.

ר' עובדיה מברטנורא

(ז) **אין תפלת המוספים אלא בחבר עיר.** בחבורת העיר, כלומר בצבור ולא ביחיד: **בחבר עיר ושלא בחבר עיר.** בין לצבור בין ביחיד:

יד אברהם

must do so (*Mishnah Berurah* 94:15).

Alternatively, the mishnah refers even to a case where one *can* determine the proper direction. Nevertheless, even though it is possible to face toward Eretz Yisrael, the mishnah does not require one to do so. The Rabbis do not obligate one to face in the proper direction when he recites the *Shemoneh Esrei* while walking or trav-

eling on a moving conveyance. Since in the case of our mishnah it is not possible to stop the boat or wagon, the mishnah does not require one to face toward Eretz Yisrael to pray. Rather, he need only visualize himself facing the Holy of Holies (*Tos. Yom Tov*, as explained by *Beur Halachah* to 94:4 s.v. היה רוכב; see also *Meiri*, first explanation).

7.

The following mishnah records a dispute regarding the extent to which the Rabbis obligated the recitation of *Mussaf*.

The *Mussaf* Prayer is fundamentally different than the Daily Prayers of *Shacharis*, *Minchah* and *Maariv*. The Daily Prayers consist of requests and supplications, whereas the text of *Mussaf* consists primarily of praises to God.[1] This distinction is a reflection of the different functions of these Prayers. Whereas the purpose of the Daily Prayers is to beseech God to provide our needs, the purpose of the *Mussaf* Prayer is to *verbally commemorate* the additional sacrifices (*mussafim*) that were offered on the Sabbath, Rosh Chodesh and Holidays (see comm. to mishnah 1 s.v. ושל מוספין). [Indeed, the Scriptural verses that describe the *mussafim* offered on a particular day are the focus of that day's *Mussaf* Prayer.] According to one opinion cited by the *Gemara* (26b), *Mussaf* and the Daily Prayers differ even in their origin: *Mussaf* was instituted by the Men of the Great Assembly to correspond to the *mussafim*, whereas the Daily Prayers originated with the Patriarchs [although the Men of the Great Assembly subsequently linked the Daily Prayers to the daily *tamid* sacrifices (see prefatory comments to mishnah 1, footnote 1)]. The singular characteristics of *Mussaf* give rise to the dispute recorded in our mishnah.

רַבִּי אֶלְעָזָר בֶּן עֲזַרְיָה אוֹמֵר: אֵין תְּפִלַּת הַמּוּסָפִין אֶלָּא בְּחֶבֶר עִיר. — *R' Elazar ben Azaryah says: The Mussaf*

Prayer is only [recited] with an assembly of the town.

I.e. with a congregation of at least

---

1. Although the versions of the Daily Prayers recited on the Sabbath and Holidays are also laudatory in nature, their corresponding weekday versions are supplicatory. [Indeed, the *Gemara* (21a) states that by rights, the Sabbath version of the three Daily Prayers should have included the supplications of the weekday version, but out of respect for the Sabbath, the Rabbis did not trouble people to recite the lengthy weekday *Shemoneh Esrei* (see *Meiri* ad loc. s.v. מי שהיה מתפלל בשבת).] See next footnote.

7. R' Elazar ben Azaryah says: The *Mussaf* Prayer is only [recited] with an assembly of the town.

YAD AVRAHAM

ten men. R' Elazar ben Azaryah maintains that, unlike the daily Prayers of *Shacharis, Minchah* and *Maariv*, the recitation of which is obligatory for individuals, the Rabbis instituted the *Mussaf* Prayer as an obligation only incumbent on a congregation (*Rav; Rashi; Rambam Comm.*).

Our translation of בְּחֶבֶר עִיר as *assembly* (lit. *group*) *of the town* follows *Rav* and *Rashi*. Others, however, while agreeing that this expression refers to the town congregation, interpret it to mean *with the sage* [חָבֵר] *of the city*. It was customary for the community to gather for services at the place of the town's greatest Torah scholar (*Rambam Comm.; Aruch* s.v. [א] חבר, cited by *Tos. Anshei Shem; see also Rashi* to *Megillah* 27b s.v. חבר). According to this interpretation, the mishnah should read בַּחֲבֵר עיר (*Kol HaRamaz*, cited by *Tos. Anshei Shem*).

Some authorities understand that the Prayer obligation of a "congregation" can only be discharged by the recitation of the *chazzan*, who represents the congregation as a whole. The prayers of the *individual members* of the congregation, however, would be considered the prayers of individuals, and not prayers of the unified congregation. According to this view, R' Elazar ben Azaryah maintains that the individual members of the congregation do not recite *Mussaf* at all. Rather, the *chazzan* who leads the service recites *Mussaf* aloud on behalf of the entire congregation, while the congregants answer "*amein*" to his blessings (*Piskei HaRid*). Others, however, maintain that the prayers of the individuals of whom the congregation consists *are* considered prayers of the congregation. According to these authorities, the members of the con-

gregation may recite *Mussaf* silently themselves, since they form the congregation upon whom there is an obligation to pray *Mussaf* (see *Bach, Orach Chaim* 592 s.v. ואח"כ; *Chazon Ish, Orach Chaim* 137:3).

R' Elazar ben Azaryah's distinction between the Daily Prayers, which he agrees are incumbent on individuals, and *Mussaf*, which he contends is incumbent only on a congregation, is the result of the different natures of these Prayers. The Daily Prayers are supplicatory in nature. Every person requires Divine assistance, so the Rabbis made these Prayers obligatory for each individual. *Mussaf*, on the other hand, is laudatory in nature (see prefatory comments). Therefore, the Rabbis deemed it sufficient for the public (i.e. a congregation) to offer these praises, and did not require it of individuals (*Rabbeinu Yonah* 20b s.v. רבי אלעזר, cited by *Tos. Yom Tov; Ritva* and *Tos. R' Yehudah Chassid* to 30a s.v. אין; *Tif. Yis.* §24).[1]

Alternatively, R' Elazar ben Azaryah maintains that *Mussaf* is obligatory only for a congregation because it was instituted by a public body (the Men of the Great Assembly). The Daily Prayers are obligatory for individuals because (in R' Elazar ben Azaryah's opinion) they were instituted by individuals — the Patriarchs [see prefatory comments] (see *Meiri; Ravya* §88).

Yet another explanation for the difference between the *Mussaf* obligation and the obligation of the Daily Prayers is that

1. This distinction applies even on the Sabbath and Holidays, when the Daily Prayers are also laudatory in nature, since they correspond to weekday Prayers that *are* supplications. Therefore, they remain individual obligations. *Mussaf*, however, has no supplicatory counterpart (*Tos. Yom Tov*, from *Rabbeinu Yonah* ibid.; *Shitah Mekubetzes*).

וַחֲכָמִים אוֹמְרִים: בְּחֶבֶר עִיר וְשֶׁלֹּא בְחֶבֶר עִיר.
רַבִּי יְהוּדָה אוֹמֵר מִשְּׁמוֹ: כָּל מָקוֹם שֶׁיֵּשׁ חֶבֶר
עִיר — הַיָּחִיד פָּטוּר מִתְּפִלַּת הַמּוּסָפִין.

ר' עובדיה מברטנורא

רבי יהודה אומר משמו. שֶׁל רבי אלעזר בן עזריה. וְאִיכָּא בֵּין תַּנָּא קַמָּא לְרבי יהודה יחיד הַדָּר
בְּעִיר שֶׁאֵין שָׁם עֲשָׂרָה לִתְנֵא קַמָּא אֲלִיבָא דְרבי אלעזר דְאָמַר לֹא תִקְּנוּה אֶלָּא בְחֶבֶר עִיר יחיד זֶה
פָּטוּר, וּלְרבי יהודה אֵין יחיד פָּטוּר אֶלָּא כְּשֶׁהוּא בְּמָקוֹם שֶׁשְּׁלִיחַ צִבּוּר פּוֹטְרוֹ. וְהִלְכָה כַחֲכָמִים:

יד אברהם

the purpose of *Mussaf* is to commemorate sacrifices that were only incumbent on the public — the *mussafim*. [The Daily Prayers, on the other hand, while *linked* to communal sacrifices, do not *commemorate* these offerings] (*Rashash* to 30a s.v. במשנה; see *Mishnah Berurah* 286:6).[1]

וַחֲכָמִים אוֹמְרִים: בְּחֶבֶר עִיר וְשֶׁלֹּא בְחֶבֶר עִיר. — *But the Sages say: [It is recited] with an assembly of the town and without an assembly of the town.*

That is, every individual is obligated to pray *Mussaf*, whether or not he is part of a congregation (*Rav*).

[The Sages maintain that despite the unique attributes of *Mussaf*, the Rabbis did not differentiate between *Mussaf* and the Daily Prayers. They established *Mussaf* as an individual obligation just like the Daily Prayers.]

Those who explain R' Elazar ben Azaryah's ruling to be based on the different origins of the various Prayers (see above s.v. רבי אלעזר בן עזריה) offer a rationale for the Sages' ruling. The Sages follow the view cited by the *Gem.* (26b) that the Daily Prayers originated with the Men of the Great Assembly as did *Mussaf*. Thus, there is no basis for differentiating between the Daily Prayers and *Mussaf*; all are incumbent on individuals (*Meiri*).

רַבִּי יְהוּדָה אוֹמֵר מִשְּׁמוֹ: — *R' Yehudah says in his name:*

I.e. in the name of R' Elazar ben Azaryah (*Rav*). [R' Yehudah reports a version of R' Elazar ben Azaryah's ruling that differs from R' Elazar ben Azaryah's ruling as cited by the *Tanna Kamma*.]

כָּל מָקוֹם שֶׁיֵּשׁ חֶבֶר עִיר — הַיָּחִיד פָּטוּר מִתְּפִלַּת הַמּוּסָפִין. — *Any place where there is an assembly of the town, an individual is exempt from the Mussaf Prayer.*

According to R' Yehudah, R' Elazar ben Azaryah exempts individuals only in places where *Mussaf* will be recited by the congregation. However, in a community whose population is too small to form a congregation of ten men, each individual is obligated to pray *Mussaf*. In contrast, the *Tanna Kamma* maintains that R' Elazar ben Azaryah exempts an individual from reciting *Mussaf* even if there is no congregation in the town (*Rav* and *Rambam Comm.*, from *Gem.* 30a).

According to R' Yehudah, individuals are technically obligated to pray *Mussaf*. However, in practice, an individual's obligation is discharged by the recitation of the *chazzan* of the congregation (*Rav*; *Rashi* to 30a s.v. יחיד), even if the individual is not present at the services (*Meiri*; see also *Melo*

1. *P'nei Yehoshua* (to 30a s.v. ראב"ע) understands this distinction to be the intent of *Rabbeinu Yonah* (cited above). This, however, seems difficult to reconcile with the words of *Rabbeinu Yonah*.

4
7

But the Sages say: [It is recited] with an assembly of the town and without an assembly of the town. R' Yehudah says in his name: Any place where there is an assembly of the town, an individual is exempt from the *Mussaf* Prayer.

HaRo'im to 30a s.v. ברש"י ד"ה יחיד in explanation of *Rashi;* cf. *Rosh Yosef* to 30a s.v. ע"ראב). Thus, if there is no congregation which prays *Mussaf,* an individual must recite it himself (*Meiri*).

The dispute between the *Tanna Kamma* and R' Yehudah has ramifications even where there is a congregation which recites *Mussaf.* According to R' Yehudah, although an individual may rely on the recitation of the *chazzan* to discharge his obligation, he may also choose to discharge his obligation by reciting *Mussaf* himself. According to the *Tanna Kamma,* who maintains that individuals were never included in the *Mussaf* obligation, an individual is *forbidden* to recite *Mussaf,* since this would be considered uttering blessings in vain (*Tzlach* to 30a s.v. רבי יהודה, cited by *Tos. Anshei Shem*).

Usually, a *chazzan* can only discharge the Prayer obligation of one who hears the *chazzan's* recitation with intent to discharge his obligation thereby [שׁוֹמֵעַ כְּעוֹנֶה]. Regarding *Mussaf,* however, R' Yehudah maintains that the recitation of the *chazzan* exempts individuals from praying *Mussaf* even though they are not present at services. This is because the Rabbis patterned the *Mussaf* Prayer on the *mussaf* sacrifices to which it corresponds. The *Kohen* who performs the sacrificial service in the Temple is, in a certain sense, an emissary for the individual who brings a particular sacrifice (see *Tosafos* to *Yoma* 19b s.v. מי איכא). With regard to communal offerings, such as the *mussaf* sacrifices, the *Kohen* is an agent for the entire

public, to discharge their obligation to offer these sacrifices. Similarly, the Rabbis instituted that the *chazzan* who leads the Prayers in the synagogue should represent the entire community, even those who are not in attendance. Thus, by his recitation of *Mussaf,* he discharges their obligation as well. However, unlike the *Kohen* in the Temple who acts on behalf of the entire nation, a *chazzan* represents only members of his community. Therefore, the *chazzan* of one community cannot discharge the obligation of the members of a different community (*Melo Haro'im* vol. I, p. 142, s.v. מוספין ביחיד).

Alternatively, it is the congregation as a whole, and not the *chazzan,* who represent those not in attendance at the service and discharge the obligation of these individuals. The members of the congregation parallel the אַנְשֵׁי מַעֲמָד, *Anshei Maamad* (lit. *the men of the standing*), who would stand by and watch as the communal sacrifices were offered. These people were emissaries of the public, who, as those upon whose behalf the sacrifice was brought, were technically obligated to be present when the sacrifice was offered (see *Taanis* 4:2). Similarly, the members of the congregation, in fulfilling *their* obligation (either through the recitation of the individual congregants or through the recitation of the *chazzan* on behalf of the congregation as a whole — see above s.v. רבי אלעזר בן עזריה אומר), are considered emissaries of the entire community, and therefore they discharge the obligation of those who are not present (*P'nei Yehoshua* to 30a s.v. במשנה).[1]

1. According to either explanation, the Rabbis only made this allowance for the *Mussaf* obligation, which commemorates the *mussaf* sacrifice and is therefore patterned after the manner in which the sacrifice was offered. The Daily Prayers, although they correspond to the communal *tamid* offerings (see prefatory comments to mishnah 1), do not *commemorate* them. Therefore, the manner in which one fulfills the Daily Prayer obligation does not parallel the *tamid* offerings.

פרק חמישי ﷽

Chapter Five

ברכות **[א] אֵין** עוֹמְדִין לְהִתְפַּלֵּל אֶלָּא מִתּוֹךְ כֹּבֶד רֹאשׁ.
חֲסִידִים הָרִאשׁוֹנִים הָיוּ שׁוֹהִים שָׁעָה
אַחַת וּמִתְפַּלְּלִים, כְּדֵי שֶׁיְּכַוְּנוּ אֶת לִבָּם לַמָּקוֹם.
אֲפִילוּ הַמֶּלֶךְ שׁוֹאֵל בִּשְׁלוֹמוֹ – לֹא יְשִׁיבֶנּוּ.

ר' עובדיה מברטנורא

פרק חמישי – אין עומדין. (א) אין עומדין. מתוך כובד ראש. הכנעה ומורא, דכתיב
(תהלים ב, יא) עבדו את ה' ביראה, ועבודה זו תפלה היא: שוהים שעה אחת. במקום שבאו להתפלל:
אפילו המלך שואל בשלומו. ודוקא מלך ישראל, אבל מלך עובד כוכבים פוסק שלא יהרגנו:

יד אברהם

1.

The following mishnah discusses the state of mind that one must assume before beginning the *Shemoneh Esrei.*

אֵין עוֹמְדִין לְהִתְפַּלֵּל אֶלָּא מִתּוֹךְ כֹּבֶד רֹאשׁ. — *One should not stand up to pray except from a state of awe.*

[That is, one should enter the *Shemoneh Esrei* only from a state of awe.] The expression כֹּבֶד רֹאשׁ translates literally as "heaviness of the head." This is understood to be a metaphor for submission and trepidation (*Rav*), or concentration and seriousness (*Rambam Comm.*).[1] That this is the proper mood for prayer is derived from the verse (*Psalms* 2:11): "Serve Hashem with awe," where the service referred to is understood to mean prayer (*Rav, Rambam Comm.* from *Gemara* 30b).

Bach (93 s.v. ובבואו) notes that the *Gemara* (31a) cites a *baraisa* that describes a different condition for entering prayer. The *baraisa* states, "One should not get up [i.e. begin] to pray from a condition of sorrow, nor from a condition of slothfulness, nor from a condition of levity, nor from a condition of chatter, nor from a condition of lightheadedness, nor from idle words, rather from the joy associated with a mitzvah." *Bach* explains that the condition of awe mentioned by our mishnah as a pre-

requisite of prayer is considered to be a מִצְוָה מִן הַמֻּבְחָר, *the optimum state* of mind for prayer. For one who cannot attain this level, the *baraisa* gives a lesser condition for entering prayer — "the joy associated with a mitzvah" (see *Mishnah Berurah* 93:4).

Aruch (s.v. כֹּבֶד) understands the mishnah's statement here to concern the physical posture a person should assume while reciting the *Shemoneh Esrei.* He explains the expression כֹּבֶד רֹאשׁ as meaning that when a person prays, his head must appear "heavy" — i.e. lowered somewhat, as a symbol of humility. Such a posture enables one to concentrate better (see also *Meiri* and *Rabbeinu Chananel,* and see mishnah 9:5, s.v. לא יקל). *Shulchan Aruch* (*Orach Chaim* 95:2) also rules that when reciting *Shemoneh Esrei,* a person should lower his head. However, his ruling is based on a statement of the *Gemara* in *Yevamos* 105b and not on our mishnah (cf. *Tif. Yis.* #1).

חֲסִידִים הָרִאשׁוֹנִים הָיוּ שׁוֹהִים שָׁעָה אַחַת וּמִתְפַּלְּלִים, — *The pious men of earlier*

---

1. For an alternative understanding of *Rambam,* see *R' Y. Kafich's* edition, where *Rambam's* words are translated as רְצִינוּת וְהִתְכּוֹנְנוּת, *seriousness and preparedness.*

<table>
<tr><td>5
1</td><td>1. **O**ne should not stand up to pray except from a state of awe. The pious men of earlier times used to wait an hour before praying, so that they could direct their thoughts toward the Omnipresent. Even if the king inquires about one's welfare, one may not reply to him [while praying].</td></tr>
</table>

YAD AVRAHAM

times used to wait an hour before praying,

These righteous people would spend an hour in preparation before commencing their prayer.[1] This time was spent clearing their minds of the activities of the day and focusing their thoughts on their Creator (*Meiri*).

The *Gemara* (32b) finds a source for this practice in the verse (*Psalms* 84:5): אַשְׁרֵי יוֹשְׁבֵי בֵיתֶךָ עוֹד יְהַלְלוּךָ סֶּלָה, "Praiseworthy are those who dwell [lit. sit] in Your house, continually they will praise You, Selah." The verse speaks of two stages — "dwelling" and then "praising." The ones meriting praise first "*dwell*" in the House of God [i.e., spend time in the synagogue preparing themselves for prayer], and only then do "they praise You" (*Rashi* 32b s.v. יושבי ביתך).

While spending an hour preparing for prayer is considered an unusually pious act of devotion, there is a minimum amount of preparation deemed proper for all. This is the time it takes to walk 8 *tefachim* [approximately 32 inches] (*Mishnah Berurah* 93:1). *Pri Migadim* (*Eishel Avraham* 93:1) suggests, however, that through the combination of waiting somewhat before prayer, saying *Pesukei D'Zimra* for close to a half-hour, and then saying *Krias Shema* with its blessings, one actually spends close

to an hour "preparing" for *Shemoneh Esrei*, thereby fulfilling the custom of the pious men of old.

כְּדֵי שֶׁיְּכַוְּנוּ אֶת לִבָּם לַמָּקוֹם. — *so that they could direct their thoughts toward the Omnipresent.*

I.e. so that they could totally immerse themselves in the service of God and remove from their minds all thoughts of earthly pleasures. The purity of thought attained by dissociating themselves from the vanities of this world and contemplating the loftiness of the Creator ensured that their prayers would be pleasing and acceptable to God (*Rabbeinu Yonah* folio 21a s.v. כדי).[2]

Some texts omit the word לַמָּקוֹם, *toward the Omnipresent.* The mishnah thus reads: "The pious men of earlier times used to wait an hour before praying so that they could direct their thoughts." Accordingly, the mishnah could be explained to mean that these pious people spent an hour in preparation so that they could concentrate on the meaning of their prayers (*Tos. Yom Tov*).

אֲפִילוּ הַמֶּלֶךְ שׁוֹאֵל בִּשְׁלוֹמוֹ — לֹא יְשִׁיבֶנּוּ. — *Even if the king inquires about one's welfare, one may not reply to him [while praying].*

The king referred to in our mishnah is a Jewish king, who presumably

---

1. Even though the term שָׁעָה, literally, a period of time, can refer to even a brief period of time, the *Gemara* 32b states clearly that these pious men would spend a full hour in preparation (*Rabbeinu Yonah* folio 21a s.v. חסידים; see *Tos. Anshei Shem* s.v. שעה א׳).

2. For the meaning of the term מָקוֹם with reference to Hashem, see *Tos. Yom Tov* to *Avos* 2:9 s.v. המקום. See also *Rambam, Moreh Nevuchim* 1:8, and *Nefesh HaChaim Shaar* 3.

ברכות וַאֲפִילוּ נָחָשׁ כָּרוּךְ עַל עֲקֵבוֹ — לֹא יַפְסִיק.

ה/ב

[ב] מַזְכִּירִין גְּבוּרוֹת גְּשָׁמִים בִּתְחִיַּת הַמֵּתִים,

─────────── ר' עובדיה מברטנורא ───────────

אפילו נחש כרוך על עקבו. דוקא נחש נהרב פעמים אינו נושך, אבל עקרב או חפעה מן הדברים
שודאי נושכים וממיתים פוסק: [ב] מזכירין גבורות גשמים. משיב הרוח, שאינו לשון בקשה
אלא לשון הזכרה ושבח. ומפני שהגשמים אחת מגבורותיו של הקדוש ברוך הוא דכתיב (איוב ה, ט-י)
עושה גדולות (עד) [ו]אין חקר [וגו'] הנותן מטר על פני ארץ, משום הכי קרי להו גבורות גשמים:

─────────── יד אברהם ───────────

would not take offense by the failure
of someone to respond while praying.
However, if a person reciting *Shemoneh Esrei* is greeted by a pagan king, he
may interrupt his prayer and respond
(*Gemara* 32b). This is because it is
likely that a pagan king would take
offense from his failure to reply and
put him to death (*Rav, Rashi* to 32b s.v.
אבל). Preserving life supersedes almost
all prohibitions (see *Sanhedrin* 74a,b).

Although in connection with reciting
the *Shema*, a previous mishnah (2:1) stated
that a person may interrupt his recitation
in order to respond to a greeting even
where there is no risk to his life (see there
s.v. ומשיב), the law for reciting *Shemoneh
Esrei* is more stringent. The difference between *Shema* and *Shemoneh Esrei* is that
when a person recites *Shema* he is talking
to himself, internalizing the principle of
God's unity. However, when a person recites *Shemoneh Esrei*, he is addressing God
directly and beseeching Him to provide his
needs (see *Meiri*). Certainly this "audience"
with the King of all kings should not be
interrupted by a response to a mortal king
(see *Gemara* 33a; see also *Rashi* to 25a s.v.
אבל לתפלה and *Rambam, Hil. Tefillah* 4:16;
see *Tosafos* 13a s.v. ובאמצע who cite a
derivation from a verse in support of this
distinction).

וַאֲפִילוּ נָחָשׁ כָּרוּךְ עַל עֲקֵבוֹ, — *And even if*

a snake is coiled around his foot,

This refers to a snake that normally
does not bite, and does not pose a
threat to the life of the person praying
(*Rav, Rambam Comm.* from *Gem.*
33a). However, if a person sees a scor-
pion or a viper approaching, he should
interrupt his prayer and move to
safety, since these creatures endanger
his life (*Rav, Rambam Comm.* and *Hil.
Tefillah* 6:9). See below.

לֹא יַפְסִיק. — *he may not interrupt.*

He may not interrupt his prayer
with speech (*Tos. Yom Tov* from
Rabbeinu Yonah folio 219 s.v. ואפילו).
Thus, he cannot call for someone to
come and remove the snake (*Meleches
Shlomo* from *Levush* 104:3). He is,
however, allowed to walk away in order to throw the snake off his foot
since walking does not constitute an
interruption (*Rabbeinu Yonah* ibid.).
Other commentaries disagree and
maintain that even walking during
Shemoneh Esrei constitutes an interruption. Accordingly, our mishnah
means that where there is no threat to
life, one may not interrupt his prayer
even by walking away (see *Beur
HaGra, Orach Chaim* 104:3; and *Beur
Halachah* 104 s.v. לא יפסיק).

2.

The following mishnah discusses the placement of three periodic additions in
the *Shemoneh Esrei*. Two of the additions are seasonal, involving rain. The

5
2
And even if a snake is coiled around his foot, he may not interrupt.

2. We mention "the Powers of Rain" in [the blessing] "The Resuscitation of the Dead,"

third is added weekly to the evening *Shemoneh Esrei* at the conclusion of the Sabbath.

מַזְכִּירִין גְּבוּרוֹת גְּשָׁמִים בִּתְחִיַּת הַמֵּתִים, — *We mention "The Powers of Rain" in [the blessing] "The Resuscitation of the Dead,"*

Every year, starting with the *Mussaf* prayer of *Shemini Atzeres* and continuing into the first day of Pesach, a clause is added to the *Shemoneh Esrei* praising God for causing the winds to blow and the rains to fall (see Mishnah *Taanis* 1:1-2). The additional clause is מַשִּׁיב הָרוּחַ וּמוֹרִיד הַגָּשֶׁם, "He causes the wind to blow and He makes the rain descend." This supplement is known as "the Powers of Rain." It is inserted into the second blessing of the *Shemoneh Esrei*, the blessing known as מְחַיֵּה הַמֵּתִים, "the Resuscitator of the Dead."

The mention of "the Powers of Rain" is not an entreaty for rain. Rather, it is a statement praising God for making the wind blow and the rain fall. As such, the appropriate place for this supplement is in the three opening blessings of the *Shemoneh Esrei*, which are laudatory, and not in the later blessings of the *Shemoneh Esrei*, which are entreaties and statements of gratitude (*Shenos Eliyahu;* see *General Introduction*). It is specifically inserted in the blessing called "the Resuscitator

of the Dead" because just as the resurrection of the dead causes the germination of life, so too does rain (*Rabbeinu Yonah*, folio 23b s.v. מתני׳ מזכירין; *Tos. Yom Tov* from *Yerushalmi* 5:2, *Shitah Mikubetzes* 33a s.v. מתני׳ מזכירין).

The *Gemara* (*Taanis* 2a) demonstrates from Scripture that rain is regarded as a manifestation of God's power. Accordingly, the formula concerning rain that is added to the second blessing of *Shemoneh Esrei* is known as "the Powers of Rain," i.e. the Divine power manifest in rain (*Rav*).

The commentators raise the question of why the expression "the Powers of Rain" is used and not "the Strength of Rain," or "the Greatness of Rain."[1] One answer given is that the expression "the Powers of Rain" was specifically adopted to correspond to the theme of the blessing into which it is inserted, "You are eternally *powerful*, Hashem" (*Tos. Taanis* 2a s.v. וכתיב).

Others explain that the term "power" and not "greatness" was used since it is a more accurate description in this context. The term "greatness" is used to describe a manifestation of the Divine that results from phenomena that are constant, such as the movement of the sun. The term "power" is used to describe a manifestation of the Divine that results from phenomena that are intermittent, such as

---

1. The question becomes more compelling upon examination of the *Gemara* (*Taanis* 2a) mentioned previously. The *Gemara* does demonstrate that rain is a manifestation of God's power. However, the verses expounded for this could just as well be describing rain as a manifestation of God's strength or greatness.

וְשׁוֹאֲלִין הַגְּשָׁמִים בְּבִרְכַּת הַשָּׁנִים, וְהַבְדָּלָה בְּחוֹנֵן הַדָּעַת. רַבִּי עֲקִיבָא אוֹמֵר: אוֹמְרָהּ בְּרָכָה רְבִיעִית בִּפְנֵי עַצְמָהּ. רַבִּי אֱלִיעֶזֶר אוֹמֵר: בְּהוֹדָאָה.

─────── ר' עובדיה מברטנורא ───────

ושאלה. ותן טל ומטר, לשון בקשה: **בברכת השנים.** מתוך שהן פרנסה קבעו שאלתן בברכת פרנסה: **והבדלה.** במוצאי שבת: **בחונן הדעת.** שהיא ברכה ראשונה של חול. ובירושלמי אמרו: מפני מה תקנו הבדלה בחונן הדעת, שאם אין דעה אין הבדלה מנין, וכן הלכה:

─────── יד אברהם ───────

the rain (see *Shenos Eliyahu*).

The mention of "the Powers of Rain" is customarily inserted in the *Shemoneh Esrei* before the words מְכַלְכֵּל חַיִּים בְּחֶסֶד, "He sustains the living with kindness." Our mishnah, however, legislates only that it be recited somewhere within the blessing of the resuscitation of the dead, without citing any specific location. Indeed, because of this, if one did not mention "the Powers of Rain" in the customary place, it suffices to add it wherever one remembers, as long as one has not concluded the blessing (*Tur Orach Chaim* 114, citing *Rosh*; see *Mishnah Berurah* 114:29,32 for details).

וְשׁוֹאֲלִין הַגְּשָׁמִים בְּבִרְכַּת הַשָּׁנִים, — *and we ask for rain in "The Blessing of the Years,"*

Starting from the seventh of Cheshvan in Israel (and from the sixtieth day after the fall equinox elsewhere),[1] and continuing until the first day of Pesach, the entreaty וְתֵן טַל וּמָטָר, "give dew and rain," is added to the ninth blessing of the *Shemoneh Esrei* (*Rav*; see Mishnah *Taanis* 1:1-2). This blessing, known as "the Blessing of the Years," is a supplication for suste-

nance. Since rain provides the basis of sustenance, the entreaty for rain is inserted into this blessing (*Rav*, based on *Gem.* 33a).

In short, there are actually two aspects to our prayer for rain: acclaim and supplication. Our acclaim of God's power in giving rain is expressed in the clause "He causes the wind to blow and He makes the rain descend." Since it is a praise of God and not a direct supplication, it was inserted by the Rabbis into the laudatory second blessing of the *Shemoneh Esrei*. The second aspect (supplication) is expressed by the entreaty "give dew and rain." Since this is a supplication, it is inserted into the supplicatory ninth blessing of the *Shemoneh Esrei*.[2]

וְהַבְדָּלָה בְּחוֹנֵן הַדָּעַת. — *and [we recite] the Havdalah [prayer] in [the blessing] "Who Graces [Man] with Understanding."*

Havdalah is the prayer said to mark the conclusion of the Sabbath. Just as there is an obligation to mark the arrival of the Sabbath by reciting *Kiddush* (lit. sanctification), so too there is an obligation to mark its departure by reciting *Havdalah* (lit. separation).[3]

1. The reason why it was legislated that this entreaty should commence specifically at this time, is explained by the *Gemara*, Taanis 10a.

2. These two aspects of the prayers for rain are evident in the different terminologies employed by the mishnah in its first and second statements. The first statement is מַזְכִּירִין גְּבוּרוֹת גְּשָׁמִים, we *mention* "the Powers of Rain," i.e., we do not *ask* for rain, rather we *acclaim* God's power. The mishnah's second statement, however, is וְשׁוֹאֲלִין הַגְּשָׁמִים, "we *ask* for rain."

3. According to some, the obligation to recite *Havdalah* is Biblical (*Rambam, Hil. Shabbos*

5	and we ask for rain in "the Blesssing of the Years," and
2	[we recite] the *Havdalah* [prayer] in [the blessing] "Who Graces [Man] with Understanding." R' Akiva says: He says it as a fourth blessing of its own. R' Eliezer says: [He says it] in [the] "Thanksgiving" [blessing].

This prayer is said in the *Maariv* service that concludes the Sabbath. The *Tanna Kamma* is of the opinion that it is incorporated into the fourth blessing of the *Shemoneh Esrei*. Since the opening three blessings of the *Shemoneh Esrei* are common to both the Sabbath version and the weekday one, the fourth blessing is the first one that can be characterized as a distinctly "weekday" blessing. Accordingly, it is the appropriate place for the *Havdalah*, which speaks of the distinction between weekday and Sabbath (*Rav* from *Gemara* 33a).

Another reason for placing *Havdalah* in the fourth blessing is that this blessing concerns the faculty of "understanding." Since "understanding" is what endows a person with the ability to be able to discern differences, it is the appropriate setting for a prayer about separating between the sacred and the mundane (*Rav*). "Understanding" is also what imbues a person with the ability to appreciate properly the value of the Sabbath day of rest and for this reason too this blessing is appropriate for this prayer (*Rabbeinu*

Yonah, folio 23b s.v. הבדלה).

רַבִּי עֲקִיבָא אוֹמֵר: אוֹמְרָהּ בְּרָכָה רְבִיעִית בִּפְנֵי עַצְמָהּ. — *R' Akiva says: He says it as a fourth blessing of its own.*

Since the *Havdalah* formula contains no (direct) connection to the blessing "He graces man with understanding," R' Akiva maintains that it is not the proper place for the *Havdalah* (*Meiri*). He therefore argues that it should be recited as an independent blessing that is inserted before the blessing concerning "understanding" (see *Meleches Shlomo*). This additional blessing is concluded with the words, "Blessed are You, Hashem, Who distinguishes between the holy and the profane" (ibid.).

רַבִּי אֱלִיעֶזֶר אוֹמֵר: בְּהוֹדָאָה. — *R' Eliezer says: [He says it] in [the] "Thanksgiving" [blessing].*

R' Eliezer is of the opinion that the *Havdalah* is incorporated into the מוֹדִים, "Thanksgiving" blessing. It is inserted before the words וְעַל כֻּלָּם, "and for all of these . . ."[1] This is also the location of other time-dependent thanksgiving prayers such as the עַל

29:1; *Rashi* to *Nazir* 4a s.v. והרי; R' *Klonymos* of Rome quoted by *Tosafos Rabbeinu Yehudah* to *Berachos* 20b s.v. נשים). According to others, the obligation to recite *Havdalah* is only Rabbinic (*Rabbeinu Tam* quoted by *Tosafos Rabbeinu Yehudah* to 20b s.v. נשים; see also *Maggid Mishneh* to *Hil. Shabbos* 29:1 and *Meiri* to 20b s.v. נתגלגל).

1. *Tos. Anshei Shem* notes that R' Eliezer was R' Akiva's teacher. As such we would expect his opinion to be mentioned before that of his student. R' Akiva's view is stated before R' Eliezer's because it more closely resembles that of the *Tanna Kamma*. The *Tanna Kamma* places *Havdalah* in the traditional fourth blessing, while R' Akiva makes it into an independent fourth blessing. R' Eliezer, however, includes the *Havdalah* only in a much later blessing of the *Shemoneh Esrei*.

הָאוֹמֵר: „עַל קַן צִפּוֹר יַגִּיעוּ רַחֲמֶיךָ",
וְ„עַל טוֹב יִזָּכֵר שְׁמֶךָ", „מוֹדִים

ר' עובדיה מברטנורא

(ג) **על קן צפור יגיעו רחמיך.** כמו שהגיעו רחמיך על לפור וגזרת (דברים כב, ו) לא תקח האם על הבנים, כן חום ורחם עלינו: **משתקין אותו.** שטועה מדותיו של הקב"ה רחמים, והן אינן אלא גזרות מלך על עבדיו: **ועל טוב יזבר שמך.** משמע על טובתך נודה לך ועל הרע לא נודה, והרי אנו חייבין לברך על הרעה כשם שמברכין על הטובה (לקמן ט, ה): **מודים מודים.** דמיחזי כמקבל

יד אברהם

הַנִּסִּים, "For the Miracles" prayer of Chanukah and Purim. R' Eliezer's reasoning is that the *Havdalah* is meant to be an expression of thanksgiving to God for having enabled us to distinguish between the sacred and mundane (*Rabbeinu Yonah* folio 23b), and for having given us the Sabbath (*Meiri*). Its proper location is therefore together with other prayers of thanksgiving.

As with many prayers and blessings, the formula for *Havdalah* was standardized by the Men of the Great Assembly (see *Gemara* 33a and *Re'ah*). [This was a body of 120 sages who flourished just before and after the construction of the Temple. It included prophets such as Chaggai, Zechariah and Malachi, and great sages such as Mordechai and Ezra.] The *Gemara* raises the following question. If the *Havdalah* was established by the Men of the Great Assembly, how could the location of the *Havdalah* be an issue of dispute by the Rabbis of the Mishnah who lived several generations later? The *Gemara* answers that the Men of

the Great Assembly originally instituted only that the *Havdalah* should be recited in the *Shemoneh Esrei*. At that point in time it was not enacted that *Havdalah* be an independent blessing recited over a cup of wine as well. This was due to the widespread poverty that existed among the Jewish people. Later in history, when economic conditions improved and wine was more readily available, *Havdalah* was removed from *Shemoneh Esrei* and reconstituted as an independent blessing recited over a cup of wine. During this "second period," *Havdalah* was not recited in the *Shemoneh Esrei* and its original location in the *Shemoneh Esrei* was forgotten. Still later in history, when the economic situation of the Jewish people again worsened, the Rabbis reinstated the *Havdalah* in the *Shemoneh Esrei*. This final enactment was to say *Havdalah* both in *Shemoneh Esrei*, and, for one who had wine, over a cup of wine (*Re'ah, Meiri* 33a). The exact point in the *Shemoneh Esrei* where it should be inserted was then disputed.

3.

The following mishnah lists forms of prayer deemed unacceptable, as well as the procedure to be followed when the one leading the congregation in prayer is unable to conclude the prayer service.

הָאוֹמֵר, „עַל קַן צִפּוֹר יַגִּיעוּ רַחֲמֶיךָ" ...
מְשַׁתְּקִין אוֹתוֹ. — *Someone who says,* "*Your mercy extends to the bird's*

nest" ... *we silence him.*

That is, he prays: "Just as Your mercy, Hashem, extends to the birds,

3. Someone who says, "Your mercy extends to the bird's nest . . .," or [who says] "For good things, may Your name be remembered," [or who says,] "We give thanks. . ., We give thanks. . ." —

YAD AVRAHAM

as manifest by the prohibition of taking a mother bird along with her young (*Deut.* 22:6,7), so too may You have mercy on us" (*Rav, Rambam Comm.*; see *Rashi* 33b s.v. האומר).

The *Gemara* (33b) offers two reasons why this prayer is unacceptable. The first is "because it instills jealousy in the works of Creation." Saying that God has mercy on birds implies that He has mercy only on birds, but not on other creations (*Rashi* to 33b s.v. שמטיל).

Meiri (to 33b s.v. האומר), however, explains this answer of the *Gemara* as meaning that the objection to this prayer is its fallacious assumption about God's Providence over creation. Saying that "God's mercy extends to the bird's nest" implies Divine Providence over individual birds (הַשְׁגָּחָה פְּרָטִית). This "instills jealousy in the works of creation," for it implies that animal life is subject to the same Divine attention as humans (see *Habbakuk* 1:14). In truth, Divine Providence for species other than man extends only to the species as a whole, not to individuals among the species.[1]

The second reason offered by the *Gemara* as to why this prayer is unacceptable is because "he renders the mitzvos of the Holy One, Blessed is He, into acts of mercy, whereas in truth they are nothing less than de-

crees" (*Gem.* 33b). Some commentators (*Rambam Comm.*; *Meiri*; *Ran to Megilah* 25a as quoted by *Tos. Yom Tov*) understand the *Gemara* here to mean that such a prayer implies that the reason for the mitzvah of sending away the mother bird before taking her young is because God has compassion on birds. This assumption is not correct, as evidenced by the permission God granted people to slaughter birds. In truth, the reason for this mitzvah is unknown to us (*Rambam Comm.*; *Ran to Megilah* 25a, as quoted by *Tos. Yom Tov*). Others explain that this mitzvah does indeed have an understandable rationale. However, it is not because God has compassion for the bird, rather the purpose of this mitzvah is to teach *us* to have compassion (see *Ramban Deut.* 22:6; *Meiri* s.v. האומר).

Others explain the *Gemara* to mean that such a prayer not only sheds a false light on this specific mitzvah, but implies a false approach to mitzvos in general. Mitzvos are not to be understood as based on God's compassion vis-a-vis a particular aspect of creation. Rather, the correct perspective on mitzvos is that they are decrees of a king to his servant (*Rav*). We need to fulfill God's decrees even when

1. This concept that animals experience Providence over the species as a whole but not over individual members of the species is mentioned explicitly by many *Rishonim*. In brief, this means that while God's knowledge certainly embraces every detail of creation, His specific manipulation of events in regard to animals only involves the species as a whole. In regard to man, however, there can be Divine manipulation of events in every detail of an individual's life (see *Moreh Nevuchim* 3:17; *Sefer HaChinuch* 169; *Rabbeinu Bachya* to *Genesis* 18:19; *Sefer Halkkarim* 4:17; *Kad Hakemach* — *Hashgachah*).

בְּרָכוֹת מוֹדִים" – מְשַׁתְּקִין אוֹתוֹ. הָעוֹבֵר לִפְנֵי הַתֵּבָה וְטָעָה,
יַעֲבֹר אַחֵר תַּחְתָּיו, וְלֹא יְהֵא סַרְבָן בְּאוֹתָהּ שָׁעָה.

ר' עובדיה מברטנורא

עליו שתי אלוהות. ומפרש בירושלמי הדא דתימא בלצבור, אבל ביחיד תחנונים הס: **ולא יהא סרבן באותה שעה.** כדרך שאר יורדים לפני התיבה שצריך לסרב פעם ראשונה, אבל זה לא יסרב כשאומרים לו לך רד, לפי שגנאי הוא שתהא התפלה מופסקת כל כך:

יד אברהם

— ,,עַל טוֹב יִזָּכֵר שְׁמֶךָ." . . . מְשַׁתְּקִין אוֹתוֹ. or [who says,] "For good things, may Your name be remembered," . . . we silence him."

This formula implies that God's name ought to be associated only with good things, not with bad. This is objectionable inasmuch as we are commanded to bless God even for things that appear to us to be bad (mishnah 9:5), not only for things whose goodness is apparent (Rav, Rambam Comm.).

— ,,מוֹדִים – מוֹדִים" . . . מְשַׁתְּקִין אוֹתוֹ. [or who says], "We give thanks ..., We give thanks ...," we silence him.

This refers to the Thanksgiving blessing (מוֹדִים) of the Shemoneh Esrei. According to Rashi (to 33b s.v. מילתא), the mishnah speaks of a case where the person recited the blessing and then repeated it. (See Mishnah Berurah 121:5 who states that according to this view, not only is repeating the full text of this blessing improper, but just repeating a full idea contained within the blessing is also objectionable.) According to Rif and Rambam (Hil. Kerias Shema 2:11), the case here is where the person repeated the word

there is no apparent reason for that specific decree (Rabbeinu Yonah, folio 23b s.v. האומר). The mitzvos demonstrate that the Jewish people are indeed God's servants and fulfill His will even in the absence of a clear rationale for certain mitzvos (Rashi s.v. מידותיו; see at length Maharal in Tiferes Yisrael Ch. 6).

The Rambam in Moreh Nevuchim (3:48) states that the view expressed by the Gemara here is the view of only some sages, who deem the mitzvos to be the incomprehensible will of God. Other sages maintain, however, that there is a rational reason for every mitzvah. However, due to our limited faculties, we may not always be able to fathom that reason. Rambam states that we follow the latter view.[1]

Yerushalmi [quoted by Meiri s.v. האומר] mentions two other explanations of why the prayer about "the bird's nest" is objectionable. One is that it seems as if the person offering the prayer is complaining to God, implying that God's mercy extends to birds but not to the person saying the prayer. Another view is that this prayer suggests a limitation of God's compassion, i.e. that God's compassion extends only until the bird's nest.

---

1. Rambam himself, however, in Hil. Tefillah 9:7 cites this reason of the Gemara without objection. See Tos. Yom Tov who notes this apparent discrepancy between Rambam's opinion in Moreh Nevuchim and his opinion in Hil. Tefilah. See also Rambam, Hil. Me'ilah 8:8 and Hil. Temurah 4:13.

5
3

we silence him. [If] someone passes before the ark and errs, another [person] should take his place. At such a time one should not refuse.

מוֹדִים, *we give thanks*, itself.[1] This practice is objectionable because it implies dualism, as if the person is worshiping two gods. *Yerushalmi* (as quoted in *Rav* and *Tosafos* 34a s.v. אמר) states that such repetitions are only objectionable in congregational prayer. Repetition of parts of prayer by an individual praying alone is considered within the parameters of the proper manner of entreaty.

מְשַׁתְּקִין אוֹתוֹ. — *we silence him.*
If the reader uses any of the above formulas, he is immediately silenced.[2]

The mishnah now continues with its second topic, the procedure to be followed if the leader of the prayer service errs.

הָעוֹבֵר לִפְנֵי הַתֵּבָה וְטָעָה, יַעֲבֹר אַחֵר תַּחְתָּיו. — *[If] someone passes before the ark and errs, another [person] should take his place.*
The expression עוֹבֵר לִפְנֵי הַתֵּבָה, *passes before the ark*, refers to the שְׁלִיחַ צִיבּוּר, the individual leading the congregational prayer (*Rambam Comm.*).

Rashi understands that the error referred to in our mishnah is where the leader skipped one of the blessings in the *Shemoneh Esrei* and is unable to return to the proper order of prayer (*Rashi* 24a s.v. מתחילת). Others explain the mistake is where the leader cannot remember the continuation of a blessing (*Meleches Shlomo* from Rabbeinu Yehonasan).[3] In such a case, another individual must be chosen to replace the original leader.

וְלֹא יְהֵא סַרְבָן בְּאוֹתָהּ שָׁעָה. — *At such a time one should not refuse.*
The mishnah's statement that at such a time one should not refuse implies that there are other times when one should refuse (*Rav, Shenos Eliyahu*). The *Gemara* (34a) says that under normal circumstances, as an expression of humility, one should not accept the first request for him to lead the congregation in prayer. In the present case however, to avoid dishonoring the prayer service by delaying it further, one should consent immediately (*Rashi* s.v. ולא יהא סרבן).

1. *Beur Halachah* 121:2 (s.v. האומר) is uncertain whether this means that the person repeated every word of the prayer or whether he repeated only the first word (מודים) twice.

2. Several *Rishonim* (*Rif, Rabbinu Yonah* and *Rosh*) include one other objectionable formula in the beginning of the text of our mishnah. According to their text, the mishnah commences: . . . הָאוֹמֵר: ,,יְבָרְכוּךְ טוֹבִים,״ הֲרֵי זוֹ דֶרֶךְ הַמִּינוּת. הָאוֹמֵר: ,,עַל קַן צִפּוֹר יַגִּיעוּ רַחֲמֶיךָ״ *If one says, "Good men shall bless you," this is heresy. If one says, "your mercy extends to the bird's nest"* . . . For a discussion of why this additional formula is objectionable, see *Megillah* 9:4.

3. It should be remembered that before the advent of printing, it was not uncommon for even the reader to recite his prayers from memory, rather than from a written copy.

מִנַּיִן הוּא מַתְחִיל? מִתְּחִלַּת הַבְּרָכָה שֶׁטָּעָה בָהּ.

[ד] הָעוֹבֵר לִפְנֵי הַתֵּבָה – לֹא יַעֲנֶה אַחַר
הַכֹּהֲנִים אָמֵן, מִפְּנֵי הַטֵּרוּף.

ר' עובדיה מברטנורא

(ד) **לא יענה אמן אחר הכהנים.** בסוף כל ברכה, כמו שֶׁאָר הַצִּבּוּר עוֹנִים: **מפני הטירוף.**
שֶׁלֹּא תִטָּרוּף דַּעְתּוֹ וְיִטְעֶה, לְפִי שֶׁהוּא שְׁלִיחַ צִבּוּר הוּא, צָרִיךְ לְהַתְחִיל בְּרָכָה שְׁנִיָּה וּלְהַקְרוֹת לָהֶן מִלָּה
בְּמִלָּה, וְאִם יַעֲנֶה אָמֵן לֹא יוּכַל לְכַוֵּן וְלַחֲזוֹר לִתְפִלָּתוֹ מַהֵר וּלְהַתְחִיל הַבְּרָכָה שֶׁרְאוּי שֶׁיַּתְחִיל:

יד אברהם

מִנַּיִן הוּא מַתְחִיל? מִתְּחִלַּת הַבְּרָכָה שֶׁטָּעָה בָהּ. — *From where does he* [the second person] *begin? From the beginning of the blessing in which* [the first person] *erred.*

The mishnah specifies that the new leader must start at the beginning of the blessing in which the first leader erred. He then continues the *Shemoneh Esrei* from that point (*Rashi* 34a s.v. מתחלקת), even if he will be repeating words that have already been said (*Meleches Shlomo*).

This rule applies when the problem arose in one of the middle blessings of the *Shemoneh Esrei*. If, however, it arose in one of the three opening blessings of the *Shemoneh Esrei*, the

new leader starts over from the beginning of the *Shemoneh Esrei*. Similarly, if the problem arose in one of the three concluding blessings, the new leader starts from רְצֵה, which is the beginning of the last section of the *Shemoneh Esrei* (*Tos. R' Akiva Eiger* from *Gem.* 34a). This is because the first three blessings, as well as the last three, are each viewed as single units, and are therefore treated like a single blessing (*Beis Yosef* 114).

Rashi had a slightly different text of our mishnah. Instead of שֶׁטָּעָה בָהּ, "in which he erred," which refers to the blessing, *Rashi* reads שֶׁטָּעָה זֶה, "that this one [i.e. the leader] erred."

4.

During the repetition of the *Shemoneh Esrei*, just before the start of the last blessing (שִׂים שָׁלוֹם), the *Kohanim* in the congregation face the worshipers from the front of the synagogue and bless them.[1] This is known as נְשִׂיאַת כַּפַּיִם, literally, the "lifting of hands," because the *Kohanim* must pronounce the blessings with raised hands (see *Sotah* 7:6).

The text of this blessing consists of three verses in *Numbers* (6:24-26): *May Hashem bless you and safeguard you. May Hashem illuminate His countenance to you and be gracious to you. May Hashem lift His countenance to you and establish peace for you.* The recitation of this blessing by the *Kohanim* fulfills a Torah commandment (see *Numbers* 6:22 and

---

1. In Eretz Yisrael, this is done every morning. In the Diaspora, this is done by Ashkenazic Jews only in the reader's repetition of the *Mussaf* prayer on Festivals (see *Rama, Orach Chaim* 128:44 and *Mishnah Berurah* 128:164). Most Sephardic congregations, however, recite the Kohanic blessing every day even in the Diaspora.

5	From where does he begin? From the beginning
4	of the blessing in which [the first person] erred.

4. The one who passes before the ark should not respond "Amen" after the [blessings of the] *Kohanim* because of the [risk of] confusion.

Rambam, Sefer HaMitzvos, Asei 26).

The manner in which these blessings are said is responsive. The leader of the service [*shliach tzibbur*] first says one word of the verse and the *Kohanim* then repeat it.[1] When the *Kohanim* finish saying each verse, the congregation answers "Amen." The process is continued until the conclusion of all three verses (*Rambam Comm.*).[2]

The following mishnah discusses the laws that apply to the leader of the service during the Kohanic blessing, and specifically addresses the case where the leader himself is a *Kohen*.

הָעוֹבֵר לִפְנֵי הַתֵּבָה – לֹא יַעֲנֶה אַחַר הַכֹּהֲנִים "אָמֵן", מִפְּנֵי הַטֵּרוּף. — *The one who passes before the ark should not respond "Amen" after the [blessings of the] Kohanim, because of the [risk of] confusion.*

"The one who passes before the ark" refers to the *shliach tzibbur*, the leader of the congregational prayer. Although the congregation answers "Amen" after the completion of each verse by the *Kohanim*, the leader does not. This is because immediately after the congregation's response of "Amen," the leader must continue with the next verse. If he too were to answer "Amen," it

was feared that he might lose his place (*Rambam Comm.*), and not be able to continue quickly (*Rav, Rashi* s.v. מפני הטרוף). Accordingly, it was ruled that the leader should not respond "Amen" to the blessing of the *Kohanim*.

Tosafos (34a s.v. לא יענה) wonder why this rationale is given when the mishnah could more simply have said that responding "Amen" constitutes an interruption of the leader's repetition of the *Shemoneh Esrei*. *Tosafos* conclude from this that responding "Amen" to the *Kohen's* blessings is considered a necessary part of the prayers and therefore is not deemed an improper extraneous interruption (see *Mishnah Berurah* 128:71).

1. There are different customs regarding the procedure for the first word of the blessing. *Shulchan Aruch* (*Orach Chaim* 128:13) rules that the *Kohanim* say this word on their own, without being prompted by the leader. *Rama*, however, states that the custom of Ashkenazic Jews is for the leader to call out this word as well.

2. *Tosafos* (34a s.v. לא יענה) say that this is based upon the *Sifrei*, which derives this halachah from *Numbers* 6:23, where Moses is commanded, "Speak to Aaron and his sons saying, so shall you bless the children of Israel, *say to them*." That is, Moses was commanded not only to tell Aaron and his children to bless the people, but also to "say to them" the exact words of the blessing for them to repeat. Likewise, each time the Kohanim recite these blessings, the prayer leader must say to them the words they are to recite. See *Rashi* (s.v. מפני הטירוף), however, who does not cite *Sifrei* as a source but a *Gemara* in *Sotah* (39b.)

וְאִם אֵין שָׁם כֹּהֵן אֶלָּא הוּא – לֹא יִשָּׂא אֶת
כַּפָּיו. וְאִם הַבְטָחָתוֹ שֶׁהוּא נוֹשֵׂא אֶת כַּפָּיו
וְחוֹזֵר לִתְפִלָּתוֹ – רַשַּׁאי.

ר' עובדיה מברטנורא

לֹא ישא את כפיו. שמא לא יוכל לכוין ולחזור לתפלתו להתחיל שים שלום, שתהא דעתו מטורפת
מאימתא דצבורא: **ואם הבטחתו.** כלומר אם בטוח הוא שלא תהא דעתו מטורפת מאימת הצבור:

יד אברהם

וְאִם אֵין שָׁם כֹּהֵן אֶלָּא הוּא – לֹא יִשָּׂא אֶת
כַּפָּיו. — *And if there is no Kohen there
except him, he should not lift up his
hands.*

If the leader is the only *Kohen* in the
synagogue, he should forgo giving
the blessing of the *Kohanim*. This is
because if the leader himself were to
bestow the blessing, he might become
confused and be unable to continue
his repetition of the *Shemoneh Esrei*
(*Rav, Rashi* s.v. לא ישא את כפיו).

וְאִם הַבְטָחָתוֹ שֶׁהוּא נוֹשֵׂא אֶת כַּפָּיו וְחוֹזֵר
לִתְפִלָּתוֹ – רַשַּׁאי. — *But if he is confident that he can lift up his hands and
resume his prayer, he is permitted [to
do so].*

If the reader is certain that he will
be able to resume his repetition of the
Shemoneh Esrei without difficulty,

then he is permitted to bestow the
blessing of the *Kohanim* (*Rav, Rashi*
s.v. ואם הבטחתו).[1]

This ruling of the Mishnah is a continuation of the previous ruling and it
refers to the case in which "there is no
Kohen there except him" to bestow
the blessing.[2] Accordingly, if there
are other *Kohanim* available to bless
the congregation, even a confident
Kohen is prohibited from joining in
bestowing the blessing (*Tos. Yom Tov
from Hagahos Maimoniyos, Hil.
Tefillah* 15:10; *Tur Orach Chaim* 128
*from Maharam Rotenberg; Darkei
Moshe* 128:12).[3]

Bach (128 s.v. כתב) explains that the reason even a confident leader does not join
other *Kohanim* in bestowing the blessing is
that there is always some risk that he may

---

1. [The mishnah's ruling was said in a time when people did not pray from *siddurim*, but
by heart. [A person reciting something by heart will often become confused if he deviates
from his memorized text.] In our days, however, since we pray using a *siddur*, every
Kohen is considered able to resume his prayer without hesitating or becoming confused
(*Mishnah Berurah* 128:76).

2. This may be seen from the fact that the mishnah does not say in its first ruling that if
the leader is a *Kohen*, he should not lift his hands *even* if there is no other *Kohen*. Rather,
the mishnah makes a separate ruling out of the case of a leader who is the only *Kohen*
("And if there is no other *Kohen* ..."). This indicates that the next ruling ("if he is
confident, etc.") is said only in regard to the particular case of the leader being the only
Kohen present and not in regard to the more general case discussed at the beginning of
the mishnah where the leader is just one of several *Kohanim* present (*Bach* s.v. כתב; *Tos.
R' Akiva*, and *Shenos Eliyahu*).

3. See, however, *Pri Chadash* (128:20) who presents an alternative explanation of the
Mishnah, according to which a confident *Kohen* would be permitted to bless the people
even if there are other *Kohanim* present.

5
4

And if there is no *Kohen* there except him, he should not lift up his hands. But if he is confident that he can lift up his hands and resume his prayer, he is permitted [to do so].

YAD AVRAHAM

in fact not be able to resume the *Shemoneh Esrei* without hesitation or confusion. Because of this, the Rabbis limited their permission for the confident leader to bestow the blessing to the case where he is the sole *Kohen*, to prevent the blessing from being omitted altogether.

Alternatively, the reason they permitted this only where he is the sole *Kohen* is because of the rule requiring the *Kohanim* who bless the congregation to do so from the platform at the front of the synagogue (see *Sotah* 38b). This requirement applies even to the *Kohen* who is presently leading the congregation in the repetition of the *Shemoneh Esrei* (*Orach Chaim* 128:20). Since in normal circumstances an individual praying the *Shemoneh Esrei* may not move from his place (see *Orach Chaim* 104:2), the mishnah only permits a *Kohen* leading the service to move if he is the sole *Kohen* present (*Mishnah Berurah* 128:72).

The mishnah states its exception for a *Kohen* who is confident only in regard to its second ruling (bestowing the blessing of the *Kohanim*), not in regard to its first ruling (answering "Amen" to these blessings). This leads some commentators to conclude that even a confident leader may not answer "Amen" to the blessings of the *Kohanim*. The reason for this distinction is based on the rationale cited above — that the Rabbis relied on the confidence of the *Kohen* only so that the Kohanic blessing should not be omitted altogether. The importance of a *Kohen* blessing the congregation outweighs the (small) risk of a subsequent delay in the continuation of the service. The leader's answering "Amen" to the blessings of the *Kohanim*, however, is not sufficiently important to outweigh that risk (*Tos. Yom Tov, Bach* s.v וכתב).

Other commentators, however, maintain that if the leader has confidence that he will not become confused, he may even answer "Amen." The reason the mishnah explicitly states this rule only in regard to bestowing the blessing is to teach us that we rely on the *Kohen's* confidence *even* to permit something as involved as blessing the congregation. It follows without saying that something less involved, such as simply saying "Amen," is also permissible (*Tos. Yom Tov* from *Midrash Rabbah* to *Deuteronomy* 26 [*Parshah* 7 sec. 1], *Tif. Yis., Pri Chadash* 128:20).[1]

[*Tos. Yom Tov* raises the issue in this context of whether halachic rulings may be derived from Midrashic sources. See *Tos. Yom Tov, Tos. R' Akiva Eiger* and *Tos. Anshei Shem* for a discussion of this matter.]

1. *Mishnah Berurah* 128:71 concludes that if the leader is using a *siddur* and has confidence that he will not become confused, he may answer "Amen." [This discussion applies solely to the "Amen" following the *Kohen's* blessing of the people. There are opinions, however, that it is prohibited for the leader to answer "Amen" to the blessing אֲשֶׁר קִדְּשָׁנוּ בִּקְדֻשָּׁתוֹ שֶׁל אַהֲרֹן וכו', which the *Kohanim* recite before bestowing the Kohanic blessing on the people. See further in *Mishnah Berurah* ibid.]

[ה] **הַמִּתְפַּלֵּל** וְטָעָה – סִימָן רַע לוֹ; וְאִם
שְׁלִיחַ צִבּוּר הוּא – סִימָן
רַע לְשׁוֹלְחָיו, מִפְּנֵי שֶׁשְּׁלוּחוֹ שֶׁל אָדָם כְּמוֹתוֹ.
אָמְרוּ עָלָיו עַל רַבִּי חֲנִינָא בֶּן דּוֹסָא כְּשֶׁהָיָה
מִתְפַּלֵּל עַל הַחוֹלִים, וְאוֹמֵר: ,,זֶה חַי״ וְ,,זֶה
מֵת״. אָמְרוּ לוֹ: ,,מִנַּיִן אַתָּה יוֹדֵעַ?״ אָמַר לָהֶם:
,,אִם שְׁגוּרָה תְפִלָּתִי בְּפִי – יוֹדֵעַ אֲנִי שֶׁהוּא
מְקֻבָּל; וְאִם לַאו – יוֹדֵעַ אֲנִי שֶׁהוּא מְטֹרָף״.

ר׳ עובדיה מברטנורא

(ה) **אם שגורה תפלתי.** סדורה בפי במרוצה ואיני נכשל בה: **שהוא מטורף.** שהחולה מטורף,
כמו אך טרוף טורף (בראשית מד, כח). פירוש אחר, לשון טורפים לו תפלתו בפניו (בגמרא לעיל
ה, ב), כלומר התפלה שהתפללו עליו מטורפת וערודה ממנו ואינה מקובלת:

יד אברהם

5.

The previous mishnah discussed regulations instituted by the Rabbis to prevent a *shliach tzibbur* from erring while he leads the congregation in prayer. The following mishnah details some implications of erring in prayer.

הַמִּתְפַּלֵּל וְטָעָה – סִימָן רַע לוֹ; — [If] *someone is praying and errs, it is a bad sign for him;*

The *Gemara* (34b) explains that an error in one's prayer is considered a bad omen only in the first blessing of the *Shemoneh Esrei* (known as אָבוֹת, *Patriarchs*). Since he is now beginning the *Shemoneh Esrei*, a mistake at this point is considered a sign that [Heaven considers] his prayer undesirable (*Rashi* s.v. באבות).

וְאִם שְׁלִיחַ צִבּוּר הוּא – סִימָן רַע לְשׁוֹלְחָיו, — *and if he is an agent of the congregation, it is a bad sign for those whom he represents,*

The term שְׁלִיחַ צִבּוּר, which refers to the individual leading the congregational prayer, literally means "the agent of the congregation," i.e., the individual who represents the entire congregation before God. If that agent errs in the opening blessing of the *Shemoneh Esrei*, it reflects negatively on those who sent him to represent them.

מִפְּנֵי שֶׁשְּׁלוּחוֹ שֶׁל אָדָם כְּמוֹתוֹ. — *because the agent of a person is like [the person] himself.*

There is a general principle that the actions of a person's agent are considered like the actions of the person himself. Accordingly, if the congregation's representative errs in the opening blessing of the *Shemoneh Esrei*, it is a sign from Heaven that this congregation's prayer is undesirable.

The rule that the actions of a person's agent are considered like his own is derived from *Exodus* 12:6, where the Torah states that the entire community of Israel should slaughter the *pesach* offering. In truth,

5 **5.** [If] someone is praying and errs, it is a bad
5 sign for him; and if he is an agent of the
congregation, it is a bad sign for those whom he
represents, because the agent of a person is like [the
person] himself. They said about R' Chanina ben
Dosa that when he would pray on behalf of the
sick, he would say, "This one will live" or, "This
one will die." They said to him: "How do you
know?" He said to them: "If my prayer is fluent in
my mouth, then I know that it is accepted; but if
not, then I know that he is rejected."

not every person actually slaughtered a
lamb; rather, people joined in groups and
shared a lamb [as the Torah itself states
in verse 4 there]. Thus, when the verse
states that everyone should slaughter a
lamb, it must mean that one person slaugh-
tering a lamb on behalf of his group is considered as if each of the members has personally slaughtered it (*Rabbeinu Yonah*
from *Kiddushin* 42a, quoted by *Tos. Yom
Tov*).

אָמְרוּ עָלָיו עַל רַבִּי חֲנִינָא בֶּן דּוֹסָא כְּשֶׁהָיָה
מִתְפַּלֵּל עַל הַחוֹלִים, וְאוֹמֵר: ,,זֶה חַי״ וְ,זֶה
מֵת.״ — *They said about R' Chanina
ben Dosa that when he would pray
on behalf of the sick, he would say,
"This one will live" or, "This one will
die."*

Some commentaries point out that
it cannot be that R' Chanina ben Dosa
actually said that the sick person
would die, since such fateful remarks
are not to be made (see *Gemara* 19a,
Shulchan Aruch Yoreh Deah 376:2,
and *Kitzur Shulchan Aruch* 33:14).
Rather, our mishnah means either that
R' Chanina ben Dosa said this in a
questioning tone (meaning "Will this
one die?"), or he said nothing at all but
it was understood from his motions

that the sick person would not live
(*Tif. Yis.*).

אָמְרוּ לוֹ: ,,מִנַּיִן אַתָּה יוֹדֵעַ״? — *They said
to him: "How do you know?"*

How do you know whether the sick
person will live or die?

אָמַר לָהֶם: ,,אִם שְׁגוּרָה תְּפִלָּתִי בְּפִי — יוֹדֵעַ
אֲנִי שֶׁהוּא מְקֻבָּל; — *He said to them: "If
my prayer is fluent in my mouth, then
I know that it is accepted;*

R' Chanina ben Dosa answered that
if he was able to pray fluently, i.e.
without mistakes (*Rav*), with his
prayers "flowing from his heart to his
mouth," enabling him to say whatever he wished to say even when he
prayed at length, then he knew that
his prayers were accepted (*Rashi* s.v.
אם שגורה). In such a case, he was certain that the person for whose health
he prayed would live.

וְאִם לָאו — יוֹדֵעַ אֲנִי שֶׁהוּא מְטֹרָף.״ — *but
if not, then I know that he is rejected."*

If R' Chanina experienced difficulty concentrating, and his prayer
did not flow fluently, then he knew
that the person for whom he was
praying had been rejected (*Rav,
Rashi*) and would not survive.

יד אברהם

Our translation of אֲנִי שֶׁהוּא יוֹדֵעַ,,
"מְטוֹרָף", "*I know that [the sick person]
has been rejected,*" follows the first
explanation of *Rav* and *Rashi* (s.v.
שהוא מטורף). According to their second explanation, these words refer not
to the sick person but to the prayer
offered on his behalf. The mishnah
would therefore translate as: "I know
that *it* [the prayer] has been rejected."
The rejection of the prayer made it
clear that the person himself would
not survive.

The *Vilna Gaon* (in *Shenos Eliyahu*) supports the first explanation. He notes that
since the word תְּפִילָה (prayer) is a feminine

noun, the word מְטוֹרָף (rejected) used to describe it should also be in the feminine
form — i.e. מְטוֹרֶפֶת, rather than מְטוֹרָף. The
use of the masculine form of the word
demonstrates that it is referring to the person, not the prayer. For further discussion
of this topic, see *Meiri* (who understands
our Mishnah to mean "the subject of the
prayer was rejected") and *Tos. Yom Tov.*

Tzlach (29b s.v. יצא בקונך המלך) comments that the Providential sign given by
R' Chanina ben Dosa is limited to someone
of his stature. For most people, one's flu-
ency or difficulty in prayer is not to be
understood as a Providential sign — except
during the first blessing in the *Shemoneh
Esrei.*

פרק ששי

Chapter Six

ברכות [א] **כֵּיצַד** מְבָרְכִין עַל הַפֵּרוֹת? עַל פֵּרוֹת
הָאִילָן אוֹמֵר: ,,בּוֹרֵא פְּרִי הָעֵץ".
חוּץ מִן הַיַּיִן, שֶׁעַל הַיַּיִן אוֹמֵר: ,,בּוֹרֵא פְּרִי הַגָּפֶן".

———————— ר' עובדיה מברטנורא ————————

פרק ששי – כיצד מברכין. (א) כיצד מברכין. חוץ מן היין. שמתוך חשיבותו קבעו
לו ברכה לעצמו, וכן הפת:

יד אברהם

1.

The mishnah now turns to the laws regarding blessings over food. As previously noted (comm. to mishnah 3:4 s.v. ועל המזון), the blessings recited before eating or drinking are Rabbinical enactments, instituted by Ezra and his contemporaries, the Men of the Great Assembly (*Rambam, Hil. Berachos* 1:5, *Hil. Kerias Shema* 1:7).[1] This Rabbinical requirement is based on the logical premise that it is appropriate for a person to acknowledge and thank the One Who created the item from which he is about to benefit. Hence, the Rabbis decreed that one must recite a blessing before eating or drinking [or when smelling an aromatic substance — see below, mishnah 6]. In the words of the *Gemara*: It is forbidden for a person to derive benefit from this world without [first reciting] a blessing (*Gem.* 35a; see *Rashi* ad loc. s.v. אלא סברא). The *Bircas HaMazon* (the Grace After Meals) recited after eating is a *Biblical* obligation, as the verse (*Deuteronomy* 8:10) states: *You will eat and you will be satisfied, and bless Hashem, your God, for the good Land that He gave you.* The other after-blessings, and the scope of the Biblical *Bircas HaMazon* obligation, will be discussed in the last mishnah of this chapter.

The other mishnayos in the chapter focus on the blessings recited before eating. The following mishnah discusses the formulas of the blessings recited over various types of food.

כֵּיצַד מְבָרְכִין עַל הַפֵּרוֹת? — *In what manner do we recite the blessings on produce?*

I.e. what are the texts of the blessings recited before eating food (see *Rambam Comm.; Tif. Yis.* §1).

Although the term פֵּרוֹת generally means "fruit," the mishnah uses the term in a very general sense, referring to all food products, including those that do not grow from the ground [see *Kiddushin* 28b with *Rashi* s.v. ופירי נמי] (*Tzlach*, cited by *Tos. Anshei Shem* s.v. על הפרות).

The mishnah's statement assumes a prior awareness of the fundamental requirement to recite a blessing before eating. *Tosafos* (to 35a s.v. כיצד, cited by *Tos. Yom Tov*) suggest that the mishnah presumes the reader is familiar with this obligation, because it is a logical requirement (see prefatory comments). Alternatively, *Tosafos* explain that the mishnah assumes the reader is aware of this obligation from an earlier mishnah (3:4), which makes reference to a *baal keri's* exemption

1. Based on his understanding of the *Gemara* on 35a, *Rabbeinu Chananel* (ad loc. s.v. ואסיקנא) maintains that the obligation to recite a blessing before eating agricultural produce *is* Biblical. However, the vast majority of authorities contend that the blessing before eating *any* type of food is a Rabbinical requirement (see *Tzlach* to 35a s.v. ודעת הפוסקים).

1. **I**n what manner do we recite the blessings on produce? On fruits of the tree one says: *". . . Who creates the fruit of the tree"*; except for wine, for on wine one says: *". . . Who creates the fruit of the vine."*

YAD AVRAHAM

from reciting the blessings before eating. *Rabbeinu Yonah* (24b s.v. כיצד, cited by *Tos. Yom Tov* ibid.) suggests that the *Tanna's* assumption is based on mishnah 1:4. Mishnah 1:4 refers to the blessings that do not conclude with the closing formula *Blessed are You, Hashem* etc., and the commentators explain this to refer to the blessings recited before eating (see comm. there, s.v. ושלא לחתום; see also *Tosafos* to 11a s.v. מקום שאמרו).

עַל פֵּרוֹת הָאִילָן אוֹמֵר: ,,בּוֹרֵא פְּרִי הָעֵץ'', — *On fruits of the tree one says: ". . . Who creates the fruit of the tree";*

The full text of the blessing is: *Blessed are You, Hashem, our God, King of the universe, Who creates the fruit of the tree.*[1] Our mishnah, which details the different blessings recited for different foods, omits this opening clause, which is common to all blessings (*Rambam Comm.*). [The criteria of a "tree" as regards the laws of blessings will be discussed in the comm. to the next mishnah s.v. ועל פרות הארץ.]

In mishnaic Hebrew, the fruit of a tree is called פְּרִי הָאִילָן ["fruit of the *ilan*"]. However, in Biblical Hebrew it is called פְּרִי הָעֵץ ["fruit of the *eitz*"] (see *Exodus* 10:15).[2] The blessing on tree fruit refers to "fruit of the *eitz*" because the text of blessings con-

forms to Biblical Hebrew (*Tos. Anshei Shem* s.v. בפה"א).

חוּץ מִן הַיַּיִן, שֶׁעַל הַיַּיִן אוֹמֵר: ,,בּוֹרֵא פְּרִי הַגָּפֶן.'' — *except for wine, for on wine one says: ". . . Who creates the fruit of the vine."*

This blessing (*Borei pri hagafen*) refers to the *specific* tree from which wine is derived. Although wine is also included in the more general category of "fruit of the tree," the Rabbis formulated a special blessing for wine because of its significance (*Rav; Rashi*). Wine has a two-fold distinction: When drunk in moderation, it satisfies one's hunger like bread; and it gladdens people [see *Psalms* 104:15] (*Tos. Yom Tov*, from *Gem.* 35b). [See comm. to next mishnah s.v. על כולם regarding whether one who recites the blessing of *Borei pri ha'eitz* on wine has discharged his obligation after the fact.]

The ultimate purpose of vines is to produce wine. Thus, although wine is only the *juice* of the grapes that grow on the vine, it is considered to be "the fruit" of the vine, and is appropriately referred to as such in the blessing. Similarly, olive oil is considered to be "the fruit" of the olive tree (see *Terumos* 11:3), because the purpose of an olive tree is to produce oil (see *Gem.* 36a with *Rashi* s.v. הכא אית ליה). [However, since olive oil does not share wine's qualities of satisfying hunger and fostering joy,

1. There is a dispute in the *Gemara* (40b) whether the words "King of the universe" (which acknowledge God's sovereignty) are an essential component of a blessing. The halachah follows the view that these words *are* critical to the validity of a blessing (see *Shulchan Aruch, Orach Chaim* 214:1).

2. The term אילן occurs only once in Scripture, in a verse (*Daniel* 4:7) which is written in Aramaic.

יד אברהם

the Rabbis did not formulate a special blessing for it. Thus, the blessing over olive oil remains *Borei pri ha'eitz* (see *Gem.* 35b).][1] Other fruit juices, however, are considered *by-products* of fruit, and not actual fruits of a tree. In the *Gemara's* (38a) words, the juice of fruit (except wine and oil) is merely the "sweat" [זֵיעָה] of fruit. Therefore, fruit juices are subject to the blessing of "...*Shehakol nihiyeh b'dvaro*," rather than the blessing of *Borei pri ha'eitz* (see *Gem.* 38a; *Shulchan Aruch, Orach Chaim* 202:8). [The *Shehakol* blessing will be discussed in mishnah 3.]

The *Borei pri hagafen* blessing was instituted only for wine. Although grapes are also "fruit of the vine," they are no more significant than other fruit, so their blessing is *Borei pri ha'eitz* (*Meiri*; see also *R' Shlomo Sirilio*, cited by *Meleches Shlomo*).

וְעַל פֵּרוֹת הָאָרֶץ אוֹמֵר: „בּוֹרֵא פְּרִי הָאֲדָמָה,״ — *And on fruits of the earth one says: "...Who creates the fruit of the ground"*;

The designation "fruits of the earth" refers to the produce of plants, i.e. grains [such as wheat and barley][2] (*Rashi*), legumes [such as beans and lentils] (*Rabbeinu Yonah* 24b s.v. ועל פירות הארץ, cited by *Meleches Shlomo*), and gourds, melons and cucumbers (*Meiri*).

Included in the classification of "fruits of the earth" is the produce of any plant which does not meet the halachic definition of a "tree" (as will be defined in the comm. to the next mishnah s.v. ועל פרות הארץ).

Although the mishnah refers to these foods as פֵּרוֹת הָאָרֶץ ("fruits of the *earth*"), the blessing uses the term פְּרִי הָאֲדָמָה ("fruits of the *ground*") because this is how Scripture refers to these "fruits" (see *Deuteronomy* 26:2), and the text of blessings conform to Biblical Hebrew (*Tos. Anshei Shem* s.v. בפה"א; see above, s.v. על פרות האילן; see also *Meiri*; see *Shenos Eliyahu* and *Aruch HaShulchan, Orach Chaim* 203:1 for a different explanation of the blessing's use of the term אֲדָמָה).

חוּץ מִן הַפַּת, שֶׁעַל הַפַּת הוּא אוֹמֵר: „הַמוֹצִיא לֶחֶם מִן הָאָרֶץ.״ — *except for bread, for on bread one says: "...the One Who brings forth bread from the earth."*

Although bread is made from grain, which is a "fruit of the earth," the Rabbis formulated a special blessing for bread because of its significance [as a staple of life] (*Rav; Rashi*). [The issue of whether one who recites the *Borei pri ha'adamah* blessing on bread has discharged his obligation (after the fact) will be discussed in the comm. to the next mishnah s.v. על כולם.]

The Rabbis also formulated a special blessing for all other grain products (e.g.

---

1. It should be noted that this blessing is only recited when one drinks olive oil as part of a mixture [in which the oil is the primary component (*Gem.* 36a), either because of its quantity (see *Rashi* ad loc. s.v. החושש בגרונו) or by virtue of its therapeutic value, for which the person drinks this mixture (see *Shulchan Aruch, Orach Chaim* 202:4 with *Mishnah Berurah* §31)]. One who drinks *plain* olive oil does *not* recite *Borei pri ha'eitz*, since this drink is harmful rather than beneficial (*Gem.* 35b.). According to *Rambam* (*Hil. Berachos* 8:2), in this case, one recites the blessing of *Shehakol*. In the opinion of *Rashi* (ad loc. s.v. אזוקי מזיק) and *Rif* (25a), *no* blessing is recited on plain olive oil. This is the view followed by *Shulchan Aruch* (loc. cit.).

2. I.e. *kernels* of wheat and barley. The blessing over *flour* is *Shehakol* (*Shulchan Aruch, Orach Chaim* 208:5; see *Gem.* 36a).

6
1

And on fruits of the earth one says: "... *Who creates the fruit of the ground*"; except for bread, for on bread one says: "... *the One Who brings forth bread from*

cereal, pasta) — the blessing of בּוֹרֵא מִינֵי מְזוֹנוֹת, *Who creates species of sustenance*. This blessing is also prescribed for the form of bread known as פַּת הַבָּאָה בְּכִיסָנִין, *kisnin*-bread. The precise definition of this term is the subject of considerable dispute (see *Shulchan Aruch* 168:7). However, there is general agreement that it is a baked good which, while related to bread, is eaten as a snack, unlike regular bread which is eaten as a staple. [However, when eaten in amounts that would constitute a meal for most people (see details in *Mishnah Berurah* 168:24), *kisnin*-bread is subject to the *Hamotzi* blessing (and *Birkas Hamazon*), like regular bread.]

It seems odd that our mishnah does not mention the *Borei minei mezonos* blessing together with the others. Possibly, this omission is because our mishnah only discusses blessings that are recited over many different species of food (for example, *Borei pri ha'eitz*, which is recited over all types of tree fruit). The *Borei minei mezonos* blessing, however, is only recited over grain products[1] (*P'nei Yehoshua* to 35a s.v. מתני׳ ביצד מברכים, cited by *Tos. Anshei Shem* s.v. ביצד).

The text of the blessing over bread (*Hamotzi*) differs in many respects from the blessings for other foods. While the other blessings refer to God as the One "Who *creates* the fruit of...," *Hamotzi* refers to Him as the One "Who *brings forth* bread." Whereas *God* creates fruits and vegetables, the making of bread — al-

though based on grain created by God — is a *human* process. Thus, we refer to God not as the *Creator* of bread, but as the One "Who *brings forth* from the ground" the means to produce bread. Alternatively, the text of the *Hamotzi* blessing is based on *Psalms* (104:14), which states: מַצְמִיחַ חָצִיר לַבְּהֵמָה וְעֵשֶׂב לַעֲבֹדַת הָאָדָם לְהוֹצִיא לֶחֶם מִן הָאָרֶץ, "He causes vegetation to sprout for the animal, and plants through man's labor, *to bring forth bread* from the earth" (*Tos. Anshei Shem*; see *Tif. Yis.* §5 and *Shenos Eliyahu* for other explanations). This verse also uses the term אֶרֶץ in reference to bread, rather than the term אֲדָמָה Scripture uses when referring to "fruits of the earth" (see above, s.v. ועל פרות הארץ). Therefore, the *Hamotzi* blessing, too, uses the term אֶרֶץ (*Meiri; Ritva; Shitah Mekubetzes* to 35a s.v. חוץ מן הפת).

Another difference between *Hamotzi* and other blessings is that the term מוֹצִיא (*motzi*) is preceded by the definite article הַ, *the*, while in the other blessings, the term בּוֹרֵא (*borei*) does not contain this prefix. *Yerushalmi* (cited by *Tosafos* to 38b s.v. והלכתא) explains that the Rabbis prefixed the term מוֹצִיא with the הַ because the preceding word, *ha'olam*, ends with the same "m" sound with which the word *motzi* begins. The Rabbis interrupted the two "m" sounds with the prefix הַ to avoid the possibility that one would merge the two consonants when reciting the blessing.[2] [Although this juxtaposition of similar sounds also occurs later in the blessing — with the

---

1. Although the *Hamotzi* blessing is also only recited over a product of grain, the mishnah lists it to demonstrate that there are exceptions to the rule that the blessing on "fruits of the earth" is *Borei pri ha'adamah*. Similarly, the mishnah mentions the blessing of *Borei pri hagafen* to show that not all "fruit of the tree" are subject to the *Borei pri ha'eitz* blessing (*P'nei Yehoshua* ibid.).

2. However, if one says "*motzi*," his blessing is valid (*Mishnah Berurah* 167:16).

The precise term used in the *Hamotzi* blessing is actually the subject of dispute in a Baraisa cited by the *Gemara* (38a). R' Nechemiah argues that the correct term is *motzi*, which connotes the past ("Who *has brought* forth"), rather than *hamotzi*, which connotes

הָאָרֶץ". וְעַל הַיְרָקוֹת אוֹמֵר: "בּוֹרֵא פְּרִי הָאֲדָמָה". רַבִּי יְהוּדָה אוֹמֵר, בּוֹרֵא מִינֵי דְשָׁאִים.

─────── ר' עובדיה מברטנורא ───────

בורא מיני דשאים. לפי שיש בכלל פרי האדמה דשא, וזרעים כגון קטניות, ורבי יהודה בעי היכר ברכה לכל מין ומין, ואין הלכה כרבי יהודה. והא דתנן על הירקות אומר בורא פרי האדמה, הני מילי ירקות שדרכן לאכלן חיין ואכלן חיין או שדרכן לאכלן מבושלים ואכלן מבושלים, אבל אותן שדרכן לאכלן חיין שאכלן מבושלים או שדרכן לאכלן מבושלים ואכלן חיין אינו מברך עליהן אלא שהכל. וירקות שאוכלין אותם בין חיין בין מבושלים, מברכין עליהן בורא פרי האדמה בין חיין בין מבושלים:

יד אברהם

words לֶחֶם מִן, *lechem min* ("bread from") — the Rabbis did not insert a prefix between the two words so the text of the blessing should conform to the verse in *Psalms*, which states: לֶחֶם מִן הָאָרֶץ (*Tosafos* ibid)[1].] The concern of merged consonants does not apply to the other blessings, where the word *ha'olam* is followed by *borei*, so no prefix was added (*Meleches Shlomo*).

— וְעַל הַיְרָקוֹת אוֹמֵר: "בּוֹרֵא פְּרִי הָאֲדָמָה". *And on greens one says: "... Who creates the fruit of the ground."*

[The term יְרָקוֹת, *greens*, refers to plants which are themselves eaten, in contrast to "fruits of the earth," which are the *produce* of the plant.] Cabbage and lettuce are examples of "greens" (*Rabbeinu Yonah* loc. cit., cited by *Meleches Shlomo* s.v. ועל פירות הארץ). This group also includes edible roots, such as carrots and beets (*Meiri*). Like the "fruits of the earth" mentioned earlier, the blessing for these foods is *Borei pri ha'adamah*.

This clause of the mishnah seems superfluous; greens could easily have

been included in the previous clause which discussed "fruit of the earth." The *Gemara* (38b) explains this seeming superfluity (see *Tos. Anshei Shem*) by stating that the mishnah mentions "greens" in a separate clause to draw a parallel between greens and the "bread" mentioned in the previous clause. Just as bread is a food that has been transformed by fire (i.e. baked), so too the mishnah refers to "greens" that have been transformed by fire (i.e. cooked). The mishnah, thus, teaches that *cooked* vegetables are also subject to the blessing of *Borei pri ha'adamah*, although they have been transformed from their natural state.

However, the blessing of *Borei pri ha'adamah* is recited on cooked vegetables only if they are *usually* eaten cooked. The blessing on a cooked vegetable that is generally eaten raw is *Shehakol* (*Rav* s.v. בורא מיני דשאים). Similarly, the blessing on a raw vegetable that is usually eaten cooked is *Shehakol* rather than *Borei pri ha'adamah*. Vegetables that are eaten both raw and cooked are subject to the *Borei pri ha'ada-*

future ("Who *will* bring forth"), since we thank God for the bread He has already "brought forth." The *Tanna Kamma* contends that the term *hamotzi* connotes the past as well as the future, and its use is therefore appropriate in the blessing. Although the *Tanna Kamma* agrees that the term *motzi* denotes the past, the *Gemara* rules that one should say *hamotzi. Tosafos* cite the aforementioned *Yerushalmi* to explain why the *Gemara* rules in favor of the disputed term over the term *motzi*, which all agree is appropriate.

1. However, one must certainly be careful not to merge the two consonants (*Levush* 167:2, cited by *Meleches Shlomo*).

6
1

the earth," And on greens one says: "... Who creates the fruit of the ground," R' Yehudah says: "... Who creates species of herbage."

mah blessing in all instances (*Rav* ibid.; *Rambam Comm.*; see further *Tosafos* to 38b s.v. משכחת). The same rules apply for tree fruit (*Tosafos* ibid.; see *Shulchan Aruch* 205:1 and *Beur Halachah* ad loc. s.v. שטובים חיים ומבושלים).

— רַבִּי יְהוּדָה אוֹמֵר: ,,בּוֹרֵא מִינֵי דְשָׁאִים". *R' Yehudah says: "... Who creates species of herbage."*

R' Yehudah disputes the *Tanna Kamma's* assertion that the blessing over greens is *Borei pri ha'adamah.* According to R' Yehudah, the correct blessing is *Borei minei deshaim.*

R' Yehudah requires a higher degree of specificity with regard to blessings. He maintains that the blessing must refer to the specific subcategory of food being eaten, rather than to the general category of "fruits of the ground" (*Rav*). Since a defining characteristic of greens is that the plant itself is eaten, greens form a subcategory to which their blessing must refer.

R' Yehudah also disagrees with the *Tanna Kamma's* ruling that the blessing on grains and legumes is *Borei pri ha'adamah.* These foods share the characteristic that the *seeds* of the plant are eaten, rather than the plant itself, and they form a separate subcategory within the general category of "fruits of the earth." According to R'

Yehudah, the correct blessing for them is בּוֹרֵא מִינֵי זְרָעִים, *Who creates species of seeds* (see *Gem.* 37a; see also *Tosefta, Berachos* 4:5).[1]

However, R' Yehudah agrees that the blessing on other "fruits of the earth" (e.g. melons, cucumbers and tomatoes) is *Borei pri ha'adamah* (*Ramban* to 40a s.v. הא דתנן; see also *Meiri*).

R' Yehudah bases his view on the verse (*Psalms* 68:20):בָּרוּךְ ה' יוֹם יוֹם, *Blessed is Hashem day [by] day.* This verse teaches that on each day, one should recite a blessing which reflects the unique nature of that day. On the Sabbath, one should incorporate into the *Shemoneh Esrei* a blessing which reflects the nature of the Sabbath; on holidays, this blessing should reflect the nature of the holiday. R' Yehudah argues that the blessings over food must reflect the specific nature of the food, as well (*Gem.* 40a).

The halachah does not follow the view of R' Yehudah. One may recite the blessing of *Borei pri ha'adamah* over all types of "fruits of the ground" (*Rav,* from *Gem.* ibid.).[2] Nevertheless, R' Yehudah's ruling does have halachic ramifications. If one recites *Borei minei deshaim* over "greens," or *Borei minei zeraim* over "seeds," he does discharge his obligation after the fact (*Birkei Yosef, Orach Chaim* 205:4, cited by *Tos. R' Akiva* §38).

1. The various species of tree fruit, however, do not have specific defining characteristics by which they can be grouped into separate subcategories. Thus, R' Yehudah agrees that all tree fruit are subject to the one blessing of *Borei pri ha'eitz.*

2. It is interesting to note that in *Succah* (46a), there is a dispute between R' Yehudah and the Rabbis as to whether one who is faced with many mitzvos to perform recites one blessing over all of them, or a separate blessing for each mitvah. R' Yehudah rules — on the basis of the verse in *Psalms* — that one recites a separate blessing for each mitzvah. In that instance, the *Gemara* rules in accordance with R' Yehudah.

─────── ר' עוֹבַדְיָה מִבַּרְטְנוּרָא ───────

(ב) בירך על פירות האילן וכו'. כל היכא דכי שקלי פירא איתיה לענף, ואותו הענף עצמו
חוזר ומוליא פרי לשנה האחרת מקרי אילן, ומברכין על פירותיו בורא פרי העץ, אבל היכא דכי

יד אברהם

2.

The following mishnah discusses the law in cases when one recites a blessing for an item other than the one prescribed by the previous mishnah.

בֵּרַךְ עַל פֵּרוֹת הָאִילָן: ,,בּוֹרֵא פְּרִי הָאֲדָמָה," יָצָא; — [If] one recited on fruits of the tree the blessing: ". . .Who creates the fruit of the ground," he has fulfilled his obligation. If one recited the blessing of Borei pri ha'adamah on fruits of a tree, rather than the pre-scribed blessing of Borei pri ha'eitz, he may eat the fruit, and no further bless-ing is needed. Essentially, tree fruit, like "fruits of the earth," grow from the ground; the tree is merely the con-duit through which the soil nourishes the fruit, like the stalk of a vegetable (see Yerushalmi 6:2 with Peirush MiBaal Sefer HaChareidim s.v. עביד). As such, the category of "fruits of the ground" includes "fruits of the earth" (e.g. "greens," "seeds," melons — see previous mishnah) as well as tree fruits. Thus, although the Rabbis as-signed tree fruit the more specific des-ignation of "fruits of the tree," the blessing of Borei pri ha'adamah suf-fices for tree fruits, as well (see Gem. 40a with Rashi s.v. דעיקר אילן; see fur-ther, comm. below).

The foregoing is the Gemara's (ibid.) in-terpretation of the ruling of our mishnah. Based on this understanding, the Gemara comments that this ruling is actually sub-ject to a dispute between R' Yehudah and the Tanna Kamma as seen in a mishnah in Bikkurim (1:6). Bikkurim are the annual first-grown fruit in Eretz Yisrael of the Seven Species for which Eretz Yisrael is praised (these are: wheat, barley, grapes,

figs, pomegranates, olives and dates). The Torah commands that bikkurim be brought to the Temple and given to a Ko-hen (see Deuteronomy 26:1-11). The Torah prescribes a passage of thanksgiving to God to be recited by the one bringing the bikkurim (ibid. v. 5 ff.). The passage con-cludes with the statement: "And now, be-hold! I have brought the first fruit of the ground which You have given me, O Hashem (ibid. v. 10)."

The mishnah (loc. cit.) cites a dispute re-garding bikkurim brought to the Temple from a tree which had meanwhile been cut down (see Rashi to 40a s.v. יבש המעיין; cf. Rash and Rav to Bikkurim ibid.). The Tanna Kamma maintains that in such a case one does not recite the bikkurim decla-ration, because he cannot refer to the fruit of "the ground You have given me"; for the tree which produced these fruit is no longer in existence. [Although the verse refers to the "ground You have given me," the intent is the item which produces the bikkurim. This, according to the Tanna Kamma, is the tree upon which the bikkurim grew.] R' Ye-hudah, on the other hand, contends that one does recite the bikkurim declaration in this case, for he considers the soil to be the primary producer of the fruit. Since the soil is still in existence, R' Yehudah maintains that the person bringing the bikkurim is still able to refer to the "ground which You have given me."

The Gemara concludes that our mish-nah, which rules that the Borei pri ha'ada-mah blessing is valid for tree fruit, follows the view of R' Yehudah that the ground is the primary producer of tree fruit. How-ever, according to the Tanna Kamma, who

2. [If] one recited on fruits of the tree the blessing:
"...Who creates the fruit of the ground,"

YAD AVRAHAM

considers the *tree* the primary producer of tree fruit, tree fruit *cannot* be categorized as "fruit of the ground." Accordingly, the *Tanna Kamma* will maintain that the blessing of *Borei pri ha'adamah* is *not* valid for tree fruit.

Since the anonymous ruling of our mishnah follows the view of R' Yehudah, the halachah is decided in his favor. It follows, then, that with regard to *bikkurim*, as well, the halachah is decided in accordance with R' Yehudah, and not the *Tanna Kamma* (see *Tosafos* to 40a s.v. רבי יהודה היא; see below, footnote 1).

However, according to one view in *Yerushalmi* (6:2, cited by *Meleches Shlomo*), even the *Tanna Kamma* of the mishnah in *Bikkurim* agrees with the ruling of our mishnah. According to this view, the *Borei pri ha'adamah* blessing is valid for tree fruit not because the fruit are *themselves* considered to grow from the soil (the issue disputed by the *Tanna Kamma* and R' Yehudah in the mishnah in *Bikkurim*), but because the *tree* which produces the fruit derives its nourishment from the soil. Thus, *by extension*, the fruits of trees can be classified as "fruits of the ground." *Rabbeinu Yonah* (28b s.v. בירך, cited by *Tos. Yom Tov* s.v. יצא and *Meleches Shlomo*) explains our mishnah according to *Yerushalmi's* interpretation. Evidently, *Rambam*, as well, follows *Yerushalmi*, for although with regard to *bikkurim*, *Rambam* (*Hil. Bikkurim* 4:12) rules in accordance with the *Tanna Kamma*, he rules (*Hil. Berachos* 8:10) that the blessing of *Borei pri ha'adamah* is valid for tree fruit. According to the interpreta-

tion of the *Gemara*, these rulings are contradictory! Apparently, *Rambam* bases his ruling on *Yerushalmi*, according to which the ruling of our mishnah is undisputed (*Kessef Mishneh, Hil. Berachos* ad loc.; for a discussion regarding *Kessef Mishneh's* assertion that *Rambam* follows *Yerushalmi*, as well as alternative interpretations of *Rambam's* ruling, see *P'nei Yehoshua* to 40a s.v. בירך; *Tzlach* s.v. מאן תנא; *Shaagas Aryeh* §23; *Yesh Seder LaMishnah*).[1] The fact that *Rav* does not note that the ruling of our mishnah reflects only the opinion of R' Yehudah indicates that he, too, follows *Yerushalmi's* interpretation that the ruling in our mishnah is unanimous (*Tos Yom Tov* loc. cit.).

The blessing of *Borei pri ha'adamah* is valid for tree fruits only after the fact (*Meiri*, printed with mishnah 1). Initially, one must recite the blessing *Borei pri ha'eitz* as prescribed by the Rabbis. If one does not know whether the appropriate blessing for an item is *Borei pri ha'eitz* or *Borei pri ha'adamah*, he may not eat that item until he ascertains its correct blessing (see *Rav* s.v. ועל כולן). However, if his doubt is due to a *halachic* uncertainty regarding the status of an item as a "fruit of the tree" or a "fruit of the earth," he may even initially rely on the blessing of *Borei pri ha'adamah* (*Shulchan Aruch, Orach Chaim* 206:1; see *Mishnah Berurah* §4; *Maadanei Yom Tov* אות ת' to *Rosh* §9).[2]

1. *Rashba* (to 40a s.v. מאן תנא) and *Beis Yosef* (*Orach Chaim* 206 s.v. בירך) cite a version of *Rambam* in which he rules that the blessing of *Borei pri ha'adamah* is *not* valid for tree fruit. According to this version, *Rambam* indeed follows the interpretation of the *Gemara*, and rules in accordance with the *Tanna Kamma* (whose view represents the majority opinion) both with regard to the laws of *bikkurim* and the laws of blessings (see *Beis Yosef* ibid.). [However, in all current editions of *Rambam*, *Rambam* rules that the *Borei pri ha'adamah* blessing *is* valid for tree fruit (see *Aruch HaShulchan* 206:1).]

2. Papayas are an example of foods of uncertain halachic status (see *R' B. Forst's The Laws of Berachos* (Mesorah Publications) p. 283).

יָצָא. וְעַל פֵּרוֹת הָאָרֶץ: „בּוֹרֵא פְּרִי הָעֵץ" – לֹא
יָצָא. עַל כֻּלָּם אִם אָמַר: „שֶׁהַכֹּל נִהְיֶה" – יָצָא.

───── ר' עובדיה מברטנורא ─────

שקלת ליה לפרי לֹא ישאר ענף שיחזור ויוציא פרי לשנה האחרת אין מברכין על הפירות אלא
בורא פרי האדמה: **ועל כולן אם אמר שהכל יצא.** ואפילו על הפת ועל היין. ומיהו
לכתחלה אין לאכול שום פרי אם אינו יודע תחלה שיצריך עליו ברכה הראויה לו:

יד אברהם

When one wishes to eat many items, all of which are subject to the same blessing, he recites a single blessing for all of them (see mishnah 4). In light of our mishnah's ruling that the blessing of *Borei pri ha'adamah* is valid (at least after the fact) for tree fruits, *Shulchan Aruch* (ibid. §2) rules that if one recites *Borei pri ha'adamah* over a "fruit of the earth" with explicit intent to discharge his obligation with regard to a tree fruit that lies before him,[1] he does not recite another blessing before eating the tree fruit. However, many authorities dispute this ruling, arguing that the ruling of our mishnah applies only when the *Borei pri ha'adamah* blessing was recited over the tree fruit (see *Shaarei Teshuvah* ad loc. §1; see also *Rashi* to 41a s.v. אבל בשאין; *Meiri*, printed with mishnah 1).

Shaarei Teshuvah (ibid.; see also *Mishnah Berurah* ad loc. §10) rules that in this case (i.e. where one had already recited the *Borei pri ha'adamah* with explicit intent to discharge his blessing obligation for the tree fruit), one should not recite an additional *Borei pri ha'eitz* blessing over the tree fruit, for many authorities do not require it, and the rule is that we are lenient in uncertainties with regard to blessings. However, to avoid this dispute, one should ideally resolve not to eat the tree fruit until later — in which case the original blessing no longer suffices in any event — so he can recite a *Borei pri ha'eitz* over it (*Shaarei Teshuvah* ibid.; *Mishnah Berurah* ad loc §10).

וְעַל פֵּרוֹת הָאָרֶץ: „בּוֹרֵא פְּרִי הָעֵץ" – לֹא יָצָא. — **But [if] on fruits of the earth [one recited the blessing]: "...Who** *creates the fruit of the tree," he has not fulfilled his obligation.*

If one recites the blessing of *Borei pri ha'eitz* over "fruits of the earth" (or "greens"), rather than the prescribed blessing of *Borei pri ha'adamah*, he may not eat the item until he recites the correct blessing. Since these items do not grow on trees, the blessing of *Borei pri ha'eitz* is inappropriate (*Rabbeinu Yonah* loc. cit., cited by *Meleches Shlomo* s.v. בירך על פירות האילן).

This ruling seems self-evident. Obviously, one has not fulfilled his obligation if he recites a blessing which bears no relation to the item he wishes to eat. The *Gemara* (40a) explains that the mishnah states this law to teach that even the produce of plants that are often referred to as "trees" are subject to the blessing of *Borei pri ha'adamah* if the plant does not meet the *halachic* criteria of a "tree."

With regard to blessings, the *Gemara* (ibid., as understood by *Rashi* ad loc. s.v. גווזא and *Rav* s.v. בירך; see also *Geonim*, cited by *Tur, Orach Chaim* 203) defines a tree as any plant (whether a tree or a bush) whose branches do not wither after the fruit has been picked, but, rather, remain capable of producing fruit year after year.

Many authorities, however, understand the *Gemara* to mean that a plant is considered a tree — and its fruits are subject to the *Borei pri ha'eitz* blessing — as long as the

---

1. See *Shaarei Teshuvah* (ad loc. §1) regarding the law if the tree fruit is *not* before him.

he has fulfilled his obligation. But [if] on fruits of the earth [one recited the blessing]: *". . .Who creates the fruit of the tree,"* he has not fulfilled his obligation. And on all of them, if one said [the blessing]: *". . . that everything came into being . . .,"* he has fulfilled his obligation.

YAD AVRAHAM

roots of the tree remain vital, and generate a new trunk year after year, even if the branches and trunk wither (*Rosh* §23; *Ri,* cited by *Tur* ibid.; see also *Tosafos* to 40a s.v. איתיה). *Shulchan Aruch* (*Orach Chaim* 203:2) follows the view of *Rashi* and *Rav* (see *Rama* ad loc.).

Bananas and strawberries are examples of produce that are considered "fruit of the earth" according to *Rav* and *Rashi,* but which the latter opinion considers "tree fruit" for which the correct blessing is *Borei pri ha'eitz* (see *Shulchan Aruch* 203:3; *Mishnah Berurah* §3).[1]

The *Gemara* (ibid.) gives a wheat stalk as an example of a plant which is referred to as a "tree," but which does not meet the halachic criterion of a tree. According to R' Yehudah, the עֵץ הַדַּעַת (*the Tree of Knowledge*) from which Adam partook (see *Genesis* 3:6) was a wheat stalk. Although the Torah refers to this plant as the *Tree of Knowledge,* wheat is *not* considered a "fruit of the tree," because wheat must be replanted every year. Thus, if one recited *Borei pri ha'eitz* on kernels of wheat, he has not discharged his obligation.

עַל כֻּלָּם, אִם אָמַר: ,,שֶׁהַכֹּל נִהְיֶה" . . . — יָצָא. — *And on all of them, if one said [the blessing] ". . .that everything came into being . . .," he has fulfilled his obligation.*

[The full text of this blessing is שֶׁהַכֹּל נִהְיֶה בִּדְבָרוֹ, *". . . that everything came into being through His word."*][2]

If one recites this blessing on any of the foods listed in the previous mishnah [even if on bread or wine (*Rav* and *Rambam Comm.,* in accordance with the opinion of R' Yochanan in *Gem.* 40b)], he may eat that item without reciting the specific blessing prescribed by the Rabbis. The *Shehakol* blessing does not refer to any defining characteristic of the food, but rather to God's creations in general ("that *everything* came into being through His word"). As such, it is appropriate for all foods.

If the general blessing of *Shehakol* suffices for wine, it would seem that the more specific *Borei pri ha'eitz* blessing would certainly suffice (at least after the fact), since wine is in the category of "fruits of the tree" (see previous mishnah). The more general nature of the *Borei pri ha'eitz* blessing (which refers to the produce of *all* trees), as opposed to the blessing of *Borei pri hagafen* (which refers specifically to vines), should not disqualify the blessing, just as the *Shehakol* blessing is valid for wine despite the general nature of the blessing. Similarly, the *Borei pri ha'adamah* blessing should suffice for bread, since the grain from which bread is produced is also a "fruit of the earth." This, in fact, is the opinion of many authorities (see *Shaarei Teshuvah, Orach Chaim* 167:4;

1. *Shulchan Aruch* refers to "muzish," which is Arabic for banana. *Mishnah Berurah* refers to "pazimkas," which is the Yiddish term for strawberries (see Forst loc. cit.).

2. There is a dispute whether the word נהיה is vowelized as נִהְיֶה, *nihyeh,* or נִהְיָה, *nihyah.* This will be discussed in detail in the comm. to the next mishnah, s.v. על דבר.

‏[ג] עַל דָּבָר שֶׁאֵין גִּדּוּלוֹ מִן הָאָרֶץ, אוֹמֵר: „שֶׁהַכֹּל." עַל הַחֹמֶץ וְעַל הַנּוֹבְלוֹת וְעַל

—————— ר' עובדיה מברטנורא ——————

‏(ג) נובלות. פירות שֶׁנפלו מִן הָאִילָן קוֹדם שֶׁנתבשלו כל צרכן:

יד אברהם

Shaar HaTziyun 208:66,67).

However, *Tosafos* (to 12a s.v. לא) imply that someone who recites *Borei pri ha'eitz* over wine does *not* discharge his obligation (see *Gilyon HaShas* ad loc.). This view is shared by other authorities, as well (see *Magen Avraham* 208:22). [Evidently, these authorities understand the terminology used in the previous mishnah ("except for wine") to *exclude* wine from the blessing of *Borei pri ha'eitz* (see *Peirush MiBaal Sefer HaChareidim* to *Yerushalmi* 6:1, s.v. מתני אמרה כן, cited by *Meleches Shlomo*).][1] However, *R' Akiva Eiger* (to *Magen Avraham* ibid., *Gilyon HaShas* ibid.) is at a loss to explain the reasoning behind this view.

Shitah Mekubetzes (to 40b s.v. ועל) maintains that the *Borei pri ha'eitz* blessing is valid for wine (after the fact), just as the *Shehakol* blessing is valid for wine (see also *Shitah Mekubetzes* to 35a s.v. חוץ). However, he raises the possibility that the blessing of *Borei pri ha'adamah* does not suffice for bread, because the Torah refers to bread by name, rather than as a fruit. As the verse (*Deuteronomy* 8:9) states: *A land where you will eat bread without poverty.* Possibly, then, the blessing for bread also cannot refer to bread as a "fruit." Moreover, it may be that in formulating a blessing for bread which makes no reference to "fruit" [unlike the special blessing formulated for wine, which *does* refer to "fruit," albeit not "fruit of the tree"], the Rabbis removed

bread from the category of fruits. Thus, bread is no longer included in a general reference to "fruits of the ground."

As with the mishnah's earlier ruling regarding one who recited *Borei pri ha'adamah* on tree fruit, the *Shehakol* blessing suffices only after the fact for items for which the Rabbis prescribed other blessings. Initially, one must recite the blessing prescribed by the Rabbis for each food (*Rav*; see further comm. above, s.v. בְּרך עַל פרות האילן).

Another example of a blessing which is valid (after the fact) for a food for which the Rabbis prescribed a different blessing is the *Borei minei mezonos* blessing. This blessing thanks God for creating "*species of sustenance,*" and was formulated for grain products other than bread, for which the prescribed blessing is *Hamotzi* (see comm. to previous mishnah s.v. חוץ מן הפת). Nevertheless, many authorities rule that if one recited *Borei minei mezonos* on bread, he has discharged his obligation, since bread is certainly a "species of sustenance" (cf. *Meiri*, printed with mishnah 1). Indeed, some maintain the blessing of *Borei minei mezonos* suffices (after the fact) for *all* food items (with the exception of water and salt), since all food provides *some* sustenance (see *Beur Halachah* to 167:10 s.v. במקום ברכת המוציא).

3.

The mishnah resumes its discussion of the blessings recited for various foods, focusing on the *Shehakol* blessing, to which the previous mishnah has referred.

עַל דָּבָר שֶׁאֵין גִּדּוּלוֹ מִן הָאָרֶץ, אוֹמֵר: „שֶׁהַכֹּל." — On something which does not grow from the earth, one says [the

blessing of] Shehakol.

The *Shehakol* blessing was formulated by the Rabbis for all foods that

———————————

1. According to *Chareidim*, this issue is the subject of a dispute in *Yerushalmi*.

3. On something which does not grow from the earth, one says [the blessing of] *Shehakol*. On wine vinegar, and on unripe fruits, and on

YAD AVRAHAM

do not fit into the more specific categories of "fruits of the ground" and "fruits of the tree."[1] This blessing gives thanks to God for causing *all* items to come into being ["that *everything* came into being through His word"]. Meat, fish and eggs are examples of items that do not grow from the ground and are therefore subject to the *Shehakol* blessing (see *Gem.* 40b).

Yerushalmi (6:1) cites a view which mandates a different blessing for foods such as fish, meat and poultry: בּוֹרֵא מִינֵי נְפָשׁוֹת ,"... *Who creates species of life.*" However, our mishnah disputes this opinion.

Although the mishnah refers to foods that do not "*grow*" from the earth," the actual criterion for this category of foods is that they do not *derive direct nourishment* from the soil. Thus, a Baraisa cited by the *Gemara* (40b) includes truffles and mushrooms in the *Shehakol* category. For although these items can be said to grow from the ground, they do not derive their nourishment from the soil [but rather, from the ground's moisture. Indeed, truffles and mushrooms can also grow on pieces of wood and utensils that are wet (see *Rashi* ad loc. s.v. מִירְבָּא רְבוּ)] (*Gem.* loc. cit., cited by *Meleches Shlomo*).

The vowelization of the word נהיה in the *Shehakol* blessing is disputed. Some au-

thorities maintain that the word should be pronounced נִהְיָה [*came* into being], in the past tense (*Magen Avraham* 167:8), since the food upon which the blessing is recited has *already* come into being (*Levushei Serad* ad loc.).[2] Others contend that it should be pronounced נִהְיֶה, a vowelization which denotes the future *as well* as the past (*Chochmas Manoach*, cited by *Magen Avraham* ibid. and 204:14; *Chayei Adam* 49:1; *Aruch HaShulchan* 204:1), for we must give thanks for what God has already created and will create in the future (see *Levushei Serad* ibid.).

עַל הַחֹמֶץ וְעַל הַנּוֹבְלוֹת וְעַל הַגּוֹבַאי אוֹמֵר: "שֶׁהַכֹּל". — *On wine vinegar, and on unripe fruits, and on locusts, one says [the blessing of] Shehakol.*

נוֹבְלוֹת, *novelos*, are fruit that fell off the tree before they matured sufficiently (*Rav; Rambam Comm.; Rabbeinu Yonah* 28b s.v. עַל החומץ; *Rabbeinu Yerucham*, cited by *Beis Yosef, Orach Chaim* 202; see further comm. below).

The blessing on locusts is obviously *Shehakol*, since they do not grow from the ground. However, since R' Yehudah maintains that no blessing at all is recited on locusts (as the mishnah will soon state), the *Tanna Kamma* stresses that one *does* recite a blessing on locusts (see *Shenos Eliyahu; Mishnah Berurah* 204:4; see also *Tif. Yis.* §14).

This clause of the mishnah introduces a new grouping of foods for

---

1. *Meiri* (printed with mishnah 1) comments that this blessing was instituted for those foods that lack defining characteristics (such that characterize agricultural produce) which can be referred to in the blessing.

2. As we have seen with regard to the *Hamotzi* blessing (see comm. to mishnah 1 s.v. חוץ מן הפת, footnote 2), the requirement that a blessing reflect the past tense is common to all food blessings. The term בּוֹרֵא, *borei*, also connotes the past (see *Aruch HaShulchan* 167:7 and 202:12).

הַגּוֹבַאי אוֹמֵר: ,,שֶׁהַכֹּל" עַל הֶחָלָב וְעַל הַגְּבִינָה
וְעַל הַבֵּיצִים, אוֹמֵר: ,,שֶׁהַכֹּל." רַבִּי יְהוּדָה אוֹמֵר,

─────── ר' עובדיה מברטנורא ───────

גּוֹבַאי. חֲגָבִים טְהוֹרִים:

יד אברהם

which Shehakol was instituted. These foods belong to categories that normally require a more specific blessing, but they are deemed insignificant compared to other members of these categories, so they are subject instead to the more general Shehakol blessing (see Meiri, printed with mishnah 1). Both wine vinegar and novelos are in categories that usually require a more specific blessing. Vinegar is derived from wine, which is subject to the blessing Borei pri hagafen. Novelos are tree fruit, and should be subject to the blessing Borei pri ha'eitz. However, since neither is of a quality suitable to its category, the Rabbis mandated the more general Shehakol blessing for them. Similarly, any food that has spoiled or has otherwise deteriorated from its usual state (e.g. moldy bread) is subject to the blessing of Shehakol rather than the blessing formulated for its category (see Baraisa cited by the Gem. loc. cit.; see also Mishnah Berurah 204:1 and Beur Halachah ad loc. s.v. ופת שעיפשה).

The Gemara (40b) defines novelos as בּוּשְׁלֵי כַּמְרָא. Rav and Rambam comm., who understand novelos to be fruit that fell from the tree before they had ripened, apparently interpret the term בּוּשְׁלֵי כַּמְרָא to mean [fruit] ripened through storing, i.e. a fruit which must be packed in straw or dirt

to ripen (see Tos. R' Akiva §39; see also Shoshanim L'David, cited by Tos. Anshei Shem s.v. נובלות; cf. Taz 204:3). According to this interpretation, these fruit are subject to the Shehakol blessing because they are not yet ripe. [It would seem that the fruit falling off the tree is irrelevant. Whether they fell off the tree or were plucked prematurely, the blessing is Shehakol (see Nishmas Adam 51:5).] This view disagrees with the opinion of Rosh (§5), who maintains that even unripe fruit are subject to the blessing of Borei pri ha'eitz (see Beur Halachah to 202:9 s.v. שבשלם).

Other commentators (Rash to Demai 1:1 s.v. נובלות; Aruch s.v. כמר; Rabbeinu Channanel, cited by Tos. HaRosh and Tos. R' Yehudah Chassid to 40b s.v. בושלי), while also interpreting בּוּשְׁלֵי כַּמְרָא as fruit ripened through storing, understand it as referring to a specific species of fruit which does not ripen on the tree, and is, therefore, picked from the tree and stored in dirt to ripen. According to this interpretation, it is the fact that this fruit cannot ripen on the tree which mandates the more general blessing of Shehakol, not simply because the fruit is unripe.[1] A fruit which would have ripened if left on the tree requires the blessing of Borei pri ha'eitz regardless when it was detached (see Mishnah Berurah 202:49,50).

Rashi (ad loc. s.v. בושלי כמרא) interprets בּוּשְׁלֵי כַּמְרָא as cooked by the heat, i.e. mature fruit that were scorched and shriveled by the heat of the sun. One recites Shehakol on these mature fruit because they are damaged.[2]

1. There is some question as to whether, according to this interpretation, the blessing on these fruit remains Shehakol even after they have been ripened in storage, or if once they have matured, one recites Borei pri ha'eitz as with other fruit (see Beur Halachah to 202:9 s.v. שבשלם).

2. However, if the state of the shriveled fruit does not represent a change for the worse (e.g.

6
3

locusts, one says [the blessing of] *Shehakol*. On milk, and on cheese, and on eggs, one says [the blessing of] *Shehakol*. R' Yehudah says:

Shulchan Aruch eschews the interpretation of *Rav* and *Rambam*, consistent with his ruling (*Orach Chaim* 202:2) that the blessing on unripe fruit is *Borei pri ha'eitz* (see *Beur Halachah* to 202:9 s.v. שבשלם). Rather, *Shulchan Aruch* (ibid. §9, 204:1) adopts the interpretation of *Rashi*, and accordingly rules that the blessing on fruit shriveled by the sun is *Shehakol*. Furthermore, *Shulchan Aruch* (202:9) rules that *Shehakol* is the blessing mandated on species of fruit that *cannot* ripen on the tree. Evidently, *Shulchan Aruch* understands that *Rash* and *Rashi* only dispute the *interpretation* of בּוּשְׁלֵי כַּמְרָא; however, both agree that either defect is reason enough to replace the *Borei pri ha'eitz* blessing with *Shehakol* (see *Shaar HaTziyun* ad loc. §57; cf. *Beur HaGra* ad loc., cited by *Shaar HaTziyun* ibid.).

The mishnah's ruling requiring a *Shehakol* on vinegar indicates that vinegar is potable, for no blessing is recited on an inedible item. *Rosh* (§23, cited by *Meleches Shlomo*) questions this implication, for the *Gemara* (36b) implies that the factor which determines the edibility of an item as regards blessings is whether or not one is liable for eating that item on *Yom Kippur*. Now, since the *Gemara* (*Yoma* 81b) rules that one is not liable for drinking vinegar on *Yom Kippur*, why does our mishnah require *any* blessing on vinegar? This difficulty leads *Rosh* to conclude that our mishnah refers to *diluted* vinegar, for which one *is* liable on *Yom Kippur* (see *Gem.* ibid.), and which, therefore, requires a blessing.

Rabbeinu Yonah (loc. cit., cited by *Meleches Shlomo.*), however, contends that our mishnah refers even to *undiluted* vinegar. He notes that the *Gemara* in *Yoma* (ibid.) rules that one who drinks a large amount of vinegar (more than a *revi'is* — between 4 and 5 ounces) *is* liable on *Yom Kippur*. Evidently, the reason one is not liable for drinking a small quantity of vinegar is not because it is not potable, but because a small amount does not alleviate one's thirst. However, one does derive *some* benefit from even a small amount of vinegar, and he must therefore recite a blessing on it (see also *Eshkol*, cited by *Shaar HaTziyun* 204:18).

Shulchan Aruch (*Orach Chaim* 204:2) rules that no blessing is recited on pure vinegar, not because pure vinegar is not potable, but because drinking it has a harmful effect on a person. The authorities comment that this ruling refers only to very strong vinegar, which bubbles when poured on the ground. Pure vinegar of lesser strength is not harmful, and, therefore, requires a *Shehakol* (*Mishnah Berurah* §24).

עַל הֶחָלָב, וְעַל הַגְּבִינָה, וְעַל הַבֵּיצִים, אוֹמֵר: ,,שֶׁהַכֹּל." — *On milk, and on cheese, and on eggs, one says [the blessing of] Shehakol.*

[Since these items do not grow from the ground, their proper blessing is *Shehakol*.]

This clause of the mishnah seems superfluous, as the mishnah already stated that any food which does not grow from the ground is subject to the *Shehakol* blessing.[1]

raisins, prunes), it requires a *Borei pri ha'eitz* blessing (see *Magen Avraham* 202:21).

1. Indeed, many versions of the mishnah — including the one printed in the *Gemara* — do not include this clause at all.

בְּרָכוֹת כָּל שֶׁהוּא מִין קְלָלָה – אֵין מְבָרְכִין עָלָיו:

[ד] **הָיוּ** לְפָנָיו מִינִים הַרְבֵּה, רַבִּי יְהוּדָה אוֹמֵר: אִם יֵשׁ בֵּינֵיהֶם מִמִּין שִׁבְעָה – מְבָרֵךְ עָלָיו.

—————————— ר' עובדיה מברטנורא ——————————

מין קללה. נובלות וגובאי על ידי קללה הן באים, ואין הלכה כרבי יהודה: **(ד) מין שבעה.** חטה ושעורה וגפן ותאינה ורמון זית ותמרים, דהני עדיפי הואיל ונשתבחה בהן ארץ ישראל:

יד אברהם

Possibly, the mishnah wishes to teach that although eggs and milk are products of the grass eaten by the animal or fowl, they are not considered products "grown from the ground" (*Tif. Yis.* §15).

רַבִּי יְהוּדָה אוֹמֵר: כָּל שֶׁהוּא מִין קְלָלָה – אֵין מְבָרְכִין עָלָיו. — *R' Yehudah says: Any [food] which is a species of curse, we do not recite a blessing on it.*

This refers to the *novelos* and locusts [mentioned earlier in the mishnah] (*Rav; Rambam Comm.*).[1] R' Yehudah disputes the ruling of the *Tanna Kamma* that one recites a *Shehakol* on these items. According to R' Yehudah, no blessing is recited at all, since these items are associated with a "curse" (i.e. a plague); they are either damaged themselves [*novelos*] or cause damage to others [locusts] (see *Tos. Yom Tov*, from *Talmidei Rabbeinu Yonah* 28b s.v. רבי יהודה).

From the comments of *Rav* and *Rambam Comm.* it appears that R' Yehudah agrees that a blessing *is* recited on vinegar, the third item listed in in the earlier clause (see *Rashash*). However, *Rashi* and *Rabbeinu Yonah* (loc. cit.; see also *Tif. Yis.* §16) include vinegar among the items on which one does not recite a blessing ac-cording to R' Yehudah [for vinegar, too, results from a "curse," i.e. the wine turning sour]. *Tos. Anshei Shem* (s.v. כל שהוא מין קללה), citing *Hon Ashir*, suggests that only *wine* vinegar is included in this ruling. Vinegar derived from other sources is not a species of curse, and R' Yehudah would agree that it requires a blessing.

Rabbeinu Yonah (ibid., cited by *Tos. Yom Tov*) cites another view which contends that R' Yehudah disputes the *Tanna Kamma* only regarding vinegar and *novelos*, since these items have undergone a change for the worse (and are therefore considered "accursed"). Locusts, however, are not damaged, and R' Yehudah does not consider them to be a "species of curse."

Presumably, R' Yehudah does not mean that these "species of curses" may be eaten without any prior blessing at all, for a Rabbinical prohibition forbids deriving benefit from any item without first thanking God for it (see prefatory comments to mishnah 1). Rather, R' Yehudah means that it is inappropriate for these items to be the objects over which a blessing of thanksgiving is recited. Instead, one should recite a *Shehakol* blessing over a different item with intent to discharge his obligation for the "species of curse," as well [see prefatory comments to next

---

1. The designation "*species* of curse" seems inappropriate for *novelos*, which (according to *Rav* and *Rambam*) are not a *species* of fruit but rather any fruit which was prematurely plucked from the tree (see comm. above s.v. על החומץ). Accordingly, *Meleches Shlomo* emends the text to read מִן קְלָלָה, "*from* a curse," i.e. an item which is *the result* of a curse or plague. This term aptly describes *novelos* (as defined by *Rav* and *Rambam*), for they were not given the opportunity to mature.

6
4   Any [food] which is a species of curse, we do not recite a blessing on it.

4. [I]f] there were many species [of food] before him, R' Yehudah says: If there is among them [one] of the Seven Species, he recites the blessing over it.

YAD AVRAHAM

mishnah] (*Tos. Anshei Shem* s.v. אין מברכין; *Mishnas Rav*).

The halachah is not in accordance with R' Yehudah. Rather, one may recite the *Shehakol* blessing on these "species of curse" (*Rav*).

4.

One who wishes to eat two or more items of food, which are all subject to the same blessing (e.g. an apple, an orange and a pear), does not recite a separate blessing on each. Rather, he recites a blessing on one, which suffices for the others, as well.[1] The blessing is recited on the most significant item.[2] The following mishnah discusses the factors that determine which item is considered more significant and, therefore, the one on which the blessing should be recited.

הָיוּ לְפָנָיו מִינִים הַרְבֵּה, — *[If] there were many species [of food] before him,*

All of which are subject to the same blessing (see *Gem.* 41a); for example, he has before him dates and apples (both of whose blessings are *Borei pri ha'eitz*), or kernels of wheat and carrots (both of which are subject to the *Borei pri ha'adamah* blessing).

The mishnah's discussion applies only when both items are before him. If the more significant item is not yet before him, he need not wait until it is brought so that he can recite the blessing on it. In this case, he may recite the blessing on the less significant item (*Mishnah Berurah* 211:31).

There is a dispute in the *Gemara* (41a) as to whether the mishnah also refers to items that are subject to *different* blessings; for example, dates and carrots, or wheat kernels and apples. This issue will be discussed in the commentary at the end of our mishnah.

רַבִּי יְהוּדָה אוֹמֵר: אִם יֵשׁ בֵּינֵיהֶם מִמִּין שִׁבְעָה, מְבָרֵךְ עָלָיו. — *R' Yehudah says: If there is among them [one] of the Seven Species, he recites the blessing over it.*

The Seven Species are the seven agricultural products for which Eretz Yisrael is praised, as the verse (*Deuteronomy* 8:8) states: *A Land of wheat, barley, grape, fig and pomegranate; a Land of oil-olives and honey.* [The honey to which the verse refers is date-honey; hence, dates are included in the Seven Species (*Rambam Comm.*).]

1. Conceptually, this is done by having in mind that the blessing recited on one item should relate to the other item, as well. However, it is not always necessary to have the other item explicitly in mind. See *Rama* 206:5; *Mishnah Berurah* ad loc. §22 and 206:22 for details. See next footnote.

2. However, if he recited the blessing over the *less* significant item, it suffices for the more significant item after the fact, provided he had the second item explicitly in mind while reciting the blessing (see *Rashba* to 41a s.v. ולענין פסק הלכה; *Meiri*; see *Rama, Orach Chaim* 211:5).

ד/ו

בְּרָכוֹת

וַחֲכָמִים אוֹמְרִים, מְבָרֵךְ עַל אֵיזֶה מֵהֶן שֶׁיִּרְצֶה.

─────────────── ר' עובדיה מברטנורא ───────────────

מברך על איזה מהם שירצה. דחביב עדיף. והלכה כחכמים:

יד אברהם

R' Yehudah maintains that the fact that Scripture praises Eretz Yisrael for these fruit attests to their overriding significance. Thus, the single blessing sufficing for all the fruit in front of the person should be recited over one of the Seven Species (*Rav*; see also *Rashi* to 41a s.v. ופליגא דרבי חנן). If one wishes to eat dates and apples, he should recite the *Borei pri ha'eitz* blessing on the date, even if he prefers to eat the apple first. [Having recited the blessing on the date, he must eat a bit of it before eating the apple (see *Rosh* §25; *Rabbeinu Yonah* 28b s.v. מחלוקת).]

The mishnah does not discuss the applicable law when *both* fruits are of the Seven Species. This matter is dealt with by the *Gemara* (41a-b, as understood by most authorities — see *Rashba* to 41a s.v. ולענין פסק הלכה; *Rabbeinu Yonah* 28b s.v. ולענין פסקא; *Shulchan Aruch* 211:1; cf. *Meiri*), which determines the significance of each of the Seven Species based on how soon it is listed after one of the two mentions of the word "Land" in the verse (see *Rashi* loc. cit.). Thus, grapes take precedence over figs, since grapes are the third item listed after the first "Land," whereas figs are the fourth food listed (see *Gem.* 41a). Olives take precedence over grapes, because olives are the first item listed after the *second* "Land" (see *Gemara* 41b). However, wheat is more significant than olives, because it is the first item listed after the *first* "Land,"

while olives are the first item listed after the *second* "Land" (*Tosafos* to 41b s.v. זה שני; the ramifications of this last point, which relates to items that are subject to different blessings, will be discussed in the commentary at the end of the mishnah). Thus, the Seven Species in descending order of significance are: wheat, olives, barley, dates, grapes, figs, pomegranates.

If *none* of the items is one of the Seven Species, R' Yehudah maintains that one recites the blessing on the item he favors most [as will be defined in the comm. below, s.v. וחכמים אומרים] (*Meiri; Rosh* loc. cit.; *Shulchan Aruch* loc. cit.).

וַחֲכָמִים אוֹמְרִים: מְבָרֵךְ עַל אֵיזֶה מֵהֶן שֶׁיִּרְצֶה. — *But the Sages say: He recites the blessing over whichever one of them he prefers.*

I.e. he should recite the blessing over the species he favors most (*Tif. Yis.,* from *Gem.* 41a; see *Rashi* ad loc. s.v. חביב עדיף).[1]

The Sages maintain that the primary factor determining a food's significance in relation to another food is one's personal preference (*Rav*, from *Gem.* loc. cit.). This determinant is so important that the preferred food is considered more significant even than a food of the Seven Species. Thus, if one prefers apples to dates, he should recite the blessing on the apples. Similarly, if the preferred food is one of the Seven Species, it is considered more

───

1. *Rosh* (§25) understands that the mishnah refers to the species a person *ordinarily* favors, even if at the moment he prefers the other item (see also *Rabbeinu Yonah* 28b s.v. מחלוקת; *Shulchan Aruch, Orach Chaim* 211:1). Thus, if he generally favors apples more than dates, he should recite the blessing on the apples, even if he prefers dates right now. According to *Rambam* (*Hil. Berachos* 8:13), however, the "one he prefers" is the species he favors *at the moment* (see *Shulchan Aruch* ibid. §2).

6
4

But the Sages say: He recites the blessing over whichever one of them he prefers.

significant than a member of the Seven Species listed closer to the word "Land" in the verse [see above, s.v. רבי יהודה אומר]. Therefore, if one prefers pomegranates (the least prominent of the Seven Species) to grapes (which ranks fifth), he should recite the blessing over the pomegranate (*Beis Yosef*, *Orach Chaim* 211 s.v. ומש"כ רבינו אפי' אם המאוחר).

However, the Sages agree that if one has no personal preference, a food of the Seven Species is deemed more significant than one that is not, and the blessing is recited on the member of that item. Similarly with regard to two foods of the Seven Species, in the absence of personal preference the blessing is recited over the item listed closest following the word "Land" in the verse listing the Seven Species [see comm. above s.v. רבי יהודה אומר] (*Rambam* ibid., as explained by *Kessef Mishneh*; *Rosh* loc. cit.; see also *Tosafos* to 41a s.v. אמר רב ירמיה; *Shulchan Aruch* ibid.).

Rav rules in accordance with the Sages that the blessing is recited over the favorite food. This is also the ruling of *Rambam* (*Comm.* and *Hil. Berachos* 8:13, as understood by *Kessef Mishneh*; see also *Shulchan Aruch* 211:2, who brings this ruling in the name of *Rambam*). However, the majority of authorities [among them *Rosh* (loc. cit.); *Tosafos* to 39a s.v. חביב; *Rashba* (loc. cit.); *Ravad* (cited by *Rashba*

ibid.); and *Rabbeinu Yonah* (28b s.v. ולענין פסקא), citing the *Geonim*)] follow the view of R' Yehudah that one recites the blessing over the item which is of the Seven Species. This ruling is also cited by *Shulchan Aruch* (ibid. §1), who implies that one should follow this view (see *Mishnah Berurah* §13).

As previously noted (see comm. above s.v. היו לפניו), one opinion in the *Gemara* (41a) understands the dispute between R' Yehudah and the Sages to involve not only two items that are subject to the same blessing, but also two items which are subject to *different* blessings (e.g. a carrot and a date). The issue in this case is which blessing is recited first. According to this view, R' Yehudah maintains that the Seven Species factor determines which of two blessings is recited first, just as it determines which item takes precedence when two foods are subject to the same blessing. Thus, one who wishes to eat a carrot and a date would first recite the *Borei pri ha'eitz* blessing on the date (which is one of the Seven Species), and then the *Borei pri ha'adamah* blessing on the carrot. Conversely, one who wishes to eat apples and wheat kernels would recite a *Borei pri ha'adamah* blessing on the wheat kernels, and then a *Borei pri ha'eitz* blessing on the apple.[1] According to the Sages, on the other hand, one first recites a blessing on the preferred item, whether or not the other item is of the Seven Species.

The other opinion in the *Gemara* contends that R' Yehudah only argues with

---

1. The question arises: Since the *Borei pri ha'adamah* blessing suffices for tree fruit, as we have seen in mishnah 2, why must he recite an additional blessing on the apple after reciting the *Borei pri ha'adamah* on the wheat kernels? The answer is that, as previously noted (see comm. to mishnah 2 s.v. בירך על פרות האילן), many authorities maintain that a *Borei pri ha'adamah* blessing only suffices for a tree fruit if it was recited on the tree fruit itself, but not if it was recited on a vegetable or other "fruit of the earth" (see *Rashi* to 41a s.v. אבל בשאין). Even according to those who maintain that a *Borei pri ha'adamah* recited on a different food suffices for a tree fruit, this is only after the fact. Initially, one should not intend to include the tree fruit in the *Borei pri ha'adamah* blessing (see *Mishnah Berurah* 206:7).

[ה] בֵּרַךְ עַל הַיַּיִן שֶׁלִּפְנֵי הַמָּזוֹן – פָּטַר אֶת הַיַּיִן שֶׁלְּאַחַר הַמָּזוֹן.

ר' עובדיה מברטנורא

(ה) **פטר את היין שלאחר המזון.** הני מילי בשבתות וימים טובים שרגילים לקבוע על
יין לאחר המזון, וכשברך על היין לפני המזון אדעתא דהכי ברך, אבל בשאר ימים שאין
רגילים לקבוע עלמן על היין שלאחר המזון, אין היין שלפני המזון פוטר היין שלאחר המזון. וכל
לאחר המזון דתנן במתניתין, היינו לאחר שסלקו ידיהם מן הפת קודם שיברכו ברכת המזון:

יד אברהם

the Sages regarding items that are subject to the same blessing. When items require separate blessings, both R' Yehudah and the Sages agree that one's personal preference takes precedence over the Seven Species factor (see Tosafos ad loc. s.v. אבל; cf. Rosh loc. cit.; see Mishnah Berurah 211:9 and Beur Halachah s.v. ויש אומרים). The halachah follows this latter view (Shulchan Aruch 211:1; see Beur Halachah ibid.). If one favors both items equally, the Seven Species factor is taken into consideration (Mishnah Berurah ad loc. §9).

However, the *types of blessings* are the most important factor determining the order in which they are recited. Hamotzi is the most significant of blessings, and it takes precedence over any other blessing (Rama 211:5).[1] All blessings take precedence over a Shehakol blessing regardless of which item the person favors [even if the Shehakol item is also one of the Seven Species — i.e date-honey (Shaar HaTziyun 211:9)]. This is because all blessings which refer to a specific category of food (e.g. "fruits of the ground," "fruits of the tree") are deemed

more significant than the Shehakol blessing, which refers to God's creations in general (Tosafos to 39a s.v. חביב and Rosh §25, based on Gem. 39a; see Shulchan Aruch 211:3 with Mishnah Berurah §14,15).[2]

The blessing of Borei pri hagafen always takes precedence over Borei pri ha'eitz and Borei pri ha'adamah, since it is more specific (referring to the subcategory of "fruit of the vine"). However, Borei minei mezonos takes precedence even over Borei pri hagafen (Rama 211:4), since it, too, refers to a specific subcategory of food ("species of sustenance," i.e. grain), and, in addition, is listed before wine ("grapes") in the verse of the Seven Species (Mishnah Berurah §24).

In brief: Regarding two items that are subject to the same blessing, the blessing is recited over the item which is a member of the Seven Species. If both items are of the Seven Species, then the blessing is recited over the item listed closest to the word "Land" in the verse of the Seven Species. If neither item is included in the Seven Species, the blessing is recited over the item one favors most.

1. A notable exception is the Borei pri hagafen for the Sabbath Kiddush wine, which must be recited before the Hamotzi blessing on the challah, since one may not eat until he recites Kiddush. Tur (Orach Chaim 271) cites Yerushalmi, which explains that we cover the challah while reciting Kiddush so the challah will "not see its shame," i.e. although Hamotzi usually takes precedence over Borei pri hagafen, in this case it does not.

2. Behag (cited by Tosafos to 41a s.v. אבל and Rosh §25) argues that by the same token the blessing of Borei pri ha'eitz (which refers to the specific category of tree fruit) takes precedence over the Borei pri ha'adamah blessing (with its reference to the broader category of "fruits of the ground," which includes both "fruit of the earth" and tree fruit, as seen in mishnah 2). Although most authorities dispute Behag in this matter, Mishnah Berurah (ibid. §18) notes the consensus of decisors that in the absence of other factors that determine the order of the blessings (i.e. personal preference or an item belonging to the Seven Species), one should indeed recite the Borei pri ha'eitz blessing before the Borei pri ha'adamah.

5. [If] one recited a blessing on the wine which precedes the meal, he has discharged [his obligation for] the wine which follows the meal.

YAD AVRAHAM

Regarding items that require separate blessings, the order of precedence is as follows: *Hamotzi; Borei minei mezonos; Borei pri hagafen; Borei pri ha'eitz* or *Borei pri ha'adamah* (depending on which is the most favored item; if both are equally favored, the order is based on the verse of the Seven Species, if applicable); *Shehakol*.

5.

The following mishnah discusses the blessing obligations for foods eaten at a meal. For the purpose of our mishnah's discussion, we note that a meal is divided into three segments: before *Hamotzi* is recited on the bread ["preceding the meal"]; the main part of the meal, during which one eats to satisfy his hunger ["during the meal"]; and after the meal has been completed,[1] but before the *Bircas HaMazon* ["following the meal"] (see *Rav* s.v. פָטַר אֶת הַיַּיִן). The first clause of the mishnah deals with the blessing obligation on wine at various points of the meal. It should be noted that although the *Hamotzi* blessing recited on bread at the beginning of the meal suffices for many of the foods and drinks during the meal, as will be seen later in the mishnah, it does not suffice for wine. Wine always requires a separate *Borei pri hagafen* blessing, because of its significance (see *Gem.* 41b-42a).

בֵּרֵךְ עַל הַיַּיִן שֶׁלִּפְנֵי הַמָּזוֹן – פָטַר אֶת הַיַּיִן
שֶׁלְּאַחַר הַמָּזוֹן. — *[If] one recited a blessing on the wine which precedes the meal, he has discharged [his obligation for] the wine which follows the meal.*

In mishnaic times it was customary to serve wine before the beginning of a meal ["the wine which precedes a meal"] (see *Gem.* 43a).[2] After the meal was completed, but before the *Bircas HaMazon*, wine would be served

again ["the wine which follows the meal"]. The mishnah teaches that it is not necessary to recite an additional *Borei pri hagafen* blessing on the postdinner wine, for this wine is included in the blessing recited over the predinner wine.

It might have been thought that since the meal intervenes between the two drinkings, the postdinner drinking is considered a new drinking, not a continuation of the previous drinking, so a new *Borei pri hagafen*

1. There are various opinions as to what constitutes the completion of the meal in this regard. Some maintain that removing the bread from the table signals the end of a meal (*Tur* 177; *Levush* ad loc.). According to others, the meal is not completed until the the table itself is removed (*Rabbeinu Yonah* 30a s.v. לא סבר; *Rashba* to 41b s.v. אמר רב פפא). [Nowadays, we do not remove the table after eating; thus, according to the latter opinion, today our meals are only completed when we recite the *Bircas HaMazon* (see *Beur Halachah* to 177:2 s.v. שאין).] In the opinion of *Tosafos* (to 41b s.v. לאחר הסעודה), the *decision* not to eat any more bread signals the meal's completion. *Tosafos* comment, however, that because today bread is generally eaten until the *Bircas HaMazon*, the meal is not considered completed until the *Bircas HaMazon* (see further comm. below, s.v. ברך על היין and footnote 1 on next page).

2. An example of "wine which precedes a meal" which is relevant today is the wine of *Kiddush* on the Sabbath and Festivals (see *Tif. Yis.* §19, from *Shulchan Aruch* 174:4).

ברכות
ו/ה

בֵּרֵךְ עַל הַפַּרְפֶּרֶת שֶׁלִּפְנֵי הַמָּזוֹן – פָּטַר אֶת
הַפַּרְפֶּרֶת שֶׁלְּאַחַר הַמָּזוֹן.

— ר' עובדיה מברטנורא —

פרפרת. כל דבר שמלפתים בו את הפת, כגון בשר ובצלים ודגים, קרויים פרפרת. ופעמים
שהיו מביאים פרפראות קודם סעודה להמשיך האכילה, וחוזרים ומביאים פרפראות אחרות
לאחר הסעודה אחר שמשכו ידיהם מן הפת:

יד אברהם

blessing is required. The mishnah therefore teaches that the *Borei pri hagafen* recited over the predinner wine suffices for the postdinner wine, as well (*Piskei HaRid* to mishnah).

The *Gemara* (42b) comments that the mishnah's ruling applies only on occasions when it is common to drink postdinner wine, such as on the Sabbath and Festivals. Since it was customary on these days to drink wine after the meal, the person presumably had postdinner wine in mind when he recited the *Borei pri hagafen* blessing on wine before the meal. At other times, however, when people do not generally drink much wine, one presumably has in mind only the wine over which he recites the blessing (*Rav; Rambam Comm.*). Thus, any wine he later decides to drink requires another blessing (see *Rashi* to 42b s.v. אלא בשבתות).

However, in places where wine is plentiful and, therefore, commonly drunk throughout the meal, one presumably also has in mind wine he drinks later. Thus, even on days other than Sabbaths and Festivals it is not necessary to recite another blessing on postdinner wine (*Hasagos HaRaavad*, 30a of *Rif* folios §1, cited by *Mishnah Berurah* 174:7). In any event, if one *specifically* intended to drink wine later, he does not need to recite another blessing over that wine (see *Tosafos* to 42b s.v. ורב ששת).

There is a dispute in the *Gemara*

(42b) whether [in a case when one did not drink wine before the meal (*Tosafos* to 42b s.v. יין)] the wine drunk after the meal is included in the blessing recited on wine *during* the meal. [As noted in the prefatory comments to our mishnah, wine is not covered by the *Hamotzi* blessing recited at the start of the meal.] Some *Amoraim* maintain that since the drinking of wine during the meal, the purpose of which is to aid in digesting the food, is not as significant as the drinking of wine before or after the meal, which is drunk for enjoyment, the blessing recited over wine *during* the meal would not suffice for the wine drunk after the meal. Other *Amoraim* do not agree with this distinction.

The halachah follows the view that a blessing on wine during the meal *does not* suffice for wine one drinks after the meal (*Rif* 30b, *Tosafos* ad loc. s.v. ורב ששת; *Rambam, Hil. Berachos* 4:12 et al.). However, *Tosafos* (ibid.) and *Rabbeinu Yonah* (30b s.v. ורב אשי) note that this ruling has no practical consequence nowadays, since our meals are not considered completed until we recite the *Bircas HaMazon* (see prefatory comments, footnote 1). Thus, any wine drunk before the *Bircas HaMazon* is considered "wine drunk *during* the meal," and is covered by the earlier *Borei pri hagafen* (see *Mishnah Berurah* 174:7).[1]

However, the blessing recited upon

1. According to the authorities who consider the meal completed when the bread is removed from the table (see prefatory comments, footnote 1), it would seem that this ruling *is* relevant today, since often the bread is removed before desserts and sweets are

<table>
<tr><td>6
5</td><td>[If] one recited a blessing over the *parperes* which precedes the meal, he has discharged [his obligation for] the *parperes* which follows the meal.</td></tr>
</table>

YAD AVRAHAM

the more significant drinking of wine *before* the meal certainly suffices for the less significant drinking of wine

during the meal (*Tosafos* ibid.; *Rabbeinu Yonah* 30b s.v. ואומר; *Meiri*; see *Shulchan Aruch* 174:4).[1]

~§ The blessing obligation on foods eaten at a meal

Although a meal may consist of many foods, each of which is normally subject to a different blessing, many do not require separate blessings when eaten as part of a meal. They are included in the *Hamotzi* blessing recited over the bread at the beginning of the meal. The basis of this law is the general rule that when one eats two foods, one of which is primary [עִקָּר] and the other secondary [טָפֵל], the subordinate food is included in the blessing he recites on the primary food (see mishnah 6). All foods eaten during the meal for sustenance, to satisfy one's hunger, are considered subordinate to bread, which is the primary food eaten for sustenance, and are therefore included in the blessing recited on the bread (see *Tosafos* to 41b-42a s.v. אי הכי and to 44a s.v. מברך על המליח). However, foods that are eaten, not for sustenance, but for their flavor (such as fruit and other dessert items), are not subordinate to bread [unless they are eaten *together* with the bread (see *Rashi* to 41b s.v. דברים הבאים מחמת הסעודה)]. In addition, any food — whether generally eaten for sustenance or for flavor — which is eaten *after* the completion of the meal, but before the *Bircas HaMazon*, requires a blessing. Since this food is eaten after the meal has been completed, it is not considered secondary to the bread.[2] [Moreover, since this food is not eaten as part of the meal, it is not included in the *Bircas HaMazon*, either.] (*Gemara* 41b, as understood by *Tosafos* ad loc. s.v. הלכתא and s.v. לאחר הסעודה[3]).

<table>
<tr><td>בֵּרַךְ עַל הַפַּרְפֶּרֶת שֶׁלִּפְנֵי הַמָּזוֹן — פָּטַר אֶת
הַפַּרְפֶּרֶת שֶׁלְּאַחַר הַמָּזוֹן. — *[If] one recited a blessing on the parperes which*</td><td>*precedes the meal, he has discharged [his obligation for] the parperes which follows the meal.*</td></tr>
</table>

brought to the table (see *Beur Halachah* cited there). However, it would seem from *Mishnah Berurah* that the view of *Tosafos* is primary.

1. There is some question in this case whether or not one must specifically intend to drink wine later, during the meal (see *Shaar HaTziyun* ad loc. §12,13).

2. *Shulchan Aruch* (177:2, cited by *Tos. Chadashim*) comments that, as with wine drunk after the meal, this law has no practical consequence nowadays, since our meals are not considered to be completed until the *Bircas HaMazon* (see comm. above s.v. ברך על היין; see *Beur Halachah* ad loc. s.v. שאין אנו רגילין).

3. It should be noted that many of the commentators have other interpretations of the *Gemara*. *Rashba* (to 41b s.v. אמר רב פפא), for example, maintains that a food generally eaten for sustenance does not require a separate blessing even if eaten after the meal (see further comm. below s.v. ברך על הפרפרת שלפני המזון). We have based our commentary on *Tosafos'* explanation because it is the one followed by *Shulchan Aruch* (177:1,2). However, in practice, the other interpretations must also be taken into consideration (see *Beur Halachah* ad loc. s.v. שאין אנו רגילין).

בֵּרֵךְ עַל הַפַּת – פָּטַר אֶת הַפַּרְפֶּרֶת; עַל הַפַּרְפֶּרֶת – לֹא פָטַר אֶת הַפַּת. בֵּית שַׁמַּאי

יד אברהם

Any food which is generally eaten together with bread during a meal is called *parperes*. Meat, eggs and fish are all examples of *parperes* [as opposed to porridge, cabbage and beans, which are usually eaten as a course by themselves (see *Rashi* to 41b s.v. שלא מחמת הסעודה)]. Occasionally, these foods would be eaten without bread as an appetizer prior to the meal [in which case they require a *Shehakol* blessing], and also as a dessert after the meal (*Rav* s.v. פרפרת, first explanation).

Alternatively, *parperes* is a preparation made from dried bread crumbs softened with soup [which, at times, was eaten as an appetizer and as a dessert]. Although the primary component of this dish is bread, its blessing is not *Hamotzi* but *Borei minei mezonos*, because the bread crumbs in this mixture no longer resemble bread [see *Gem.* 37b] (*Rav*, second explanation, s.v. מעשה קדירה; *Rabbeinu Channanel*, cited by *Tosafos* to 42a s.v. ברך על הפת; see further comm. below s.v. על הפרפרת).

As the mishnah will presently rule, when this dish is eaten *during* the meal, it is covered by the *Hamotzi* recited on the bread [since it is generally eaten for sustenance] (see prefatory comments above). However, when it is eaten after the meal's conclusion it does require a blessing, since the

Hamotzi blessing does not cover foods eaten after the completion of the meal (see *Meiri*; see prefatory comments). Nevertheless, if one ate this dish as an appetizer before the meal [i.e. before reciting *Hamotzi* on the bread, in which case it required a blessing], the blessing he recited then [whether a *Shehakol* or a *Borei minei mezonos*] suffices for the dessert, as well.

Rashba (to 41b s.v. אמר רב פפא) rejects the notion that our mishnah refers to a food generally eaten for sustenance. *Rashba* argues that such foods are included in the *Hamotzi* blessing even when eaten after the meal. According to *Rashba*, only foods eaten for their flavor require a separate blessing (see prefatory comments above, footnote 3). Rather, our mishnah refers to *kisnin*-bread (see comm. to mishnah 1 s.v. חוץ מן הפת). Since *kisnin*-bread is generally eaten for its sweet flavor rather than for sustenance, it is not included in the *Hamotzi* blessing when eaten after the meal. However, unlike other foods eaten for flavor, *kisnin*-bread does not require a separate blessing when eaten *during* the meal. Since *kisnin*-bread is a form of bread [albeit not one which normally requires a *Hamotzi* blessing], it *is* included in the *Hamotzi* blessing when eaten during the meal.[1] This definition of *parperes* is shared by *Meiri*, who finds support for it from *Yerushalmi* (6:5). For yet another definition of *parperes*, see *Rashi* to our mishnah.

בֵּרֵךְ עַל הַפַּת – פָּטַר אֶת הַפַּרְפֶּרֶת; — *[If] one recited a blessing on the bread, he*

---

1. It should be noted that many authorities — among them *Tosafos* (to 41b s.v. אלא פת הבאה בכיסנין; see *Tos. R' Akiva* §40) — dispute *Rashba's* assertion, and contend that *kisnin*-bread *does* require a separate blessing even during the meal (see *Shulchan Aruch* 168:8), unless one eats it to satisfy his hunger [in which case it is treated like any food eaten for sustenance], or in amounts that would subject it to the *Hamotzi* blessing were it eaten by itself [in which case it is treated like bread; see comm. to mishnah 1 loc. cit.] (*Mishnah Berurah* ad loc. §42). See *Beur Halachah* (ad loc. s.v. טעונים ברכה) for the practical halachah.

[If] one recited a blessing on the bread, he has discharged [his obligation for] the *parperes*; [but if one recited a blessing] on the *parperes*, he has not discharged [his obligation for] the bread. Beis Shammai

has discharged [his obligation for] the parperes;

This clause of the mishnah refers to *parperes* eaten *during* the meal. *Parperes* served *after* the meal is *not* included in the *Hamotzi* blessing, as previously noted [see comm. above s.v. ברך על הפרפרת שלפני המזון (*Tosafos* to 42a s.v. ברך על הפת; *Meiri*).[1]

According to *Rashba*, who defines *parperes* as *kisnin*-bread (see comm. above s.v. ברך על הפרפרת שלפני המזון), the *Hamotzi* blessing covers *parperes* eaten during the meal even when the *parperes* is eaten for its flavor rather than for sustenance (see prefatory comments above). According to *Tosafos* (cited in prefatory comments above), however, the *parperes* eaten during the meal is included in the *Hamotzi* blessing only because it is eaten for sustenance. If it is eaten purely for its flavor, it would require a separate blessing (see *Tos. R' Akiva* §40).

The mishnah obviously refers to a case in which *parperes* was not served prior to the meal. If *parperes* had been eaten before the meal, it would not be necessary to rely on the *Hamotzi* blessing for the *parperes* served during the meal, as the mishnah has just ruled for the postdinner *parpares* (*Meiri*).

עַל הַפַּרְפֶּרֶת — לֹא פָּטַר אֶת הַפַּת. *[but if one recited a blessing] on the parperes, he has not discharged [his obligation for] the bread.*

[If one eats *parperes* before the meal, its blessing does not suffice for the bread he will eat during the meal.]

Tosafos (to 42a s.v. ברך) ask: According to those who define *parperes* as fish or meat (see comm. above s.v. ברך על הפרפרת שלפני המזון), what is the novelty of the mishnah's ruling? Obviously, the *Shehakol* blessing for these items is inappropriate for bread! Because of this difficulty, *Tosafos* adopt the interpretation of *Rabbeinu Chananel* (cited in comm. ibid.) that the mishnah refers to a preparation of dried bread crumbs soaked in broth, which is subject to the blessing of *Borei minei mezonos*. The mishnah teaches that although the primary ingredient of this mixture is bread (albeit not in a form that requires the blessing of *Hamotzi*), its blessing does not suffice for regular bread. See also *Rav* s.v. מעשה קדירה.

However, *P'nei Yehoshua* (to *Tosafos* ibid.; see also *Piskei HaRid* to 42b s.v. פיס ברך) comments that even if the blessing for *parperes* is *Shehakol*, the mishnah's ruling is not obvious at all! One might have thought that the *Shehakol* blessing recited on the *parperes* indeed *does* suffice for bread, since one who recites the *Shehakol* blessing on *any* food has discharged his obligation (see mishnah 2). The reason the blessing on the *parperes* in fact does *not* include bread is because, according to many authorities, the *Shehakol* blessing suffices for a food subject to a different blessing only if it is recited on that food (see comm. to mishnah 2 s.v. ברך על פרות האילן). In the case of our mishnah, however, the *Shehakol* blessing was recited not on the

---

1. Interestingly, neither *Rav* nor *Rashi* comments that this clause of the mishnah refers to *parperes* eaten during the meal. *Tiferes Yisrael* (§23) interprets their silence to imply that the mishnah is referring to *parperes* eaten *after* the meal. *Tiferes Yisrael* finds this implication difficult, for the mishnah has previously ruled that *parperes* eaten after the meal is only exempt from a blessing because of the predinner *parperes*. For an explanation of *Rav* and *Rashi*, see *Boaz* §7.

ר' עוֹבַדְיָה מִבַּרְטֵנוּרָא

מעשה קדרה. כגון הריפות וגרס כרמל וקמח שנתבשל במים כגון הלביבות וכיוצא בהן. ואית דמפרשי פרפרת דמתניתין, פת הבאומה בקטרה שאין בה מראה לחם, דמברכיס עלה בורא מיני מזונות. והשתא ניחא דאילטריך לאשמעינן ברך על הפרפרת לא פטר את הפת אף על גב דהיא נמי מין פת, אבל מעשה קדרה פטר. ובית שמאי סברי, כשם שאם ברך על הפרפרת לא פטר את הפת כך לא פטר מעשה קדרה. ואין הלכה כבית שמאי:

יד אברהם

bread but on the *parperes*. Therefore the bread is not included in the blessing. [Even according to those who contend that a *Shehakol* recited over one item *does* suffice for another item for which a different blessing is prescribed, this is only after the fact. Initially, one should not intend to include that other item in the *Shehakol* blessing (see comm. to mishnah 2 s.v. ברך על פירות האילן). Thus, the mishnah teaches that the blessing on the *parperes* does not suffice — at least initially — for the bread.]

— בֵּית שַׁמַּאי אוֹמְרִים: אַף לֹא מַעֲשֵׂה קְדֵרָה.
Beis Shammai say: [He has] not even [discharged his obligation] for porridge.

I.e. not only is the blessing on *parperes* insufficient for bread, it does not suffice for porridge, either. The *Tanna Kamma*, on the other hand, implies that although the blessing on *parperes* does not suffice for bread, it *does* suffice for porridge (*Rav and Rambam Comm.*, from *Gem.* 42b; see further comm. below).

It would seem from this case of the mishnah that the *parperes* of the mishnah is not an item which is subject to the blessing of *Shehakol* [as *Rav* maintains in his first explanation]. For how can the *Tanna Kamma* rule that a *Shehakol* blessing on *parperes* suffices for porridge, which is subject to the blessing of *Borei minei mezonos*? Rather, the mishnah's *parperes* must be an item which also is subject to the blessing of *Borei minei mezonos*. Hence, the *Tanna Kamma's* implied ruling that this blessing suffices for porridge as well (*Meiri*).

However, if the mishnah refers to a food

which requires a *Borei minei mezonos* blessing, the ruling of Beis Shammai presents difficulties. Since *parperes* and porridge are both subject to the blessing of *Borei minei mezonos*, why do Beis Shammai argue that the blessing on *parperes* does not suffice for porridge? *Meiri* explains that, indeed, if one had the porridge explicitly in mind when reciting the blessing on the *parperes*, the porridge would not require a separate blessing. However, our mishnah deals with a case in which one did not specifically have the porridge in mind when reciting the blessing on *parperes*. Beis Shammai argue that without specific intent, the blessing on *parperes* does not include porridge, because porridge is not as prominent as *parperes*, which is a form of bread [whether it is *kisnin*-bread, as *Meiri* and *Rashba* maintain, or dried bread crumbs soaked in broth, as *Tosafos* explain (see comm. above s.v. ברך על הפת and s.v. על הפרפרת)]. For other explanations of Beis Shammai, see *Rashba* (to 42b s.v. או דילמא) and *Tos. Anshei Shem* s.v. מעשה קדירה.

The interpretation of *Rav* and *Rambam Comm.*, according to which Beis Shammai dispute a ruling implied in the *Tanna Kamma's* last statement, is but one of two possible interpretations suggested by the *Gemara* (loc. cit.). According to the other interpretation of this dispute, Beis Shammai disagree with the *previous* statement of the *Tanna Kamma*, in which he rules that the *Hamotzi* blessing on bread suffices for *parperes*. Beis Shammai argue that not only is the *Hamotzi* blessing insufficient for *parperes*, it does not include

say: [He has] not even [discharged his obligation] for porridge.

YAD AVRAHAM

porridge, either. The *Gemara* does not decide between these two possible interpretations.

The *Gemara's* uncertainty relates not only to the opinion of Beis Shammai (whose view is not followed by halachah in any event — see *Rav* s.v. מעשה קדרה), but also to the opinion of the *Tanna Kamma*. If Beis Shammai argue that the blessing on *parperes* does not suffice for porridge, then perforce the *Tanna Kamma* maintains that it *does* suffice (and the halachah would be decided accordingly). However, if Beis Shammai argues that the blessing on the *bread* does not suffice for porridge, we can only infer that the *Tanna Kamma* maintains that the *Hamotzi* blessing on the bread suffices for porridge. There is no reason to assume that a blessing on *parperes* suffices for porridge according to the *Tanna Kamma*. Rather, all would agree

that a blessing on *parperes* does not include porridge, just as it does not include bread, and the halachah would be decided accordingly (see *Divrei Chamudos* §96, cited by *Tos. Anshei Shem* s.v. מעשה קדרה; *Tos. Chadashim* s.v. בית שמאי אומרים; see also *Kessef Mishneh* and *Lechem Mishneh*, *Hil. Berachos* 4:6; cf. *Tos. Chadashim*).

Many authorities rule in accordance with the interpretation according to which the *Tanna Kamma* maintains that the blessing over *parperes* does exempt porridge (*Rashba* to 42b s.v. או דילמא; see also *Meiri*; *Rama* 176:1; cf. *Rambam*, *Hil. Berachos* 4:6; *Rabbeinu Yonah* 30a s.v. בית שמאי, as emended by *Chiddushei Anshei Shem* §2). Presumably, the reason *Rav* and *Rambam Comm.* only cite this interpretation of the dispute is because they, too, rule in accordance with this view (*Divrei Chamudos* loc. cit., cited by *Tos. Anshei Shem* s.v. מעשה קדרה).

6.

There is a general rule that one may discharge his blessing obligation by listening to someone else's recitation [the principle of שׁוֹמֵעַ כְּעוֹנֶה, *one who listens is like one who responds*] (see *Succah* 38b). Indeed, it is *preferable* for blessing obligations to be discharged in this manner, for when many people recite God's praises as one (by means of שׁוֹמֵעַ כְּעוֹנֶה), God's glory is manifested to a greater extent than if each person praised Him individually, as the verse (*Proverbs* 14:28) states: בְּרָב עָם הַדְרַת מֶלֶךְ, *a multitude of people is a king's glory* (see *Ramach*, cited by *Kessef Mishneh*, *Hil. Berachos* 1:12; *Beur Halachah* to 167:11 s.v. אחד מברך לכולם). However, with regard to the blessings on food (both before and after eating), the use of this mechanism is limited to situations in which the various people who are subject to the blessing obligation eat together as a collective group, rather than as separate individuals. If a number of unrelated individuals happen to eat together at the same time, each one must recite the blessings himself.[1] The following mishnah discusses when one may recite the blessings over food on behalf of others, and when each person must recite the blessings himself.

1. However, if one is *incapable* of reciting the blessing himself, he may discharge his obligation by listening to another recite the blessing, even if he is not part of a group (see *Shulchan Aruch* 193:1; *Mishnah Berurah* 213:9).

The requirement that the people eat together as a group is a Rabbinical enactment; Biblical law makes no distinction between people eating as a *group* and people eating as *individuals* (see *Or Zerua* §150, cited by *Shaar HaTziyun* 167:56).

הָיוּ יוֹשְׁבִין לֶאֱכֹל – כָּל אֶחָד וְאֶחָד מְבָרֵךְ לְעַצְמוֹ. הֵסֵבּוּ – אֶחָד מְבָרֵךְ לְכֻלָּן.

ר' עובדיה מברטנורא

(ו) **הָיוּ יוֹשְׁבִים.** בְּלֹא הֲסִיבָה, וְסִימָן הוּא שֶׁלֹּא נִתְוַעֲדוּ לֶאֱכֹל יַחַד, שֶׁרְגִילִים הָיוּ כְּשֶׁמִּתְוַעֲדִים חֲבוּרוֹת אֲנָשִׁים לֶאֱכֹל שֶׁהָיוּ מְסוּבִּין עַל הַמִּטּוֹת וְאוֹכְלִים וְשׁוֹתִים בַּהֲסִבַּת שְׂמֹאל: **כָּל אֶחָד מְבָרֵךְ לְעַצְמוֹ.** שֶׁלֹּא הָיָה לָהֶם קֶבַע סְעוּדָה בְּלֹא הֲסִיבָה. וּמִיהוּ אִם אָמְרוּ נֵיזִיל נִיכוּל נַהֲמָא בְּדוּכְתָּא פְּלָן, אַף עַל פִּי שֶׁלֹּא הֵסֵבּוּ כְּהֵסֵיבוּ דָמֵי, וְאֶחָד מְבָרֵךְ לְכוּלָּם וּמִצְטָרְפִין נַמִי לְזִמּוּן:

יד אברהם

הָיוּ יוֹשְׁבִין לֶאֱכֹל — *[If] they were sitting [together] to eat,*

A group of several people were eating a meal [containing bread]. They were *sitting* rather than *reclining* on couches (*Rav; Rashi*).

כָּל אֶחָד וְאֶחָד מְבָרֵךְ לְעַצְמוֹ. — *each and every one recites the blessings for himself.*

I.e. each individual is required to recite the *Hamotzi* blessing before eating the bread, and the *Bircas HaMazon* afterward (see *Tosafos* to 42a s.v. הסבו).

In mishnaic times, a group of people who gathered to share a fixed [bread] meal would recline while eating, whereas one would merely *sit* for an insignificant snacklike meal. Someone eating a snack is regarded as being at the table only temporarily, and cannot be considered part of a group. Hence, if a number of people eat in a sitting position, they indicate that they are not eating the meal as a group, but are, rather, a collection of individuals who happen to be eating at the same time. Therefore, each must recite the relevant blessings himself [see prefatory comments] (see *Rav* s.v. היו יושבים and s.v. כל אחד; *Rashi* s.v. כל אחד).

Rabbeinu Channanel (cited by *Rosh* §33) understands the case of the mishnah to be when the group had originally sat down together to engage in other activities. While they were sitting, food was brought to them, and so it emerged that they ate the meal together. Since they did not originally sit down for the purpose of eating, their sitting together does not establish a common bond for eating. However, if they *initially* sat down to eat, they would, in fact, be considered a group sharing a common meal, and one would recite the blessings on behalf of the entire group.[1]

הֵסֵבּוּ – אֶחָד מְבָרֵךְ לְכֻלָּן. — *[If] they reclined, one recites the blessings for all of them.*

By reclining at the meal, the members of the group demonstrate that they are eating a fixed meal. Consequently, they are viewed as a collective group sharing a common meal [even if each eats from his own loaf of bread (see *Gem.* 42b)], rather than as a temporary collection of individuals. Therefore, one recites the blessings on behalf of the entire group (see *Rav* and *Rashi*, cited in comm. above s.v. כל אחד), both the *Hamotzi* blessing before eating bread, and the *Bircas HaMazon* at the end of the

---

1. This interpretation cannot be reconciled with our version of the mishnah, which states "If they were sitting *to eat* etc.," implying that their purpose in sitting down *is* to eat. Apparently, *Rabbeinu Channanel's* version of our mishnah did not contain the word לֶאֱכֹל, *to eat*. The version of the mishnah printed in the *Gemara* also does not contain this word, and it is evident from the comments of many of the commentators that this was their reading, as well (see *Meleches Shlomo*).

6. [If] they were sitting [together] to eat, each and every one recites the blessings for himself. [If] they reclined, one recites the blessings for all of them.

YAD AVRAHAM

meal (*Tosafos* loc. cit.).[1]

Rav Hai Gaon understands the term הֵסֵבּוּ to mean *[if] they sat in a circle* (a conjugation of the verb לְסַבֵּב, *to surround* or *to encircle*). According to this definition, the term יוֹשְׁבִים refers to a number of people who are sitting at random locations, in which case they are considered unrelated individuals. However, if they are all sitting in a circle around the food, they are viewed as a collective group sharing a common meal, even if they do not recline (*Rabbeinu Yonah* 30b s.v. מתני, cited by *Meleches Shlomo*; *Rashba* to 42a s.v. מתניתן).

The *Gemara* (43a) adds that if a number of people designate a location at which to eat a meal, they are considered a united group sharing a common meal, even if they do not recline (*Rav*).

Tosafos (loc. cit.) comment that nowadays, when it is no longer the practice to recline while eating, the mishnah's distinction between reclining and sitting no longer applies. Rather, the participants at a meal establish themselves as a collective group sharing a common meal simply by sitting together at the same table (see *Shulchan Aruch* 167:11).

The mishnah only discusses a meal containing bread. Other foods, however, were not eaten while reclining; therefore, the fact that a group of people do not recline when eating these foods does not indicate that they are eating a temporary snacklike

meal. Possibly, then, a number of people eating these foods can be considered a collective group, and one may recite the blessings on behalf of the entire group, simply by virtue of their *sitting* together (see *Shulchan Aruch* 213:1 with *Mishnah Berurah* §5). On the other hand, it may be that since these foods, by their very nature, do not constitute a significant, fixed meal, the assembled are always viewed as eating an insignificant snacklike meal, in which case each individual is regarded as being at the table only temporarily (see comm. above s.v. כל אחד). Accordingly, they would not be considered a unified group, even if they recline.

These two possibilities are implied in the two versions cited by the *Gemara* (43a) of a dispute between the *Amoraim* Rav and R' Yochanan regarding wine. In the first version of the dispute, Rav maintains that if a group gathers together to drink wine, one may recite the *Borei pri hagafen* blessing on behalf of the group even if the assembled do not recline. This is because people do not necessarily recline while engaged in a drinking session, and therefore *sitting* does not indicate that the assembled are a mere collection of individuals. R' Yochanan, however, argues, that fixed drinking sessions *are* held while reclining, and therefore the participants are only considered a unified group if they recline. According to this version, it emerges that other foods do not require reclining,

---

1. It should be noted that with regard to the *Bircas HaMazon*, the mishnah's ruling only applies [at least initially — see *Mishnah Berurah* 193:2] to a group of *three* or more people (see *Gem.* 45b). For the blessings recited *before* eating, however, even a group of two suffices (*Tosafos* to 45a s.v. אם רצו לזמן; cf. *Rashi* to 45b s.v. מצוה ליחלק). The reason for this distinction is that after the group has finished eating, its members intend to disband. Therefore, only three or more people are considered a collective group at this time. Alternatively, the reason the *Bircas HaMazon* requires a group of three is because the Rabbis were more stringent regarding the Biblically mandated *Bircas HaMazon* than with the blessings recited before eating, which are a Rabbinical obligation (*Tosafos* ibid.). See further below (footnote 2 on next page) concerning the other after-blessings.

ברכות
ו/ו
בָּא לָהֶם יַיִן בְּתוֹךְ הַמָּזוֹן – כָּל אֶחָד וְאֶחָד מְבָרֵךְ
לְעַצְמוֹ; לְאַחַר הַמָּזוֹן – אֶחָד מְבָרֵךְ לְכֻלָּם. וְהוּא

──────────── ר' עובדיה מברטנורא ────────────

בא להם יין בתוך המזון כל אחד מברך לעצמו. הואיל ואין בית הבליעה פנוי ואין לב
המסובים פונה אל המברך אלא לבלוע מה שבפיהם. אי נמי, חיישינן שמא יחנק כשבא לענות אמן:

יד אברהם

With regard to wine, the halachah is that one may recite the blessing on behalf of the entire group, provided they are reclining (in accordance with either version of R' Yochanan). However, the law regarding other foods is disputed by the authorities. Some follow the first version cited by the Gemara and rule that one may recite the blessings on foods (other than wine and bread) on behalf of others [provided the assembled are all sitting, as noted above] (Rambam, Hil. Berachos 1:12; Rosh ibid.; Ramban, cited by Rosh).[2] Others, however, follow the second version and rule that each individual must recite the blessings on these foods himself (Hasagos HaRaavad to Rambam ibid.).

Shulchan Aruch (213:1) follows the view that one may recite a blessing over other foods on behalf of others, however, cites the other ruling, according to which each individual must recite the blessing himself. Rama concludes that, on the basis of this view, the custom is for each person to recite his own blessing on fruit and other such items.[3]

since all agree that these foods are customarily eaten while sitting.

In the second version of the dispute, Rav maintains that drinking sessions do not constitute a significant fixed gathering, as evident from the fact that they are not held in a reclining position. Therefore, the assembled are always regarded as a collection of individuals present at the table only temporarily, and each must recite the blessings himself. R' Yochanan argues that drinking sessions *are* held while reclining, and are therefore significant enough to allow the participants to be regarded as a unified group (provided they recline). Consequently, one may recite the blessing on behalf of the entire group. According to this version, all agree that even reclining does not suffice for other foods, since these foods do not constitute a significant meal, as indicated by the fact that they are eaten in a sitting position. [However, if these foods are eaten as part of a significant bread meal at which the participants were reclining, the bond forged by reclining at the meal suffices for these foods, as well (see Gem. ibid.).][1]

---

1. The above is the understanding of *Rosh* (§33) and *Rashba* (ad loc. s.v. ולענין פסק) of the *Gemara*, according to which both versions of the dispute imply that other foods are not treated like bread; either it is not necessary to recline for other foods (first version) or reclining does not suffice to create a commonality among the assembled (second version). Other commentators, however, understand the *Gemara*, and hence the law regarding other foods, differently (see *Ritva* ad loc. s.v. אמר רב and s.v. אמר רבי יוחנן; *Shitah Mekubetzes* ad loc. s.v. אמר רב; see also *Teshuvos HaRambam*, cited by *Kessef Mishneh*, *Hil. Berachos* 1:11). We have followed *Shulchan Aruch* (213:1) in explaining the *Gemara* according to *Rosh* and *Rashba*.

2. However, even these authorities agree that the *after*-blessings for these less significant foods must be recited individually (see *Chullin* 106a with *Tosafos* s.v. ושמע מינה; *Shulchan Aruch* 213:1).

3. *Mishnah Berurah* (ad loc. §12) notes that we very rarely discharge our blessing obligation (even for bread and wine) by listening to the recitation of a member of a group [notable exceptions being the *Kiddush* and *Hamotzi* of the Sabbath meals], although a group blessing is preferable to individual blessings (see prefatory comments). *Mishnah*

6
6

[If] wine was brought to them during the meal,
each and every one recites the blessing for himself; [if wine was brought] after the meal, one
recites the blessing for all of them. And he

בָּא לָהֶם יַיִן בְּתוֹךְ הַמָּזוֹן — — *[If] wine
was brought to them during the meal,*

And they had not been served wine
prior to the meal; thus, the wine served
during the meal requires a *Borei pri
hagafen* blessing (*Meiri;* see comm. to
previous mishnah s.v. בֵּרֵךְ עַל הַיַּיִן).

Alternatively, the mishnah refers to the
blessing of הַטּוֹב וְהַמֵּטִיב, *Hatov v'hameitiv,*
a blessing of praise, which is recited upon
drinking a second wine of different
vintage (see *Tosafos* to 43a s.v. הואיל;
Shulchan Aruch 175:5).

כָּל אֶחָד וְאֶחָד מְבָרֵךְ לְעַצְמוֹ; — *each and
every one recites the blessing for himself;*

Although the participants are
viewed as a collective group sharing a
common meal, one may not recite the
blessing on behalf of the entire group,
as was done for the *Hamotzi* blessing
and will be done for the *Bircas HaMazon* (see *Rabbeinu Yonah* 30b s.v. בא
להם). The *Gemara* explains that this is
because "the throat is not clear [of
food]" during the meal. This means
that since the people are preoccupied
with their eating, there is concern that
they will not pay proper attention to

the one reciting the *Borei pri hagafen*
blessing on their behalf [in which case
they cannot discharge their obligation
with his recitation] (*Rav*, first explanation; *Rashi* to 43a s.v. הואיל).

Alternatively, the *Gemara* means
that the Rabbis were concerned that
having one recite the blessing aloud for
all of the assembled might cause one of
the listeners to choke on his food while
answering "Amen."[1] Therefore, the
Rabbis instituted that each individual
recite the *Borei pri hagafen* blessing
himself, after he swallows the food in
his mouth (*Rav*, second explanation;
Rambam Comm.; Rosh §34; for the
ramifications of these two interpretations, see *Shulchan Aruch* and *Rama*
174:8 with *Mishnah Berurah* §43).

Others explain the *Gemara* to mean that
since one who is swallowing food is unable
to drink at that moment, his blessing obligation for the drink cannot be fulfilled at
that moment, either (*Re'ah* and *Shitah
Mekubetzes* to 43a s.v. אמר להם הואיל).[2]

לְאַחַר הַמָּזוֹן — אֶחָד מְבָרֵךְ לְכֻלָּם. — *[if
wine was brought] after the meal, one
recites the blessing for all of them.*

After they have finished eating,

Berurah posits that we do not rely on another's recitation out of concern that we will not
pay proper attention to the words being recited.

1. Although, strictly speaking, one discharges his obligation even if he does not answer
"Amen" to the other's blessing, the Rabbis were concerned that one would answer
"Amen" anyway (*Rosh* §34; see *Tos. R' Akiva* §42; see also *Tif. Yis.* §28).

2. According to this explanation, one does not discharge his obligation in this manner
even *after the fact.* According to the other explanations, it would seem that one who hears
the blessing from another *has* discharged his obligation after the fact, although he has
violated a Rabbinical institution. However, *Tosafos* (to 43a s.v. הואיל) imply that as a
result of the Rabbis' institution, one does not discharge his obligation [even after the fact]
in any event (see *Shaar HaTziyun* 174:50).

אוֹמֵר עַל הַמֻּגְמָר, אַף עַל פִּי שֶׁאֵין מְבִיאִין אֶת הַמֻּגְמָר אֶלָּא לְאַחַר הַסְּעֻדָה.

ר' עוֹבַדְיָה מִבַּרְטְנוּרָא

וְהוּא אוֹמֵר עַל הַמּוּגְמָר. הַמְבָרֵךְ בִּרְכַּת הַמָּזוֹן הוּא מְבָרֵךְ עַל הַמּוּגְמָר בּוֹרֵא עֲצֵי בְשָׂמִים. וְאַף עַל גַּב דַּאֲכִילָא דַּעֲדִיף מִינֵּיהּ אֲפִילוּ הָכִי כֵּיוָן דְּאַתְחִיל בַּחֲדָא עָבִיד לְאִידָךְ: **לְאַחַר הַסְּעוּדָה.** לְאַחַר בִּרְכַּת הַמָּזוֹן, דִּהֲשַׁתָּא לָאו מִלְּרַכֵּי הַסְּעוּדָה הוּא, אֲפִילוּ הָכִי כֵּיוָן שֶׁהִתְחִיל בְּבִרְכוֹת אַחֲרוֹנוֹת גּוֹמְרָן: **מוּגְמָר.** רְגִילִין הָיוּ לְהָבִיא אַחַר הַסְּעוּדָה עֲצֵי בְשָׂמִים בְּמַחְתָּה עַל הָאֵשׁ לְרֵיחַ טוֹב:

יד אברהם

there is no longer any concern that [they will not pay attention to the one reciting the blessing, or that] they will endanger themselves by answering "Amen." Therefore, one recites the blessing on behalf of the others (*Rabbeinu Yonah* 30b s.v. לאחר המזון).	*Mazon* to create a pleasant fragrance. Upon smelling burning incense, one must recite the blessing בּוֹרֵא עֲצֵי בְשָׂמִים, *Who creates fragrant woods* (*Rav* and *Rashi*, from *Gem.* 43a; see *Gem.* 43b for a Scriptural allusion to the requirement to recite a blessing on fragrances).[1] The mishnah teaches that although there may be a more prominent individual at the meal to whom it would seem more appropriate to accord the honor of reciting the blessing, the honor is reserved for the one who recited the *Bircas HaMazon*. Since he has already discharged the obligation of the others in one matter (the *Bircas HaMazon*), he is given the honor of reciting the blessing on the incense, as well (*Rav; Rambam Comm.*).

Although it was also customary to eat *parperes* after the meal (see comm. to previous mishnah s.v. ברך על הפרפרת שלפני המזון; *Rashi* to 42a s.v. ברך על היין), the small amount of *parperes* that is eaten does not give rise to the same concerns that exist during the meal, when people eat larger quantities of food to satisfy their hunger (*Tzlach* to 43a s.v. הואיל).

וְהוּא אוֹמֵר עַל הַמֻּגְמָר, — *And he says [the blessing] on the incense,*

That is, the one who recited the *Bircas HaMazon* on behalf of the entire group [to whom the mishnah has earlier alluded — see comm. above s.v. הסבו (see *Pri Chadash*, cited by *Tos. Chadashim*)] is the one who recites the blessing on the incense brought out after the meal (*Rav; Rambam Comm.*).

In mishnaic times, it was customary to burn incense after the *Bircas Ha-*

Alternatively, the mishnah refers not to the one who recited the *Bircas Hamazon*, but to the one who recited the *Borei pri hagafen* blessing on the wine after the meal [before the *Bircas Hamazon*] (*Rashi; Tosafos* to 42b s.v. ואע״פ). [The fact that the mishnah has just mentioned this person would seem

---

1. Our versions of the *Gemara* actually conclude that the blessing *Borei atzei besamim* is inappropriate for burning incense, since we do not smell the wood itself, but rather the *smoke* of the burning wood. According to these versions, the proper blessing is בּוֹרֵא מִינֵי בְשָׂמִים, *Who creates species of fragrances* (see *Rashi* ad loc. s.v. ועל ההדס). However, the commentators cite with approval a variant text of the *Gemara*, according to which the *Gemara* rules that the correct blessing is, in fact, *Borei atzei besamim* (see *Tosafos* ad loc. s.v. ועל ההדס).

6
6

says [the blessing] on the incense, even though
they do not bring the incense until after the meal.

to support this understanding of the pronoun "he" to refer to this individual (see *Tos. Yom Tov*; cf. *Pri Chadash* cited in comm. above).]

אַף עַל פִּי שֶׁאֵין מְבִיאִין אֶת הַמֻּגְמָר אֶלָּא לְאַחַר הַסְּעוּדָה. — *even though they do not bring the incense until after the meal.*

That is, until after the *Bircas HaMazon* (*Rav; Rashi; Rambam Comm.*).

Since the incense was brought out after the *Bircas HaMazon*, it is not associated with the meal at all. Accordingly, it might have been thought that the honor of reciting the blessing on the incense need not be given to the individual who recited the blessings associated with the meal (i.e. the *Bircas HaMazon* or the *Borei pri hagafen* — see comm. above s.v. והוא). The mishnah, therefore, teaches that this individual is, in fact, awarded the honor of reciting the *Borei atzei besamim* blessing (*Rav; Rashi*).

Tosafos (loc. cit.) — who, like *Rashi*, un-

derstand the mishnah to be referring to the one who recited the *Borei pri hagafen* blessing on the wine (see comm. above s.v. והוא אומר) — explain that the novelty of the mishnah's ruling is that the honor of reciting the blessing is awarded to this individual even though the *Bircas HaMazon* intervened between the drinking of the wine and the burning of the incense.

According to either interpretation, the mishnah discusses incense burned after the *Bircas HaMazon*. However, *Rabbeinu Yonah* (30b s.v. והוא אומר) cites a version of *Rashi* which understands the mishnah to be referring to incense which was brought out *before* the *Bircas HaMazon*. According to this understanding, the mishnah explains that although incense is usually brought out after the *Bircas HaMazon*, in which case it is not associated with the meal and the honor of reciting the *Borei atzei besamim* blessing is in fact not given to the one who recited the earlier blessings, in the event that it was brought out *before* the *Bircas HaMazon*, it *is* associated with the meal, and the individual who had earlier recited the *Borei pri hagafen* blessing is the one who recites the *Borei atzei besamim* blessing, as well.

7.

When a person eats two foods, one of which is primary and the other secondary, the blessing he recites on the primary food covers the subordinate food, as well. Olives eaten to blunt the sharpness of radishes are an example of a food subordinate to a different food. Since the olives are only eaten because of the radishes, the *Borei pri ha'adamah* blessing recited on the radishes is also effective for the olives [which normally require a *Borei pri ha'eitz* blessing] (see *Gem* 41a). We have seen an application of this principle in mishnah 5, where the mishnah rules that the *Hamotzi* blessing on bread also covers *parperes* eaten during the meal, because all foods eaten for sustenance [during the meal] are secondary to bread. By the same token, the *Bircas HaMazon* covers the *parperes*, as well (see comm. to mishnah 5, prefatory comments preceding s.v. ברך על הפת). The following mishnah discusses a case in which *bread* is considered a secondary food (see *Tosafos* to 44a s.v. מברך על המליח, cited by *Tos. Yom Tov* s.v. שהפת טפלה לו; *Rabbeinu Yonah* 31b s.v. הביאו לפניו; *Meiri*).

[ז] הֵבִיאוּ לְפָנָיו מָלִיחַ בַּתְּחִלָּה וּפַת עִמּוֹ – מְבָרֵךְ עַל הַמָּלִיחַ וּפוֹטֵר אֶת הַפַּת, שֶׁהַפַּת טְפֵלָה לוֹ. זֶה הַכְּלָל:

— ר' עובדיה מברטנורא —

(ז) מליח. כל דבר מלוח: שהפת טפלה לו. מי שאכל אכילה גסה מפירות מתוקים ביותר אוכל אחריו דבר מליח לחתך הליחות הנדבקות בגופו מחמת רוב הפירות, ומפני שאינו

יד אברהם

הֵבִיאוּ לְפָנָיו מָלִיחַ בַּתְּחִלָּה וּפַת עִמּוֹ, — *[If] they brought before [someone] a salted food first, and bread with it,*

I.e. the salted food is eaten before the bread (*Tif. Yis.* §32). [The significance of this point will be discussed in the comm. below, s.v. שהפת טפלה לו.]

The noun מָלִיחַ (from the root מֶלַח, *salt*) is a general term used to describe any salty food (*Rav; Rashi*). Examples of מָלִיחַ are salted fish (see *Tif. Yis.; Rambam, Hil. Berachos* 3:7) and salted olives (*Meiri*). Our mishnah refers to a food which is so salty that bread is eaten afterward to blunt its saltiness.

מְבָרֵךְ עַל הַמָּלִיחַ וּפוֹטֵר אֶת הַפַּת, — *he recites a blessing on the salted food and discharges [the blessing obligation for] the bread,*

[Unlike the case in mishnah 5, in which one recites a *Hamotzi* blessing on the bread and thereby discharges his obligation for other foods, in our mishnah's case, a blessing is recited on the salty food, which also suffices for the bread, as the mishnah will explain.]

שֶׁהַפַּת טְפֵלָה לוֹ. — *because the bread is subordinate to it.*

Since the bread is eaten only to offset the saltiness of the salted food, it is considered secondary to the salted food (see *Rav*). Therefore, the bread is in-

cluded in the blessing recited on the primary food (the salted food), in accordance with the law that the blessing on a primary food suffices for a secondary food (see prefatory comments). In contrast, the bread in mishnah 5 is eaten for sustenance, and, therefore, all foods that are similarly eaten to satisfy one's hunger are subordinate to the bread. Thus, the *Hamotzi* blessing on the bread covers those foods.

Presuming that the mishnah refers to a salted food eaten to satisfy one's hunger, the *Gemara* (44a) asks: How can bread — the staple of sustenance — ever be considered secondary to another food eaten for sustenance? The *Gemara* (as understood by *Rav* s.v. שהפת טפלה לו; *Rambam Comm.*) explains that our mishnah refers to a case in which one had previously eaten a large quantity of extremely sweet fruit. To counteract the harmful effects of the extreme sweetness, he eats a food so salty that it must be eaten with bread. Since the salted food is not eaten for sustenance, it is not automatically subordinate to the bread; on the contrary, the bread is subordinate to the salted food (see *Bach, Orach Chaim* 212 s.v. ומ״ש כגון שאכל דג מליח).[1]

Others understand the *Gemara* to

---

1. *Tosafos* (ad loc. s.v. באוכלי פירות גנוסר, cited by *Tos. Yom Tov* s.v. שהפת) wonder why, in this case, both the salted food and the bread are not subordinate to the *fruit*. *Tosafos* answer that the mishnah refers to a person who left the place where he recited the blessing on the fruit, thus necessitating another blessing on the other foods [see *Shulchan Aruch*

6
7

7. **[I**f] they brought before [someone] a salted food first, and bread with it, he recites a blessing on the salted food and discharges [the blessing obligation for] the bread, because the bread is subordinate to it. This is the rule:

mean that the *fruit* is the salted item to which the mishnah refers. Since these fruit are exceptionally sweet, they can only be eaten if they are salted to offset the sweetness (*Rabbeinu Yonah* 32a s.v. באוכלי פירות גנוסר; *Shitah Mekubetzes* ad loc. s.v. באוכלי פירות גנוסר). These sweet fruit are not considered secondary to the bread because they are so exceptional that they are deemed more significant even than bread (*Rashi* to 44a s.v. פירות גנוסר; see *Rashash* ad loc. s.v. רש"י ד"ה פירות גנוסר).

[Alternatively, since fruit that are eaten during a meal are eaten for their flavor rather than for sustenance, they are, therefore, not automatically subordinate to the bread (see comm. to mishnah 5, prefatory comments preceding s.v. ברך על הפת).]

The *Gemara's* question implies that bread can never be considered secondary to another food eaten for sustenance. Thus, if one eats salted fish as a meal, and he eats bread to blunt the saltiness of the fish, he would recite a *Hamotzi* blessing to cover both the bread and the fish, although it is the *fish* which is intended to satisfy his hunger rather than the bread. From the comments of *Rav* (loc. cit.) and *Rambam Comm.* it appears that they subscribe to this view (see *Shaar HaTziyun* 212:9).

However, *Tur* and *Shulchan Aruch* (212:1) imply that if one eats bread only to

offset the saltiness of the fish, he recites a blessing on the fish, not the bread. According to these authorities, as long as one did not eat the bread to satisfy his hunger, it is secondary to the food (the salted fish) which is the focus of his meal. Evidently, these authorities understand the *Gemara's* answer to be simply an example of bread which is not eaten for sustenance (see *Shaar HaTziyun* ibid.).

As noted in the comm. above (s.v. הביאו לפניו), the mishnah refers to a case in which the salted food is eaten before the bread. *Tos. Yom Tov* explains that the mishnah chooses such a case because only when the secondary item is eaten *after* the primary food, or *together* with it, is it unnecessary to recite a blessing on the secondary food. However, if the secondary food is eaten *before* the primary food, a blessing must be recited on it, since no blessing had yet been recited on the primary food.

The precise blessing required in this case (or in other cases where a blessing is needed for the secondary food — see footnote 1 above; *Mishnah Berurah* 212:4) is the subject of a dispute among the authorities. Some maintain that the blessing on a secondary food (when required) is always *Shehakol*, regardless of the food's normal blessing. Since a secondary item is subordinate to the primary food, it has no intrinsic significance, and it, therefore, loses its

and *Rama* 178:1 with *Mishnah Berurah* §12] (see *Tos. Yom Tov* ibid., *Tos. R' Akiva* §44 and *Tif. Yis., Boaz* §9 for the exact circumstances of this case). Alternatively, *Tosafos* answer that the person had not realized that he would need to eat salted food and bread to offset the extreme sweetness of the fruit. Thus, he did not have these foods in mind when he recited the *Borei pri ha'eitz* blessing on the fruit, so they cannot be covered by that blessing.

כָּל שֶׁהוּא עִקָּר וְעִמּוֹ טְפֵלָה – מְבָרֵךְ עַל הָעִקָּר וּפוֹטֵר אֶת הַטְּפֵלָה.

ר׳ עובדיה מברטנורא

יכול לאכול המליח לבדו אוכל מן הפת טמא. אבל המליח לבדו עיקר והפת טפלה לו:

יד אברהם

mary, and [there is] a subordinate [food] with it, he recites a blessing on the primary [food] and discharges [the obligation for] the subordinate [food].

[The mishnah's ruling regarding bread eaten with a salted food is not unique. It is a consequence of a general rule concerning primary and secondary foods.]

Usually, when a mishnah cites a general rule after a specific example, it is to teach an aspect of the law which would not otherwise have been apparent. *Tos. R' Akiva* (§43) explains that one might have thought that the blessing recited on the salted food suffices for the bread only because that blessing is one which always suffices (after the fact) for bread (i.e. the *Shehakol* blessing — see mishnah 2). By citing the general rule, the mishnah teaches that the secondary food is included in the blessing of the primary food no matter which blessing is recited.[2]

Thus far, the illustrations we have seen of the principle that a secondary food is subordinate to the primary food involve two separate and distinct items (bread and *parperes*, bread and salted foods). There is, however, another application of this law — the case of a single dish containing many different ingredients, each of which is normally subject to a different blessing;

original blessing. Thus, in the mishnah's case of bread and salted food, if the bread is eaten first, it requires only a *Shehakol* (see *Terumas HaDeshen* §31; *Rama* 212:1; see *Mishnah Berurah* §10).[1] Others, however, contend that in cases where a secondary food requires a separate blessing, one must recite the blessing to which it is usually subject. According to these authorities, the blessing on bread eaten before the salted food is its regular *Hamotzi* (see *Beis Yosef* 212 s.v. כתב בתרומת הדשן). See *Magen Avraham* ad loc. §4 (cited by *Tif. Yis.* §33) for yet another opinion.

Alternatively, *Tos. Yom Tov* suggests that the mishnah gives an example of a primary food which is eaten first to teach a *leniency*, viz. that the secondary food is subordinate to the primary food even if the two foods are not eaten at the same time. As long as the secondary food is eaten because of the primary food, the blessing on the primary food suffices for both. [However, this does not explain why the mishnah stresses that the primary food was eaten *first* (see *Tos. Chadashim*).]

זֶה הַכְּלָל: כָּל שֶׁהוּא עִקָּר וְעִמּוֹ טְפֵלָה – מְבָרֵךְ עַל הָעִקָּר וּפוֹטֵר אֶת הַטְּפֵלָה. — *This is the rule: Whenever [a food] is pri-*

---

1. According to this view, the mishnah could have easily illustrated the concept that a secondary food is subordinate to the primary food with a case in which the bread is eaten *before* the salted food, by ruling that the blessing on the bread in this case is *Shehakol*. However, our mishnah chooses not to give this example because it wishes to demonstrate that at times, no blessing at all is required for the secondary food (*Tif. Yis.* §33).

2. Note that this explanation presumes that the salted food of the mishnah is fish or other such foods that are subject to the *Shehakol* blessing. However, according to those who understand the salted food of the mishnah to be fruit (see comm. above s.v. שהפת טפלה לו), the mishnah cannot have intended to teach this law with this statement, for the blessing on these fruit [*Borei pri ha'eitz*] does not normally suffice for bread (see *Rashash*).

6
7
Whenever [a food] is primary, and [there is] a subordinate [food] with it, he recites a blessing on the primary [food] and discharges [the obligation for] the subordinate [food].

YAD AVRAHAM

for example, a stew containing meat and vegetables. In this case, as well, the rule of our mishnah dictates that one does not recite a separate blessing for each component. Rather, he only recites the blessing appropriate for the primary ingredient. [Gener-ally, the primary component is the food which is present in the largest quantity. However, in certain cases, other factors determine which is considered the primary component. See *Shulchan Aruch* 204:12 and 212:1 with commentators for details.]

8.

The mishnah now discusses the blessings recited after eating. There is a Biblical requirement to bless God after eating certain foods. Foods that are not included in the Biblical obligation are subject to a *Rabbinically* mandated after-blessing (see comm. below s.v. רבי עקיבא אומר). The source of the Biblical obligation is a verse at the end of the Scriptural passage which declares the praises of Eretz Yisrael (*Deuteronomy* 8:8-10): "(8) A Land of wheat, barley, grape, fig and pomegranate; a Land of oil-olives and honey: (9) a Land where you will eat bread without poverty — you will lack nothing there; a Land whose stones are iron and from whose mountains you will mine copper: (10) *You will eat and you will be satisfied, and bless Hashem, your God, for the good Land that He gave you.*" Three blessings are indicated in the last verse of the passage: "*You will eat and you will be satisfied* and bless Hashem, your God" implies a blessing giving thanks to God for the food He provides; the phrase "and bless Hashem, your God, *for the . . . Land*" implies a blessing of thanksgiving to God for granting us Eretz Yisrael; "for the *good* Land" alludes to a supplicatory blessing concerning Jerusalem, which is described elsewhere (*Deuteronomy* 3:25) as "this *good* mountain (see *Sifrei* and *Rashi* ad loc.). The three blessings that were formulated in fulfillment of this Biblical obligation are known as בִּרְכַּת הַזָּן, *Bircas HaZan* [lit: *the blessing of sustenance*]; בִּרְכַּת הָאָרֶץ, *Bircas HaAretz* [lit: *the blessing of the Land*]; and בּוֹנֵה יְרוּשָׁלַיִם, *Bonei Yerushalayim* [lit: *the Builder of Jerusalem*], which, in its present form, is a supplicatory blessing beseeching God to rebuild Jerusalem and the Temple[1] (*Rav* s.v. מברך אחריהן, from *Gem.* 48b). These three blessings are collectively known as the *Bircas HaMazon*.[2] Later, somewhat after

1. Although the requirement to recite blessings referring to these three concepts is Biblical, the Torah does not mandate a specific text to be recited (see *Rashba* to 48b s.v. הא דאמרינן). The texts of these blessings were composed by Moses [*Bircas HaZan*], Joshua [*Bircas Ha'Aretz*], and David and Solomon [*Bonei Yerushalayim*] (*Gem.* 48b).

   As originally composed by David and Solomon, *Bonei Yerushalayim* contained a plea that God bless the Land with tranquility. After the destruction of the Temple and the exile, the blessing was modified to embody a prayer for the return of the Land and the rebuilding of Jerusalem and the Temple (see *Rashba* ibid.).

2. Biblically, one is required to recite the *Bircas HaMazon* only if he ate sufficient food to satisfy his hunger, as the verse implies ["you will eat and you *will be satisfied*"] (see

ברכות [ח] אָבַל תְּאֵנִים וַעֲנָבִים וְרִמּוֹנִים – מְבָרֵךְ אַחֲרֵיהֶן שָׁלשׁ בְּרָכוֹת, דִּבְרֵי רַבָּן גַּמְלִיאֵל. וַחֲכָמִים אוֹמְרִים, בְּרָכָה אַחַת מֵעֵין שָׁלשׁ.

ר' עובדיה מברטנורא

(ח) **מברך אחריהן שלש ברכות.** דכל שהוא משבעת המינים מברך אחריו שלש ברכות, דסבירא ליה לרבן גמליאל דואכלת ושבעת וברכת לאו אלהם בלבד קאי אלא אכל אכל אלא מאמין המוחכרים לעיל בפרשה. ובהאי קרא שלש ברכות רמיזי, וברכת זו ברכת הזן, על הארץ זו ברכת הארץ, הטובה זו בונה ירושלים, וכן הוא אומר (דברים ג, כה) ההר הטוב הזה: **וחכמים אומרים ברכה אחת.** מעין שלש ברכות. אם ענבים תאנים רימונים זיתים ותמרים אכל, מברך על העץ ועל פרי העץ ועל ארץ חמדה טובה וכו', וחותם על הארץ ועל הפירות. ובארץ ישראל חותם על

יד אברהם

the destruction of the Second Temple, the Rabbis instituted a fourth blessing, known as the blessing of הַטּוֹב וְהַמֵּטִיב, *Hatov Vehameitiv* [lit: *Who is good and Who confers good [on others]*] (see *Gem.* ibid.). [The recitation of this blessing is a Rabbinical requirement (see *Gem.* 49a with *Tosafos* s.v. מאן דאמר).]

The verse does not explicitly state which foods are included in the Biblical obligation of an after-blessing. This issue is the subject of dispute in the following mishnah.

אָבַל תְּאֵנִים וַעֲנָבִים וְרִמּוֹנִים — *— [If] one ate figs, or grapes, or pomegranates,*

One ate figs, grapes or pomegranates, or one of the other members of the Seven Species for which Scripture praises Eretz Yisrael [i.e. wheat, barley, olives and dates — see *Deuteronomy* 8:8] (see *Rav*; *Rambam Comm.*; *Rashi*, from *Gem.* 37a; see *Meleches Shlomo*).

מְבָרֵךְ אַחֲרֵיהֶן שָׁלשׁ בְּרָכוֹת, דִּבְרֵי רַבָּן גַּמְלִיאֵל. — *he recites after them the Three Blessings. [These are] the words of Rabban Gamliel.*

That is, he recites the *Bircas HaMazon*. [The mishnah refers to the *Bircas HaMazon* as "the Three Blessings" because it originally consisted of three

blessings — see prefatory comments] (*Rambam Comm.*).

Rabban Gamliel maintains that the verse mandating the *Bircas HaMazon* (*Deuteronomy* 8:10) refers to the Seven Species mentioned earlier in that Scriptural passage (ibid. v. 8; see prefatory comments). Hence, there is a Biblical obligation to recite the *Bircas HaMazon* after eating any of the Seven Species[1] (*Rav*; *Rashi* to 44a s.v. וברכת).

However, as will be seen in the comm. below (s.v. וחכמים אומרים), even according to Rabban Gamliel, kernels of wheat and barley are not subject to the *Bircas HaMazon*, even though they are members of the Seven Species.

וַחֲכָמִים אוֹמְרִים: בְּרָכָה אַחַת מֵעֵין שָׁלשׁ. — *But the Sages say: [He recites] one*

Mishnah Berurah 184:22 and *Beur Halachah* ad loc. s.v. בכזית). However, Rabbinically there is a requirement to recite the *Bircas HaMazon* after eating an amount of food the size of an olive (see *Rambam, Hil. Berachos* 1:1; *Shulchan Aruch* 184:6).

1. This includes spelt [which is considered a form of wheat], and oats and rye [which are types of barley] (see *Pesachim* 35a).

8. [**I**f] one ate figs, or grapes, or pomegranates, he recites after them the Three Blessings. [These are] the words of Rabban Gamliel. But the Sages say: [He recites] one blessing which is an abridgment of the Three [Blessings].

YAD AVRAHAM

blessing which is an abridgment of the Three [Blessings].

According to the Sages, the *Bircas HaMazon* is only recited after eating bread.[1] For other members of the Seven Species, or for nonbread products of wheat and barley, one recites a one-blessing abridgment of the *Bircas HaMazon*. This single blessing alludes to the four blessings of the full version.

The *Gemara* (44a) cites the text of the blessing for fruit of the Seven Species: *Blessed are You, Hashem, our God, King of the universe, for the tree and the fruit of the tree, and for the produce of the field* (this segment summarizes the *Bircas Hazan* of the unabridged *Bircas HaMazon*); *and for the desirable, good and spacious land that You gave our forefathers as a heritage, to eat from its fruit and to be satisfied from its goodness* (this segment alludes to the *Bircas Ha'Aretz*). *Have mercy, Hashem, our God, on Israel, Your people, and on Jerusalem, Your city; and on Your Temple; and on Your Altar. And may You rebuild Jeru-*

salem, Your holy city, speedily in our days, and bring us into it and gladden us with it (this is an allusion to the blessing of *Bonei Yerushalayim*). *For You, Hashem, are good and You do good to all* (this summarizes the blessing of *Hatov Vehameitiv*). *Blessed are You, Hashem, for the Land and for the fruits.* In Eretz Yisrael, the concluding formula is "for the Land and for *its* fruits" [since the blessing is being recited on the fruit of the Land of Eretz Yisrael itself]. For grain products (other than bread), the opening phrase *for the tree and the fruit of the tree* is replaced by *for the nourishment and the sustenance*, and the concluding phrase with *for the land and for the nourishment.* With regard to wine, *Rav* and *Tosafos* (to 44a s.v. על העץ) state that just as the blessing recited before drinking wine refers to the specific tree from which wine is derived ("Who creates the fruit of the *vine*" — see mishnah 1 with comm. s.v. חוץ (מן היין), so should its after-blessing. Therefore, the phrase *for the tree and the fruit of the tree* is replaced by *for the vine and the fruit of the vine.*[2]

1. This includes *kisnin*-bread (see comm. to mishnah 5 s.v. ברך על הפרפרת שלפני המזון), if one eats an amount which would constitute a meal for most people (*Tif. Yis.* §37, from *Shulchan Aruch* 168:6). Bread made from spelt, oats or rye is also subject to the *Bircas HaMazon* obligation (see *Gem.* 37b with *Rashi* s.v. ולא מין דגן). However, bread made from rice or millet requires neither the *Bircas HaMazon* nor the one-blessing abridgment. Rather, its after-blessing is *Borei Nefashos* (see *Gem.* 37a; *Shulchan Aruch* 208:7). [The *Borei Nefashos* blessing will be discussed in the comm. below s.v. רבי עקיבא אומר.]

2. *Tosafos* (see also *Rav* s.v. וחכמים אומרים and *Tos. Yom Tov* s.v. ברכה אחת) maintain that the *concluding* formula for wine is the same as for fruit. Others, however, contend that the after-blessing for wine concludes with the phrase *for the Land and the fruit of the vine.* *Shulchan Aruch* (208:11) implies that either version is acceptable. However, *Mishnah Berurah* (§56) notes the consensus of the authorities is to conclude the blessing with the phrase *for the Land and the fruit of the vine.*

It should be noted that the text we customarily recite differs somewhat from the text cited by the *Gemara* (see *Mishnah Berurah* 208:50 with *Shaar HaTziyun* §50).

רַבִּי עֲקִיבָא אוֹמֵר: אֲפִלּוּ אָכַל שֶׁלֶק וְהוּא מְזוֹנוֹ,
מְבָרֵךְ אַחֲרָיו שָׁלֹשׁ בְּרָכוֹת.

—————— ר' עובדיה מברטנורא ——————

הָאָרֶץ וְעַל פֵּירוֹתֶיהָ. וּבְרָכָה זוֹ עַל מַה שֶּׁמְּבָרֵךְ עַל הַיַּיִן אֶלָּא שֶׁפּוֹתֵחַ בָּהּ עַל הַגֶּפֶן וְעַל פְּרִי הַגָּפֶן.
וְעַל כָּל דָּבָר הַנַּעֲשֶׂה מֵחֲמֵשֶׁת מִינֵי דָגָן, בִּמְקוֹם עַל הָעֵץ וְעַל פְּרִי הָעֵץ אוֹמֵר עַל הַמִּחְיָה וְעַל
הַכַּלְכָּלָה וְחוֹתֵם עַל הָאָרֶץ וְעַל הַמִּחְיָה: אֲפִלּוּ אָכַל שֶׁלֶק. שֶׁל יָרָק, וְהוּא מְזוֹנוֹ, שֶׁסּוֹמֵךְ עָלָיו לְמָזוֹן
מְבָרֵךְ שָׁלֹשׁ בְּרָכוֹת, דּוּכְלַלָּה וּשְׁבַעַת אָכַל [מַאן] [מַאן] דְּאָכַל קָאֵי. וַהֲלָכָה כַּחֲכָמִים שֶׁאֵין מְבָרְכִין שָׁלֹשׁ
בְּרָכוֹת אֶלָּא אָלֶחֶם אָלֶחֶם, וְעַל שֶׁבַעַת הַמִּינִין בְּרָכָה אַחַת מֵעֵין שָׁלֹשׁ, וְעַל כָּל שְׁאָר דְּבָרִים בּוֹרֵא נְפָשׁוֹת
רַבּוֹת וְחֶסְרוֹנָן. פֵּירוּשׁ חֶסְרוֹנָן כְּמוֹ לֶחֶם וּמַיִם שֶׁאִי אֶפְשָׁר לְהִתְקַיֵּים בְּלֹא הֵם, וְעַל כָּל מַה שֶּׁבָּרָא
לְהַחְיוֹת בָּהֶם נֶפֶשׁ כָּל חַי, כְּלוֹמַר עַל כָּל מַה שֶּׁבָּעוֹלָם שֶׁגַּם אִם לֹא נִבְרְאוּ יְכוֹלִין הַבְּרִיּוֹת לְהִתְקַיֵּים,
וְלֹא נִבְרְאוּ כִּי אִם לְתַעֲנוּג וּלְתוֹסֶפֶת טוֹבָה. וּמִפְּנֵי שֶׁיֵּשׁ בַּבְּרָכָה זוֹ שְׁנֵי עִנְיָנוֹת הָיִיל בְּרָכָה אֲרוּכָה
וּפוֹתֵחַת בְּבָרוּךְ וְחוֹתֶמֶת בְּבָרוּךְ, כִּדְאִיתָא בִּירוּשַׁלְמִי שֶׁחוֹתְמִים בָּהּ בָּרוּךְ אַתָּה ה' חֵי הָעוֹלָמִים:

יד אברהם

The Sages dispute Rabban Gamliel's assertion that the verse obligating the *Bircas HaMazon* refers to the Seven Species. They argue that since verse 9 intervenes between the verse of the Seven Species (v.8) and the verse of the *Bircas HaMazon* (v.10), verse 10 cannot be referring to the Seven Species. Rather, it refers to the bread mentioned in verse 9 ["A Land where you will eat *bread* without poverty"] (*Tos. Yom Tov* and *Tif. Yis* §37, from *Gem.* 44a).

Rabban Gamliel, on the other hand, contends that the Torah's reference to bread in verse 9 is not to teach that bread is the *only* food requiring the *Bircas HaMazon*; indeed, all Seven Species are included in the *Bircas HaMazon* obligation. Rather, the reference to bread is to *qualify* the *Bircas HaMazon* requirement as not applying to wheat and barley (which are included in the Seven Species) unless they have been processed by baking or cooking, like bread. *Kernels* of wheat or barley are not subject to the *Bircas*

HaMazon requirement (*Gem. ibid.*). They require only the one-blessing abridgment of the *Bircas HaMazon* (*Rabbeinu Yonah* 32a s.v. ונראה למורי; cf. *Rashba* to 44a s.v. ורבנן).[1]

It would seem that the obligation to recite the one-blessing abridgment is Rabbinic, since the foods that are subject to it (whether the Seven Species according to the Sages, or only kernels of grain according to Rabban Gamliel) are not included in the verse which is the source for the Biblically obligated after-blessing. Many authorities subscribe to this view (see *Rambam, Hil. Berachos* 8:12 with *Kessef Mishneh; Rabbeinu Yonah* loc. cit.; see also *Shulchan Aruch* 209:3 with *Mishnah Berurah* §10).

However, others maintain that the requirement to recite the one-blessing abridgment after eating these foods is *Biblical*. These authorities understand that the reference to bread (in v. 9) is not intended to *exclude* the Seven Species (or kernels of grain according to Rabban Gamliel) from a Biblically mandated after-blessing, but to indicate that they are subject to a *modified* version of the *Bircas HaMazon*, i.e. one that consists of a single blessing rather than the

1. The Sages also dispute this assertion, contending that the after-blessing for kernels of wheat and barley is *Borei nefashos* (*Rabbeinu Yonah* ibid.; *Shulchan Aruch* 208:4; see *Tosafos* to 37a s.v. הכוסס). [See further comm. below s.v. רבי עקיבא אומר regarding the blessing of *Borei nefashos*.]

R' Akiva says: Even if one ate a cooked vegetable and it is his sustenance, he recites after it the Three Blessings.

YAD AVRAHAM

full three-blessing version alluded to in the verse [see prefatory comments] (*Ramban* to 49b s.v. ר' מאיר; *Rashba* and *Ritva* to 44a s.v. ורבנן; *Tur* 209; see also *Rashba* to 35a s.v. הכי גרסינן; *Rabbeinu Yonah* 24b s.v. ובגמ' נחלקו; *Mishnah Berurah* loc. cit.).[1]

רַבִּי עֲקִיבָא אוֹמֵר: אֲפִלּוּ אָכַל שֶׁלֶק וְהוּא מְזוֹנוֹ, מְבָרֵךְ אַחֲרָיו שָׁלשׁ בְּרָכוֹת. — *R' Akiva says: Even if one ate a cooked vegetable and it is his sustenance, he recites after it the Three Blessings.*

R' Akiva maintains that if one makes a meal out of even a cooked vegetable, he is Biblically obligated to recite the *Bircas HaMazon* (*Rav; Rashi*). According to R' Akiva, the verse of *"you will eat and you will be satisfied and you will bless Hashem . . ."* refers to *any* food that is the basis of one's meal (*Rav*), as long as it satisfies his hunger (see *Rashba* to 37a s.v. ונתן ר"ו רשות, in the name of *Tosafos*).

The *Gemara* (44b) identifies the cooked vegetable to which the mishnah refers as the stalk of a cabbage, which is the only vegetable which satisfies one's hunger. It seems odd that *Rav* does not make this distinction, implying that R' Akiva refers to *all* vegetables (*Tos. Chadashim*).

The halachah is in accordance with the Sages, who maintain that the *Bircas HaMazon* is recited only for bread. The Seven Species (including grain products other than bread) require the one-blessing abridgment of the *Bircas HaMazon*. All other foods [including kernels of grain (see comm. above s.v. וחכמים אומרים, footnote 1 on previous page)] are subject to the [Rabbinically mandated] after-blessing of *Borei Nefashos* (*Rav*).

The *Borei nefashos* blessing is the standard after-blessing formulated by the Rabbis for foods that are not subject to a Biblically mandated after-blessing.[2] Its text is: *Blessed are You, Hashem, our God, King of the universe, Who creates numerous living things with their deficiencies; for all that You have created with which to maintain the life of every being. Blessed is He, the life of the worlds.*[3] The term *deficiencies* refers to a person's need for bread and water, items without which one cannot survive. *All that You have created with which to maintain life* refers to those items that are not essential for life, but which God created for the enjoyment of His creatures (*Rav; Tosafos* to 37a s.v. בורא נפשות).

1. The question whether or not the single-blessing abridgment is a Biblical obligation has a practical consequence in the case of someone who is uncertain whether he recited it. If this after-blessing is a Biblical requirement, he must recite the blessing in order to remove the doubt; if it is Rabbinical, he does not recite it (*Meiri* to 44b s.v. מי שנסתפק; *Tif. Yis.* §37; *Tur Orach Chaim* 209).

2. According to those who maintain that the one-blessing abridgment of *Bircas HaMazon* recited for the Seven Species is a Rabbinical obligation (see comm. above s.v. וחכמים אומרים), we must say that the Rabbis formulated a special after-blessing for the Seven Species, patterned on the *Bircas HaMazon*, because of the significance of these foods (see *Mishnah Berurah* 208:1 and *Shaar HaTziyun* §1).

3. It should be noted that there are various disputes regarding the text of *Borei Nefashos*. For example, some maintain that the blessing concludes "Blessed *are* You, Hashem, the life of worlds" (see *Rav; Tosafos* to 37a s.v. בורא נפשות). The version we have cited is the one given by *Mishnah Berurah* 207:3.

הַשּׁוֹתֶה מַיִם לִצְמָאוֹ, אוֹמֵר: ,,שֶׁהַכֹּל נִהְיָה בִּדְבָרוֹ". רַבִּי טַרְפוֹן אוֹמֵר: ,,בּוֹרֵא נְפָשׁוֹת רַבּוֹת".

ר' עובדיה מברטנורא

השותה מים לצמאו. דוקא, מברך שהכל. אבל השותה מים לבלוע מאכל שנתחב לו בגרונו וכיוצא בזה, אינו מברך: **רבי טרפון אומר בורא נפשות רבות.** מברך לפני שתיית המים. ואין הלכה כרבי טרפון, אלא לפניהם מברך שהכל ולאחריהם בורא נפשות רבות:

יד אברהם

הַשּׁוֹתֶה מַיִם לִצְמָאוֹ, אוֹמֵר: שֶׁהַכֹּל נִהְיָה בִּדְבָרוֹ". — *One who drinks water to [quench] his thirst says [the blessing of] "...that everything came into being through His word."*

[This refers to the blessing recited *before* drinking water. Since water does not grow from the ground, its proper blessing is *Shehakol* (see mishnah 3).]

The mishnah teaches that a blessing is recited on water only if one drinks to quench his thirst. If one drinks water to dislodge something stuck in his throat [or for any purpose other than quenching thirst, e.g. to aid in swallowing medicine (see *Beur Halachah* to 204:7 s.v. השותה מים)], he does not recite a blessing (*Rav*, from *Gem.* 44b-45a), neither a pre-blessing nor an after-blessing (*Rosh* §43; *Shulchan Aruch* 204:7; see *Tosafos* to 45a s.v.

דחנקתיה). Since water is tasteless, it is only beneficial when it quenches one's thirst. Therefore, when water is drunk for other purposes, it does not require a blessing. However, other liquids *do* require a blessing even when they are drunk to dislodge something stuck in one's throat, since the person derives benefit from their taste (*Tosafos* loc. cit., based on *Gem.* 36a; *Meiri*; *Tif. Yis.* §39 et al.).

רַבִּי טַרְפוֹן אוֹמֵר: ,,בּוֹרֵא נְפָשׁוֹת רַבּוֹת". — *R' Tarfon says: [He says the blessing of] "...Who creates numerous living things."*

R' Tarfon maintains that the blessing one recites *before* drinking water is *Borei nefashos* (*Rav*; *Tosafos* to 45a s.v. רבי טרפון; *Rashi* to *Eiruvin* 14b s.v. רבי טרפון אומר; cf. *Meiri*). [As noted above, this blessing was formulated by the Rabbis as the standard after-

6
8
One who drinks water to [quench] his thirst says [the blessing of] "... that everything came into being through His word." R' Tarfon says: [He says the blessing of] "... Who creates numerous living things ...."

blessing for foods other than bread and members of the Seven Species. According to R' Tarfon, it was also formulated as a *pre-blessing* for water.]

R' Tarfon contends that water, which provides no nourishment (see *Gem.* 35a), does not even warrant the general *Shehakol* blessing, which was formulated for foods and drinks that provide some nourishment. Rather, one recites the *Borei nefashos* blessing, which thanks God for providing our "deficiencies" [i.e. water — see comm. above s.v. רבי עקיבא אומר] (*Re'ah*; *Ritva* and *Shitah Mekubetzes* to 44b s.v. השותה מים).

Alternatively, R' Tarfon reasons that the general *Shehakol* blessing is *insufficient* for water, because of water's critical function in sustaining life. Rather, one should recite the blessing of *Borei nefashos*, which specifically refers to the essential necessities of life (*Sefer HaMichtam* to 44b s.v. ר' טרפון).

As noted in the comm. above (s.v. רבי עקיבא אומר), the standard after-blessing for items other than bread and members of the Seven Species is *Borei nefashos*, and this would seem to be true of water, as well. However, it seems strange that R' Tarfon would mandate the same blessing both before *and* after drinking water. Some commentators explain that, in fact, R' Tarfon requires no after-blessing at all for water, since it does not provide sustenance (*Ritva* to 44b s.v. השותה מים; see also *Tos. HaRosh* and *Tos. R' Yehudah Chassid* to 45a s.v. רבי טרפון). [This view is not unprecedented. The *Gemara* (44b) cites one *Amora* who maintains that water requires no after-blessing; another *Amora* is of the opinion that even vegetables do not require an after-blessing, since they provide little sustenance (see *Ritva* ad loc. s.v. ועל הקופרא; *P'nei Yehoshua* ad loc. s.v. אמר רבי יצחק בר אבדימי).] Others, however, maintain that indeed R' Tarfon requires the *Borei nefashos* blessing both before and after drinking water (*Rashba* to 45a s.v. רבי טרפון).

The halachah is not in accordance with R' Tarfon. Rather, one recites the *Shehakol* blessing before drinking water. The blessing of *Borei nefashos* is recited *after* drinking water (*Rav*; see *Gem.* 45a).

פרק שביעי ~§
Chapter Seven

After one eats bread, he is Biblically required to recite *Bircas HaMazon*, the Grace After Meals. This consists of three Biblical blessings and one blessing that is a Rabbinic requirement (*Gemara* 48b).

This chapter focuses on an additional requirement — the laws of זִימוּן, *zimmun* — the collective blessing. This is the manner in which the *Bircas HaMazon* is recited after a company of at least three people have eaten bread together. One of the three is appointed the leader and, following a prescribed formula (see mishnah 3), summons the others to participate in saying the *Bircas HaMazon* together. In essence, it is an *invitation* (לְזַמֵן, *to invite*) to the others of the group to join him in praising God and thereby offer a collective blessing (see *Rashi* to 45a ד"ה שלשה שאכלו; *Ritva* and *Meiri* ibid.; *Mishnah Berurah* 192:1, 194:1).

Originally, the leader of the *zimmun* recited the entire *Bircas HaMazon* aloud on behalf of the entire group, who fulfilled their obligation by carefully listening in silence to the leader's recitation. This is the ideal form of *zimmun*. Nowadays, however, since people find it difficult to listen to and concentrate on every word of the leader's recitation, we are concerned that inattention will cause them to fail to fulfill even the basic *Bircas HaMazon* obligation. It has therefore become customary for each individual to recite the entire *Bircas HaMazon* himself, with at least the first blessing said quietly along with the leader (see *Shulchan Aruch Orach Chaim* 183:7 with *Taz* 6 and *Mishnah Berurah* 27-28).

The Halachic authorities disagree as to whether the collective blessing is a Biblical or Rabbinic obligation. Most authorities seem to hold that it is Rabbinic (*Pri Megadim* quoted by *Mishnah Berurah, Shaar HaTziyun* 197:16).[1]

---

1. Among the early authorities, *Ravad* (quoted by *Tur Orach Chaim* 188; *Hasagos* to *Baal HaMaor* Ch. 9 s.v. שאין דנין דנין והורגין) and *Tur* (ibid.) [as understood by *Chazon Ish* (*Orach Chaim* 31:1)] hold that *zimmun* is a Biblical obligation. *Re'ah* (to 45a s.v. אמר רב אסי), *Meiri* (ibid. s.v. וענין הזמון), *Rashba* (to 50a s.v. וליברכו) and *Ritva* (*Hilchos Berachos* 5:19;19) hold that it is a Rabbinic obligation.

[א] **שְׁלֹשָׁה** שֶׁאָכְלוּ כְּאֶחָד חַיָּבִין לְזַמֵּן.
אֲבָל דְּמַאי, וּמַעֲשֵׂר רִאשׁוֹן

—————— ר' עובדיה מברטנורא ——————

פרק שביעי – שלשה שאכלו. (א) **שלשה שאכלו. לזמן.** להזדמן יחד, לברך בלשון
רבים נברך שאכלנו משלו: **דמאי.** פירות עמי הארץ קרויים דמאי, כלומר דא מאי, מטושרין
הן או לא. לפי שהם חשודים על המעשרות ואסרו חכמים לאכול מפירותיהן עד שיעשר. ואם
אכל ולא עשר מברך עליו ולא הוי מצוה הבאה בעבירה דרוב עמי הארץ מעשרים הם:

—————— יד אברהם ——————

1.

The following mishnah first defines the basic obligation of *zimmun*, then enumerates foods for which *zimmun* may or may not be obligatory, and concludes by listing those individuals who may be included or must be excluded from the quorum of three necessary for *zimmun*. This list is continued in the next mishnah.

שְׁלֹשָׁה שֶׁאָכְלוּ כְּאֶחָד חַיָּבִין לְזַמֵּן. — *Three people who ate together are obligated [to say] the blessing collectively.*

That is, three people who have eaten bread together are required to designate a leader to recite the *Bircas HaMazon* on their behalf. He formally summons the others to participate collectively by calling to them נְבָרֵךְ שֶׁאָכַלְנוּ מִשֶּׁלּוֹ, "*Let us bless [He] from Whose [food] we have eaten*" (*Rav; Rashi*).

The *Gemara* (45a) establishes that the quorum for a collective blessing is three people from one of the following verses:

a. גַּדְּלוּ לַה' אִתִּי וּנְרוֹמְמָה שְׁמוֹ יַחְדָּו — *Declare (plural) the greatness of Hashem with me, and let us exalt His Name together (Psalms 34:4).*

b. כִּי שֵׁם ה' אֶקְרָא הָבוּ גֹדֶל לֵאלֹהֵינוּ — *When I call out the Name of Hashem, ascribe (plural) greatness to our God (Deuteronomy 32:3).*

In each of these verses, one person is calling out to two others to participate in exalting the Name of Hashem together (*Rashi*). From this, the Sages derived that the minimum number of participants necessary for *zimmun* is three (*Tos. Yom Tov*).

There is a difference of opinion as to whether eating "together" means that the three people must be united from the very start of the meal, as in the mishnah above, 6:6, or whether it is sufficient that they eat together at some point during the meal and finish eating at the same time even if they did not start together; for although they did not constitute a group for the *Hamotzi* blessing, they nevertheless are united as a group for the *Bircas HaMazon* (see *Talmidei Rabbeinu Yonah* folio 32b s.v. שלשה and *Rosh* 7:1.) However, if one joined two others who were already eating but they did not finish eating at the same time, those who finished first may recite the *Bircas HaMazon* individually. *Orach Chaim* 193:2 with *Mishnah Berurah* 19. See also *Shaar HaTziyun* 17.

One who eats forbidden foods is ineligible to join in *zimmun* (see below s.v. אֵין מְזַמְּנִין עֲלֵיהֶם). The mishnah will now enumerate foods that appear to be prohibited for consumption which nevertheless do not disqualify one from *zimmun*.

1. Three people who ate together are obligated [to say] the blessing collectively. [If] one ate [bread] of *demai*, or [of] first tithe whose

YAD AVRAHAM

To clearly comprehend many of the cases about to be listed by this mishnah, a brief outline of the obligatory tithes that one must separate from agricultural produce is in order.

Tithes are separated only during the first six years of the seven-year *shemittah* cycle [produce of *shemittah*, the Sabbatical year, is exempt of all tithes (see *Rosh Hashanah* 15a, Rashi s.v. אבייל א״)]. *Terumah gedolah* (usually about 2 percent) is separated every year of the six and is given to a *Kohen*. This is followed by *maaser rishon*, the first tithe (10 percent of the remainder), which is also separated every year and is given to a Levite. In the first, second, fourth and fifth years, *maaser sheini*, the second tithe (10 percent), is then separated from the remaining produce. This is taken to Jerusalem and eaten by its owner or his guests, or if this should prove impractical, it is redeemed with money and the money is then taken to Jerusalem where food is purchased with it and eaten there. During the third and sixth years, *maaser anni*, the pauper's tithe (10 percent), replaces the second tithe; it is given to the poor (*Rambam Comm.*).

In addition to the above, the Levite must separate 10 percent of the first that he receives and give it to the Kohen as *terumas maaser.*

אָכַל דְּמַאי, — *[If] one ate [bread] of demai,*

"Demai" is a term used for agricultural produce that was acquired from the general, unlearned populace (עַמֵּי הָאָרֶץ), who were not necessarily scrupulous in their separation of the obligatory tithes. It is a contraction of the two words דָּא, *this*, מַאי, *is what*? I.e. is this produce tithed or not? (*Rav*).

The *Gemara* (*Sotah* 48a) relates that Yochanan the High Priest commissioned a national survey regarding observance of the tithing laws. He discovered that although everyone was careful to separate *terumah*, some were lax in separating all the other tithes. He therefore instituted that all produce acquired from an *am haaretz* must be assumed to be untithed and forbidden for consumption until the tithes in question have been separated (see *Demai* 2:2).

The mishnah will soon teach that

an individual who has eaten forbidden food cannot be included in *zimmun*. Thus, one might have concluded that a person who ate *demai* without separating the obligated tithes is disqualified from participating in *zimmun*, for he has transgressed Yochanan's enactment. The mishnah therefore teaches that this is not so, because the majority of the general populace, although unlearned, nevertheless did indeed separate the required tithes. Yochanan's enactment was instituted only to protect against the minority who were lax (*Tosafos to Shabbos* 13a s.v. רבא). Hence, if one ate *demai* without first tithing it, he is not considered to have eaten forbidden food and may participate in the collective blessing (*Rav*).

The *Gemara* (47a) elaborates on this and further explains that although it is indeed Rabbinically forbidden to eat *demai* without first separating the appropriate tithes,

שֶׁנִּטְלָה תְּרוּמָתוֹ, וּמַעֲשֵׂר שֵׁנִי וְהֶקְדֵּשׁ שֶׁנִּפְדּוּ,

---

ר' עובדיה מברטנורא

שנטלה תרומתו. ואף על פי שלא נטלה ממנו תרומה גדולה, כגון בן לוי שהקדים את הכהן ולקח המעשר בשבלים קודם שנטל הכהן תרומה גדולה, והכהן היה לו ליטול תרומה גדולה תחלה אחד מחמשים, דרחמנא קרייה ראשית, נמצא תרומה גדולה של כהן בתוך המעשר הזה אחד מחמשים שבו, לבד מתרומת מעשר שעל הלוי להפריש תרומה ממעשרו. ואשמעינן מתניתין דהכא דפטור הלוי מלהפריש ממנו תרומה גדולה דכתיב (במדבר יח, כו) והרמתם ממנו תרומת ה' מעשר מן המעשר, מעשר מן המעשר אמרתי לך ולא תרומה גדולה ותרומת מעשר מן המעשר: **ומעשר שני והקדש שנפדו.** כגון שנתן את הקרן ולא נתן את החומש, שהבעלים מוסיפים חומש. וקמשמע לן תנא דאין חומש מעכב:

יד אברהם

there are certain exceptions to this rule (since the majority of the general populace did separate the required tithes) particularly that it is permitted to feed the poor with *demai* (*Demai* 3:1 — see *Rashi* to *Shabbos* 127b s.v. מאכילין). Since a person can at any time declare all his belongings ownerless, everyone is potentially a poor person permitted to eat *demai*. Accordingly, eating *demai*, which is potentially permitted, is not treated like eating forbidden foods, which is absolutely prohibited (*Tos. Yom Tov;* see *Rishon LeTziyon*).

וּמַעֲשֵׂר רִאשׁוֹן שֶׁנִּטְלָה תְּרוּמָתוֹ, — *or* [*of*] *first tithe whose terumah has been taken,*

The mishnah cannot be stating that one who ate bread made from first tithe whose *terumas maaser* has been separated may participate in the *zimmun,* for this would be teaching the obvious. If all the required tithes have been separated, it is perfectly permissible food and there is no reason to think that one who partakes from it cannot participate in the *zimmun!* The *Gemara* (47a) therefore explains that the mishnah is referring to a unique case where the *terumas maaser* has been separated from the first tithe but

the general *terumah* — *terumah gedolah* — has not been separated, and need not be separated.

Ordinarily, an owner first separates *terumah* from his produce for the Kohen and *then* separates *maaser rishon* for the Levite.[1] If the owner reversed the order and first separated *maaser rishon* and only then separated *terumah gedolah* for the Kohen, the Levite's *maaser rishon* contains within it the *terumah gedolah* — two percent — that should have been separated from the owner's produce prior to *maaser rishon.* The Levite should therefore be required to separate it and give it to a Kohen (in addition to the *terumas maaser* he must always give).

However, the obligation to separate *terumah* and *maaser* commences only after the grain has been threshed, winnowed, piled into heaps and then smoothed down [a process known as מֵרוּחַ] (see *Maasros* 1:6). Prior to this procedure, there is no obligation to tithe. At this stage, then, if the Levite prevails upon the owner to give him *maaser rishon* before the *terumah* has been separated, the Levite is *not* re-

---

1. The Torah refers to *terumah gedolah* as רֵאשִׁית, *the first* (*Deuteronomy* 18:4), stipulating that the Kohen's *terumah* must be separated before the Levite's *maaser rishon* (*Rav* — see *Terumos* 3:7).

terumah has been taken, or [of] second tithe
or consecrated produce that were redeemed,

YAD AVRAHAM

quired to separate *terumah gedolah* from it. He is only required to separate *terumas maaser*.[1]

Our mishnah is referring to this case. This grain is not *tevel* and is permissible for consumption as long as the *terumas maaser* has been separated from it — even though *terumah gedolah* was never taken from it! Accordingly, the mishnah is teaching that if one ate bread made of this grain, although it may resemble forbidden food, he may be included in the collective blessing (*Rav; Rambam Comm.*).

וּמַעֲשֵׂר שֵׁנִי וְהֶקְדֵּשׁ שֶׁנִּפְדּוּ, — *or [of] second tithe or consecrated produce that were redeemed,*

As explained in the introduction, second tithe may be redeemed with money. Once redeemed, the produce loses its consecrated status and may be eaten anywhere. The sanctity that had been attached to the produce becomes transferred to the coins, and then to the food that is purchased with these coins in Jerusalem. Similarly, if one consecrated food as a contribution to the Temple, it must be redeemed [since it is not fit for sacrifice]. Once it has been redeemed, it loses its consecrated status, and its sanctity is transferred to the money or movable objects (see *Bechoros* 51b; *Rambam Hil. Arachin* 7:1)

by which it was redeemed.

When one redeems *his own* second-tithe produce or produce that he himself had consecrated, he must add an additional "fifth" to the original value of the item (see *Bava Metzia* 4:8 and *Gemara* there for how this "fifth" is calculated).

Clearly, the mishnah cannot be stating that one who ate bread outside of Jerusalem made of *maaser sheni* that had been properly redeemed may be included in the *zimmun*, for this would be obvious. Redeemed produce is perfectly permissible food! The *Gemara* (47b) therefore explains that the mishnah is referring to a case where the owner redeemed these items according to their proper value but failed to add the additional fifth while making the exchange. The mishnah is teaching that failure to include the additional fifth does not prevent the redemption from taking effect. Consequently, although the owner still owes the additional fifth, the produce is nevertheless redeemed and permitted to be eaten. One who has eaten bread of this produce may be included in the collective blessing (*Rav; Rambam Comm.*).

The mishnah now lists individuals who are eligible to participate in *zimmun* despite certain shortcomings.

1. This exemption is derived from the verse וַהֲרֵמֹתֶם מִמֶּנּוּ תְּרוּמַת ה' מַעֲשֵׂר מִן הַמַּעֲשֵׂר, *and you shall separate from it Hashem's terumah, maaser from the maaser* (Numbers 18:26). The verse does not merely state *and you shall separate from it maaser from the maaser;* it obligates the Levite to separate *Hashem's terumah* and then describes the *terumah* as *maaser from the maaser* (*Rashi* to *Beitzah* 13b). This description is understood to be exclusionary, teaching that the Levite is required to give only the *terumah* identified as *maaser from the maaser*, i.e, *terumas maaser*, but he is exempted from repaying the *terumah gedolah* to the Kohen (*Rav* from *Gemara* 47a).

ברכות וְהַשַּׁמָּשׁ שֶׁאָכַל כַּזַּיִת, וְהַכּוּתִי – מְזַמְּנִין עֲלֵיהֶם.
ז/א אֲבָל אָכַל טֶבֶל, וּמַעֲשֵׂר רִאשׁוֹן שֶׁלֹּא נִטְּלָה

────────── ר' עובדיה מברטנורא ──────────

והשמש שאכל כזית. דמהו דתימא כיון שהשמש אין לו קביעות אלא בא והולך אלא אין מזמנין עליו
קא משמע לן. ובכל הני אשמעינן דאף על גב דדמו לאיסור אין כאן ברכה בעטיה: **והכותי.** מן
העובדי כוכבים שהביא מלך אשור מכותא ומשאר ארצות ויושב אותם בערי שומרון, ונתגיירו מאימת
האריות שהיו אוכלים בהם כמפורש בספר מלכים (ב, יז), והיו שומרים תורה שבכתב, וכל מצוה
שהחזיקו בה מדקדקים בה יותר מישראל, לפיכך היו מחמינים בהם בקלת המלות, עד שבדקו אחריהם
ומלאו להם דמות יונה בראש הר גריזים הר גריזים שהיו עובדים אותה, ומאז עשאום כעובדי כוכבים גמורים
לכל דבריהם, הלכך האידנא אין מזמנין ממנו תרומה ומעשרות
קרוי טבל. ופירוש טבל, טב לא. ואין צריך לומר טבל דאורייתא, אלא אפילו טבל דרבנן כגון דגן
שלא צמח בעפין [שאינו נקוב] שאינו טבל אלא אלא מדרבנן, אין מזמנין עליו: **ומעשר ראשון שלא ניטלה**
תרומתו. לאו תרומת מעשר קאמר דהאי טבל גמור הוא, אלא כגון שהקדים לוי את הכהן בכרי
לאחר שנתמרח והוקבע לתרומה מן התורה ונטל מעשר ראשון תחלה, ואחד מחמשים שבו היא ראויה
לתרומה גדולה לכהן, וכל זמן שלא נתן ממנו תרומה גדולה זו אף על פי שהספרים תרומת מעשר אין

────────── יד אברהם ──────────

וְהַשַּׁמָּשׁ שֶׁאָכַל כַּזַּיִת, — or [if] an attendant who ate an olive's volume,

If a man was waiting on two people who were eating together, he may complete the necessary quorum and participate in the *zimmun* provided that he has eaten a *kezayis*, an olive's volume, of bread[1] with them. Although one who eats without remaining seated usually is ineligible to join in *zimmun*, for he is not considered to be eating a proper meal, a waiter is different. Since this is the manner in which a waiter normally eats, he is deemed to be eating a proper meal and is eligible to join in *zimmun* (*Rav* from *Gemara* 47b; *Rosh* 7:1; *Shulchan Aruch* 193:2 and *Mishnah Berurah* 193:22; see also *Shitah Mekubetzes* to 47b s.v. והשמש).

וְהַכּוּתִי — or a Cuthean

The Cutheans were a pagan people who were transplanted by the Assyrian emperor from their native Cutha to Samaria to replace the exiled Ten Tribes. Inspired by an outbreak of lion attacks, they converted en masse to Judaism (see *II Kings* Ch. 17). Their religious observance consisted only of commandments that are written in the Torah but not of those that were taught orally. Nevertheless, those laws that they did observe, they followed meticulously. The legitimacy of their conversion was a matter of dispute throughout the Tannaic period (see *Kiddushin* 75b, *Bava Kamma* 38b). Eventually, it was discovered that they continued to profess pagan beliefs and even maintained an idolatrous house of worship on Mt. Gerizzim. It was then unanimously decided that they

1. This is the opinion of *Rambam* (*Hil. Berachos* 5:8). *Rif* (folio 35b) and *Rashba* (to 48a s.v. ולענין from *Yerushalmi* 7:2) hold that one may join in the collective blessing if he ate an olive's volume of דָּגָן *grain*, in some other form. *Tosafos* (to 48a s.v. תשעה), *Rabbeinu Yonah* (folio 35b s.v. ואפי׳) and *Rosh* (7:21) hold that one may join even if he ate an olive's volume of any kind of food. The custom nowadays is to follow this last opinion (*Mishnah Berurah* 197:22).

or [if] an attendant who ate an olive's volume, or a Cuthean — the collective blessing is recited on their account. But if one ate *tevel*, or first tithe whose *terumah* had not been taken,

should be treated in all respects as non-Jews (*Rav, Rambam Comm.* to *Mishnah* 8:8 based on *Chullin* 6a; see *Tos. Anshei Shem* and *Tos. Chadashim*).

Our mishnah, which states that a Cuthean may be included in *zimmun*, predates this final resolution and reflects the Tannaic opinion of Rabban Shimon ben Gamliel who regarded them as full-fledged Jews (*Meleches Shlomo* from *Yerushalmi*). However, once it was ruled that Cutheans are non-Jews, they, like all gentiles, are not to be included in the collective blessing (*Rav, Rambam Comm.* to 8:8).

מְזַמְּנִין עֲלֵיהֶם. — *the collective blessing is recited on their account.*

[In all of the above cases, a collective blessing is in order since the food in question is in fact permitted for consumption or since the person in question is eligible for inclusion. In the cases which follow, this is not so and a collective blessing is not warranted.]

אֲבָל אָכַל טֶבֶל, — *But if one ate tevel,*

"*Tevel*" is produce from which the *terumah* and tithes have not yet been separated. It is absolutely prohibited for consumption (see *Sanhedrin* 83a). It is a contraction of the two Aramaic words טב, *good*, and לא, *not*, i.e., "not good," for it is not fit for consumption (*Rav, Rambam Comm.*).

If the mishnah were referring to Scriptural *tevel*, it would be teaching the obvious — for if the consumption of *tevel* is prohibited, no *zimmun* is possible — see below s.v. אֵין מְזַמְּנִין. The *Gemara* (47a) therefore explains

that the mishnah is teaching that even one who ate bread made of Rabbinically prohibited *tevel* cannot be included in the collective blessing (*Rav, Rambam Comm.* from Gemara 47a).

Under Biblical law, only produce of the Land of Israel that draws its nourishment from the ground is subject to tithing. This includes both produce grown in the actual ground and produce grown in a perforated flowerpot, for it too draws its nourishment from the ground through its perforation (*Demai* 5:10; see *Rabbeinu Yonah* cited by *Tos. Yom Tov* s.v. טבל). The Rabbis, however, ordained that even produce grown in an unperforated pot is also subject to the laws of tithing. Accordingly, produce that has been grown in an unperforated pot is Rabbinically prohibited as *tevel*. Thus, one who has eaten bread of this produce cannot participate in the collective blessing (*Rav, Rambam Comm.*).

וּמַעֲשֵׂר רִאשׁוֹן שֶׁלֹּא נִטְּלָה תְרוּמָתוֹ, — *or first tithe whose terumah had not been taken,*

The mishnah cannot be referring to first-tithe food whose requisite *terumas maaser* had not been separated, for it would then be teaching the obvious — since this is actual *tevel*, it is prohibited food and does not warrant a collective blessing! The *Gemara* (47b) therefore explains that the mishnah is referring to a unique case where the *maaser rishon* was uncharacteristically subject to both the standard *terumas maaser* that the Levite must always

תְּרוּמָתוֹ, וּמַעֲשֵׂר שֵׁנִי וְהֶקְדֵּשׁ שֶׁלֹּא נִפְדּוּ,
וְהַשַּׁמָּשׁ שֶׁאָכַל פָּחוֹת מִכַּזַּיִת, וְהַנָּכְרִי —

───────── ר' עובדיה מברטנורא ─────────

מזמנין עליו, ואם היה מקדימו בשבלים קודם שתתמרח שלא היה צריך להפריש תרומה גדולה כדכתבינן
לעיל: **ומעשר שני והקדש שלא נפדו.** אין צריך לומר שלא נפדו דהא כלל מילתא דפשיטא
היא, אלא שנפדו ולא נפדו כהלכתן, כגון שפדה מעשר שני בגרוטואות של כסף או במטבע שאין
עליו צורה, ורחמנא אמר (דברים יד, כה) וצרת הכסף בדבר שיש בו צורה. והקדש שחללו על גבי
קרקע ולא פדאו בכסף, ורחמנא אמר ונתן את הכסף: **והשמש שאכל פחות מכזית.** משנה
שאינה צריכה היא, אלא חיידי דהדר לרובא לטורך הדר נמי להא: **ועובד כוכבים.** בגר שמל ולא
טבל מיירי. ואשמעינן דכל כמה דלא טבל עובד כוכבים הוא, ולעולם אינו גר עד שימול ויטבול:

───────── יד אברהם ─────────

separate for the Kohen from the *maaser rishon* he receives, as well as the general *terumah* — *terumah gedolah*.

As explained previously in this mishnah (s.v. וּמַעֲשֵׂר רִאשׁוֹן שֶׁנִּטְּלָה תְּרוּמָתוֹ), the obligation to separate *terumah* and *maaser* commences only after the grain has been piled into heaps and then smoothed down — the process known as מֵרוּחַ. After this process, the owner ordinarily separates *terumah gedolah* for the Kohen and then separates *maaser rishon* for the Levite. However, the mishnah is dealing with a case where the Levite preempted the Kohen and took *maaser rishon* after the מֵרוּחַ process but before the *terumah gedolah* has been separated. The Levite is therefore obligated to separate both the standard *terumas maaser* and the general *terumah* which belong to the Kohen.

The mishnah is teaching that unlike the previous case (first tithe whose *terumah* had been taken), where the Levite took his *maaser rishon* prior to the מֵרוּחַ process and is only obligated to separate *terumas maaser*, this case is dealing with a situation where the מֵרוּחַ process had already taken place, thus already subjecting the produce to the separation of the general *terumah*. Until both portions of *terumah* are separated, one is prohibited from eating this *maaser rishon*. Therefore, one who ate bread of this *maaser rishon* cannot be included in the quorum for the *zimmun* (*Rav; Rambam Comm;* see *Tos. Yom Tov*).[1]

In the present case, since both the *terumah gedolah* and the *terumas maaser* must be separated from the first tithe, the Mishnah refers to both as *terumah* of the first tithe — thus, the expression "first tithe whose *terumah* was not separated" refers to the general *terumah* as well. In the earlier case (s.v. וּמַעֲשֵׂר רִאשׁוֹן) since only the *terumas maaser* had to be separated, only *terumas maaser* was referred to as תְּרוּמָתוֹ, *whose terumah* (*Tos. Yom Tov* from *Talmidei Rabbeinu Yonah* folio 32b s.v. וּמעשר ראשון).

וּמַעֲשֵׂר שֵׁנִי וְהֶקְדֵּשׁ שֶׁלֹּא נִפְדּוּ, — *or [of] second tithe or consecrated produce that was not redeemed,*

The mishnah cannot be referring to second tithe (*maaser sheini*) or

───────────

1. This is derived from the verse מִכֹּל מַתְּנֹתֵיכֶם תָּרִימוּ אֵת כָּל תְּרוּמַת ה׳, *from all your gift portions you shall separate all of Hashem's terumah* (Numbers 18:29). The word "all" includes both *terumas maaser* and *terumah gedolah*. Thus, Scripture teaches that the Levi must at times separate *terumah gedolah* as well as *terumas maaser*.

or [of] second tithe or consecrated produce
that was not redeemed, or [if] an attendant ate
less than an olive's volume, or a gentile —

YAD AVRAHAM

consecrated produce that have not been redeemed *at all,* for it would then be teaching the obvious. Unredeemed second tithe (outside Jerusalem) or consecrated foods are unquestionably prohibited for consumption and therefore do not warrant a collective blessing! The *Gemara* (47b) explains that the mishnah is referring to a case where the second tithe and consecrated produce have indeed been redeemed, albeit improperly.

Maaser-sheini produce may be redeemed only with minted coins, i.e. coins that have an image stamped on them. This is derived from the verse וְצַרְתָּ הַכֶּסֶף בְּיָדְךָ, *and you shall bind the money in your hand* (*Deuteronomy* 14:25). The use of the verb וְצַרְתָּ, *you shall bind,* rather than וְנָתַתָּ, *you shall put,* leads the *Gemara* (47b) to associate this term with the word צוּרָה, *image* (*Meleches Shlomo*). Hence, an unminted metal slug cannot be used for redemption. When the Mishnah speaks of unredeemed second tithe, it is referring to a case of second-tithe grain that was improperly redeemed with an unminted metal slug.

The *Gemara* (47b) also derives from Scripture (*Leviticus* 27:19[1]) that consecrated produce may be redeemed only onto coins or movable property [מְטַלְטְלִין] but not onto real property [קַרְקַע]. When the mishnah speaks of unredeemed consecrated food, it is re-

ferring to a case where consecrated grain was improperly redeemed with real property and then made into bread.

The mishnah thus teaches that in both these instances, the redemption procedure is completely ineffective, and the prohibitions on consuming these products remain in force. Consequently, their consumption is not eligible for a collective blessing (*Rav, Rambam Comm.* based on *Gem.* 47b).

וְהַשַּׁמָּשׁ שֶׁאָכַל פָּחוֹת מִכַּזַּיִת, — *or [if] an attendant ate less than an olive's volume,*

It is obvious that a waiter who ate less than a *kezayis,* an olive's volume, cannot participate in the collective blessing since this reservation applies to anyone, even to those sitting and eating together! Why then, did the mishnah teach the specific case of the attendant? (*Tif. Yis.*) The *Gemara* (47b) explains that this statement is in fact obvious (see *Tos. Anshei Shem* s.v. והשמש) and is included only for reasons of stylistic symmetry, i.e., so that every case mentioned in the first clause of this mishnah will have its counterpart in the later clause (*Rav*).

וְהַנָּכְרִי — *or a gentile*

The mishnah cannot be teaching that a non-Jew cannot participate in the collective blessing because that would be teaching the obvious, since

---

1. The *Gemara* (47b) cites the verse ונתן הכסף וקם לו, *and he shall give the money, and it will pass to him,* as the source for this rule. Actually, there is no such verse in the Torah. The *Gemara* is merely paraphrasing *Leviticus* 27:19: וְיָסַף חֲמִישִׁית כֶּסֶף עֶרְכְּךָ עָלָיו וְקָם לוֹ, *and he shall add a fifth of the money- assessment to it, and it shall pass to him* — see *Tosafos* to *Shabbos* 128a s.v. ונתן.

[ב] נָשִׁים, וַעֲבָדִים, וּקְטַנִּים – אֵין מְזַמְּנִין

ר' עובדיה מברטנורא

(ב) וקטנים אין מזמנין עליהם. דוקא קטנים שאין יודעים למי מברכין, אבל קטן היודע למי מברכין מזמנין עליו. ואיכא מרבוותא דאמרי דלא אמרו קטן היודע למי מברכין מזמנין עליו אלא בבן שלש שלש עשרה שנה ויום אחד שלא הביא שתי שערות והוא הנקרא קטן פורח, אבל בצעיר מהכי אין מזמנין עליו, ואפילו יודע למי מברכין. ובירושלמי מייתי הלכה למעשה, דאין מזמנין על הקטן כלל עד שיגדל ויביא שתי שערות. ונשים מזמנות לעצמן ועבדים מזמנין לעצמן, אבל נשים עם עבדים לא משום פריצותא: **עד כזית.** וכן הלכה, ולא כרבי יהודה דאמר עד כביצה:

יד אברהם

the *mitzvah* of *zimmun* does not apply to him. The *Gemara* (47b) therefore explains that the mishnah is referring to a non-Jew who is in the process of converting to Judaism.

The conversion process requires the convert to undergo circumcision (in the case of a man), and immersion in a *mikveh*. In the mishnah's case, the convert had undergone circumcision, but had not yet immersed in a *mikveh*. The mishnah is teaching that although his conversion process has started, he is nevertheless a non-Jew until he has immersed in a *mikveh* and completed the conversion process (*Rav, Rambam Comm.* from *Gem.* 47b).

אֵין מְזַמְּנִין עֲלֵיהֶם. — *the collective blessing is not recited on their account.*

In all of the above cases — eating

prohibited food, even if only forbidden Rabbinically, eating less than a *kezayis*, or a non-Jew who ate — the person listed is ineligible to participate in the collective blessing and thus, cannot be included in the quorum of three.[1]

The mishnah has ruled that someone who ate prohibited food cannot participate in *zimmun*. Some authorities maintain that he is even ineligible to recite his own personal *Bircas HaMazon*, for one does not recite any blessing when eating prohibited food, not the blessings prior to its consumption nor those recited afterwards (*Rambam, Hil. Berachos* 1:19[2]; *Rashba* to 45a s.v. אבל טבל; *Shulchan Aruch, Orach Chaim* 196:1; see below mishnah 8:6 s.v. אין מְבָרְכִין). Their reasoning is that the blessings for food are an expression of thanksgiving to God, acknowledging that He has given us this food to sustain us. However, when one recites a blessing over food that

---

1. This ruling applies only if one ate a meal that included prohibited bread among other permissible dishes. However, if the bread was permissible, and only the side dishes were forbidden, he would be eligible to participate in the collective blessing; for it is the bread that necessitates the obligation to say *Bircas HaMazon* and not the other foods (*Meiri* 47a s.v. ויראה לי).

2. Some Rishonim point out that the Mishnah's mention of "an attendant who ate less than a *kezayis*" may support *Rambam's* position. It is unanimously agreed that *Bircas HaMazon* (and all other after-blessings) is not recited for eating less than a *kezayis* (*Rif* folio 27b; *Rambam, Hil. Berachos* 1:2 and 3:12). Thus, it is clear that the attendant who ate less than a *kezayis* is not merely excluded from the collective blessing; he does not recite *Bircas HaMazon* at all. Likewise, in the mishnah, where prohibited food was consumed, the exclusion is not only from *zimmun*, but from the basic *Bircas HaMazon* as well (see *Re'ah* 45a s.v. שלשה; see also *Shitah* to 45a s.v. ומעשר).

the collective blessing is not recited on their account.

2. [I]n the case of] women, slaves, and minors —
the collective blessing is not recited on

YAD AVRAHAM

God has prohibited us to eat, the blessing has been brought through a transgression and is considered blasphemous (see *Rashi* 45a, s.v. והשמש; *Beis Yosef, Orach Chaim* 196 s.v. כתב הרמב״ם). Others explain that the mishnah only excludes him from participating in the collective blessing but not from reciting *Bircas HaMazon* (*Hasagos HaRavad* to *Hil. Berachos* 1:19; *Rosh* 7:2); for although he did eat prohibited food and transgressed the law, he nevertheless derived pleasure from the food, obligating him to recite the *Bircas HaMazon*. The collective blessing, however, is recited only when three people eat a proper meal together. Prohibited food cannot be considered a proper meal. It is merely as if a group of three ate fruit or a snack together (*Hasagos HaRavad* to *Hil. Berachos* 1:19). Accordingly, even if three people deliberately sat down together to share a meal of prohibited food, the meal is not considered a proper meal but has the status of a snack for which there is no *zimmun*. They do, however, each recite the *Bircas HaMazon* individually (*Meiri* to 47a s.v. המשנה השנית in explanation of *Ravad*).

Ravad's wording implies that one who eats prohibited food must recite the blessings both before and after he eats. *Taz* (*Orach Chaim* 196:1), however, suggests that *Ravad* obligates a blessing only where the forbidden food was eaten inadvertently, for then his blessing cannot be considered blasphemous (*Mishnah Berurah* 196:4). If the forbidden food was eaten deliberately, even *Ravad* would agree that the blessing is not recited. Accordingly, *Ravad's* rule of reciting a blessing for the consumption of forbidden food can only be referring to the *Bircas HaMazon* blessing and cannot be referring to the blessing recited before eating. This ruling is adopted by *Mishnah Berurah* (ibid.).

If one must eat forbidden food due to illness or the danger of starvation, he must recite a blessing both before and after he eats (*Orach Chaim* 204:9). The food is no longer considered forbidden but is reclassified as permitted food due to the dangerous circumstances. Furthermore, by eating the ''forbidden'' food, he fulfills the *mitzvah* of saving his life [וָחַי בָּהֶם] (*Mishnah Berurah* 197:5).

2.

The following mishnah continues discussing who may be counted towards the quorum for a collective blessing, as well as the quantity of food one must eat to participate.

נָשִׁים, וַעֲבָדִים, וּקְטַנִּים — אֵין מְזַמְּנִין עֲלֵיהֶם.
— [*In the case of*] *women, slaves, and minors, the collective blessing is not recited on their account.*

Although the mishnah groups women, slaves, and minors together and disqualifies them from participating in the collective blessing, these groups are subject to different levels of disqualification based on the separate reasons for their disqualification.

The quorum of three necessary for conducting *zimmun* may not consist of a group of men and women together. However, three women who have eaten together are qualified to conduct their own collective blessing (*Rav* from *Gemara* 45b; *Arachin* 3a). According to some, they are obligated to do so (*Rabbeinu Yonah* — folio 33a s.v. ונראה; *Rosh* 7:4); according to others, it is merely optional for them to do so (*Tosafos* 45b s.v. שאני). Similarly, three Canaanite slaves are qualified to form their own *zimmun;* they are disqualified only from being counted as part of a *zimmun* with free men.

The *Gemara* does not explain the reason that a mixed group of men and women is disqualified. Some commentators explain it is because the association of men and women together in one group is inappropriate (*Rashi* cited by *R' Yonah*, ibid.) for it may lead to promiscuous behavior (*Ran, Megillah* folio p. 6b of *Rif*, Vilna edition). Others maintain that the obligation of conducting *zimmun* was never imposed on women (*Tosafos* 45b s.v. שאני) because they were generally unfamiliar with its text (*Mishnah Berurah* 199:16). Although they may elect to conduct *zimmun* by themselves, they may not complete the quorum of three together with men because their association is undignified and inappropriate (ibid. 199:17). However, a woman who ate together with three men is obligated to participate in the *zimmun* with them (*Tiferes Yisrael* from *Orach Chaim* 199:7). This is neither inappropriate nor undignified since the quorum has been satisfied without relying on the woman (*Mishnah Berurah* 199:17).

Similarly, Canaanite slaves cannot join with one or two men to form the required quorum of three because slaves are generally promiscuous and are suspect of homosexuality (*Rabbeinu Yonah* cited by *Tos. Yom Tov* s.v. ועבדים). Consequently, their association with nonslave men in a single group is considered undignified and inappropriate (*Mishnah Berurah* 199:12).[1]

Although a group of three slaves who have eaten together may elect to conduct their own *zimmun*, they may not include women in their group due to their promiscuous behavior and low moral standards (*Rav*).

Minors may not join with one or two men to form the required quorum necessary for *zimmun*, only if they are very young, and do not yet understand that the blessing is directed to God. However, an older child who knows that the *Bircas HaMazon* is directed to God may be included (*Rav*, from *Rambam Comm.* and *Hil. Berachos* 5:7, from *Gem.* 48a; see also *Rif*, folio 35b). Others maintain that any minor is disqualified [because he is not yet obligated to perform *mitzvos*]. Only an adult male of at least thirteen years old may be included. Ordinarily, one is considered an adult only if he has reached the age of thirteen, and in addition, has sprouted two pubic hairs. However, to be included in the collective blessing, it is sufficient that he be thirteen years old, even if he has not yet sprouted two pubic hairs, provided that he understands that the blessing is directed to God (*Rav*, from *Tosafos* to 47b s.v. קטן, *Rashba* to 48a s.v. ולית, cf. *Maadanei Yom Tov* [to *Rosh* 7:20] #90, and see also *Talmidei Rabbeinu Yonah*, folio 35a s.v. קטן).

Nevertheless, *Yerushalmi* writes that in actual practice only a thirteen-year-old who has sprouted two pubic hairs can be included in the *zimmun* quorum, thereby disqualifying *any* minor (*Rav*, from *Rosh* 7:20, *Maharik*

1. Actually, the *Gemara* does not disqualify a quorum formed by free *men* and slaves due to promiscuous behavior. It only disqualifies a group of *women* and slaves for this reason (see *Tos. Chadashim*). *Rabbeinu Yonah*, however, disqualifies the group due to promiscuous behavior (see *Shaar HaTziyun* 199:3).

7
2

their account. How much [food must one eat in order] to participate in the collective blessing? At least an olive's volume. R' Yehudah says: [At least] an egg's volume.

YAD AVRAHAM

#49). This is the position adopted by *Rama* to *Orach Chaim* 199:10.

עַד כַּמָּה מְזַמְּנִין? עַד כַּזַּיִת. — *How much [food must one eat in order] to participate in the collective blessing? At least an olive's volume.*

Most commentators understand the *Tanna* to be teaching that *eligibility* for *zimmun* depends on the consumption of a *kezayis*, an olive's volume,[1] by each of the three members of the group. [They differ, however, as to whether all three members of the group must eat a *kezayis* of bread (*Rambam, Hil. Berachos* 5:8), or whether only two are required to eat bread but the third participant may eat a *kezayis* of any food that requires the blessing of *borei minei mezonos* (*Rif* folio 35b, *Rashba* to 48a s.v. ולעניין from *Yerushalmi* 7:2), or even a *kezayis* of vegetables (*Tosafos* to 48a s.v. תשעה; *Talmidei Rabbeinu Yonah* folio 35b s.v. ואפי'; *Rosh* 7:21).] Others maintain that the *Tanna* is teaching that although one who sits and eats together with a group *may* join in a *zimmun* upon eating less than a *kezayis* (unlike the waiter in the previous mishnah), nevertheless, eating a *kezayis* of bread *obligates* one to join in a *zimmun* and this amount makes one eligible to lead the *zimmun* and recite the *Bircas HaMazon* on behalf of the others (*Rashi* as explained by *Pnei Yehoshua* and *Rashash*).

רַבִּי יְהוּדָה אוֹמֵר: עַד כַּבֵּיצָה. — *R' Yehudah says: At least an egg's volume.*

Although the dispute between the *Tanna Kamma* (R' Meir — see *Gemara* 49b) and R' Yehudah seems to be simply regarding the obligation of reciting *zimmun*, it actually centers around the basic obligation of reciting *Bircas HaMazon* itself. The *Tanna Kamma* holds that one is obligated to recite *Bircas HaMazon* after eating just a *kezayis* of bread, whereas R' Yehudah holds that this obligation is incurred only after one consumes an egg's volume. Their dispute regarding *zimmun* is merely an extension of their dispute regarding *Bircas HaMazon*. The *Gemara* (49b) cites the verse (*Deuteronomy* 8:10): וְאָכַלְתָּ וְשָׂבָעְתָּ וּבֵרַכְתָּ אֶת ה' אֱלֹהֶיךָ, *And you shall eat and be satisfied and bless Hashem, Your G-d,* as R' Yehudah's source, since an egg's volume is the minimum quantity that satiates. The *Tanna Kamma*, however, maintains that the words *and you shall be satisfied* refer to eating accompanied by drinking. Accordingly, the words *and you shall eat* mentioned in the verse is referring to the minimum quantity that can be described as eating, namely, eating an olive's volume. Although the *Gemara* (48b) cites this verse to teach the basic obligation of reciting *Bircas HaMazon* after a meal of bread, the same holds true regarding *zimmun*; for the same minimum amount that obligates one to recite *Bircas HaMazon* obligates a group of three to participate in *zimmun* (*Tos. Yom Tov* from *Tosafos* 49b s.v. עד).

---

1. Although this was taught in the previous mishnah (see comm. there s.v. וְהַשַּׁמָּשׁ), it is reiterated here to introduce the dissenting opinion of R' Yehudah, which follows (*Piskei HaRid* to 49b s.v. מתני' עד כמה).

[ג] **כֵּיצַד** מְזַמְּנִין? בִּשְׁלֹשָׁה, אוֹמֵר:
„נְבָרֵךְ"; בִּשְׁלֹשָׁה וְהוּא,
אוֹמֵר: „בָּרְכוּ". בַּעֲשָׂרָה, אוֹמֵר: „נְבָרֵךְ
לֵאלֹהֵינוּ"; בַּעֲשָׂרָה וְהוּא, אוֹמֵר: „בָּרְכוּ".

───── ר' עובדיה מברטנורא ─────

(ג) בשלשה והוא אומר ברכו. דהא בלאו דידיה איכא זימון, וכן כולם:

יד אברהם

The halachah follows R' Meir, that the minimum quantity for both *Bircas HaMazon* and *zimmun* is an olive's volume (see *Orach Chaim* 184:6 and 196:4).

Since the dispute in our mishnah is based on Biblical exegesis, it would seem that one is *Biblically* required to recite the *Bircas HaMazon* when eating an olive's volume according to R' Meir or an egg's volume according to R' Yehudah. Indeed, many *Rishonim* (*Hasagos HaRavad, Hil. Berachos* 5:15; *Rambam, Milchamos Hashem,* folio 12a s.v. ונשים בברכת המזון; *Rashba* to 20b s.v. אלא) rule that one who has eaten a *kezayis* of bread is *Biblically* obligated to recite *Bircas HaMazon.* Most *Rishonim*

(*Rashi* to 20b s.v. שיעורא, 48a s.v. עד; *Tosafos* to 48a s.v. עד, 49b s.v ורבי מאיר; *Rosh* 7:24; *Baal HaMaor* folio 12a s.v. ונשים; *Rambam Hil. Berurah* 7:1, 5:16), however, dispute this and maintain that under Biblical law one is obligated to recite *Bircas HaMazon* only if he has eaten a portion that truly satisfies him [שֶׁאָכַל וְשָׂבַע מַמָּשׁ], an amount that varies from person to person (*Sefer HaChinuch, Mitzvah* 430 — see also *Shaar HaTziyun* 144:25). The *Bircas HaMazon* requirement when eating an olive's volume or egg's volume is merely a Rabbinic enactment (see *Gemara* 20b). The verses cited as sources for the rulings of R' Meir and R' Yehudah are merely *asmachtos,* Scriptural support for the Rabbinical law (*Tosafos* 49b s.v. ורבי מאיר, *Rosh* 7:24).

3.

The following mishnah describes the formulas used to summon a group for the collective blessing. These formulas consist of a convocation, recited by the leader, and a response returned by the participants.[1]

The leader begins the formal convocation and calls out:[2] נְבָרֵךְ שֶׁאָכַלְנוּ מִשֶּׁלוֹ, "Let us bless He of Whose [bounty] we have eaten." This is the basic *zimmun* formula (see *Gemara* 50a; *Rambam, Hil. Berachos* 5:2), but it is modified according to the number of participants. The others then respond: בָּרוּךְ שֶׁאָכַלְנוּ מִשֶּׁלוֹ

1. Nowadays, a customary introductory exchange has been added to the original formula. The leader begins by announcing רַבּוֹתַי נְבָרֵךְ, "*Gentlemen, let us bless,*" to which the others respond: יְהִי שֵׁם ה' מְבֹרָךְ מֵעַתָּה וְעַד עוֹלָם, "Blessed be the Name of Hashem, from this time and forever" (*Psalms* 113:2). The leader then repeats this verse. This introductory exchange has been added to the *zimmun* because it is proper for one who performs a sanctification service to express that he is preparing for it (*Zohar* to *Devarim,* cited by *Magen Avraham* in his preface to *Orach Chaim* 192; *Mishnah Berurah* 192:2).

2. In the currently used formula, this summons is preceded by the words בִּרְשׁוּת מָרָנָן וְרַבָּנָן וְרַבּוֹתַי, "*with the permission of the distinguished people present.*" This is done as a matter of etiquette, requesting permission of the members of the group to initiate the collective blessing (*Orchos Chaim, Hil. Bircas HaMazon* #16).

3. How do we perform *zimmun*? When there are three, he says: "Let us bless." When there are three besides him, he says: "Bless." When there are ten, he says: "Let us bless our God." When there are ten besides him, he says: "Bless."

YAD AVRAHAM

וּבְטוּבוֹ חָיִינוּ, "Blessed is He of Whose [bounty] we have eaten and through Whose goodness we live."[1] The leader then repeats this response and proceeds to recite the *Bircas HaMazon* aloud.

כֵּיצַד מְזַמְּנִין? בִּשְׁלשָׁה אוֹמֵר: ,,נְבָרֵךְ''; — *How do we perform zimmun? When there are three, he says: "Let us bless."*

In a group that consists of exactly three people, the leader must include himself in the summons to bless by saying: "Let *us* bless." He cannot simply call on the *others* to bless by saying: . . . בָּרְכוּ, *"Bless"* [as in the next case], for to do so might suggest that the two who were addressed by the leader are considered a valid quorum, when in fact the minimum group for *zimmun* is three. He must therefore use a formula that clearly requests of the others that they *join him* in creating the quorum of three necessary for *zimmun*. Thus, he declares: . . . נְבָרֵךְ, "Let *us* bless Him of Whose [bounty] we have eaten."

בִּשְׁלשָׁה וָהוּא, אוֹמֵר: ,,בָּרְכוּ''. — *When there are three besides him, he says: "Bless."*

If the group is comprised of more than the three people necessary for the quorum, the leader can instruct those assembled to bless Hashem's Name rather than request that they *join him* in reciting the blessing. He therefore says: "Bless Him of Whose [bounty] we have eaten," since there is a valid quorum without him (*Rav, Rashi*).

The *Gemara* (49b-50a) explains that the mishnah does not mean to disqualify the formula, "Let us bless. . .," for a group of more than three. Rather, it is teaching that since there is a quorum without the leader, he is not bound to the previously mentioned formula but may instead choose to say, "Bless . . . "

Although a group of more than three may choose either of the two *zimmun* formulas, it is unclear whether they are both of equal preference. Most commentators agree that "Let us bless . . . " is the preferred formula (*Rashi*, 50a s.v. אף; *Rambam* comm; *Tosafos* 50a s.v. אלא according to *Bach, Orach Chaim* 192 s.v. ואם; *Rav* s.v. במאה, *Ravad* cited by *Shitah* 50a. According to *Maharsha*, however, *Tosafos* hold that both "Let us bless . . ." and "Bless . . ." are of equal preference). For as Shmuel said: "One should never exclude himself from the group" (*Gemara* 49b). This is in fact the common practice (*Magen Avraham* 192:2).

בַּעֲשָׂרָה, אוֹמֵר: ,,נְבָרֵךְ לֵאלֹהֵינוּ''; בַּעֲשָׂרָה וָהוּא, אוֹמֵר: ,,בָּרְכוּ''. — *When there are ten, he says: "Let us bless our God." When there are ten besides him he says "Bless."*

Sacred declarations are recited only in the presence of a *minyan*, a quorum of ten males (*Megilah* 23b). The public recitation of God's Name by the leader

1. The mishnah does not give the full text of the leader's convocation, and we have concluded it according to the currently used formula. According to the mishnah (see below s.v. כְּעִנְיָן), the formula concludes with the words "for the food we have eaten." The conclusion used today is based on a text referred to in the *Gemara* 50a.

אֶחָד עֲשָׂרָה וְאֶחָד עֲשָׂרָה רִבּוֹא.
בְּמֵאָה, אוֹמֵר: „נְבָרֵךְ לַיָי אֱלֹהֵינוּ; בְּמֵאָה
וָהוּא, אוֹמֵר: „בָּרְכוּ". בְּאֶלֶף, אוֹמֵר: „נְבָרֵךְ לַיָי
אֱלֹהֵינוּ אֱלֹהֵי יִשְׂרָאֵל"; בְּאֶלֶף וָהוּא, אוֹמֵר:
„בָּרְכוּ". בְּרִבּוֹא, אוֹמֵר: „נְבָרֵךְ לַיָי אֱלֹהֵינוּ
אֱלֹהֵי יִשְׂרָאֵל אֱלֹהֵי הַצְבָאוֹת יוֹשֵׁב הַכְּרוּבִים עַל
הַמָּזוֹן שֶׁאָכַלְנוּ"; בְּרִבּוֹא וָהוּא, אוֹמֵר: „בָּרְכוּ".

─────── ר' עובדיה מברטנורא ───────

אחד עשרה ואחד עשר רבוא. הך רישא רבי עקיבא היא, דאמר מה מלינו נצבית
הכנסת משהגיעו לעשרה אין חילוק בין רבים למועטים, הכא נמי אין חילוק: **במאה אומר נברך**
לה' אלהינו. הך סיפא כולה רבי יוסי הגלילי היא, דאמר לפי רוב הקהל הן מברכין, שנאמר
במקהלות ברכו אלהים. ופסק הלכה, משלשה ועד עשרה, ואין עשרה בכלל, המברך אומר
נברך שאכלנו משלו וכולן עונים ברוך שאכלנו משלו ובטובו חיינו. ועשרה או מעשרה ולמעלה,
המברך אומר נברך לאלהינו שאכלנו משלו, וכולן עונים ברוך אלהינו שאכלנו משלו ובטובו חיינו:

יד אברהם

of the *zimmun* falls into this category (ibid.). Thus, for a group of exactly ten, the leader uses the formula "Let us bless our God of Whose [bounty] we have eaten." For a group of more than ten, the leader can use either the same formula, or "Bless our God of Whose [bounty] we have eaten" (see above s.v. בשלשה והוא).

Although three women who have eaten together may conduct their own *zimmun* (see mishnah 2 s.v. נָשִׁים), a group of ten women cannot invoke God's name in their collective blessing, since they cannot be counted in the quorum necessary for a *minyan* (*Rambam, Hil. Berachos* 5:7; *Meiri* to 47b s.v. המשנה השלישית).

The standard text of the mishnah has נְבָרֵךְ לֵאלֹהֵינוּ with the preposition ל, "to" (i.e. "Let us recite blessings to our God"). *Tosafos* (to 49b s.v. נברך) writes that the ל should be deleted since we do not find that Scripture uses the verb בָּרֵךְ, followed by the preposition ל (see *Tos. Yom Tov* and *Tos. Anshei Shem*). Others, however, point out that in *Nechemiah* 11:2 and *I Chronicles* 29:20 there is Biblical precedent for the

verb בָּרֵךְ followed by the preposition ל (*Rashash;* see *Hagahos R' Elazar Moshe Horowitz* to 49b s.v. תוד"ה מברך). Nonetheless, *Shulchan Aruch* (*Orach Chaim* 192:1) rules that the ל should be deleted (see *Mishnah Berurah, Shaar HaTziyun* 192:6). And the leader should say: . . . . נְבָרֵךְ אֱלֹהֵינוּ, "*Let us bless our God . . .*"

אֶחָד עֲשָׂרָה וְאֶחָד עֲשָׂרָה רִבּוֹא. — *[It is all] one [formula] whether there are ten or ten myriads.*

The form of collective blessing used for ten people is used for any larger number of people as well — even for ten myriads (a myriad is ten thousand).

בְּמֵאָה, אוֹמֵר: „נְבָרֵךְ לַה' אֱלֹהֵינוּ"; בְּמֵאָה וָהוּא, אוֹמֵר: „בָּרְכוּ". — *When there are a hundred, he says: "Let us bless Hashem, our God." When there are a hundred besides him, he says: "Bless."*

The Gemara (50a) explains that the previous anonymous ruling represents the view of R' Akiva, who holds that the *zimmun* formula is identical for any group of more than ten. The rest of this mishnah gives the view of R'

7
3

[It is all] one [formula] whether there are ten or ten myriads.

When there are a hundred, he says: "Let us bless Hashem, our God." When there are a hundred besides him, he says: "Bless." When there are a thousand he says: "Let us bless Hashem our God, the God of Israel." When there are a thousand besides him, he says: "Bless." When there are ten thousand, he says: "Let us bless Hashem our God, the God of Israel, the Lord of Hosts, Who dwells by the Cherubim, for the food that we have eaten." When there are ten thousand besides himself, he says: "Bless."

Yose HaGlili, who maintains that the *zimmun* formula changes according to the number of people participating, as the mishnah will state below (*Rav, Rambam Comm.* based on *Gem.* 50a; cf. *Shenos Eliyahu* and see *Rashash*).

R' Yose HaGlili holds that for a group of a hundred up to a thousand people, the collective blessing is expanded to read *"Hashem, our God."* Following the pattern established earlier, if the group consists of exactly one hundred people, the leader opens with the words "Let us bless." If the group is larger than one hundred people, he may summon them with "Bless."

בְּאֶלֶף, אוֹמֵר: ,,נְבָרֵךְ לַה' אֱלֹהֵינוּ אֱלֹהֵי יִשְׂרָאֵל". בְּאֶלֶף וָהוּא, אוֹמֵר: ,,בָּרְכוּ". — *When there are a thousand, he says: "Let us bless Hashem, our God, the God of Israel." When there are a thousand besides him, he says: "Bless."*

For a group of a thousand or more, R' Yose HaGlili holds that the collective blessing is expanded to read *"Hashem, our God, the God of Israel."*

בְּרִבּוֹא, אוֹמֵר: ,,נְבָרֵךְ לַה' אֱלֹהֵינוּ אֱלֹהֵי יִשְׂרָאֵל אֱלֹהֵי הַצְּבָאוֹת יוֹשֵׁב הַכְּרוּבִים עַל הַמָּזוֹן שֶׁאָכַלְנוּ". בְּרִבּוֹא וָהוּא, אוֹמֵר: ,,בָּרְכוּ". — *When there are ten thousand, he says: "Let us bless Hashem, our God, the God of Israel, the Lord of Hosts, Who dwells by the Cherubim for the food we have eaten." When there are ten thousand besides him, he says "Bless."*

According to R' Yose HaGlili, if the group consists of ten thousand people or more, the expression "the Lord of Hosts, Who dwells by the Cherubim," is added.

In some versions of the mishnah, the addition to the formula for a group of ten thousand is only "the Lord of Hosts" without "Who dwells by the Cherubim." Some suggest that the expression "Who dwells by the Cherubim" is added only for a group of ten myriads, i.e. one hundred thousand people (*Tos. R' Akiva* from *Teshuvos HaRama Mifano* #7).

[The formula used by the mishnah has the leader conclude with the words עַל הַמָּזוֹן שֶׁאָכַלְנוּ, *"for the food we have eaten."* The formula in use today concludes: שֶׁאָכַלְנוּ מִשֶּׁלּוֹ, *"He of Whose [bounty] we have eaten"* (see *Meleches Shlomo*).]

כְּעִנְיָן שֶׁהוּא מְבָרֵךְ, כָּךְ עוֹנִין אַחֲרָיו: ״בָּרוּךְ יְיָ אֱלֹהֵינוּ אֱלֹהֵי יִשְׂרָאֵל אֱלֹהֵי הַצְּבָאוֹת יוֹשֵׁב הַכְּרוּבִים עַל הַמָּזוֹן שֶׁאָכַלְנוּ״. רַבִּי יוֹסֵי הַגְּלִילִי אוֹמֵר: לְפִי רֹב הַקָּהָל הֵן מְבָרְכִין, שֶׁנֶּאֱמַר [תהלים סח, כז]: ״בְּמַקְהֵלוֹת בָּרְכוּ אֱלֹהִים, יְיָ מִמְּקוֹר יִשְׂרָאֵל.״ אָמַר רַבִּי עֲקִיבָא: מַה מָּצִינוּ בְּבֵית הַכְּנֶסֶת, אֶחָד מְרֻבִּין וְאֶחָד מוּעָטִין אוֹמֵר: ״בָּרְכוּ אֶת יְיָ״.

יד אברהם

כְּעִנְיָן שֶׁהוּא מְבָרֵךְ, כָּךְ עוֹנִין אַחֲרָיו: ״בָּרוּךְ ה׳ אֱלֹהֵינוּ אֱלֹהֵי יִשְׂרָאֵל אֱלֹהֵי הַצְּבָאוֹת יוֹשֵׁב הַכְּרוּבִים עַל הַמָּזוֹן שֶׁאָכַלְנוּ״. — *In the same manner in which he makes the blessing, so do they respond after him: "Blessed is Hashem, our God, the God of Israel, the Lord of Hosts, Who dwells by the Cherubim, for the food we have eaten."*

The participants respond to the leader with a formula that parallels the one used by the leader. Thus, for a company of ten thousand, their response includes the expression "God of Israel, the Lord of Hosts, Who dwells by the Cherubim."

Although R' Akiva differs with R' Yose HaGlili and maintains that the *zimmun* formula does not change for any group comprised of more than ten people, he nevertheless does agree that the response of the participating group should parallel the leader's convocation. If the leader calls out, נְבָרֵךְ אֱלֹהֵינוּ שֶׁאָכַלְנוּ מִשֶּׁלּוֹ, "Let us bless our God of Whose [bounty] we have eaten," one would expect the participants to respond: בָּרוּךְ אֱלֹהֵינוּ שֶׁאָכַלְנוּ מִשֶּׁלּוֹ, *"Blessed is our God of Whose [bounty] we have eaten."* In fact, however, the collective response adds several words and reads: בָּרוּךְ אֱלֹהֵינוּ שֶׁאָכַלְנוּ מִשֶּׁלּוֹ וּבְטוּבוֹ חָיִינוּ, *"Blessed is our God Whose bounty we have eaten and **through Whose goodness we live**"* (Rambam, Hil. Berachos 5:4).

Many authorities maintain that the leader does indeed introduce the *zimmun* with the words נְבָרֵךְ שֶׁאָכַלְנוּ מִשֶּׁלּוֹ וּבְטוּבוֹ חָיִינוּ, to which the participants then respond with a parallel formula (Levush, Orach Chaim 192, cited by Meleches Shlomo; Ritva, Hil. Berachos). Bach (Orach Chaim 192 s.v. וכל) writes that this was the prevalent custom in many European communities until it was discontinued by Maharal of Prague.

רַבִּי יוֹסֵי הַגְּלִילִי אוֹמֵר: לְפִי רֹב הַקָּהָל הֵן מְבָרְכִין, שֶׁנֶּאֱמַר: ״בְּמַקְהֵלוֹת בָּרְכוּ אֱלֹהִים יְיָ מִמְּקוֹר יִשְׂרָאֵל.״ — *R' Yose HaGlili says: They recite the blessing in accordance with the size of the assemblage as it is stated (Psalms 68:27): "In assemblages, bless God, Hashem, from the source of Israel."*

According to R' Yose HaGlili, the plural form of *assemblages* [מַקְהֵלוֹת] implies that a different blessing is to be recited by each type of assemblage; for as the size of the assemblage increases, so does its sanctity (Maharsha; see also Tiferes Yisrael, Boaz 6). Although R' Yose HaGlili's name is not mentioned in the mishnah until this point, the opinion stated earlier (that the *zimmun* formula changes according to the number of participants) is indeed his — see above s.v. בְּמֵאָה. The mishnah must be viewed as if the text reads

7
3

In the same manner in which he makes the blessing so do they respond after him: "Blessed is Hashem our God, the God of Israel, the Lord of Hosts, Who dwells by the Cherubim, for the food we have eaten." R' Yose HaGlili says: They recite the blessing in accordance with the size of the assemblage as it is stated (*Psalms* 68:27): "In assemblages, bless God, Hashem, from the source of Israel." R' Akiva says: What do we find in the synagogue? Whether many or few, he says: "Bless Hashem."

שֶׁרַבִּי יוֹסֵי הַגְלִילִי אוֹמֵר, *"for so did R' Yose HaGlili say"* (*Tiferes Yisrael* #20).

Following on his thesis that there is a difference between a group of ten thousand and a group of a hundred thousand (see above s.v. ברבוא), *R' Menachem Azarya of Fano* points out that the six different categories for *zimmun* listed by R' Yose HaGlili — three, ten, a hundred, a thousand, ten thousand, and a hundred thousand — correspond to the six words in *Psalms* 68:27, בְּמַקְהֵלוֹת בָּרְכוּ אֱלֹהִים ה', מִמְקוֹר יִשְׂרָאֵל the verse upon which R' Yose HaGlili bases his position (*Teshuvos HaRama Mifano* #7).

R' Akiva maintains that the מְקוֹר, *source*, mentioned in this verse is *the womb*. The word מַקְהֵלוֹת, *assemblages*, at the beginning of the verse, is referring to the fetuses that were in their mothers' womb. The *entire verse*, then, is teaching that every Jew acknowledged the miracle of the splitting of the Red Sea, even the fetuses in their mothers' womb (*Tos. Yom Tov* from *Gem.* 50a). Accordingly, this verse cannot teach that there are various assemblages for *zimmun*. R' Akiva therefore taught that when there are ten or more people in a *zimmun* group, the formula of the collective blessing should be modeled on a

similar prayer recited in the synagogue, as the mishnah now continues to explain. [R' Yossi HaGlili, however, maintains that this is derived specifically from the word מְקוֹר, *source*. The exposition that the *zimmun* text enhances in accordance with the size of the assemblage is derived from the word בְּמַקְהֵלוֹת, *assemblages*.]

אָמַר רַבִּי עֲקִיבָא: מַה מָּצִינוּ בְּבֵית הַכְּנֶסֶת, אֶחָד מְרֻבִּין וְאֶחָד מוּעָטִין אוֹמֵר: ,,בָּרְכוּ אֶת ה'." — *R' Akiva says: What do we find in the synagogue? Whether many or few, he says: "Bless Hashem."*

The prayer בָּרְכוּ אֶת ה', *"Bless Hashem,"* is recited during the services [before בִּרְכוֹת קְרִיאַת שְׁמַע, the blessings preceding *Shema*, and before the reading of the Torah (*Meleches Shlomo*)] when there is a quorum of at least ten men present. The text of this prayer remains the same regardless of the size of the congregation. This, argues R' Akiva, disproves R' Yose HaGlili's position regarding *zimmun*. For the prayer service is also an "assemblage to bless Hashem," and yet the formula for doing so does not change with the size of the crowd. By the same token, then, the text should remain the same for

ברכות   רַבִּי יִשְׁמָעֵאל אוֹמֵר: ,,בָּרְכוּ אֶת יְיָ הַמְבֹרֶךְ".

ז/ד

[ד] **שְׁלֹשָׁה** שֶׁאָכְלוּ כְּאֶחָד אֵינָן רַשָּׁאִין לַחֲלֵק, וְכֵן אַרְבָּעָה, וְכֵן חֲמִשָּׁה. שִׁשָּׁה נֶחֱלָקִין, עַד עֲשָׂרָה. וַעֲשָׂרָה

—— ר' עובדיה מברטנורא ——

רבי ישמעאל אומר ברכו את ה' המבורך. והלכה כרבי ישמעאל: **(ד) אינן רשאים לחלק.** מכיון שחלה עליהם חובת זימון: **וכן ארבעה וכן חמשה.** אין השלשה מזמנין לעצמן והיחיד יחלק מהן, דאיהו נמי אקבע בחובת זימון: **ששה נחלקים.** כדי זמון לכאן וכדי זמון לכאן, עד עשרה, אבל עשרה אין נחלקים דאתחייבו להו בזמון שיש בו הזכרת השם, עד שיהיו עשרים, ואז יחלקו לשתי חבורות אם ירצו:

---

zimmun as well regardless of the size of the assemblage.

R' Yose HaGlili agrees that the synagogue prayer text does not vary according to the size of the congregation, but he attributes that to the nature of synagogue attendance. Since people are always entering and leaving, the rabbis did not impose upon the reader the additional task of calculating the number of people present. They therefore did not vary the formula of the synagogue prayer. However, it is much easier to know the number of people that have eaten together since they have all been sitting together and do not leave until after they have recited *Bircas HaMazon*. He therefore argues that it is necessary to adjust the formula according to the numbers of people (*Tos. Yom Tov* from *Tosafos* 49b s.v. אמר).

רַבִּי יִשְׁמָעֵאל אוֹמֵר: ,,בָּרְכוּ אֶת ה' הַמְבֹרֶךְ". — *R' Yishmael says: "Bless Hashem,*

the blessed One."

R' Yishmael does not refer to the collective *zimmun* blessing but to the synagogue prayer, cited by R' Akiva in his proof (*Tif. Yis.*). He has the reader add הַמְבֹרֶךְ, *the blessed One*, to this prayer. He thereby includes himself among those offering blessings, since the reader calls on the others to bless Hashem Who is blessed by all, including himself (*Rif* folio 36b, from *Yerushalmi*, cited by *Tos. Yom Tov* s.v. נברך). This text is preferable to the formula mentioned by R' Akiva ("Bless Hashem"), which does not include the reader among those offering blessings. R' Yishmael's formula is in fact that which is used in synagogues today.

R' Akiva does not dispute the validity of R' Yishmael's formula; he merely states that even his "Bless Hashem" formula suffices (*Rashi* to 50a s.v. בהדי).

4.

If the conditions for *zimmun* are satisfied, its recitation is not merely optional; it is obligatory. Therefore, if a group has become obligated to conduct a collective blessing, the members of that group may not disperse until they have fulfilled this obligation and recited the collective blessing. The following mishnah elaborates on this rule.

4. Three who ate together are not permitted to separate. And so too for four, and so too for five. Six may separate, up to ten. But ten

YAD AVRAHAM

שְׁלשָׁה שֶׁאָכְלוּ כְּאֶחָד אֵינָן רַשָּׁאִין לֵחָלֵק, — Three who ate together are not permitted to separate.

Since they are obligated to recite a collective blessing, the members of this group may not recite *Bircas HaMazon* separately and individually (*Rabbeinu Yonah* folio 36b s.v. מתני׳ שלשה), but must conduct a collective blessing and recite *Bircas HaMazon* together in one group (*Rav, Rashi*).

Although the ruling of this mishnah seems to be a repetition of mishnah 1, the *Gemara* (50a) explains that on the basis of the first mishnah one may have thought that "eating together" means eating from the same loaf of bread. This mishnah was therefore taught to emphasize that *whenever* three people eat together as a group, even if each eat from separate loaves, they may not disband without conducting a collective blessing (*Tos. Yom Tov*).

Alternatively, this mishnah teaches that although each member of the group has not yet eaten the minimal *kezayis* which actually obligates him to recite *Bircas HaMazon* and the *zimmun* blessing, the rabbis ruled that since they began their meal together, they may not disband. They must remain together and ultimately conduct a collective blessing (*Tosafos Rabbeinu Yehudah* to 50a s.v. קמ״ל; *Rosh* 7:29; see also *Rabbeinu Yonah* folio 37a s.v. הכי קתני).

וְכֵן אַרְבָּעָה, וְכֵן חֲמִשָּׁה. — And so too for four, and so too for five.

The obligation to participate in *zimmun* is the personal obligation of every member of the group that ate together. Therefore, even if three people of the original group will remain to conduct *zimmun*, the fourth and fifth members

may not separate and recite the *Bircas HaMazon* on their own (*Rav; Rashi* — see *Magen Avraham* 193:3).

שִׁשָּׁה נֶחֱלָקִין, עַד עֲשָׂרָה. — Six may separate, up to ten.

A group consisting of six, seven, eight or nine people may separate into groups of three or more people, since each group of three will have its own quorum (*Rav, Rashi*).

Ravad (cited by *Shitah* to 50a s.v. והנוקדנין) maintains that not only is a group of six *permitted* to split into two groups, it is *required* to do so.

According to *Ravad*, the נְבָרֵךְ formula is preferred to the בָּרְכוּ formula, for it includes the leader in the *zimmun* blessing together with the other members of the group (see mishnah 3, s.v. בִּשְׁלשָׁה וָהוּא). Since a group of three people *must* use the נְבָרֵךְ formula (mishnah 3, s.v. כֵּיצַד), while a group of more than three may opt to use the בָּרְכוּ formula too, splitting into groups of three assures that the preferred נְבָרֵךְ formula will be used.

Others however argue that even though it is *permissible* for a group of six to divide into two groups of three, it is *desirable* not to do so since Scripture (*Proverbs* 14:28) teaches that the larger the group that participates in a *zimmun* blessing, the greater the honor to Hashem [בְּרָב עָם הַדְרַת מֶלֶךְ, a multitude of people is a King's glory] (*Meleches Shlomo* from *Levush* 193; *Darkei Moshe, Orach Chaim* 193:2; see *Mishnah Berurah, Shaar HaTziyun* 193:8-9).

אֵינָן נֶחֱלָקִין, עַד שֶׁיִּהְיוּ עֶשְׂרִים.

[ה] שְׁתֵּי חֲבוּרוֹת שֶׁהָיוּ אוֹכְלוֹת בְּבַיִת אֶחָד: בִּזְמַן שֶׁמִּקְצָתָן רוֹאִין אֵלּוּ אֶת אֵלּוּ, הֲרֵי אֵלּוּ מִצְטָרְפִין לְזִמּוּן; וְאִם לָאו, אֵלּוּ מְזַמְּנִין לְעַצְמָן, וְאֵלּוּ מְזַמְּנִין לְעַצְמָן.

―――――――― ר' עובדיה מברטנורא ――――――――

(ה) ואם לאו אלו אלו מזמנין לעצמן. ובזמן שמשמש אחד משמש לשתי החבורות, אף על פי שאין

יד אברהם

A third opinion maintains that although a single collective blessing conducted by a group of six enhances the honor to Hashem, it is evenly balanced by the two blessings conducted by two groups of three, since twice the amount of blessings are recited. Accordingly, there is no preference one way or the other (*Taz, Orach Chaim* 193:3).

וַעֲשָׂרָה אֵינָן נֶחֱלָקִין, — *But ten may not separate,*

As explained in mishnah 3, the *zimmun* formula for a group of ten includes the Name of Hashem. Since the *zimmun* formula for a group of three does not, a group of ten may not separate into smaller groups. Although the smaller groups will also conduct *zimmun*, nevertheless, their formula will not include mention of Hashem's Name, and is therefore considered inferior to the *zimmun* of a group of ten (*Rav, Rashi*).

עַד שֶׁיִּהְיוּ עֶשְׂרִים. — *up to twenty.*

Although a group numbering from ten through nineteen people cannot split into smaller groups, since their *zimmun* formula does not mention the Name of Hashem, a group of twenty, however, may split into two groups. Since both of the smaller groups will consist of ten people, they both can conduct the *zimmun* blessing with the Name of Hashem, as the original group of twenty (*Rav, Rashi*).

Pri Megadim (*Orach Chaim, Mishbetzos Zahav* 193:3) suggests that even if a group of six may divide into two groups of three (see above), it is certainly preferable that a group of twenty conduct a single *zimmun* blessing as one large group rather than two groups of ten. The rule of בְּרָב עָם הַדְרַת מֶלֶךְ, *a multitude of people is a king's glory* (*Proverbs* 14:28), is particularly relevant to the *zimmun* blessing of a group of ten or more, since the formula actually mentions Hashem's name. Accordingly, a group of twenty shows more honor than two groups of ten, and is to be preferred.

5.

The first part of the following mishnah discusses the criteria necessary for uniting different groups so that they all may recite one collective blessing together. The second part discusses the blessing over wine.

שְׁתֵּי חֲבוּרוֹת שֶׁהָיוּ אוֹכְלוֹת בְּבַיִת אֶחָד: — *[If] two groups were eating in one house:*

That is, if two groups of people

were eating in the same house, each at a different table (*Meiri* to 50a s.v. המשנה הששית).

There is a difference of opinion as to the

may not separate, up to twenty.

5. **[** [I]f **]** two groups were eating in one house: When some of them can see each other, they may combine for a collective blessing; but if not, these conduct a collective blessing by themselves, and these conduct a collective blessing by themselves.

YAD AVRAHAM

size of these groups. Some explain that this ruling applies even where each group consists of less than three people, and each group is not presently obligated in a *zimmun* blessing. The mishnah teaches that when certain conditions are satisfied, the groups may combine to *form* the three-man quorum needed for the standard *zimmun*. Likewise, the mishnah teaches that when these conditions are met, groups of less than ten may combine in order to recite the enhanced *zimmun* (*Meiri* to 50a s.v. המשנה הששית).

Others argue that the ruling of the mishnah applies only where the groups are comprised of at least three people, and each independent group is currently obligated to conduct *zimmun* (*Ritva, Hil. Berachos* 7:15; see *Hagahos R' Akiva Eiger* to *Shulchan Aruch Orach Chaim* 195:1). The two groups may join together and form one large group to recite one single collective blessing rather than two separate blessings of smaller groups. However, if the groups consisted of less than three people and were not obligated to conduct *zimmun*, they cannot join together to form a three-man quorum. Similarly, two groups of more than three people but less than ten cannot join together to recite the enhanced *zimmun* formula that includes the Name of Hashem (*Rashbash* resp. 37 [quoted in editor's note to *Rabbeinu Aharon HaLevi*, p. 159, n.82]; see also *Mishnah Berurah, Beur Halachah* 195:1 s.v. שתי חבורות).

בִּזְמַן שֶׁמְּקְצָתָן רוֹאִין אֵלוּ אֶת אֵלוּ, הֲרֵי אֵלוּ מִצְטָרְפִין לְזִמּוּן; — *When some of them can see each other, they may combine for a collective blessing;*

If some of the members of one group are able to see some of the members of

the other group, the groups may combine to act as one group for *zimmun*. For example, if two people are eating in one corner of the house, and two others are eating together in another corner, and one person of one group can see one person from the other, the two groups may combine to form a quorum and conduct the *zimmun* blessing (*Meiri*).

Rashba maintains that this rule applies only when the parties involved entered the house with the intent of eating in areas where they see each other, for it is then considered as if they sat down to eat together. However, if this was not their intent, they may not combine for *zimmun*.

Many authorities rule that this applies even if the two groups are in *different houses*; provided they entered those houses with the intent of eating in areas where they are visible to each other (see *Shulchan Aruch* 195:1; see also *Mishnah Berurah* 195:6).

Alternatively, the case of the mishnah is where there are *three* people in each group. The mishnah is teaching that if anyone of one group is in sight of anyone of the second group, a single recitation of the collective blessing exempts both groups from their obligation (*Rashbash* resp. 37; see above s.v. שתי).

וְאִם לָאו, אֵלוּ מְזַמְּנִין לְעַצְמָן, וְאֵלוּ מְזַמְּנִין לְעַצְמָן. — *but if not, these conduct a collective blessing by themselves, and these conduct a collective blessing by themselves.*

If no member of one group is visible

אֵין מְבָרְכִין עַל הַיַּיִן עַד שֶׁיִּתֵּן לְתוֹכוֹ מַיִם; דִּבְרֵי
רַבִּי אֱלִיעֶזֶר. וַחֲכָמִים אוֹמְרִים: מְבָרְכִין.

───────── ר' עובדיה מברטנורא ─────────

רוֹאִים אֵלּוּ אֶת אֵלּוּ, הַשַּׁמָּשׁ מְצָרְפָן: **אֵין מברכין על היין.** בּוֹרֵא פְּרִי הַגֶּפֶן: **עד שיתן לתוכו**
מים. לְפִי שֶׁהָיָה יֵינָם חָזָק מְאֹד וְלֹא הָיָה רָאוּי לִשְׁתִיָּה בְּלֹא מַיִם, הִילְכָךְ אַכַּתִּי לֹא אִישְׁתַּנִּי לְמַעֲלִיוּתָא
וְלֹא זַז מִבִּרְכָתוֹ הָרִאשׁוֹנָה וּמְבָרְכִין עָלָיו בּוֹרֵא פְּרִי הָעֵץ כְּעֲנָבִים. וְאֵין הֲלָכָה כְּרַבִּי אֱלִיעֶזֶר:

יד אברהם

to any member of the other group, the two groups cannot combine for a joint collective blessing. However, the *Gemara* (50b) adds, that even where they cannot see each other, if both groups are being served by the same waiter, they can combine for *zimmun* even if the waiter did not eat with them (*Rav, Rambam Comm.*; see *Ohr Same'ach* to *Hil. Berachos* 5:12).

Tif. Yis. (#27) questions the superfluous wording of this section of the mishnah. The mishnah could have simply stated that where they do not see each other "they do not combine for *zimmun*." The wording of the latter section of the mishnah would then parallel the first section. He suggests that the mishnah wishes to emphasize that even though each respective group consists of a valid quorum to conduct *zimmun* [so that each group will in any case be subject to a collective blessing], they may not *combine* for a collective blessing since they do not see each other [*Tif. Yis.* is following *Meiri's* approach (see s.v. בזמן

שמקצתן רואין), i.e. where the groups view each other, they may combine even to form the minimum quorum].

The following dispute, at first glance, seems to be out of place in this chapter (see below).

אֵין מְבָרְכִין עַל הַיַּיִן עַד שֶׁיִּתֵּן לְתוֹכוֹ מַיִם; דִּבְרֵי רַבִּי אֱלִיעֶזֶר. — *We do not recite a blessing over wine until water is added to it; [these are] the words of R' Eliezer.*

The wine of the mishnaic period was very strong and was not fit for drinking until diluted with water. R' Eliezer rules that prior to dilution it is not yet classified as wine, and therefore does not qualify for the *Borei pri hagafen* blessing. For those who wish to drink it undiluted, it retains the blessing it had as a grape: *Borei pri ha'eitz* (*Rav, Rambam Comm.*).

וַחֲכָמִים אוֹמְרִים: מְבָרְכִין. — *But the Sages say: We recite the blessing.*

We do not recite a blessing over wine until water is added it; [these are] the words of R' Eliezer. But the Sages say: We recite the blessing.

The Sages say that even prior to dilution it is considered wine, and its blessing is *Borei pri hagafen* (*Gem.* 50b from *Tosefta* 4:3). Although undiluted wine is not really considered a drinkable beverage, it was nevertheless the primary ingredient in a potion called קוֹרְיַיטֵי, *koraytei* (*Gem.* 50b). [This is a generic term for the beverages known in Tannaic literature as אֲנוּמְלִין, *anumlin*, and אֲלוּנְתִית, *aluntis* (*Rashi*). These are made, respectively, from full-strength wine, honey and pepper, and from full-strength wine, clear water and balsam oil (see *Avodah Zarah* 30a; see also *Rashi* to *Chullin* 6a s.v. לתת לתוך המורייס).] It is therefore considered to have been transformed for the better (from its original state) and merits the *Borei pri hagafen* blessing by one who desires to drink it full strength (*Tosafos* to 50b s.v. למאי; cf. *Rashba* to 50b s.v. למאי).

It would seem more appropriate to include this dispute in Chapter 6, where the mishnah deals with the blessings recited over food and drink. Why then was it placed here with the laws of *Bircas HaMazon*?

Furthermore if R' Eliezer is in fact discussing the *Borei pri hagafen* blessing, why does he not mention it? He should have said "We do not recite the blessing *Borei pri hagafen* until water is poured into the wine"! Similarly, why do the Sages not mention the blessing? The mishnah should have stated: "But the Sages say: We do recite the *Borei pri hagafen* blessing (*Tzlach* to 50b s.v. ת"ר).

These difficulties suggest that this dispute is not regarding the *Borei pri hagafen* blessing generally recited over wine, but regarding the cup of wine that is poured for the recitation of the *Bircas HaMazon* (see Chapter 8 mishnahs 5 and 8). The term מְבָרְכִין of the mishnah refers to the blessings of *Bircas HaMazon*. Thus, R' Eliezer says that *Bircas HaMazon* is not recited over a cup of undiluted wine, while the Sages say that it is (*Tos. Anshei Shem* s.v. אין; *Tzlach* to 50b s.v. ת"י).

Although this approach answers many difficulties, it seems directly contradicted by the *Gemara* (50b) where R' Yose ben R' Chanina states clearly that although the Sages dispute R' Eliezer concerning the recitation of *Borei pri hagafen* over undiluted wine, they agree that for the *Bircas HaMazon*, the cup of wine must be diluted. See however *Tos. Anshei Shem* (s.v. אין) and *Tzlach* (to 50b s.v. ת"ר).

פרק שמיני ⤳
Chapter Eight

Having completed its treatment of the *Bircas HaMazon* and its related laws, the mishnah now lists disputes that pertain to the rituals that either precede or follow a meal (*Tosafos HaRosh* to 51b s.v. אלו). The chapter begins with *Kiddush* (mishnah 1), continues with *netilas yadayim* [washing the hands before eating bread] (mishnahs 2-3), *mayim acharonim* [washing the hands after the meal, before reciting *Bircas HaMazon*] (mishnah 4), and then goes on to *Havdalah* [the blessing recited over a cup of wine to mark the departure of the Sabbath] (mishnah 5).[1] Having introduced the topic of *Havdalah*, the mishnah elaborates several laws concerning *Havdalah* (mishnah 6). It then discusses the law for someone who finished his meal and forgot to recite *Bircas HaMazon* (mishnah 7), and laws regarding the recitation of the *Bircas HaMazon* over a cup of wine (mishnah 8). The chapter concludes with a discussion of laws regarding "Amen," the response uttered upon hearing the recitation of a blessing (mishnah 8). In most of these cases, the mishnah's focus is on the disputes between Beis Shammai and Beis Hillel in regard to these matters.

---

1. The mishnah is discussing a particular case in which the *Havdalah* is recited in conjunction with *Bircas HaMazon* following the last meal of the Sabbath.

[א] אֵלּוּ דְבָרִים שֶׁבֵּין בֵּית שַׁמַּאי וּבֵית
הִלֵּל בַּסְעוּדָה: בֵּית שַׁמַּאי אוֹמְרִים:
מְבָרֵךְ עַל הַיּוֹם וְאַחַר כָּךְ מְבָרֵךְ עַל הַיַּיִן. וּבֵית
הִלֵּל אוֹמְרִים: מְבָרֵךְ עַל הַיַּיִן וְאַחַר כָּךְ מְבָרֵךְ
עַל הַיּוֹם.

ר' עובדיה מברטנורא

פרק שמיני – אלו דברים. (א) אלו דברים. בתחלה קדוש היום
ואחר כך מברך על היין בורא פרי הגפן, שתחלה קדש היום ואחר כך בא היין על השלחן
בשביל היום, וכשם שקדם לכניסה כך קודם לברכה: **מברך על היין.** תחלה, והוא הדין למקדש
על הפת, שהיין או הפת גורמים לקדוש היום, שאם אין לו יין או פת לא יקדש:

יד אברהם

1.

The following mishnah discusses *Kiddush*, the blessing generally recited over
a cup of wine at the start of the first meal of the Sabbath or a Festival. The
Kiddush consists of two blessings. One blessing declares the sanctity of the day
(on the Sabbath, this is the lengthy blessing that concludes with the words מְקַדֵּשׁ
הַשַּׁבָּת, "Who sanctifies the Sabbath," and on the Festivals it is the blessing that
concludes with מְקַדֵּשׁ יִשְׂרָאֵל וְהַזְּמַנִּים, "Who sanctifies Israel and the festive
seasons"). The other blessing is the blessing always recited over wine — *Borei
pri hagafen*. The dispute which follows concerns the order in which these
blessings are recited.

אֵלּוּ דְבָרִים שֶׁבֵּין בֵּית שַׁמַּאי וּבֵית הִלֵּל
בַּסְעוּדָה: — *These are the matters [of
dispute] between Beis Shammai and
Beis Hillel [with respect to] meals.*

That is, with respect to the laws
pertaining to meals (*Rashi*).

Beis Shammai and Beis Hillel also

dispute other laws concerning meals
that are not listed in this chapter.[1]
They are omitted here because our
chapter lists only those disputes that
relate to matters that either precede or
follow the meal, not to those of the
meal itself (*Tosafos HaRosh* to 51b s.v.

---

1. The *Tanna Kamma* of mishnah 6:5 (identified in *Yerushalmi* 6:5 as Beis Hillel; cf. *Meiri*
to 51b s.v. ובאמת) holds that if one recited the *Mezonos* blessing before the meal on a
peripheral dish of *kisnen*-bread, he is not discharged of his obligation to recite *Hamotzi*
over actual bread. Beis Shammai maintain that he is not even discharged of the obligation
to recite the *Mezonos* blessing over the porridge that he will later eat *during* the meal —
see *Gemara* 42b.
    Gemara 43b cites another dispute in a baraisa. If fragrant oil and a cup of wine are
brought, Beis Shammai say that the oil is held in the right hand and the wine in the left.
The blessing is then recited first over the oil (because the pleasure derived from its
fragrance is immediate) and then over the wine. Beis Hillel disagree and maintain that the
wine is held in the right hand and the blessing is first said over the wine and then over
the fragrant oil (because the wine — which is consumed by the body — is more significant
than the oil, which is merely smelled).

1. **T**hese are matters [of dispute] between Beis Shammai and Beis Hillel [with respect to] meals. Beis Shammai say: One recites the blessing over the [sanctity of] the day [first], and recites the blessing over the wine afterwards. But Beis Hillel say: One recites the blessing over the wine [first], and recites the blessing over [the sanctity of] the day afterwards.

YAD AVRAHAM

אֵלוּ but see *Rashba* to 51b s.v. אֵלוּ).

בֵּית שַׁמַּאי אוֹמְרִים: מְבָרֵךְ עַל הַיּוֹם, וְאַחַר כָּךְ מְבָרֵךְ עַל הַיַּיִן. — *Beis Shammai say: One recites the blessing over the [sanctity of] the day [first], and recites the blessing over the wine afterwards.*

Beis Shammai say that *Mekadeish haShabbos,* the blessing that declares the sanctity of the day, precedes the *Borei pri hagafen* blessing that is recited over the wine. They base their position on two arguments (see *Gemara* 51b). The first is שֶׁהַיּוֹם גּוֹרֵם לַיַּיִן שֶׁיָּבֹא, *that the day causes the wine to be brought.* That is, the sanctity of the day is what necessitates taking a cup of *Kiddush* wine (*Rashi*), and were it not for the sanctity of the Sabbath [or Festival], we would have no need for this cup of wine (*Rambam Comm.*). Consequently, it is the blessing that declares the sanctity of the day that is the main point of this exercise, and it therefore takes precedence (*Rabbeinu Yonah,* folio 38b s.v. שהיום).

Secondly, the day becomes sanctified before the wine is brought to the table. The Sabbath or Festival begins either from the time one accepts the Sabbath upon himself, or with night-

fall (*Rashi* 51b s.v. וכבר), whereas the *Kiddush* wine is not brought until later, when the evening meal is about to begin. Since chronologically, the day attains its sanctity before the arrival of the wine, it is only proper that the blessing over the sanctity of the day precede the blessing over the wine (*Rav,* based on *Gemara* 51b).

Tos. Yom Tov points out that *Rav's* wording here is meant to convey both reasons stated in the Baraisa. *Rav* writes: "For the day becomes sanctified first, and only later does the wine come to the table, *on account of the day."* See *Tos. R' Akiva Eiger.*

וּבֵית הִלֵּל אוֹמְרִים: מְבָרֵךְ עַל הַיַּיִן, וְאַחַר כָּךְ מְבָרֵךְ עַל הַיּוֹם. — *But Beis Hillel say: One recites the blessing over the wine [first], and recites the blessing over [the sanctity of] the day afterwards.*

Beis Hillel argue that since it is the wine that makes the recitation of the *Kiddush* possible (for without wine, one may not recite the *Mekadeish haShabbos* blessing), the blessing over the wine takes precedence and is recited before the blessing of *Mekadeish haShabbos* (*Rav, Rambam Comm.* based on *Gem.* 51b).[1]

Additionally, Beis Hillel base their

---

1. Actually, if there is no wine, the *Kiddush* may be recited over bread (see *Pesachim* 106b). In that case, Beis Hillel's logic would apply to the blessing over the bread. The point is that *Kiddush* is recited only over certain substances, and in the absence of those

position on the general rule governing precedence between mitzvos: תָּדִיר וְשֶׁאֵינוֹ תָּדִיר תָּדִיר קוֹדֵם, *[when] that which is frequent [contends] with that which is not [as] frequent, that which is [more] frequent takes precedence (Tos. Yom Tov* from *Gem.* 51b; see Mishnah *Zevachim* 10:1). Now the *Borei pri hagafen* blessing is a more frequently encountered obligation than the blessing over the sanctity of the day because it appears in all recitals of *Kiddush,* as well as in *Havdalah,* and the wedding blessings (see *Rashi* to 40b s.v. חוץ), whereas the *Mekadeish haShabbos* blessing of *Kiddush* is encountered only once per Sabbath (*Shaagas Aryeh* #21 s.v. וי"ל).[1] Accordingly, the *Borei pri hagafen* blessing has precedence over the *Mekadeish haShabbos* blessing and is recited first.

Most authorities maintain that the obligation to recite *Kiddush* is Biblical, whereas the obligation to recite it specifically over wine or bread is only Rabbinic (*Rambam, Hil. Shabbos* 29:1,6; *Tosafos* to *Nazir* 4a s.v. מאי; see *Tosafos* to *Pesachim* 106a s.v. זוכרהו). Accordingly, *Tzlach* (to 51b s.v. שהיין גורם) challenges the assertion that it is the wine that brings about the recitation of the *Kiddush.* Although this might be so on the Rabbinic level, on the Biblical level, one who does not have wine or bread recites *Kiddush* without them. Furthermore, it stands to reason that a Biblical obligation should have precedence over one that is Rabbinic even if the latter is more frequent.

If so, why do Beis Hillel give precedence to the Rabbinically obligated *Borei pri hagafen* blessing over the Biblically obligated *Mekadeish ha'Shabbos* blessing?

Tzlach (to 52a s.v. תוס' ד"ה ור"י) therefore argues that Beis Hillel make their argument based on the common case where the person reciting *Kiddush* has already prayed *Maariv,* the Sabbath evening prayer. One who intends to fulfill his *Kiddush* obligation during the Sabbath *Shemoneh Esrei* prayer of *Maariv* satisfies his Biblical obligation to sanctify the day with this prayer (see *Beur Halachah* 271 s.v. מיד). In this case, his subsequent *Kiddush* over wine is only a Rabbinic obligation. Since both his *Kiddush* obligation and the obligation to recite *Kiddush* over wine are now only Rabbinic, the usual rules of precedence according to frequency apply. Therefore, the *Borei pri hagafen* blessing has precedence. By the same token, since the *Kiddush* is now only Rabbinically obligated, it is in fact necessitated only because of the presence of wine, since the Rabbinically obligated *Kiddush* is not said in the absence of wine [or bread].

It should follow from this that where a person recites *Kiddush* before he has prayed *Maariv* — in which case his obligation to recite *Kiddush* is Biblical — the *Mekadeish haShabbos* blessing should precede the *Borei pri hagafen* even according to Beis Hillel![2] *Tzlach,* however, concludes that the *Borei pri hagafen* comes first even in this case, because the standard formula of *Kiddush* is determined by the most common case of *Kiddush.* Since most people recite *Kiddush* after having prayed *Maariv,* the formula for all *Kiddush* recitals was

substances *Kiddush* is not recited. Thus, if bread is used, its blessing precedes the *Mekadeish haShabbos* blessing (*Rashi* 51b s.v. שהיין).

1. *Shaagas Aryeh* argues that the fact that one is permitted to drink wine every day (which would lead him to make its blessing each day), whereas one is not permitted to recite *Mekadeish haShabbos* every day, does not give *Borei pri hagafen* precedence. In order for something frequent to precede something that is less frequent, it must be demonstrated that the former is more frequently *obligated* than the latter. See there for his proofs, and see *Zevachim* 91a.

2. The same rule should apply in the case of a woman who does not usually pray *Maariv* but is nonetheless Biblically obligated in *Kiddush.*

established based on this scenario. There-fore, the *Borei pri hagafen* blessing *always* precedes *Mekadeish hashabbos* (according to Beis Hillel).

It should also be noted that the assumption that a Biblical obligation has prece-dence over a Rabbinic one, even when the Rabbinic one is more frequent, is not unan-imously held (see *Shaagas Aryeh* §22 and *Kunteres Acharon* to *Shaagas Aryeh* §2 s.v. ד"ה עוד הביא ראיה; see also *Aruch LaNer* (to *Succah* 56a s.v. שהיין גורם).

2.

The following mishnah deals with *netilas yadayim*, the Rabbinical obliga-tion to wash one's hands before partaking of bread. To understand the mishnah properly, an introduction to the laws of *tumah* transference is in order.

◆§ Degrees of *Tumah*

An אַב הַטּוּמְאָה [*av hatumah*], *a primary source of tumah* (see *Keilim* Ch. 1 for a listing), transfers *tumah* to a person or object by contact (and, depending on the source, in certain other ways as well). The contaminated person or object can in turn transmit that *tumah* further. When *tumah* is transmitted from one bearer to another, it generally becomes weakened, with the recipient acquiring a lower degree of *tumah* than that of the transmitter. Thus, a person or object that contracts *tumah* from an *av hatumah* is known as a רִאשׁוֹן לְטוּמְאָה, *rishon le'tumah* — i.e. one who is contaminated with *the first degree of [derived] tumah*. The *rishon le'tumah*, in turn, creates a שֵׁנִי לְטוּמְאָה, *sheni le'tumah* — i.e. one contaminated with *the second degree of [derived] tumah*. [These terms are often shortened simply to *rishon* and *sheni*.] A *sheni* is the weakest form of *tumah* that can be acquired by objects that are *chullin*. Thus, in most cases, an *av hatumah* will create a *rishon*, which in turn can create a *sheni*. *Terumah*, however, can acquire yet another degree of *tumah* — a *shlishi* (third degree).

Not every item can contract all levels of *tumah*. Under Biblical law, persons and utensils can contract *tumah* only from an *av* (or a human corpse, which is an even more powerful source of *tumah*). Thus, a person or utensil can only become a *rishon*; if a *rishon* touches them, however, they remain *tahor*, and certainly they are *tahor* if they are touched by a *sheni*. The only items that a *rishon* can make into a *sheni* are foods and beverages. Foods and beverages that are *tamei* as a *sheni* cannot convey *tumah* to other *chullin* foods at all. Thus, if a *sheni* touches unsanctified food, that food acquires no degree of *tumah* whatsoever.

◆§ *Tumah* of Liquids

The Sages, however, instituted an exception to this last rule. They decreed that when a *sheni* touches a beverage ("beverage" in this context refers to the seven liquids listed in *Machshirin* 6:4: water, wine, bees' honey, olive oil, milk, dew and blood), the beverage becomes a *rishon*, and is invested with the capacity to convey tumah to foods (*Parah* 8:7). There was also a decree that *tamei* beverages can transmit *tumah* to utensils (see *Shabbos* 14b).

◆§ *Tumah* of Hands

A person's hands are active and they are apt to touch things without the person being aware. Thus, it is quite likely that without his knowing, one touched parts of his body that are full of perspiration or otherwise unclean. Were he then to touch *terumah*, the holy food would become repugnant or even

[ב] **בֵּית** שַׁמַאי אוֹמְרִים: נוֹטְלִין לַיָּדַיִם,
וְאַחַר כָּךְ מוֹזְגִין אֶת הַכּוֹס. וּבֵית

ר' עובדיה מברטנורא

(ב) **בית שמאי אומרים נוטלין לידים ואחר כך מוזגין את הכוס.** שאם אתה אומר מוזגין
את הכוס תחלה, גזרה שמא יטמאו משקים שנפלו באחורי הכוס מחמת הידים, שהידים קודם נטילה
תורת שני לטומאה יש להן ומטמאים את המשקים להיות תחלה, ויחזרו המשקים ויטמאו את אחורי
הכוס, שהמשקים שנטמאו מטמאים כלים מדרבנן, אלא שהקילו בטומאה זו שכלי שנטמאו אחוריו

יד אברהם

inedible. To avoid such irreverent treatment of *terumah*, the Rabbis forbade it
to be touched with unrinsed hands (*Rashi, Shabbos* 14a עסקניות ד"ה).[1] They
strengthened the prohibition by declaring that unrinsed hands are *tamei* in the
degree of *sheni* (see *Zavim* 5:12 and *Shabbos* 14a). Thus, they disqualify *terumah* on contact. This enactment is known as the decree of סְתָם יָדַיִם ("*ordinary
hands*," i.e. unrinsed hands). They also extended this prohibition to eating even
ordinary (i.e. non-*terumah*) bread with such hands (see *Chullin* 106a and
Mishnah Berurah 157:1).

Hands can be cleansed of this *tumah* by rinsing them in the prescribed
manner. This is known as נְטִילַת יָדַיִם, *netilas yadayim*. Once rinsed, they
remain *tahor* as long as the person does not divert his attention from them (הֶסַח
הַדַּעַת, *diversion of attention*) and is mindful of what he touches. Generally, one
is mindful of what his hands touch during a meal. Consequently, once the meal
is completed, one's hands are again rendered *tamei*.

The mishnah (*Parah* 8:7) states: *Anything that invalidates terumah* [i.e. a
sheni, which can contaminate *terumah* but not *chullin*] *contaminates liquids to
be a beginning of tumah* [i.e. it makes the liquids a *rishon*]. Thus, when unwashed hands, which have the status of a *sheni*, come in contact with a liquid
that spilled over onto the outside of a cup, that liquid will become a *rishon* and
will in turn transmit *tumah* to the outside of the cup. For as we said above, the
Rabbis decreed that *tamei* beverages contaminate utensils.[2]

From the above it follows that if *tahor* wine is touched by *tamei* hands, the
wine becomes a *rishon le'tumah*. If this wine touches the outside of the cup, the
outside becomes *tamei*, while the interior remains *tahor*. Since the cup acquires
its *tumah* from a *rishon le'tumah*, the exterior of the cup is a *sheni le'tumah*.
If other wine that is *tahor* wine now touches the *tamei* exterior of this cup, this

---

1. *Rashi* also mentions a different explanation of this decree in the name of his teachers,
namely, that the person may have touched something that was actually *tamei*. *Rashi*
himself rejects their view, but see *Rambam Comm.* to *Tohoros* 7:8 which espouses it.

2. In order to stress that the cup is only Rabbinically *tamei*, the Rabbis distinguished
between the interior and the exterior of the utensil and decreed that the *tumah* of liquids
affect only the exterior of the utensil and not its interior (*Keilim* 25:6; *Bechoros* 38a).

Rashi (*Berachos* 52a s.v. כלי) notes that we are only discussing a cup made from metal
or wood, which contracts *tumah* through contact with its outside. Earthenware, however,
does not contract *tumah* from its outside at all, even when a Biblical *tumah* is involved.

2. Beis Shammai say: We wash [our] hands [first], and pour the cup [of wine] afterwards.

YAD AVRAHAM

wine too becomes a *rishon le'tumah* — and it will render the hands of a person who washed *netilas yadayim* a *sheni*.[1] As a result, he will now have to repeat *netilas yadayim* to eat bread.

The *Gemara* (52b) states that there is a difference of opinion between Beis Shammai and Beis Hillel as to whether one who has washed *netilas yadayim* is permitted to use a cup whose outside is *tamei*. Beis Shammai forbid this out of concern that some of the liquid contained inside the cup might splash onto the outside of the cup, thereby contracting *tumah* from the outside of the cup and transmitting it to the hands. Beis Hillel permit using such a cup because it is uncommon for liquid to splash onto the outside of the cup, and thus unlikely that the hands will become contaminated.[2] The dispute of our mishnah is an outgrowth of this dispute.

בֵּית שַׁמַּאי אוֹמְרִים: נוֹטְלִין לַיָּדַיִם, וְאַחַר כָּךְ מוֹזְגִין אֶת הַכּוֹס. — *Beis Shammai say: We wash [our] hands [first], and pour the cup [of wine] afterwards.*

The mishnah is referring to a cup of wine that one wishes to drink prior to the start of his meal. This might be the cup of wine used for *Kiddush* that one drinks at the start of his Sabbath meal (*Rif* folio 38b; *Rambam Comm.*), or simply a cup of wine that one wishes to drink prior to the start of his weekday meal (*Rashi*; see above mishnah 6:5 and *Gemara* 43a).

According to Beis Shammai, if one intends to drink wine and eat bread, he first washes *netilas yadayim* for the bread, pours his cup of wine, recites the *Borei pri hagafen* blessing, drinks the wine, and only then recites the *Hamotzi* blessing and eats his bread. Thus, pouring the cup of wine, reciting its blessing and drinking from it intervene between his *netilas yadayim* and the *Hamotzi* he recites over the bread.

Beis Shammai hold that it is forbidden to use a cup whose exterior is *tamei*, as explained in the preface to this mishnah. It follows, then, that the case of the mishnah is where both the interior and exterior of the cup are *tahor*. However, if the drinking of the wine prior to the meal were to take place before *netilas yadayim* (i.e. with *tamei* hands), there is the concern that some of the liquid in the cup might splash out and wet the exterior of the cup. These droplets would then contract *tumah* from the unwashed hands of the one holding the cup, and they would in turn render the exterior of the cup *tamei*. The person who would continue to use this cup after washing his hands for the meal would thus end up drinking during the meal from a cup whose exterior is *tamei* — which Beis Shammai forbid. To prevent this, Beis Shammai rule that he must wash his hands prior to pouring the wine, so that his hands will be *tahor* when he

---

1. However, in the absence of droplets, touching the outside of the cup itself would have no effect on his hands, since a *sheni le'tumah* cannot render hands that come in contact with it a *sheni* (see *Yadayim* 3:1,2).

2. Our explanation of this matter follows *Rav* and *Rashi*. See *Rabbeinu Yonah* (folio 38a s.v. אלו) for a somewhat different explanation of the concern.

הִלֵּל אוֹמְרִים: מוֹזְגִין אֶת הַכּוֹס, וְאַחַר כָּךְ
נוֹטְלִין לַיָּדָיִם.

[ג] **בֵּית** שַׁמַּאי אוֹמְרִים: מְקַנֵּחַ יָדָיו
בַּמַּפָּה, וּמַנִּיחָהּ עַל הַשֻּׁלְחָן.

ר' עובדיה מברטנורא

במשקים טמאים לא נטמא תוכו ולא ידיו ולא אוגנו, וסברי בית שמאי אסור להשתמש בכוס שאחוריו
טמאות אף על פי שלא נטמא תוכו, גזרה שמא ינתזו נצוצות מתוכו על אחורי הכוס ויקבלו המשקין
טומאה מחמת אחוריו ויטמאו את הידים. וכיון דאסור להשתמש בכלי שאחוריו טמאות, נוטלין לידיס
תחלה ואחר כך מוזגין את הכוס, כדי שלא יקבלו המשקים שאחורי הכלי טומאה מחמת ידים ונמלאו
אחורי הכלי טמאים מחמת אותן משקים ומשתמש בו באיסור. ובית הלל סברי אין אסור להשתמש
בכלי שאחוריו טמאות, הלכך מוזגין את הכוס תחלה ואחר כך נוטלין לידיס, שאם אתה
אומר נוטלין לידיס תחלה ואחר כך מוזגין את הכוס גזירה שמא יהיו אחורי הכוס טמאים, שמותר
להשתמש בכלי שאחוריו טמאים, ולא יהיו ידי נגובות יפה וגמלא אוכל בידים מסואבות, ואותן
משקין שנעשו תחלה יחזרו ויטמאו את הידים וגמלא אוכל בידים מסואבות: (ג) **מקנח ידיו במפה.**
מנטילת מים ראשונים, ומניחה על השלחן ומקנח בה ידו תמיד מזוהמת התבשיל, ולא יניחנה על

---

pours and thus incapable of transmitting *tumah* to the cup even if some
wine should splash (*Rav; Rashi*).

וּבֵית הִלֵּל אוֹמְרִים: מוֹזְגִין אֶת הַכּוֹס, וְאַחַר
כָּךְ נוֹטְלִין לַיָּדָיִם. — *But Beis Hillel say:
We pour the cup [first], and wash
[our] hands afterwards.*

Unlike Beis Shammai, Beis Hillel
permit the use of a cup whose exterior
is *tamei* and interior is *tahor*, as explained in our prefatory remarks.
Consequently, if a person using such a
cup first washes *netilas yadayim* and
then drinks from this cup of wine, it
raises the concern that the outside of
the cup may transmit *tumah* to the
water on his hands (which are wet
from washing *netilas yadayim*). This
would in turn transmit *tumah* to his
hands and thereby invalidate the previous washing. If he were to proceed
to eat bread on the basis of the washing performed prior to the pouring of
the cup, he would be eating with

hands that are *tamei*! This would de-
feat the purpose of the *netilas yadayim*, which was to remove the *tumah* from his hands. Beis Hillel
therefore rule that one should first
drink the cup of wine and then wash
netilas yadayim (*Rav; Rambam
Comm.* from *Gemara* 52a).

The concern of Beis Hillel that water
that remained on the hands from *netilas
yadayim* might contract *tumah* from the
outside of the cup, and thereby make his
hands *tamei*, would seem to exist even during the meal. How is it allayed by drinking
from the cup before washing *netilas yadayim*? *Tosafos* answer that since it is prohibited to eat bread with hands that were
not properly dried (see *Sotah* 4b), we are
not concerned that he will fail to dry his
hands properly before eating the bread.
Beis Hillel are therefore concerned only
that he will take hold of a cup while his
hands are still wet *before* the meal, when
they might contract *tumah* from the cup.
(*Tosafos* 52a s.v. גזירה).

The *Gemara* (52b) cites a Baraisa in

But Beis Hillel say: We pour the cup [first], and wash [our] hands afterwards.

3. Beis Shammai say: He wipes his hands with the cloth and [then] places it on the table.

YAD AVRAHAM

which Beis Hillel put forward yet another argument to Beis Shammai. Granted, they said, that you prohibit using a cup whose exterior surface is *tamei* during a meal, and you are concerned that pouring the wine before washing *netilas yadayim* might lead to the exterior of the cup becoming *tamei*, it is still better to pour the cup and then wash. For there is a rule that the meal should follow immediately after washing *netilas yadayim*, and pausing after *netilas yadayim* to pour the cup of wine would disrupt this immediacy. This should be of greater concern to you than the possibility of *tumah* resulting from splashing droplets.

3.

It was common for the towel used to dry the hands from *netilas yadayim* to also be used as a napkin during the meal. If this napkin was still damp, its moisture would be considered a liquid,[1] and would become *tamei* if touched by something *tamei*. Since liquids contaminated by *tumah* always become a *rishon* (as we saw in the previous mishnah), the liquid absorbed in the napkin would in turn contaminate the hands of the person, rendering them a *sheni* and requiring the person to repeat *netilas yadayim* (*Rav; Rashi*). The mishnah therefore considers where the damp napkin should be kept during the meal so as to avoid this problem.

בֵּית שַׁמַּאי אוֹמְרִים: מְקַנֵּחַ יָדָיו בַּמַּפָּה, וּמַנִּיחָהּ עַל הַשֻּׁלְחָן. — *Beis Shammai say: He wipes his hands with the cloth, and [then] places it on the table.*

The cloth one used to dry his hands from *netilas yadayim* should be placed on the table to be used for wiping one's hands during the meal (*Rav, Rashi*).

Beis Shammai hold that it is forbidden to eat on a table that is *tamei*, even if the table is only a *sheni le'tumah*, which cannot transfer *tumah* to foods that are *chullin*.[2] Hence, the table at which the person is eating is *tahor*. Thus, there is no concern that the damp napkin will contract *tumah* from the table. The napkin may therefore be placed on the table.

1. [The *Gemara* (25a,b) discusses in another context how damp something must be for the liquid absorbed in it to be considered a "liquid." The *Gemara* concludes that there is a Tannaic dispute whether it must be merely damp enough to dampen an object that touches it (טוֹפֵחַ), or whether it must be damp enough to make the object touching it wet enough to dampen yet another object (טוֹפֵחַ עַל מְנָת לְהַטְפִּיחַ). The same yardstick would presumably apply here as well (see *Rashi*).]

2. Although a *sheni* cannot transmit *tumah* to *chullin* to render it a *shelishi*, it can transmit *tumah* to *terumah* that comes in contact with it, rendering it *pasul* and subject to being burned (see prefatory remarks to mishnah 2). Beis Shammai prohibit using a *tamei* table for *chullin* out of concern that it may inadvertently be used for *terumah* as well.

וּבֵית הִלֵּל אוֹמְרִים: עַל הַכֶּסֶת.

--- ר' עובדיה מברטנורא ---

הכסת שהוא יושב בה, גזירה שמא יהיה הכסת ראשון לטומאה ויהיה משקה טופח במפה מחמת נגוב הידים, ואותו משקה כשנוגע בכסת נעשה ראשון, דלעולם המשקים נעשות תחלה, וחוזר ומטמא את הידים כשמקנח בה תמיד בתוך הסעודה. אבל בשלחן ליכא למגזר הכי, שאסור להשתמש בשלחן שהוא שני לטומאה. ובית הלל סברי מותר להשתמש בשלחן שהוא שני לטומאה, הלכך לא יניח המפה על השלחן, שמא יטמאו המשקים שבמפה מחמת השלחן ויחזרו ויטמאו את האוכלים, ואם יניחנה על הכסת אין לחוש כי אם שמא יטמאו ידיו, מוטב שיטמאו ידים שאין להם עיקר מן התורה, דהא נטילת ידים לחולין מן התורה, ולא יטמאו אוכלים שיש להם עיקר מן התורה, דראשון עושה שני בחולין מן התורה:

--- יד אברהם ---

Beis Shammai, however, prohibit placing the napkin on the cushion upon which the person is reclining. This is because Beis Shammai permit eating a meal while reclining on a cushion that is a *rishon* or a *sheni le'tumah*. If one were to place the damp napkin on such a cushion, the moisture in it would contract *tumah* from the cushion and would become a *rishon*, as explained in the preface to this mishnah. If the person were to then wipe his hands on this napkin during the meal, the moisture in the napkin, being a *rishon*, would render his hands a *sheni*, thereby invalidating the prior *netilas yadayim*. Beis Shammai therefore rule that the napkin should be placed on the table [which is certainly *tahor*] and not on the cushion [which might be *tamei*] (*Rav, Rashi* to 52b s.v. משקין).

Where the cushion is a *rishon le'tumah*, the hands can become *tamei* simply by touching it. Nonetheless, Beis Shammai permit eating while reclining on such a cushion because they maintain that a person will be careful to avoid touching the cushion with his hands and there is no need to legislate against using it (see *Tos. Yom Tov* s.v. ומניחה).[1] The napkin, however, is specifically intended for wiping one's hands. Accordingly, Beis Shammai promulgated precautionary legislation aimed at preventing the moisture in the napkin from becoming a *rishon le'tumah*. For if the moisture in the napkin were to become a *rishon*, it would, in turn, convey the *tumah* to the hands.

וּבֵית הִלֵּל אוֹמְרִים: עַל הַכֶּסֶת. — *But Beis Hillel say: On the cushion.*

Beis Hillel's view is the very opposite of Beis Shammai's. According to Beis Hillel, the cloth used to dry the hands should be placed on the cushions and *not* on the table.

Beis Hillel hold that it is permitted to eat *chullin* on a table that is a *sheni le'tumah* [for a *sheni* cannot create a *shlishi* in the case of *chullin*].[2] Consequently, if one were to place the damp napkin on the table, the moisture in the napkin would contract *tumah* from the table and become a *rishon le'tumah*. It could then potentially

1. They do not, however, permit using a cushion that is an *av hatumah*. Since an *av hatumah* Biblically conveys *tumah* to humans and utensils, Beis Shammai do not rely on the person to remember throughout the meal that the cushion is *tamei* and that he must avoid touching it with his hands (*Tos. Yom Tov* s.v. ומניחה).

2. Beis Hillel maintain that those who eat *terumah* are conscientious and will not inadvertently use a table that is *tamei* for *terumah* food. They therefore see no reason to decree against using for *chullin* a table that is a *sheni* (*Tos. Yom Tov* s.v ומניחה from *Gemara* 52b).

convey *tumah* to the food on the table. Beis Hillel therefore rule that the damp napkin should not be placed on the table, in case the table should be *tamei*. The napkin may, however, be placed on the cushion. Since food is not placed on the cushion, even if the cushion is *tamei* there is no concern that the damp napkin will transmit *tumah* to any food. Although if the cushion is *tamei*, *tumah* will be transmitted from the cushion to his hands through the moisture of the napkin, there is no Biblical source for *tumah* of hands. It is therefore better, in Beis Hillel's opinion, to place the napkin on a cushion and risk the hands contracting *tumah* than to place the napkin on a table and risk contaminating the food (*Rav*).

Under Biblical law, a person's hands are not a separate entity. Rather, they are a part of the person's entire body which, like the rest of the body, can contract *tumah* only from an *av hatumah* and not from a *rishon* (see prefatory remarks to mishnah 2). It is only under Rabbinic law that hands are treated as a separate entity that contracts *tumah* from a *rishon* and requires *netilas yadayim*.

Foods of *chullin*, however, do contract *tumah* under Biblical law from a *rishon* and are rendered a *sheni*. Therefore, although the actual *tumah* that will be transmitted from the table to the foods through the moisture in the damp napkin is only Rabbinic (due to the Rabbinic decrees rendering a liquid touched by a *sheni le'tumah, tamei* in the degree of *rishon*), Beis Hillel are still more concerned about the *tumah* of the foods than about the transmission of *tumah* to the person's hands (*Rav* from *Gemara* 52b).

4.

The following mishnah delineates the dispute between Beis Shammai and Beis Hillel regarding the Rabbinic requirement of *mayim acharonim* (literally, the final waters).

In addition to washing the hands prior to eating bread, the Rabbis instituted that one must also wash his hands after the meal and cleanse them before reciting *Bircas HaMazon*. The *Gemara* (*Berachos* 53b) links this requirement to the verse וְהִתְקַדִּשְׁתֶּם וִהְיִיתֶם קְדֹשִׁים, *You shall sanctify yourselves and you shall become holy* (*Leviticus* 11:44). The *Gemara* explains that the words *sanctify yourselves* refer to *mayim rishonim*, the first waters, i.e. the purification of our hands prior to eating bread. The words *and you shall become holy* refer to *mayim acharonim*, the cleansing of our dirtied hands after the meal, in preparation of the recitation of *Bircas HaMazon*.

The *Gemara* (*Chullin* 105a; *Eruvin* 17b) gives an additional reason for washing *mayim acharonim*. The Rabbis advised that salt should be eaten after a meal (*Berachos* 40a). Now, there is a certain type of salt, known as Sodomite salt, which is dangerous to the eyes. Should a person rub his eyes with this salt on his fingers, he might cause serious injury to them, even blindness. The Rabbis therefore made it obligatory to wash *mayim acharonim* to remove all traces of this salt so that one will not inadvertently injure his eye.[1]

---

1. Some justify the common practice of not washing *mayim acharonim* on the basis that Sodomite salt is not commonly found today or on the basis that it is no longer customary

בְּרָכוֹת [ד] **בֵּית** שַׁמַּאי אוֹמְרִים: מְכַבְּדִין אֶת הַבַּיִת,
וְאַחַר כָּךְ נוֹטְלִין לַיָּדָיִם. וּבֵית הִלֵּל
אוֹמְרִים: נוֹטְלִין לַיָּדַיִם וְאַחַר כָּךְ מְכַבְּדִין אֶת הַבָּיִת.

ר' עובדיה מברטנורא

(ד) בית שמאי אומרים מכבדין את הבית. מקום שאכלו שם מכבדים אותו משיורי אוכלים
שנתפררו עליו ואחר כך נוטלים לידים מים אחרונים, דפעמים שהשמש עם האחר ומניח הפירורים
שיש בהם כזית, ואם אתה אומר נוטלים לידים תחלה, נמצא אתה מפסיד את האוכלים, שמים
אחרונים נתזים עליהם ונמאסים. ובית הלל סברי אסור להשתמש בשמש עם הארץ, ושמא תלמיד
חכם אינו מניח פירורים שיש בהן כזית אלא מסיר אותם, ואם נתזים המים על גבי פירורים שאין

יד אברהם

בֵּית שַׁמַּאי אוֹמְרִים: מְכַבְּדִין אֶת הַבַּיִת,
וְאַחַר כָּךְ נוֹטְלִין לַיָּדָיִם. — *Beis Shammai
say: We [first] sweep the house and
afterwards we wash [our] hands.*

Beis Shammai hold that the area
where the meal was eaten must be
cleared of leftover food prior to washing *mayim acharonim* (*Rav*). [The
word בַּיִת, which literally means *house*,
is often used to refer to a room (see
Gemara 17b; mishnah 7:5).] If they ate
while reclining on the floor, the floor
must be swept. If they ate while seated
at a table, the leftover food must be
cleaned off the table (*Rashi* 51b s.v.
מכבדין). Only afterwards may they begin washing *mayim acharonim*.

The reason for this is that it is forbidden to destroy pieces of food that
are the size of an olive or larger. Beis
Shammai are concerned that if the
floor is not swept until after washing

mayim acharonim, some of that water
might splash on olive-sized pieces of
bread that had fallen, which would
render them repulsive (*Rav*).[1] Although it is the responsibility of the
waiter to pick up large pieces of food
that fall during the meal and put them
away (*Rabbeinu Aharon HaLevi* to
52b s.v. בש״א), the *Gemara* (52b) explains that we are concerned that the
waiter may be an unlearned person
(עַם הָאָרֶץ) who may be unaware of the
prohibition to destroy olive-sized
pieces. If the master of the house is not
required to clean up prior to washing
mayim acharonim, these pieces will
be destroyed.

וּבֵית הִלֵּל אוֹמְרִים: נוֹטְלִין לַיָּדַיִם, וְאַחַר כָּךְ
מְכַבְּדִין אֶת הַבָּיִת. — *But Beis Hillel say:
We [first] wash [our] hands, and afterwards we clean the house.*

Beis Hillel hold that it is forbidden

to dip one's fingers into salt after the meal (*Tosafos* 53b s.v. והייתם). Others maintain that
although Sodomite salt is not commonly found today, there is nevertheless the danger of
using a different salt with similar hazardous qualities (*Rambam, Hil. Berachos* 6:3, cited by
Beis Yosef 181).

Although many rely on the lenient view, the *Gra* (181:12), *Magen Avraham* (181:10),
Maharshal (*Yam Shel Shlomo, Chullin* 8:10), and *Birkei Yosef* (181:7) adopt the more strin-
gent view and insist that one must wash *mayim acharonim* after the meal. See *Mishnah
Berurah* 181:1,22,23.

1. There is no risk that the water will be poured directly onto the food, since the water from
mayim acharonim is collected in a bowl. However, there is still a risk that water might spray
onto the food (*Tos. Anshei Shem*).

8
4

4. **B**eis Shammai say: We [first] sweep the house, and afterwards we wash [our] hands. But Beis Hillel say: We [first] wash [our] hands, and afterwards we clean the house.

to use an unlearned person as a waiter.[1] Since the waiter is a Torah scholar, he knows that he must remove the olive-sized crumbs before *mayim acharonim* is begun and place them where they will not be ruined. As for the smaller crumbs, there is no concern that the *mayim acharonim* may splatter on them for they may even be deliberately destroyed. This being the case, there is no reason to postpone the washing until after the sweeping. Accordingly, Beis Hillel rule that "we first wash our hands and clean the house afterwards" (*Rav, Rashi, Rambam Comm.* based on *Gem.* 52b).

Beis Hillel do not mean that one *must* wash *mayim acharonim* before sweeping the eating area, but only that one *may* do so (*Shenos Eliyahu*). Nor do Beis Hillel mean that the eating area must be swept clean immediately after washing *mayim acharonim*. Their point is only that the washing can precede the sweeping. The washing of *mayim acharonim* can then immediately be followed by the recitation of the *Bircas HaMazon*, with the final sweeping being done afterwards (*Pnei*

Yehoshua to 52b s.v. בגמרא).[2]

The preceding interpretation understands the concern of Beis Shammai and Beis Hillel as how to prevent *mayim acharonim* water from splattering and ruining olive-sized crumbs. Others, however, explain the concern to be whether an unlearned waiter can be relied upon to remove large crumbs. If washing *mayim acharonim* is permitted before the waiter sweeps the eating area, there is the possibility of the master of the household reciting *Bircas HaMazon* and leaving before the waiter removes the olive-sized crumbs. Free of his master's surveillance, the waiter might not bother to collect these pieces, and they will thus be left around, only to be trodden upon and disgraced. By insisting that the house be swept before washing *mayim acharonim*, Beis Shammai ensures that the servant's cleaning will be supervised. Beis Hillel do not share this concern because in their opinion one may not use an unlearned waiter, and a learned one may be relied upon to remove and properly store olive-sized crumbs (see *Rashba* 52b s.v. מותר, *Meiri* ibid. s.v. המשנה הרביעית).

The *Gemara* (52b) rules that in all the cases mentioned in this chapter the halachah follows the view of Beis Hillel, except in this case, where the view

1. *Meiri* states that an unlearned person in this context is one who is not knowledgeable of the laws of meals.

2. Although it is permitted to destroy pieces of food smaller than an olive, it is not permitted to step on them, as stepping on food is a greater disgrace of the food than destroying it. Indeed, the *Gemara* states in *Chullin* (105b) that one who steps on crumbs brings poverty upon himself. It is for this reason that, although one removed the pieces that are an olive size or more prior to *mayim acharonim*, he must nevertheless sweep up the remaining pieces after *mayim acharonim* (as ruled by Beis Hillel in the mishnah). For although we are not concerned about the smaller pieces being rendered repulsive by the *mayim acharonim*, we are concerned that they not be stepped upon (*Tosafos*, according to *Magen Avraham* 180:3; cf. *Beis Yosef* and *Shulchan Aruch, Orach Chaim* 180:4).

—————————— **ר' עובדיה מברטנורא** ——————————

בהם כזית אין בכך כלום, דפירורים שאין בהם כזית מותר לאבדן ביד. והלכה כבית שמאי בזה, שמותר להשתמש בשמש עם הארץ: **(ה) נֵר וּמָזוֹן.** מי שאכל בשבת במנחה ומשכה לו ועדיין לא גמר סעודתו ואין לו יין אלא שיעור [כוס] אחד, בית שמאי אומרים נר ומזון בשמים והבדלה. דכולי עלמא הבדלה בסוף, דאפוקי יומא מחחרינן ליה כי היכי דלא ליהוי עליה כמשאוי. לא נחלקו אלא על הנר ועל הבשמים, דבית שמאי אומרים נר ומזון ואחר כך בשמים, ובית הלל אומרים נר ובשמים כי הדדי, דברכות שאנו יכולים לעשותם דלא מיחזי כמשאוי כגון נר ובשמים מקדמין להו לברכת המזון:

יד אברהם

of Beis Shammai prevails (Rav, Tos. Yom Tov). We are therefore permitted to use a waiter who is unlearned and we must therefore sweep up the left-overs prior to washing *mayim acharonim*. See *Shulchan Aruch, Orach Chaim* 180:3 with *Mishnah Berurah* §9.

5.

Generally, when one concludes the last Sabbath meal (סְעוּדָה שְׁלִישִׁית), he recites the *Bircas HaMazon* over a cup of wine and later uses a different cup of wine for the recitation of the *Havdalah* blessing. Since he has two available cups of wine, it is not proper to "bundle mitzvos together" and recite *Bircas HaMazon* and *Havdalah* over the same cup (*Ravad, Hil. Shabbos* 29:12 cited by *Tos. Anshei Shem*).[1] However, one who has only one cup of wine recites the *Bircas HaMazon* and *Havdalah* over the single cup of wine. The blessings over fragrant spices (*besamim*) and the flame, generally recited over the cup of wine together with the *Havdalah* blessing (see *Pesachim* 54a), are also recited over this cup of wine. Thus, four blessings are recited over a single cup of wine. The following mishnah delineates the order in which these blessings are said.

בֵּית שַׁמַּאי אוֹמְרִים: נֵר, וּמָזוֹן, וּבְשָׂמִים, וְהַבְדָּלָה. — *Beis Shammai say: [The blessing over] the flame [is first, followed by] Bircas HaMazon, [the blessing over] fragrant spices, and [then] Havdalah.*

The mishnah deals with a case where one began his third Sabbath meal near the end of the Sabbath but did not complete his meal until after nightfall, and he has only one cup of wine available for the recitation of both *Bircas HaMazon* and *Havdalah*

(*Rav; Rambam Comm.; Rabbeinu Nissim Gaon* cited by *Rabbeinu Yonah*; see also *Yerushalmi* cited by *Rif*). Beis Shammai and Beis Hillel dispute the proper sequence for reciting the four blessings.

Two versions of this dispute are presented in the *Gemara*, one by R' Yehudah (52a) and one by R' Meir (52b). The *Gemara* establishes that the version of the dispute recorded in our mishnah follows R' Meir (*Tos. Yom Tov* from *Gemara* 52b). According to

1. *Rambam, Hil. Shabbos* 29:12, however, maintains that both *Bircas HaMazon* and *Havdalah* may always be recited over one cup of wine, even if two cups are available.

5. **B**eis Shammai say: [The blessing over] the
flame [is first, followed by] *Bircas HaMazon*,
[the blessing over] fragrant spices, and [then]

YAD AVRAHAM

this version, Beis Shammai and Beis Hillel agree that the blessing over the flame is recited first and the *Havdalah* last. The dispute concerns *Bircas HaMazon* and the blessing over fragrant spices. Beis Shammai maintain that *Bircas HaMazon* is recited before the blessing over fragrant spices, whereas Beis Hillel rule that the blessing over fragrant spices is recited before *Bircas HaMazon*.

R' Yehudah disputes this version of the dispute. According to his version, there is no disagreement between Beis Shammai and Beis Hillel regarding *Bircas HaMazon* and *Havdalah*. Both agree that *Bircas HaMazon* is recited first, and *Havdalah* last. They disagree only concerning the sequence of the blessings over the flame and fragrant spices. Since our mishnah follows the view of R' Meir, we will explain the mishnah according to his view, and explain R' Yehudah's view at the end of this section of the mishnah.

All agree that the blessing over the flame is recited first. This is because the benefit derived from its light is immediate, as soon as the lamp is brought in (*Tos. Yom Tov* from *Rabbeinu Yonah* folio 38b s.v. מתני׳ ב״ש אומרים נר). All agree that the *Havdalah* blessing is recited last. This is so that we may delay marking the departure of the Sabbath as long as possible, so that the Sabbath not appear as a burden upon us which we are eager to dispatch (*Gem.* 52a).

As for the remaining two benedictions, the *Bircas HaMazon* and the blessing over the fragrant spices, Beis Shammai argue that since the obligation to recite *Bircas HaMazon* is for food already eaten, it precedes the blessing over the spices, whose fragrance has not yet been smelled (*Tos. Yom Tov* from *Rabbeinu Yonah* ibid.; *Tif. Yis.* #12).

Our explanation of the mishnah as dealing with a case of someone who extended his final Sabbath meal beyond nightfall follows the commentaries of *Rav, Rambam,* et al. *Rabbeinu Yonah* (folio 38b s.v. ויש), however, cites others who reject this explanation. Instead, they argue that the mishnah is dealing with a case of one who *begins* his meal after the Sabbath has ended, but before he has recited *Havdalah*. Ordinarily, it is forbidden for one to eat anything after the Sabbath prior to reciting *Havdalah* (*Pesachim* 105a, 107a). However, where one has only a single cup of wine, if he recites *Havdalah* before eating he will not have wine over which to recite the *Bircas HaMazon* after his meal. In this particular case, the Rabbis permitted him to delay *Havdalah* until after he has eaten, and thereby make maximum use of his cup of wine. This explanation is also given by *Ravad* (quoted by *Rashba* to 52a s.v. הנכנס), *Rosh,* and seems to have been *Rashi's* understanding as well (see 51b s.v. נר ומזון).

Meiri (to 52b s.v. המשנה החמישית), however, challenges this interpretation. If we are discussing a case of one who has not yet eaten, then he has not yet become obligated to recite the *Bircas HaMazon*. With the arrival of nightfall and the departure of the Sabbath, however, he has already become obligated to recite the *Havdalah*. How then can the existing obligation of *Havdalah* be set aside to fulfill an obligation (to recite the *Bircas HaMazon* over a cup of wine) that has not yet materialized?

Despite this objection, *Tur* and *Shulchan Aruch* rule in accord with this latter explanation of the mishnah (*Orach Chaim* 296:3).

וְהַבְדָּלָה. וּבֵית הִלֵּל אוֹמְרִים: נֵר, וּבְשָׂמִים, וּמְזוֹן,
וְהַבְדָּלָה.
בֵּית שַׁמַּאי אוֹמְרִים: „שֶׁבָּרָא מְאוֹר הָאֵשׁ".
וּבֵית הִלֵּל אוֹמְרִים: „בּוֹרֵא מְאוֹרֵי הָאֵשׁ".

―――――――――― ר' עובדיה מברטנורא ――――――――――

בית שמאי אומרים שברא מאור האש. סברא דמשמע לשעבר, ולא בורא דמשמע
להבא. מאור האש ולא מאורי האש, דחדא נהורא איכא בנורא: **ובית הלל אומרים בורא.**
נמי משמע לשעבר: **מאורי האש.** שהרבה גוונים יש בשלהבת, אדומה לבנה וירקרוקת:

―――――――――――――――― יד אברהם ――――――――――――――――

וּבֵית הִלֵּל אוֹמְרִים: נֵר, וּבְשָׂמִים, וּמְזוֹן,
וְהַבְדָּלָה. — *But Beis Hillel say: [The
blessing over] the flame [is first, followed by the blessing over] fragrant
spices, Bircas HaMazon, and [then]
Havdalah.*

Beis Hillel argue that the blessing recited over fragrant spices should follow the blessing recited over the flame
(rather than *Bircas HaMazon*) because
they are both connected to the departure of the Sabbath (*Tos. Yom Tov
from Rabbeinu Yonah*). The blessing
over fire at the conclusion of the Sabbath was instituted as a remembrance
of the creation of fire after the first
Sabbath. At that time, God gave Adam
the instinctive understanding to rub
two stones together and bring forth
fire (*Pesachim 54a*). The reason for
smelling the fragrance of spices after
the Sabbath is to comfort ourselves
over the loss of the departing *neshamah yeseirah*, the additional Sabbath
soul that arrives and departs together
with the Sabbath (see *Beitzah 16a*).
Since the blessings recited over the
flame and fragrant spices are both connected to the departure of the Sabbath,
it makes sense for them to be recited
together and not be interrupted by the

Bircas HaMazon. And since unlike the
Havdalah, these two blessings do not
explicitly mention anything about the
departure of the Sabbath, reciting
them before *Bircas HaMazon* does not
demonstrate any eagerness to end the
Sabbath (*Rav*). Accordingly, Beis Hillel rule that the blessing over the fragrant spices should follow the blessing
over the flame and precede *Bircas
HaMazon*.

It emerges from our mishnah's version
of the dispute that both Beis Shammai and
Beis Hillel agree that the blessing over the
flame precedes the blessing over the fragrant spices. The accepted practice, however, is to recite the blessing over the fragrant spices first. This is because there is
another version of the dispute between Beis
Shammai and Beis Hillel, as mentioned
above. According to R' Yehudah, all agree
that *Bircas HaMazon* is the first of the
blessings, and *Havdalah* is the last. The
dispute concerns the order to be followed
for the blessings over the fragrant spices
and the flame. Beis Shammai say that the
blessing over the flame is recited first,
while Beis Hillel say the blessing over the
fragrant spices should be recited first. It is
Beis Hillel's opinion according to this version of the dispute that is accepted in practice (see *Tosafos* to 52b s.v. נהגו).[1]

The reason Beis Shammai maintain that

1. The mishnah makes no mention of the *Borei pri hagafen* blessing for the cup of wine.
This is because both Beis Shammai and Beis Hillel agree that this blessing must come after

8
5
Havdalah. But Beis Hillel say: [The blessing over] the flame [is first, followed by the blessing over] fragrant spices, *Bircas HaMazon*, and [then] *Havdalah.*

Beis Shammai say: [The blessing is worded] "... Who created the illumination of fire." But Beis Hillel say: [It is worded] "... Who creates the illuminations of fire."

the blessing over the flame should come first, according to this version, is that its benefit comes immediately, and therefore so too should its blessing. Beis Hillel maintain that the blessing over the fragrant spices should come first because smelling the spices honors the Sabbath [by demonstrating our need for consolation at its departure], whereas the flame commemorates a secondary matter, the creation of fire (*Ritva* 52b).

The mishnah moves on to consider the proper wording of the blessing over the flame.

בֵּית שַׁמַּאי אוֹמְרִים: ,,שֶׁבָּרָא מְאוֹר הָאֵשׁ."
— *Beis Shammai say: [The blessing is worded:]"... Who created the illumination of the fire."*

Beis Shammai say that the text of the blessing over the flame reads, "Blessed are You, Hashem, our God, King of the universe, Who created the illumination of fire." In this formulation the verb בָּרָא, *created*, is in the past tense. Beis Shammai consider this more appropriate because the blessing is praising Hashem for having created fire in the past, on the first night after the Sabbath (*Rashi* 52b). The illumination of fire is referred to in the singular [מְאוֹר] because there is but one light in fire (*Rav* from *Gemara* 52b).

— וּבֵית הִלֵּל אוֹמְרִים: ,,בּוֹרֵא מְאוֹרֵי הָאֵשׁ."
But Beis Hillel say: [It is worded:]"... Who creates the illuminations of fire."

Beis Hillel's version of this blessing differs from Beis Shammai's in two ways. It uses the present tense of the verb *create*, בּוֹרֵא, *Who creates*, and it also speaks of the light of the flame in the plural, מְאוֹרֵי הָאֵשׁ, *the illuminations of fire* (*Rav*). Beis Hillel agree that the blessing for the flame refers to the original creation of fire. However, since the word בּוֹרֵא, *creates*, can be understood to include past, present and future, it is an acceptable wording for this blessing (*Rav* from *Gemara* 52b). Beis Hillel prefer it over the past-tense form because we find several Scriptural verses that describe God's act of creation using this form of the word [בּוֹרֵא חֹשֶׁךְ, *Who creates darkness* (Isaiah 45:7), בֹּרֵא רוּחַ, *Who creates winds* (Amos 4:13), בּוֹרֵא הַשָּׁמַיִם, *Who created the heavens* (Isaiah 42:5)] (*Tos. Yom Tov* from *Tosafos* to 52b s.v. בברא).

Bircas HaMazon, because *Bircas HaMazon* would surely constitute an interruption between the *Borei pri hagafen* and the drinking of the wine.

Accordingly, the blessing on the wine must be linked to the *Havdalah* blessing said at the end, and whether it comes before or after that blessing has already been disputed by Beis Shammai and Beis Hillel in the first mishnah of this chapter (*Tos. Anshei Shem* s.v. נר ומזון; cf. *Shenos Eliyahu* to mishnah 8:8 from *Yerushalmi*).

[ו] אֵין מְבָרְכִין לֹא עַל הַנֵּר וְלֹא עַל הַבְּשָׂמִים שֶׁל עוֹבְדֵי כּוֹכָבִים,

(ו) לֹא עַל הַנֵּר וְלֹא עַל הַבְּשָׂמִים שֶׁל עוֹבְדֵי כּוֹכָבִים. נר משום דלא שבת, שהעובד כוכבים עשה מלאכה לאורו, וקיימא לן אור שלא שבת אין מברכין עליו הואיל ונעבדה בו עבירה. ובשמים של עובדי כוכבים, בבשמים שהם במסבה שעובדי כוכבים מוסבים בה לסעודה מיירי. והא דתנן בסיפא ולא על הנר ולא על הבשמים של עבודת כוכבים, מה טעם קאמר, מה טעם אין מברכין על בשמים של עובדי כוכבים לפי שסתם מסבת עובדי כוכבים לעבודת כוכבים ואין מברכין על בשמים של עבודת כוכבים:

יד אברהם

The *Gemara* (52b) thus concludes that although Beis Shammai use the word שֶׁבָּרָא, *Who created*, and Beis Hillel use בּוֹרֵא, *Who creates*, this is not truly a subject of dispute, inasmuch as both agree that either word may be used to refer to the original creation of fire. Each school simply selected the phrase it was accustomed to using (*Tos. HaRosh* to 52b s.v. בברא). They do, however, disagree regarding the words מְאוֹר and מְאוֹרֵי. Beis Shammai hold that there is but one light in a flame and therefore the singular form of מְאוֹר הָאֵשׁ, *the illumination of fire*, should be used in the text of the blessing. Beis Hillel, however, contend that since there are several colors that appear in a flame — red, white, blue-green — it is more appropriate to refer to the light cast by a flame in the plural, מְאוֹרֵי הָאֵשׁ, *the illuminations of fire* (*Rav* from *Gem.* 52b).

The *Gemara's* conclusion seems problematic. First, how can the *Gemara* say that Beis Shammai and Beis Hillel do not disagree concerning בָּרָא and בּוֹרֵא, when the mishnah explicitly states that Beis Sham-

mai hold that one must say בָּרָא, *Who created*, and Beis Hillel say that one must say בּוֹרֵא, *Who creates*? Secondly, how can Beis Shammai say that there is only one color in flame — anyone can see with his own eyes that this is not the case!

Shenos Eliyahu explains that there are two aspects of fire upon which it is possible to make a blessing — the fire that we are able to create at any time, and the original, first source of fire. While it is true that a flame has many colors, the original source of fire had but one. Thus, he explains that Beis Shammai and Beis Hillel dispute to which aspect of the fire the blessing refers. According to Beis Shammai, we thank Hashem for the original creation of fire; therefore, we say מְאוֹר, in the singular, for it had but a single color. We therefore also say בָּרָא (past tense), because the original creation took place in the past. Beis Hillel, however, maintain that we bless Hashem for the fire that we are able to create *now*, whose source is that original fire. Thus, we say מְאוֹרֵי, in the plural, for the light of *our* flames indeed burns in multiple colors. We also say בּוֹרֵא (present tense), for all agree that the word בּוֹרֵא connotes both past and present creation. [See *Boaz* §3 for a similar explanation.]

6.

The following mishnah lists a series of rulings regarding the blessings recited over the flame and fragrant spices of the *Havdalah* service.

אֵין מְבָרְכִין לֹא עַל הַנֵּר וְלֹא עַל הַבְּשָׂמִים שֶׁל עוֹבְדֵי כּוֹכָבִים, — *We do not recite* the blessings over the flame or the fragrant spices of idolaters,

The blessing recited over the flame during the *Havdalah* service may not be recited over a fire that did not rest [from prohibited work] on the Sabbath, because a transgression has been performed with it (*Rav*). Since an idolater surely used its light to perform some type of work prohibited for Jews on the Sabbath, we may not recite the blessing over his flame (*Rav, Rashi* to 52b s.v. משום). [Therefore, even if the idolater lit the lamp before the start of the Sabbath, and the lamp burned until after the Sabbath had departed, the blessing over fire may not be recited over the flame of his lamp.] One who recited the *Borei me'orei ha'eish* blessing over an idolater's flame did not fulfill his obligation and must repeat the blessing over a different flame (*Rashba* cited by *Beis Yosef Orach Chaim* 297 [end of s.v. ואין מברכין] and *Meleches Shlomo*).

Others explain that the reason a blessing may not be recited over a flame lit by an idolater is because the idolater is assumed to have kindled, or at least adjusted, the flame on the Sabbath [thereby performing a forbidden labor with the flame itself] (*Tos. Yom Tov* from *Rabbeinu Yonah*, folio 38b s.v. מתני׳ אין מברכין). Although the idolater has done nothing wrong by

lighting the flame, for he is not bound by the Sabbath laws, his kindling of the flame is referred to as having been done impermissibly because had it been kindled by a Jew, it would have constituted a transgression.[1]

The fragrant spices of idolaters referred to by the mishnah are those used by them at a banquet. Such gatherings were generally celebrated for idolatrous purposes. Since it is forbidden to derive any pleasure from fragrant spices used for idols (see further in this mishnah), no blessing may be recited over them (*Rav* from *Gemara* 52b).[2]

Accordingly, though the mishnah groups both rulings together, the reasons behind them differ. A blessing may not be recited over the flame of an idolater because it did not rest from prohibited work on the Sabbath. A blessing may not be recited over the fragrant spices used at a banquet of idolaters because they presumably served idolatrous purposes. *Rambam* (*Hil. Shabbos* 29:25), however, prohibits reciting a blessing over the flame of an idolater for the same reason as it is prohibited over their spices, because the flame too was used at a banquet serving idolatrous purposes (see *Maggid Mishneh* there).

1. One may, however, recite a blessing over a flame that was kindled on the Sabbath by a Jew for someone dangerously ill [or by a gentile for someone whose illness is not life threatening (*Magen Avraham* 298:7, *Taz* 298:5)]. Although the fire did not rest, it nevertheless *rested from prohibited work*, since it was permitted to light the flame for these purposes (*Tos. Anshei Shem* from *Gemara* 53a; *Shulchan Aruch, Orach Chaim* 298:5).

2. It should emerge from this that if the idolater's spices were not from a banquet, one would be permitted to recite the blessing over them. For a discussion of this point, see *Taz, Orach Chaim* 298:5 and *Mishnah Berurah* 297:5.

וְלֹא עַל הַנֵּר וְלֹא עַל הַבְּשָׂמִים שֶׁל מֵתִים, וְלֹא
עַל הַנֵּר וְלֹא עַל הַבְּשָׂמִים שֶׁלִּפְנֵי עֲבוֹדָה זָרָה.
אֵין מְבָרְכִין עַל הַנֵּר עַד שֶׁיֵּאוֹתוּ לְאוֹרוֹ.

[ז] **מִי** שֶׁאָכַל, וְשָׁכַח וְלֹא בֵרַךְ, בֵּית שַׁמַּאי

ר' עובדיה מברטנורא

ולא על הנר של מתים. דלא אתעביד לאורה אלא לכבוד בעלמא: **ולא על בשמים של
מתים.** דלעטורי ריחא עבידי: **ולא על נר ובשמים.** דעבודת כוכבים, לפי שאסורין בהנאה:
עד שיאותו לאורו. שיהנו מאורו, ולא שיהנו ממש אלא שקרוב לו כל כך שיוכל ליהנות אם ירצה:

יד אברהם

וְלֹא עַל הַנֵּר וְלֹא עַל הַבְּשָׂמִים שֶׁלִּפְנֵי עֲבוֹדָה
זָרָה. — *nor over the flame or fragrant
spices [placed] before an idol.*

It is forbidden to derive any benefit
from items that have been used in the
service of idols. This is learned from the
verse (*Deuteronomy* 13:18): וְלֹא יִדְבַּק
בְּיָדְךָ מְאוּמָה מִן הַחֵרֶם, *no part of the
banned property may adhere to your
hand* (*Rambam Comm.*). It is therefore
prohibited to make use of lights illumi-
nating the area around an idol, or to
smell the fragrance of spices placed
near one. Accordingly, it is also prohibited to recite blessings over them (*Rav*).

This statement of the mishnah warrants clarification. The first ruling of
the mishnah already taught that fragrant spices used at a banquet of idolaters are excluded from the blessing,
due to probable idolatrous association
[see above s.v. אין מברכין]. What then is
this last ruling of the mishnah adding?
It too excludes fragrant spices that
were used in the service of an idol from
the blessing! The *Gemara* (52b) explains that this latter statement must
be understood as an explanation of the
reason for the first ruling. The mishnah is in effect saying that the earlier
ruling that spices from a dinner gathering of idolaters may not be used for

וְלֹא עַל הַנֵּר וְלֹא עַל הַבְּשָׂמִים שֶׁל מֵתִים,
— *nor over the flame or fragrant spices
of the dead,*

We do not recite the blessing over a
lamp that is placed near a corpse because it is not placed there for illumination but to honor the deceased (*Rav
from Gem.* 53a). The *Borei me'orei
ha'eish* blessing is recited only over fire
that is used for illumination. Similarly,
the blessing for the fragrant spices is
recited only over spices whose fragrance is designated for smelling. We
therefore do not recite a blessing over
fragrant spices that were placed near a
corpse, because they were placed there
to mask the odor of the decaying corpse
(*Rav*) rather than to be smelled for their
fragrance (*Tos. Yom Tov* from *Rashi*).

If the lamp serves the twofold purpose of
both honoring the deceased and illuminat-
ing the funeral procession, some authorities
maintain that a blessing may be recited over
its flame, even though the deceased was a
distinguished person for whom lights
would be lit during the day (*Ritva* 53a).
Others maintain that a blessing is not recited over a lamp lit for a deceased for
whom lights would be lit during the day,
even when the lamp serves the twofold purpose of honoring the deceased and illumi-
nating the funeral (see *Rabbeinu Yonah* folio 39b, and *Beur Halachah* to 298:11 נר ד"ה
בית הכנסת).

8
7
nor over the flame or fragrant spices of the dead, nor over the flame or fragrant spices [placed] before an idol.

We do not recite the blessing over the flame until benefit is derived from its light.

7. One who ate, and forgot and did not recite *Bircas HaMazon*, Beis Shammai say:

YAD AVRAHAM

the blessing is *because* "we do not recite blessings over the fragrant spices placed before an idol" (*Rav*).

The *Gemara* (*Beitzah* 39a) states that since a flame is an intangible object, one may derive benefit from it even if it was lit for idolatry. Benefit is prohibited from a flame only when it emanates from a tangible object, such as a coal, that has become forbidden by being lit for idolatry. Our mishnah prohibits reciting a blessing over a flame lit for an idol because it speaks of a flame emanating from a coal [or lamp] lit for that purpose (*Rosh, Beitzah* 5:10, cited by *Tos. R' Akiva Eiger*). If, however, one lit another lamp from the flame of that coal, the flame emanating from that lamp would be permitted for benefit, and one could therefore recite the blessing over it (*Tif. Yis.*; see *Mishnah Berurah* 298:19).

אֵין מְבָרְכִין עַל הַנֵּר עַד שֶׁיֵּאוֹתוּ לְאוֹרוֹ — *We do not recite the blessing over the flame until benefit is derived from its light.*

The intent of the mishnah is that we do not recite a blessing over a *Havdalah* flame unless its illumination is suitable for use. That is, that one must stand close enough to the light to be *able* to derive benefit from its illumination, if he wishes. One need not actually derive benefit from its light, as a simple reading of the mishnah would suggest (*Rav; Hasagos HaRavad* to *Baal HaMaor* folio 39b). Others maintain that to recite the blessing over the flame, one must actually benefit from its illumination, at least to the extent of distinguishing between two similar coins (*Baal HaMaor* folio 39b).

The custom is to derive benefit from the *Havdalah* flame by looking at one's fingernails and distinguishing between the nail and the surrounding flesh, for this is akin to distinguishing between two coins (*Tos. HaRosh*). Fingernails were chosen because they are part of the body and are thus always readily available. Furthermore, fingernails constantly grow, and growth is in itself a sign of blessing (*Rabbeinu Yonah* folio 39a s.v. ולא).

7.

Bircas HaMazon must be recited in the place where one ate his meal. The following mishnah cites a dispute between Beis Shammai and Beis Hillel regarding the law for one who forgot to recite *Bircas HaMazon* at the site of his meal, and remembered after he had gone somewhere else.

מִי שֶׁאָכַל, וְשָׁכַח וְלֹא בֵרַךְ, — *One who ate, and forgot and did not recite Bircas HaMazon,*

That is, if he ate a meal in a particular place, and then forgot to recite *Bircas HaMazon*. He realized his omission only after leaving the place where he had eaten.

אוֹמְרִים: יַחֲזוֹר לִמְקוֹמוֹ וִיבָרֵךְ. וּבֵית הַלֵּל
אוֹמְרִים: יְבָרֵךְ בַּמָּקוֹם שֶׁנִּזְכָּר. עַד אֵימָתַי הוּא
מְבָרֵךְ? עַד כְּדֵי שֶׁיִּתְעַכֵּל הַמָּזוֹן שֶׁבְּמֵעָיו.

━━━━━ ר' עוֹבַדְיָה מִבַּרְטֶנוּרָא ━━━━━

(ז) **שיתעכל המזון שבמעיו.** כל זמן שאינו רעב מחמת אותה האכילה הוא שלא נתעכל
המזון. ודוקא בשכח אמרי בית הלל דאינו חוזר, אבל במזיד דברי הכל יחזור למקומו ויברך:

━━━━━━━━━━ **יד אברהם** ━━━━━━━━━━

The dispute between Beis Shammai and Beis Hillel that follows pertains only to a case where he *forgot* to recite *Bircas HaMazon* before leaving the place where he ate. However, if he intentionally left the place without reciting *Bircas HaMazon*, all agree that he must return to that place to recite *Bircas HaMazon* (*Rav* from *Gem.* 53b).

The *Rishonim* dispute whether the requirement of reciting an after-blessing in the place where one ate is unique to *Bircas HaMazon* or not. *Rashba* (below, 53b ד"ה מחלוקת) and *Hagahos Maimoniyos* (*Hil. Berachos* 4:1) maintain that it is unique to *Bircas HaMazon*. *Tosafos* (to *Pesachim* 101b ד"ה אלא) and *Rosh* (*Pesachim* 10:6; see *Madanei Yom Tov* to *Rosh* here, 8:5), however, maintain that the rule taught below applies to any dish that requires an *Al ha'michyah* blessing, namely, one made of any of the five species of grain. *Rashbam* (to *Pesachim* 101b) and *Rambam* (*Hil. Berachos* 4:1) go even further and state that it applies whenever the one-blessing abridgment of the Three Blessings is recited. Thus, one who drank wine or ate any of the seven species of fruit for which the Land of Eretz Yisrael is praised must recite the after-blessing in the place where he ate. All agree, however, that one is not required to recite *Borei nefashos* in the place where he ate.

Mishnah Berurah 178:45 cites the opinion of the *Gra* that the halachah accords with *Tosafos* and the *Rosh*, that only *Bircas HaMazon* and *Al ha'michyah* must be recited in the place where one ate.

— בֵּית שַׁמַּאי אוֹמְרִים: יַחֲזוֹר לִמְקוֹמוֹ וִיבָרֵךְ.
Beis Shammai say: He should return to his place and recite Bircas HaMazon.

Beis Shammai say that when one realizes that he forgot to recite *Bircas HaMazon*, he cannot recite it wherever he may happen to be. Rather, he must return to the place where he ate his meal and recite the *Bircas HaMazon* in that place.

However, if he failed to return and recited the *Bircas HaMazon* where he was, he has fulfilled his obligation (*Tur, Orach Chaim* 184, as explained by *Beis Yosef*; see *Rama* 184:1; cf. *Beur HaGra* and *Bach* loc. cit.).

— וּבֵית הַלֵּל אוֹמְרִים: יְבָרֵךְ בַּמָּקוֹם שֶׁנִּזְכָּר.
But Beis Hillel say: He may recite Bircas HaMazon in the place where he remembered.

Beis Hillel rule that one need not return to his original place of eating to recite the *Bircas HaMazon*. Rather, he may recite it wherever he is. They concede, however, that although one is not obligated to do so, it is admirable for him to return to the place and recite the *Bircas HaMazon* there (*Tosafos* to 52b s.v. בכוליה; *Rabbeinu Yonah* folio 40a s.v. חד).

There is a corollary to this dispute. As mentioned above, one who intentionally leaves the site of his meal without reciting *Bircas HaMazon* must, according to all opinions, return to that site to recite *Bircas HaMazon* (*Gemara* 53b). If he did not return, but recited *Bircas HaMazon* where he was,

8
7

He should return to his place and recite *Bircas HaMazon*. But Beis Hillel say: He may recite *Bircas HaMazon* in the place where he remembered. Until when can he recite *Bircas HaMazon*? Until the food in his stomach has been digested.

Beis Shammai and Beis Hillel differ as to whether he has fulfilled his obligation. Beis Shammai hold that he has not fulfilled his obligation, whereas Beis Hillel hold that although he is required to return to his original place of eating, if he did not do so, he had fulfilled his obligation (*Tur, Orach Chaim* 184, as explained by *Beis Yosef*; see *Shulchan Aruch, Orach Chaim* and *Rama* 184:1).

There is a dispute among the *Rishonim* whether the halachah follows Beis Shammai or Beis Hillel in this matter. A number of *Geonim* (*Rav Amram* cited by *Rosh*; *R' Shmuel bar Chofni*, cited by *Rabbeinu Yonah*) rule in favor of Beis Shammai's view. *Rambam* (*Hil. Berachos* 4:1), however, rules in accord with Beis Hillel. See *Shulchan Aruch* and *Rama, Orach Chaim* 184:1; and *Mishnah Berurah* there §5.

עַד אֵימָתַי הוּא מְבָרֵךְ? — *Until when can he recite Bircas HaMazon?*

For how long after a meal may one recite *Bircas HaMazon*?

The mishnah's question is relevant for both one who left a meal without reciting *Bircas HaMazon*, and for one who remains at the table long after he finishes eating without reciting *Bircas HaMazon* (*Halachos Gedolos* [Jerusalem: *Mekitzei Nirdamim*], vol. 1 p. 133; cf. *Rabbeinu Chananel* quoted by *Raavya, Berachos* sec. 142). The commandment to recite *Bircas HaMazon* is consequent upon eating and "being satiated" (*Deuteronomy* 8:10). Once the satiation generated by a meal has passed, *Bircas HaMazon* may no longer be recited (*R' Moshe Mi-*

Trani, Kiryas Sefer to *Hil. Berachos* Ch. 2).

עַד כְּדֵי שֶׁיִּתְעַכֵּל הַמָּזוֹן שֶׁבְּמֵעָיו. — *Until the food in his stomach has been digested.*

As long as one has not become hungry after eating a meal, the food of that meal is not considered digested (*Rav, Rambam Comm.* following the view of R' Yochanan in *Gem.* 53b). The first sensations of hunger mark the beginning of digestion (*Rabbeinu Yonah* folio 40a s.v. כל זמן; *Orach Chaim* 184:5). The mishnah does not mean until the food in his stomach is completely digested but only until digestion begins.[1]

The *Gemara* (53b) also cites the view of Reish Lakish, who distinguishes between large meals and small ones. He states that the time of digestion for one is "until a person no longer feels thirsty as a result of the food he ate," whereas the time of digestion for the other is "the time it takes to walk four *mil*" (seventy-two, ninety, or ninety-six minutes, depending on the different opinions). There is a disagreement between *Rashi* (to 53b s.v. אכילה מרובה) and *Tosafos* (s.v. באכילה) as to whether the time limit of "until a person is no longer thirsty" is longer or shorter than the time it takes to walk four *mil*. Accordingly, they differ over which time limit applies to which meal. Clearly, the time limit for reciting *Bircas HaMazon* after a large meal is the longer time limit. According to *Rashi*, the time limit for a large meal is the time that it takes to walk four *mil*. It follows, then, that the time limit after a small meal is until he is no longer thirsty, which is a shorter period. According to *Tosafos*, the

---

1. However, R' Yaacov Chagiz understands that the digestion referred to by the mishnah means complete digestion, (*Halachos Ketanos* I:145).

[ח] **בָּא** לָהֶם יַיִן לְאַחַר הַמָּזוֹן וְאֵין שָׁם
אֶלָּא אוֹתוֹ הַכּוֹס, בֵּית שַׁמַּאי
אוֹמְרִים: מְבָרֵךְ עַל הַיַּיִן וְאַחַר כָּךְ מְבָרֵךְ עַל
הַמָּזוֹן. וּבֵית הִלֵּל אוֹמְרִים: מְבָרֵךְ עַל הַמָּזוֹן
וְאַחַר כָּךְ מְבָרֵךְ עַל הַיַּיִן.

ר' עובדיה מברטנורא

(ח) **מברך על היין ואחר כך מברך על המזון.** שאין ברכת המזון טעונה כוס. ובית הלל
סברי ברכת המזון טעונה כוס:

יד אברהם

four-*mil* time limit that Reish Lakish gives is for a small meal. The time limit for a large meal is until the person is no longer thirsty which must therefore be a longer period.

Although the law follows R' Yochanan (*Rif* folio 40a, *Rosh* 8:5), there is a difference of opinion among the *Poskim* whether R' Yochanan disputes only the dependent-on-thirst time limit, or whether he also disputes the four-*mil* time limit (see *Magen Avraham* 184:9 and *Taz* 184:2.) Thus, according to *Rashi*, R' Yochanan disputes Reish Lak-

ish in regard to a small meal, but he may perhaps agree with him that after a large meal, the time limit for reciting *Bircas HaMazon* is the time it takes to walk four *mil*. According to *Tosafos*, R' Yochanan definitely disputes Reish Lakish in regard to a large meal, but he may perhaps agree with him in regard to a small meal that the time limit is four *mil*. See *Shulchan Aruch*, *Orach Chaim* 184:5, *Mishnah Berurah* 184:;18,20 and *Beur Halachah* ד"ה אם אינו יודע.

8.

There is a difference of opinion among the commentators as to what issue the following mishnah is addressing. According to *Rav*, the mishnah considers whether or not *Bircas HaMazon* must be recited over a cup of wine. *Rashba* advances a different approach. We will explain the mishnah according to *Rav* and then discuss *Rashba's* understanding of it.

בָּא לָהֶם יַיִן לְאַחַר הַמָּזוֹן, וְאֵין שָׁם אֶלָּא אוֹתוֹ הַכּוֹס, — *[If] wine was brought to them after the meal, and there is no other [wine there] but that cup,*

The mishnah is discussing a regular weekday meal (*Tos. Yom Tov* from *Rashi* to 52a s.v. בא), in which the participants did not have any wine to drink during the meal, and it was only after they finished eating [before they recited *Bircas HaMazon*] that a single cupful of wine was brought (*Rashi* to 52a s.v. אחר המזון).

Rif (folio 40a), *Baal HaMaor* (folio 39a s.v. הא) and others have a variant reading:

בָּא לָהֶם יַיִן בְּתוֹךְ הַמָּזוֹן, "[If] wine was brought to them *in the middle of* the meal," instead of לְאַחַר הַמָּזוֹן, "after the meal." The significance of this variant reading will be discussed below; see s.v. ובית הלל.

בֵּית שַׁמַּאי אוֹמְרִים: מְבָרֵךְ עַל הַיַּיִן, וְאַחַר כָּךְ מְבָרֵךְ עַל הַמָּזוֹן. — *Beis Shammai say: He [first] recites the blessing over the wine, and then recites Bircas HaMazon afterwards.*

I.e. one may drink the wine first and then recite *Bircas HaMazon* without a cup of wine. [Since he did not drink any wine during this meal, if he drinks wine now he is required to say a *Borei*

8
8

8. **[**If] wine was brought to them after the meal, and there is no other [wine] there but that cup, Beis Shammai say: He [first] recites the blessing over the wine, and then recites *Bircas HaMazon* afterwards. But Beis Hillel say: He [first] recites *Bircas HaMazon* for the food, and then recites the blessing over the wine afterwards.

pri hagafen blessing.] Hence, Beis Shammai refer to drinking the wine as "reciting the blessing over the wine." Beis Shammai are of the opinion that there is no requirement to recite *Bircas HaMazon* over a cup of wine (*Rav*). Accordingly, even though a cup of wine is available, it need not be saved for the recitation of *Bircas HaMazon*. The person may therefore drink the wine and then recite *Bircas HaMazon* without a cup of wine. Beis Shammai's ruling should thus be understood to mean, "He *may* [first] recite the blessing over the wine and then recite *Bircas HaMazon* afterwards" (*Tos. Yom Tov* from *Rashi* to *Rif*, folio 40a s.v. בית שמאי). Accordingly, the drinking of the wine is referred to by Beis Shammai as *reciting the blessing over the wine* (see above mishnah 6:5).

In mishnah 5 of this chapter we learned that if someone has but a single cup of wine at the conclusion of the Sabbath, he recites both *Havdalah* and *Bircas HaMazon* over it. Although Beis Shammai and Beis Hillel disagree over the order in which the various blessings are said, all agree that both *Havdalah* and *Bircas HaMazon* are said over that single cup of wine. This suggests that Beis Shammai *do* require *Bircas HaMazon* to be recited over a cup of wine, contrary to what we have just learned in this mishnah! One answer is that even if Beis Shammai do not require *Bircas HaMazon* to be recited over a cup of wine, they consider it com-

mendable to do so. Beis Shammai therefore prescribe a procedure to be used by a person who wishes to act commendably and has only one cup of wine to use for both *Bircas HaMazon* and *Havdalah* (*Rashba* to 52a s.v. תרי).

Another answer is given by *Tos. Yom Tov*. He notes that the Gemara (53a) concludes that there is a dispute of Tannaim as to whether Beis Shammai require a cup of wine for *Bircas HaMazon*. Accordingly, the contradiction between our mishnah and mishnah 5 may be explained as reflecting two different views of Beis Shammai's position.

וּבֵית הָלֵּל אוֹמְרִים: מְבָרֵךְ עַל הַמָּזוֹן וְאַחַר כָּךְ מְבָרֵךְ עַל הַיַּיִן. — *But Beis Hillel say: He [first] recites Bircas HaMazon for the food, and then recites the blessing over the wine afterwards.*

Beis Hillel hold that *Bircas HaMazon* must be recited over a cup of wine. Consequently, if a single cup of wine was brought just before *Bircas HaMazon*, it must be saved for the recitation and may not be drunk beforehand (*Rav, Rashi* to *Rif*, folio 40a s.v. בית שמאי, *Baal HaMaor*, folio 39a s.v. הא).

Alternatively, Beis Hillel agree that there is no *obligation* to recite *Bircas HaMazon* over a cup of wine. Nevertheless, it is desirable to do so, for then the *mitzvah* will be performed in a choice manner. However, one need not search for wine to use for *Bircas HaMazon* (*Ramban, Milchamos Hashem* folio 39a; see also *Meiri* to 52a

1. [We noted above that even Beis Shammai, who do not consider it an obligation to recite

──────── ר' עובדיה מברטנורא ────────

עונין אמן אחר ישראל המברך. ואף על פי שלא שמע הזכרת השם אלא סוף הברכה,
דמסתמא לשמים ברך: אלא אם כן שמע כל הברכה. שמא ברך להר גריזים:

יד אברהם

s.v. ולענין).[1] Some suggest that according to this approach, Beis Hillel may distinguish between a case in which wine was brought during the main course of the meal, and the case in which wine was brought after the meal just prior to *Bircas HaMazon* (see the textual variants cited above s.v. בָּא). In the latter case, Beis Hillel would say that since reciting *Bircas HaMazon* over wine is desirable, the cup of wine should not be drunk before *Bircas HaMazon*, but should be used for the recitation. In the former case, however, where the wine was brought during the meal, saving it for *Bircas HaMazon* rather than drinking it with the meal would not be required. Hence, in such a case, Beis Hillel would agree that one may drink the wine with the meal and need not save it for *Bircas HaMazon* (*Shitah* to 52a s.v. גבי מתניתין; see, however, *Milchamos Hashem* ibid.).

A different approach to our mishnah is advanced by *Rashba* (52a s.v. ולענין, and *Teshuvos* I:342 quoted by *Tos. R' Akiva* #50). The Torah (*Deuteronomy* 8:10) states: וְאָכַלְתָּ וְשָׂבָעְתָּ וּבֵרַכְתָּ, "*And you shall eat, and you shall be satisfied, and you shall bless* ... [i.e. recite *Bircas HaMazon*]." Beis Shammai understand that the word וְשָׂבָעְתָּ, *and you shall be satisfied*, is a reference to drinking. Hence, according to Beis Shammai, one is not Biblically required

to recite *Bircas HaMazon* unless he first quenches his thirst. It is this rule that Beis Shammai is teaching in our mishnah. One who had no wine during the meal, and then was brought wine before he had recited *Bircas HaMazon*, *must* drink the wine so that he may "be satisfied" and recite *Bircas HaMazon* on the Biblical level. He does not have the option of saving it for *Bircas HaMazon*, since quenching one's thirst is a precondition for reciting *Bircas HaMazon*, and the wine of *Bircas HaMazon* is not drunk until after *Bircas HaMazon* is recited (*Tos. R' Akiva* #50).

Beis Hillel dispute this understanding of וְשָׂבָעְתָּ and maintain that one may indeed recite *Bircas HaMazon* even without drinking during his meal. In addition, they hold that one is not required to recite *Bircas HaMazon* over a cup of wine. Consequently, if a cup of wine is brought before *Bircas HaMazon*, the person has the option to either drink the cup of wine before *Bircas HaMazon* [and recite *Bircas HaMazon* without wine] or, if he wishes, to recite *Bircas HaMazon* over the cup of wine. Thus, in contrast with Beis Shammai who say that the person *must* drink before reciting *Bircas*

Bircas HaMazon over a cup, agree that it is commendable to do so. Since according to this explanation Beis Hillel also agree that it is preferable, but not obligatory, to recite *Bircas HaMazon* over a cup, we must say that the dispute between Beis Shammai and Beis Hillel concerns the degree of preference attached to this practice. Beis Hillel maintain that it is not merely commendable but preferable to recite *Bircas HaMazon* over a cup. Therefore, they urge the person to save the cup of wine for this purpose. Beis Shammai, however, leave it to the person to do as he wishes (see *Milchamos Hashem* ibid.).]

8

8 One answers "Amen" after the blessing of an Israelite, but one does not answer "Amen" after the blessing of a Cuthean unless he hears the entire blessing.

HaMazon, Beis Hillel say that if he wants, he can recite *Bircas HaMazon* over the wine, and drink it afterwards. [Note that according to *Rashba's* approach, neither Beis Hillel nor Beis Shammai require *Bircas HaMazon* to be recited over a cup of wine.]

The Mishnah in *Eduyos* (Chapters 4-5) lists all the disputes in which Beis Shammai are more lenient than Beis Hillel. According to the approach of *Rav* to our mishnah, Beis Shammai do not require *Bircas HaMazon* to be recited over a cup of wine while Beis Hillel do. This would then seem to be a dispute in which Beis Shammai is more lenient than Beis Hillel; hence, it should be recorded in *Eduyos.* It is therefore curious that this dispute is not listed there. According to *Rashba's* approach, however, the dispute in our mishnah is that Beis Shammai require drinking as a precondition for reciting *Bircas HaMazon* whereas Beis Hillel do not. If so, then this is a typical dispute in which Beis Shammai is more stringent, and this accounts for its omission from the list of disputes in which Beis Shammai is more lenient (*Tos. R' Akiva #50*).

The next section of the mishnah discusses when it is appropriate to answer "Amen" after a blessing, and when it is not.

עוֹנִין אָמֵן אַחַר יִשְׂרָאֵל הַמְבָרֵךְ, — *One answers "Amen" after the blessing of an Israelite,*

One who hears the conclusion of a blessing is obligated to answer "Amen" (*Rambam, Hil. Berachos* 1:13; cf. *Tur Orach Chaim* 215 and see *Taz, Orach Chaim* 215:2). Even if he did not hear the first part of the blessing that mentions Hashem's Name, he must still respond "Amen" (*Rav, Rashi* to

51b s.v. עונין, from *Gem.* 53b). Therefore, if one heard *Borei pri hagafen* but did not hear *Baruch atah Hashem Elokeinu melech ha'olam,* he still answers "Amen." Although the listener did not hear the mention of Hashem's Name, we assume that Jews who recite blessings have the correct intentions, and direct their blessings to Hashem and not to some idol (*Rav*).

Others maintain that one does need to hear the mention of Hashem's name in order to respond with "Amen," even though he need not hear the entire blessing (*Rabbeinu Yonah,* folio 40a s.v. עונין אמן; *Rosh* 8:5). Therefore, if a person enters a room in time to hear the words *Hashem Elokeinu melech ha'olam borei pri hagafen,* he answers "Amen" even though he did not hear the beginning of the blessing.

One is required to answer "Amen" at the conclusion of the recitation of a blessing even if he is not himself obligated to make that blessing. Thus, for example, if Reuven, Shimon and Levi are together, and Reuven and Shimon want to drink wine and are hence both obligated to make a *Borei pri hagafen,* but Levi does not want to drink and is not obligated in the blessing, when Reuven makes the blessing in order to discharge both his obligation and Shimon's, both Shimon and Levi must respond "Amen." Shimon, however, even if he answers "Amen," cannot be exempted unless he hears the entire blessing from beginning to end.

וְאֵין עוֹנִין אָמֵן אַחַר הַכּוּתִי הַמְבָרֵךְ עַד שֶׁיִּשְׁמַע כָּל הַבְּרָכָה. — *but one does not answer "Amen" after the blessing of a Cuthean unless he hears the entire blessing.*

The Cutheans (see above mishnah

יד אברהם

7:1 s.v. והכותי), even before they were conclusively demonstrated to be idolaters, were suspected of worshiping an idol on Mt. Gerizim. Thus, if someone heard only the conclusion of a blessing recited by a Cuthean, he had no way of knowing whether the blessing was made to Hashem, or to a pagan deity on Mt. Gerizim. Accordingly, the mishnah teaches that when hearing a blessing recited by a Cuthean, one responds "Amen" only if he hears the entire blessing, and therefore knows that the blessing was made to Hashem (*Rav* from *Gem.* 53b).

According to the view of *Rabbeinu Yonah* cited above, that one never answers "Amen" to a fragment of a blessing unless he hears the name of Hashem, the mishnah means to teach that a Cuthean is suspected even of using the name Hashem with reference to his pagan deity. If, however, he recites the entire blessing according to its accepted text, then he is no longer suspected of intending it for his pagan deity. Therefore, if one hears a Cuthean utter an entire blessing, one should respond "Amen" (see *Rabbeinu Yonah* and *Meleches Shlomo*).

The mishnah has spoken of a Cuthean but not a gentile. *Rama* rules that one who hears a gentile's blessing says "Amen" to it provided he hears an entire blessing from him (see *Rama, Orach Chaim* 215:2 with *Mishnah Berurah*).

פרק תשיעי ﷽
Chapter Nine

The final chapter of the tractate lists various blessings formulated by the Rabbis to be recited on particular occasions.

[א] **הָרוֹאֶה** מָקוֹם שֶׁנַּעֲשׂוּ בוֹ נִסִּים לְיִשְׂרָאֵל, אוֹמֵר: "בָּרוּךְ שֶׁעָשָׂה נִסִּים לַאֲבוֹתֵינוּ בַּמָּקוֹם הַזֶּה".

— ר' עובדיה מברטנורא —

פרק תשיעי – הרואה. (א) הרואה מקום שנעשו בו ניסים. כגון מעברות ים סוף ונחלי ארנון ומעברות הירדן ואבן שישב עליה משה כשנצחו הסלום כשנעשה מלחמה בעמלק ודומיהן. ואניסא דרבים כגון הני דאמרינן מחייבי כולי עלמא לברוכי, אבל אניסא דיחיד כגון הרואה מקום שנעשה לו בו נס, איהו חייב לברוכי ברוך שעשה לי נס במקום הזה, ובנו ובן בנו חייבים לברך ברוך שעשה גם לאבותי במקום הזה. וכל הני ברכות דמתניתין בטו הזכרת שם

יד אברהם

1.

הָרוֹאֶה מָקוֹם שֶׁנַּעֲשׂוּ בוֹ נִסִּים לְיִשְׂרָאֵל, — *[If] one sees a place where miracles were performed on behalf of Israel,*

The mishnah refers to the sites of miracles that involved the entire nation of Israel [or a majority of the nation (*Rabbeinu Yonah* 43a s.v. אניסא דרבים; *Tif. Yis.* §1)]. Examples of such locations are the place where the Jews crossed the Red Sea [see *Exodus* 14:15-31]; where they traversed the canyons of Arnon during their subsequent travels in the Wilderness [see *Numbers* 21:15; for a description of the miracle which occurred at this site see *Rashi* ad loc., *Gem.* 54a-b]; where they crossed the Jordan river in miraculous fashion [see *Joshua* 3:15-4:19]; and the stone upon which Moses sat when the Jews did battle with Amalek [see *Exodus* 17:8-13] (*Rav, Rashi* and *Rambam Comm.*, from *Gem.* 54a). Upon seeing these places, one must recite a blessing thanking God for performing miracles, the text of which the mishnah cites presently (see *Gem.* ibid. for a list of other locations that warrant a blessing).

Magen Avraham (218:1) comments that a common characteristic of the aforementioned locations is that the sites themselves memorialize the miraculous occurrences that took place there. Observing the waters of the Red Sea or the waters of the Jordan River, for example, brings to mind the miraculous splitting of these waters. Thus, the Rabbis deemed it appropriate upon seeing these places to recite a blessing of thanksgiving for these miracles. However, the mere fact that a miracle occurred at a particular location does not warrant a blessing upon seeing that site. Thus, one would not recite a blessing, for example, upon seeing the environs of Jerusalem, although God performed a great miracle there in the times of King Hezekiah, when He destroyed the army of the Assyrian king Sannacherib (see *II Kings* Ch. 19), since the site itself does not evoke the memory of that miraculous event.

Some authorities maintain that, in the context of our mishnah, a miracle is defined as an act of Divine providence which *supersedes* the laws of nature. Others, however, include any unlikely occurrence (see *Beur Halachah* to 218:9). *Meiri* differentiates between the site of a miracle involving the entire nation and the site of a miracle involving individuals [for which there also exists a blessing obligation, as will be discussed in the comm. below s.v. בָּרוּךְ שֶׁעָשָׂה נִסִּים]. The former warrants a blessing only if the event was supernatural. In the case of the latter, a blessing is required even if the occurrence conformed to the laws of nature.

אוֹמֵר: "בָּרוּךְ שֶׁעָשָׂה נִסִּים לַאֲבוֹתֵינוּ בַּמָּקוֹם

1. [If] one sees a place where miracles were performed on behalf of Israel, he says: "Blessed ... Who performed miracles for our forefathers at this place."

הַזֶּה"." — *he says: "Blessed ... Who performed miracles for our forefathers at this place."*

The full text of the blessing is: "Blessed *are You, Hashem, our God, King of the universe,* Who performed miracles for our forefathers at this place." Similarly, all the blessings listed in this chapter include the phrase *are You, Hashem, our God, King of the universe.* Indeed, failure to include this phrase *invalidates* the blessing, for reference to the Name of God and to His universal sovereignty are essential components of any blessing [see *Gem.* 40b] (*Rav, Rambam Comm., Tosafos* to 54a s.v. הרואה, et al.; see *Yerushalmi* 9:1).[1]

Ravad (*Hasagos* to *Baal HaMaor* 44a of folios of *Rif,* §2; see also *Rashba* to 54a s.v. הרואה and to 49a s.v. ברוך) disputes the assertion that the blessings enumerated in this (and the following) mishnah require the mention of God's Name and reference to His sovereignty. *Ravad* argues that בִּרְכוֹת הָרְאִיָּה, *blessings made on things seen* (e.g. the site of a miracle), are not subject to this requirement, because they are blessings of praise and thanksgiving (see *Beis Yosef* 218 s.v. ומה שכתב רבינו) rather than set obligations (one is not *obligated* to seek out locations of miraculous events; the

blessing is incumbent on him only if he happens to come across these sites). According to *Ravad,* then, the mishnah's version of these blessings is complete.

The requirement to recite a blessing upon seeing the place where a miracle occurred is derived from the actions of Jethro. As related in Scripture (*Exodus* 18:10), Jethro declared, upon hearing Moses' account of God's miraculous deliverance of the Jews from the hands of the Egyptians: *Blessed is Hashem, Who has rescued you from the hands of Egypt and from the hand of Pharaoh, Who has rescued the people from under the hand of Egypt* (*Gem.* 54a).[2]

Jethro did not recite this blessing at the *site* of the miracles of the Exodus, in Egypt, but in the *Wilderness,* where he had gone to meet Moses (see ibid. v. 5). Nevertheless, his blessing serves as the source for the blessing obligation upon seeing the *location* of a miraculous event, for seeing the beneficiary of a miracle (in Jethro's case, Moses and the Jewish Nation) is tantamount to seeing the place where the miracle occurred (*Ritva* and *Shitah Mekubetzes* to 54a s.v. מנא הני מילי; see also *Meiri* ad loc. s.v. ובמשנה and s.v. כל; see *Rama* 218:6 for the halachic ramification of this explanation; see *Maharsha* ad loc. s.v. ברוך ה' for a different explanation).

1. According to *R' Nachshon Gaon* (cited in *Otzar HaGeonim*), the mishnah *intentionally* omits the middle segment of the blessings enumerated in this chapter, to prevent an inadvertent uttering of God's Name while studying these laws (see also *Magen Avraham* 215:5; cf. *Sheilas Yaavetz* I:81).

2. *Maharsha* (to 54a s.v. ברוך ה') points out that Jethro's blessing makes no apparent mention of God's sovereignty, which, according to most authorities, is an essential component of this blessing (see comm. above). *Maharsha* explains that mentioning God's rescue of the Jewish people from Egypt is the equivalent of mentioning His sovereignty, since the Exodus demonstrated God's omnipotence.

מָקוֹם שֶׁנֶּעֶקְרָה מִמֶּנּוּ עֲבוֹדַת כּוֹכָבִים, אוֹמֵר:
„בָּרוּךְ שֶׁעָקַר עֲבוֹדָה זָרָה מֵאַרְצֵנוּ".

ר' עובדיה מברטנורא

וּמַלְכוּת, דְּכֹל בְּרָכָה שֶׁאֵין בָּהּ הַזְכָּרַת הַשֵּׁם וּמַלְכוּת אֵינָהּ בְּרָכָה:

יד אברהם

This blessing is only recited if one has not seen the site of the miracle within the past thirty days (*Tosafos* to 54a s.v. הרואה; *Shulchan Aruch* 218:3). Similarly, the other blessings listed in this chapter for particular landmarks [e.g. places from which idolatry was uprooted (mishnah below), mountains, rivers (mishnah 2)] are recited only if one has not seen them within the past thirty days (*Rosh* §1; *Meiri* to 58b s.v. ועל הזוועות; *Mishnah Berurah* 228:2; see comm. to next mishnah s.v. בִּזְמַן שֶׁרוֹאֶה).[1]

According to some, a blessing is obligatory only the first time one sees the site of a particular miracle. Subsequently, the blessing is optional (*Ravad*, cited by *Rashba* to 54a s.v. הרואה and *Meiri* to 54a s.v. ברכה זו; see also *Hasagos HaRavad* to *Baal HaMaor* loc. cit.). According to others, the blessing is obligatory each time one sees the place of the miracle [after a lapse of at least thirty days, as noted above] (*Meiri*; see also *Beis Yosef* 218 s.v. אבל אדוני אבי, who concludes that this is also the opinion of *Tosafos* and *Rosh*, and, accordingly, follows this view in *Shulchan Aruch* 218:3).

The mishnah only discusses the obligation to recite a blessing upon seeing the location of a miracle involving a majority of the nation (see comm. above s.v. הָרוֹאֶה). This obligation is incumbent on every Jew. If only an individual experienced a mir-

acle, others are not obligated to recite a blessing at the site of the miracle. However, the individual himself *is* required to recite a blessing (*Gem.* 54a). The formula of this blessing is: "Blessed ... Who performed a miracle *for me* at this place" (*Shulchan Aruch* 218:4). This obligation is also incumbent on his children and his children's children (*Rav*; *Rif* 43a; *Rambam, Hil. Berachos* 10:9; *Meiri*; from *Gem.* ibid. as emended by *Hagahos HaGra*; see *Rosh* §1). Others include *all* his descendants in this obligation (*Rashba* to 54a s.v. הרואה; *Shulchan Aruch* ibid. §4). See *Shulchan Aruch* ibid. with *Mishnah Berurah* §17 and *Shaar HaTziyun* §8 regarding the formula recited by one's descendants.

A miracle which generated a public sanctification of God's Name (e.g. Daniel's rescue from the lions' den) is treated like a miracle involving the entire nation, and every Jew must recite a blessing upon seeing the site of the miracle (*Rosh* §1; *Rashba* ibid. from *Yerushalmi* 9:1; see *Gem.* 57b). Similarly, a miracle involving a person famous throughout the entire nation (e.g. David's general Yoav; see further *Beur Halachah* to 218:7 s.v. על נס מסויים) is treated like a national miracle (*Rosh* ibid.; *Rashba* ibid.). The text of the blessing is: "Blessed Who performed miracles *for the righteous ones* at this place" (*Shulchan Aruch* ibid. §7; see *Gem.* ibid. as

---

1. *Magen Avraham* (ad loc. §4) is uncertain whether this thirty-day interval includes or excludes the days of the previous and current sightings. In accordance with the principle that halachic doubts regarding blessings are decided leniently, *Mishnah Berurah* (ad loc. §11) rules that one should not recite a blessing unless thirty days have elapsed exclusive of the two sightings (see *Shaar HaTziyun* §3).

[If one sees] a place from which idolatry was uprooted, he says: "Blessed . . . Who uprooted idolatry from our land."

YAD AVRAHAM

emended by *Hagahos HaGra* §2).

One must also recite a blessing upon seeing a place where a miracle occurred to his [primary — *Mishnah Berurah* ibid. §20] teacher (*Rashbah* ibid.; *Re'ah*; *Shulchan Aruch* ibid. §6). The text of this blessing is: "Blessed Who performed a miracle *for my master* at this place." This obligation is due to the honor one must accord his teacher, and is, therefore, only incumbent on the student himself, but not on his descendants (see *Mishnah Berurah* ibid.).

מָקוֹם שֶׁנֶּעֶקְרָה מִמֶּנּוּ עֲבוֹדַת כּוֹכָבִים, אוֹמֵר: בָּרוּךְ שֶׁעָקַר עֲבוֹדָה זָרָה מֵאַרְצֵנוּ. — *[If one sees] a place from which idolatry was uprooted, he says: "Blessed . . . Who uprooted idolatry from our land."*

The mishnah refers to a place in Eretz Yisrael from which an idolatrous shrine was eliminated. Hence, the reference in the blessing to *our land*, i.e. Eretz Yisrael. *Yerushalmi* (9:1, cited by *Rosh* §5 and *Tos. Yom Tov;* see also *Rabbeinu Yonah* 42b s.v. הרואה; *Tif. Yis.; Shulchan Aruch* 224:2) states that upon seeing such a location *outside* Eretz Yisrael, one recites ". . . Who uprooted idolatry from *this place.*" In either case, one continues: *And just as it* [i.e. idolatry] *has been uprooted from this place, so may it be uprooted from all places of Is-*

rael,[1] *and bring back the hearts of those who serve them* [i.e. idols] *to serve You* (see *Gem.* 57b; *Rabbeinu Yonah* ibid.).

Tosafos (to 54a s.v. שעקר עכו״ם, cited by *Meleches Shlomo*) cite a version of this *Yerushalmi* according to which *Yerushalmi's* ruling refers to locations *in* Eretz Yisrael. According to *Tosafos'* version of *Yerushalmi*, the formula "Who uprooted idolatry *from our land*" is recited only if there are no other idolatrous shrines in Eretz Yisrael. If idolatry still exists in the land, however, this formula is inappropriate [for the words "uprooted idolatry from our land" imply that the *entire* land has been cleansed of idolatry]. Rather, one recites the formula which praises God for "uprooting idolatry *from this place,*" i.e. from this particular location. According to *Tosafos, Yerushalmi* does not refer at all to locations *outside* Eretz Yisrael. [However, even according to this approach, the formula "Who uprooted . . . *from this place*" would seem to be proper outside Eretz Yisrael (see *Chidushei Hagahos* to *Tur* 224 §1).]

Interestingly, although our editions of *Yerushalmi* contain *Tosafos'* version, the halachic authorities cite, without qualification, the formula "from *the land*" as the blessing recited in Eretz Yisrael[2] (see *Mishnah Berurah* 224:4 and *Shaar HaTziyun* §2).

---

1. Note that the halachic authorities omit the words *of Israel* from this formula (see *Rambam, Hil. Berachos* 10:9; *Shulchan Aruch* 224:2; see next footnote).

2. *Tos. Chadashim* (see also *Meiri*) suggests that we do not follow *Tosafos* in this regard because even if we grant *Tosafos'* version of *Yerushalmi* our *Gemara* does not agree with this *Yerushalmi's* distinction. For the *Gemara* on 57b (cited above) states that after reciting the blessing "Who . . . from *our land*," one prays, *"And just as it has been uprooted from this place, so may it be uprooted from all places of Israel."* The phrase "from all places *in Israel"* implies that there are still places in Eretz Yisrael where idolatry exists, yet one recites the blessing "Who . . . from *our land.*" [However, as noted in the previous footnote, many authorities omit the words *of Israel* from the text of this prayer.]

ברכות ט/ב

[ב] **עַל** הַזִּיקִין, וְעַל הַזְּוָעוֹת, וְעַל הַבְּרָקִים,
וְעַל הָרְעָמִים, וְעַל הָרוּחוֹת, אוֹמֵר:
„בָּרוּךְ שֶׁכֹּחוֹ וּגְבוּרָתוֹ מָלֵא עוֹלָם".
עַל הֶהָרִים, וְעַל הַגְּבָעוֹת, וְעַל הַיַּמִּים, וְעַל

ר' עובדיה מברטנורא

(ב) **זיקים.** כוכב הנראה כמו שפותח הרקיע ויורה כחץ ממקום למקום. אי נמי, כוכב
שנראה כמו שיש לו זנב ארוך: **זועות.** שהארץ מזדעזעת ורועשת: **רעמים.** קול הנשמע ברקיע
מעננים שׁושׁופכים מים מזה לזה, כמה דתימא (ירמיה נא, טז) לקול תתו המון מים בשמים:
ועל הרוחות. שבאים בסערה וחעף, ואינם מליוית אלא לפרקים: **ברוך שכחו מלא עולם.**
ואי בעי מברך ברוך עושה מעשה בראשית, שכל אלו מעשה בראשית הם דכתיב (תהלים קלה,
ז) ברקים למטר עשה. אבל על ההרים ועל הגבעות וכו' אומר עושה מעשה בראשית דוקא,
דלא מצי לברוכי עלייהו שכחו מלא עולם, שאינן נראים ברוב העולם אלא כל אחד ואחד במקומו:

יד אברהם

2.

The following mishnah lists the blessings that are recited on a variety of striking natural phenomena and formations.

עַל הַזִּיקִין, — *Upon [seeing] meteors,*

[Upon seeing this striking natural phenomenon, one must recite a blessing acknowledging the might and power of its Creator, the text of which the mishnah will cite presently.]

Our translation of זִיקִין, *zikin,* as *meteors* is based on *Rav* (first explanation) and *Rashi* (to 58b s.v. כוכבא דשביט; see also *Rabbeinu Yonah* 42b s.v. על הזיקים), who describe *zikin* as heavenly bodies that shoot across the sky like an arrow, seemingly "tearing the fabric" of the sky. This is an apt description of a shooting star (or, more correctly, a meteor).

Rav, in his second explanation, defines *zikin* as a starlike heavenly body with a long tail, i.e. a comet. This is also the definition given by *Rambam Comm.* and *Rav Hai Gaon* (cited in *Hagahos Maimoniyos, Hil. Berachos* 10:14 and *Rishon LeTziyon*; see also *Tif. Yis.* §4).[1]

Shulchan Aruch, like *Rashi,* defines *zikin* as *meteors.* However, *Mishnah Berurah* (§1), after citing the definition of *Rambam Comm.,* notes the consensus of authorities that *both* these phenomena warrant a blessing (see *Shaarei Teshuvah* ad loc. §1; cf. *Rishon LeTziyon* s.v. על הזיקין). Indeed, although *Rambam Comm.* defines *zikin* as *comets,* in his code (*Hil. Berachos* 10:14) he rules that one must recite a blessing both on meteors *and* comets.

וְעַל הַזְּוָעוֹת — *and earthquakes,*

Our translation of זְוָעוֹת as *earthquakes* is based on *Rav* and *Rashi* (to 59a s.v. גוהא). *Rambam* (*Comm.* and *Hil. Berachos* 10:14) defines זְוָעוֹת as a very loud noise which occasionally occurs in nature.

---

1. *Meiri* (to 58b s.v. המשנה השלישית) defines *zikin* as a bright light in the sky resulting from "the flaming of the atmosphere." This is an apparent reference to the *aurora borealis* (the Northern Lights), which is produced in the ionosphere when atomic particles strike and excite atoms.

2. Upon [seeing] meteors, and earthquakes, and lightning, and thunder, and tempests one says: "Blessed . . . Whose strength and might fill the world." Upon [seeing] mountains, and hills, and seas, and

YAD AVRAHAM

According to *Rabbeinu Yonah* (loc. cit., cited by *Meleches Shlomo*) the mishnah refers to hurricane winds that are accompanied by rain. [These are distinct from the רוחות, tempests, the mishnah will soon present. The latter are violent winds unaccompanied by precipitation.]

וְעַל הַבְּרָקִים וְעַל הָרְעָמִים — *and lightning, and thunder,*

The mishnah refers to lightning which is accompanied by thunder [resulting from a storm], not lightning generated by heat, such as is common in the summer (*Mishnah Berurah* 227:3).

וְעַל הָרוּחוֹת, — *and tempests,*

I.e. winds that blow with great violence (*Rav*, from *Gem.* 59a) [for example, hurricanes[1] and tornadoes].

אוֹמֵר: ,,בָּרוּךְ שֶׁכֹּחוֹ וּגְבוּרָתוֹ מָלֵא עוֹלָם". — *one says: "Blessed . . . Whose strength and might fill the world."*

On experiencing any of the aforementioned natural events, one must recite this blessing, which acknowledges God's might (see further comm. below s.v. אוֹמֵר בָּרוּךְ עוֹשֶׂה). These phenomena are manifestations of the power of God, Who formulated the laws of nature that produce these remarkable events. Indeed, the purpose of these events is to fill people with awe of the Creator (see *Avudraham*, cited by *Mishnah Berurah* 227:7; see *Gem.* 59a).

The blessing refers to God's power "filling the world." This is because these phenomena are visible or audible across vast distances (see *Rashi* to 54a s.v. מלא עולם; *Meiri* to 58b s.v. ועל; cf. *Rav* s.v. ברוך, as understood by *Tos. Yom Tov* s.v. מלא עולם).

עַל הֶהָרִים, וְעַל הַגְּבָעוֹת, — *Upon [seeing] mountains, and hills,*

The mishnah refers to mountains and hills that possess extraordinary features (for example, their size), through which one discerns the might of the Creator (*Avudraham*, cited by *Beis Yosef* 228 s.v. כתב רד"א; *Shulchan Aruch* 228:3). *Aruch HaShulchan* (ad loc. §1) gives as examples the Pyrenees mountains and Mt. Ararat.

וְעַל הַיַּמִּים, וְעַל הַנְּהָרוֹת, — *and seas, and rivers,*

Here, too, the mishnah refers only to exceptionally large or mighty rivers (*Avudraham*, cited by *Beis Yosef* ibid.). [For example, the Rhine or the Volga (see *Aruch HaShulchan* ibid. §2).]

Tosafos (to 54a s.v. על) comment that the mishnah refers to the four rivers mentioned in the Torah's account of Creation [i.e. the Pishon (commonly identified as the Nile), the Gichon, the Chidekel (identified as the Tigris) and the Peras (Euphrates) — see *Genesis* 2:11-14)]. *Shulchan Aruch* (228:2), apparently on the basis of *Tosafos'* comment, mentions only these four rivers as warranting a blessing. However, *Magen Avraham* (ad loc §3) understands *Tosafos* merely to be giving examples of extraordinary rivers (see *Machatzis HaShekel* ad loc.). *Mishnah Berurah* (ad loc. §4) accordingly rules that one recites a blessing on seeing any exceptional river.

---

1. Note that according to *Rabbeinu Yonah* (cited in the comm. above s.v. וְעַל הַזְּוָעוֹת), hurricanes are in the category of זְוָעוֹת, because they are accompanied by rain.

הַנְּהָרוֹת, וְעַל הַמִּדְבָּרוֹת, אוֹמֵר: „בָּרוּךְ עוֹשֶׂה
מַעֲשֵׂה בְרֵאשִׁית".
רַבִּי יְהוּדָה אוֹמֵר: הָרוֹאֶה אֶת הַיָּם הַגָּדוֹל,
אוֹמֵר: „בָּרוּךְ שֶׁעָשָׂה אֶת הַיָּם הַגָּדוֹל",

ר' עובדיה מברטנורא

הים הגדול. ים אוקינוס שמקיף העולם: **ברוך שעשה הים הגדול.** שמתוך גדלו וחשיבותו

יד אברהם

וְעַל הַמִּדְבָּרוֹת, — *and deserts,*

The term מִדְבָּר is commonly translated as *desert*. However, some seem to understand the mishnah to be referring to a wilderness [i.e. any wild and uninhabited region] (see *Eishel Avraham* [*Botchatch*] to *Orach Chaim* 228).

אוֹמֵר: בָּרוּךְ עוֹשֶׂה מַעֲשֵׂה בְרֵאשִׁית. — *one says:* Blessed . . . Who makes the work of Creation.[1]

Upon witnessing any of the aforementioned landmarks, one must recite this blessing of praise to God. These formations, which hark back to Creation, warrant a blessing because they inspire us to stand in awe of God the Creator. If His creations yet endure, certainly He does! (*Avudraham*; see also *Mishnah Berurah* 228:1).

Accordingly, this blessing is not recited on formations that have been altered in some way from their original state. One does *not* recite a blessing, for example, upon seeing a river which has been diverted from its original course by human efforts [although a blessing *is* warranted on the portion of the river that remains in its original path] (see *Gem.* 59b; *Shulchan Aruch* ibid. §2). Similarly, if a sea was artificially extended and connected with an-other sea, one does not recite a blessing upon seeing the extension. For example, one would not recite a blessing upon seeing the Suez Canal (*Mishnah Berurah* §6 with *Shaar HaTziyun*).

Although these landmarks attest to the power of God Who formed them, they do not warrant the blessing "Whose strength and might fill the world" (see *Gem.* 59a). This is because each of these landmarks is set in place, and is not seen across vast distances. [Thus, they do not manifest God's power throughout the world] (*Rav* s.v. ברוך שכחו; *Rashi* ad loc. s.v. על ההרים; *Meiri* to 58b s.v. ועל הזוועות; cf. *Rabbeinu Yonah* 42b s.v. על).

The mishnah implies that this blessing is reserved for the aforementioned landmarks. It is not an appropriate blessing, however, for the natural phenomena listed earlier in the mishnah (meteors, earthquakes, lightning, thunder and tempests). The *Gemara* (59a) wonders why this should be so. After all, those phenomena are also works of Creation! Rava answers that the mishnah should not be understood to imply that the blessing "Who makes the work of Creation" is limited to these landmarks.

---

1. It should be noted that the version of our mishnah printed in the *Gemara* does not include the word מַעֲשֵׂה, *the work of.* This seems to have been the reading of *Rambam* as well, for in his code (*Hil. Berachos* 10:15) he presents the text of the blessing as בָּרוּךְ עוֹשֶׂה בְרֵאשִׁית, *Blessed Who makes Creation. Shulchan Aruch* (ibid §1), however, follows our reading of the mishnah.

rivers, and deserts, one says: "Blessed ... Who makes the work of Creation."

R' Yehudah says: [If] one sees the Great Sea he says: "Blessed ... Who made the Great Sea."

YAD AVRAHAM

Indeed, the blessing is appropriately recited upon seeing the natural events listed earlier. Rather, the mishnah means that the *only* suitable blessing for these formations is "Who makes the work of Creation." The blessing "Whose strength and might fill the world," however, is *not* appropriate for landmarks (as explained in the comm. above).

There is a dispute among the authorities as to the meaning of Rava's answer. According to *Rav, Rambam* (*Comm.* and *Hil. Berachos* 10:14) and *Tosafos* (to 59a s.v. רבא), Rava means that *either* blessing is acceptable for extraordinary natural events. However, one would not recite *both* together. *Rashi* (to 59a s.v. כרוך), *Ravad* (*Hasagos* to *Rambam* ad loc.) and *Rashba* (to 59a s.v. רבא), however, understand Rava to mean that one must recite *both* blessings upon witnessing these events.

Shulchan Aruch (227:1) rules in accordance with *Rambam* that only one blessing is recited (see *Mishnah Berurah* §6). He implies that one should preferably recite the blessing "Who makes the work of Creation," although, if one wishes, he may recite the blessing "Whose strength and might fill the world" instead.

It has become customary to recite the blessing "Who makes the work of Creation" upon seeing lightning, and the blessing "Whose strength and might fill the world" on hearing thunder (though either blessing is certainly acceptable). Although there is no basis in the mishnah or Gemara for this distinction, it has become the practice because people wish to praise God with many different types of bless-

ings (see *Machatzis HaShekel* to *Magen Avraham* 227:1). Given the choice between thunder and lightning, the blessing "Whose strength and might fill the world" is more appropriate for thunder, since thunder manifests God's power to a greater degree than does lightning (*Taz* 227:1; *Mishnah Berurah* §5).

However, one may only recite both blessings when two blessings are necessary (e.g. one recited a blessing on lightning and then heard thunder). If one both sees lightning and hears thunder before he recited any blessing, he may not recite both blessings (according to *Rambam* and *Shulchan Aruch*), since the first blessing he recites (whether "Who makes ..." or "Whose strength ...") covers both events (see *Magen Avraham* 227:1; see *Mishnah Berurah* ibid.; *Aruch HaShulchan* ad loc. §2; cf. *Eliyah Rabbah* ad loc §4).

רַבִּי יְהוּדָה אוֹמֵר: הָרוֹאֶה אֶת הַיָּם הַגָּדוֹל — 'R אוֹמֵר: ,,בָּרוּךְ שֶׁעָשָׂה אֶת הַיָּם הַגָּדוֹל", *Yehudah says: [If] one sees the Great Sea he says, "Blessed ... Who made the Great Sea."*

R' Yehudah maintains that one does not recite the same blessing ("Who makes the work of Creation") for the Great Sea as for other seas. Because of the size and significance of the Great Sea, R' Yehudah assigned it a special blessing which refers specifically to it (*Rav; Rashi*), just as the Rabbis assigned special blessings for bread and wine because of their significance [see mishnah 6:1 with comm. s.v. חוּץ מִן הַיַּיִן and חוּץ מִן הַפַּת] (*Rashash*).

Alternatively, R' Yehudah's ruling here is based on his stated view that one should render praise to God corresponding to the specific blessings He bestows on him [see

בִּזְמַן שֶׁרוֹאֶה אוֹתוֹ לִפְרָקִים.
עַל הַגְּשָׁמִים, וְעַל הַבְּשׂוֹרוֹת הַטּוֹבוֹת, אוֹמֵר:

─────────── ר' עובדיה מברטנורא ───────────

קוֹבֵעַ בְּרָכָה לְעַצְמוֹ: **לִפְרָקִים.** מִשְׁלשִׁים יוֹם לִשְׁלשִׁים יוֹס: **עַל הגשמים וכו'.** מְבָרֵךְ הַטּוֹב
וְהַמֵּטִיב, וְהוּא דְּאִית לֵיהּ אַרְעָא בְּשׁוּתָּפוּת עִם אַחֲרִינֵי, דְּהָכִי מַשְׁמַע הַטּוֹב וְהַמֵּטִיב הַטּוֹב לְדִידֵהּ

יד אברהם

<table>
<tr><td>

[רבי יהודה אומר .mishnah 6:1 with comm. s.v
(*Beur HaGra* to 228:1).

It is not altogether clear whether or not
the *Tanna Kamma* disputes R' Yehudah's
ruling. *Gra's* comments imply that the
Tanna Kamma does disagree with R' Yehu-
dah [just as he disputes R' Yehudah's view
regarding the degree of specificity required
for other blessings — see mishnah ibid. (see
Rashash)]. *Rambam Comm.* also under-
stands the *Tanna Kamma* here to disagree
with R' Yehudah, for *Rambam* states that
the halachah is not in accordance with R'
Yehudah. However, in his halachic code
(*Hil. Berachos* 10:15), *Rambam* rules that one
does recite R' Yehudah's blessing on seeing
the Great Sea. This indicates that the *Tanna
Kamma* (whose view is presumably fol-
lowed in halachah) does *not* disagree with R'
Yehudah's assertion (*Kessef Mishneh* ad
loc., cited by *Meleches Shlomo*; see *Kessef
Mishneh* ibid. for another possible justifica-
tion of *Rambam's* ruling; cf. *Tur* 228). This
is also the understanding of *Rosh* (*Teshuvos*
4:4), who cites the ruling of *Rambam's* code
in support. In any event, *Shulchan Aruch*
(228:1) follows *Rambam's* code and rules in
accordance with R' Yehudah.

If one nevertheless recited the blessing
"Who makes the work of Creation" upon
seeing the Great Sea, he has discharged his
obligation, just as the more general *She-
hakol* blessing suffices (after the fact) for
foods for which the Rabbis formulated a
more specific blessing [see mishnah 6:2
with comm. s.v. ועל כולן] (*Beur Halachah* to
Shulchan Aruch ibid. s.v. ועל הים הגדול).

The identity of the "Great Sea" to
which R' Yehudah refers is the subject

</td><td>

of debate among the commentators. In
Scripture, the designation יָם הַגָּדוֹל, *the
Great Sea*, is given to the Mediter-
ranean Sea (see, for example, *Num-
bers* 34:6), and it would therefore seem
that the mishnah is referring to the
Mediterranean. However, many com-
mentators understand our mishnah to
be referring to "Oceanus" (*Rav;
Shenos Eliyahu; Teshuvos HaRosh*
loc. cit., cited by *Meleches Shlomo*, as
explained by *Divrei Chamudos* 9:37).
[Oceanus is a term used to describe the
vast body of water encircling the
globe, including all the world's
oceans.] This would also seem to be
the understanding of *Rashi*, who ex-
plains the prominence of the Great Sea
in terms of its size.

R' Yosef Karo cites the aforemen-
tioned *Teshuvos HaRosh* in *Beis Yosef*
(228 s.v. ומה שתמה). Nevertheless, in
Shulchan Aruch (228:1) he applies R'
Yehudah's ruling to "the sea which
one traverses when traveling to Eretz
Yisrael and Egypt," i.e. the Mediter-
ranean Sea. [According to this under-
standing, the prominence of the Great
Sea lies not in its size (for Oceanus is of
much greater size) but in the fact that it
washes the shore of the Holy Land[1]
(*Tif. Yis.* §9; *Mishnah Berurah* §2).]
Divrei Chamudos (ibid.) comments
that R' Yosef Karo had a corrupted
version of *Teshuvos HaRosh*, which

</td></tr>
</table>

1. Scripture similarly refers to the Euphrates as "the Great River" because of its relation
to Eretz Yisrael (see *Rashi* to *Genesis* 15:18 s.v. עד הנהר הגדול).

9

[But only] when he sees it at intervals.

2

On rains and on [hearing] good tidings, one says:

led him to misinterpret *Rosh's* intent.[1]

בִּזְמַן שֶׁרוֹאֶה אוֹתוֹ לִפְרָקִים. — *[But only] when he sees it at intervals.*

One does not recite this blessing if he has recently seen the Great Sea. The *Gemara* (59b) defines this as within the past thirty days (*Rav*).

As noted in the comm. to the previous mishnah (s.v. אוֹמֵר בָּרוּךְ שֶׁעָשָׂה נִסִּים), the requirement of a thirty-day interval also applies to the blessings recited upon viewing the landmarks listed in this and the previous mishnah. Thus, for example, one would not recite a blessing on a mountain if he had seen that mountain within the past thirty days (see *Mishnah Berurah* 228:2). However, if he saw a different mountain, he *would* recite another blessing (see *Magen Avraham* 224:10). By the same token, one would recite a blessing upon experiencing an earthquake (or any of the other natural phenomena listed earlier) even if he had witnessed an earthquake within the past thirty days, since the earthquake of today is not the same earthquake as the one he had previously experienced (*Ritva; Re'ah* to 59a; *Sefer HaMichtam* to 59b; see also *Mishnah Berurah* 218:13).[2]

However, with regard to thunder and lightning, there is one further qualification. Although each clap of thunder and flash of lightning is new, one recites blessings for thunder and lightning only once for a single storm. [In this context, a storm is not considered to end until the sky clears (*Yerushalmi* 9:2, cited by *Rosh* §13; *Tif. Yis.* §10, from *Shulchan Aruch* 227:2).] However, if the storm continues into the next

day, one is required to recite the blessings again (*Yerushalmi* ibid., cited by *Rosh* ibid.; *Mishnah Berurah* 227:8).

עַל הַגְּשָׁמִים, וְעַל הַבְּשׂוֹרוֹת הַטּוֹבוֹת, אוֹמֵר: "בָּרוּךְ הַטּוֹב וְהַמֵּטִיב." — *On rains and on [hearing] good tidings* [lit. *good things reported*], *one says: "Blessed ... Who is good and does good."*

[This blessing acknowledges God as the Source of all good fortune.] Examples of tidings that warrant this blessing are news of the birth of a son, and reports that one has acquired an inheritance (see *Gem.* 59b; see further comm. below).

The mishnah refers to a rainfall which comes after a sustained period of drought. At these times, rainfall is an event calling for a formal expression of thanksgiving (see *Shulchan Aruch* 221:1; see there further for details regarding the amount of rain required in order to recite the blessing).

Rama (ad loc.) notes that it is not customary to recite this blessing for rain. He explains that this is because we live in countries where it rains regularly. Thus, we do not usually experience the drought which makes rainfall a particularly joyous event. However, in the event of a drought, one must certainly recite the blessing upon rainfall, regardless of where he lives (*Mishnah Berurah* §2). It is also possible that in areas that are blessed with rainfall only at set seasons of the year (e.g. Eretz Yisrael), one must recite this blessing when the rains

---

1. Interestingly, the unique terminology *Shulchan Aruch* employs to refer to the Mediterranean ("the sea which one traverses when traveling to Eretz Yisrael and Egypt") is taken verbatim from *Teshuvos HaRosh*. This would seem to indicate that *Shulchan Aruch's* ruling is based on (his understanding of) *Rosh*.

2. There is, however, one natural event to which the thirty-day interval does apply. Comets are usually visible for many days at a time. One does not recite a blessing upon seeing a comet he has seen within the past thirty days (*Mishnah Berurah* 227:1).

„בָּרוּךְ הַטּוֹב וְהַמֵּטִיב"; וְעַל שְׁמוּעוֹת רָעוֹת אוֹמֵר: „בָּרוּךְ דַּיַּן הָאֱמֶת":

ר' עובדיה מברטנורא

והמטיב לאחריני, אבל כי לית ליה ארעא כלל אומר מודים אנחנו לך ה' אלהינו על כל טיפה וטיפה שהורדת לנו וכו', ואם יש לו קרקע לבדו מברך שהחיינו:

יד אברהם

begin in their proper time, although there had been no drought (see *Mishnah Berurah* §1 and *Beur Halachah* s.v. היו אם at length).

The mishnah's reference to "rain" cannot mean *tidings* of rain. Reports of rain after an extended period of drought undoubtedly qualify as "good tidings," and it would not be necessary for the mishnah to specifically mention tidings of rain as a cause to recite the blessing. Rather, the mishnah refers to one who actually *experiences* the rainfall (*Gem.* 59b, as explained by *Rashba* ad loc. s.v. ואידי אידי אלא). Similarly, events the *tidings* of which obligate this blessing also warrant the blessing if one witnesses them himself (see *Mishnah Berurah* 223:1).

With regard to rain, this blessing is recited to thank God for causing crops to grow. Accordingly, it is only recited by a landowner, whose crops flourish as a result of the rains. One who does not own land does not benefit from rain in the same way as a landowner, and this blessing is not warranted in his case. Rather, he recites a prayer of thanksgiving, the general text of which is cited in the *Gemara* (see *Rav*; see *Shulchan Aruch* 221:1 for the exact text of this prayer).

The *Gemara* (59b) notes that the next mishnah mandates a different blessing to be recited on joyous occasions (such as acquiring a house) — *Shehecheyanu*. Why, then, does our mishnah mandate the blessing of *Hatov Ve'hameitiv* for rainfall (and good tidings)? The *Gemara* explains that the blessing of *Hatov Ve'hameitiv*, which

makes a double reference to God's Attribute of Goodness ("Who *is good* and *does good*"), was formulated for occasions when others share in the good fortune of the one reciting the blessing. Hence, the blessing speaks of God as *being* good to the reciter, and *doing* good for others (see *Rav*). However, if one is the sole beneficiary of the good fortune, he does not recite the blessing of *Hatov Ve'hameitiv*, but rather *Shehecheyanu*. Accordingly, one recites the blessing of *Hatov Ve'hameitiv* on receiving an inheritance only if there are other heirs who share in the estate. If one is the sole heir, he recites the *Shehecheyanu* blessing (see comm. to next mishnah s.v. בָּרוּךְ אוֹמֵר regarding the view of *Yerushalmi*). In the words of the *Gemara*: [The blessing of *Hatov Ve'hameitiv*] is recited when one has a partnership with others (who therefore share in his good fortune); [the *Shecheyanu* blessing] is recited when one has no partnership with others (and is, therefore, the sole beneficiary of the good fortune).

With regard to the birth of a son, one's spouse also shares in the joy. Therefore, the blessing of *Hatov Ve'hameitiv* is warranted (see *Gem.* ibid.). However, if one's wife died in childbirth, or the husband dies before the child was born, the surviving parent recites the blessing of *Shehecheyanu*, since he (or she) is the sole beneficiary of the joyous good fortune (*Rama* 223:1; see *Mishnah Berurah* ad loc. §4).

Many commentators (*Rav*; *Rif* 43b;

"Blessed ... Who is good and does good." And on [hearing] bad tidings, one says: "Blessed ... the true Judge."

YAD AVRAHAM

Rambam, Hil. Berachos 10:5; see also *Meiri* to 59b s.v. מה שאמר במשנה and s.v. היה לו קרקע) understand the *Gemara's* reference to "partnership" to be referring to the blessing recited for rainfall, i.e. that one recites *Hatov Ve'hameitiv* on rain only if he is a partner in a field with others. In this case, the particular good fortune for which he recites the blessing — the beneficial effect of the rain on his field — is shared by others. However, if one is the sole owner of a field, he recites the *Shehecheyanu* blessing. For although the rain certainly benefits other field owners as well, they are not sharing in *his* good fortune, but, rather, are beneficiaries of their own good fortune.

However, others (*Rashi* to 59b s.v. ה"ג; *Rashba* to 59b s.v. והא דאמרינן; see also *Rosh* §14, cited by *Tos. Yom Tov*) maintain that even the sole owner of a field recites *Hatov Ve'hameitiv*. These authorities argue that it is not necessary for others to share in one's *particular* benefit, as long as the event is cause for them to rejoice. According to this view, the *Gemara's* reference to a "partnership with others" applies to the building of a house or other such joyous events, in which case two people share the good fortune only because they are partners in the same endeavor. With regard to rain, however, *all* landowners are "partners" in good fortune.

Shulchan Aruch (221:2) follows *Rambam* and *Rif*, and rules that one recites *Hatov Ve'hameitiv* on rain only if he shares ownership of a field with others.

However, *Mishnah Berurah* (§4) notes the view of many authorities that even according to *Shulchan Aruch*, the sole owner of a field may recite *Hatov Ve'hameitiv* if he is married with children, since his family also shares in his particular good fortune [see comm. above] (see *Shaar HaTziyun* §2).

וְעַל שְׁמוּעוֹת רָעוֹת אוֹמֵר: ,,בָּרוּךְ דַּיַּן הָאֱמֶת." — *And on [hearing] bad tidings* [lit. *bad things heard*] *one says:* "*Blessed . . . the true Judge.*"

[This blessing expresses our faith that, ultimately, God's every decree is just. The obligation to bless God for misfortune will be elaborated on below, mishnah 5.]

The mishnah refers to tidings of a *loss* which causes one anguish. For example, news of someone's death (see *Mishnah Berurah* 223:8 for details), or of a monetary loss. However, if the tidings inform him not of a loss but of the lack of expected gain [e.g. a poor harvest], a blessing is not warranted (see *Beur Halachah* to 222:2 s.v. דיין האמת).

The mishnah refers to bad tidings as שְׁמוּעוֹת, something *heard*, whereas good tidings are called בְּשׂוֹרוֹת, something *reported*. *Shenos Eliyahu* explains the subtle difference in phrasing: It is meritorious to be the bearer of good news. Thus, if there is any good news, there will be many individuals who will hasten to *report* it. However, in regard to bad news Scripture (*Proverbs* 10:18) states: *he who utters a negative word is a fool* (see *Pesachim* 3b). Thus, no one will want to report bad news to a person. Rather, he will have to *listen* for it if he is to find out (see also *Tif. Yis.* §13; cf. *Meleches Shlomo* s.v. ועל שמועות, who cites a version of the mishnah which reads בְּשׂוֹרוֹת הָרָעוֹת).

[ג] **בָּנָה** בַּיִת חָדָשׁ, וְקָנָה כֵלִים חֲדָשִׁים,
אוֹמֵר: ,,בָּרוּךְ שֶׁהֶחֱיָנוּ".

ר' עובדיה מברטנורא

(ג) בנה בית חדש וקנה כלים חדשים. בין יש לו כיוצא בהן בין אין לו כיוצא בהן מברך שהחיינו:

יד אברהם

3.

The following mishnah continues the discussion of the previous mishnah about blessings recited on joyous and sad occasions. The mishnah concludes with a general principle concerning prayer.

בָּנָה בַיִת חָדָשׁ וְקָנָה כֵלִים חֲדָשִׁים, — *[If]
one built a new house, or purchased
new utensils,*

[Building a house (or buying one — *Mishnah Berurah* 223:11; see further comm. below) or acquiring new utensils are occasions for rejoicing. Accordingly, they warrant a blessing of thanksgiving (see previous mishnah).]

In mishnaic Hebrew, the term כֵּלִים generally refers to clothing (see, for example, *Kesubos* 5:8). Some commentators (cited by *Meleches Shlomo*) understand our mishnah, too, to be using the term in this sense, and accordingly rule that only the purchase of clothing warrants a blessing. In the view of these authorities, one would not recite a blessing on a purchase of eating utensils or similar items. However, *Meleches Shlomo* argues that there seems no reason to limit the ruling of the mishnah specifically to clothes, since other purchases also engender joy. According to *Meleches Shlomo*, our mishnah uses the term כֵּלִים in the broader sense of *utensils* (see also *Teshuvos Radvaz* I:395, III:412; *Mishnah Berurah* 223:13). Our translation reflects this approach.

Tosafos (to 59b s.v. ורבי יוחנן) comment that our mishnah refers to the purchase of consequential items, just as the house mentioned previously is an item of significance. The acquisition of such items, which one does not purchase on a regular basis, presumably brings joy to the purchaser, which warrants a formal expression of thanksgiving (see *Meiri; Tif. Yis.* §14). However, the purchase of insignificant items, such as

shoes or a shirt, is not a particular occasion for rejoicing, and does not warrant a blessing. *Rosh* (§16) opines that this issue is subjective, depending entirely on the particular purchaser: A poor person for whom the purchase of shoes is a joyous event must recite a blessing even for shoes; a wealthy person must recite a blessing only for acquisitions that bring *him* joy. In practice, *Rama* (223:6) rules that even a pauper should not recite a blessing on shoes (see *Mishnah Berurah* ad loc. §23 for *Rama's* reason).

In the context of our mishnah, "new" utensils does not mean that they are *newly manufactured*. Even used utensils are considered "new," since they are new to the *purchaser*, and are included in the mishnah's ruling mandating a blessing (*Yerushalmi* 9:3, cited by *Rosh* loc. cit.; see also *Shoshanim LeDavid*, cited by *Tos. Anshei Shem*). So too, one recites a blessing when he buys a house which has already been lived in (*Meiri*). Rather, the term "new" in the mishnah excludes a utensil [or house] which the purchaser had owned at one time and then sold. If he buys this item back, he does not recite a blessing (*Ravad*, cited by *Rashba* to 59b s.v. בנה; see also *Shulchan Aruch* 223:3).

Yerushalmi (9:3, cited by *Rosh* §16) implies that the blessing should be recited immediately upon acquiring the item, when one feels the most joy at his acquisition. [One's joy at an acquisition naturally

3. [I]f] one built a new house, or purchased new utensils, he says: "Blessed ... Who has kept us alive."

YAD AVRAHAM

lessens as the novelty of his purchase wears off (see *Mishnah Berurah* 223:15).]

There is some question whether one recites a blessing on the purchase of an item similar to one he already owns. According to one version cited by the *Gemara* (59b-60a), the *Amora* R' Yochanan maintains that one who did not acquire the first item through *purchase* (e.g. he received it as an inheritance) must recite a blessing on the second item, since it is the first time he has *purchased* such an item. However, if one had also purchased the first item, there is no element of "newness" in the current purchase, so a blessing is not warranted. According to a second version cited by the *Gemara*, R' Yochanan is of the opinion that even a second *purchase* warrants a blessing. As regards the halachah, many authorities rule according to the first version of R' Yochanan's ruling that purchasing the second item does not warrant a blessing if the first item was similarly purchased (*Rambam, Hil. Berachos* 10:1, as understood by *Kessef Mishneh* ad loc.; see also *Rashba* to 60a s.v. לישנא אחרינא). *Rav* also implies this ruling (see *Meleches Shlomo*). However, others follow the *second* version of R' Yochanan and rule that even a second *purchase* warrants a blessing (*Rif* 44a; *Tosafos* to 59b s.v. ורבי יוחנן; *Rosh* §16; *Meiri;* see *Shulchan Aruch* 223:3 with *Mishnah Berurah* §14; see also *Teshuvos HaRashba* I:245).

אוֹמֵר: ,,בָּרוּךְ שֶׁהֶחֱיָנוּ.'' — *he says: "Blessed ... Who has kept us alive."*

The complete text of this blessing is: *Blessed are You, Hashem, our God,*

King of the universe, Who has kept us alive, sustained us and brought us to this season. This blessing, which is also recited on Festivals and upon performing seasonal mitzvos (e.g. taking a *lulav* on Succos) and seeing [or eating — see *Shulchan Aruch* 225:3] seasonal fruit, is often referred to simply as בְּרְכַּת הַזְּמַן, *Bircas HaZeman* (*the blessing of the season*).

The previous mishnah states that the blessing recited on joyous occasions is *Hatov Ve'hameitiv.* However, as we have seen (comm. there s.v. עַל הַגְּשָׁמִים), the *Hatov Ve'hameitiv* blessing is limited to occasions where there are multiple beneficiaries of the joyous event. Our mishnah refers to a case in which only *one* person (the purchaser) benefits from the purchase, and, therefore, the *Hatov Ve'hameitiv* blessing is inappropriate (see *Gem.* 59b). However, if others will also benefit from his purchase — for example, his family will live in the new house — he must recite the blessing *Hatov Ve'hameitiv* (*Tif. Yis.* §15).

Yerushalmi (9:3, cited by *Tosafos* to 59b s.v. ורבי יוחנן), makes a different distinction: If one *purchases* an item (as is the case in our mishnah), he recites the *Shehecheyanu* blessing; if the item is given to him as a *gift*, he recites *Hatov Ve'hameitiv. Tosafos* (ibid.) understand *Yerushalmi* to mandate the *Hatov Ve'hameitiv* blessing even in instances where only the recipient of the gift benefits from it. *Tosafos* puzzle over this distinction, for our *Gemara* mandates the *Hatov Ve'hameitiv* blessing only when there are *multiple* beneficiaries. *Rosh* (§16) explains that the giver also benefits from giving a gift. If the recipient is needy, the giver fulfills the mitzvah of charity. If

מְבָרֵךְ עַל הָרָעָה מֵעֵין הַטּוֹבָה, וְעַל הַטּוֹבָה מֵעֵין הָרָעָה.

על הרעה מעין הטובה. מפרש בגמרא כגון שלפו מים על חרמו ושטפו תבואתו של שנה זו, אף על פי שרוו המים פני האדמה ונעשית שדהו משובחת לשנים הבאות, השתא מיהא רעה היא ומברך דיין האמת: **ועל הטובה מעין הרעה.** כגון דאשכח מליאה, אף על גב דרעה היא דאי שמע בה מלכא חובטו במכות ויסורין ושקיל לה מיניה, השתא מיהא מיהא טובה היא ומברך הטוב והמטיב:

the recipient is a prominent individual, the giver rejoices that such a respected person accepted his gift [see *Kiddushin* 7a]. Hence, there are always multiple beneficiaries when one gives a gift, so the *Hatov Ve'hameitiv* blessing is *always* warranted. [According to this understanding, an *inheritance* is like a purchase; at times, it will not warrant the blessing *Hatov Ve'hameitiv*, but rather *Shehecheyanu*.]

However, *Gra* (*glosses to Rosh ad loc., Beur HaGra to Shulchan Aruch* 223:5) disputes the assertion of *Rosh* that the giver is considered a beneficiary of the gift. Were this so, argues *Gra*, the giver would also be required to recite a blessing, and *Yerushalmi* does not indicate that such an obligation is incumbent on the giver. [Evidently, only the receipt of *material* benefit obligates a blessing (see *Mishnah Berurah* ad loc. §21).] Rather, *Gra* explains, *Yerushalmi* indeed disagrees with our *Gemara*. According to *Yerushalmi*, the factor determining the appropriate blessing is not the *number* of beneficiaries, but whether the beneficiary of the joyous event received the benefit *gratis*. If he did not have to give something in return (e.g. he received a gift), the *Hatov Ve'hameitiv* blessing is warranted, for he has been granted a benefit. However, if he had to *pay* for the benefit (i.e. he purchased the utensil, or the building materials to build the house), *Hatov Ve'hameitiv* is not an appropriate blessing;

he has not been *granted* anything, he merely exchanged one item (money) for another (the purchase). Thus, although his acquisition is an occasion for joy which warrants a formal expression of thanks, the proper blessing is *Shehecheyanu*.[1] [According to *Gra's* understanding of *Yerushalmi*, an inheritance is treated like a gift, since the inheritor received it for free.]

The authorities dispute whether there is an *obligation* to recite the *Shehecheyanu* blessing upon experiencing the joyous events described by our mishnah, or if is discretionary. Those who maintain that it is discretionary base their opinion on the *Gemara* in *Eruvin* (40b), which states that one must recite the *Shehecheyanu* blessing on the joyous occasion of Festivals because they occur at set annual intervals (and, therefore, obligate a blessing thanking God for "bringing us to *this season*"). These authorities understand the *Gemara* to mean that the *Shehecheyanu* blessing is obligatory *only* for events that occur at annual intervals. Events such as the joyous occasions described by our mishnah do not fulfill this criterion, for they are not bound to a specific time of year. Accordingly, the *Shehecheyanu* blessing our mishnah prescribes for

---

1. Interestingly, *Gra* in *Shenos Eliyahu* explains that *Yerushalmi* does not argue with our *Gemara's* distinction, but rather *qualifies* it. According to *Yerushalmi*, even if two people materially benefit from an event, the blessing of *Hatov Ve'hameitiv* is only warranted if they receive the benefit for free.

One recites a blessing on a calamity which has an aspect of good, and on a favorable occurrence which has an aspect of bad.

YAD AVRAHAM

joyous events is perforce only discretionary (see *Rav Shereira Gaon*, cited by *Tosafos* to *Succah* 46a s.v. העושה [ב] סוכה).[1] Others, however, dispute the understanding of the *Gemara* as *limiting* the blessing obligation to annual events. In their opinion, *any* event which causes joy obligates the *Shehecheyanu* blessing which thanks God for allowing us to experience this time of joy (see *Beis Yosef* 223 s.v.כתבו התוס'; *Darkei Moshe* ad loc. §4; *Beur Halachah* to 223:1 s.v. ויש שכתבו).

Rama (223:1) notes that many are not scrupulous to recite the *Shehecheyanu* blessing on occasions of good fortune. He ascribes this custom to reliance on the view that in such cases the blessing is not obligatory. However, in *Darkei Moshe* (ibid.), *Rama* writes that in practice, one should be careful to recite the *Shehecheyanu* blessing in these instances, since many authorities consider it obligatory (see *Mishnah Berurah* §7).

מְבָרֵךְ עַל הָרָעָה מֵעֵין הַטּוֹבָה, — *One recites a blessing on a calamity which has an aspect of good,*

I.e. one recites the blessing prescribed for misfortune — *Dayan Ha'Emes* (see previous mishnah) — even if much good will eventually result from the event. For example, if one's field is flooded and his crops ruined, he must recite the *Dayan Ha'Emes* blessing even though his field is now well irrigated, and will be more fertile in the future. Although ultimately the benefit to his field will outweigh the loss of his crops (see *Rabbeinu Yonah* 44a s.v. על הרעה מעין הטובה), *at the present time* the event represents a calamity, and warrants a blessing for occasions of misfortune (*Gem.* 60a, as understood by *Rav*).

וְעַל הַטּוֹבָה מֵעֵין הָרָעָה — *and on a favorable occurrence which has an aspect of bad.*

One should recite the appropriate blessing for good fortune (whether *Hatov Ve'hameitiv* or *Shehecheyanu*) even if the occurrence has the potential to turn into a calamity. For example, a person finds a treasure — obviously a favorable occurrence — but someone else learns of his find. If the latter reports the find to the king, the king will confiscate the treasure [and possibly even punish the finder for withholding it (see *Rav*; *Rosh* §17)], in which case finding the treasure will have been cause for *sorrow*, not for rejoicing (see *Gem.* ibid.). Nevertheless, *at the present time* finding the treasure is a favorable occurrence, and one must recite the blessing appropriate to his good fortune without considering potential unfavorable consequences (*Gem.* ibid., as understood by *Rav*).

Rambam Comm. has a different understanding of the mishnah's principle. According to *Rambam*, we do not take future

1. The concept of a discretionary *Shehecheyanu* blessing is not unprecedented. The *Gemara* in *Eruvin* (ibid.) clearly states that the *Shehecheyanu* blessing recited on seasonal fruit is merely discretionary. [The blessing being discretionary, however, does not detract from the importance of reciting it. *Mishnah Berurah* (225:9) comments that although it is not an obligation, one should be scrupulous to recite a *Shehecheyanu* on new seasonal fruit.]

הַצּוֹעֵק לְשֶׁעָבַר – הֲרֵי זוֹ תְּפִלַּת שָׁוְא.
כֵּיצַד? הָיְתָה אִשְׁתּוֹ מְעֻבֶּרֶת, וְאָמַר: "יְהִי
רָצוֹן שֶׁתֵּלֵד אִשְׁתִּי זָכָר" – הֲרֵי זוֹ תְּפִלַּת
שָׁוְא. הָיָה בָא בַדֶּרֶךְ וְשָׁמַע קוֹל צְוָחָה בָּעִיר,
וְאָמַר: "יְהִי רָצוֹן שֶׁלֹּא יִהְיוּ אֵלּוּ בְּנֵי בֵיתִי" –

ר' עובדיה מברטנורא

הַצּוֹעֵק לְשֶׁעָבַר. הַמִּתְפַּלֵּל עַל מַה שֶׁכְּבָר הָיָה הֲרֵי זוֹ תְּפִלַּת שָׁוְא, דְּמַאי דַּהֲוָה הֲוָה:

יד אברהם

consequences into account in defining a particular event as good or bad because the potential consequences of the event might not materialize. For example, it is possible that one's field will *not* benefit from the flood. Since the unfavorable aspect of the flood is certain (his crops were definitely ruined), while the potential favorable aspect is uncertain, the event is defined as one of misfortune, which warrants the blessing *Dayan Ha'Emes.* Similarly, while the favorable aspect of finding a treasure is certain, the unfavorable consequences are not definite; perhaps the king will not hear of it and will do him no harm. Therefore, the event is defined as a favorable occasion, and one must recite the appropriate blessing for good fortune. However, if the eventual calamity is not a matter of speculation but of *certainty* (e.g. the king himself saw him find the treasure), one would not recite a blessing appropriate for a joyous event, since the event will definitely result in misfortune (see *Tos. Yom Tov; Chiddushei Maharich;* see also *Aruch HaShulchan* 222:4).

Certain events contain elements of good and evil at the *time of occurrence.* For example, the death of one's father is certainly a cause for sorrow. On the other hand, there is an aspect of the event for which the son must render thanks to God, viz. he inherits his father's property (see comm. to previous

mishnah s.v. עַל הַגְּשָׁמִים). In this case, both the blessing for misfortune and the blessing for favorable events are warranted. Therefore, when one's father dies, the son must recite *two* blessings: the blessing *Dayan Ha'Emes* for the actual death, and a blessing of thanksgiving for the inheritance he receives thereby [either *Hatov Ve'hameitiv* or *Shehecheyanu,*[1] depending on whether or not he is the sole heir — see comm. ibid.] (see *Gem.* 59b.; *Shulchan Aruch* 223:2).

הַצּוֹעֵק לְשֶׁעָבַר, הֲרֵי זוֹ תְּפִלַּת שָׁוְא. — *[If]* one prays* [lit. cries out] *regarding the past, this is a prayer in vain.*

I.e. if one prays that God alter a past occurrence, his prayer is in vain, for the past cannot be changed (*Rav; Rambam Comm.*). [Certainly one can (and should) pray regarding the *future* effects of a past event. The past event *itself,* however, is immutable.].

This principle is so self-evident that it seems unnecessary for the mishnah to mention it. Obviously, one cannot pray that a particular event should not have occurred! (see *glosses of R' Eliyahu Guttmacher*). However, the mishnah wishes to teach that certain prayers, although they might be construed as regarding the future, are in

---

1. *Mishnah Berurah* (§6,9) comments that in cases where the *Shehecheyanu* blessing is warranted, *Dayan Ha'Emes* should be recited first, since all agree it is obligatory, whereas some maintain that the *Shehecheyanu* recited for joyous events is discretionary (see comm. above s.v. אומר ברוך).

9
3

[If] one prays regarding the past, this is a prayer in vain. How so? [If] one's wife was pregnant, and he said, "May it be [God's] will that my wife give birth to a male," this is a prayer in vain. [If] one was coming along the road, and he heard the sound of screaming in the city, and he said, "May it be [God's] will that those [who are screaming] not be [members of] my household,"

YAD AVRAHAM

fact considered prayers regarding the past, and are, therefore, uttered in vain (see *Tos. Anshei Shem* s.v. היה בא בדרך).

כֵּיצַד? — *How so?*

[I.e. what are examples of prayers that might be thought to refer to the future, but are actually considered prayers regarding past events? The mishnah cites two examples, each of which, for a different reason, is understood to refer to the past.]

הָיְתָה אִשְׁתּוֹ מְעֻבֶּרֶת וְאָמַר ,,יְהִי רָצוֹן שֶׁתֵּלֵד אִשְׁתִּי זָכָר" — *[If] one's wife was pregnant, and he said, "May it be [God's] will that my wife give birth to a male,"*

[The gender of a fetus is usually determined at the moment of conception. In certain cases, it is only set forty days into the pregnancy (see *Gem.* 60a).] Our mishnah refers to a prayer recited after the gender of the fetus has been fixed.

הֲרֵי זוֹ תְּפִלַּת שָׁוְא. — *this is a prayer in vain.*

[Although the prayer refers to the *future* birth of the child, it actually relates to an event which has already occurred, for the gender of the fetus has previously been fixed. It is, therefore, a prayer in vain.]

Certainly, God can abrogate the

laws of nature at will, and can change the gender of a female fetus. However, one should not request of Him that He perform a supernatural miracle (see *Gem.* ibid.). According to the laws of nature, one gives birth to a male only if the original gender of the fetus was male. Thus, the mishnah teaches, a prayer for one's wife to give birth to a male is really a request that the fetus originally be male. Since the gender has already been determined, it is a prayer seeking to change the past (see *Shoshanim LeDavid*, cited by *Tos. Anshei Shem* s.v. היה בא בדרך; *Shenos Eliyahu*).

הָיָה בָא בַדֶּרֶךְ, וְשָׁמַע קוֹל צְוָחָה בָּעִיר, — *[If] one was coming along the road, and he heard the sound of screaming in the city,*

[A calamity had occurred somewhere in the city, and the screams of the victims reached him.]

וְאָמַר: ,,יְהִי רָצוֹן שֶׁלֹּא יִהְיוּ אֵלּוּ בְּנֵי בֵיתִי" — *and he said, "May it be [God's] will that those [who are screaming] not be [members of] my household,"*

[This prayer seeks to change that which has already occurred, for the calamity has already befallen those who are screaming. If the victims were members of his household, his prayer cannot change that fact.]

[329] THE MISHNAH/BERACHOS — Chapter Nine: *Haro'eh*

הֲרֵי זוֹ תְּפִלַּת שָׁוְא:

[ד] הַנִּכְנָס לַכְּרַךְ – מִתְפַּלֵּל שְׁתַּיִם, אַחַת בִּכְנִיסָתוֹ וְאַחַת בִּיצִיאָתוֹ. בֶּן עַזַּאי אוֹמֵר: אַרְבַּע, שְׁתַּיִם בִּכְנִיסָתוֹ וּשְׁתַּיִם בִּיצִיאָתוֹ;

ר' עובדיה מברטנורא

(ד) שתים בכניסתו ושתים ביציאתו. בכניסתו אומר שתכניסני לכרך זה לשלום, נכנס אומר מודה אני לפניך שהכנסתני לכרך זה לשלום, הרי (זה) שתים בכניסתו. בקש לצאת אומר שתוליאני

יד אברהם

הֲרֵי זוֹ תְּפִלַּת שָׁוְא. — *this is a prayer in vain.*

Although this prayer could be considered a plea that the members of his household be saved from harm, a matter pertaining to the present, it was not formulated as such. Were he to *explicitly* pray that the people involved in the calamity escape unharmed, indeed it would be a valid prayer (see *Meiri* to 60a s.v. הצועק; *Meleches Shlomo*). However, because in its present form it relates to past events, it is a prayer in vain, and is not accepted as a request to save his family from harm (*Shoshanim LeDavid*, cited by *Tos. Anshei Shem* ibid.).

R' Eliyahu Guttmacher understands our mishnah to be teaching a different principle regarding prayer. It is an axiom of Prayer that no properly recited prayer ever goes to waste. Even if God does not see fit, for some reason, to grant the specific request of his prayer, God will grant him some other advantage as a consequence of this prayer. For example, one's prayer that he be successful in his business affairs might result in God granting him and his family health and longevity. The exception to this rule is a prayer concerning matters of the past; such prayers are not accepted at all. Not only is the specific request not granted, but the prayer will also not be beneficial in any other way, either. Such a prayer is truly uttered "in vain."

4.

We have seen that whenever one feels the need for Divine aid, he should offer a supplicatory prayer requesting heavenly assistance (see mishnah 4:2 with comm. s.v. רַבִּי נְחוּנְיָא בֶּן הַקָּנָה). The following mishnah discusses a dangerous situation which warrants such a prayer.

הַנִּכְנָס לַכְּרַךְ מִתְפַּלֵּל שְׁתַּיִם, — *One who enters a city should pray twice,*

The term כְּרַךְ connotes a large, fortified city (*Tos. Yom Tov*). In the past, such cities were often governed by corrupt rulers, who would seek pretexts to libel those passing through their domain [so they could execute them and confiscate their property — see *Gem.* 60a] (*Rashi* to 54a s.v. הנכנס לכרך; *Tif.*

Yis.). Obviously, these cities were extremely dangerous for travelers, and, therefore, one who must travel has good reason to beseech God for protection. *Two* prayers are called for, as the mishnah will presently explain.

The *Gemara* (60a) cites two versions of a ruling defining the type of city in which our mishnah's ruling applies. According to the first version, these prayers are warranted

this is a prayer in vain.

4. **O**ne who enters a city should pray twice, once upon his entry and once upon his departure. Ben Azzai says: [He should pray] four [times], twice upon his entry and twice upon his departure.

YAD AVRAHAM

only when entering cities in which people are executed without a hearing. Since the accused is not given an opportunity to defend himself, strangers in such cities are particularly susceptible to false accusations. However, in a city where punishment is meted out only after a trial, the ruler is not likely to falsely accuse strangers. As long as a traveler is careful not to violate the laws of the city, he will not be in danger (see *Rashi* to 60a s.v. לית לן בה). Therefore, these prayers are not necessary when entering such cities. According to the second version of the *Gemara's* ruling, prayers are warranted even in cities where the accused is allowed a hearing. For even with a trial, a stranger will often be unable to find a lawyer who can prove his innocence. Hence, the traveler is in a precarious situation even in such cities.

Some authorities follow the first version of the *Gemara's* ruling, and authorize these prayers only in places where punishment is meted out without a trial (see *Baal HaMaor* 44a of *Rif* folios, s.v. והא; *Shitas Rivav* ad loc. s.v. ת״ר בכניסתו). Most authorities, however, follow the second version and require these prayers even in cities where the accused would have a hearing (see *Milchamos Hashem* ad loc. s.v. אמר הכותב). According to *Meiri*, the prayers are *obligatory* when traveling through a city in which no trial is granted; in cities where a trial is granted, these prayers are optional. According to *Ravad* (*Hasagos to Baal Hamaor* ad loc. §2), the mishnah's prayers are *always* optional.

אַחַת בִּכְנִיסָתוֹ וְאַחַת בִּיצִיאָתוֹ. — *once upon his entry and once upon his departure.*

Before entering the city, the traveler recites a supplicatory prayer that he enter the city safely. Before leaving the

city, he recites a supplicatory prayer that he depart in safety (*Rashi* to 54a s.v. אחת and s.v. ביציאתו; *Meiri*). [The texts of these prayers will be presented in the comm. below s.v. בֶּן עַזַאי.]

Alternatively, his prayer upon leaving the city is one thanking God for protecting him from harm during his stay (*Rambam Comm.*).

בֶּן עַזַאי אוֹמֵר: אַרְבַּע, שְׁתַּיִם בִּכְנִיסָתוֹ וּשְׁתַּיִם בִּיצִיאָתוֹ, — *Ben Azzai says: [He should pray] four [times], twice upon his entry and twice upon his departure.*

Ben Azzai requires two prayers in addition to the ones mandated by the *Tanna Kamma*, a total of *four* prayers. Before entering the city, the traveler must recite a supplicatory prayer that he be granted safe entry. Upon entering safely [i.e. after arriving safely at his place of lodging (see *Tif. Yis.* §19)], he must recite a prayer of thanks for his safe entry. Before departing, he must recite a supplicatory prayer that he depart in safety. After safely departing, he must recite a prayer of thanks for his safe departure (*Rav*, from *Gem.* 60a).

According to *Rashi* (cited in the comm. above s.v. אַחַת בִּכְנִיסָתוֹ), the additional prayers required by Ben Azzai are the two prayers of thanksgiving, recited after entering and departing the city. According to *Rambam* (cited in comm. ibid.), one of Ben Azzai's additional prayers is the prayer of thanksgiving upon entering the city safely, and the other is the supplicatory prayer recited before departing (see further comm. below s.v. וְנוֹתֵן הוֹדָאָה).

The *Gemara* (60a) cites a Baraisa

וְנוֹתֵן הוֹדָאָה לְשֶׁעָבַר, וְצוֹעֵק לֶעָתִיד לָבֹא:

[ה] חַיָּב אָדָם לְבָרֵךְ עַל הָרָעָה כְּשֵׁם שֶׁהוּא מְבָרֵךְ עַל הַטּוֹבָה, שֶׁנֶּאֱמַר

—————————— **ר' עובדיה מברטנורא** ——————————

מברך זה לשלום, לאחר שיצא אומר מודה אני לפניך שהוצאתני מכרך זה לשלום. וכל כך למה,
מפני שצריך ליתן אדם הודאה לבוראו על מה שעבר עליו מן הטוב ויתפלל על העתיד שתבא
לו טובה: **(ה) חייב אדם לברך על הרעה.** כשמברך דיין האמת על הרעה, חייב לברך

—————————— **יד אברהם** ——————————

(quoted in part by *Rav*) which presents the texts of these prayers: As he enters [the city], what does he say? *May it be Your will, Hashem, my God, that You bring me into this city safely.* [After] entering, he says, *I thank You, Hashem, my God, for having brought me into this city safely.* When he prepares to leave, he says, *May it be Your will, Hashem, my God and the God of my forefathers, that You bring me out of this city safely.* [After] he has left, he says, *I thank You, Hashem, my God, for having brought me out of this city safely. And just as You have brought me out toward peace, so should You lead me toward peace, uphold me toward peace and emplace my footsteps toward peace. And may You rescue me from the hand of every foe and ambush along the way.*

The second half of the prayer recited after leaving the city is strikingly similar to the תְּפִלַּת הַדֶּרֶךְ, *the wayfarer's prayer*, recited every day of a journey (see *Gem*. 29b), but there are some differences. The prayer after departing from a dangerous city is recited immediately upon leaving the city limits, whereas the *wayfarer's prayer* is recited only once the traveler is well on his way. In addition, the *wayfarer's prayer* concludes with the formula of a blessing, *Blessed are You, Hashem, Who hears Prayer,* and the aforementioned Baraisa does not include this closing formula in its prayer. However, *Shulchan Aruch* (230:1) *does* include the

formula *Blessed are You, Hashem, Who hears Prayer* in the text of the prayer recited after leaving a dangerous city, and comments that this prayer is, indeed, the *wayfarer's prayer*. *Mishnah Berurah* (§3) explains that *Shulchan Aruch* does not mean that this *entire* prayer is the *wayfarer's prayer* recited on any journey, for the standard text of the *wayfarer's prayer* does not include a prayer of thanks for the past (see *Shulchan Aruch* 110:4). Moreover, the *wayfarer's prayer* is usually recited only after one is well on his way, and not immediately after leaving the city. Rather, the *second* part of the prayer cited by the Baraisa is the *wayfarer's prayer*, which, in the case of one traveling through a dangerous city, the Rabbis mandated be recited together with the prayer of thanks this person recites immediately after leaving the city. *Shulchan Aruch* informs us that since the second half of the prayer is, in fact, the *wayfarer's prayer*, one is not required to recite it after leaving the dangerous city if he has previously discharged his obligation to recite the *wayfarer's prayer*. He need only recite the segment of the prayer cited by the Baraisa which gives thanks to God for protecting him during his stay in the city.

— וְנוֹתֵן הוֹדָאָה לְשֶׁעָבַר, וְצוֹעֵק לֶעָתִיד לָבֹא. *He should give thanks for the past, and pray for what will come in the future.*

This is part of Ben Azzai's statement (see *Meleches Shlomo*). Ben Azzai explains his rationale for requiring two additional prayers: A principle of prayer is that one must not only peti-

He should give thanks for the past, and pray for
what will come in the future.

5. A person is obligated to recite a blessing for the
bad just as he recites a blessing for the good,

YAD AVRAHAM

tion God for assistance in the future, he
must also give thanks for that which
has already transpired (*Rav*; see also
Rashi to 54a s.v. ארבע). Therefore, besides the two supplicatory prayers
mandated by the *Tanna Kamma* (see
Rashi, cited in comm. above s.v. אַחַת
בְּכְנִיסָתוֹ), one must also utter prayers
thanking God for granting him safe
entry into, and departure from, the city.

According to *Rambam Comm.*, the *Tanna
Kamma* also subscribes to this principle, for
one of the *Tanna Kamma's* two prayers

thanks God for granting him safe entry into
the city (see comm. above s.v. בֶּן עַזַּאי). Accordingly, this last part of Ben Azzai's statement must be understood as a *description* of
his two additional prayers, not as an *explanation* of the rationale for his requirement.
Ben Azzai describes his additional prayers
as (1) one that "gives thanks for the past,"
i.e. the prayer of thanksgiving upon entering the city safely; and (2) one "prayer for
what will come in the future," i.e. the prayer
of supplication upon preparing to depart
[see comm. above s.v. בֶּן עַזַּאי אוֹמֵר] (see *Tos.
Chadashim; Chiddushei Maharich*).[1]

5.

The final mishnah of the tractate refers to several different topics. First, the
mishnah elaborates on the obligation, taught in mishnah 2 of this chapter, to
recite a blessing for misfortune. The mishnah then discusses the laws of respect
for the Temple (the connection between these two themes will be discussed
below), which leads to a discussion concerning the formula used for blessings
recited in the Temple. Finally, the mishnah discusses the proper formula of a
greeting. [As will be seen in the comm. below (s.v. וְהִתְקִינוּ שֶׁיְּהֵא אָדָם), the mandated greeting consists of a blessing (or prayer) that God support and grant peace
to the recipient of the greeting. It was, therefore, deemed appropriate for the
present tractate, which focuses on the laws of blessings and Prayer.]

חַיָּב אָדָם לְבָרֵךְ עַל הָרָעָה כְּשֵׁם שֶׁהוּא מְבָרֵךְ
עַל הַטּוֹבָה, — *A person is obligated to
recite a blessing for the bad just as he
recites a blessing for the good,*

I.e. one must recite the blessing
Dayan Ha'Emes for misfortune [see
mishnah 2] with the same sincerity
and good cheer with which he recites

1. As seen in the Baraisa (cited in comm. ibid.), the supplicatory prayer is recited before the
prayer of thanks in each of the two prayer sequences (i.e. upon entering the city and upon
departing). It seems strange, therefore, that Ben Azzai mentions the requirement of prayers
of thanks before mentioning the prayers of supplication. This would seem to corroborate
the understanding of *Rambam Comm.* that Ben Azzai *describes*, rather than *explains* the
rational for, his additional prayers. Thus, Ben Azzai first describes his additional prayer of
thanksgiving, uttered after entering the city ("he should give thanks for the past"), since
it is the first of his two additional prayers recited; he then describes the other additional
prayer, the supplicatory prayer ("and pray for what will come in the future") recited later,
before departing the city (*Tos. Chadashim; Chiddushei Maharich*).

[דברים ו,ה]: ,,וְאָהַבְתָּ אֵת ה' אֱלֹהֶיךָ בְּכָל
לְבָבְךָ וּבְכָל נַפְשְׁךָ וּבְכָל מְאֹדֶךָ''. ,,בְּכָל
לְבָבְךָ'' — בִּשְׁנֵי יְצָרֶיךָ, בְּיֵצֶר טוֹב וּבְיֵצֶר רָע.
,,וּבְכָל נַפְשְׁךָ'' — אֲפִילוּ הוּא נוֹטֵל אֶת נַפְשֶׁךָ.

ר' עובדיה מברטנורא

בשמחה ובלב טוב, כשם שמברך בשמחה הטוב והמטיב על הטובה:

יד אברהם

the blessing *Hatov Ve'hameitiv* on happy occasions [see mishnah ibid.] (*Rav*, from *Gem.* 60b; see also *Rashi* ad loc. s.v. לקבולינהו בשמחה). He must suppress his natural distress at his calamity, and compose himself to recite the blessing with joy (*Rambam Comm.*).

One can never be certain that a seemingly calamitous event is in fact a misfortune. Often, apparent misfortune actually results in positive developments, just as many joyful events have negative consequences (*Rambam Comm.*). Moreover everything God brings about — even pain and suffering — is ultimately for one's good (see *Gem.* ibid.). Suffering is comparable to a painful operation necessary to heal a serious physical disorder. The operation itself is painful, but it certainly cannot be regarded as bad, for it restores the patient to good health. Similarly, pain and suffering cleanse a person of his sins (*Aruch* s.v. טב, cited by *Rishon LeTziyon*; see *Rabbeinu Yonah* 44b s.v. חייב, cited by *Tos. Yom Tov*; see also *Mishnah Berurah* 222:4). Therefore, one must praise God and thank Him for bad events with the same enthusiasm and sincerity as on favorable occasions.

Tur (222; see also *Shulchan Aruch* ad loc. §3) takes a different approach: The loving acceptance of pain and suffering demonstrated by the *Dayan Ha'Emes* blessing is a form of Divine service, for the Torah commands us to accept God's judgment with love, as the mishnah will presently state. Thus, the actual pain is cause to recite the *Dayan Ha'Emes* blessing joyfully, for it enables him to fulfill this aspect of Divine service.

שֶׁנֶּאֱמַר: ,,וְאָהַבְתָּ אֵת ה' אֱלֹהֶיךָ בְּכָל לְבָבְךָ וּבְכָל נַפְשְׁךָ וּבְכָל מְאֹדֶךָ'' — *as it says* (*Deuteronomy* 6:5): *And you shall love Hashem, your God, with all your heart, with all your soul, and with all your resources.*

The mishnah expounds the last phrase of this verse (*with all your resources*) in support of its teaching. Before progressing to the proof, however, the mishnah expounds the entire verse (see *Tif. Yis* §23; cf. *Meiri*).

,,בְּכָל לְבָבְךָ''; בִּשְׁנֵי יְצָרֶיךָ, בְּיֵצֶר טוֹב וּבְיֵצֶר רָע. — *With all your heart; with both your inclinations, with the good inclination and with the evil inclination.*

[The Sages interpret the heart as a metaphor for the seat of craving and aspiration.] The word לְבָבְךָ, *your heart*, could have been written לִבְּךָ. Homiletically, the extra ב indicates a second heart. Thus, the verse teaches that one should love God with *both* his hearts (*Re'ah*; *Tif. Yis.*). I.e. he should manifest his love of God by serving Him with both inclinations.

9
5
as it says (*Deuteronomy* 6:5): *And you shall love Hashem, your God, with all your heart, with all your soul, and with all your resources. With all your heart;* with both your inclinations, with the good inclination and with the evil inclination. *And with all your soul;* even if He takes your life.

YAD AVRAHAM

One serves God with both inclinations by utilizing his good inclination to perform the mitzvos, and by rejecting the evil inclination to sin. Alternatively, the "good inclination" refers to inherently positive attributes, such as mercy. The "evil inclination" refers to negative attributes, such as hardness of heart. In the service of God, there are times when mercifulness is appropriate, and there are times when harshness is appropriate, i.e. when dealing with wicked people. One must use each inclination appropriately for each situation (*Rabbeinu Yonah* 44b s.v. בכל לבבך, cited by *Meleches Shlomo*).

According to *Rambam Comm.*, the mishnah refers to one's anger and distress, the source of which is the "evil inclination." The verse teaches that one must demonstrate his love of, and belief in, God even during times of personal anger and frustration.

Another interpretation: One should harness even his baser instincts, which are identified with the evil inclination [which utilizes them to lead people to sin], for the sake of Heaven. For example, one should pursue his business activities so that he can serve God by giving charity and supporting Torah scholars, not to accumulate wealth (see *Meiri; Tif. Yis.* §22; see also *Tos. Anshei Shem,* quot-ing *Rambam Comm., introduction to Avos*).

"וּבְכָל נַפְשְׁךָ"; אֲפִילוּ הוּא נוֹטֵל אֶת נַפְשֶׁךָ. — *And with all your soul; even if He takes your life* (lit. *your soul*).

The obligation to love God requires that one be prepared to sacrifice his life for His sake rather than commit certain transgressions (see *Rambam, Hil. Yesodei HaTorah* Chap. 5 and *Shulchan Aruch, Yoreh Deah* 157 for details regarding this law).

From this verse, the *Gemara* (*Sanhedrin* 74a; see *Rambam, Hil. Yesodei HaTorah* 5:7 with *Kessef Mishneh*) derives the specific obligation to sacrifice one's life rather than commit idolatry, which is the antithesis of love of God (see *Rashi* ad loc. s.v. ואהבת). However, other occasions also call for martyrdom (see *Gem.* ibid. at length). One must be prepared to demonstrate his love of God with the ultimate sacrifice whenever the situation calls for it.

It would seem more appropriate for the mishnah to write "even if *they* take your life," rather than "even if *He* takes away your life," for it is not God but those who attempt to force the Jew to transgress who kill him. The mishnah's terminology reflects the assurance that when one allows himself to be killed rather than transgress, God, as it were, takes his soul [נֶפֶשׁ] and covets and honors it. Thus, the martyr dies secure in the knowledge that his ultimate sacrifice is not in vain (*R' Moshe Alshich,* cited by *Meleches Shlomo*).

„וּבְכָל מְאֹדֶךָ" – בְּכָל מָמוֹנֶךָ. דָּבָר אַחֵר:
„בְּכָל מְאֹדֶךָ" – בְּכָל מִדָּה וּמִדָּה שֶׁהוּא מוֹדֵד
לְךָ הֱוֵי מוֹדֶה לוֹ בִּמְאֹד מְאֹד.
לֹא יָקֵל אָדָם אֶת רֹאשׁוֹ כְּנֶגֶד שַׁעַר הַמִּזְרָח,

ר' עובדיה מברטנורא

דבר אחר בכל מאדך. בכל מדות המדודות לך, בין מדה טובה בין מדת פורענות: **לא יקל**
אדם ראשו. לא ינהג קלות ראש: **כנגד שער המזרח.** חוץ להר הבית אשר בחומה הנמוכה
אשר לרגלי הבית הבית למזרח, לפי שהוא מכוון, שכל השערים מכוונים זה כנגד זה, שער מזרח שער
עזרת נשים ושער עזרת ישראל ופתח האולם ופתח האולם והיכל ובית קדש הקדשים בימי בית ראשון:

וּבְכָל מְאֹדֶךָ"; בְּכָל מָמוֹנֶךָ. — *And with all*
your resources; with all your wealth.

There are times when love of God
requires that one sacrifice all his money.
Specifically, one must give up all his
possessions rather than transgress any
negative commandment (see *Shulchan*
Aruch 656:1; *Rama, Yoreh Deah* 157:1;
see *Beur HaGra* to *Rama* ad loc.).

דָּבָר אַחֵר: בְּכָל מְאֹדֶךָ"; בְּכָל מִדָּה וּמִדָּה
שֶׁהוּא מוֹדֵד לְךָ הֱוֵי מוֹדֶה לוֹ בִּמְאֹד מְאֹד. —
An alternative interpretation: With
all your resources (me'odecha);

whatever measure (midah) He metes
out to you, praise (modeh) Him very
much (me'od).

[I.e. one must praise God] whether
He sends him good fortune or suffering (*Rav; Rashi* to 54a s.v. ד"א בכל).
This interpretation corroborates the
mishnah's ruling that one must recite
the blessing for unfavorable events
with the same sincerity and frame of
mind as he recites the blessing for favorable occasions (*Tif. Yis.;* cf. *Tos.*
Anshei Shem s.v. חייב).

◄§ Respect for the Temple

In addition to the obligation to love God, there is a parallel obligation to fear
Him (see *Deuteronomy* 6:13). One of the ways in which one displays fear of God
is by demonstrating reverence for the Temple which hosts the Divine Presence
(see *Yevamos* 6a-b). Accordingly, having elaborated on the obligation to love
God, the mishnah proceeds to discuss the obligation to demonstrate respect for
the Temple (*Tos. Yom Tov*).

The obligation to display a particular reverence for the Temple is derived from
the verse (*Leviticus* 19:30), which states: *and you shall revere My Holy Temple.*
This commandment applies even after the Temple's destruction (*Yevamos* ibid.),
for the site of the Temple retains its sanctity even after the destruction (see
Rambam, Hil. Beis HaBechirah 7:7). The obligation to demonstrate respect for
the Temple prohibits inappropriate behavior in and around the Temple
precincts. The mishnah now lists these forbidden activities.

לֹא יָקֵל אָדָם אֶת רֹאשׁוֹ כְּנֶגֶד שַׁעַר הַמִּזְרָח,
— *A person may not behave light-*
headedly (lit. *lighten his head*) *oppo-*

site the eastern gate [of the Temple],
I.e. the gate in the eastern wall surrounding the Temple Mount (*Rav;*

9
5

And with all your resources; with all your wealth. An alternative interpretation: *With all your resources;* whatever measure He metes out to you, praise Him very much.

A person may not behave lightheadedly opposite the eastern gate [of the Temple], for it is

Rashi to 54a s.v. כנגד שער מזרחי; *Tif. Yis.;* see further comm. below). The laws of respect for the Temple dictate that one behave with particular deference while standing opposite this gate, although he is not standing within the Temple precincts, or, indeed, within the city limits of Jerusalem (see *Meiri*). [The mishnah will soon explain the significance of the area opposite the eastern gate.] Therefore, it is forbidden to behave in a lightheaded fashion opposite this gate. Examples of lightheaded behavior include engaging in laughter or frivolous conversation (*Rambam Comm.*), standing naked (*Shitah Mekubetzes* to 61b s.v. לא יקל; *Meiri*), cutting one's hair or beard, and urinating (*Meiri*).

Aruch (s.v. [1]קל) defines קלות ראש (which we have translated as *lightheadedness*) as walking with one's head held high. According to *Aruch*, our mishnah forbids acting in a pompous manner opposite the eastern gate. Rather, one must walk with his head lowered, expressing humility before God, Who dwells, as it were, in the Temple.

The *Gemara* (61b) qualifies the mishnah's ruling: This law applies [opposite the eastern gate] until a place called Tzofim [which is the farthest place from which the Temple Mount is visible (*Rashi* ad loc. s.v. מן הצופים)]; it applies only when one actually sees the Temple Mount [but not when he is standing in a depression in the ground which prevents him from seeing the

Temple (*Rashi* ad loc. s.v. וברואה), or when he is facing a different direction (*Meiri*); it does not apply if a wall interposes between the person and the Temple; nor does it apply after the Temple's destruction (in contrast to other laws regarding respect for the Temple, which apply even today — see prefatory comments above).

Our commentary has thus far reflected the understanding of *Rav* and *Rashi*, according to whom the mishnah refers to the eastern gate of the Temple Mount. Accordingly, the mishnah's prohibition against exhibiting lightheadedness opposite this gate applies *outside* the Temple Mount, as is, indeed, evident from the *Gemara* (ibid.), which states that displaying lightheadedness is forbidden until Tzofim (see comm. above). However, *Rambam* (*Comm.* and *Hil. Beis HaBechirah* 7:5) understands our mishnah to be referring to the Gate of Nikanor, which was the gate in the eastern wall surrounding the Temple *courtyard.* According to *Rambam*, the mishnah's prohibition applies only *within* the Temple precincts [i.e. within the area of the Temple Mount] (see *Kiryas Sefer* ad loc.). Moreover, in his halachic code (ibid. §7), *Rambam* rules that this prohibition remains in force even *after* the Temple's destruction, in apparent contradiction to the *Gemara*, which forbids displays of lightheadedness only while the Temple is standing. Furthermore, while *Rambam does* rule that displays of lightheadedness are forbidden until Tzofim while the Temple is standing (ibid. §8), *Rambam's* source is evidently not our mishnah's ruling, for he does not limit the prohibition to areas directly opposite

שֶׁהוּא מְכֻוָּן כְּנֶגֶד בֵּית קָדְשֵׁי הַקֳּדָשִׁים. לֹא יִכָּנֵס
לְהַר הַבַּיִת בְּמַקְלוֹ, וּבְמִנְעָלוֹ, וּבְפֻנְדָּתוֹ, וּבְאָבָק
שֶׁעַל רַגְלָיו, וְלֹא יַעֲשֶׂנּוּ קַפַּנְדַּרְיָא, וּרְקִיקָה מִקַּל
וָחֹמֶר.

ר' עובדיה מברטנורא

באפונדתו. חֲזוֹר חָלוּל שֶׁנּוֹתְנִים בּוֹ מָעוֹת. פֵּרוּשׁ אַחֵר, בֶּגֶד שֶׁלּוֹבֵשׁ עַל בְּשָׂרוֹ לְקַבֵּל הַזֵּיעָה
שֶׁלֹּא לְטַנֵּף שְׁאָר בְּגָדִים, וּנְגַנֵּי לָאָדָם לָצֵאת בְּאוֹתוֹ בֶּגֶד לְבַדּוֹ: **קפנדריא.** לִיכָּנֵס בְּפֶתַח זֶה
וְלָצֵאת בְּפֶתַח שֶׁכְּנֶגְדּוֹ כְּדֵי לְקַצֵּר הִלּוּכוֹ דֶּרֶךְ שָׁם. וּלְשׁוֹן קַפַנְדַרְיָא, אַדְמַקִּיפְנָא אַדְרֵי בָתֵּי אַעוּל בְּהָא, כְּלוֹמַר
בְּעוֹד שֶׁאֲנִי צָרִיךְ לְהַקִּיף שׁוּרוֹת שֶׁל בָּתִּים אַקֵּצֵר מַהֲלָךְ וְאֶכָּנֵס דֶּרֶךְ כָּאן: **ורקיקה.** אֲסוּרָה בְּהַר הַבַּיִת:
מקל וחומר. מִמִּנְעָל, וּמַה מִּנְעָל שֶׁאֵינוּ דֶּרֶךְ בִּזָּיוֹן אָסוּר, רְקִיקָה שֶׁהִיא דֶּרֶךְ בִּזָּיוֹן לֹא כָּל שֶׁכֵּן:

יד אברהם

the eastern gate (i.e. the Gate of Nikanor) as our mishnah states (see *Minchas Chinuch* §254). Apparently, *Rambam* understands the mishnah and the *Gemara* to be discussing two *separate* prohibitions. The mishnah's prohibition against lightheadedness applies (according to *Rambam*) only within the Temple precincts, opposite the Gate of Nikanor. Moreover, it applies even after the Temple's destruction, due to the continued sanctity of the Temple site [see prefatory comments above]. The *Gemara*, however, discusses a separate prohibition against displays of lightheadedness *anywhere* within sight of the Temple Mount. This prohibition is Rabbinic in nature (for the Biblical obligation to demonstrate respect for the Temple refers to the actual Temple precincts), and was limited by the Rabbis to the time when the Temple is standing (see *Kiryas Sefer* to *Hil. Beis HaBechirah* ibid.; *Bechor Shor* to 54a).

שֶׁהוּא מְכֻוָּן כְּנֶגֶד בֵּית קָדְשֵׁי הַקֳּדָשִׁים. — *for it is aligned opposite the chamber of the Holy of Holies.*

The gate in the eastern wall of the Temple Mount was in a direct line with both the eastern gate of the Outer Courtyard of the Temple [עֲזָרַת נָשִׁים] and that of the Inner Courtyard [עֲזָרַת יִשְׂרָאֵל]. These gates in turn were positioned directly opposite the doorway

at the antechamber of the Temple [אוּלָם], the gate of the Temple itself [הֵיכָל], and the opening to the Holy of Holies (*Rav; Rashi* to 54a s.v. כנגד שער מזרחי). Hence, one standing opposite the eastern gate of the Temple Mount would be in exact alignment with the entrance to the Holy of Holies. [Thus, one behaving lightheadedly opposite the eastern gate of the Temple Mount is in effect doing so opposite the Holy of Holies!]

R' Yehonasan MiLunel writes that the prohibition against lightheaded behavior opposite the eastern gate only applied in the First Temple, in which the partition between the Holy of Holies and the rest of the Temple took the form of a wall, in which there was an opening across which a curtain was drawn (see *Rashi* ibid.). In the Second Temple, however, the partition before the Holy of Holies consisted of a pair of curtains. These curtains were drawn across the width of the Temple from North to South; the outer one was folded back at its southern end, the inner one at its northern end. These curtains were never opened. Rather, one wishing to enter the Holy of Holies (e.g. the *Kohen Gadol* on *Yom Kippur*) would enter the space between the edge of the outer curtain and the southern wall of the Temple, walk through the

9
5
aligned opposite the chamber of the Holy of Holies. One may not enter the Temple Mount with his staff, with his shoe, with his money belt, or with the dust that is upon his feet. And one may not make it a shortcut. And spitting [is forbidden there] on account of a *kal vachomer* [argument].

passage formed by the two curtains, and enter the Holy of Holies through the space between the edge of the inner curtain and the northern wall (see *Yoma* 51b-52b). Since these curtains were never opened, they were considered an actual wall between the Holy of Holies and the rest of the Temple. Accordingly, the injunction against lightheaded behavior did not apply [just as the *Gemara* (cited in comm. above s.v. לֹא יָקֵל) rules that the prohibition does not apply if a wall intervenes between the person and the Temple]. Both *Rashi* and *Rav* specifically mention the opening in the wall which stood before the Holy of Holies in the First Temple. Some commentators understand this to imply that both *Rav* and *Rashi* concur with *R' Yehonasan MiLunel's* assertion that the prohibition against displays of lightheadedness only applied in the First Temple, when there was such an opening.

לֹא יִכָּנֵס לְהַר הַבַּיִת בְּמַקְלוֹ, וּבְמִנְעָלוֹ, וּבְפֻנְדָתוֹ, וּבְאָבָק שֶׁעַל רַגְלָיו. — *One may not enter the Temple Mount with his staff, with his shoe, with his money belt, or with the dust that is upon his feet.*

It is disrespectful to enter the Temple Mount while carrying one's staff or money belt, or without washing one's feet. Wearing shoes is not disrespectful; nevertheless, the great sanctity of the Temple Mount dictates that it be entered barefoot, as God commanded Moses to approach the Burning Bush [see *Exodus* 3:5] (*Gem.* 62b).

Our translation of פֻנְדָתוֹ as *money belt* is based on *Rashi* (to 54a s.v. בפונדתו) and the first interpretation of

Rav. In his second interpretation, *Rav* follows *Rambam Comm.* in defining the term פֻנְדָתוֹ as an absorbent undergarment (i.e. an undershirt). Since people do not generally wear this as an outer garment, it is inappropriate to do so on the Temple Mount.

וְלֹא יַעֲשֶׂנּוּ קַפַּנְדַּרְיָא, — *And one may not make it a shortcut.*

That is, one may not enter the Temple Mount simply to shorten his route (*Rav* and *Rambam Comm.*, from *Gem.* 62b). One may only enter the Temple for matters associated with the worship of God (*Rambam, Comm.* and *Hil. Beis HaBechirah* 7:2).

This law also applies to a synagogue. One may not use a synagogue as a shortcut (see *Gem.* ibid.; see *Shulchan Aruch, Orach Chaim* 151:5 for details).

וּרְקִיקָה מִקַּל וָחֹמֶר. — *And spitting [is forbidden there] on account of a kal vachomer [argument].*

One may certainly not *spit* while on the Temple Mount. This prohibition is derived from a *kal vachomer* (*a fortiori*) argument as follows: If wearing *shoes* is forbidden on the Temple Mount, although wearing them does not show disrespect (see comm. above s.v. לֹא יִכָּנֵס), certainly spitting, which *is* disrespectful behavior, is forbidden! (*Rav*, from *Gem.* 62b). If a person must spit while on the Temple Mount, he should do so into a cloth (*Rambam, Hil. Beis HaBechirah* 7:2).

כָּל חוֹתְמֵי בְרָכוֹת שֶׁהָיוּ בַּמִּקְדָּשׁ הָיוּ אוֹמְרִים: „מִן הָעוֹלָם". מִשֶּׁקִּלְקְלוּ הַמִּינִין, וְאָמְרוּ, אֵין עוֹלָם אֶלָּא אֶחָד, הִתְקִינוּ שֶׁיְּהוּ אוֹמְרִים: „מִן הָעוֹלָם וְעַד הָעוֹלָם".

─────── ר' עוֹבַדְיָה מִבַּרְטְנוּרָא ───────

כל חותמי ברכות שבמקדש. המברך אומר בסוף כל ברכה ברוך ה' אלהי ישראל מן העולם ועד העולם חונן הדעת וכן בכולם, והטעונין אומרים ברוך שם כבוד מלכותו לעולם ועד, שאין עונין אמן אחר כל ברכה שבמקדש, דכתיב בעזרא (נחמיה ט, ה) קומו ברכו את ה' אלהיכם מן העולם עד העולם, ואומר אחר כך ויברכו שם כבודך, כלומר שעונים ברוך שם כבוד מלכותו לעולם ועד. ואשמעינן הכא דבמקדש ראשון לא היו אומרים אלא אלהי ישראל מן העולם ולא יותר ולא היו אומרים ועד העולם: **משקלקלו המינים.** שאין מאמינים בתחיית המתים ואמרו אין עולם אלא זה, התקינו עזרא ובית דינו שיהו אומרים מן העולם ועד העולם, לומר שני עולמות יש, העולם הזה והעולם הבא, להוציא מלב המינים שכופרים בתחיית המתים:

─────── **יד אברהם** ───────

◆§ **The expanded formula of blessings and responses in the Temple**

The listeners' response to blessings recited in the Temple differed from our standard response of "Amen." In the Temple, the response to a blessing was: בָּרוּךְ שֵׁם כְּבוֹד מַלְכוּתוֹ לְעוֹלָם וָעֶד, *Blessed is the Name of the glory of His kingship forever* [lit. *for the World*] *and ever* (*Rav* s.v. כל חותמי ברכות; *Rashi* to 54a s.v. כל; see *Gem.* 63a for the Scriptural source of this law). This formula reflects God's providence throughout the entire world (see *Tif. Yis.* §29). To match this lengthier response, the concluding formula of the blessing itself was made longer (see *Gem.* ibid., as explained by *Shitah Mekubetzes* ad loc. s.v. כל and *Tif. Yis.* ibid.; see also *Rav* ibid.). Originally, this addition consisted of the phrase מִן הָעוֹלָם, *from the world.*[1] For example, whereas our version of the first of the intermediate blessings of the *Shemoneh Esrei* concludes with the words בָּרוּךְ אַתָּה ה' חוֹנֵן הַדָּעַת, *Blessed are You, Hashem, gracious Giver of wisdom*, in the Temple, this blessing would conclude: בָּרוּךְ ה' אֱלֹהֵי יִשְׂרָאֵל מִן הָעוֹלָם חוֹנֵן הַדָּעַת, *Blessed [is] Hashem, God of Israel, from the World, gracious Giver of wisdom* (*Rav* ibid.; *Rashi* ibid.).[2] Subsequently, at the beginning of the Second Temple era, Ezra and his court, the Men of the Great Assembly, saw a need to revise this concluding formula, as the mishnah will explain. They added the words וְעַד הָעוֹלָם, *until the world*, to the phrase מִן הָעוֹלָם. Thus, after this revision, a blessing would conclude *Blessed [is] Hashem, God of Israel, from the world until the world, gracious Giver of wisdom.*

1. According to some versions of our mishnah (including the one printed in the *Gemara*), the additional phrase was עַד הָעוֹלָם, "until the world," rather than "from the world." *Ritva* (to 63a) maintains that *either* wording was acceptable.

2. According to *Rashi*, the blessing concluded: בָּרוּךְ אַתָּה ה' אֱלֹהֵי יִשְׂרָאֵל... בָּרוּךְ חוֹנֵן הַדָּעַת, "Blessed are You, Hashem, God of Israel . . . Blessed [is] the gracious Giver of wisdom." The *Gemara* (*Taanis* 16b) omits the word אַתָּה, *are You*, but does include the second *Blessed*.

9
5

[Originally] all those who would conclude blessings in the Temple would say: "from the world."
When the heretics corrupted [the faith], and said
there is but one world, [the Rabbis] instituted that
they should say: "from the world until the world."

כָּל חוֹתְמֵי בְרָכוֹת שֶׁהָיוּ בַּמִּקְדָּשׁ הָיוּ אוֹמְרִים:
„מִן הָעוֹלָם." — *[Originally] all those
who would conclude blessings in the
Temple would say: "from the World."*

I.e. throughout the First Temple era,
before the revision instituted by Ezra
and the Men of the Great Assembly
(see prefatory comments above), the
expanded concluding formula for
blessings in the Temple only consisted
of the words *from the world* (see *Rav;
Rashi* ibid.).

As previously noted (see prefatory comments above), the expanded concluding
formula of blessings in the Temple was enacted to parallel the lengthier response to
the blessing. However, it is evident from
Nehemiah 8:6 that at times the "Amen" response was also used in the Temple. *Ravad*
(cited by *Rashba* to 63a s.v. ת"ר and by
Meiri to 63a s.v. המשנה העשירית; see also
Shitah Mekubetzes ibid.) explains that the
lengthier response — and so too the lengthier concluding formula mentioned by our
mishnah — was only used for blessings that
were part of the Prayer service.[1] The blessing referred to in *Nehemiah* 8:6, however,
was not part of the Prayer service, but
rather a blessing recited before reading the
Torah. The conventional formulas were
used for such blessings even in the Temple.

מִשֶּׁקִּלְקְלוּ הַמִּינִין, וְאָמְרוּ אֵין עוֹלָם אֶלָּא אֶחָד,
— *When the heretics corrupted [the
faith], and said there is but one world,*

These heretics said there is only one

world — the present one (*Rashi*). They
denied the cardinal beliefs of תְּחִיַּת
הַמֵּתִים, *the Resurrection of the Dead*
(*Rav*), and the existence of the World
to Come (*Rambam Comm.*). This took
place during the time of Ezra and his
court (the Men of the Great Assembly)
at the beginning of the Second Temple
era (see *Rav; Rashi*). When these
heretics began to spread their heresy...

The version of our mishnah printed in the
Gemara reads: מִשֶּׁקִּלְקְלוּ הַצְּדוֹקִים, "when the
Sadducees corrupted etc." (see also *Rambam
Comm.*, ed. Vilna), a reference to the infa-
mous sect which denied the validity of the
Oral Torah and the authority of the Sages.
This seems strange, for the founder of the
Sadducee sect, Tzadok, an errant disciple of
Antigonus of Socho (see *Rambam Comm.* to
Avos 1:3), lived many years after the passing
of Ezra and the Men of the Great Assembly.
Maharatz Chayes (to 54a s.v. משקלקלו) explains that although the sect was not formed
until the times of Tzadok, there existed even
in the days of Ezra individuals who es-
poused this heresy. The [*Gemara's* version
of the] mishnah refers to these heretics by
the name of the well-known sect which subsequently adopted their philosophy.

הִתְקִינוּ שֶׁיְּהוּ אוֹמְרִים: „מִן הָעוֹלָם וְעַד
הָעוֹלָם." — *[the Rabbis] instituted that
they should say: "from the world until the world."*

To combat the spread of the hereti-
cal philosophy of the nonbelievers,

1. Both in the First and Second Temples. Although the *Gemara* (33a) states that formal
Prayer was established by the Men of the Great Assembly (at the beginning of the Second
Temple period), there was a standard prayer that was recited before then, also (see *Otzar
HaGeonim-HaTeshuvos* to *Berachos* 33a sec. 203).

וְהִתְקִינוּ שֶׁיְּהֵא אָדָם שׁוֹאֵל אֶת שְׁלוֹם חֲבֵרוֹ בַּשֵּׁם,
שֶׁנֶּאֱמַר [רות ב,ד]: ,,וְהִנֵּה בֹעַז בָּא מִבֵּית לֶחֶם,
וַיֹּאמֶר לַקּוֹצְרִים׳ עִמָּכֶם, וַיֹּאמְרוּ לוֹ, יְבָרֶכְךָ ה׳ ".
וְאוֹמֵר [שופטים ו,יב]: ,,ה׳ עִמְּךָ גִּבּוֹר הֶחָיִל".
וְאוֹמֵר [משלי כג:כב]: ,,אַל תָּבוּז כִּי זָקְנָה אִמֶּךָ".

ר' עובדיה מברטנורא

שיהא אדם שואל בשלום חבירו בשם. בשמו של הקדוש ברוך הוא, ולא אמרינן מזלזל
הוא בכבודו של מקום בשביל כבוד הבריות להוליא שם שמים עליו. ולמדו מבועז שאמר
לקולרים ה' עמכם (רות ב, ד). וכי תימא בועז מדעתיה דנפשיה קעבד ולא גמרינן מיניה, תא
שמע מן המלאך שאמר לגדעון ה' עמך גבור החיל (שופטים ו, יב), וכי תימא לא שאל המלאך
בשלום גדעון ולא ברכו, אלא בשליחותו של מקום הודיעו שהשכינה עמו, ולא גמרינן מיניה, תא
שמע ואומר (משלי כג, כב) אל תבוז כי זקנה אמך, אל תבוז את בעז לומר שמדעתו עשה אלא
למוד מזקני אומתך כי יש לו על מי להסמך שנאמר (תהלים קיט, קכו) עת לעשות לה' הפרו תורתך:

יד אברהם

Ezra and his court revised the extended concluding formula used by those reciting blessings in the Temple, adding the words *until the world.* Thus, throughout the Second Temple era, the concluding formula was lengthier than in the First Temple (see *Rav; Rashi* loc. cit.). This affirmation of God's providence (see prefatory comments above) in *two* worlds — "from the world (i.e. this world) to the world (i.e. the world to Come)" — reinforced belief in the existence of the World to Come, and was intended as a rejection of the heretics' denial of the Resurrection of the Dead (*Rav; Rashi* to 54a s.v. התקינו).

וְהִתְקִינוּ שֶׁיְּהֵא אָדָם שֶׁיְּהֵא שְׁלוֹם חֲבֵרוֹ בַּשֵּׁם, — *And they instituted that a person should greet his fellow with the Name [of God].*

The Rabbis also enacted that one should include the Name of God in a greeting. [For example, one should greet another by saying, "May Hashem endow you with peace" (*Rivan* to *Makkos* 23b s.v. ושאילת שלום בשם).]

Although one thereby uses God's Name to show honor to a mere mortal, we do not consider this to be disrespectful of God (*Rav; Rashi* to 54a s.v. שיהא אדם).

This enactment was instituted because a greeting containing God's Name [which is essentially a blessing that God grant one's colleague peace and support] spreads friendship and goodwill among men (see *Rav* s.v. רבי נתן אומר; *Rashi* to 54a s.v. עת ואומר לעשות). Alternatively, the Rabbis sought to reinforce the concept that God is the source of peace and blessing (*Meiri*; see also *Shitah Mekubetzes* to 63a s.v. ת"ש).

Rivan (to *Makkos* 23b s.v. ושאילת) cites two opinions regarding this enactment. According to the first view, the enactment *permits* the use of God's Name in a greeting, but does not require it. According to the second view, the Rabbis *obligated* the use of God's Name in a greeting.

Our standard greeting, *shalom aleichem* ("peace unto you"), reflects this Rabbinical enactment, for the term *Shalom* is one of the Names of God (*Rivan* ibid., from *Shab-*

9
5
And they instituted that a person should greet his fellow with the Name [of God], for it is stated (*Ruth* 2:4): *And behold, Boaz came from Bethlehem, and he greeted the harvesters, "Hashem is with you!": And they said to him, "May Hashem bless you." And [a verse] states (Judges 6:12): Hashem is with you, mighty man of valor. And [a verse] states (Proverbs 23:22): Do not shame [her], though your mother be old.*

bos 10b; see also *Rambam Comm.; Aruch* s.v. עת).

שֶׁנֶּאֱמַר: ,,וְהִנֵּה בֹעַז בָּא מִבֵּית לֶחֶם וַיֹּאמֶר לַקּוֹצְרִים ה' עִמָּכֶם, וַיֹּאמְרוּ לוֹ יְבָרֶכְךָ ה' ''. — *for it is stated (Ruth 2:4): And behold Boaz came from Bethlehem, and he greeted the harvesters, "Hashem is with you!": And they said to him, "May Hashem bless you."*

This verse, which describes the exchange of greetings between Boaz and his workers, was the Scriptural precedent the Rabbis followed in instituting that God's Name be part of any greeting (*Rav; Rashi* to 54a s.v. שיהא אדם).

וְאוֹמֵר: ,,ה' עִמְּךָ גִּבּוֹר הֶחָיִל.'' — *And [a verse] states (Judges 6:12): Hashem is with you, mighty man of valor.*

This verse, which contains the greeting extended to Gideon by the angel when he instructed Gideon — in the Name of God — to wage war against Midian [see *Judges* ibid. s.v.14-16], also serves as a Scriptural source on which the Rabbis based their enactment of including God's Name in greetings (*Rashi* ibid.).

This additional source is necessary because one might argue that the greeting used by Boaz cannot serve as a Scriptural basis. [The verse does not *authorize* this form of greeting, it merely describes the greeting Boaz used.] Perhaps Boaz was acting on his own [without a halachic basis]. Accordingly, we may not rely on his actions to institute an enactment which apparently shows lack of respect toward God (*Rav*, from *Gem.* 63a). [The angel's greeting, however, *can* serve as a Scriptural basis for the Rabbinical enactment, for the angel certainly did not act contrary to God's wishes.]

וְאוֹמֵר: ,,אַל תָּבוּז כִּי זָקְנָה אִמֶּךָ.'' — *And [a verse] states (Proverbs 23:22): Do not shame [her], though your mother be old.*

I.e. do not shame the elders of Israel (*your mother*) by refusing to rely on their practices, for their practices are based on Scripture (see *Rav*), and may certainly serve as valid precedents (*Rashi* to 54a s.v. ואומר אל תבוז).

The mishnah cites this verse in reference to Boaz, to refute the argument that he might have acted improperly by greeting his workers with the Name of God, and that his actions thus cannot serve as a basis for the Rabbinical enactment. We must not shame Boaz by casting aspersions on his behavior, claiming that he acted on his own, for he was one of the elders of Israel; without question, his greeting had a valid Scriptural source, as the mishnah will soon demonstrate (*Rav; Rashi* to 63a s.v. תא שמע).

וְאוֹמֵר [תהלים קיט,קכו]: „עֵת לַעֲשׂוֹת לַה׳ —
הֵפֵרוּ תוֹרָתֶךָ". רַבִּי נָתָן אוֹמֵר: „הֵפֵרוּ תוֹרָתֶךָ"
— „עֵת לַעֲשׂוֹת לַה׳".

סְלִיק מַסֶּכֶת בְּרָכוֹת

ר' עובדיה מברטנורא

רבי נתן אומר הפרו תורתך. פעמים שמבטלים דברי תורה כדי לעשות לה׳, אף זה המתכוין
לשאול בשלום חברו, וזהו רצונו של מקום שנאמר (תהלים לד, טו) בקש שלום ורדפהו, מותר להפר
תורה ולעשות דבר הנראה אסור:

יד אברהם

The mishnah returns to its original
proof from Boaz, because one might
possibly argue that no precedent can
be derived from the greeting the angel
extended to Gideon. His words might
have been neither a greeting nor a
blessing; rather, as a messenger of
God, he was *informing* Gideon of
God's assurance that He would support Gideon in the forthcoming war
(*Rav*, from *Gem.* ibid.).

וְאוֹמֵר: „עֵת לַעֲשׂוֹת לַה׳ הֵפֵרוּ תוֹרָתֶךָ".
*And [a verse] states (Psalms 119:126):
It is a time to act for Hashem; they
have nullified Your Law.*

The mishnah cites this verse as the
Scriptural basis for Boaz's behavior
[see comm. above s.v. וְאוֹמֵר אַל תָּבוּז]

(*Rav* s.v. שואל אדם שיהא; *Rashi* to 63a
s.v. תא שמע; cf. *Tif. Yis.* §33). According to its simple interpretation, the
second half of the verse ("they have
nullified Your Law") refers to evildoers who violate the Torah's commandments. However, according to its
homiletic interpretation, which the
mishnah cites presently, the verse
teaches the halachic principle upon
which Boaz based his actions, in seeming disrespect for the Name of God.

**רַבִּי נָתָן אוֹמֵר: „הֵפֵרוּ תוֹרָתֶךָ" — עֵת
לַעֲשׂוֹת לַה׳".** — *R' Nassan says: They
have nullified Your law [because] it is
a time to act for Hashem.*

R' Nassan explains how this verse
serves as the basis for the actions of

9
5

And [a verse] states (*Psalms* 119:126): *It is a time to act for Hashem; they have nullified Your Law.* R' Nassan says: *They have nullified Your Law* [because] *it is a time to act for Hashem.*

Boaz (see *Tos. Yom Tov* s.v. נתן רבי; cf. *Tif. Yis.* §34). The verse is expounded by reversing the order of its two phrases. According to this exposition, the verse refers not to evildoers but to the leaders of the generation. They have seemingly nullified certain laws of the Torah *because* it is time to act for Hashem, i.e. because by doing so they uphold His wishes (see *Gem.* 63a). The verse thus teaches that in order to fulfill God's will, the Rabbis are permitted, at certain times, to act in a manner which *appears* to be a nullification of the Law. Greeting one with the name of God spreads goodwill among men (see comm. above s.v. וְהִתְקִינוּ שֶׁיְּהֵא אָדָם), in accordance with God's wishes, as it says (*Psalms* 34:15): *seek peace and pursue it* (*Rav; Rashi* to 54a s.v. ואומר עת לעשות). [Similarly, it achieves the purpose of reinforcing the belief that God is the source of all

blessing (see comm. ibid.).] Thus, although it might appear disrespectful of God, Boaz specifically utalized such a greeting.

Rambam Comm. explains the last part of the mishnah differently. According to *Rambam*, the mishnah's citation of the verse in *Proverbs* marks the start of a discussion regarding respect for, and compliance with, Rabbinic enactments in general. The mishnah cites the verse "Do not shame [her], though your mother be old" to teach that one should not disparage Rabbinic enactments as being antiquated, and unsuitable for the modern era. Moreover, states the mishnah, one who scorns Rabbinic enactments and violates them can expect to be punished. R' Nassan's expositions is understood as follows: *They have nullified Your Law,* i.e. those who violate Rabbinic enactments have transgressed *God's Law.* There will come *a time for Hashem to act,* i.e. a time when God will punish these evildoers for their violation of both Biblical and Rabbinic commands.

⚜ תפלה אחר למוד משניות על הנפטר ⚜

It is customary to recite this prayer whenever Mishnayos are studied
in memory of a deceased.

אָנָּא יהוה מָלֵא רַחֲמִים, אֲשֶׁר בְּיָדְךָ נֶפֶשׁ כָּל חַי, וְרוּחַ כָּל בְּשַׂר
אִישׁ.[1] יִהְיֶה נָא לְרָצוֹן לְפָנֶיךָ תוֹרָתֵנוּ וּתְפִלָּתֵנוּ בַּעֲבוּר נִשְׁמַת
(deceased's Hebrew name) בֶּן/בַּת (father's Hebrew name). וּגְמוֹל נָא עִמָּהּ
בְּחַסְדְּךָ הַגָּדוֹל, לִפְתּוֹחַ לָהּ שַׁעֲרֵי רַחֲמִים וָחֶסֶד, וְשַׁעֲרֵי גַן עֵדֶן.
וּתְקַבֵּל אוֹתָהּ בְּאַהֲבָה וּבְחִבָּה, וְשָׁלַח לָהּ מַלְאָכֶיךָ הַקְּדוֹשִׁים
וְהַטְּהוֹרִים, לְהוֹלִיכָהּ וּלְהוֹשִׁיבָהּ תַּחַת עֵץ הַחַיִּים, אֵצֶל נִשְׁמַת
הַצַּדִּיקִים וְהַצִּדְקָנִיּוֹת, חֲסִידִים וַחֲסִידוֹת, לֵהָנוֹת מִזִּיו שְׁכִינָתֶךָ,
לְהַשְׂבִּיעָהּ מִטּוּבְךָ הַצָּפוּן לַצַּדִּיקִים. וְהַגּוּף יָנוּחַ בַּקֶּבֶר בִּמְנוּחָה
נְכוֹנָה, בְּחֶדְוָה וּבְשִׂמְחָה וְשָׁלוֹם, כְּדִכְתִיב: יָבוֹא שָׁלוֹם, יָנוּחוּ עַל
מִשְׁכְּבוֹתָם, הֹלֵךְ נְכֹחוֹ.[2] וּכְתִיב: יַעְלְזוּ חֲסִידִים בְּכָבוֹד, יְרַנְּנוּ עַל
מִשְׁכְּבוֹתָם.[3] וּכְתִיב: אִם תִּשְׁכַּב לֹא תִפְחָד, וְשָׁכַבְתָּ וְעָרְבָה שְׁנָתֶךָ.[4]

for a female:	for a male:
וְתִשְׁמוֹר אוֹתָהּ מֵחִבּוּט הַקֶּבֶר, וּמֵרִמָּה וְתוֹלֵעָה. וְתִסְלַח וְתִמְחוֹל לָהּ עַל כָּל פְּשָׁעֶיהָ, כִּי אָדָם אֵין צַדִּיק בָּאָרֶץ, אֲשֶׁר יַעֲשֶׂה טּוֹב וְלֹא יֶחֱטָא.[5] וּזְכוֹר לָהּ זְכִיּוֹתֶיהָ וְצִדְקוֹתֶיהָ אֲשֶׁר עָשָׂתָה. וְתַשְׁפִּיעַ לָהּ מִנִּשְׁמָתָהּ לְדַשֵּׁן עַצְמוֹתֶיהָ בַּקֶּבֶר מֵרֹב טוֹב הַצָּפוּן לַצַּדִּיקִים, דִּכְתִיב: מָה רַב טוּבְךָ אֲשֶׁר צָפַנְתָּ לִּירֵאֶיךָ,[6] וּכְתִיב: שֹׁמֵר כָּל עַצְמוֹתָיו, אַחַת מֵהֵנָּה לֹא נִשְׁבָּרָה.[7] וְתִשְׁכּוֹן בֶּטַח בָּדָד[8] וְשַׁאֲנָן מִפַּחַד רָעָה, וְאַל תִּרְאֶה פְּנֵי גֵיהִנֹּם. וְנִשְׁמָתָהּ תְּהֵא צְרוּרָה בִּצְרוֹר הַחַיִּים,[9] וּלְהַחֲיוֹתָהּ בִּתְחִיַּת הַמֵּתִים עִם כָּל מֵתֵי עַמְּךָ יִשְׂרָאֵל בְּרַחֲמִים. אָמֵן.	וְתִשְׁמוֹר אוֹתוֹ מֵחִבּוּט הַקֶּבֶר, וּמֵרִמָּה וְתוֹלֵעָה. וְתִסְלַח וְתִמְחוֹל לוֹ עַל כָּל פְּשָׁעָיו, כִּי אָדָם אֵין צַדִּיק בָּאָרֶץ, אֲשֶׁר יַעֲשֶׂה טּוֹב וְלֹא יֶחֱטָא.[5] וּזְכוֹר לוֹ זְכִיּוֹתָיו וְצִדְקוֹתָיו אֲשֶׁר עָשָׂה. וְתַשְׁפִּיעַ לוֹ מִנִּשְׁמָתוֹ לְדַשֵּׁן עַצְמוֹתָיו בַּקֶּבֶר מֵרֹב טוֹב הַצָּפוּן לַצַּדִּיקִים, דִּכְתִיב: מָה רַב טוּבְךָ אֲשֶׁר צָפַנְתָּ לִּירֵאֶיךָ.[6] וּכְתִיב: שֹׁמֵר כָּל עַצְמוֹתָיו, אַחַת מֵהֵנָּה לֹא נִשְׁבָּרָה.[7] וְיִשְׁכּוֹן בֶּטַח בָּדָד[8] וְשַׁאֲנָן מִפַּחַד רָעָה, וְאַל יִרְאֶה פְּנֵי גֵיהִנֹּם. וְנִשְׁמָתוֹ תְּהֵא צְרוּרָה בִּצְרוֹר הַחַיִּים,[9] וּלְהַחֲיוֹתוֹ בִּתְחִיַּת הַמֵּתִים עִם כָּל מֵתֵי עַמְּךָ יִשְׂרָאֵל בְּרַחֲמִים. אָמֵן.

⸰{ PRAYER AFTER THE STUDY OF MISHNAH FOR THE DECEASED }⸰

It is customary to recite this prayer whenever Mishnayos are studied
in memory of a deceased.

אָנָּא Please, O Hashem, full of mercy, for in Your hand is the soul of all the living and the spirit of every human being.[1] May You find favor in our Torah study and prayer for the soul of (deceased's Hebrew name) son/daughter of (father's Hebrew name) and do with it according to Your great kindness to open for it the gates of mercy and kindness and the gates of the Garden of Eden. Accept it with love and affection and send it Your holy and pure angels to lead it and to settle it under the Tree of Life near the souls of the righteous and devout men and women, to enjoy the radiance of Your Presence, to satiate it from Your good that is concealed for the righteous. May the body repose in the grave with proper contentment, pleasure, gladness and peace, as it is written: "Let him enter in peace, let them rest on their beds — everyone who has lived in his proper way."[2] And it is written: "Let the devout exult in glory, let them sing joyously upon their beds."[3] And it is written: "If you lay down, you will not fear; when you lay down, your sleep will be sweet."[4] And protect him/her from the tribulations of the grave and from worms and maggots. Forgive and pardon him/her for all his/her sins, for there is no man so wholly righteous on earth that he does good and never sins.[5] Remember for him/her the merits and righteous deeds that he/she performed, and cause a spiritual flow from his/her soul to keep his/her bones fresh in the grave from the abundant good that is concealed for the righteous, as it is written: "How abundant is Your goodness that You have concealed for Your reverent ones,"[6] and it is written: "He guards all his bones, even one of them was not broken."[7] May it rest secure, alone,[8] and serene, from fear of evil and may it not see the threshold of Gehinnom. May his/her soul be bound in the Bond of Life.[9] And may it be brought back to life with the Resuscitation of the Dead with all the dead of Your people Israel, with mercy. Amen.

---

(1) Cf. *Job* 12:10. (2) *Isaiah* 57:2. (3) *Psalms* 149:5. (4) *Proverbs* 3:24. (5) *Ecclesiastes* 7:20.
(6) *Psalms* 31:20. (7) ibid. 34:21. (8) Cf. *Deuteronomy* 33:28. (9) Cf. *I Samuel* 25:29.